Contents

 Chapter I   Growing Up in Society   1

 Chapter 2   The Family Shapes the Child   34

Chapter 3   The Rich Diversity of Family Forms   72

Chapter 4   Routes to Parenting   101

Chapter 5   Child Rearing   145

 Chapter 6   Family Strengths and Stresses   179

 Chapter 7   Early Education and Child Care: New Challenges   202

Supporting Children in their Home, School, and Community

Dorothy Holin Sailor

Fullerton College

PEARSON

A and *B*

Boston ■ New York ■ San Francisco
Mexico City ■ Montreal ■ Toronto ■ London ■ Madrid ■ Munich ■ Paris
Hong Kong ■ Singapore ■ Tokyo ■ Cape Town ■ Sydney

Dedication

To my late husband, Danton, who unfailingly supported my work on
this book and my work with children over the years
To my three sons, Kevin, Timothy, and Dorton
To my colleagues

Series Editor: Traci Mueller
Editorial Assistant: Krista E. Price
Marketing Manager: Elizabeth Fogarty
Production Editor: Kathy Smith
Editorial-Production Service: Chestnut Hill Enterprises, Inc.

Composition Buyer: Linda Cox
Manufacturing Buyer: JoAnne Sweeney
Cover Administrator: Linda Knowles
Cover Designer: Studio Nine
Electronic Composition: Omegatype Typography, Inc.

For related titles and support materials, visit our online catalog at www.ablongman.com

Between the time Website information is gathered and then published, it is not unusual for
some sites to have closed. Also, the transcription of URLs can result in typographical errors.
The publisher would appreciate notification where these errors occur so that they may be
corrected in subsequent editions.

Photo credits appear on page xvi, and are considered an extension of this copyright page.

Library of Congress Cataloging-in-Publication Data

Sailor, Dorothy Holin.
    Supporting children in their home, school, and community / Dorothy Holin Sailor.
        p.   cm.
    Includes bibliographical references and index.
    ISBN 0-205-36092-0
    1. Child development. 2. Socialization. 3. Child rearing. 4. Children—
Family relationships. 5. Children—Services for. 6. Children—United States—
Social conditions. 7. Family—United States. I. Title.

HQ767.9.S23   2004
305.231—dc22   2003050043

Printed in the United States of America

10 9 8 7 6 5 4   07

Chapter 8 Schooling   242

Chapter 9   Siblings, Peers, and Friends   287

Chapter 10   Mass Media and Technology   322

Chapter 11   Violence in the Lives of Children and Peaceful Alternatives   349

Chapter 12 Effects of Government and All Social
Policies on Children and Families 374

 Chapter 13 Community: Its Influence on Children 395

 Appendix Piaget's Stages of Cognitive Development 423

Foreword

*W*hether we call it a community, a village, a neighborhood, or a context, we know that children grow and learn and mature influenced by the environment that surrounds them. In this book you will find a comprehensive yet a very readable look at the factors in our families and in our society that influence our children as they grow.

Dorothy Sailor provides us with a perspective that is based on her many years of parenting, teaching, researching, observing, and traveling around the world learning about parenting children and teaching children in many countries. Her wealth of knowledge provides an approach to supporting children and families that is both practical and scholarly.

Teachers, caregivers, and all professionals who work with children and families do themselves come from varied backgrounds, value systems, and teaching philosophies. It is important for us as professionals to absorb as much information as possible about those factors relevant to growing up in this society. In this book Professor Sailor presents concise and yet thorough information on this myriad of societal, family, school, and community influences. She poses questions, presents data and current trends, and identifies successful models of supporting children and families. The author's sensitivity and respect for the broad cultural context of rearing and supporting children comes from her rich multicultural experiences both in America and around the world. Her approach is sensitive to both intergenerational and global influences.

The format of this book facilitates both learning opportunities and readability. The key points, critical thinking questions, and the resources and references contribute to its use for the individual reader as well as its use for group discussions. Additionally, the format of the book serves as a launching point for seeking additional information.

What will it take in the years ahead to support children who are diverse in so many ways? Certainly it will take an understanding of the broad array of influences that contribute to the home, school, and community context of their growing years. This book addresses those influences and makes a unique contribution to our understanding of what it really takes to support children in a way that will foster positive relationships and a sense of belonging. That support will facilitate the cooperation and communication necessary to live in a more peaceful world, a world filled with hope for the future.

Cheryl L. Foster
Central Arizona College, Governing Board Member, National Association
for the Education of Young Children, 1998-2002

Introduction

Topics

Supporting Children in Their Family, School, and Community promotes the values and examines the challenges of raising and educating children in a pluralistic society. Because the understanding of differences is so important, the book covers a variety of cultures, family forms, learning styles, and physical and mental abilities. The access to high-quality child care, education, and health care, and safety in neighborhoods varies greatly.

The first chapters provide a foundation for understanding society at large and the family. Various family forms and different styles of parenting and cultural values provide information helpful to those working with children. The family is examined in terms of characteristics found in healthy families and those that appear in dysfunctional families as well as ways to cope with stress and crises in the lives of children and families. Children learn to handle stresses differently. Some children, referred to as resilient children, are able to cope with some damaging conditions in positive ways.

The middle chapters focus on the role of child care, schools, and peers in the development of children. The various types of early care and education, the degrees of quality, and the short- and long-term effects on the child are examined. The multiple roles of schools and teachers, school choice, technology, the essentials for children with special needs, and for those who are homeless provide a broad view of schooling. The ultimate question is, how can schools provide a quality education for all children so that they will graduate from high school with adequate reading, math, and general skills to function successfully in society?

The final chapters provide information about the roles of the broader community and society on children's development. Mass media, violence, and peaceful alternatives, and all social policies affect children and their families either directly or indirectly. The influence of citizens as child advocates and the work of advocacy groups help students understand the role of child advocacy. The final chapter on the community compares services and conditions for children in cities, suburbs, and rural areas. A look at health care in America includes the lack of adequate mental health care and alarming conditions such as child obesity. The text ends with a look at some delightful parks and programs for all children and families.

As an educator and researcher of thirty years in the fields of early education and child care, child development, and parenting education, I am acutely aware of the challenges today to those working with children and the tremendous rewards available through helping children develop into healthy adolescents and adults.

Approach to This Book

Researchers study the child from many perspectives including biology, psychology, history, medicine, and education. This book is oriented toward a sociological and ecological approach reflecting the works of Bandura and Bronfenbrenner. However, because the child is an individual and lives with other individuals, psychological research is incorporated. In particular, theories of development as described by Erikson, Piaget, Kohlberg, Vygotsky, and Selman are considered.

Supporting Children offers practical tips for teachers, parents, and those working with children. The message to the reader is one hope: that through knowledge and working together, we can make a real difference in the lives of *all* our children.

Pedagogical Features

Critical thinking questions at the end of each chapter help students become actively involved in their learning.

Photos and children's art visualize ideas and topics for readers.

Success stories and model projects help motivate and inform readers.

Tables, charts, and graphs help visualize key information.

Quotations throughout the book from well-known people help inspire readers.

Cross-cultural materials are an integral part of the book.

Current and classical research are an integral part of the book.

Coverage of issues of gender, race/ethnicity, and socioeconomic class give the book a broad perspective.

Practical information is included to help parents, teachers, and people from the community work together.

Information on ways to help and change conditions detrimental to children and families enables citizens to become child advocates at various levels.

Key points present a detailed summary for each chapter.

Resources, including references, related readings, and Web sites are listed at the end of each chapter.

About the Author

The author began her work with children as a graduate student assistant in the Child Development Lab at the University of Illinois. She has worked with children, college students, and parents in child study laboratories and taught a variety of child development and family living classes at Fullerton College for thirty years. She has published articles in national and international journals. She has been active in community projects involving children, homeless families, and a variety of school issues.

She brings a global perspective to her work. She has lived and worked overseas on four different occasions and traveled and researched the educational systems in many areas of the world. Her commitment to children internationally began in 1977 with the World Organization for the Education of Young Children (OMEP), a nongovernmental agency with consultative status to UNESCO and UNICEF. Recently she served six years on the OMEP World Executive Committee as Vice President for North America and the Caribbean, and currently serves on the Board for the U.S. National Committee for OMEP.

Acknowledgments

I am grateful for the contributions and support of so many colleagues and friends. I want to thank Dorothy Hewes for her support at various stages of this book, Cheryl Foster for reading every chapter and for valuable resources, Neva Root for her critical eye and her ability to look at the big picture, Tom Chiaromonte for his support, Chris Lamm for her resources on teaching peace, Patti Green for the multicultural pictures, and for the views of our students at Fullerton College.

The generous support of my son Kevin, a cognitive psychologist, of my research and his expert job of critiquing the materials during various stages of writing were crucial to the completion of this text. I want to thank my son, Dorton, for his professional help with photographs and his technical advice.

I appreciate the efforts of William Evans, who reviewed each chapter from a layperson's viewpoint and the talents of Ralph Kuttner in recreating many of my tables and graphs. I want to thank the librarians at Fullerton College for their assistance.

I want to thank the following reviewers of the book for their meticulous reading of the chapters and valuable comments. Eileen Donahue Brittain, Truman College; Dorothy Hewes, San Diego State University; Suzanne Krogh, Western Washington University; Linda Medearis, Texas A&M International University; Christine Osgood, Mesa Community College; Peggy Pearl, Southwest Missouri State University; and Maria Elena Reyes, University of Alaska, Fairbanks.

Growing Up
in Society

Our most basic link is that we all inhabit this planet. We all breathe the same air. We all cherish our children's future.

— John F. Kennedy

*C*hildren are born into a family living in a society and a nation, each representing one or more cultures. Through social interactions, individuals develop a self or identity that includes a personality and self-concept. Children may learn that they are loved or just tolerated and that adults can be trusted or cannot be relied on.

A four-year-old boy returned from a visit to his aunt. Enthusiastically he said to his mother, "Aunt Joan loves me."

Obviously he had a good time and his extended family affirmed that he was loved.

Socialization is a life process of learning how to feel, think, and act in each social context. Every social experience makes some impact, but in the early years these experiences are crucial to the child's development. For example, the type of attachment a child forms to the mother and/or major caregivers in the early years affects emotional and social relationships during childhood and later in life. Some research even relates the type of romantic relationship in adulthood with the kind of attachment formed during infancy (Ainsworth, 1989; Ainsworth and Bowlby, 1991; Shaw and Vondra, 1995). Of all experiences, those in the family during the early years are the most crucial and lasting.

Primary socialization occurs in childhood. The child learns how to interact with others according to society's expectations. Schools are vital in teaching behaviors that are appropriate in settings outside the family, such as the classroom, peer groups, and in larger society. All through childhood, children continue to learn what is expected of them and to assume new responsibilities. As adults, they learn the values and the norms expected of adults in their various and changing roles in society.

Resocialization is learning a new set of behaviors, values, and beliefs. It occurs when a specific behavior of an individual is changed. It could be alcoholism, abusive behavior, or overeating. In prisons, there is an attempt to resocialize inmates so that their behavior will be acceptable to society.

Socialization involves absorbing the culture or cultures of the society and the particular settings where one is living. Through the process of socialization, society passes its culture from one generation to another. Today's society is built on the actions and values of previous generations. Each new generation makes its own adaptations. All societies stress both tradition and new ideas but to differing degrees. In the United States, the dominant culture places high priority on the individual. For example, in teaching the child how to fit into the family and society, the dominant culture emphasizes each child's temperament, interests, and talents. In some minority cultures, such as Hispanic or many Asian American cultures, more emphasis is placed on tradition and support of the family and less on the interests of the individual.

Society

A society is a group of people sharing a common territory, culture, and social structure. Members of a society are relatively independent of people in other societies. However, in the twenty-first century the actions within one society increasingly affect other societies. The foundation of a society is kinship, although family structure varies considerably over cultures. A society usually exists within a nation. A nation is a political entity within borders. The United States can be referred to both as a society and as a nation.

Societies differ due to their *technology, modes of thinking,* and *division of labor.* From the plow to the computer, technological advances have forced societies to change. Some changes, such as the development of new ideas, behaviors, or material products, emerge from invention. The telephone, and more recently the Internet, have changed the ways individuals communicate. Change also occurs from discovering something not recognized or fully understood before. This usually emerges through scientific research, although some discoveries are accidental. Change also grows out of diffusion when cultural traits of one society are spread to others or exchanged in the process.

Some forces for change, like globalization, come from outside the society and produce changes in many societies. In the United States, many manufacturing or production jobs have moved to less developed societies where labor costs are much lower and government regulations may be more favorable. United States workers have lost their jobs and local workers in these less developed countries are employed, helping their economy. However, environmental conditions may not be good for their workers.

The diffusion of cultures within a society brings about changes. For example, in the United States many companies are responding to the large number of Spanish-speaking customers by making information available in Spanish.

Tradition brings stability while change causes disruption, reorganization, and adjustments. The results of change can be both beneficial and detrimental to some or all members of a society. Changes due to technological advances have improved the quality of life and increased longevity for many. However, some changes have been responsible for ecological damage and other changes for greater destruction through the lethal weapons used in wars.

Agrarian Societies

About 7,000 years ago, agrarian societies emerged in various areas in the world with the planting and sustaining of crops. Farms became more productive with the invention of the plow pulled by an animal, irrigation of the land, and other technological innovations (Mackay, Hill, and Buckler, 1988). This created greater diversity and social inequality. In hunting and gathering societies, women held high status for producing most of the food. In agrarian societies, men produced food and had social dominance over women. Slavery existed. As production increased, excess crops were available for distribution. Some workers were no longer needed on the farm and found work in town. Many became artisans and craftsmen. Although most families lived and worked together on farms, towns and cities emerged.

Industrial Societies

The Industrial Revolution, which began around 1750, changed the structure of societies. Social experiences and expectations for behavior varied according to occupation, age groups, gender, race, and ethnicity. Population shifted to the cities, where employment was often related to manufacturing goods and products in factories. Industrialists overshadowed or replaced the landed aristocracy and industrial technicians, administrators, and white-collar workers became the new middle class (Ware Panikkar, and Romein, 1966). In contrast to an agricultural society, in an industrial society:

1. People earned their living from their employment as individuals and not as a family group.
2. Employment and promotions were largely based on individual ability and competence rather than on the wishes or needs of family members.
3. Mobility was needed for employment and other pursuits.
4. The development of public and private services and institutions, such as schools, banks, and hospitals, allowed individuals to live apart from the control and support of their kin.
5. Relationships were more formal, often limited to the area of interaction such as the workplace.
6. Culture was more diverse.

Postindustrial Societies or Information Economies

The United States and other industrialized societies have entered a new era due to technological advancements. This includes Canada, most of Europe, Japan, Australia, and New Zealand. David Bell (1973, 1989) coined the term *postindustrialism* to refer to technology supporting the information economy. Production has been moving from material-based products to the creation and distribution of highly technological products. Emphasis is on service industries, information production, and economic consumption (Bell, 1973; Beniger, 1993). The vast majority of employment positions are related to teaching, information processing, and related services. Assembly-line and production work are going to the developing countries.

In a postindustrial society compared to an industrial society:

1. Members of a society no longer depend solely on the economy and policies of their nation but are a part of a *global society*. The national economy is affected by events around the world, such as a major stock market fluctuation in Asia, cheap labor in a third world country, or one country's import tariffs on another country's goods.

2. *Flexibility* is required if industries or individual workers are going to survive. Increasing numbers of workers are able to work from their home at least part of the week.

3. *Education for life* is essential to gain knowledge for future jobs, health, recreation needs, and for longevity. More people earn a living from intellectual skills and education than physical skills and brawn. These workers need a knowledge of the computer and its expanding capabilities, satellite systems, and facsimile machines. Workers increasingly will be using advanced skills in mathematics, critical thinking, and technology.

4. *Long-range planning and delayed gratification* are essential abilities because of the complexity of our lives. It takes longer to learn to understand and operate the equipment in our homes as well as in the workplace.

5. *Decision-making skills* are essential as more choices are available in our personal lives and our work lives.

6. Control moves from *centralization,* with control at the highest level of the government or an organization, to *decentralization,* with greater control at the lower or local levels. For example, the trend is for more school decisions to be made at the local level and for parents to have a greater voice in these decisions.

7. *Networking* is the current approach to work. Groups of people work together to share ideas, information, and resources to improve products or conditions. Members work together as *equals* rather than members working according to different ranks in position as in *hierarchies.*

Culture

Culture represents a shared way of life. It includes the beliefs, values, traditions, behavior, and material objects shared by a group of people that enable them to live together. A group may be defined in terms of national origin, race, language, religion, or by other categories. The culture of any group is constantly evolving in response to what is occurring in the environment. Some cultures are more static and change less than others. Culture, by its very nature, limits its members by providing standards for behavior and a set of values. However, individuals work to shape and reshape various aspects of their culture and society in an attempt to meet their needs and dreams. In some societies, members are freer to be creative and make changes than in others.

Individuals and families often belong to more than one cultural group at the same time. Sociologists estimate that five to six thousand distinctive cultures have existed on Earth. Although the cultural diversity of the world has been decreasing, at least one thousand cultures still remain (Durning, 1993). The United States is a multicultural society representing hundreds of cultures brought by immigrants to this country along with numerous Native American cultures.

Components of Culture

Despite the many differences among cultures, there are five major components of all cultures: symbols, language, values, norms, and material objects.

SYMBOLS   Symbols are the most important component of culture because they are the basis for human environment. Symbols represent any action or object that has a particular meaning to people who share the same culture. Cultural symbols change over time. The power of a symbol can be seen when someone misuses it. Burning a U.S. flag during a political protest brings a flood of emotions to many citizens. A recent flag-burning episode brought pressure from some citizens to seek a law prohibiting the burning of the flag. This never materialized because such a law violates the First Amendment rights of citizens.

The same symbol can carry very different meanings for people from different cultures. Looking someone in the eye during a conversation may be a sign of listening in one culture and a lack of respect in another culture. One must be careful not to offend someone of another culture consciously or unconsciously.

Cultural relativism judges other people from the perspective of their culture and not from the perspective of one's own culture. Looking at their norms, values, and customs in terms of their distinctive culture helps one to understand differences. It does not mean that one must accept every cultural variation. **Ethnocentrism** is judging people in terms of one's own culture. Ethnocentrism can be very damaging to mutual understanding and good relationships.

LANGUAGE   Language is a system of symbols that allows individuals to communicate directly with those who have the same language or through an interpreter with those who speak another language. **Language is essential in order to think, work, and live together in a broader community.** It also transmits culture from generation to generation. Children learn their home language through interactions with family members. In families where more than one language is used regularly, children often acquire more than one home language. As children develop language, they begin to understand their parents' values. When children enter school with little or no English, it is difficult for them to learn English well enough to think and learn in this new language. It is important for them to be able to speak English in their home and other settings as well to maintain their native language.

VALUES AND BELIEFS   Values are culturally defined standards by which people judge desirability, goodness, and beauty and which serve as broad guidelines for living (Macionis, 1997). Values are guidelines for choosing goals and judging behaviors. Beliefs are the conceptions people have about what is true in the world that may or may not be proven. Beliefs are specific standards for behavior. When beliefs are given moral significance, they also become values. Young children learn values and beliefs from those close to them. As children increase in cognitive skills and social experiences, they begin to accept certain values and beliefs as their own.

United States society is so diverse that it is impossible to come up with a definitive list of values. Individuals may belong to one or more subgroups, each with overlapping and different values. Often two individuals or groups have conflicting values. For example, children and parents or employees and employers may strongly disagree about something. The process of value clarification involves all parties examining both sets of values and beliefs, looking at the alternatives and then making a joint decision. This process becomes increasingly important as individuals with different cultures or ideas interact more frequently.

IDEAL VALUES OF THE U.S. CULTURE   A few mainstream values and beliefs that have helped to shape our society have remained constant over time, although the ways that we define them may have changed (Sullivan, 1995). A review of twenty-seven different descriptions of basic values in the United States, including the writings of anthropologist Margaret Mead, reports values similar to those of sociologist Robin Williams (Devine, 1972). The following ten values are most central to life in America (Williams, 1970).

1. **Equal opportunity.** Every individual should have an equal opportunity to succeed based on talent and hard work regardless of social status at birth. This does not mean that everyone will end up with the same achievements.
2. **Achievement and success.** Competition is encouraged whether it is in academics, in sports, or in the workplace. For example, a new record may appear in the Guinness' Book of Records. Success is admired by others, but it also improves one's self-image.
3. **Material comfort.** Much emphasis is placed on material objects such as a new bicycle, car, house, swimming pool, recreational objects, special clothing like designer jeans, and labor-saving devices. This may not be a yardstick for judging happiness, but it certainly is a measure for judging success.

4. **Activity and work.** Hard work is considered virtuous. Action is preferred to reflection. Activities are encouraged whether they are for economic gain, recreation, health, social improvement, or political reasons.

5. **Practicality and efficiency.** To achieve one's goal in a fast efficient way is rewarded. Both cost-effectiveness and time efficiency are desirable goals.

6. **Progress.** A new model, product, or innovation is considered better than its predecessor. This may or may not be true. Advertisers often say, "the new improved" or "the latest advancement." Of course, there are always some who say, "Remember the good old days."

7. **Science.** Knowledge and scientific discoveries improve our lives. Scientific facts often take precedence over emotional beliefs. The discovery of the Dead Sea Scrolls provides scientific documentation of religious beliefs.

8. **Democracy and free enterprise.** Each individual has a right to make choices and affect governmental policies. Our free elections allow citizens to vote for their political leaders. Individuals make choices in their daily lives that affect future products or conditions. By watching certain TV shows, people are supporting that type of programming. For example, if people truly do *not* want certain types of violence on children's television programs, they do not watch those shows or support their advertisers and they try to find others who agree with them. Free enterprise allows individuals to provide a service or product that is largely regulated by public acceptance. Free enterprise is encouraged and in some cases protected by antimonopoly laws.

9. **Freedom.** The United States has laws and values based on the rights of individuals. These are in the Bill of Rights, which was attached to our Constitution in 1791. This idea of individual rights was made clear to the author when visiting preschools and research centers in the 1970s and early 1980s in many of the former Soviet Union countries. Invariably, one of her host's first statements was, "Remember, we teach our children that the group comes first and the individual second." In the United States, individuals are encouraged to pursue personal goals, although group and social responsibilities are also important.

10. **Racism and group superiority.** Most people value certain groups or individuals differently based on gender, ethnicity, religion, and socioeconomic status (Williams, 1970).

When the gap between the ideal value and the real value becomes too large, these contradictions cause tensions in people's lives. Eventually pressures to reduce these discrepancies bring about change. For example, the contrast between the ideal value of equality and equal opportunity for all and the practice of denying equal opportunities to racial minorities, women, and individuals with disabilities became unacceptable to many people. This resulted in the 1960s protests that eventually brought about legal changes protecting the rights of various groups. The ideal value of equal rights and opportunity for all was extended *legally* to more individuals in the United States.

There are inconsistencies even among these generally accepted values. For example, the values of racism and group superiority clash with the value of equal opportunity for all. Even within a specific value, there may be exceptions. For instance, equal opportunities for all excludes gays in the military who acknowledge their sexual orientation. Many times, actual behavior varies from U.S. ideals. Some of these inconsistencies occur because cultural patterns are influenced by age, education, race, ethnicity, religion, and social class. People who have attained success and some wealth are more likely to believe that there is equal opportunity based on the individual's responsibility to achieve. Those who are less successful may disagree and feel that they are victims of the system. They believe that they did not have equal educational and other opportunities and now receive unequal monetary compensation and status for their particular type of work (Schaeffer, 2002).

Inconsistencies in values also occur because of changes in society. One current trend involves the issue of responsibility for a situation or a condition. This condition could be poverty, unemployment, or addiction to a drug or habit such as gambling. Who is responsible, the individual, the company, or society?

THE NEW CULTURE OF VICTIMIZATION OR "THE BLAME GAME"   Sociologist Irving Horowitz coined the term *culture of victimization* to designate a society in which everyone is a victim and no one accepts responsibility for anything. Many individuals claim to be victims of various addictions. The term *addiction* now covers more than drugs. It includes an array of indulgences and abuse such as uncontrolled shopping sprees, gambling, and sex.

The value *that individuals are responsible for what befalls them* is eroding based on three factors. *First,* the public has a greater awareness of scientific information showing how conditions in society affect people's lives. *Second,* successful lawsuits on behalf of victims suing for damages have escalated in the last two decades. For example, the courts have ordered various tobacco companies to pay certain victims of tobacco smoking large settlements. Victims can include those who pay for the smokers' treatments. *Third,* the number of "rights" groups has increased. They have expanded their agenda and improved their effectiveness. Issues today include the rights of opposing groups such as the environmentalists protecting trees and the lumber industry, the rights of nonsmokers and of smokers, and the hotly contested issue on the rights of women to control their body and the rights of the unborn. The concern is to what extent this may be eroding our responsibilities to society (Etzioni, 1991; Hollander, 1995; Macioni, 1997; Taylor, 1991).

COLLEGE STUDENTS' VALUES   What do college students value? Over the last thirty years, entering first-year college students in the United States have become more concerned with becoming "very well off financially" and less concerned with developing "a meaningful philosophy of life." Each year since 1966, 350,000 entering college students across the nation have filled out questionnaires reporting their attitudes on specific issues, beliefs, and life goals. The value "being financially well off" has shown the strongest gain, rising from 44 percent in 1967 to 74 percent in

FIGURE 1.1   LIFE GOALS OF COLLEGE STUDENTS FROM 1966–2001.

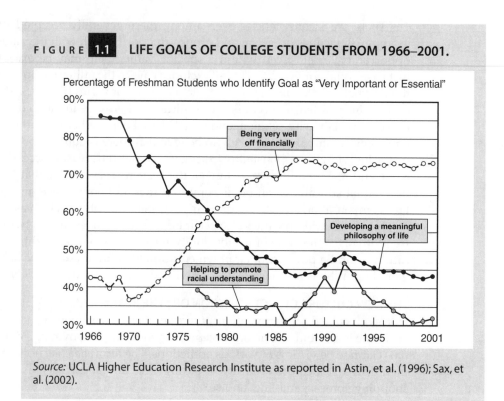

Source: UCLA Higher Education Research Institute as reported in Astin, et al. (1996); Sax, et al. (2002).

1998. The value "developing a meaningful philosophy in life" has had the greatest decline. It was the most popular value in 1967, but had fallen to sixth place in 2001 with only 38 percent of the students stating that "influencing social values" was essential or very important. In 2001, over 30 percent of the students rated "helping to promote racial understanding" essential or very important while five years earlier in 1992, 42 percent of students had rated this high (see Figure 1.2). Although the popularity of various values has changed, they all still remain on students' lists of important issues, beliefs, and life goals.

NORMS   Another component of culture involves norms or rules and expectations for the behavior of individuals. In contrast, values involve general preferences. Norms can be **formal** or **informal.** Formal norms are usually written and include specific penalties for violators. Formal norms include laws and other rules and regulation such as graduation requirements. *Proscriptive* norms mandate what should not be done, while those labeled *prescriptive* tell what should be done. How close we stand when talking to a friend or acquaintance, how we dress for various social functions, and how we seek justice when someone has cheated us are examples of rules that guide our lives and help us know what to expect from others.

For example, in the U.S. mainstream culture, the distance to be maintained during a conversation is from six to eighteen inches unless it is an intimate relationship. Among some cultures, conversations take place within that smaller zone and standing outside that zone may be considered an insult. When relating to people of different cultures, it is crucial to determine the distance to be maintained or their comfort zone. Of course, within a culture individuals vary somewhat in their comfort zone.

Some norms are always the same while others are specific to a particular situation or setting. For example, you would usually greet a friend differently when meeting on the street, at a party, or in your home. Having an accepted standard for acting in each situation helps you to know what to expect and provides order and stability in everyday life. When this does not occur, there is confusion and annoyance. For example, being on time for an appointment is an accepted rule in the dominant U.S. culture, but not as important in some subcultures in the United States. Delaying gratification is more important among middle-class families than among working or lower classes.

MORES AND FOLKWAYS Norms are also classified in terms of their relative importance. Norms that have greater moral significance are referred to as mores (pronounced more'-ays). They are necessary for the welfare of the group and people feel very strongly about them. Violations usually result in sanctions. These social rules include taboos against theft, public nudity, first cousins marrying, and sexual relations among close kin.

Folkways are norms having less moral significance and govern everyday behavior. This would include behavior that is customary and generally accepted, such as being quiet during a sermon, a lecture, or at the theater. The use of a cell phone in a restaurant is often annoying to others. Breaking a folkway is mildly upsetting to others and involves only minor consequences. This behavior may be termed rude or inappropriate.

With values and beliefs, behavior represents the *real* norms which may differ from *ideal* norms. Sometimes a particular behavior representing the real norm is so common that the ideal norm changes to narrow the gap. Other times, enough people are so upset with the common behavior that they try to force others to change. Some people believe that the ideal value of equality and equal opportunity for all is still being denied in subtle ways to many members of racial minorities, women, and individuals with disabilities. In the last few decades, major efforts have brought about many changes in practices.

SOCIAL CONTROL Society uses various methods to pressure its members and its institutions to conform to its norms. Conformity can be limiting but also provides predictability and a basis for safety. Some norms are so vital to a society that they become laws, are enforced, and offenders are punished.

There are many sanctions, both formal and informal. Rewards and punishments are used to influence behavior. The use of grades in school represents a formal reward or punishment while a car bumper sticker saying "my child is an honor roll student" is an informal reward for a specific achievement.

TABLE 1.1	Social Controls	
	Formal Sanctions	**Informal Sanctions**
Positive	Good Grades	Smile
	Awards, Medals	Complement, Bumper Sticker Message
	Monetary	Cheers
Negative	Retention or Demotion	Frown
	Expulsion	Humiliation
	Jail or Juvenile Hall	Belittling

As soon as children develop a conscience, a sense of guilt occurs when they behave contrary to their values and beliefs. The extent to which a sense of guilt affects behavior is discussed in the next chapter. Some people resist a particular temptation to deviate because they do not want to be embarrassed by others seeing their inappropriate behavior. Ideally, individuals internalize their cultural norms, making them a part of their personal beliefs and code of behavior. This means that their feelings and actions in a situation will be based more on their own value system and less on external forces.

MATERIAL CULTURE AND TECHNOLOGY   Material culture refers to the tangible objects that reflect the values and norms of a society as well as its technology. Scientists use resources from the physical environment to invent tools, machines, medicines, and materials that change people's lives. Because technological progress is one of our recognized values, we like to think that these inventions and discoveries have improved our lives and even extended life for many. However, this is not always true. Changes in the ozone layer and smog have resulted from technology. Industrial wastes pollute our waterways affecting fish, wildlife, and the health of humans.

Subcultures

Subcultures are formed when groups of individuals have certain patterns of behavior or characteristics that set them apart from the major culture. These differences can be based on race, ethnicity, religion, national origin, age, geographical area, occupation, socioeconomic status, or sexual orientation. Sometimes people judge individuals in a group only in terms of the characteristics of that group, ignoring the fact that they are members of other groups and society at large.

Groups such as the homeless or welfare recipients are particularly vulnerable to stereotypes. The stereotypes of alcoholic men and bag ladies are far from true for many homeless. Today one-third of all the homeless are families with children. To say that welfare recipients are lazy, or could get a job if they would try, can be hurtful and far from the truth. With the downsizing of industry and business failures, many parents have lost their jobs and are unable to earn enough money for housing and other essentials for their families.

The dominant culture in the United States has been white, northern European, and often Protestant. This group has most of the power, wealth, and privileges. The United States has many minority groups. The subcultures or minority groups often represent the disadvantaged in U.S. society. Some groups, like the descendants of the Mayflower, are not treated as a minority. When sociologists refer to minority groups, they usually refer to those groups with less economic or political power or that, in general, have little power. This hierarchy of groups often is a source of conflict. Tensions often occur around religion and ethnicity. Sometimes the strong beliefs of a subgroup are accompanied with such hatred or disapproval of opposing subgroups that violence ensues. The American Civil War is one example.

Some hatred results in the genocide or deliberate killing of a group of people. During World War II, Nazi Germany's extermination of six million European Jews and members of other minorities is one example. In the United States, the Native Americans were victims of genocide in the nineteenth century. In 1800, the Native American population was approximately 600,000; in 1850 it was reduced to 250,000 because of warfare with the cavalry, disease, and forced relocation to inhospitable environments (Schaefer, 2002).

Counterculture

Individuals or small groups of people who strongly disagree with the establishment have always existed. Their ideas and behavior often provoke members of mainstream society. Their differing values are usually reflected in their music, dress, and general lifestyle. Some adolescents, in their search for a personal philosophy, join a counterculture, usually for a brief period of time.

Other countercultures represent all ages. The Ku Klux Klan and other white supremacist groups are active today. They promote violence and hatred against Catholic, Jewish, and nonwhite members of society in order to spread and protect what they call "real American values."

High Culture and Popular Culture

The word *culture* comes from the same Latin root that the word *cultivate* does. Culture is defined both as 'cultivation' and 'the act of developing by education, discipline, and training.' High culture includes classical painting, literature, music, and dance. These complex art forms require study in order to understand and appreciate them. When referring to a person as "cultured," it indicates that this individual has cultivated the "finer" things in life. Not everyone has access to this process, which is more available to the elite.

Popular culture refers to the ways of life for the majority of the population, who usually have a lower social standing than the elite. The art forms of ordinary people are known as folk art. These artists usually have no formal training. If one wanted to put a value judgment on high culture art forms versus popular culture art or mass-produced items, there would be disagreement even within the same group.

In the United States and other technological societies, many cultural objects or products are created, mass-produced, mass-distributed, and mass-consumed (Hall and Neitz, 1993). These objects compete with works of the individual artist or artisan. Mass culture includes information and ideas communicated through the media, reaching large numbers of people at the same time and affecting their tastes and purchases.

In general, when the term *culture* is used in this book and by sociologists, it refers to the ways of life of all members. This includes differences within individual groups in a culture.

Multicultural or Anti-Bias Environment

In the past, U.S. society promoted the idea of immigrants coming to this country and eventually blending into one great society. George Washington, the first president, believed that future immigrants would learn the ways of this new nation and become "one people" (Gray, 1991). However, our culture stressed Anglo-European values,

The Many Faces of America

No single race or ethnic group will ultimately be in the majority in the United States, so the next generation will need "to move beyond the injustice, intolerance, resentment, and anger that has been such weighty baggage in United States history" (Children of 2010, Washington and Andrews, 1998).

law, and norms. Our institutions were and still are based on British traditions. Instead of melting into one culture, the pressure has always been to become anglicized. Social status and opportunities favored the British, followed by descendants of northern Europeans. Proponents of a multicultural view call this Eurocentrism.

A multicultural environment supports the understanding and valuing of all cultures. Each culture is given equal opportunity for support and success in institutions—educational, economic, and political. More broadly speaking, a multicultural environment demands equal valuing and opportunity for all individuals regardless of race, ethnicity, gender, age, physical ableness, and mental or emotional ability.

Another approach to providing an environment in which each individual is accepted, valued, and supported is termed anti-bias. In an anti-bias environment, each child has a right to develop a positive self-image, respecting his or her gender, race, ethnicity, religion, physical ableness, and mental or emotional ability. Each child should value and respect those who differ in any of these categories. Children should earn that judging someone on the basis of one of these traits is prejudice and damaging to all. Children and adults should stand up against bias and prejudicial treatment of others (Derman-Sparks, 1991, see Chapter 7).

AFFIRMATIVE ACTION   Affirmative action was initiated in the early 1960s by the Kennedy administration to give equal opportunity to disadvantaged groups for jobs and special educational programs. Under the G.I. bill, initiated during World War II, college education was funded for veterans of all races. Many African American men and women earned a college degree, but did not find appropriate employment. The affirmative action law required employers and college admission officers to solicit applications from all races, ethnic groups, and both genders. The selection process and future promotion processes were supportive of minorities. In recent years, the courts have rejected a quota system that requires the hiring or acceptance in programs of the best minority applicants rather than the best applicant. The law supports preferential treatment if the minority individual is qualified or sometimes even qualifiable for the job or educational program. For example, some minority medical school applicants with lower scores than their nonminority counterparts have been accepted into the program. In the early 1990s, the quota system was hotly debated and accused by many as leading to reverse discrimination. In 1996, California voters passed the California Civil Rights Initiative that prohibits any program that gives preference to women and minorities in college admissions, hiring, promotion, or in government contracts. In 1998, voters in Washington State also passed an anti-affirmative measure.

Social Classes in the United States

It is a myth that the United States is a classless society. Various groups of people have unequal amounts of the wealth, power, education, and resources. Their socioeconomic status (SES) is affected by ancestry, income, education, occupation, and gender, as well as talent and hard work. However, the lines for social classes are somewhat blurred. There is mobility for some families or individuals, especially within and from the middle class. This is usually accomplished through education and hard work, but on occasion by a successful idea, invention, investment, or having the winning lottery ticket. There are many success stories of athletes, computer entrepreneurs, jazz musicians, rock stars, or famous authors who grew up in poverty. An example of the latter is Frank McCourt, author of *Angela's Ashes*, who grew up in dire poverty in Ireland. The book and subsequent movie were based on a story of his childhood.

It is also true that status inconsistences exist, especially in the middle of the class system. One may have high power at work, such as that of a top level bureaucrat, but receive low pay and have moderate status outside of work. Perhaps a member of the clergy would have high prestige in the community but relatively low pay.

Most individuals and families in the United States fall into one of four broad classes: upper class, middle class, working class, or lower class. Levine and Levine (1996) diagram the social classes that are generally used to represent social stratification in the United States (Figure 1.2). The upper-upper class represents about 1 percent of the population, with much of their wealth and their position in society inherited (Rossides, 1997). Those in the lower-upper class (2 percent) are the newly rich who have earned income as their primary source of wealth. They are not fully accepted in the world of the old rich or "blue bloods."

The middle class represents about 56 percent of the population. The upper-middle class members (22 percent) have higher paying and more prestigious jobs and more schooling than do members of the lower-middle class (34 percent). They are affluent, hard-working, and value achievement. The lower-middle class families earn less but have many of the same values. Most middle-class families have social advantages and good-quality living standards. The working-class members comprise about 41 percent of our population. The upper working class (32 percent) represents lower-paid white-collar workers, skilled tradespersons, factory workers, and other hourly workers. The lower working class (18 percent) has mostly unskilled laborers. They live at or below the official poverty threshold.

A growing number of families who were part of the lower working class are now identified by many as the underclass (Benson, 1997; Blau, 1992). This includes many ethnic minority families who have fallen into poverty (Children's Defense Fund, 1997). Most underclass families are on welfare or government assistance, have marginal or no housing, lack adequate health care and nutrition, and may be involved with drugs and/or crime. Both homeless and itinerant families are a growing part of this category. These families are harder to support because of their mobility and inadequate attention from society.

The economic growth from 1999 to 2000 was the largest single-year increase ever recorded (www.bea.doc.gov). In 1999, over 47 percent of family income went to the wealthiest one-fifth of the families while approximately 4 percent went to the poorest one-fifth of the families. The top 5 percent of the population in 1998 had a yearly average income of $246,846, with many individuals' income consid-

FIGURE **1.2**   **SOCIAL CLASS STRUCTURE IN THE UNITED STATES**

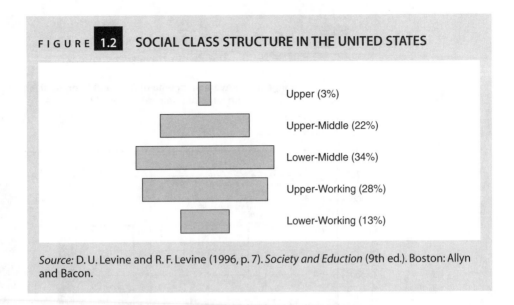

Upper (3%)

Upper-Middle (22%)

Lower-Middle (34%)

Upper-Working (28%)

Lower-Working (13%)

Source: D. U. Levine and R. F. Levine (1996, p. 7). *Society and Eduction* (9th ed.). Boston: Allyn and Bacon.

erably higher (Children's Defense Fund, 2000). In 2000, the median income for a family with children was $53,286 (U.S. Bureau of Census 2002).

Over the last twenty years (1979–1999), the income in constant dollars for the wealthiest one-fifth of U.S. families rose 42 percent, the middle one-fifth gained 11 percent, and the poorest one-fifth actually lost 4 percent. This widening of the economic gap has not always been the case. Between 1949 and 1979, the economic growth was shared more equally: incomes for families from all economic groups more than doubled (see Figure 1.3).

Family Characteristics and Options for Children

The conditions that help determine a family's social status also affect their children's options in life. Ancestry, wealth, education, race, ethnicity, and family form help to determine children's choices. For example, the family's living conditions, its access to adequate health care and quality child care, nutritious or essential foods, and the type and years of education for its children are all affected by family resources such as available money. Of course, children also play a role in their socialization and opportunities in life. Temperament, talents, hard work, and other traits affect children's relationships with others and, consequently, their opportunities.

Upper Class and Lower Class

A child who is born into a family of either extreme wealth or poverty is likely to carry on with that tradition as an adult. These conditions affect the child's self-image, future schooling, adult occupation, and income. The wealth of approximately half

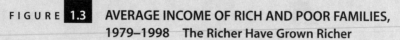

FIGURE **1.3**   **AVERAGE INCOME OF RICH AND POOR FAMILIES,
1979–1998   The Richer Have Grown Richer**

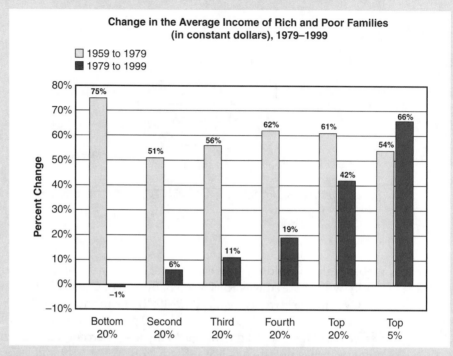

Note: The Census Bureau adjusted these figures for inflation using an inflation measure, called the CPIU-X1, which is more conservative than the official inflation measure. If the figure had been adjusted using the official measure of inflation, they would have shown deeper losses or smaller gains.

Source: U.S. Department of Commerce, Bureau of the Census, Historical Income Tables, at http:/www.census.gov/hhes/income/histinc/f03.html
Calculations by Children's Defense Fund.

of the individuals with hundreds of millions of dollars is due primarily to inheritance (Thrurow, 1987; Queenan, 1989). Family heritage, etiquette, established standards of behavior, and proper schooling are stressed. Children of upper-class families most often attend special private schools, including prestigious colleges or universities. They compete with children from similar backgrounds. Their education, often liberal arts, prepares them for high-paying prestigious jobs that are secured often by their family and school connections. Their careers frequently are in a family enterprise or in public service.

Poverty for many families is also passed on from one generation to the next. Many of these children at some period in their lives lack adequate food, health care, shelter, or appropriate play opportunities. In addition, language modeling and limited environmental experiences often put these children at risk for not doing well in school. Head Start and similar high-quality comprehensive infant–toddler and preschool programs help those young children and families who are fortunate enough to attend; even so, a high percentage of poor children drop out of school before graduating from high school. Those who remain in school often study courses related to manual and semi-skilled jobs. Only a small percentage attend college.

Another problem for the poor is a prevailing negative attitude in society toward them and resentment by some citizens about tax money spent on entitlement programs. One of our U.S. values is equal opportunity for all. If you work hard, you can succeed. People with lower incomes usually see poverty as caused by the socioeconomic system (Schaefer, 2002). However, some poor believe that their personal shortcomings are responsible for their condition in society. This low self-image is damaging to adults and their children (Sennett and Cobb, 1973). Male and female roles in such families are traditional.

Middle Class and Working Class

Middle-class families vary in the types of behavior they teach their children and the amount of education that they believe is important. Most parents have gained their status through education and hard work. Relationships are more often egalitarian with husband and wife in partnership in their roles. White-collar workers, who have more education, income, and status than working-class parents, usually encourage their children to develop thinking skills, to question or evaluate rules, and consider the intentions of those involved. Guidance is more through reasoning rather than physical punishment. Middle-income family values are similar to public school values and many parents are involved in and/or support the schools.

Working-class families often differ in some of their values from those of their children's school, but will participate on specific projects to support it (Barbour and Barbour, 2001). Working-class families have close ties to the extended family and emphasize respect for elders. Patriarchal or traditional roles rather than egalitarian roles predominate unless the father is not in the home. Living for the present and issues of security and survival take precedence over delayed gratification and achievement. Working-class parents teach their children to follow the rules and obedience because these qualities are required in their jobs (Kohn, 1977). Each approach sets the stage for very different types of educational experiences and future occupations.

Underclass

Parents may be so overwhelmed with survival that they are unable to give their children the nurturance, emotional support, safe and challenging environments, and other essentials for healthy development. Most of these families are living below the poverty level. Poverty is a risk factor, especially for children. Children of families that have inadequate education, health care, and nutrition, and are socially unstable, have little hope of breaking the cycle of poverty. Only massive social support can change this.

Race and Ethnicity

Race is a biological distinction referring to skin color and general appearance. There are no pure races. A century ago, the three broad racial groups identified were Caucasian, Mongolian, and Negroid. Confusion and inconsistencies over race have increased with the growing numbers of interracial births, transracial adoptions, and immigrants with mixed racial heritage. Race is also a socially constructed label affecting status and prospects in U.S. society and elsewhere. On the other hand, **ethnicity** refers to shared cultural heritage and not to biology. A person may identify with a group on the basis of national origin, culture, race, or religion. Ethnicity is less visible than racial difference. This contributes to the fact that stratification along racial lines is more resistant to change than along ethnic lines (Schaefer, 2002).

A Jewish student was offended to read the word Jewish *used to describe one of a child's four grandparents of diverse racial/ethnic backgrounds. She thought* Jewish *only referred to a religious affiliation.*

Each ethnic group has some differences in its approach to life and the socialization of children. Differences can be seen in choices of food, housing or neighborhood. Its members also differ in how they relate to each other and family, how they perceive time, and their goals for children. Some members of an ethnic group become "Americanized" or take on some of the values and behaviors of the dominant culture. Their degree of assimilation into the dominant culture varies. It is important to avoid labeling individuals according to their ethnicity, although an understanding and appreciation of an ethnic group is valuable.

Throughout U.S. history, Anglo Americans have acquired most of the wealth and power. In 2000, White Americans and Asian Americans earned far more money, had fewer families living in poverty, a lower unemployment rate, and completed more years of education than Hispanic Americans and Black Americans. Only the median family income was available for Native Americans (U.S. Bureau of Census, 2002).

Gender

Women's participation in the workforce steadily increased during the last half of the twentieth century, but their social position as a group remains lower than that of men. Their income is less, they accumulate less wealth, and their occupations have lower prestige (Bernard, 1981; Lengermann and Wallace, 1985). In 1997, women accounted for 46 percent of the workforce but held very few of the higher-

TABLE 1.2	Social and Economic Profiles of Selected Racial and Hispanic (of any race) Origin Populations for 2000			
Characteristics	Median Family Income	Percentage of Families Below Poverty Level	Percentage of Unemployment Rate[1]	Percentage with Bachelor's Degree Age 25 and Older
White	$53,256	6.9	2.3	26.1
Asian American	NA (2000) $49 105 (1998)	8.8[2]	2.6	43.9
Hispanic any race	$35,054	18.5	NA (2000) 5.3 (1998)	10.6
Black	$34,192	19.1	5.0	16.5
Native American	NA (2000) $21,619 (1998)	NA	NA	NA

NA: not available
[1] Civilians 16 years and older in labor force
[2] Native Hawaiian and other Pacific Islanders included
Source: U.S. Census Bureau, *Statistical Abstract of the United States, 2002,* Tables 35, 36, 37. *Statistical Abstract of the United States, 1998,* Tables 51, 52, 54, 55.

paying jobs and most of the lower-paying jobs. For example, women represented only 10 percent of the engineers, 17 percent of the dentists, 26 percent of the physicians, and 29 percent of the computer systems analysts. On the other hand, 99 percent of all dental hygienists, 98 percent of secretaries, 97 percent of child-care workers, and 96 percent of receptionists were women (U.S. Bureau of Census, 1998, 418–421). According to a recent study of the *Fortune 1000* largest corporations, women held only 9 percent of the seats on their boards of directors, and sixteen of these corporations did not have one single woman on their board (Catalyst, 1999).

In 1999, according to the median weekly earnings of full-time employees, women earned approximately 77 percent of what men earned. Women are in far greater danger of poverty than men, and some women also suffer from racial and ethnic stratification (U.S. Bureau of Labor Statistics News, 2000). This is why the increase in single-parent female-headed families has resulted in more children living in poverty.

Ways Children Are Socialized

Children learn through all of their senses—sight, hearing, touch, smell, and taste—as well as through their cognitive capabilities. How parents help children learn acceptable ways of feeling, thinking, and behaving are discussed in Chapter 6 under child rearing.

Affective methods involve relationships. The most basic is the attachment process, discussed in Chapter 2. How children interpret the responses of others to them affects their self-image, feelings about others, and their values. This influences their responses to those with whom they have a relationship and their basic feelings of trust or distrust of others. Children's emotions also affect their responses to other socialization methods.

Operant methods involve actions and reactions. Children's actions are followed by a response from others. If the action is followed by a favorable response, the likelihood of this behavior being repeated is increased; if the action is ignored or the response unfavorable, it is decreased. The principles of reward, punishment, and extinction are fundamental to this method.

Observational methods involve children observing the behavior of others with its consequences and processing these actions for their future use. This means they have to be able to see its applicability in a different situation. Children model behavior that they believe elicits a desirable outcome. The behavior may be prosocial or antisocial. Television cartoon heroes are often seen using violence to achieve their goal.

Cognitive methods involve thinking. Children learn from being told what to do. This is more effective if it is followed by a reason. A child's level of reasoning or interpreting cause and effect depends on age and experience. Giving a child the requirements for reaching an appropriate goal helps the child understand and succeed. An example would be for a teacher to state the requirements for an A on a project (see Chapters 5 and 10).

Sociocultural methods involve conforming. Children experience various types of pressure from their family, community, and social groups to conform or behave according to their norms. Significant people have great influence on children's actions, but so do others around the individual. In addition, the traditions, rituals, and symbols of the culture help the individual to conform to sociocultural expectations.

An Ecological Model

The ecological approach to human development and socialization provides a broad perspective for understanding human behavior and finding solutions rather than a simple cause–effect approach. For example, in the case of parental child abuse, one looks not only at the parent–child interactions, but at the characteristics of the neighborhood or community and also at social policies that might influence abusive behavior. A neighborhood and its support systems can contribute or deter child maltreatment. When a neighborhood has incidents of violence, such as drive-by shootings or fighting, the neighborhood would be assessed as high-risk for child abuse. Policies that provide parenting classes for at-risk parents reduce the incidences of abusive behavior. Social policies that affect employment or health care options, for example, not only affect the children's quality of life but increase or minimize stresses on parents.

The ecological or systems approach to human development grew out of the work of European gestalt psychologists. They emphasized the unity and the integration of the whole person. Gestalt psychologists looked at the whole person adapting to the environment rather than the behaviorist's approach of studying the different parts of human behavior (stimuli and responses) reacting to the environment.

Human ecology studies the relationships between human beings and their environment. According to ecological or systems theories, human development is affected by:

1. the person, the person's contributions to a particular situation or stage of development, and the results;
2. the environment or the settings that are available to the child in a particular situation or stage of life, and what they contribute. This would include the family, child-care facility, school, neighborhood, and community;
3. the reciprocal nature of the interaction between the person and the environment.

Bronfenbrenner developed a model for studying human interactions and their relationships (1979, 1989, 1995). The model is like a system of Russian nesting dolls with the child in the center. Human development is studied in natural settings rather than in artificial or laboratory settings. The environment includes the immediate or smaller settings, the interaction of these settings, and larger settings, including the culture. In each of these structures, three dimensions are present:

1. the physical space and materials;
2. human relationships;
3. individual or joint activities.

Bronfenbrenner divided the environment into four structural levels. The first structure, the **microsystem** (*micro* means "small"), includes the activities and relationships of the child and the significant people in a particular place. This includes the family and home, teachers and children in a child-care setting or school, peers, an area in the community, such as a neighborhood or a library, and the media, which include television, videos, movies, books, magazines, computers, and the Internet. Bronfenbrenner places the media in the exosystem because it is in not a small interactive setting, but Berns (2001) views it as part of the microsystem because it is such a powerful socializer. Children spend so much time in front of the TV, experiencing so many different ideas and values, that television becomes a powerful influence on their attitudes and behavior. Even computers, with interactive software and the exchange of e-mails, affect social relationships as well as provide information and entertainment (Berns, 2001).

The second basic structure, the **mesosystem** (*meso*, a combining form meaning, "in the middle"), includes the interrelationships between or among two or more microsystems. For example, interactions of the child's home and the school, or the school and the community library, or social agencies and the family, all affect the socialization of the child. If the parents support the child's teacher by supervising their child's homework, valuing the curriculum, or cooperating with the teacher, both the child's academic performance and value of the educational experience will be increased. If parents do not take time to participate in the child's school experience, or downgrade its importance, the child will not perform as well and will pick up the parents' attitudes about school (see Chapter 9).

The third basic structure, the **exosystem** (*exo*, "outside"), includes settings where the children are not present, but their relationships, activities, and policies affect the lives of the children. Certainly the parent's workplace and the working conditions affect children. Other exosystems include school boards, city councils, community services such as sanitation and garbage control, traffic regulations, and regulatory agencies such as the Federal Communication Commission.

The fourth structure, the **macrosystem** (*macro*, "large"), consists of the society and its ideology in which the child grows up. Society refers to the group at large and to groups within this larger setting such as one's cultural group, socioeconomic class, and ethnic, racial, or religious groups. A macrosystem directs how exosystems, mesosystems, and microsystems shall interact. The values, attitudes, and beliefs of society and its subgroups affect the lives of children and their families. A change in the macrosystem will cause adaptations in the other structures. For example, changes caused by economic conditions, war, technology, new roles for women and men, or legal rights affect children, their families, and all groups or institutions.

Agents of Socialization

Social agents within a society help children acquire the attitudes, values, skills, and behaviors that they and society consider desirable and/or appropriate. Children learn society's rules by observing and interacting with people. Some messages sent to children are intentional but children also receive many unintentional messages.

Children don't want to be told, they want to be shown. It is difficult to undo the effects of one [un]wise action.

Family, Child Care, School, Peers, Media, Government, and Community

Although there are numerous settings in which socialization occurs, the **family** is the most important. In the beginning, it may be the child's whole social world. The family is responsible for bringing children into society and for helping them learn how to live in society and become healthy productive members. The child's experiences within the family are crucial. For example, a recent study showed that the importance of the mother in the mother–infant attachment process was far greater than the child-care experiences (NICHD Early Child Care Research Network, 1997). However, characteristics of the child-care experiences did affect the child in many other ways.

Children in **child care** experience an expanding social world quite early. Infants in high-quality centers are able to develop strong secondary attachments to their consistent caregivers along with their strong maternal attachment (Clarke-Stewart, Allhusen, and Clements, 1995; Honig, 1993). Experiences in child-care settings influence children's behavior, attitudes, values, and identity at all ages, but especially in the younger years. Rules, discipline, activities, and degrees of acceptance in child care vary to some extent from those within the family. It is important for parents and teachers to work together to reinforce desired responses and feelings. Children in child care are with adults and children from different backgrounds. These experiences can help them learn to value those who differ from them in some way and, at the same time, develop a positive self-identity.

Schools teach children a wide range of information and skills but, beyond this, they teach important cultural values of society. Schools reflect the values of the community as well as the larger society. Ideas, values, norms, and discipline may vary significantly from the family. Some children learn to function under two sets of rules and expectations. Because society is changing so rapidly, schools cannot know exactly what skills or information children will need for the future. Most agree that children will need to be flexible and adaptable to cope with changes. Is a more general education preferable to a more specialized one? Schools continue to play an important role in expanding the child's experiences with social diversity.

The **peer group** allows children to relate to and learn from those close to their own age and interests in settings relatively free from adult supervision. Children learn about themselves and how to understand and relate to others and to society at large. Peers help shape a child's self-esteem.

Mass media bring information and entertainment to vast audiences. Advertisers believe that this has an effect on individuals' behavior. As mentioned earlier in this chapter, television is an important socializing agent because of the number of children who view television daily for one or more hours. Television provides entertainment and information in many areas including gender roles, problem solving, and events in the world. The print media, the computer, the Internet, movies, videos, and music also affect children's views about themselves and the world.

Government policies on the local, state, and national levels directly and indirectly affect conditions for children and families through the legislative, administrative, and judicial systems. Government support for families, child-care facilities, schools, health care, social services, libraries, and parks and recreational programs affects what services or activities are available for many children. How successfully children are protected from violence, environmental hazards, and unsafe foods and drugs depends on laws, regulatory agencies, and moneys allocated for education, prevention, and enforcement. Economic conditions and foreign policies also impact conditions for families.

The **neighborhood and community** at large can facilitate or limit the child's experiences and affect the child's overall growth and development. The kinds and quality of resources and activities available for children and families are crucial. Health care, libraries, parks and recreational programs, transportation, and schools as well as protection from crime, disaster, and pollution are a few essential services. The community and neighborhood send messages to children through their actions. Children may learn that they are very important or just tolerated. Conditions in society under which children live affect their growth, development, and socialization. Some conditions support healthy growth and development while others do not. Future chapters will explore, in more depth, these important agents of socialization.

Religion

Religion is part of the macrosystem, which affects the microsystem, mesosystem, and exosystem. Religion affects the values, beliefs and morals of individuals, families, and communities. Religious beliefs influence gender roles, sexual behavior, marriage, divorce, birth rates, and child-rearing practices. Religious doctrine may prescribe appropriate dress, diet, alcohol consumption, health care, and social interactions. Religion helps its followers to understand or accept devastating events or crises in their lives.

Religion gives identity to one's life. Rituals and formal ceremonial activities help people to celebrate a supreme being and remind them of their responsibilities. Rituals include prayers, tithing, handling sacred objects, wearing certain clothing, eating or avoiding certain foods, or fasting at specific times. Each religion has its special holidays to celebrate important events.

Religion also plays a role in a nation's politics and policies. In the United States, Christian Protestant ethics are still a part of the nation's value system. For example, an ideal person is individualistic, thrifty, self-sacrificing, efficient with time, strong in personal responsibility, and productive. The United States continues to have more people of diverse cultures and religions, and their values are gradually being reflected in the national values.

The six world religions, Christianity, Islam, Judaism, Hinduism, Buddhism, and Confucianism represent approximately three-quarters of all humanity. In the United States 58 percent of the population report that they are Protestant, 25 percent Catholic, 2 percent Jewish, 2 percent Latter-Day Saints, and 1 percent Orthodox. According to a Gallop Poll in 2000, 68 percent of Americans said they were members of a church or synagogue, about the same percentage for the last sixty years.

Civil religion is not a specific doctrine but incorporates many traditional religious beliefs into the political system of a secular society. Quasi-religious loyalty binds one to country, elicits patriotism, and promotes citizenship. Most people in the United States consider their way of life to be moral. After the terrorist attacks of September 11, 1999, displays of patriotism escalated. Flags were everywhere as was the message, "God Bless America."

Childhood: Yesterday and Today

Societies view the first twelve years of life differently. In past centuries, the idea of childhood as a special stage of life did not exist. By the 1800s, children in the United States and Europe shared many of the burdens of the adults such as working long hours in mills and factories. Children of the very poor were often indentured servants. The novel *Oliver Twist,* by Charles Dickens (1837–1839), depicts conditions for some children in London in the early nineteenth century.

Even today, childhood in the developing nations is very different from childhood in the industrialized nations. In the poorer nations, children work for survival. Many young children are selling items in the markets and on the streets. In some countries, such as Thailand, child prostitution thrives. In North America, it is estimated that 80 percent of children in the sex trade are victims of abuse (Lobe, 1999).

In response to the detrimental conditions affecting many children in the world, the United Nations, after ten years of work by over forty countries, passed the **Convention on the Rights of the Child** in 1989. This Convention (like a treaty) contains forty-three articles on the basic human rights of all children. One of its articles is *the right to primary education for all children including girls* (UNICEF, 2002). This is not occurring today for many children, especially girls, in a number of developing nations (Lobe, 1998). In 2002, every country, except for the United States and Somalia (which does not have a legal government), has ratified the UN Convention, making its forty-three articles the law of their land (UNICEF, 2002). This does not mean that the articles are always followed.

In contrast to developing nations, the more technological societies do not need children's labor for survival. Here, childhood is considered a time for nurture and protection from adult burdens. Ideally, this allows time for biological and emotional maturity and for the necessary education required for future technological jobs. Unfortunately, this is not true for all children in these societies.

Childhood: A Time to Play

This 4-year-old is swinging from a tree limb in a botanical garden. For most children in the developed nations, like the United States, childhood is a time to play and to learn.

In the United States, childhood is the first twelve years of life followed by adolescence, a transitional period between childhood and adulthood. Play is valued for children, as is education. Young children learn through both. There are child labor laws protecting children. Childhood is usually considered a time for children to grow and develop in a nurturing environment. The majority of children are loved, healthy, and doing well today in the United States.

Since the 1970s, a number of changes within the family have taken place, including large numbers of mothers in the workforce and heading one-parent families. This means that more infants and young children are being cared for in child-care centers, family child-care homes, and by other people while their parents are at work. Child care costs are high. The average child-care cost for a four-year-old in an urban area is more than the average annual cost of public college in most states (Schulman, 2000).

Lifestyles in the 1970s also brought pressures for children to grow up fast (Elkind, 1988; Winn, 1977). Some of these conditions exist today. Many children come home after school to an empty house, often with the responsibility of caring for younger siblings. Nearly one in ten children ages five to eleven went home to an empty house after school one or more days every week (Children's Defense Fund, 2001). According to a Census Bureau report released in 2000, almost seven million children from seven to fourteen years of age cared for themselves after school on a regular basis, without adult supervision (Children's Defense Fund, 2001).

Today, children are exposed to information on sex and violence. With television sets in 99 percent of the homes in the United States, children view programs with messages on sexuality, violence, discrimination, quick-fix-it solutions to problems, and a view of today's world as unsafe. David Elkind (1988) labeled this the "hurried child."

The high divorce rate has burdened many children with adult problems. These children are suffering stress and grief from losing one parent in the household. Other problems associated with divorce are less income and poverty for many children and their families. Parents living in poverty have additional stresses when they attempt to provide adequate nutrition, health care, and housing for their children, and to find sufficient free time to spend with them.

Many parents, especially affluent ones, encourage their young children to read and master other academic skills. In 1994, Elkind reported that children were under stress to achieve more in school and to conform to the needs of the adults. Many children are given the responsibility of self-care for short periods of time. Elkind sees families as less child-centered than in the recent past (1994).

At the beginning of the twenty-first century, many are concerned over the pervasive violence in society and the failure of schools to teach effectively many of our children. National Goals for Education 2000 are still not met (see Chapter 8). Many children have problems in school both in learning and in their behavior. Despite special programs, a number of children do not acquire basic reading skills. *Only 31 percent of fourth graders read at or above the Proficient Level according to a national assessment (Children's Defense Fund, 2001).* Too many youths, especially minority youths, do not graduate from high school. *Only 62 percent of Hispanic students complete high school, while 89 percent of Black students and 93 percent of White students graduate. Children in the poorest families are five times more likely to drop out of high school as are students in wealthier families (Children's Defense Fund, 2001).* Parents and all citizens are being asked to assume more responsibility for all children.

The 2001 bi-partisan education reform bill made more money available for education. Efforts to reduce the class size for the first years in elementary school, to improve teacher quality, and to establish new academic standards and testing are facing tough changes due to current budget deficits. Politicians and citizens are pressuring the schools to enable all of their students to achieve high levels of competence in reading, writing, and mathematics. These levels of competence are measured at the fourth, eighth, and twelfth grades. There is much controversy over the effects of required testing and especially the use of a single test to assess competencies.

Drugs are found on elementary school grounds, approximately 135,000 guns are brought to school each day, and 100,000 children are homeless each night. Many of these homeless children are unable to attend school regularly (Children's Defense Fund, 1996, 2000). The private sector and government are working jointly to improve these conditions.

In the United States, children are more likely to be poor than are children in other industrialized countries. Children also have a greater chance of dying before their first birthday. In 1999, the United States had the largest percentage of poor children and one of the smallest percentages of children lifted out of poverty compared to twenty industrialized countries. The United States was the only one of these countries *not* to provide universal health insurance/health care, paid maternal/paternal leave at childbirth, and family allowance/child dependency grants. The

TABLE 1.3   U.S. Children: Victims of Poverty
Hungry; Lacking Basic Health Care; Homeless
16.9% of children under 18 live in poverty.
18% of children under six live in poverty.
6.6% of children live at less than half of the poverty level.
33⅓% of children will be poor at some time.
Every 44 seconds a baby is born into poverty, over 1,000,000 babies a year.
Every 4 minutes a baby is born to a mother who had no or late prenatal care.
Every minute a baby is born without health insurance.
Every 24 seconds a baby is born to an unmarried mother.
Every 37 minutes a baby is born to a mother who is not a high school graduate.

(Children's Defense Fund, *The State of America's Children Yearbook 2001* (Washinton, DC: Children's Defense Fund, 2001.)

United States ranked twenty-third among these industrialized countries in infant mortality rates (Children's Defense Fund, 2001).

There are both short- and long-term consequences for children of poverty. For some, it means their life, while for others it is hunger, inadequate diets, increased illness, decreasing learning capabilities, homelessness, unsafe neighborhoods, greater chance of drug abuse, inadequate schooling, inadequate health care, neglect or abuse, and continued poverty as adults.

War on Poverty

Under former President Johnson, a "war on poverty" was launched in 1964 to attack the problem of poverty in the United States. A formula was established for determining a poverty threshold or annual income required to sustain basic family needs. Below this poverty level, an individual or a family is entitled to certain benefits. In 1999, the poverty base line for a family of *four* in an urban area was $17,029. About 42 percent of poor children are living below half of the established poverty level (Children's Defense Fund, 2000, 2001). A few children are living in absolute poverty or under conditions that are life-threatening, such as living on the streets.

Although productivity almost doubled in thirty years, the percentage of poor children today is approximately the same as it was at the beginning of the "war on poverty." In contrast, from 1970 to 1988, poverty for senior citizens was cut in half (Vedder and Gallaway, 1990). Why can't society do at least this well for its children, whose futures and the quality of society are at risk?

To reduce poverty for children, families must be helped. This is costly, but the costs of adequate prenatal care, basic and preventive health care, and adequate nutritious food in the early years are a fraction of the costs of special education, learning disabilities, drugs, violence, early pregnancies, school dropouts, and unemployment, which will occur later in their lives (Keniston, 1977; Children's Defense Fund, 2001). For example,

- ✔ a dollar invested in good early childhood programs for low-income children saves $7.00;
- ✔ a dollar invested in immunizations against diphtheria, tetanus, and whooping cough saves $23.00;
- ✔ a dollar spent in Women's, Infants, and Children (WIC) nutritional programs saves $3.07 during a baby's first year;
- ✔ every year that a child grows up in poverty costs $9,000 in lost future productivity over the child's working life (Children's Defense Fund, 2001).

● Current Trends

American society is turning to grassroot efforts to improve conditions for children. The number of partnerships involving government, business, philanthropic groups, and citizen activists continues to grow. When each entity helps with the funding and contributes ideas from different perspectives, the method of attacking problems shifts from a competitive approach to cooperative efforts and networking.

Unless safety nets increase for poor families, the gap between the rich and the poor will continue to increase and our underclass will grow. Progress is being made to reduce the number of children without health-care insurance. The number of children eligible for programs such as Early Start and Head Start will continue to grow, so more programs will have to be established to serve these children. Current facilities cannot accommodate many children even today.

Childhood is still a valued time for children to play, grow, develop, and learn. However, many children are living with increased responsibilities and stress because of recent changes in society. Parents, professionals working with children, and citizens must find ways for all children to become healthy adults. If society fails to support its children effectively, many of them, as adults, may not be able to support themselves, their children, or their parents or those who are in their declining years.

Key Points

1. Socialization is a life-long process of learning how to behave, think, and act in each social context.
2. Children grow up in a society that is a group of people interacting in organized ways, sharing a culture, and living within specific boundaries, often the same as a nation.
3. Culture refers to a shared way of life. All cultures have their own symbols, language, values, norms, and material objects.
4. The United States is a multicultural nation. Multicultural or anti-bias programs support the understanding and valuing of all people regardless of race, ethnicity, gender, or physical or mental abilities.
5. Social class is determined by ancestry, wealth, occupation, talent, education, and effort. A family's social class has an influence on how children learn to solve problems and think, the type of education and length of schooling, and their future occupation.

6. Children are socialized by the individual actions and the interactions of the family, child-care programs, schools, peers, mass media, community, and the government.
7. Children in the United States are more likely to be poor and have a greater chance of dying before their first birthday than children in other industrialized countries.

Critical Thinking Questions

1. How do the values and beliefs of one's culture, either the dominant culture or a family's cultural group, affect a child's socialization? Reflect on your own culture and its impact on your life today.
2. To what extent does a parent's education, income, and occupation affect a child's options in life?
3. What do you think are the advantages and disadvantages of an ecological approach to child development?

Resources and References

■ Web Sites

Children's Defense Fund
   http://www.childrensdefense.org
U.S. Bureau of the Census
   http://www.census.gov/
U.S. Bureau of Labor Statistics
   http://www.bls.gov
U.S. Committee for UNICEF
Office of Public Policy and Advocacy
Full text of The Convention on the Rights of the Child
   http://www.unicef.org

■ Related Readings

Washington, V., and Andrews, J. D., Eds. (1999). *Children of 2010*. Washington, DC: National Association for the Education of Young Children.

■ References

Ainsworth, M. D. (1989). Attachments beyond infancy. *American Psychologist, 44,* 709–716.

Ainsworth, M. D., and Bowlby, J. (1991). An ethological approach to ethological development. *American Psychologist, 46,* 333–341.

Astin, A., Korn, W., Sax, L., and Mahoney, K. (1996). *The American freshman: National goals for fall 1995*. Los Angeles: U.C.L.A. Higher Education Research Institute.

Barbour, C., and Barbour, N. H. (2001). *Families, schools, and communities*. Upper Saddle River, NJ: Merrill Prentice-Hall.

Bell, D. (1973). *The coming of post-industrial society*. New York: Basic Books.

Bell, D. (1989). The third technological revolution. *Dissent, 36* (Spring), 164–176.

Beniger, J. R. (1993). The control revolution. In Albert H. Teich (Ed.), *Technology and the future,* (6th ed.), New York: St. Martin's Press.

Benson, P. (1997). *All kids are our kids*. San Francisco: Jossey-Bass.

Bernard, J. (1981). *The female world*. New York: Free Press.

Blau. J. (1992). *The visible poor: Homelessness in the United States*. New York: Oxford University Press.

Berns, R. (2001). *Child, Family, School, Community*. Fort Worth, TX: Harcourt College Publishers, Fort Worth, TX.

Bronfenbrenner, U. (1979). *The ecology of human development*. Cambridge, MA: Harvard University Press.

Bronfenbrenner, U. (1989). Ecology systems theory. In R. Vasta (Ed.), *Annals of child development* (Vol. 6). Greenwich, CT: JAI Press.

Bronfenbrenner, U. (1995). Developmental ecology through space and time: A future perspective. In P. Moen, G. H. Elder, Jr., and K. Luscher (Eds.), *Examining lives in context: Perspectives on the ecology of human development*. Washington, DC: American Psychological Association.

Catalyst. (1999). *1999 Catalyst census of women board of directors of the Fortune 1000*. New York: Author.

Children's Defense Fund. (1996). *The state of America's children: Yearbook 1996*. Washington, DC: Author.

Children's Defense Fund. (1997). *The state of America's children: Yearbook 1997*. Washington, DC: Author.

Children's Defense Fund. (2000). *The state of America's children: Yearbook 2000*. Washington, DC: Author.

Children's Defense Fund. (2001). *The state of America's children: Yearbook 2001*. Washington, DC: Author.

Clarke-Stewart, K. A., Allhusen, V. D., Clements, D. C. (1995). Nonparenting caregiving. In M. H. Bornstein (Ed.), *Handbook of parenting, 3*. Mahwah, NJ: Lawrence Erlbaum.

Derman-Sparks, L. (1991). *Anti-bias curriculum: Tools for empowering young children*. Washington, DC: National Association for the Education of Young Children.

Devine, D. (1972). *Political culture of the United States: The influence of member values on regime maintenance*. Boston: Little, Brown.

Durning, A. T. (1993). Supporting indigenous peoples. In Lester R. Brown, et al., (Eds.), *State of the world, 1993: A Worldwatch Institute report on progress toward a sustainable society*. (pp. 80–100). New York: Norton, 1993.

Elkind, D. (1988). *The hurried child: Growing up too fast too soon*. (Rev. ed.). Reading, MA: Addison-Wesley.

Elkind, D. (1994). *Ties that stress: The new family imbalance*. Cambridge, MA: Harvard University Press.

Etzioni, A. (1991). Too many rights, too few responsibilities. *Society, 48*(2), 41–48.

Gray, P. (1991). Who's America? *Time,* 137, no. 27 (July 8): 12–17.

Hall, J. R., and Neitz, M. J. (1993). *Culture: Sociological perspectives.* Englewood Cliffs, NJ: Prentice-Hall.

Hollander, P. (1995). We are all (sniffle, sniffle) victims now. *Wall Street Journal,* January 18, A14.

Honig, A. S. (1993). Mental health for babies: What do theory and research teach us? *Young Children,* 48(3), 69–76.

Keniston, K. (1977). *All our children: The American family under pressure.* New York: Harcourt Brace Jovanovich.

Kohn, M. L. (1977). *Class and conformity: A study in values.* (2nd ed.). Homewood, IL: Dorsey Press.

Lengermann, P. M., and Wallace, R. A. (1985). *Gender in America: Gender control and gender change.* Englewood Cliffs, NJ: Prentice-Hall.

Levine, D. U., and Levine, R. F. (1996). *Society and education* (9th ed.). Boston: Allyn and Bacon.

Lobe, T. Awad. (1998). *A right world.* Columbus, Ohio: Ohio Youth Advocate Program Village Press.

Macionis, J. J. (1997). *Sociology.* (6th ed.). Upper Saddle River, NJ: Prentice-Hall.

Mackay, J. P., Hill, B. D., and Buckler, J. (1988). *A history of world societies.* (22nd ed.).

Massey, D. S., and Denton, N. A. (1993). *American apartheid: Segregation and the making of the underclass.* Cambridge, MA: Harvard University Press.

NICHD Early Child Care Research Network. (1997). The effects of infant child care on infant–mother attachment security: Results of the NICHD study of early child care. *Child Development,* 68(5), 860–879.

Queenan, J. (1989). The many paths to riches. *Forbes,* 144(9), 149.

Regensburger, L. (2001). The American family: A changing nation. Farmington Hills, MI: Gale Group.

Rossides, D. W. (1997). *Social stratification: The interplay of class, race, and gender,* 2nd ed. Upper Saddle River, NJ: Prentice-Hall.

Sax, L., Astin, A., Korn, W., and Mahoney, K. (2002). *The American freshman: National goals for 1995–2001.* Los Angeles: U.C.L.A. Higher Education Research Institute.

Schaefer, R. T. (2002). *Sociology: A brief introduction.* (4th ed.). New York: McGraw-Hill.

Schulman, K. (2000). *Issue brief: The high cost of child care puts quality child care out of the reach for many families.* Washington, DC: Children's Defense Fund.

Sennett, R., and Cobb, J. (1973). *The hidden injuries of class.* New York: Vintage.

Shaw, D. S., and Vondra, J. I. (1995). Infant attachment security and maternal predictors of early behaviors: A longitudinal study of low-income families. *Journal of Abnormal Child Psychology, 23,* 335–335.

Sullivan, T. (1995). *Sociology: Concepts and Application for a diverse world.* 4th ed. Boston, MA: Allyn and Bacon.

Taylor, J. (1991). "Don't blame me: The new culture of victimization." *New York Magazine,* June 3, 28–34.

Thrurow, L. (1987). A surge in equality. *Scientific American, 256*(5), 30–37.

United Nations. (2002). *Convention on the Rights of the Child,* passed in 1989. New York: UNICEF.

U.S. Bureau of Census. (1993). Washington, DC: U.S. Government Printing Office.

U.S. Bureau of Census. (1998). *Statistical abstract of the United States, 1998.* Washington, DC: U.S. Government Printing Office.

U.S. Bureau of Census. (2002). *Statistical abstract of the United States,* 2002, Tables 35, 36, 37. Washington, DC: U.S. Government Printing Office.

U.S. Bureau of Labor Statistics. (1998). *Employment status of the civilian population by race, sex, age, and Hispanic origin.* Washington, DC: U.S. Government Printing Office.

U.S. Bureau of Labor Statistics News. (2000, May). *Highlights of women's earnings in 1999.* Washington, DC: U.S. Department of Labor.

Vedder, R., and Gallaway, L. (1990). Youthanasia: The plight of the rising generation. *The Family in America* (July).

Ware, C., Panikkar, K., and Romain, J. (1966). *The twentieth century, History of mankind: Cultural and scientific development,* vol 6, pp. 99–100. New York: Oxford University Press.

Washington, V., and Andrews, J. (Eds.). (1998). *Children of 2010.* Washington, DC: National Association for the Education of Young Children.

Williams, R. M., Jr. (1970). *American society: A sociological interpretation* (3d ed., p. 70). New York: Alfred A. Knopf.

Winn, M. (1977). *The plug on drug.* New York: Bantam.

The Family Shapes the Child

2

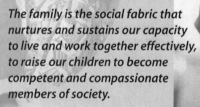

The family is the social fabric that nurtures and sustains our capacity to live and work together effectively, to raise our children to become competent and compassionate members of society.

— Urie Bronfenbrenner (1979)

*C*hapter 2 is devoted to children growing up in the family. Understanding the roles of the family in society and in the lives of children are basic to exploring different family structures and the healthy functioning of families.

Every child is born into a family, whether it consists of mother and child or includes a father, siblings, or other members. The infant's entire universe is centered in the family, which provides food, clothing, and shelter essential for physical survival, and confers legal and social status. The family plays an equally crucial role in laying the child's psychic foundations. It transforms the newborn, a biological organism, into a member of society and assures the continuity of that society.

In primitive societies, the family performs all these necessary tasks. In complex societies, like that of the United States, other institutions assume or share some of these tasks. An institution is an organized system of human relationships with its own set of values, established ways of behaving, and responsibilities. The family has its own set of norms and responsibilities. These institutions are also referred to as social agencies or social agents.

Today's families share many tasks with other institutions, such as economic production, health care, education, religious training, recreation, and even physical sustenance for family members. How well children function in these settings is affected by the involvement and relationship of the parent or parents with the children's health-care professionals, teachers, friends, and community workers (e.g., the mesosystem). How do parents and teachers work together? Do they agree on common goals for the child's education and socialization? Do the children's friends play at their home and are they included in some family activities? Do parents support their children's recreational programs with time, money, and/or interest? The interrelationships between the family and other institutions are as important in children's development as are the activities and relationships within the family (Bronfenbrenner, 1979).

How Forces in Society Affect Family Life

The quality of life and the interactions within the family are affected by other segments of society. How the family raises its children is influenced by a large range of values and beliefs within society, but particularly those of its ethnic and racial grouping (e.g., the macrosystem). For example, some ethnic groups teach their children that the needs of the group or the family come before the individual's interests. Others stress the needs of the individual, personal worth, and freedom over the interests of the group. Most families try to meet both individual and family needs.

The family's socioeconomic status (e.g., the macrosystem) affects the options children have. The conditions of parents' employment (e.g., the exosystem) such as work hours, medical and dental plans, and income affect the time and care parents are able to give their children. The quality, affordability, and availability of child care, schools, health care, transportation systems, libraries, parks, and, indeed, all of the community's resources influence the child's growth and development and overall quality of life. These topics are discussed in detail in later chapters.

In modern society, governmental policies at local, state, and national levels affect the quality of life for every family member. All levels of government provide a range of protective services. Taxes and allocation of funds, interest rates, declaration of war, and court decisions represent a few ways by which governmental policies affect the quality of life for families (see Chapter 12).

Even though other institutions provide vital services for family members, the family remains irreplaceable for the survival of the young. It is only the family that can give the child the love that is necessary for emotional well-being. For the child and adult, this shared love and a sense of belonging are of ultimate importance. No one has said it better than Urie Bronfenbrenner: "A child (to develop normally) needs the enduring, irrational involvement of one or more adults in the care of and in joint activity with him. Somebody has to be crazy about the kid and have time to devote to him." (Bronfenbrenner, 1979).

Children need their families not just for survival, but to reach their optimal physical, emotional, social, moral, and intellectual development. Society needs the family for the love and humanizing experiences that only it can offer the citizens of tomorrow, its children.

Family: A Facilitating Environment

The fortunate child is born into a family that will provide nurturing, protection, and an environment that promotes healthy physical and psychological growth and development. This means that the family establishes a home where the child is valued and accepted as a person regardless of behavior or accomplishments and the child feels this sense of belonging. If this sense of belonging and stability is missing from the beginning, the child will face psychological handicaps that may never be overcome. In addition, the family strongly influences its children's intellectual and moral development.

In the family, children form their essential attachment to one or more adults. This attachment enables them to develop a healthy personality, an appropriate gender identity, and fruitful relationships both within the family and larger society. A healthy family will help the child grow and develop by offering appropriate models and responsible rules for living in society with consistency, fairness, and stability.

The Family Provides Emotional Attachment

The newborn's psychological needs are best met by at least one consistent caregiver. The baby's need for love and stimulation is so strong that babies placed in an institution without a consistent caregiver, withdrew, lost weight, and had difficulty sleeping in their new setting (Spitz, 1946).

Forming an attachment is a gradual process according to Bowlby (1969). In the **preattachment phase,** from birth to 6 weeks, infants send a variety of signals to the adult for contact, including grasping, crying, or gazing into the adult's eyes. The adult responds in many ways such as cuddling or talking softly to the infant. Infants direct their smiles, looks, and vocalizations more to people than to inanimate objects, but respond to familiar and unfamiliar people alike. Infants recognize their mother's smell and voice but are not yet attached to her. In the **second phase,** from 6 weeks to 6 to 8 months, infants' signals intensify and the recipients more often are their caregivers rather than a stranger. They are still relatively friendly to strangers, but respond differently to familiar caregivers than to a stranger (Barrera and Maurer, 1981; Watson, Hayes, Vietze, and Becker, 1979). As attachment increases during the **third phase,** infants from 6 to 8 months to 18 months to 2 years take a more active part in seeking and following their caregivers. Infants often show **separation anxiety** or become upset when a parent or familiar person leaves. Infants use their mother or their attachment figure as a secure base for exploration and show an intense preference for their significant attachment figures over strangers, especially when distressed. During the **fourth phase,** from 18 months to 2 years and on, infants form reciprocal relationships with their parents and significant people in their life. They have increased their language skills and are better able to understand their parents' routines, especially their patterns of coming and going. Their separation protests decline. They are better able to negotiate with their parents or caregivers on issues such as bed or nap time.

During these phases of attachment, children form an emotional bond to their parent(s) that provides support in their parents' absence. Children construct a set of expectations as to how available the major attachment figures are and how they comfort or support them in times of stress. These experiences and their relationship or bond to their parent(s) also serve as a basis for future close relationships (Bretherton, 1992).

Infants' First Attachments

Traditionally it was believed, especially by Freudians (Freud, 1953) and ethologists (Bowlby, 1969), that there was an innate bias for the infant to become attached to a single figure, the mother. It was only after this primary attachment that the infant could reach out to form secondary attachments. More recent research shows that infants begin to establish attachments with more than one figure simultaneously. This may include mother, father, siblings, grandparents, and caregivers. These attachments differ in scope and degree. For example, in times of illness, fatigue, or distress, infants will show a decided preference for one figure over another (Ainsworth, 1979).

Infants will attach to their mother and father at the same time, but the quality of the infants' attachments to each differs. When mother, father, and infant are alone in a relaxed, nonstressful environment, infants show a preference to be with their father by sending more distal signals, such as smiling, vocalizing, and looking more toward their father. However, when a threat or stress is introduced into the scene, such as the appearance of a stranger, the infants show a decided preference for mothers over fathers, approaching and staying close to their mother (Lamb, 1976a, 1976b).

It is interesting to speculate on the cause of this pattern. Is it biological or does it arise from the type of interactions infants experience with each parent? Fathers may be more novel to infants, may play with them more, or have a more engaging style of stimulating them (such as rougher play). Perhaps mothers are a preferred source of solace when stress arises because of habit, but there is a lack of research on situations like this in which mothers and fathers have reversed roles.

Infants can also become attached to siblings. In one study (Samuels, 1980), 23-month-old infants were observed twice a week in the back yard of a home. Each infant was observed first with his or her mother and an older sibling present and the second time with only the mother. When siblings were present, the infants ventured farther from their mother, exploring objects with greater manipulation, crying less, and wanting to go home less.

Infants often become attached to an object called a "security blanket." Most adults can recall some child's dependence on a particular stuffed animal or perhaps a cloth that was soft and comfortable. A group of two-year-old children attached to a "security blanket" was observed in a novel laboratory setting. When these toddlers were alone, there was distress and little exploration, but when either their mother or their security blanket was present, their distress signs disappeared and exploration continued. However, when the situation was made more threatening, such as dimming the lights or weird noises, only the mother was able to ease the distress (Passman and Weisberg, 1975). A particular object is used by some children as a security symbol in the transition from dependence on the attachment figure to increased independence.

Characteristics of Interactions Affecting Attachment

The amount of time required for a mother or any individual to interact with an infant for attachment to occur is surprisingly low. Infants attach to their mothers even when they spend much of their waking time with the child care worker. The type of attachment to their mother varies, however, from very insecure to quite secure.

Secure and Insecure Attachments

The stability of attachment patterns between 1 and 2 years of age varies greatly and appears to be influenced by certain conditions. Most infants from secure and stable middle socioeconomic families maintain a stable secure attachment. Infants who were insecurely attached but had mothers who were well adjusted by the time they reached 1 year of age, and also had positive family and/or friendship relationships, were securely attached from 1 to 2 years of age. On the other hand, infants from lower socioeconomic families, with many daily stresses and little social support, were insecurely attached to their mother at age 1. Either their attachments had moved from secure to insecure or, for most of these children, from one form of insecurity to another (Berk, 2002; Owen, Easterbrooks, Chase-Lansdale, and Goldberg, 1984; Vaughn, Egeland, Stroufe, and Waters, 1979; Vondra, Hommerding, and Shaw, 1999).

The quality of the mother's and the family's life affects the nature of the infant's attachment. When a mother is chronically stressed, suffering depression after childbirth, feeling dissatisfaction with her marriage, or lacking social support, the infant is more likely to be insecurely attached (Owen and Cox, 1997; Isabella and Belsky, 1991).

The behavior of mothers of securely attached infants differs in four ways from those of infants classified as insecure. **First,** the mothers of secure infants respond more quickly and consistently to their infants' bids for attention, especially distress signals (DeWolf and Ijzendoorn, 1997). **Second,** these mothers show more sensitivity in interpreting and responding to their infants' signals than do mothers of insecure infants (Blehar, Lieberman, and Ainsworth, 1977). Mothers of secure infants are concerned about feeding, diaper changing, playful exchanges, and other activities in a way that is comfortable for the infant. **Third,** mothers of secure infants express their affection for their infants more consistently and in different ways than the other mothers. For example, there is more affectionate touching, smiling, and verbal communication by mothers with securely attached infants (Clarke-Stewart, 1973). **Finally,** mothers of securely attached infants maintain higher standards of physical care for their infants. Egeland and Sroufe (1981) found that the more times a mother neglected her infant, the more likely the infant was classified anxious/resistant.

When parents are inconsistent in responding to their young children's bids for attention, their children often show intense, anxious, attention-seeking behavior. This was found across a rather broad age span (Macoby 1980). Around 24 months of age, securely attached children make fewer contacts with their mother during play, while insecurely attached children increase their contacts with their mother.

Insecure attachments can be reversed if the patterns of interaction between parent and child change, taking on more of the characteristics found between securely attached infants and their mothers. An intervention program teaching mothers how to respond more sensitively to their irritable 6-month-old infants was effective in strengthening their infants' attachment security, exploration skills, cooperation, and sociability. This remained present at 3½ years of age (Van den Bloom, 1995).

Attachment Failure and Loss

Are there irreversible consequences for children who fail to form a specific attachment by a particular age? Will they ever be able to form an attachment or be free from serious psychological problems later in life? Will children who fail to become attached lack a secure base from which to explore the world? Will they remain fearful and demanding of attention?

The critical age for attachment is of concern to many but of particular importance to adoptive parents and agency workers. Two 10-year studies following infants adopted at various ages showed no long-range affects on children adopted as late as 19 months. The first study compared infants placed in their adoptive homes under 6 months of age with those adopted after 6 months. They found no long-range group differences in personality, adjustment, and competence 10 years later, even though the initial intensity of separation distress was greater in the older group of infants (Yarrow and Goodwin, 1973; Yarrow, Goodwin, Manheimer, and Milowe, 1973). Macoby (1980) concluded that the child's long-range adjustment is determined by the quality of the child's relationships with the new caregivers rather than by the separation itself.

Children who fail to attach or are late in forming attachments appear to be more aggressive and demand more attention than securely attached children. Rutter (1979) reviewed several longitudinal studies of English children raised in institutions by multiple caregivers. As toddlers and preschoolers they demanded attention not only from their housemothers but also from strangers. At age 8 most children still in the institution had not formed a preferential attachment with one of their housemothers and still demanded attention. At school, they were restless, disruptive, disobedient, and not accepted by their peers. Their social overtures were inappropriate. However, those children in the study who were adopted as late as 4 years of age did develop deep bonds with their adoptive parents but were still having social problems in school. The behavior of these children resembled that of insecurely attached children in their demands for attention and in their uncooperative and noncompliant style of interaction.

The Family Provides Nurturing

In the process of forming attachments, children experience nurturing. While attachment is a physical bonding between parent (or another person) and child, nurturing is a broader concept involving love, emotional security, and a sense of acceptance and well-being.

Nurturing involves intimacy. From the moment of birth, the family is the place where the child comes to understand the meaning of intimate relationships. The mother holds her baby closely, looks into the baby's eyes and croons, "You are won-

Look, I'm Driving

Nurturing involves both psychological and physical care. These parents help their son to have special experiences with their adult friends.Wearing the life jacket insures their child's physical safety.

derful, you are the love of my life." She is providing the baby with a love message that will be played back when the child becomes an adult and begins his or her own love relationships (Fraiberg, 1977).

Nurturing helps children feel loved. It is crucial that the parent recognize the baby's signals and respond appropriately. A nurturing parent tries to identify and support the interests, talents, and particular needs of each child. It is important that parents give their children unconditional positive regard, which means that children are accepted and loved for themselves and not for their behavior.

Nurturing includes supporting children in understanding and expressing their emotions. As children develop, they experience an increasing range of emotions. Distress reactions in infancy gradually evolve into emotions such as disgust, anger, fear, and jealousy. Positive delight reactions gradually become more specific emotions such as elation, affection, and joy (Camras, 1992).

Children need help in learning acceptable ways for expressing their feelings. The development of pleasant emotions can be stimulated and reinforced by positive experiences such as holding, touching, or feeding the child as well as by stimulating games that parents play with young children. Unpleasant feelings and destructive impulses need to be channeled. Parents and caregivers can provide children with acceptable releases for these feelings through guidance and by example. Temper tantrums, for instance, often can be ignored so as not to encourage their repetition. In any case, when children have regained control or calmed down, parents can help them identify and deal with the frustration. Children need to learn various acceptable ways to release these feelings. In the process, it is important for adults to stay with them until their frustrations and actions have been successfully channeled into more acceptable behavior.

Children need to acquire socially acceptable ways to gain attention, affection, and approval. Adults' expectations for children's behavior change with age. A baby may cry to gain attention whereas a two-year-old needs to respond differently in order to please an adult. Smiling, verbalizing, and crawling up on a lap are more acceptable responses. In a healthy family, all members are able to express love, fear, and anger without the threat of losing love. These feelings are accepted and the parents' task is to help their children understand the cause (if possible) as well as to learn ways to release and live with their feelings.

Parents nurture a child from the security of their own feelings of being loved and wanted. When family members are living with stress and conflict among significant adults, it is more difficult for a family to offer the child sufficient nurturing.

Children come to know that the family is where they belong. A nurturing family is a safe place to retreat and recover from hurt feelings, an emotional refuge from the outside world. This nurturing frees children to use their energies for growth and development in the broader environment.

Qualities of Temperament

The ways in which the family responds to an infant are influenced by that baby's temperament. Temperament also affects the infant's initial response to her or his environment. Temperament is a broad term that includes an individual's predisposition to certain moods and reaction styles. Babies appear to be born with these constitutionally based biases. Doctors and nurses as well as parents and researchers are able to see signs of temperament within a few hours after birth.

Temperament is the foundation of personality development and includes such qualities as emotional responses, activity level, sociability, and impulsiveness. Thomas and Chess (1986) believe temperament is established by the first two or three months of life. Researchers continue to study the genetic influences as well as the effect of the environment on temperament. Does the child's environment affect modest changes in his or her temperament over time?

Is an infant's temperament relatively stable throughout life, supporting the theory of genetic determination? In studying these and other questions, Thomas and Chess (1986) have identified nine qualities of temperament that are present in children at birth. The following traits were researched for ten years beginning in 1968:

1. Activity level
2. Approach or withdrawal (when confronted by new experiences)
3. Adaptability to change
4. Quality of mood or irritability
5. Attention span or persistence
6. Distractability
7. Rhythmicity (regularity)
8. Sensitivity to stimuli (how much noise to wake the baby)
9. Intensity of reaction

Because these characteristics appeared in clusters, Thomas and Chess (1986) classified temperament in babies according to three styles: "easy," "slow to warm up," and "difficult." However, 35 percent of the infants did not fit into any category.

1. **Easy to warm up babies**—40 percent. Positive disposition, regular body functions, adaptable, curious, moderate to low intensity of emotions.

2. **Slow-to-warm-up babies**—15 percent. Inactive or calm reactions to the environment, withdraw from new situations.
3. **Difficult babies**—10 percent. More negative moods; babies withdraw or are slow to adapt to new situations.

In studying various characteristics in children from infancy through age seven, Thomas and Chess found relatively little change in their basic styles. For example, a large number of babies classified as "difficult" were found to have more serious emotional problems at age seven than babies in the other two groups. However, other research showed both stability and changes in various temperament dimensions throughout childhood. Many studies found that children who showed high or low extremes in attention span, irritability, sociability, or shyness were likely to score much the same throughout childhood and sometimes into adulthood (Caspi, Henry, McGee, Moffit, and Silva, 1995; Kochanska and Radke-Yarrow, 1992). Other studies found that some characteristics such as shyness or sociability can change over time and only appear to be stable if a child is extremely shy or sociable (Kerr, Lambert, Statin, Klachenberg-Larsson, 1994; Sanson, Pedlow, Cann, Prior, and Oberklaid, 1996).

A longitudinal study by Guerin and Gottfried (1994) on developmental stability and change in temperament from ages 2 to 12 showed that most changes occurred in the first five years, with no significant changes during the years from ages 5 to 12. These changes were found for five of the nine dimensions: rhythmicity, mood, persistence, threshold, and intensity. Temperamental difficulties during infancy foreshadowed adverse temperamental qualities such as slow adaptability and negative mood as well as behavioral problems during childhood (Guerin, Gottfried, and Thomas, 1997). Boys and girls were found to be more alike in temperament than different (Guerin and Gottfried, 1994).

An important factor in determinating children's behavior involves the principle of **bidirectionality.** The reactions of the baby affect the responses of the adult, which in turn influence the baby's next response.Thus, smiling, cuddling, content babies will encourage parents and other people to smile with them and enjoy their company. Fretful babies who cry easily may be upsetting to parents and caregivers, resulting in interactions producing frustrations and less joy. A parent or parents without a support system are particularly vulnerable to the stresses of living with a difficult or unresponsive baby. However, parents who respond to a difficult or fretful baby with warmth and consistency are more likely to have a child who later avoids problems that other irritable babies have (Belsky, Fish, and Isabella, 1991; Crockenberg, 1986). It is tempting to assume certain patterns of behavior are a product of a child's temperament, but the principle of bidirectionality needs to be considered.

As early as the first weeks of life, the infant has an influence on the caregiver. One mother, who welcomed motherhood and wanted to do her best, felt rejected by her infant, who alternated between uncontrollable intense screaming and crying and heavy sleep. The mother was so depressed by the rejection that she sought therapy (Thomas and Chess, 1986). Another mother whose daughters were in their thirties describes it this way:

> *The oldest daughter would stiffen and rear back her head when I attempted to cuddle her, while the younger one would snuggle contentedly in my arms. I still feel the sense of rejection the oldest daughter caused me.*

When parents consider the child's temperament and respond appropriately to their child's behavior, they help to modify behavior that some parents might assume to be "natural" for the child.

The family's culture and/or the dominant culture of the community also influence the way in which the family reacts to a child's behavior. Do certain values or beliefs in the culture complement the child's temperament? For example, an irritable infant in the East African Masai culture in Kenya may thrive better there than if raised in the United States. The Masai mother breastfeeds a baby who is crying, giving this baby additional nutrition and comfort (M. V. deVries, 1984). The Masai mother is *not* told to let the baby cry.

Effective caregiving is seen in terms of cultural values. In Western nations, adults consider children who are very shy to have a social problem. In contrast, Chinese adults consider their shy children to be advanced in social maturity and understanding. In a study comparing Canadian and Chinese children, Canadian mothers reported that they punished and protected their shy children and showed less acceptance and encouragement of their achievements. In contrast, Chinese mothers of shy children responded with less protection and rejection and greater acceptance and encouragement (Chen, Hastings, Rubin, Chen, Cen, and Stewart, 1998).

The Family Facilitates Personal and Social Development

With temperament as the foundation, children develop their personal and social traits or their personality largely in the family. Because personality traits are present in complex degrees and blends, they are much more difficult to measure than many physical traits. Personality includes the traits that distinguish or characterize each person as an individual. This involves an individual's behavior, thinking, and feelings.

The debate continues as to whether nature or nurture or both determine the development of an individual's personality. Biological determinism claims that an individual's personality is an outgrowth of an individual's genetic makeup, while behaviorism states that all behavior is learned. Nurture sees the physical and social environments as determining a child's personality. Most modern researchers believe that personality has both genetic and social roots and are more concerned with how nature and nurture work together (deWall, 1999).

INTERACTION OF GENETICS AND ENVIRONMENT: All personality traits are influenced by both genetics and the environment. A child's genetic behavioral characteristics will help direct the way a family and others respond to him or her. This is reciprocal, for a "good" baby tends to make a "good" mother who encourages these positive responses in her baby. Most traits are modified, especially in the early years, by the responses of parents and significant others to the child. Children who are loved, touched, talked to, and listened to, and who have their physical and psychological needs met tend to be loving, caring, and cooperative in return. Children who feel rejected at home, by peers, or at school react accordingly and do not feel good about themselves. For example, if children are unable to receive attention or success through cooperation, they often find disruptive ways to receive this needed attention. A sense of failure in school will alter a child's established behavior and feelings of self-worth.

Goodness of Fit

Thomas and Chess (1977) proposed this "goodness-of-fit" model to explain how a child's temperament and environment can work together to provide a healthy setting for the child's growth and development. It is important that children grow up in a family, child-care setting, and school, where the environment facilitates their development. Some children are fortunate to be in a family where the family's interests, schedules, activities, and rules are comfortable for them.

When children are struggling to conform, how can they be helped? Perhaps a child is having difficulty with a required task and may benefit by approaching the task differently. The task might be too long and needs to be presented in smaller parts. As mentioned earlier, the daily schedule could be altered slightly to meet the child's ability to feel comfortable. Some children may need a different explanation for clarity while others may see the reasons given as very clear. Parents may feel that they give all children in the family the same stimulation and love, but one child, perhaps overly sensitive by nature, may feel a lack of love on the parents' part.

It is important for parents to observe their child's responses to different conditions to determine what is best for that child. What features in the environment complement the child's temperament? Do the demands of the environment fit the child's capabilities and interests or do they require a constant struggle on the part of the child? High-activity children may do best with some directions for their high energy, whereas low-activity children may do best if allowed to pursue and explore activities largely on their own (Bornstein and Lamb, 1992; Mangelsdorf, Gunnar, Kestenbaum, Lang, and Andreas, 1990; Thomas and Chess, 1977, 1980). Slight adjustments to current patterns of child rearing may allow the child to thrive and still fit into the family's schedule. Maybe the child does not handle change well.

Minimizing changes in the daily schedule and giving advance notice when change is necessary would help the child adapt to the family's schedule.

Because each child has a unique genetic response to the environment as well as a personal history (e.g., a set of experiences), the child benefits when the environment, if feasible, is adapted or altered to help accommodate his or her individual needs.

Social Cognition

Social cognition is the knowledge of social relationships and interactions. How do children come to understand themselves, their relationships with others, and the personality and psychological functioning of others? How do children come to understand the rules involved in social relationships and in social group membership? Their understandings are based on both their cognitive maturity and social experiences.

Children under age 7, according to Piaget's stage of concrete operational thinking, would have difficulty in taking another person's point of view and, therefore, difficulty in understanding what the other person is thinking. Children in the concrete operational stage of thinking are able to reason using concrete facts but not able to distinguish between hypotheses or abstract thoughts and actual facts, so they still make errors in judgment. Not until children reach logical abstract thinking, from ages 11 to adulthood or never, are they able to include logical and abstract thinking in their judgments. The family and significant others in the lives of children have great influences on their development of social cognition. (See Appendix I on Piaget.)

Social cognitive development is viewed differently by cognitive development theorists such as Piaget and social learning theorists such as Bandura. According to Piaget (1963), children and adults learn by taking in new information and fitting this information into existing schemas (categories). Piaget calls this process assimilation. The next time information is taken in that conflicts with the existing schemas, the individual makes an adjustment, called accommodation, in order to make sense out of the old and new knowledge. The successful assimilation or accommodation of new information produces a state of equilibrium or balance. Children's social concepts become more numerous and complex as they mature.

Social cognitive skills are developed as children interact with others, exchange thoughts, share experiences, and adjust attitudes. According to Selman (1973), the child's ability to assume another person's point of view develops in stages. Role-taking ability begins with only an egocentric perspective and progresses through various levels of mutual role-taking. These five stages of role-taking ability are discussed under moral development in this chapter.

Piaget believed that the way in which children perceive experiences depends on their underlying thought structures or more basic ways of processing and organizing information. According to Piaget, children pass through four qualitatively different stages of cognitive development from birth through adolescence (see Appendix I). Social and other schemas are limited by the child's stage of cognitive development as well as being affected by his or her experiences.

Social learning theorists, such as Bandura, believe that children learn about themselves, others, and social relationships from their social experiences rather than according to their underlying thought structures. Children are forced constantly to make sense out of social interactions and the complex social rules under which such interactions are conducted. These contingency rules motivate their behavior. However, Bandura's more recent work emphasizes so strongly how children think about themselves and others that he calls it a social-cognitive, rather than a social learning, approach (1986, 1989, 1992).

Social cognition, according to social learning theorists, is further complicated by the fact that both the rules and the child are constantly changing, particularly as the child's social experiences expand. New attachments or heroes such as a teacher, club leader, or an entertainment figure may encourage new or different behaviors.

Acquiring a Sense of Self

One of the most important tasks in the area of social cognitive development is to understand one's own self and psychological functioning. The family has the initial, and by far the greatest, influence on a child's self-concept development. Self-concept is the individual's understanding of who she or he is. Self-esteem is the evaluative component by which a child measures her or his self-worth, The development of self-concept is a gradual process.

The infant's first major social task is to recognize him- or herself as separate from the environment. Most children are around 18 months old before they form a clear mental image of their face (Berthenthal and Fischer, 1978; Lewis and Brooks-Gunn, 1981). As they gain in cognitive maturity and social experience, they undergo changes in their self-concept. Infants are unable to see themselves as different from anyone else. As children become older, they are able to view themselves in different areas of their life, forming a self-concept in each area.

What Fun!

This 23-month-old child is developing a sense of self by exploring her body through her senses. Between 17 and 24 months most children are able to distinguish themselves from others and are aware of some of their capabilities.

Children also form an opinion about their self-worth, known as self-esteem. Family and other important people in their lives influence the outcome.

Self as Observable Surface Attributes

Young children describe themselves in terms of surface attributes. This includes physical characteristics, possessions, house, family, friends, and favorite activities (Eder, 1989; Livesley and Bromley, 1973; Peevers and Secord, 1973). Four-year-old Scott says to a new child at preschool, "I am tall and I have cowboy boots, a fire engine, and a puppy." Preschool age children usually have an unrealistic or inflated view of what they can do. Scott may also say to a friend even after an unsuccessful attempt, "I can kick the ball farther than you can" (Damon and Hart, 1988).

Psychological Self

During their elementary school years, children begin to see themselves less in terms of physical or external traits and more in terms of psychological or internal traits. Children as young as age three may comment on something inside themselves that others cannot see. The child points to his head when asked, "Where do you think?" The child also answers, "No, you cannot see me thinking in there." However, it is not until age eight or nine that most children describe themselves in terms of stable personality traits such as lazy, funny, or serious (Maccoby, 1980). This supports Piaget's view that children must be in the concrete operational stage of thinking before they can understand psychological attributes (see Appendix 1).

Children with concrete operational thinking capacities no longer are limited by a generalized self-concept and self-esteem, but are able to view and evaluate themselves separately in different domains. They are able to recognize that they may be good in sports but not in math. Experiences at school become part of their academic self-concept. Getting along with peers and having friends and relation-

TABLE 2.1	School-Age Children and Multiple Self-Concepts	
Self-Concept	**Children's Views of Self**	
Academic	Based on skills in reading, language, history, math and/or science	
Social	Based on relationships with peers and significant others	
Emotional	Based on emotional states (behavior)	
Physical	Based on physical abilities and acceptance of physical appearance	

ships with parents and teachers help form their social self-concept. They also form an emotional self-concept and a physical self-concept. Each of these components has distinct differences as well as some overlap. These components become more refined with age (Marsh, 1990; Marsh, Craven, and Debus, 1998). School-age children are able to combine their separate evaluations into a general psychological image of themselves (Harter, 1998, 1999). Not all of these components have equal weight in forming a general self-concept. One area may not be as important to an individual as another. It is interesting to note that, although children have individual and age differences in what they see as most important, the vast majority of children perceive physical appearance as the most important factor in determining their satisfaction with themselves (Harter, 1998; Hymel, LeMare, Ditner, and Woody, 1999).

Determinants of Self-Concept

How do children develop their self-concept? All children use similar processes in attempting to understand who they are, who they would like to be, and what they are capable of doing. However, there are great differences in children's experiences that affect the outcome of the self.

The "Looking-Glass Self"

In the early 1900s Charles Cooley observed that children learn who they are by interacting with others, which he termed "the looking-glass self." Cooley saw the process of developing a self-identity as having three phases. First, individuals imagine how they present themselves to others. Next, they imagine how *others* are evaluating them, and, finally, children develop an overall feeling about themselves from these impressions (Cooley, 1902/1964). They can feel good about who they are or have negative feelings such as shame or stupidity or not being capable.

Before children are able to construct a self-concept, they must learn the rules and what behavior or responses are wanted as well as what is unacceptable. It helps when parents and teachers are consistent and have similar rules and expectations. How parents feel about a child and how they communicate these feelings to the child are crucial to the developing self-concept. For the development of a healthy self-concept, it is important that a child feels loved, valued, and capable. For example, according to Erikson's stages of development, a child has specific tasks to master during each stage. If a child does not successfully fulfill the requirements of the current stage, progressing to the next stage is more difficult. Therefore, when a toddler struggles to achieve autonomy and fails, the result is a feeling of shame and doubt. This struggle for autonomy or independence may continue, thus thwarting the move to the next stage to seek initiative. During the initiative stage, a child moves on to master new tasks and test his or her power in the world. (Erikson's stages are discussed in Chapter 5.)

Verbal Attribution

Adults can encourage certain traits in a child if they attribute these characteristics to the child. Behavior showing kindness such as sharing a toy or displaying sadness if someone is hurt can be seen in preschool children. When adults label a child as helpful or a troublemaker, the child is likely to respond accordingly. However, the child must be able to understand the concept. If character traits such as kindness, honesty, empathy, or their counterparts are not understood until age 8 or 9, when is it effective to begin to promote such traits? An interesting study done by Grusec and Redler (1980) examined the display of altruistic behavior in a new situation for 5-year-olds and 8-year-olds. Each child in the project was told that he or she was a nice person and one who would help others. Later, these children were given a chance to collect craft materials for a hospitalized child. The 8-year-olds were much more responsive than the 5-year-olds. These differences showed that verbal attribution increased the altruistic behavior in a new setting for 8-year-olds but not for 5-year-olds. The 5-year-old children did not understand the traits of empathy and kindness as well as the older children and most younger children were unable to transfer this behavior to a new setting to be expressed in a different way. Prosocial behavior in younger children can be encouraged by telling them they are good sharers, but they are *not* likely to see the relationship of that trait in a new and very different setting.

Much has been written about constructive and destructive praise and criticism. Praising or criticizing the personality can be damaging to the individual's self-image. In the case of labeling the person as good or generous, it can cause anxiety or fear of not living up to the label as well as regression in moral development. Criticism of the person's self can be very damaging. It is much better to deal with a person's actions rather than the personality (Ginott, 1965). To be told that your behavior is wrong or hurtful is easier to adjust to or defend than hearing that you are stupid, lazy, or dishonest.

Self-Observation

Children's observations of their behavior and the outcome through their own eyes are crucial to self-concept development. Children reflect on both past and present behavior in deciding what kind of a person they are. This becomes part of their self-concept. Older children increasingly evaluate the results of their behavior with peers as well as with adults. For example, when peers or adults listen to them, they learn that they can influence important events. This helps children to develop an internal locus (source) of control. They tend to assume responsibility for their own behavior rather than relying on external sources to determine it. Feelings of being respected by their peers and being responsible for their own actions are reflected in their self-concept.

Causal Attribution of Behavior

In trying to understand what kind of a person they are, children make critical conclusions about themselves based on the motivation of their behavior. If they really sacrificed to give something to a friend, they would consider that action more noble or kind than sharing a duplicate or undesirable object. If they made the present all by themselves rather than with someone's help, they would think of themselves more highly. Children are looking at their actions internally rather than on the basis of external forces.

Parents can distort this process by being overly helpful, solving children's problems, always telling them what to do, and not allowing them to make decisions and assume responsibility for themselves. In these situations, children see parents and not themselves as the source of power. This would also reinforce external control for behavior rather than encourage the child to develop internal control. For example, in Erikson's stages, developing a sense of autonomy or independence is important for toddlers and the need to learn how to solve problems continues throughout life.

Social Comparison

Children's self-concept is influenced by a constant process of social comparison. Children measure their behavior, their abilities, and their attitudes with those around them. In school, for example, children decide how well they read by comparing themselves to their classmates. In listening to young children playing, a 4-year-old child can be heard to say, "My block tower is taller than yours . . . I'm stronger than you . . . Look at what I can carry." Although children make social comparisons at an early age, Ruble, Boggiano, Feldman, and Loebl (1980) found that these comparisons are not accurate estimates of their abilities until age 7 or 8. This is the typical age for the beginning of self-attribution of traits.

Acquiring a Sense of Others

The social self emerges as children increasingly become involved with other people. While children are refining their self-concepts, they are becoming more skilled at processing information about others. The process of defining self in terms of one's group takes place at the same time as they are defining self as unique from others. It is like two sides of a coin. Children learn that various social groups may place different expectations on their members. Children may need to adapt some personal values to be accepted by the group. In doing so, the private self yields in part to the requirements of the group. When children struggle with social rules that conflict with their personal values, they often experience great psychic or emotional costs. Guilt can occur when the child alters a rule or value for social approval.

There are obvious parallels between person-perception and self-perception. Preschool children tend to perceive other people in terms of their surface appearance, possessions, and activities, whereas older children are more likely to think of people in terms of their psychological functioning and enduring dispositions. Adolescents are even more sophisticated in their perceptions. They distinguish between a trait occurring under all conditions or only under certain conditions. An example would be, "She is only quiet around boys she does not know."

Causal Attribution

Children try to determine the causes for other children's actions in order to respond more effectively. "Was it an accident or intentional? Was it because I did something to make Joe mad or was he in a bad mood? Did Sally do something nice because she wants a favor from me?"

In the development of causal attribution, children develop schemas (categories) that help them detect the causes of events, to differentiate between accidental and intentional acts, to distinguish among intentional actions on the basis of the person's motive, and to decide whether to hold a person responsible for his or her behavior. Young children, ages 4 to 6 or 7, will find a cause that may or may not be accurate. Until children realize that certain properties of an object remain the same despite changes in the object's appearance, their answers will be based on intuition. In most cases, their answers are poised somewhere between fact and fiction.

Perspective Taking

Still, another aspect of social cognitive functioning is role-taking or learning to consider the other person's perspective. To understand another person, their feelings, and needs, individuals must temporarily put aside their egocentrism and consider the situation from that person's point of view. Piaget (1963) believed that children younger than age 7 or 8 were too egocentric to be capable of role-taking (see Appendix 1). Other researchers have found preschoolers capable of a simple form of role-taking based on their own experiences and those of others close to them, for example, "Mommy likes earrings, so she will be happy if I give her earrings for her birthday."

According to Piaget, role-taking develops into the social and conventional role-taking stage beginning around age 12. At this stage, children can view the social system as a result of shared perspectives of many members. They compare their own views with those of their friends, and sometimes they do not agree. Some of their friends may take a candy bar from a store and justify it with, "everybody does it" or "the shopkeeper doesn't care." This discrepancy in perspectives disturbs children, especially if they are close friends.

> *A 5-year-old child plays shortstop and sees the job as standing between second and third base and catching the ball.*
>
> *A 12-year-old would see a broader picture of the role of shortstop. He or she would keep an eye on the batter but also on any players at second or third base and be prepared to catch the ball and throw it quickly to the appropriate base or home plate to put an opponent out.*

According to Selman (1973), the quality of perspective-taking changes as children grow and develop. Children and youths interpret a situation differently, perhaps each having different information, but young children will only view the situation from their egocentric perspective. As children mature, they will be able to look at each others' perspective and say, "I thought you would think that." Between ages 10 to 15, many children look at two people's responses at the same time and apart from their view. Finally, youths and adults may consider societal values along with the views of others.

Children who are the same age vary greatly in their role-taking skills. The ability to take another person's perspective is influenced by cognitive maturity and social experiences. When adults and peers explain the reasons behind their view-

TABLE 2.2	**Selman's Stages of Role-Taking Ability**	
Stage 0	3 to 6 years	Children are egocentric, but may recognize others can have different thoughts.
Stage 1	4 to 9 years	Children accept that others have different perspectives and understand intentions.
Stage 2	7 to 12 years	Children develop reciprocal awareness. Each can look at the other's point of view.
Stage 3	10 to 15 years	Children can view a two-person conflict from an outsider's or third-person perspective.
Stage 4	14 years and later	Individuals can be influenced by societal values in their third-party perspective taking. (Selman, 1973)

point, it helps children to understand and accept rules and expectations in the family, at school, and in playing with peers.

Self-Esteem

The mature self-concept is comprised of several elements, one of which is the evaluative component known as self-esteem. Before age 7, children have a generalized negative or positive self-evaluation (Harter, 1990a; Marsh and Shavelson, 1985). As mentioned earlier, around this age children begin to differentiate and to form a self-evaluation for a particular situation as well as an overall self-evaluation. How children feel about themselves affects their ability to perform tasks, their inclination to attempt new tasks, their relationships with others, and their overall satisfaction with life. In a longitudinal study by Coppersmith (1967), high self-esteem children were participants rather than listeners, were assertive, were free to express their opinions even under criticism, were more resistant to irrational peer pressures, approached new tasks with greater confidence, made friends more easily, and were less preoccupied with their personal problems than low self-esteem children. In addition, Coopersmith found that an individual's sense of self-worth was generally stable by the end of the elementary school years. It is interesting to note that there are more differences in self-esteem among members of the same gender as there are between the genders.

High Self-Esteem and Violence and Aggression

Improving children's self-esteem has been seen as a way to help children become successful in school and reduce their behavior problems. In particular, raising children's self-esteem is said to reduce aggression, violence, and antisocial behavior (California Task Force, 1990). Recent research has shown that this is not always true and *very* high self-esteem can increase aggression and violence.

According to a large survey of research from a number of disciplines, very high self-esteem is often associated with aggression and violence (Baumeister, Smart, and Boden, 1996). When individuals with unusually high self-esteem are challenged, they often use aggressive means to maintain their high self-esteem. Those with lower self-esteem do not usually respond aggressively, perhaps because they feel the criticism is accurate. Researchers also report that these perpetrators have an inflated view of themselves (Feldman, 1998). This relationship to aggression does not mean that having high self-esteem is always bad. It depends more on the type of success needed to feel great and how this high level of self-esteem is maintained. Self-worth could be based on many things such as exceptional strength, athletic ability, high grades, valuable service on school committees, having and caring for friends, or the ability to work with others. Each requires different skills and behavior. When this esteem is based on unrealistic levels of performance, it can be dangerous. Will this person turn to aggression and violence toward others in order to maintain his or her high level of self-esteem?

Race/Ethnicity and Self-Esteem

Racial awareness is evident at an early age. Many toddlers can distinguish between dark and fair skin colors. By 3 or 4 years of age, children identify Black Americans and White Americans and attach some social significance to each.

For many decades, studies reported that members of minority groups who experienced prejudice and discrimination had a poorer self-image than members of the majority group. The effect of this prejudice was particularly true for African Americans (Deutsch, 1967). An early study by Clark and Clark (1947) reported that African American girls preferred white dolls over black ones. Today, this is not necessarily true. Research has shown that members of a minority group can have just as high self-esteem as majority group members if they view the negative attitudes and discrimination against them as unjustified and see a possibility to change the status and power structure (Duckitt, 1994; Gabarino, 1985; Harter, 1990b). Rather than feeling responsible for the discrimination and prejudice, they blame the perpetrators. Perhaps the increased recognition in recent decades of the many contributions of minority groups has contributed to more positive feelings of self-esteem for their members.

Cultural Identity and Self-Esteem

Cultural identity affects the child's self-esteem. It is important that parents value their culture but also appreciate others whose cultures differ. Parents are influenced by their culture in teaching children their values on basic issues such as punctuality, the type and amount of space needed for comfort in various settings, and the pace or tempo of daily living. There are differences in how parents expect their children to reason or solve problems and in their verbal messages, social roles in the family and community, the types of interpersonal relationships, and social organization. Various cultures approach these issues differently (Bennett, 2003). Some children will encounter different views on some of these issues, possibly in their child-care facility, school, or peer group.

Does the squeaky wheel get the grease or does the nail that stands out get pounded down? In the dominant culture, which is based on European cultures, an individualistic orientation stresses the uniqueness of each person and individual achievement. Families and schools often reward an individual who stands out, especially if accompanied by a particular achievement. In most Asian cultures and among many Asian American families, a collectivist orientation emphasizes contributing to and blending into the group. There are variations within a culture and certainly within subcultures. The degree of assimilation into the dominant culture affects the values and norms of a minority family. Children tend to view and evaluate themselves in terms of their family's cultural values.

Moral Development

Moral judgments are guides to how we should behave toward one another. They emerge along with cognitive development. Based on principles of justice and concern for others, moral judgments are taught by families, schools, religious institutions, peer groups, and the media. How are these rules and customs acquired and how are they internalized so that children will behave accordingly? These crucial questions have been debated through the ages.

There are three distinct aspects of morality. **Moral reasoning** involves an individual's ability to refine and understand the moral rules based on a personal standard of good or evil. **Self-evaluation** reflects an individual's sense of success or failure to adhere to his or her moral standards and thus the amount of guilt an individual feels. Finally, the **behavioral aspect** of morality is reflected in one's ability to resist temptation. Two individuals can break the same code of conduct, but only one of them may feel guilty about the behavior. Yet, they both may evaluate the act as equally immoral. Two people may also behave the same way in a similar situation, but their reasons for the action could be based on different principles or levels of moral behavior.

Social learning theorists and attribution theorists study how individuals make moral decisions, but much research is based on the investigations of Piaget and Kohlberg. Piaget, and years later Kohlberg, showed that children's views on moral judgments were dependent on their level of cognitive development. As the ego develops and the intellect matures, their moral judgments change. Egocentrism diminishes, allowing them to see things from another person's point of view. With the onset of abstract logical thinking, individuals are able to think about possibilities of justice. Both Piaget and Kohlberg agree that moral development takes place within moral interactions.

Piaget's research shows children moving through several stages of moral development. The initial stage of moral development, from ages 4 to 7, is **heteronomous morality:** the rules are unchangeable and each child sees only one way to play the game. Everyone does his or her own thing. As children move into the **incipient cooperation stage,** ages 7 to 10, they learn the formal rules of the game with others and play according to shared rules. However, these rules are still largely unchangeable. It is not until the **autonomous stage,** around age 10, that children can grasp that people have different perspectives on moral issues and that intentions, along with the outcomes, are considered in judging behavior (Piaget, 1965).

Piaget defined morality as the understanding and following of the rules because of one's own desire to do so. He believed that, by age 12, children's moral conceptions were similar to those of most adults. At this point, they were able to understand the nature of the rules and had moved from literal conceptions of justice to a much more flexible approach, taking into consideration intentions, circumstances, and differential needs (Piaget, 1965).

Kohlberg began his work thirty years after Piaget's studies on moral development were published (Kohlberg, 1984). Based on Piaget's research, Kohlberg argued that morality was not a fixed trait but rather a **decision-making** capacity. It was the way an individual reasoned about the moral problem and not the response that determined the level of moral maturity. In 1964, he summarized several studies that showed no relationship between parental demands, religious training, and overt behavior. Kohlberg also argued that strength of will or **ego strength** affected moral behavior rather than the superego, as Freud said. Furthermore, Kohlberg stated that a strong conscience did not keep individuals from behaving poorly, but it did make them feel guilty.

In addition, children's moral behavior is based on their cognitive stage of development, ability to delay gratification (to choose long-term goals over short-term

TABLE 2.3	Kohlberg's Stages of Moral Reasoning (Piaget's Stages of Cognitive Development)

Level 1: Preconventional Morality (ages 4 to 10)—Actions based on rewards and punishments. External control

> **Stage 1: Based on reward and punishment.** Individuals follow the rules to avoid punishment.
>
> (Piaget: Preoperational and early concrete operational)
>
> **Stage 2: Rules are followed for personal benefit.** "You scratch my back and I'll scratch yours."
>
> (Piaget: Concrete operational)

Level 2: Conventional Morality (ages 10–13)—Conformity to social rules is necessary for a good society and the need to please others.

> **Stage 3: "Good boy, good girl" morality.** Individuals want to maintain the respect of others. They are able to take another person's viewpoint and understand the Golden Rule, Do unto others what you would have them do unto you.
>
> (Piaget: Early formal operational)
>
> **Stage 4: Authority and social-order maintaining morality.** Individuals conform to society's rules, believing that they are right and must be obeyed under all circumstances.
>
> (Piaget: Formal operational (see Appendix I)

Level 3: Postconventional morality (age 13, early adulthood, or never)— Individuals follow moral principles determined by abstract principles and values applying to all societies.

> **Stage 5: The social contract morality.** Individuals follow laws and rules that are supportive of individual rights and the interests of the majority, but support changing laws that are unjust.
>
> **Stage 6: The universal ethical principle morality.** This is the highest level of morality. Individuals follow laws that are based on universal ethical principles and disobey laws that violate these principles. (Kohlberg, 1969)

objectives), and self-esteem. Children with high self-esteem are less likely to behave immorally and are less vulnerable to pressure from their peers.

Kohlberg's Stages of Moral Reasoning

According to Kohlberg's research, it is important for adults to realize that children cannot perceive things in the same way as adults (Kohlberg, 1968). Behavior that is dependent on the understanding of laws cannot be expected of young children. They only understand behavior that they can process in terms of reward and punishment rather than any beliefs about right and wrong. The behavior of young children may be the same as older children, such as not "snitching" a cookie, but the reasoning behind it is quite different. A 5-year-old will not take something for fear of getting caught, whereas an adolescent or an adult might not do it because it is breaking a rule or custom. Even adults operate at different levels of reasoning. The following example shows that the behavior may be the same, but the moral reasoning for that behavior differs.

The person is driving the legal speed on a street in front of the college. Why?

  a. *The driver already has two tickets and does not want another one.*
  b. *The driver is obeying the law.*
  c. *The driver is concerned that he might accidently hit a student or another car.*
  d. *The driver is being ecologically responsible by conserving fuel.*

Not only is movement to a higher stage a gradual process, but the rate at which change takes place varies among individuals. Kohlberg's studies showed that the many individuals do not reach the stage based on rules and/or laws until their mid-twenties. Only a small percentage of adults in the United States reason at the next stage based on principled morality. Reasoning at a higher stage does not mean that an individual reasons at that level all, or even most, of the time. Also, reasoning at a higher level does not always mean behaving at that level (Malinowski and Smith, 1985).

Family's Influences on Moral Development

Child-rearing methods have enormous impact on moral development. Parents who use authoritative child-rearing methods and who are warm, nurturing, and exemplify and expect high standards of morality help children greatly in their moral development. These parental characteristics are associated with internalized moral standards and high self-esteem in their children (Denham, Renwick, and Holt, 1991; Parke and Buriel, 1998; Steinberg, Darling, and Fletcher, 1995). Children need practice in making decisions. Parents help their children by encouraging them to learn to delay gratification, a process that can begin in the preschool years. For example, children who save money for a desirable toy rather than spending money on an immediate impulse are learning to wait to achieve more desirable goals.

It is important that children have an explanation of rules and for how their behavior affects others. To reach the higher stages of moral development, children must first learn to control their own behavior as opposed to being controlled by others, such as parents or other authority figures (see Chapter 5).

Our society believes that, as we grow older, we should be better able to make moral judgments. Our juvenile justice system was formed to give children a chance to learn how to make moral decisions and follow society's laws. Their records are sealed so as not to penalize them as adults. (The juvenile justice system is covered in Chapter 12.)

Sex Differences and Gender Identity

Basic to one's self-concept is one's name and an understanding of one's gender. Parents give the child a name that is usually appropriate for the child's gender. Naming their child begins a process of socializing the child as a female or a male. One of the most fundamental things a child learns in the family is how to deal with sexuality. Families teach children the acceptable behavior expected for a boy or a girl. This is called gender role development or gender stereotyping. The sex of a child is biologically determined but the gender role is determined by social experiences and is learned. Gender identity is a person's psychological awareness of his or her sex. The term *gender* will be used to describe role identity and behavior of males and females. In order to understand males and females, physiological, psychological, and sociological differences need to be considered. What differences between the genders are due to biology and what traits come from their socialization?

Many differences between the genders can be observed in personality and social development. Boys and girls have different play preferences, peer relations, interactions with parents, and scholastic achievement. Some stereotypes such as boys being more aggressive than girls have been substantiated. Others, such as girls being more dependent are debatable. Studies have shown boys to be more sociable than girls (Lott, 1978; Roper and Hinde, 1978), while girls are shown to be more nurturing. Boys have greater spatial ability while girls have greater verbal skills. Girls are *not* more suggestible than boys and boys do *not* have a higher achievement motivation nor are they more analytical (Maccoby and Jacklin, 1974; Fagot, 1995; Ruble and Martin, 1998). Gender differences are greater within each gender than between them.

Biological Determinants

There is increasing evidence that biological factors such as genetics, hormones, neurology, muscularity, and temperament contribute to certain gender differences.

Some psychological gender differences are partially rooted in biology. The issue is not which is responsible but how nature and nurture can work together.

HORMONE AND CEREBRAL LATERALIZATION   Hormones are special chemicals secreted by glands or organs that stimulate activity in various parts of the body. Androgens are male hormones such as testosterone. Estrogen and progesterone are female hormones. Both genders have these hormones in various concentrations. High levels of androgens are associated with aggression in either gender, as reported in the following studies by Money and Eghardt (1972). Boys whose bodies could not make full use of androgens were quieter and less competitive. Another example involved girls whose mothers took a synthetic hormone similar to androgen to prevent a miscarriage during pregnancy. These girls were born with ambiguous genitals that were later corrected by surgery. Even though these girls were genetically female, they still showed more masculine traits, such as being aggressive and more competitive, than a comparable group of females who showed more female traits such as nurturing and dependence. In cross-cultural studies of a number of traits, such as dependency, nurturing, and compliance, aggression was the only behavior with sufficient evidence of biological roots. In almost every culture and species the male is more aggressive (Maccoby and Jacklin, 1974).

Some researchers believe that differences in brain organization may account for certain general discrepancies in problem-solving abilities between boys and girls. If the hemispheres of male brains are more specialized or lateralized than those of females, then those with a highly lateralized right hemisphere should be better in solving visual/spatial problems (Bianci, 1993). However, some of these differences could be due to environmental influences such as giving boys toys, like Legos, that involve spacial and visual relationships.

Gender Development

Cognitive developmental theory views gender role development as part of the child's total cognitive development. There are stages involved in gender constancy and each stage is influenced by the child's interactions with the environment. About age 5 or 6, children understand the concept of male and female and adopt the behavior appropriate for their biological sex. Parents give children "appropriate" toys, activities, clothes, and help them to express their emotions as a boy or girl should. Some parents allow their children more freedom in their choices than other parents. Children's peers, child-care personnel, school teachers, and the characters in the media also contribute to their gender role development (Kohlberg, 1966).

The gender schema theory proposes that children learn how they are to behave and feel through their social experiences and cognitive development (Bem, 1981; Martin, Wood, and Little, 1990; Ruble, 1988). Children develop a schema or a pattern of beliefs about gender expectations that changes with their stage in cognitive development.

Most children go through three stages in gender development (Shepherd-Lock, 1982). The earliest form is **gender identity,** the ability to label oneself and others. This ability generally occurs between ages 2 and 3 (Huston, 1983). Young preschoolers determine gender by surface attributes. For example, while dressed up in male clothes, the child is a boy. A mother asked her 3-year-old whether the new child who moved in next door was a girl or a boy. The child said, "I don't know cause it didn't have any clothes on."

In the next stage, children develop **gender preferences** as to which gender they wish to be. Gender preferences for toys and activities are seen around age three, while preferences for appropriate personal qualities come later. About age 5 or 6, most children think that boys are strong and girls are dependent.

As young as age 2, children will associate specific toys or activities with a certain gender, and, by age 3 or 4, children have acquired many gender stereotypes. Three-year-olds are more likely to choose a male doll for hitting activities and a female doll for statements of affection (Kuhn, Nash, and Brucken, 1978). Preschool and early elementary school children hold more rigid stereotypes than do older children. This is compatible with Piaget's theory of moral development: older children are less rigid in their judgments because they take other things like intentions into consideration. On the other hand, gender-based affiliation increases with age. It does vary, however, with the extent to which the child is "gender-typed" for traditional gender role adoption.

Gender constancy comes when the child recognizes that gender remains permanent over the years. A little girl now will tell you that she will grow up to be a mommy. Gender constancy involves a motivational component. Children realize that they cannot change gender simply by willing it. They also understand that their appearance or activities do not affect their gender, even temporarily. Boys may play with dolls or dress like a girl without becoming a girl. Although gender constancy first appears around age 4 or 5, it is not until ages seven to nine that it becomes stable for most children (Emmerich and Sheppard, 1982). Finally, it is not until children are 8 or 9 that they refer to the biological differences of the genitals as the reason for gender constancy and understand the gender concepts of masculinity and femininity (Martin, et al., 1990; Emmerich, Goldman, Kirsh, and Sharaconaghy, 1977; McConaghy, 1979). Brighter or more socially aware children progress through these stages more rapidly (Gouze and Nadelman, 1980). All three of these stages contribute to both a child's gender role and understanding of the behaviors expected by society for each gender.

Family Influences on Gender Role Acquisition

Many parents treat girls and boys differently from birth (Fagot, 1995). Parents respond more quickly to demanding, fussy behavior from baby sons than their baby daughters (Feiring and Lewis, 1979; Hutt, 1977) and to distress in male infants more quickly than daughters (Corter and Bow, 1976). Parents stop feeding a baby boy when he spits up food or coughs sooner than a girl (Parke and Sawin, 1981). Do parents treat their sons with more respect than daughters? Do they value boys more than girls, or do boys have a way of getting their parents to attend to them more?

The way in which parents and the media socialize children encourages differences between the genders. Parents have been found to reward gender-appropriate behavior and punish cross-gender activity (Langlois and Downs, 1980). In a study of toddlers, parents reinforced girl toddlers for dancing, playing with dolls, asking for help, and following parents around the house, while sons at the same age were praised for playing with blocks. Their daughters were criticized more than sons for manipulating objects, running, jumping, and climbing, while their sons were rebuked for playing with dolls and asking for or volunteering help (Fagot, 1978). Parents of older preschool and younger school-age children assign household chores that are usually gender appropriate. In general, parents reward boys for traditional male traits such as assertiveness, emotional reserve, and independence. They praise girls for being cooperative, dependent, nurturing, and emotionally expressive (Fagot and Hagan, 1991; Lytton and Romney, 1991).

Toys, activities, clothing, and the environment of children's bedrooms often show gender stereotyping. Rheingold and Cook (1975) went into the homes of children under age 6. Boys' rooms had more transportation vehicles, machines, army equipment and soldiers, animal furnishings, educational art materials, spatial-temporal toys, and sport equipment. Girls' rooms contained more baby dolls, girl dolls, floral patterns, and ruffled furnishings. In general, boys had a greater variety of toys that dealt with activities outside the home while girls' toys encouraged activities in housekeeping and caring for children.

Fathers are more active than mothers in socializing their children (Ruble and Martin, 1998). This is especially true for their sons. Fathers will reward children more for gender-appropriate activities and punish them for play with cross-gender toys (Lytton and Romney, 1991; Fagot, 1978; Lansky, 1967). At preschools, fathers can be seen hugging their daughters more than their sons but mothers tend to behave the same to both genders in their greetings and departures. Fathers may act this way to preserve male power or because they have been under more pressure since childhood than women to conform to traditional gender roles. Whatever the reason, boys are more traditionally gender-typed than girls (Faulkender, 1980; Kleinke and Nicholson, 1979).

Fathers play a very important part in developing masculine traits in boys and feminine traits in girls. Boys with warm, nurturing but masculine fathers tend to show more masculine traits. Fathers teach daughters how to relate to the opposite gender and encourage them to develop their nurturing role. Highly feminine gender-typed girls have fathers who are masculine yet affectionate and who praised them for feminine behavior (Johnson, 1977). See Chapter 5 for more information on personality traits of parents and their children's gender roles. The effects of the father's absence on boys' and girls' gender roles are discussed in Chapter 3.

Traditional Roles and Androgynous Roles

Traditional roles can be classified as "instrumental" for males and "expressive" for females (Parsons, 1955). The traditional masculine role includes that of decision maker, leader, protector, breadwinner, and being assertive and competitive. The traditional female role encompasses emotionality, nurturing, kindness, cooperation, and concern for interpersonal harmony. In androgynous roles, the masculine and feminine traits are blended to varying degrees.

Androgynous gender roles hold some advantages for both genders. Girls with some masculine traits have a more positive self-image, are more accepted by their peers, and better in mathematics than girls who see themselves exclusively in feminine terms (Hall and Haberstadt, 1980; Massad, 1981). As adults, both men and women with some traits of the other gender appear to have higher self-esteem and receive more respect from others compared to highly gender-typed adults (Hall and Haberstadt, 1980; Massad, 1981; Major, Carnevale, and Deaux, 1981). However, good mental health and personal adjustment are associated with high masculine traits. Individuals of either gender who are highly feminine are more likely to have lower self-esteem and poorer social adjustments (Bem, 1975; Major, et al. 1981).

Today, children experience conflicting messages regarding what behavior is expected of their gender. The roles for women have changed in many ways. Women contribute to their family's income. Increasing numbers of women have a college education and are assuming professional roles that once were left largely to men. Our laws have changed in an attempt to establish gender equity. In 1972, Congress passed the Title IX Education Amendment prohibiting discrimination on the basis of gender. This has affected textbooks, course requirements in schools, sports programs, gender balance on staffs, and other aspects of life in the United States. However, efforts to enact the Equal Rights Amendment failed.

Room to Grow

Gender stereotyping is under attack. A leading critic, Bem (1975, 1981) argues that this produces a gender-schematic person who is reluctant to display a traditionally cross-gender attribute even when it appears beneficial. Rigidly gender-typed people only feel comfortable with behaviors consistent with their role. Androgynous individuals are able to act in cross-gender ways when desirable or beneficial to them. Traditional masculine men show the greatest preference for gender-congruent tasks even when tempted by rewards (Helmreich, Spence, and Holahan, 1979). Another study, using Bem's Sex Role Inventory, showed that previously unacquainted adults got along better when one of the test couples was androgynous than when they both had traditional gender roles (Ickes and Barns, 1978).

In the last three decades, early childhood educators and their professional organizations have been active in the movement to provide young children with a nonsexist preschool environment allowing girls and boys to grow and develop according to their talents and interests (Bredekamp and Copple, 1997). Early childhood

Trophy Time: Grandpa Supported Each Grandchild at Individual Practices and Games.

Each child, regardless of gender, has an opportunity to explore his or her interests and talents. In androgynous roles, traditional masculine, and female traits are blended to varying degrees.

professionals continue to advocate for young children to experience literature showing women and men in many roles. This encourages them to engage in a variety of play activities, not just those that have been traditionally accepted for their gender. Many feel it is important for boys to be able to express all their emotions and to be able to nurture as well as be strong and assertive. On the other hand, girls should be encouraged to show leadership and be assertive along with being kind, sympathetic, and cooperative. Both girls and boys need practice in visual spatial activities. The belief is that children and society at large will benefit when children have room to grow and develop according to their talents and not only those based on traditional gender roles.

There are many questions yet to be answered. How do families socialize children for their gender so that they will feel secure and comfortable yet fulfill themselves as individuals? What traits in men and women will society need when today's children become adults? How can parents socialize their children to adopt different gender roles from some that they are modeling? Will American society modify its socialization goals for gender roles so as to minimize gender differences in the future? Will females and males have a broader range of ways to utilize their talents and interests both in the family and the workplace?

 A Child's Membership in the Family

Family membership gives a child identity and establishes the child's place in society. At birth, the child acquires identity as a family member and becomes a legal member of society. He is John's son or she is the Smiths' daughter. As mentioned in Chapter 1, the place the child has in society is largely determined by the family's status in the community. Status is based on honor and prestige and includes such factors as ancestry, occupation, income, education, race/ethnicity, and lifestyles. Chapter 1 discusses the effects of socioeconomic status on children.

There is also status within the family. A child has a social place in the family as the oldest, youngest, middle, or the only child. This birth order will shift as new children enter the family. Their gender as well as their personality may also affect their place in the family. The family sets the stage for possibilities, property, and power for the next generation.

In a family, children learn the rights, privileges, and obligations of family members and the family's standards for behavior, or norms and values. These may be as simple as "Children do not talk back to their parents" or as complex as "Family members are expected to be good citizens." Families prepare children for society by transmitting their language, morals, laws, and culture. They teach children how to live with other people and function in group situations. As a member of the family, children learn about the larger society. Through kin, neighbors, employers, and general family connections, children gain an expanding view of the outside community.

Ideally, family membership is for life, even though children's status within the family changes as they become adults. Not only do adults view the family they grew up in with some degree of nostalgia, they often use it as a refuge from the world in times of trouble. Young adults, furthering their education or seeking employment, and adults with their own family in crisis, often turn to their parents or siblings for support.

Children: Society's Future

The future of society is in its children. Margaret Mead once said, "As the family goes, so goes the nation," meaning that strong and healthy families provide the backbone of a nation. The family needs support from other institutions and individuals in order to provide adequately for its children. Poverty and inadequate nutrition, lack of health care, and insufficient education are just a few conditions that can be very costly both in human and monetary terms. Society needs healthy successful children to become future citizens who will ensure a quality environment and productive society for coming generations.

Key Points

1. The family assures the continuity of society by giving birth to children, conferring legal status, socializing them, and providing for their physical and psychological development.
2. Nurturing involves love, emotional security, and a sense of belonging that only the family can adequately provide.
3. Personality includes the traits that distinguish each person and involves an individual's behavior, thinking, and feelings.

4. Social cognition is the knowledge of social relationships including an understanding of the self and of others.
5. Self-concept development is a gradual process involving an understanding of one's own personality and psychological functioning overall and in specific areas. Self-esteem is the evaluative component.
6. Morality involves an individual's judgment of acts, self-evaluation, and one's behavior. According to Kohlberg, moral development occurs in stages paralleling cognitive development and

is influenced by social relationships. Moral behavior comes from ego strength and decision-making ability rather than from the strength of one's conscience.

7. Sex refers to the physiological differences between males and females while gender is the psychological awareness of one's sex and is learned. This text uses gender for both terms.

8. Androgynous roles allow children to develop according to their talents, temperament, and interests, rather than to be limited by traditional gender roles.

9. Families need support in order to provide adequately for their children, ensuring a healthy society in the future.

Critical Thinking Questions

1. In what ways might a baby's temperament affect the infant's attachment to a parent, siblings, and significant others?

2. In what ways do you see your gender role as enhancing and limiting your options in life?

3. Within the family, how can parents help each of their children to feel better about themselves?

Resources and References

American Academy of Pediatrics
www.aap.org

■ References

Ainsworth, M. (1979). Infant–mother attachment. *American Psychologist, 34,* 932–937.

Ainsworth, M., Blehar, M. C., Waters, E., and Wall, S. (1978). *Patterns of attachment.* Hillsdale, NJ: Erlbaum.

Bandura, A. (1986). *Social foundation of thought and action: A social cognitive theory.* Englewood Cliffs, NJ: Prentice-Hall.

Bandura, A. (1989). Social cognitive theory. In Vasta (Ed.), *Annals of child development* (Vol. 6), pp. 1–60. Greenwich, CT: JAI Press.

Bandura, A. (1992). Perceived self-efficacy in cognitive development and functioning. *Educational Psychologist, 28,* 117–118.

Barrera, M. E., and Maurer, D. (1981). The perception of facial expressions by the three-month-old. *Child Development, 53,* 203–206.

Baumeister, R. F., Smart, L., and Boden, J. M. (1996). Relation of threatened egotism to violence and aggression: The dark side of high self-esteem. *Psychological Review, 105,* 5–33.

Belsky, J., Fish, M., and Isabella, R. (1991). Continuity and discontinuity in infant negative and positive emotionality: Family antecedents and attachment consequences. *Developmental Psychology, 27,* 421–431.

Bem, S. (1975). Sex role adaptability: One consequence of psychological androgyny. *Journal of Personality and Social Psychology, 31,* 634–643.

Bem, S. L. (1981). Gender schema theory: A cognitive account of sex typing. *Psychological Review, 88,* 354–364.

Bem, S. L. (1989). Genital knowledge and gender constancy in preschool children. *Child Development, 60,* 649–662.

Bennett, C. (2003). *Comprehensive multicultural education: Theory and Practice.* (5th ed.). Boston: Allyn and Bacon.

Berk, L. E. (2002). *Infants, children, and adolescents.* (4th ed.). Boston: Allyn and Bacon.

Bertenthal, B. and Fischer, K. (1978). Development of self-recognition in the infant. *Development Psychology, 14,* 77–91.

Bianci, V. (1993). *Mechanisms of brain lateralization.* Philadelphia: Gordon and Beach.

Blehar, M., Lieberman, C., and Ainsworth, M. (1977). Early face-to-face interaction and its relation to later infant-mother attachment. *Child Development, 58,* 182–194.

Bornstein, M. H., and Lamb, M. E. (Eds.). 1992. *Developmental psychology: An advanced textbook.* Hillsdale, NJ: Erlbaum.

Bowlby, J. (1969). *Attachment and loss:* Vol. 1: Attachment. New York: Basic Books.

Bredekamp, S., and Copple, C. (Eds.). (1997). *Developmentally appropriate practice in early childhood programs.* Washington, DC: National Association for the Education of Young Children.

Bretherton, I. (1992). The origins of attachment theory: John Bowlby and Mary Ainsworth. *Developmental Psychology, 28,* 759–775.

Bronfenbrenner, U. (1979). *The ecology of human development*. Cambridge, MA: Harvard University Press.

California Task Force to Promote Self-Esteem and Personal and Social Responsibility. (1990). *Toward a state of self-esteem*. Sacramento, CA: California State Department of Education.

Camras, L. A. (1992). Expressive development and basic emotions. *Cognitions and Emotion, 6,* 267–283.

Caspi, A., Henry, B., McGee, R. O., Moffitt, T. E., and Silva, P. A. (1995). Temperamental origins of child and adolescent behavior problems: From age three to age fifteen. *Child Development, 66,* 55–68.

Chen, X., Hastings, P., Rubin, K., Chen, H., Cen, G., and Stewart, S. (1998). Child-rearing attitudes and behavioral inhibition in Chinese and Canadian toddlers: A cross-cultural study. *Developmental Psychology, 34,* 677–686.

Chen, X., Rubin, K., and Li, Z. (1996). Social functioning and adjustment in Chinese children: A longitudinal study. *Developmental Psychology, 31,* 531–539.

Clark, K. B., and Clark, M. P. (1947). Radical identification and preference in Negro children. In T. M. Necomb and E. L. Hartley (Eds.), *Readings in social psychology*. New York: Holt, Rinehart and Winston.

Clark-Stewart, K. (1973). Interactions between mothers and their young children. *Monographs of the Society for Research in Child Development, 38,* 1–153.

Cooley, C. H. (1902). *Human nature and the social order*. New York: Scribner's. (Reprinted in 1964.)

Coppersmith, S. (1967). *The antecedents of self-esteem*. San Francisco: Freeman.

Corter, C., and Bow, J. (1976). The mother's response to separation as a function of her infant's sex and vocal distress. *Child Development, 47,* 872–876.

Crockenberg, S. B. (1986). Are temperamental differences in babies associated with predictable differences in caregiving? In J. V. Lerner and A. C. Peterson (Eds.), *Temperament and social interaction in infants and children* (pp. 75–88). San Francisco: Jossey-Bass.

Damon, W., and Hart, D. (1988). *Self-understanding in childhood and adolescence*. New York: Cambridge University Press.

Denham, S. A., Renwick, S. M., and Holt, R. W. (1991). Working and playing together: Prediction of preschool social-emotional competence from mother–child interaction. *Child Development, 62,* 242–249.

de Vries, M. W. (1984). Temperament and infant mortality among the Masai of East Africa. *American Journal of Psychiatry, 141,* 1189–1194.

Deutsch, M. (1967). *The disadvantaged child: Selected papers of Martin Deutsch and associates*. New York: Basic Books.

deWall, F. B. M. (1999). The end of nature versus nurture. *Scientific American, 281*(6), 94–99.

DeWolf, M. and Ijzendoorn, M. (1997). Sensitivity and attachment: A meta-analysis on parental antecedents of infant attachment. *Child Development, 68,* 571–591.

Duckitt, J. (1994). Conformity to social pressure and racial prejudice among white South Africans. *Genetic, Social, and General Psychology Monographs, 120,* 121–143.

Eder, R. (1989). The emergent personologist: The structure and content of 3½-, 5½-, and 7½-year-olds' concepts of themselves and other persons. *Child Development, 60,* 1218–1228.

Egeland, B. and Sroufe, L. (1981). Attachment and early maltreatment. *Child Development, 52,* 44–52.

Emmerich, W., Goldman, K. S., Kirsh, B., and Sharaconaghy, R. (1977). Evidence for a transitional phase in the development of gender constancy. *Child Development, 48,* 930–936.

Emmerich, W., and Sheppard, K. (1982). Development of sex-differentiated preferences during late childhood and adolescence. *Developmental Psychology, 18,* 407–417.

Fagot, B. I. (1978). The influence of sex of child on parental reactions to toddler children. *Child Development, 49,* 458–465.

Fagot, B. I. (1995). Parenting boys and girls. In M. H. Bornstein (Ed.), *Handbook of parenting* (Vol. 1). Mahwah, NJ: Erlbaum.

Fagot, B. I., and Hagan, R. (1991). Observation of parent reaction to sex-stereotyped behaviors: Age and sex effects. *Child Development, 62,* 617–628.

Fagot, B. I., and Leinbach, M. D. (1989). The young child's gender schema: Environmental input, internal organization. *Child Development, 62,* 617–628.

Fagot, B. I., Leinbach, M. D., and O'Boyle, C. (1992). Gender labeling, gender stereotyping, and parenting behaviors. *Developmental Psychology, 28,* 225–230.

Faulkender, P. (1980). Categorical habituation with sex-typed toy stimuli in older and younger preschoolers. *Child Development, 51,* 515–519.

Feiring, C., and Lewis, M. (1979). Sex and age differences in young children's reactions to frustration: A further look at the Lewis and Goldberg subjects. *Child Development, 59,* 848–853.

Feldman, R. (1998). *Child Development,* p. 188. Upper Saddle River, NJ: Prentice Hall.

Fraiberg, S. (1977). *Insights from the blind: Contemporary studies of blind and sighted infants.* New York: Basic Books.

Freud, S. (1953). *A general introduction to psychoanalysis.* (J. Riviere, Trans.). New York: Permabooks. (Original work published 1935).

Garbarino, J. (1985). *Adolescent development: An ecological perspective.* Columbus, OH: Merrill.

Ginot, H. (1965). *Between parent and child.* New York: Avon.

Gouze, K. R., and Nadelman, L. (1980). Constancy of gender identity for self and others between the ages of three and seven. *Child Development, 51,* 275–278.

Grusec, J., and Redler, E. (1980). Attribution, reinforcement, and altruism: A developmental analysis. *Developmental Psychology, 16,* 525–534.

Guerin, D. W., and Gottfried, A. W. (1994). Developmental stability and change in parent reports of temperament: A 10-year longitudinal investigation from infancy through preadolescence. *Merrill-Palmer Quarterly, 40,* 334–355.

Guerin, D. W., Gottfried, A. W., and Thomas, C. W. (1997). Difficult temperament and behaviour problems: A longitudinal study from 1.5 to 12 years. *International Journal of Behavioral Development, 21*(1), 71–90.

Gunnar, M. R., Porter, F. L., Wolf, C. M., Rigatuso, J., and Larson, M. C. (1995). Neonatal stress activity: Predictions to later emotional temperament. *Child Development, 66,* 1–3.

Hall, J. A., and Haberstadt, A. G. (1980). Masculinity and femininity in children: Development of the Children's Attributes Questionnaire. *Developmental Psychology, 16,* 270–280.

Harter, S. (1990a). Identity and self development. In S. Feldman and G. Elliott (Eds.), *At the threshold: The developing adolescent.* Cambridge, MA: Harvard University Press.

Harter, S. (1990b). Issues in the assessment of self-concept of children and adolescents. In A. LaGreca (Ed.), *Through the eyes of a child.* Boston: Allyn and Bacon.

Harter, S. (1998). The development of self-representations. In N. Eisenberg (Ed.), *Handbook of Child Psychology: Vol. 3: Social, emotional, and personality development* (5th ed., pp. 553–618). New York: Wiley.

Harter, S. (1999). *The construction of self: A developmental perspective.* New York: Guilford.

Helmreich, R. L., Spence, J. T., and Holahan, C. K. (1979). Psychological androgyny and sex-role flexibility: A test of two hypotheses. *Journal of Personality and Social Psychology, 37,* 1631–1644.

Huston, A. C. (1983). Sex-typing. In P. Mussen (Ed.), *Handbook of child psychology* Vol. 4, New York: Wiley.

Hutt, C. (1977). Sex differences in human development. In E. M. Hetherington and R. D. Parke (Eds.), *Contemporary readings in child psychology.* New York: McGraw-Hill.

Hymel, S., LeMare, L., Ditner, E., and Woody, E. Z. (1999). Assessing self-concept in children: Variations across self-concept domains. *Merrill-Palmer Quarterly, 45,* 602–623.

Ickes, W., and Barns, R. D. (1978). Boys and girls together—and alienated: On enacting stereotyped sex roles in mixed-sex dyads. *Journal of Personality and Social Psychology, 36,* 669–683.

Isabella, R. and Belsky, J. (1991). Interactional synchrony and the origins of infant-mother attachment: A replication study. *Child Development, 62,* 373–384.

Johnson, M. M. (1977). Fathers, mothers, and sex-typing. In E. M. Hetherington and R. D. Parke (Eds.), *Contemporary readings in child psychology.* New York: McGraw-Hill.

Kerr, M., Lambert, W. W., Statin, H., and Klachenberg-Larsson, I. (1994). Stability of inhibition in a Swedish longitudinal sample. *Child Development, 65,* 138–146.

Kleinke, C. L., and Nicholson, T. A. (1979). Black and white children's awareness of de facto race and sex differences. *Developmental Psychology, 15,* 84–86.

Kochanska, G., and Radke-Yarrow, M. (1992). Inhibition in toddlerhood and the dynamics of the child's interaction with an unfamiliar peer at age five. *Child Development, 63,* 325–335.

Kohlberg, L. (1966). A cognitive-developmental view of sex-role development. In E. Maccoby (Ed.). *The development of sex differences.* Stanford, CA: Stanford University Press.

Kohlberg. L. (1968, April). The child as a moral philosopher. *Psychology Today,* 25–30.

Kohlberg. L. (1969). Stage and sequence: The cognitive-developmental approach to socialization. In D. Goslin (Ed.), *Handbook of socialization theory and research.* Chicago: Rand McNally.

Kohlberg, L. (1984). *The psychology of moral development: Essays on moral development (2).* San Francisco: Harper and Row.

Kuhn, D., Nash, S. C., and Brucken, L. (1978). Sex role concepts of two- and three-year-olds. *Child Development, 49,* 445–451.

Lamb, M. E. (1976a). Effects of stress and cohort on mother– and father–infant interaction. *Developmental Psychology, 12,* 435–433.

Lamb, M. E. (1976b, Ed.). *The role of the father in child development.* New York: Wiley.

Langlois, J., and Downs, A. (1980). Mothers, fathers, and peers as socialization agents of sex-typed behaviors in young children. *Child Development, 51,* 1217–1247.

Lansky, L. M. (1967). The family structure also affects the model: Sex role attitudes in parents of preschool children. *Merrill-Palmer Quarterly, 13,* 139–150.

Lewis, M. and Brooks-Gunn, J. Self, other, and fear: The reactions of infants to people. In E. M. Hetherington, and R. Parke (Eds.), *Contemporary readings in child psychology.* New York: McGraw-Hill.

Livesley, W. J., and Bromley, D. R. (1973). *Person perception in childhood and adolescence.* London: Wiley.

Lott, B. (1978). Behavioral concordance with sex role ideology related to play areas, creativity, and parental sex typing. *Journal of Personality and Social Psychology, 36,* 1087–1100.

Lytton, H., and Romney, D. M. (1991). Parents' differential socialization of boys and girls: A meta analysis. *Psychological Bulletin, 109*(2), 267–303.

Maccoby, E. E. (1980). *Social development: Psychological growth and the parent–child relationship.* New York: Harcourt Brace Jovanovich.

Maccoby, E. E., and Jacklin, C. (1974). *The psychology of sex differences.* Stanford, CA: Stanford University Press.

Major, B., Carnevale, P. J. D., and Deaux, K. (1981). A different perspective on androgyny: Evaluations of masculine and feminine personality characteristics. *Journal of Personality and Social Psychology, 41,* 988–1001.

Malinowski, C. I., and Smith, C. P. (1985). Moral reasoning and moral conduct: An investigation prompted by Kohlberg's theory. *Journal of Personality and Social Psychology, 49,* 1016–1037.

Mangelsdorf, S., Gunnar, M., Kestenbaum, R., Lang, S., and Andreas, D. (1990). Infant proneness-to-distress temperament, maternal personality, and mother–infant attachment: Association and goodness of fit. *Child Development, 61,* 820–831.

Marsh, H. W. (1990). The structure of academic self-concept: The Marsh/Shavelson model. *Journal of Educational Psychology, 82,* 623–636.

Marsh, H. W., Craven, R., and Debus, R. (1998). Structure, stability, and development of young children's self-concepts: A multicohort-multioccasion study. *Child Development, 69,* 1030–1053.

Marsh, H. W. and Parker, J. W. (1984). Determinants of student self-concept: Is it better to be a relatively big fish in a small pond even if you don't learn to swim as well? *Journal of Personality and Social Psychology, 47,* 213–231.

Marsh, H. W., and Shavelson, R. (1985). Self-concept: Its multifaceted, hierarchical structure. *Educational Psychologist, 20,* 107–123.

Martin, C. L., Wood, C. H., and Little, J. K. (1990). The development of gender stereotype components. *Child Development, 61,* 1891–1904.

Massad, C. M. (1981). Sex role identity and adjustment during adolescence. *Child Development, 52,* 1290–1298.

McConaghy, M. J. (1979). Gender permanence and the genital basis of gender: Stages in the development of constancy of gender identity. *Child Development, 50,* 1223–1226.

Mead, M. (1934). *Mind, self, and society.* Chicago: University of Chicago Press.

Money, J., and Eghardt, A. A. (1972). *Man and woman, boy and girl: The differentiation and dimorphism of gender identity from conception to maturity.* Baltimore: Johns Hopkins University Press.

Moss, H. A. (1967). Sex, age, and state as determinants of mother–infant interaction. *Merrill-Palmer Quarterly, 13,* 19–36.

Owen, M. T., Easterbrooks, M. A., Chase-Lansdale, L., and Goldberg, W. A. (1984). The relationship between maternal employment status and the stability of attachment to mother and father. *Child Development, 55,* 1894–1901.

Owen, W., and Cox, M. (1997). Marital conflict and the development of infant-parent attachment relationships. *Journal of Family Psychology, 11,* 152–164.

Parke, R. D., and Buriel, R. (1998). Socialization in the family: Ethnic and ecological perspectives. In N. Eisenberg, (Ed.), *Handbook of child psychology: Vol. 3: Social, emotional, and personality development* (5th ed., pp. 463–552). New York: John Wiley and Sons.

Parke, R. D., and Sawin, D. B. (1981). Father–infant interaction in the newborn period. A reevaluation of some current myths. In E. M. Hetherington and R. D. Parke (Eds.), *Contemporary readings in child psychology.* New York: McGraw-Hill.

Parsons, T. (1955). Family structure and the socialization of the child. In T. Parsons and R. F. Bales (Eds.), *Family socialization and interaction process.* Glencoe, IL: Free Press.

Passman, R. H., and Weisberg, P. (1975). Mothers and blankets as agents for promoting play and exploration by young children in a novel experiment: The effects of social and nonsocial attachment objects. *Developmental Psychology, 11,* 170–177.

Pedlow, R., Sanson, A., Prior, M., and Oberklaid, F. (1993). Stability of maternally reported temperament from infancy to 8 years. *Developmental Psychology, 29,* 998–1007.

Peevers, B. H., and Secord, P. F. (1973). Developmental changes in attribution of descriptive concepts of persons. *Journal of Personality and Social Psychology, 27,* 120–128.

Phillips, S., King. S., and Dubois, L. (1978). Spontaneous activities of female versus male newborns. *Child Development, 49,* 590–597.

Piaget, J. (1963). *The origins of intelligence in children.* New York: Norton.

Piaget, J. (1965). *The moral judgement of the child.* New York: Free Press. (Original work published in 1932.)

Roper, R., and Hinde, R. A. (1978). Social behavior in a play group: Consistency and complexity. *Child Development, 49,* 570–579.

Rheingold, H. L., and Cook, K. V. (1975). The content of boys' and girls' rooms as an index of parents' behavior. *Child Development, 46,* 459–463.

Ruble, D. N. (1988). Sex-role development. In M. H. Berstin and M. E. Lamb (Eds.), *Social cognitive development.* Hillsdale, NJ: Erlbaum.

Ruble, D. N., Boggiano, A. K., & Feldman, N. S., and Loebl, J. H. (1980). Developmental analysis of the role of social comparison in self-evaluation. *Developmental Psychology, 16,* 105–115.

Ruble, D., and Martin, C. L. (1998). Gender development. In W. Damon (Ed.), *Handbook of Child Psychology* (vol. 3 5th ed.). pp. 000. New York: Wiley.

Rutter, M. (1979). Maternal deprivation, 1972–78: New findings, new concepts, new approaches. *Child Development, 50,* 283–305.

Samuels, H. R. (1980). The effect of an older sibling on infant locomotor exploration of a new environment. *Child Development, 51,* 607–609.

Sanson, A. V., Pedlow, R., Cann, W., Prior, M., and Oberklaid, F. (1996). Shyness ratings: Stability and correlates in early childhood. *International Journal of Behavioural Development, 19,* 705–724.

Sanson, A. V., Smart, D. F., Prior, M., and Pedlow, R., 1994. The structure of temperament from 3 to 7 years: Age, sex and sociodemographic influences. *Merrill-Palmer Quarterly, 40,* 233–252.

Schlesinger, H. (1980). The impact of deafness on lifestyle. In J. M. Stack (Ed.), *The special child.* New York: Human Sciences Press.

Selman, R. L. (1973, March). *A structural analysis of the ability to take another's social perspective: Stages in the development of role-taking ability.* Paper presented at the meeting of the Society for Research in Child Development, Philadelphia.

Sheppard-Look, D. (1982). Sex differentiation and the development of sex roles. In B. Walman (Ed.). *Handbook of Developmental psychology.* Englewood Cliffs, NJ: Prentice-Hall.

Spitz, R. (1945). Hospitalism: An inquiry into the genesis of psychiatric conditions in early childhood. *Psychoanalytic Study of the Child, 1,* 113–117.

Spitz, R. (1946). Anaclitic depression. *Psychoanalytic Study of the Child, 2,* 313–342.

Steinberg, L., Darling, L. E., and Fletcher, A. C. (1995). Authoritative parenting and adolescent development: An ecological journey. In P. Moen, G. H. Elder, and K. Luscher (Eds.), *Examining lives in context* (pp. 423–466). Washington, DC: American Psychological Association.

Tajfel, H. (1982). *Social identity and intergroup relations.* London: Cambridge University Press.

Thomas, A., and Chess, S. (1977). *Temperament and development.* New York: Brunner-Mazel.

Thomas, A., and Chess, S. (1980). *The dynamics of psychological development.* New York: Brunner-Mazel.

Thomas, A., and Chess, S. (1986). The New York Longitudinal Study: From infancy to early adult life. In R. Plomin and J. Dunn (Eds.), *Changes, continuities, and challenges.* Hillsdale, NJ: Erlbaum.

Thompson, S. (1975). Gender labels and early sex role development. *Child Development, 46,* 339–347.

Van den Bloom, D. C. (1995). Do first year intervention effects endure? Follow-up during toddlerhood of a sample of Dutch irritable infants. *Child Development, 66,* 1798–1816.

Vaughn, B. E., Egeland, B. R., Stroufe, L. A., and Waters, E. (1979). Individual differences in infant–mother attachment at twelve and eighteen months: Stability and change in families under stress. *Child Development, 50,* 971–975.

Vondra, J. I., Hommerding, K. D., and Shaw, D. S. (1999). Stability and change in infant attachment in a low-income sample. In J. I. Vondra and D. Barnett (Eds.), *Atypical attachment in infancy and early childhood among children at developmental risk. Monographs of the Society of Research in Child Development, 64,* 3, Serial No. 258, 119–124.

Watson, J. S., Hayes, L. A., Vietze, P., and Becker, J. (1979). Discriminative infant smiling to orientations of talking faces of mother and stranger. *Journal of Experimental Child Psychology, 28,* 92–99.

Yarrow, M. J., and Goodwin, M. S. (1973). The immediate impact of separation reactions of infants to a change in mother figures. In L. J. Stone, H. T. Smith, and L. B. Murphy (Eds.), *The competent infant.* New York: Basic Books.

Yarrow, M. J., Goodwin, M. S., Manheimer, H., and Milowe, I. D. (1973). Infancy experience and cognitive and personality development at ten years. In L. J. Stone, H. T. Smith, and L. B. Murphy (Eds.), *The competent infant.* New York: Basic Books.

The Rich Diversity of Family Forms

3

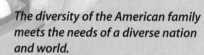

The diversity of the American family meets the needs of a diverse nation and world.
— **Judith Stacey and Arlene Skolnick**

*T*his chapter looks at the history of the family and examines the different family forms in which children grow up. Expanded lifestyle choices for both men and women in recent decades have led to dual-career families, cohabitation or unmarried couples living together with or without children, nuclear families, single-parent families, blended families, extended families, and gay or lesbian families (Davidson and Moore, 1992). Children grow up in different family forms with many children living in more than one family during their childhood.

During the twentieth century, most members of American society defined the family as a social group of two or more individuals based on blood, marriage, or adoption who usually live together (Macioni, 1997). The pluralism of contemporary lifestyles has forced new definitions. It is difficult to form a consensus because many individuals view the family according to the type(s) in which they grew up. The challenge is to find a definition broad enough to include groups recognized by many as families. The family may ultimately be described as a small group of people who are bound by a mutual feeling of belonging and caring. Most children grow to maturity within a family where, ideally, their most basic needs are met, and the lives of all its members are deeply affected.

Origin of the Family

The family, now considered vital for the survival of society, is very recent in human evolution. For approximately two to three million years, human beings lived in groups moving from place to place, hunting and gathering (McKay, Hill, and Buckler, 1988). During this period, almost every kind of relationship, adult-to-adult, male-to-female, adult-to-child, was shared broadly within the entire group.

The Paleolithic era lasted about 400,000 years, ending around 7,000 years ago. For at least part of this period, the basic social unit was probably the family, but it was enmeshed with a number of other families living in a tribe. Members of the tribe considered themselves descendants of a common ancestor. They were led by a male or patriarch (McKay, Hill, and Buckler, 1988). The formation of the family as we know it today was linked closely with the economic revolution in which human beings gave up hunting and foraging for agriculture. This provided both male and female adults and children more physical and emotional security. It was not until the Neolithic Age, approximately 3,000 to 7,000 years ago, that the family became well established (Buckler, 1988).

Most authorities believe that the extended family is the original family form, a refinement of precivilized human groups. Until the eighteenth century, the majority of families in the United States were extended families. This family included the husband and wife and their children plus any of their relatives living in the same household or in close proximity. It usually involved three generations. Extended families were suited to an agricultural society in which many individuals were needed to work the land.

The nuclear family, consisting of father, mother, and their children, is a product of modern times. With the rise of capitalism and resulting wealth, individuals were less economically bound to an extended family. Industrialization and ensuing social changes made the nuclear family better suited than the extended family to meet the demands of the workplace and society. The nuclear family is more flexible and freer to move to the job (see Chapter 1).

Contemporary Families

The family continues to change. In the traditional family of Western civilization, the bonds between members were considered more important than the wishes and needs of the individuals. Today, the needs of individual family members are emphasized. In addition, increasing affluence means that marriage partners can select each other less for economic reasons and more for romantic love. This trend in Western society has reached the point where the quest for romantic love relationships has almost submerged the economic basis for marriage. In a survey of college students in the United States, only 4 percent said they were willing to marry without romantic love (Levine, 1993). Along with the right to marry for love has come the right to dissolve a relationship. Divorce and separation have become common.

Today's families are small, averaging 3.14 members per household (U.S. Bureau of Census, 2000). Fewer members than in the past are needed to sustain a household. Families are mobile. Most children live in more than one house or apartment during their childhood. In addition, increasing numbers of families with children are homeless for some period during each year.

Children, once considered an economic asset, today are an economic liability. Although accounts vary, the cost of raising a child from birth to age seventeen averages $149,000 (Bamford, 1996). This figure approximately doubles if the child attends college (U.S. Department of Agriculture, 1993). The average annual income for a family raising children is about $49,940 a year (U.S. Bureau of Census, 2000). Poverty affects many families with children. This increased risk for poverty is especially true for African American, Hispanic American, and Native American children. Along with poverty, the risk of violence is a concern for many families.

How should these changes be viewed? Optimists such as Judith Stacey (1990) and Arlene Skolnick (1991) see adaptability as one of the strengths in the contemporary family. Its diversity meets the needs of a diverse nation and world. They feel that the high divorce rate, which has stabilized in recent years, is normal for advanced industrialized societies such as the United States. On the other hand, pessimists see the collapse of the two-parent family over the last three decades as the disintegration of the family. They believe that this has contributed to or been responsible for increased crime, drug abuse, and other serious social problems (Popenoe, 1993).

A popular romantic focus may be on dreams of family harmony and fulfill-ment but this is far from true for many families.

Extended Families

Extended families today include the parent or parents and children plus any rela-tives who are living with or close to the family and are bound together for emo-tional and economic reasons. However, some families, especially those who are not living near relatives, consider certain close friends to be their "extended family." In African American families, certain community members, who are involved in the life of the family, may be considered extended family just as blood relatives might be. Because the emphasis is on the family and not on the individual, extended families can last over generations.

Extended families vary as to who has the major authority and responsibility for the family. In most parts of the world, the extended family is patriarchal or based on the father's authority and that of his family. In China, traditionally the bride moves in with her husband's family. In matriarchal families, the mother's side of the family is responsible for socialization and authority. In the Navajo Native American family, the mother traditionally heads the household and the husband and children belong to the mother's side of the family tree (see Chapter 7). Extended families in the United States are largely egalitarian. This means that support can come from either or both sides of the family. Legally, both sets of grandparents would have equal legal rights to visitation after a divorce or to cus-tody after parental death or abandonment.

In the United States today, the extended family is formed largely for economic and/or cultural reasons. Certain ethnic groups often prefer living in an extended family. This is true for many Native Americans, Mexican Americans, and Asian Americans (Soldier, 1992; Branham, 1992; Ahmeduzzman and Roopnarine, 1992). Some teen mothers and their babies live with their parents, the baby's grandpar-ents, for both financial and emotional support. This is called a subfamily rather than extended because the grandparents are the head of the household and not the parent with the child.

The Nuclear Family

The nuclear family is composed of husband, wife, and their unmarried children living in the same household. Many people in the United States consider the nuclear family to be the normal family model, yet less than half (49 percent) of the children under age eighteen are living in a family with two parents, including step-parents (U.S. Census Bureau, 2000). The nuclear family has declined in numbers in recent decades while alternative family forms have increased.

Family Structure: Organization, Roles of Parents and Children

The basic organizational patterns of each family form and the roles of its members are covered under family structure. Certain comparisons to other family forms are also mentioned. A traditional family, in which the father is the breadwinner and the mother stays home with the children, has not been the norm since 1970. In 1999, both spouses worked in more than half (53 percent) of married-couple families. Only the husband worked in 19.5 percent of married-couple families (U.S. Bureau of Labor, 2000).

Today, most nuclear families are less involved with the extended family than in the past. However, some nuclear families maintain very strong kinship support and involvement. These nuclear families, sometimes labeled **modified extended families,** are less self-contained than the private nuclear families.

The nucleus or heart of the nuclear family is the husband-and-wife relationship, independent of their parents, and freely formed out of love and mutual needs. Nuclear families make decisions primarily on the needs of their family unit rather than the kinship group. Within the family, the focus is on each individual. Today's families seek privacy in their housing with fences and private patios. In the past, front porches and fewer fences provided opportunities for neighbors to interact.

ROLES OF PARENTS   As with all institutions, changes in the roles and tasks of family members are inevitable as conditions in society change. The nuclear family is no exception. Roles are more egalitarian with a wider range in the division of roles. Since both parents are in the home, the adults usually make the major decisions.

In the past two or three decades, roles for women and men have become less clearly defined. Increasingly, the father and mother share the roles of authority figure and economic providers. In over half of the nuclear families (65 percent of married mothers with children less than six years old), the mother is contributing to the family income, although her wages are generally much less than that of her spouse (U.S. Census Bureau, 1998).

In many families, the father is now expected to assume a more nurturing role than in the past. Some fathers take an active part during the prenatal development of their child. They attend birthing classes that prepare both parents for the delivery of their child. The father's presence in comforting the mother and greeting the newborn allows him to bond early with the baby. Many fathers assume some child-care tasks besides the traditional role of playing with their child. Women working outside the home have been forced to give up many hours of child-care to relatives, child care providers, or to the father.

The task of housework is still generally seen as women's work, in spite of enormous social changes in gender roles during the last three decades. The woman also

TABLE 3.1	Child Care and Housework for Men and Women						
HOURS IN CHILD CARE				**HOURS IN HOUSEWORK**			
Workdays	Men	Women		Workdays	Men	Women	
1977	1.8	3.3		1977	1.2	3.7	
1997	2.3	3.0		1997	2.2	3.1	
NON-WORKDAYS				**NON-WORKDAYS**			
1977	5.2	7.3		1977	4.2	7.2	
1997	6.4	8.3		1997	5.1	6.1	

Source: Bond, Galinsky, and Swanberg. 1998.
The 1997 National Study of the Changing Workforce, 40–41, 44–46. © Families and Work Institute. Reprinted by permission.

assumes the major responsibility for managing the care of the children. However, since the late 1960s, men have slowly assumed more responsibilities in both categories. In the 1970s men spent approximately 13½ hours in child care per week while women spent over 22 hours. In housework, men spent approximately 14½ hours a week while women spent almost 33 hours. In 1997, men spent 11½ hours a week in child care while women spent over 14½ hours; in housework, men spent 21 hours a week while women spent over 27½ hours.

In addition to this, employed women spend time (much more time than employed men) in invisible labor such as thinking, planning, and organizing the household tasks and the care and schedules for the children (Walzer, 1996; Hochschild, 1989, 1990; DeVault, 1987; Mederer, 1993). Based on national studies, Hochschild reports that women who are productive wage earners spend fifteen fewer hours per week than men in leisure activities and in a year work an extra month of twenty-four-hour days. This reflects their second work shift of household and child-care duties and family management (Hochschild, 1989, 1990). These conditions produce stress on the women and on the whole family. The journal article, "Whistle While You Work: The Effect of Household Task Performance on Women's and Men's Well-Being," says it all. Men are more likely to call attention to the housework they do while taking what women do for granted (Robinson and Spitze, 1992).

Traditional roles still exist in some nuclear families, especially when the mother stays home with the children. The husband has the responsibility for financial support and is the major authority figure while the wife has the responsibility for maintaining the household and for child care.

Traditional Roles	Contemporary Roles
Major authority figure—Father	Authority figures—Father and Mother
Decision maker—Father for major decisions	Decision makers—Father and Mother
Economic provider—Father	Economic providers—Father (earning more money) and Mother
Nurturer—Mother	Nurturer—Mother major role with Father's role increasing
Child care—Mother	Child care—Mother major role with Father's role increasing
Household chores—Mother	Household chores—Mother major role and Father minimal role
Household repairs and yard maintenance—Father	Household repairs and yard maintenance—Father

ROLES OF CHILDREN   The children, depending on their age and ability, participate in minor decisions that often involve daily activities. Readers may remember negotiating with their parents to stay up late to watch their favorite TV show, but they probably did not choose which family car to buy or house to live in. Parents determine the monies allocated for major items in the budget such as rent, food, clothing, transportation, and annual vacations. Weekend activities, some television shows, lunch menus, snack food, toys, and choice of personal clothing will be influenced by the children. Children are responsible for their homework and parents assist to varying degrees.

Today, most children less than twelve years old do not work outside the home. In the home, children under age nineteen average only three to six hours a week on household tasks. Children from nuclear families spend less time on household tasks than children in blended or single-parent homes (Demo & Acock, 1993). Children more often will share household chores similar to those of the same gender parent. If all children are the same gender, chores are less gender stereotyped. Children are often responsible for picking up or cleaning their own room.

In families where both parents work, parents have less time for activities and tasks at home, and children are given more responsibilities. For example, young children are encouraged to dress themselves if possible.

> Johnny, please put on your trousers and mommy will button them. We are going to be late for your preschool and my work . . . Will you carry out Susie's diaper bag, my hands are full. You are such a great help to mommy.

Older children who spend a couple of hours at home waiting for a parent to arrive have the responsibility of managing this time, whether it is doing homework, viewing television, or watching a younger school-age sibling.

Challenges of Nuclear Families

In this trend toward privacy and autonomy, the nuclear family has often severed kinship ties and not formed bonds within the neighborhood. Consequently, in times of need, the nuclear family must look elsewhere for help. Indeed all families, often have difficulty finding social agencies to provide affordable and adequate support.

> The mother came home from the hospital with the new baby. One grandmother worked full-time and the other lived in another state. There were no other relatives and she didn't know any of her neighbors. The baby was fussy. To whom could she turn to for help?

Another vulnerability of the nuclear family is its foundation, which is based on the intimate relationship between the husband and wife. If one parent leaves, the family undergoes drastic financial and emotional changes and must be reorganized. In the traditional family, where kinship ties are strong, extended family members and the community tend to support and encourage couples to stay together despite their problems. As Skolnick (Skolnick and Skolnick, 1983) put it:

> In traditional family systems, the inevitable tensions of marriage are contained by kin and community pressure, as well as by low expectations concerning the romance or happiness to be found in marriage.

Many people feel that the family, and particularly the nuclear family, is crucial to a healthy society. This means a society with less violence, drugs, and divorce. This places the nuclear family under intense pressure to remain healthy and intact.

Strengths of This Family Form

Children have both their parents in the home for support and role modeling. Children have not gone through the stress of family divorce or death of a parent. The family income is generally higher than that of single-parent or blended families. There remains the widespread belief in society at large that children of healthy nuclear families have the best opportunity to develop values and emotional strengths that will make them successful adults.

Single-Parent Families

Over one out of every four (27.7 percent) children lives in a single-parent home with one parent and possibly siblings (U.S. Bureau of the Census, 2000). The number of children living in single-parent families has grown from 12 percent of all families in 1970 to 27.7 percent in March 2000 (U.S. Bureau of the Census, 1982; U.S. Bureau of the Census, 2000). Although the vast majority of these families are headed by a mother, the number of single father-headed families is also increasing. It has gone

FIGURE **3.1**   **CHILDREN AND FAMILY FORM**

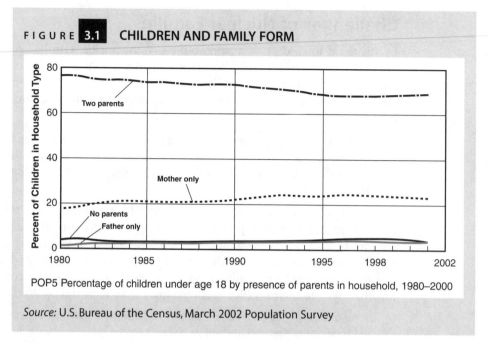

POP5 Percentage of children under age 18 by presence of parents in household, 1980–2000

Source: U.S. Bureau of the Census, March 2002 Population Survey

- ✔ 23 percent of American children lived with only their mothers;
- ✔ 4 percent lived with only their fathers and 4 percent with neither parent;
- ✔ in 2002, 69 percent of American children lived with two parents including stepparents;
- ✔ since 1996, the percentage of children living with only one parent has not changed significantly, but the percentage of births to unmarried mothers has increased

from less than 3 percent in 1988 (Bianchi, 1990) to 4 percent in 1998 (U.S. Bureau of the Census, 2000). These changes reflect the following trends:

1. the doubling of the divorce rate between 1965 and 1990;
2. more women are financially able to become single parents;
3. single adults are giving birth to and adopting children. The first adoption to a single parent in the United States was granted in Los Angeles County in 1965 (Schlesinger, 1978);
4. changing legal attitudes reflect the increase in father-headed single-parent families. Only in recent years have the courts stopped routinely giving custody of the children to the mother.

Family Structure

Single-parent families vary in their origin, race, and ethnicity. Parents who have never married form their family with the birth or adoption of a child. Other families emerge with the death of a parent or a divorce or separation. The number of children living with a mother who has never married has escalated from 7 percent of all single-parent families in 1970 to 40.3 percent in 1998. The chances of a child living with a divorced parent or a parent who has never married are about the same (U.S. Bureau of the Census, 1994, 1998). Single parents also vary in age and in education. Parents with babies range in age from the teen years to the early forties and in education from less than a high school diploma to a graduate degree. All of these conditions affect the parenting skills, income, and lifestyle of a family.

The percentages of children in single-parent homes vary according to their race or ethnic group. African American children are much more likely to be living in a single-parent family than Asian American or White children. Only 20 percent of all Asian American families and 17 percent of White families live in single-parent families compared to 31 percent of Hispanic families and 52 percent of all African American families (U.S. Bureau of the Census, 2000).

ROLES OF PARENTS   The parent–child relationship is at the heart of the single-parent family. The roles of parents and children are less clearly defined than in the nuclear family. The adult is ultimately responsible for all family decisions, but as soon as children are able they participate in many of these decisions. Some parents assume the role of friend or even peer to their children, avoiding the parental role of authority and discipline. Parents without custody have varying degrees of contact with and influence on their children. In cases of joint custody, both parents share more equally in the responsibility and in making decisions for the care of their children.

With no other adult in the home, the single parent must assume most of the responsibilities of both father and mother. These include the jobs of economic provider, disciplinarian, nurturer, and adult role model. Some help may be given by the noncustodial parent or other support systems.

Single parents frequently suffer from the stress of task/role overload (Clarke-Stewart, 1989; Colletta, 1983; Hetherington, Cox, and Cox, 1978; Weiss, 1979). The burden of assuming the roles of both parents, the lack of adequate economic resources (especially for women), reconciling a personal social life with the family's social needs, and finding adequate quality child care and transportation can be overwhelming. In addition, single parents cope with such temporary problems as illness of family members.

> Sally's two-year-old daughter has a viral infection and is running a fever. The doctor said it could last one week. Sally took sick leave from work the first day. The family day-care provider said she could not take Susie until the doctor said she was no longer contagious. Sally's employer was upset and finally said if he had to look for temporary help too often, he would have to find someone who would be able to do the job. He was very sorry, but he had to run a business. He also said he could not pay her sick leave for those days.

ROLES OF CHILDREN   Children often participate in more of the family decisions than children in two-parent families. Children in general are given more responsibilities because there is only one parent in the home. They may have to assume a task or role that typically would fall to an adult. Older siblings often help with the care of younger siblings. Children in single-parent families are usually more independent than those in two-parent families.

Challenges

Many single-parent families may still be dealing with the crisis of death or divorce. A large body of literature suggests that it takes from two to five years after a divorce for the new family to deal with grief, define and adjust to new roles and lifestyle, and attain stability and balance in family functioning (Hetherington, Cox, and Cox, 1978, 1979; Wallerstein and Kelly, 1980). When a parent becomes involved in a new relationship in the first year or two, the parent may not have dealt sufficiently with the various emotions relating to the divorce or death. In addition, the child probably has not been able to work through the different stages for dealing with the crisis such as anger, denial, bargaining, possible depression, and finally acceptance. In addition, young children, in the egocentric stage, may feel guilt that in some way they caused the divorce or death (Piaget, 1965). If young children remember saying, doing, or wishing something bad about the parent, they often believe that they have caused the parent to leave the home or to die.

A major problem for single parents is a sense of social isolation (Hetherington, et al., 1978; Wallerstein and Kelly, 1980). There is often no one with whom to talk out problems. Should my child go to the doctor? Is my child ready to start school? How should discipline problems be handled? How can my child be helped to understand and accept my basic values for living? With all these tasks, the single parent often lacks freedom for adult socialization or time to be alone. In addition, there may be a sense of loneliness in a "couples' society" (Shaw, Emery, and Tuer, 1993).

Even though society has broadened its definition of what constitutes a family, the single-parent family is still frequently referred to as incomplete, dysfunctional, or a family with great potential for problems in child rearing (Kissman and Allen, 1993). Society still implies that the two-parent family is ideal and may see any variation of this form as flawed (Richards and Schmiege, 1993). Certainly most of the research has focused on the problems rather than the strengths of the single-parent family, and particularly the problems for children (Glen and Kramer, 1985; Krein, 1986; Wallerstein and Blakeslee, 1989; Whitehead, 1993). In addition, the majority of past literature has not taken into account the diversity and complexity of single-parent families. Placing single-parent families into one category makes it more difficult to identify their particular needs and find appropriate support for an individual family (Richards and Schmiege, 1993).

In comparing single-parent families to nuclear families, many variables need to be considered. The socioeconomic status (SES) of the family and the frequency or regularity of contact with the noncustodial parent are crucial factors. The time elapsed since the crises of death or divorce and the remarriage or living arrangements of the noncustodial parent should also be considered.

CHALLENGES FOR SINGLE-MOTHER-HEADED FAMILIES The economics of single-parenthood is particularly disastrous for many single women and their children.

About one-third of all families headed by White women are poor. This figure increases to almost half for those of African American and Hispanic ancestries (Hogan and Kitagawa, 1985; U.S. Bureau of the Census, 1993). Overall, half of all the children living in single-parent families in 1997 were poor compared to only 1 in 10 children in two-parent families (Children's Defense Fund, 1997 and 1999). Money is also a concern for middle-class single mothers. When they were asked to name their three worst problems, one mother responded, "Money, money, and money" (Richards and Schmiege, 1993)!

A number of factors lead to single-parent mothers' low income. Education makes a big difference for staying out of poverty. Only 2.4 percent of custodial mothers with a bachelor's degree or more are living below the poverty line compared to 41.3 percent of those who did not finish high school (U.S. Bureau of the Census, 1999). The majority of women are concentrated in the lower paying jobs, sometimes referred to as "pink collar" jobs (U.S. Bureau of the Census, 1999). Lower wages are sometimes due to the classification given women's jobs. Whatever the reasons, the median weekly earnings of women working full-time are only 77 percent of what men working full-time earn (U.S. Bureau of Labor, 2000). In addition, less than half of single-parent mothers receive regular child-support payments from the fathers of their children. According to a report from the U.S. General Accounting Office, only 20 percent to 40 percent of families in states with early back-to-work welfare requirements had any child support collected during the past year of their welfare help (Children's Defense Fund, 1999). The *Federal Child Support Performance and Incentive Act of 1998* and the *Deadbeat Parents Punishment Act of 1998* are helping this situation.

CHALLENGES FOR SINGLE-FATHER-HEADED FAMILIES   Less research data on single-father families is available because their numbers are still small. Men appear to have some problems different from those of women. Most men were not socialized to be as nurturing as most women were or to be the primary caregiver for their children (Kissman and Allen, 1993). Conventionally, men are inexperienced in performing many of the daily household chores and in establishing and meeting the routines for the children. Finding flexible child-care arrangements and/or an understanding and adaptable employer is particularly difficult, and sometimes impossible. However, fathers' financial resources can open doors to various child-care arrangements.

Some fathers find it harder to raise daughters than sons, while the opposite is true for single mothers. Some men find it difficult to ask for assistance when problems arise. Perhaps this is because traditionally men are to protect women and children and solve problems. Some men are getting support from their female relatives. New parenting books for fathers are available. Fathers are writing about their experiences and sharing their ideas and encouragement with other fathers. Despite their difficulties, many single fathers report that they enjoy parenting and feel quite competent to raise their children (Hanson, 1988).

Two major differences between mother- and father-headed families are money and acceptance by society. Although some (14.5 percent) single-father headed families are living below the poverty line, this is the exception (U.S. Bureau of the

New Addition to This Single-Parent Family: Dad and Daughters with New Puppy

Single parents frequently suffer stress from dealing with all of the parenting tasks. Men often find it difficult to arrange transportation for school-age children to their various after-school activities, summer programs, and to provide child care on short school days. In this family, his parents are helping.

Census, 1999). According to U.S. Bureau of the Census (2000), the median income in 1999 for single fathers was **$41,838,** almost double that of single mothers (**$24,566**). Custodial fathers are often able to maintain the same house, avoiding the trauma of moving (Hansen, 1988). However, society looks at fathers heading a household differently from mothers. Some people think of fathers as less involved or committed than mothers in raising children. Almost half of the fathers in this study reported that they felt like oddities (Richards and Schmiege, 1993). Custodial fathers certainly are not the norm and neither are noncustodial mothers. Family and society often look at noncustodial mothers with hostility and some see them as abandoning their children. Fathers are not subject to the same degree of blame and guilt (Clay, 1995; Chesler, 1986).

CHALLENGES FOR CHILDREN Some social authorities tend to view single-parent children as having special problems. For most children, there is the initial trauma of the loss through death or divorce of a parent with whom they had been living, grown to love, and to depend on. The grieving may continue for two or more years, affecting their behavior and learning both at home and school (Astone and McLanahan, 1991; Hetherington, Cox, and Cox, 1985; Wallerstein and Kelly, 1980).

It is preferable for the child to maintain a healthy relationship with the absent parent. Children need accurate, positive information about this parent. Children also are affected by the parenting relationship between the two parents. It is damaging to children when they are used as pawns by the parent(s) to hurt or gain information about their former spouse. If one parent rejects the other, children often feel rejected too. When one parent uses the visits to entertain the child, such as outings to Disneyland, and/or rarely helps with homework or normal discipline problems, it makes the other parent as the enforcer and not as much fun.

Some children assume adult responsibilities at an early age (Glenwick, et al., 1986). When the job requires judgment and skills that they do not have, negative consequences occur. A child faced with caring for a sibling may use inappropriate or harmful discipline in an attempt to control behavior. On the other hand, many children benefit from assuming additional responsibilities.

EFFECTS ON GENDER ROLE DEVELOPMENT   How does the absence of one parent from the family affect the development of a girl's or a boy's gender role identity? As discussed in Chapter 1, the process of learning the culturally appropriate feelings, thoughts, and behaviors begins in infancy. Gender constancy, or realizing that one's gender will never change does not occur until age four or five and is well established by ages seven to nine. Research shows that many variables can influence the outcomes. These include the gender of the child, the ages of the children during their father's absence from the home, the length of his absence, his availability, regularity of visits, the socioeconomic level, and the presence of a father figure. Separation from the father early in life appears to have a greater effect on both boys and girls than when they are older (Frost and Pakiz, 1990; Hetherington and Clingempeel, 1992; Wallerstein and Corbin, 1989). Empirical research has failed to show that boys need a male parent to establish a masculine identity (Pleck, 1995).

Gender role orientation for young adult males is affected by the father's nurturance, education, and parenting style during childhood. Close and nurturing father–son relationships and the father's high education level are related to the son's egalitarian or nontraditional roles, higher orientations to parenting, and lower orientations to work as a young adult. From this and other studies, it appears that **the nature of fathering has less effect on the development of gender roles for girls than for boys** (Hardesty, Wenk, and Morgan, 1995; Cochran, Larner, Riley, Gunnarsson, and Henderson, 1990).

Little research is available concerning the effects on children raised by their father. Boys in these families have more contacts with opposite gender role models, such as caregivers and teachers, than do boys raised by their mother. Some research shows an advantage for children living with the same-sex parent. Boys who live with their father are less demanding, more mature and sociable, and have higher self-esteem than boys living with their mothers. The same is true for girls living with their mothers compared to girls living with their fathers (Santrock and Warshak, 1986; Santrock, Warshak and Eliot, 1982). However, a study of more than 3,400 eighth graders living in mother-only families and more than 400 eighth graders in father-only families reports no significant benefits to the children living with the same-sex parent. These researchers state that other variables, like the quality of the relationship and the degree of nurturing, are more important to a child's adjustment than the same parent–child gender (Downey and Powell, 1993).

Girls and boys gain valuable insights by being around both sexes. Surrogate role models are especially important for children missing the same-sex parent. Relatives, close friends, and groups like "Big Brothers," "Big Sisters," and "Parents Without Partners" can be very beneficial to these children in their social behavior and school progress and possibly in developing a healthy self-image (Coley, 1998).

Children are affected by the dating relationship of either of their parents. This person often gives children an opportunity to do interesting things and simply to have some extra adult attention. It is particularly true if the relationship lasts for a period of time so that children can feel the stability of another caring person in their life. However, when children bond to the new partner, they may be devastated if the relationship breaks up.

A parent's dating behavior can be confusing and even damaging to children. This new person takes their parent's time and attention. Particularly damaging is the exposure to sexual knowledge and behavior. In a traditional marriage relationship, parents normally do not display overt sexual behavior in the presence of their children. The sexual activity of the single parent, in the courtship stage, is often expressed in much more kissing and caressing, culminating many times in the new partner staying overnight. Older children recognize this as a full sexual relationship and it is deeply troubling and disturbing for most of them. It is particularly destructive if they see this as infidelity to the divorced parent, creating deep resentment against both the custodial parent and the new partner.

It is important that parents are sensitive to their children's feelings when introducing them to a romantic partner. As the relationship gains intensity, the children may feel increasingly jealous of the time and affection that their own parent lavishes on this outsider. Sometimes children try to destroy the relationship, but eventually most children realize that their parent needs company and a social life (Kissman and Allen, 1993).

EFFECTS ON SCHOOL PERFORMANCE   The research comparing the school performance of children from single-parent and two-parent families shows that children from single-parent families are at higher risk for problems. A study comparing children from intact, blended, and single-parent families found that children from single-parent families ranked the lowest in grade-point average and the highest in absenteeism, tardies, poor citizenship, and disinterested attitudes (Featherstone, Cundick, and Jensen, 1992). This study did not include socioeconomic or other factors.

Regardless of education, income, or race/ethnicity, fathers in single-parent homes who were highly involved in their children's schools had children who did well in school, in extracurricular activities, and were rarely suspended or expelled (Nord, 1998; Nord, Brimhall, and West, 1997).

A recent study of third and fourth graders living in single-mother families found that social experiences with their absent father or father substitute affected their school behavior and/or performance. The presence of warmth and control by their father related to better academic achievement, and control from nonparental men was related to fewer behavior problems in school and better peer acceptance. All girls and Black children were *more* positively affected by relations with their fathers and father figures than were all boys and White children. Interestingly, fathers' control and discipline predicted improved behavior for Black children and more problems for White children which agrees with other studies (Coley, 1998). Another study of elementary age children found that, when male relatives were involved in activities with boys, these boys tended to improve their academic performances (Gauze, Burowski, Aquan-Assee, and Sippola, 1996)

YOUTH ORGANIZATIONS   It is important for all children to be able to participate in organizations like scouting, YMCA, YWCA, and 4-H. In a recent study of 4-H clubs, it was found that single-parent families were the most underrepresented family form with blended families being next. Part of the problem was the way the club and its activities were organized. Although the organization had been working on diversity for years, the staff had not been consciously aware of meeting the needs of diverse family forms (Ganong, 1993). Organizations need to examine their policies to see if they are reaching out to all family forms.

LONG-TERM EFFECTS   According to several studies, adults who were raised in single-parent families compared to intact families have lower educational and economic achievements (Amoto and Keith, 1991; Keith and Finlay, 1988; Krein and Beller, 1988). These adults also are more likely to have trouble forming lasting relationships with partners (Wallerstein and Blakeslee, 1989), which results in a higher percentage of this group becoming single-parent families themselves (Glenn and Kramer, 1987; McLanahan, 1988; Mueller and Cooper, 1986). Because these studies do not adjust for the socioeconomic status of the families, the negative results may be linked to the financial difficulties faced by most single-parent families (Acock and Kiecolt, 1989; Demo, 1993; McLanahan, 1985).

Strengths of This Family Form

Because the single-parent family is based on the parent–child relationship, there is an opportunity for children to enjoy a sense of greater importance and a heightened self-image. Participation in decisions ranging from simple events such as, "shall we go to the park or beach Saturday?" to major decisions such as "what kind of a car shall we buy?" contribute to the child's feeling of importance. Additional family responsibilities can bring competencies to these children that children from two-parent families may not learn.

Despite all the potential problems of the single-parent family, it is increasingly clear from a series of studies over the years that children do better in a peaceful single-parent family than in a two-parent family that is filled with strife and turmoil (Emery, 1982; Goodman, Brogan, Lynch, and Fielding, 1993; Gottman and Katz, 1989; Raschke and Raschke, 1979).

Although there are many stressful aspects of single parenting, there are also rewards such as learning to handle new situations successfully. Parents find satisfactions in developing new healthy family relationships and in managing the household. In a study of seventy-one successful single-parent families, most women and men listed parenting skills as their greatest strength. They felt that they were supportive and proud of their children. They helped them to cope in life and become more independent. Many felt that their children had a good self-image. The second most frequently mentioned strength was family management skills. These included being dependable and well organized. They were able to coordinate everyone's schedules. Good communication was another strength. They listened to their children, gave them choices, and allowed them to make decisions. Another strength was their own personal growth. They were proud of their ability to cope, overcoming initial self-doubts and dealing with the complexity and constant challenges of the task. Women felt pride in their ability to provide financially for their family (Richards and Schmiege, 1993). Gaining a sense of independence can be a positive force in children's and parents' self image and in their ability to deal with life constructively.

There is a growing understanding and acceptance of the single-parent family. During the 1980s and 1990s, more television specials and series, magazine articles, and books depicting this family in a less sterotyped way were available. Community groups such as "Parents Without Partners," "Big Brothers" and "Big Sisters" provide support. Religious organizations often have programs for single parents, and many school districts offer regular or extended day classes on parenting, financial matters and other related topics.

A mentoring system in which experienced single parents share information with less experienced or struggling single parents could prove very valuable. Such a self-help mentoring group would be even more beneficial if professional therapists were involved (Stewart, 1990).

Studies are needed to examine the relationships within single-parent families, understanding their differences, and finding effective ways for support. It is essential that society supports single-parent families and all families if society's goal is to have healthy, well-adjusted, and well-educated children growing up to become the next generation of productive adults.

Blended Families   *An Instant Family*

What outwardly appears to be a nuclear family may instead be a blended or step-family in which one of the parents is not the biological or legal parent. When a stepparent adopts a child, the family becomes a nuclear adoptive family, but the Census Bureau still counts them as stepfamilies. These families are also called reconstituted or recoupled. For the husband or wife, this may be a first or second marriage and the children may legally be his, hers, or theirs. Blended families may also take the form of a remarried parent and stepparent with whom children are living or visiting, as well as a parent in a long-term relationship with an unmarried partner. Many of these children continue to share their lives with both of their biological parents. In all situations, children's lives are greatly affected.

Evidence of this growing lifestyle is seen at airports at holiday times when children wait to board airplanes, going from the home of one parent to another. In 1980, 14.8 percent of all children under eighteen were living in a blended family with only 1.5 percent of these children with a stepmother and biological father. (U.S. Bureau of the Census, 1995). The government stopped reporting the number of stepchildren or stepfamilies after 1990, but projections based on earlier data show that 23 percent of children live in legally married stepfamilies and another 7 percent with a cohabiting parent. It is estimated that two-thirds of all women and 30 percent of all children are likely to spend some time in a stepfamily, which includes cohabitating couples (Bumpass, Raley, and Sweet, 1995; U.S. Bureau of the Census, 1998).

Stepfamilies are not new in history and have often been portrayed in a negative fashion. Fairy tales like Hansel and Gretel, Cinderella, and Snow White are examples of this (Coleman and Ganong, 1987). The word *step* itself comes from the Old English prefix *step-* meaning 'bereaved' or 'orphaned.' *Step* originally meant a substitute for the parent who had died.

At the beginning of the twentieth century, the stepparent was almost always a replacement for a parent who had died. Today most stepparents are a result of divorce and remarriage. Approximately two-thirds of divorced parents remarry but approximately 60 percent of these marriages end in divorce (Glick and Lin, 1987; Parke and Buriel, 1998). However, after five years, blended families are about as stable as nuclear families of the same duration in their divorce rate (Rutter, 1994).

Family Structure

The blended family is an "instant" family. The developmental stages of courting and marriage may be present, but certainly there is no nine-month period awaiting a child's birth. The child arrives partially grown with her or his own personality and needs.

> The young couple had just married and rented a one-bedroom apartment. Before they had time to unwrap their wedding gifts, his first wife called and demanded that he take custody of their child. 'I've had him on my hands for eight years and now it is your turn. He's arriving on the five o'clock bus.'

The addition of a planned or unplanned child can be highly disruptive to a relationship still in the honeymoon stage. The role of stepparent comes more easily when the children in the new family ease into the relationship with short and frequent visits. Stepfathers and biological mothers form the majority of blended families.

The blended family is a more complex unit than the nuclear family. A child or children from the previous family(ies) may move in immediately or may join them at different times. This complex family form is part of a meta-family structure composed of former spouses, grandparents, stepparents, aunts, uncles, and significant others. These may include a child with a stepaunt, stepcousins, siblings of stepsiblings, and the stepparent's former spouse. All this leads to a situation in which the emotional components of the blended family are the most complex of any family structure. For example, it is holiday time. At whose home or homes will this occasion be celebrated? Should all members of the immediate blended family be together? Which parent does the stepchild visit? All this has to be negotiated.

ROLES OF PARENTS   Each parent may have previously established roles and expectations for family life that contradict the other parent's views. Obviously, adaptations must be made for the healthy functioning of the family. Flexibility and open communications are particularly crucial in the early stages of this family. As the blended family grows in family cohesiveness, members' roles often are redefined.

Some stepfathers are as involved as most biological fathers with the children, while others try to be only minimally involved. Stepmothers are more involved with the children because of their child-care and housekeeping duties. It is difficult for new stepparents immediately to assume the role of disciplinarian. First, they need to establish a sense of trust between themselves and their new stepchild. It is best if the major disciplining and child monitoring is assumed by the natural parent. Stepparents need to feel respected and slowly assume some degree of authority. It is a measure of the success of the relationship and the marriage when a stepparent is able to assume more child-care responsibilities.

ROLES OF CHILDREN   When children first enter the family, their previous family roles will need to be adapted to this new family structure. In general, children from single-parent homes have participated in many decisions and assumed a share of the family's responsibilities. With two adults in the family, more of the decisions are being made by the adults. A child may have assumed the role of the absent parent in the previous family, but the new stepparent is taking on this role. Children may also find their position in the family changes due to new stepsiblings. The child who previously was the oldest, and given more responsibilities than the other siblings, may now find herself or himself with an older stepsibling assuming this role. The youngest child may now be the middle child with more responsibilities and fewer indulgences. When changes are made slowly and the children take part in the decisions, they accept them more easily.

As members of the blended family adjust to their new family, children's roles become better defined. Children's roles, along with the roles of the stepparent will change, hopefully into a more cooperative and comfortable relationship.

Challenges of Parents and Children

PARENTS   Members of this family find that what was considered normal and expected in their previous family may not be normal in blended families. This is especially true in the beginning. Role ambiguity, loyalty conflicts, stepparent–stepchild discipline problems, and conflict or lack of closeness between stepchild and stepparent are typical experiences for all blended families at some point.

Members of blended families have usually suffered a primary relationship loss. Spouses may be hurt, angry, and feel deserted as a result of their previous experiences. There are ghosts from former relationships that may haunt each member of the new family.

Roles for stepparents are poorly defined and often contradictory. Some literature tells the stepparent to let the biological parent do the disciplining in the beginning (Pasley, 1985) while other studies report that biological parents frequently complain that the stepparent is inadequately involved in the parenting process (Furstenberg, 1987; Furstenberg, Nord, Peterson, and Zill, 1983). The stepparent can use a child's first name but still may have some adjustment referring to her as a "daughter" or "stepdaughter." Stepmothers are expected to provide nurturing. This may be difficult when much of the child's affection is directed toward the biological mother. Stepfathers are expected to share financially in the child's support and participate in the stepchild's education and socialization, but legally they are not responsible for their stepchild.

Medical and legal problems can be complicated. Legally a stepparent cannot sign emergency forms or school permission slips, but may be the responsible adult available most of the time. However, the stepparent may, as can any adult, carry a special consent-for-treatment form signed by the parent enabling the stepparent to sign for emergency medical treatment for the child.

An essential determinant of the *quality of the marriage* is the *quality of the stepparent–stepchild relationship* (Pasley, Dollahite, and Ihinger-Tallman, 1993). The two outsiders need time and help if they are going to form a healthy relationship. One suggestion, besides deferring the discipline and child monitoring to the legal parent, is for the stepparent occasionally to side with the child on an issue (Pasley, et al., 1993). Perhaps the parent's policy needs altering. This stepparent–stepchild coalition could be strengthened by working together without undermining the parent–child relationship.

Newly formed step families may have to deal with competing developmental needs of a child. For example, this family needs to bond, to develop cohesiveness, and at the same time an adolescent child needs to break away and become more independent. In an intact or bonded family, this would not be the same problem.

The stepfamily has to function at times with the lack of support and recognition from other institutions. Stepparents are often ignored by schools when holiday gifts are made, when tickets are given out for graduation or school events, or when family conferences are called. Stepparents may not be included in a family wedding. Most cultural forms and rituals are related to the nuclear family. Evidence of this lack of recognition is seen in greeting cards. Until recently there were no cards saying, "Happy Mother's Day to My Stepmother." Even today, cards for any step relationship are difficult to find. However, there are an increasing number of books available for children and adults about stepfamilies. A friend recently saw a Father's Day card that said, "To the man my mother married." There are also some television programs and a few movies portraying stepfamilies. The Stepfamily Association of America has information on their Web site: http://www.step.org

CHILDREN   Children enter these families with previous loyalties, experiences, and various expectations. Family activities, and often rules for behavior, change. For example, when a behavior or expressed feeling is not as appropriate in this new family as it was in the previous one, it causes confusion, and even resentment. Building a relationship with a new stepparent takes time, especially regarding discipline. A stepchild may say to the stepparent, "You can't tell me what to do. You are not my real parent!" There are few social precedents to guide children in addressing or responding to their new stepparent. Children have their own "Mom" or "Dad" and the stepparent may resent being addressed on a first name basis. When changes are made slowly and children take part in making the decisions, they accept them more easily.

Children may still be mourning the loss of a parent, either by death or separation. As mentioned earlier, not only may young children feel guilty, thinking that they have been the cause of that divorce or death, but may worry that they might be responsible for a second divorce. Guilt breeds anger and resentment.

Activities and times alone with their parent will be fewer than before. In addition, some children report that they feel disloyal to their biological parent when they are close to their stepparent. A story book shows the boy sitting on his birth dad's lap saying, "How would you feel if I called Tim 'Dad?'" In this instance, his birth dad said, "That's just fine. You can have two dads."

Younger children seem better able to adjust and eventually attach to a competent and caring stepparent. It is more difficult for older children, but particularly hard for young adolescents because of their developmental needs. Stepfathers who form a relationship on warmth, mutual concern, and friendly involvement rather than on parental authority are more likely to be accepted by adolescent boys, but not necessarily by girls. Young teen girls have a difficult time with the mother's remarriage (Giles-Sims and Crosbie-Burnett, 1989; Hetherington, 1989; Vuchinich, Hetherington, Vuchinich, and Clingempeel, 1991).

Children may be visiting or living with their stepsiblings. This involves building relationships, sharing parents, and dealing with jealousies. At least half of these children will have to cope with a new stepsibling, a baby, joining their family (Kantrowitz and Wingert, 1990). When their biological parent and their stepparent have a baby, additional jealousy often occurs because the baby has a full-blooded relationship with both parents rather than their half-blooded relationship (Francke,

Blended Family Enjoying Dining Out

Blended families offer children a complex assortment of relationships.

1983, Rutter; 1994). For real or imagined reasons, a child may say to the stepparent or parent, "You love her more and let her do more things because she is your baby!"

Strengths of Blended Families

Ideally, this family has a husband and wife in love, sharing the parenting tasks and household chores. The biological parent should have more time now for nurturing and other needs of the children than when she or he was a single parent. The income or available money should be greater because two households have merged. This is especially true for the single-female parent who marries. Children benefit from the flexibility of this family in working together.

The children now have another "parent" figure and gender role model in the home. Children should also be freed of some previous responsibilities. With two adults in the home, crises are more easily managed. Children can benefit from new relationships, ideas, and broader experiences.

Current Trends

Many children continue to experience life in more than one family form during their childhood. The percentages of nuclear, single-parent, and blended families has remained approximately the same for the last few years. However, the number of father-headed households has increased. Society has become more accustomed to divorce and remarriage.

All families need sufficient money, support, and recognition, but this is particularly true for many single-parent families. Many single-parent and single-mother headed families need sufficient money to stay out of poverty, support to prevent emotional and task overload, and recognition by society that it is a viable family form for raising healthy productive children.

Studies are needed to examine the relationships within a particular family form and find effective ways to support these families. It is essential that society support all families if society's goal is to have healthy, well-adjusted, and well-educated children growing up to become the next generation of productive adults.

 Key Points

Families, Origin, Contemporary, Extended, and Nuclear

1. A family traditionally is defined as two or more individuals, usually living together, based on blood, marriage, and legal ties such as adop-

tion. With increased diversity in family forms, a broader definition of family is a small group of people who are bound together by a mutual feeling of belonging and caring.

2. The extended family in the United States is egalitarian or both sides of the family share in

support and legal rights. It is formed out of economic and/or cultural needs.

3. The nuclear family, consisting of husband and wife and their children, accounts for fewer than half of all families.

4. Today's nuclear family is private, less involved with kin, neighbors, and people at work than nuclear families in the past.

5. Generally the roles of husband and wife are overlapping, but wives, even when employed, spend far more time on housework, family management, and child care than their husbands.

6. There still is the widespread belief that the healthy nuclear family provides the best environment for a child's growth and development.

Critical Thinking Questions

1. What are the advantages and/or disadvantages of each family form you have experienced?

2. What do you see as the benefits and/or advantages of growing up in a nuclear family?

Key Points

Single-Parent Families

1. Over 27 percent of children live in a single-parent family, usually with their mother. Over half of these children live in or near poverty compared to one in ten children in two-parent families.

2. Single parents assume all the parenting roles in the home, often resulting in emotional overload. It takes from two to five years for a single-parent family to stabilize after the crisis of a divorce or death.

3. Children assume more responsibilities and have more input in major decisions compared to children from two-parent families.

4. Children have a higher percentage of learning and behavioral problems, but those who have regular contact with their noncustodial parent and are from emotionally stable families with

higher socioeconomic status do as well in school as other children.

5. Community support groups such as "Parents Without Partners," "Big Brothers," and "Big Sisters" provide needed role models and enriching activities.

6. Single-parent families need sufficient money to stay out of poverty, support to avoid task overload, and recognition by society as a viable family from.

Critical Thinking Questions

1. How might children and their parent support each other and reduce some of their stresses and how could teachers help?

2. Is it more appropriate to view divorce as normal or dysfunctional and why?

3. What would be the implications for the single-parent family if society viewed divorce as a normal part of our marriage system.

Key Points

Blended Families

1. It is estimated that 23 percent of children live in a blended family, usually with their mother and stepfather.

2. All blended families as some point experience role ambiguity, loyalty conflicts, stepparent-stepchild discipline problems, and lack of closeness.

3. Stepparents need to establish a sense of trust with a stepchild before attempting major disciplining. A good stepparent-stepchild relationship is key to the success of the marriage.

4. Initially, children must adjust to different family roles and expectations for behavior. They are adapting to a new parent figure and often stepsiblings. They may be still mourning the loss of a parent through death or divorce.

5. Children benefit from a stable, caring stepfamily with two gender role models, increased income, rewarding relationships, and a broader view of the world.

Critical Thinking Questions

1. How might a stepchild or stepparent deal with hurt feelings or concerns in a constructive way?
2. How do you think the knowledge of a child's family form could help a teacher facilitate the child's acquisition of social and academic skills?
3. What might be the challenges for a teacher from a nuclear family in relating to parents from single-parent or blended families?

Resources and References

Families and Work Institute
   http:/www.familiesandworkinst.org/
National Council on Family Relations
   http://lists.ncfr.org
National Parent Information Network/ERIC
   http://www.ericpsed.uiuc.edu/npin/
Stepfamily Foundation
   http://www.stepfamily.org/

■ Related Readings

Barnett, R. C., and Rivers, C. (1996). *She works, he works.* Cambridge, MA: Harvard University Press.
Hareven, T. (1999). *Families, history, and social change: Life course and cross-cultural perspectives.* Boulder, CO: Westview Press.

■ References: Families, Origin, Contemporary, Extended, Nuclear

Ahmeduzzman, M., and Roopnarine, J. (1992). Sociodemographic factors, functioning style, and fathers' involvement with preschoolers in African American families. *Journal of Marriage and Family, 54,* 699–707.
Bamford, J. (1996). *Raising your quarter-million dollar baby.* Washington, DC: U.S. Department of Agriculture.
Berger, B., and Berger, P. L. (1983). *The war over the family: Capturing the middle ground.* Garden City, NY: Doubleday.
Branham, A. M. (1992). Hispanic culture interwoven into American life. *Children's Horizons,* Fall, Phoenix, AZ: The Governor's Office for Children.

Children's Defense Fund. (1996). *The state of children in America Yearbook 1996.* Washington, DC: Author.
Coverman, S., and Sheley, J. F. (1986). Change in men's housework and child care, 1965–1975. *Journal of Marriage and the Family, 48,* 413–422.
Davidson, J. K., Sr. and Moore, N. B. (1992). *Marriage and family.* Dubuque, IA: William C. Brown.
Demo, D. H., and Acock, A. C. (1993). Family diversity and the division of labor. How much have things really changed? *Family Relations, 42,* 323–331.
DeVault, M. L. (1987). Doing housework: Feeding and family life. In N. Gerstel and H. E. Gross (Eds.), *Families and work* (pp. 178–191). Philadelphia: Temple University Press.
Hochschild, A. R. (1990). The second shift: Are women putting in another day of work at home? *Utne Reader, 38,* March–April, 66–73.
Hochschild, A. R., with Anne Machung (1989). *The second shift: Working parents and the revolution at home.* New York: Viking-Penguin.
Laslett, B. (1973). The family as a public and private institution: An historical perspective. *Journal of Marriage and the Family, 35,* XXX.
Levine, R. V. (1993). Is love a luxury? *American Demographic, 15,* (2), 27–28.
Macioni, J. J. (1997). *Sociology* (6th ed.). Upper Saddle River, NJ: Prentice-Hall.
McKay, J., Hill, B., and Buckler, J. (1988). *A History of World Societies,* 2nd ed. Boston: Houghton Mifflin Company.
Mederer, H. (1993). Division of labor in two-earner homes: Task accomplishment versus household management as critical variables in perceptions about family work. *Journal of Marriage and the Family, 55,* 133–145.
Nord, C., Brimhall, D., and West, J. (1997). *Fathers' involvement in their children's schools* (NCES 98–99). Washington, DC: National Center for Educational Statistics.
Popenoe, D. (1993). Scholars should worry about the disintegration of the American family. *Chronicle of Higher Education,* April 14: Sec.A, 48.
Regensburger, L. (2001). *The American family: Reflecting a changing nation.* Farmington Hills, MI: Gale.
Skolnick, A. S., and Skolnick, J. H. (1983). *Family in transition (4th ed.).* Boston: Little, Brown.
Skolnik, A. (1991). *Embattled paradise: The American family in an age of uncertainty.* New York: Garland.

Soldier, L. (1992). Building optimum learning environments for Navajo students. *Childhood Education, Spring,* 145–148.

Stacey, J. (1990). *Brave new families: Stories of domestic upheaval in late twentieth-century America.* New York: Basic Books.

U.S. Bureau of the Census. (1991). *Population Profile of the United States: 1991.* Current Population Reports. Series P-23, No. 173. Washington, DC: U.S. Government Printing Office.

U.S. Bureau of the Census. (1998). *Current population reports* by L. M. Casper and K. Bryson. Series P-20-515. Washington, DC: U.S. Government Printing Office.

U.S. Bureau of the Census. (2000). *Current population reports.* Series P-20-515. Washington, DC: U.S. Government Printing Office.

U.S. Bureau of Labor. (2000). *Statistics News 2000.* Washington, DC: Government Printing Office.

U.S. Department of Agriculture. (1993). Agriculture Research Service. Family Economics Research Group. *Expenditures on a child by families, 1992.* Hyattsville, MD: The Group.

Vuchinich, S., Hetherington, E. M., Vuchinich, R. A., and Clingempeel, W. G. (1991). Parent–child interaction and gender differences in early adolescents' adaptation to stepfamilies. *Developmental Psychology, 27* (4), 618–626.

Walzer, S. (1996). Thinking about the baby: Gender and divisions of infant care. *Social Problems, 43,* 219–234.

■ References: Single-Parent Families

Acock, A. C., and Kiecolt, K. J. (1989). Is it family structure or socioeconomic status? Family structure during adolescence and adult adjustment. *Social Forces, 68,* 553–571.

Amato, P. R., and Keith, B. (1991). Separation from a parent during childhood and adult adjustment. *Social Forces, 70,* 327–337.

Astone, N. M., and McLanahan, S. S. (1991). Family structure, parental practices, and high school completion. *American Sociological Review, 56,* 309–320.

Becker, G. S. (1981). *A treatise on the family.* Cambridge, MA: Harvard University Press.

Bianchi, S. (1990). America's children: Missed prospects. *Population Bulletin,* June 4–5 (1), 7–10.

Bumpass, L. (1984). Children and marital disruption: A replication and update. *Demography, 21,* 71–82.

Chesler, P. (1986). *Mothers on trial.* New York: McGraw-Hill.

Children's Defense Fund. (1997). *The state of America's children: Yearbook 1997.* Washington, DC: Author.

Children's Defense Fund. (1999). *The state of America's children: Yearbook 1999.* Washington, DC: Author.

Clay, R. A. (1995). Courts reshape image of "the good mother." *APA Monitor,* (December), 31.

Cochran, M., Larner, M., Riley, D., Gunnarsson, L., and Henderson, C. R. (1990). *Extending families: The social network characteristics of parents and their children.* New York: Cambridge University Press.

Coley, R. L. (1998). Children's socialization experiences and functioning in single-mother households: The importance of fathers and other men. *Child Development, 69*(3), 219–230.

Colletta, N. D. (1983). Stressful lives: The situation of divorced mothers and their children. *Journal of Divorce, 6*(3), 19–31.

Demo, D. (1993). The relentless search for the effects of divorce: Forging new trails or tumbling down the beaten path? *Journal of Marriage and the Family, 55,* 42–45.

Downey, D. B., and Powell, B. (1993). Do children in single-parent households fare better living with same-sex parents? *Journal of Marriage and the Family, 55,* 55–71.

Duncan, G. (1984). *Years of poverty, years of plenty.* Ann Arbor, MI: Institute for Social Research.

Emery, R. E. (1982). Interparental conflict and the children of discord and divorce. *Psychological Bulletin, 92,* 310–330.

Featherstone, D. R., Cundick, B. P., and Jensen, L. C. (1992). Differences in school behavior and achievement between children from intact, reconstituted, and single-parent families. *Adolescence, 27* (105), 5–11.

Frost, A. K., and Pakiz, B. (1990). The effects of marital disruption on adolescents: Time as a dynamic. *American Journal of Orthopsychiatry, 60,* 544–555.

Ganong, L. H. (1993). Family diversity in a youth organization. *Family Relations, 42,* 286–292.

Gauze, C., Burowski, W. M., Aquan-Assee, J., and Sippola, L. K. (1996). Interactions between family environment and friendship and associations with self-perceived well-being during early adolescence. *Child Development, 67,* 2201–2216.

Glenn, N. D., and Kramer, K. B. (1985). The psychological well-being of children of divorce. *Journal of Marriage and the Family, 47,* 905–912.

Glenn, N. D., and Kramer, K. B. (1987). The marriages and divorces of children of divorce. *Journal of Marriage and the Family, 49,* 811–825.

Glenwick, D. S., and Mowrey, J. D. (1986). When parent becomes peer: Loss of intergenerational boundaries in single-parent families. *Family Relations, 35,* 57–62.

Glick, Paul C. (1986). How American families are changing. In Ollie Pocs (Ed.), *Marriage and Family 86/87* (12th ed., pp. 23–26). Clifford, CT: Dushkin. *Family environment and delinquency.* Boston: Houghton Mifflin.

Gottman, J. M., and Katz, L. F. (1989). Effects of marital discord on young children's peer interaction and health. *Developmental Psychology, 25,* 373–381.

Goodman, S. H., Brogan, D., Lynch, M. E., and Fielding, B. (1993). Social and emotional competence in children of depresses mothers. *Child Development, 64,* 516–531.

Grief, G. L. (1985). *Single fathers.* Lexington, MA: D.C. Heath.

Hanson, S. (1986). Healthy single-parent families. *Family Relations, 35,* 125–132.

Hanson, S. M. H. (1988). Divorced fathers with custody. In P. Bronstein and D. P. Cowan (Eds.), *Fatherhood today: Men's changing role in the family.* New York: Wiley.

Hardesty, C., Wenk, D., and Morgan, C. S. (1995). Paternal involvement and the development of gender expectations in sons and daughters. *Youth and Society, 26*(3), 283–297.

Hetherington, E. M., and Clingempeel, W. (1992). Coping with marital transitions: A family systems perspective. *Monographs of the Society for Research in Child Development, 57* (2–3, Serial No. 227).

Hetherington, E. M., Cox, M., and Cox, R. (1978). The aftermath of divorce. In J. H. Stevens and M. Matthews (Eds.), *Mother–child, father–child relations* (pp. 149–176). Washington, DC: National Association for the Education of Young Children.

Hetherington, E. M., Cox, M., and Cox, R. (1979). Stress and coping in divorce: A focus on women. In J. Gullahorn (Ed.), *Psychology and women in transition* (pp. 95–128). Washington: V. H. Winston; [New York] distributed by Halsted Press, 1979.

Hetherington, E. M., Cox, M., and Cox, R. (1985). Long-term effects of divorce and remarriage on the adjustment of children. *Journal of the American Academy of Child Psychiatry, 24,* 518–530.

Hoffert, S. L. (1985). Updating children's life course. *Journal of Marriage and the Family, 47,* 93–115.

Hogan, D. P., and Kitagawa, E. M. (1985). The impact of social status and neighborhood on the fertility of black adolescents. *American Journal of Sociology, 90,* 825–855.

Howe, L. K. (1977). *Pink collar workers.* New York: G. P. Putnam's Sons.

Keith, V. M., and Finlay, B. (1988). The impact of divorce on children's educational achievement, marital timing, and likelihood of divorce. *Journal of Marriage and the Family, 50,* 97–80.

Kissman, K., and Allen, J. A. (1993). *Single-parent families.* Newbury Park, CA: Sage.

Krein, S. F. (1986). Growing up in a single-parent family: The effects on education and earning on young men. *Family Relations, 35,* 161–168.

Krein, S. F., & Beller, A. H. (1988). Educational attainment of children from single-parent families: Differences by exposure, gender, and race. *Demography, 25,* 221–234.

McGrab, P. R. (1978). For the sake of the children: A review of the psychological effects of divorce. *Journal of Divorce, 1,* 233–244

McLanahan, S. (1985). Family structure and the reproduction of poverty. *American Journal of Sociology, 90,* 873–901.

McLanahan, S. (1988). Family structure and dependency: Early transitions to female household headship. *Demography, 25,* 1–15.

Mueller, D. P., and Cooper, P. W. (1986). Children of single-parent families: How they live as young adults. *Family Relations, 35,* 169–176.

Nord, C. (1998). *Non-residential fathers can make a difference in children's school performance.* Washington, DC: National Center for Education Statistics.

Nord, C., Brimhall, D., and West, J. (1997). *Fathers' involvement in their children's schools: National Household Education Survey.* Washington, DC: National Center for Education Statistics.

Office of Child Support Enforcement. (1988). *Twelfth annual report to Congress for the period ending September 29, 1987.* Washington, DC: U.S. Government Printing Office.

Piaget, J. (1965). *The moral judgment of the child.* New York: Free Press. (Original work published 1932).

Pleck, J. H. (1995). The gender role strain paradigm: An update. In R. F. Levant and W. S. Pollack (Eds.), *A new psychology of men.* New York: Basic Books.

Raschke, H. J., and Raschke, V. J. (1979). Family conflict and the children's self-concepts. *Journal of Marriage and the Family, 41,* 367–374.

Regensburger, L. (2001). *The American family: A changing nation.* Farmington Hills, MI: Gale.

Richards, L. N., and Schmiege, C. J. (1993). Problems and strengths of single-parent families: Implications for practice and policy. *Family Relations, 42,* 277–285.

Rosenthal, K. M., and Keshet, H. F. (1981). *Fathers without partners.* Totowa, NJ: Rowman & Littlefield.

Santrock, J. W., and Warshak, R. A. (1986). Development, relationships, and legal/clinical considerations in father-custody families. In M. E. Lamb (Ed.), *The father's role: Applied perspectives.* NY: Wiley.

Santrock, J. W., Warshak, R. A., and Eliot, G. L. (1982). Social documents and parent–child interaction in father-custody and stepmother families. In M. E. Lamb (Ed.), *Nontraditional families.* Hillsdale, NJ: Erlbaum.

Schlesinger, B. (1978). Single-parent fathers: A research review. *Children Today, 7*(3), 12.

Shaw, S. (1991). The conflicting experiences of lone parent-hood. In M. Hardy & G. Crow (Eds.), *Lone parenthood* (pp. 143–155). Toronto: University of Toronto Press.

Stewart, M. J. (1990). Professional interface with mutual-aid self-help groups: A review. *Social Science Medicine, 31,* 1143–1158.

U.S. Bureau of the Census. (1982). *Marital status and living arrangements, March, 1982: Current population reports,* Series, P-20. Washington, DC: U.S. Government Printing Office.

U.S. Bureau of the Census. (1992). *Statistical abstract of the United States: 1992,* No. 68 & 69 (112th ed.), Washington, DC: U.S. Government Printing Office.

U.S. Bureau of the Census. (1993). *Family form in the U.S. in 1992.* Washington, DC: U.S. Government Printing Office.

U.S. Bureau of the Census. (1994). *Statistical abstract of the U.S., 1994,* no. 76 and series P70, no. 38. Washington, DC: U.S. Government Printing Office.

U.S. Bureau of the Census. (1998). *Household and Family Characteristics: March Update.* In *Current Population Reports: P20-515.* Washington, DC: Government Printing Office.

U.S. Bureau of the Census. (1999). *Child support for custodial mothers and fathers: 1995. Current Population Reports,* P60-196, March, 1999, by Lydia Scoon-Rogers.

U.S. Bureau of the Census. (2000). *Household and Family Characteristics: March Update.* In *Current Population Reports: P20-515.* Washington, D.C.: Government Printing Office.

U.S. Bureau of the Census. (2000). *Money income in the United States: 1999.* Washington, DC: Government Printing Office.

U.S. Bureau of Labor Statistics. (1994). *Employment and earnings, 41*(1). Washington, DC: U.S. Government Printing Office.

U.S. Bureau of Labor Statistics News. (June 2000). *Employment characteristics of families in 1999.* Washington, DC: U.S. Department of Labor.

U.S. Department of Labor. (1991). *Employment in perspective: Women in the labor force.* (Bureau of Labor Statistics, Report No. 822). Washington, D.C.: U.S. Government Printing Office.

Wallerstein, J. S. (1985). The overburdened child: Some long-term consequences of divorce. *Social Work, 30,* 116–123.

Wallerstein, J. S., and Blakeslee, S. (1989). *Second chances: Men, women and children a decade after divorce.* New York: Ticknor & Fields.

Wallerstein, J. S., and Corbin, S. B. (1989). Daughters of divorce: Report from a ten-year follow-up. *American Journal of Orthopsychiatry, 59,* 593–604.

Wallerstein, J. S., and Kelly, J. (1980). *Surviving the breakup: How children and parents cope with divorce.* New York: Basic Books.

Weiss, R. (1979). *Going it alone: The family life and social situation of the single parent.* New York: Basic Books

Whitehead, B. D. (1993). Dan Quayle was right. *The Atlantic,* 47–84.

■ References: Blended Family

Ahrons, C. R., and Wallisch, L. (1987). Parenting in the bi-nuclear family: Relationship between biological and stepparents. In K. Pasley and M. Ihinger-

Tallman (Eds.), *Remarriage and stepparenting: Current research and theory* (pp. 225–256). New York: Guilford.

Bray, J. H., Berger, S. H., and Boethel, C. L. (in press). Role integration and marital adjustment in stepfather families. In K. Pasley and M. Ihinger-Tallman (Eds.), *Stepparenting: Issues in theory, research and practice.* Westport, CT: Greenwood.

Bray, J. H., Berger, S. H., Silverblatt, A. H., and Hollier, A. (1987). *Family process and reorganization during early marriage: A preliminary analysis.* In J. P. Vincent, (Eds.), *Advancements in family intervention, assessment, and theory* (pp. 253–279). Greenwich, CT: JAI Press.

Bumpass, L., Martin, T. C., and Sweet, J. (1989). The impact of family background and early marital factors on marital disruption. *Journal of Family Issues, 12,* 22–42.

Bumpass, L. L., Raley, R. K., and Sweet, J. A. (1995). The changing character of stepfamilies: Implications of cohabitation and nonmarital childbearing. *Demoography, 32,* 425–436.

Clarke-Stewart, K. (1989 January). Single-parent families: How bad for children? *NEA Today,* 60–64.

Clingempeel, W. G., Brand, E., and Ievoli, R. (1984). Stepparent–stepchild relationships in stepmother and stepfather families: A multimethod study. *Family Relations, 33,* 465–473.

Clingempeel, W. G., Brand, E., and Segal, S. (1987). A multilevel-multivariable-developmental perspective for future research on stepfamilies. In K. Pasley and M. Ihinger-Tallman (Eds.), *Remarriage and stepparenting: Current research and theory* (pp. 65–93). New York: Guilford.

Coleman, M., and Ganong, L. (1987). The cultural stereotyping of stepfamilies. In K. Pasley and M. Ihningrt-Tallman (Eds.), *Remarriage and stepparenting: Current research and theory* (pp. 19–41). New York: Guilford.

Francke, L. B. (1983). *Growing up divorced.* New York: Fawcett/Crest.

Furstenberg, F. F., Jr. (1987). The new extended family: The experience of parents and children after remarriage. In K. Pasley and M. Ihinger-Tallman (Eds.), *Remarriage and stepparenting: Current research and theory* (pp. 42–61). New York: Guilford.

Furstenberg, F. F., Jr., Nord, C. W., Peterson, J. L., and Zill, N. (1983). The life course of children of divorce: Marital disruption and parental contact. *American Sociological Review, 48,* 656–668.

Giles-Sims, J. (1984). The stepparent role: Expectations, behavior, sanctions. *Journal of Family Issues, 5,* 116–130.

Giles-Sims, J., and Crosbie-Burnett, M. (1989). Adolescent power in stepfather families. *Journal of Marriage and the Family, 51,* 1065–1078.

Glick, P. (1989). Remarried families, stepfamilies, and stepchildren: A brief demographic analysis. *Family Relations, 38,* 24–27.

Glick, P. C., and Lin, S. L. (1987). Remarriage after divorce: Recent changes and demographic variation. *Sociological Perspectives 30*(2), 162–167.

Goodman, S. H., Brogan, D., Lynch, M. E., and Fielding, B. (1993). Social and emotional competence in children of depressed mothers. *Child Development, 64,* 516–531.

Guisinger, S., Cowan, P. A., and Schuldberg, D. (1989). Changing parent and spouse relations in the first years of remarriage of divorced fathers. *Journal of Marriage and the Family, 51,* 445–456.

Hetherington, E. M. (1988). Family relations six years after divorce. In K. Pasley and M. Ihinger: Tallman (Eds.), *Remarriage and stepparenting: Current research and theory* (pp. 185–205). New York: Guilford.

Hetherington, E. M. (1988). Divorce: A child's perspective. *American Psychologist, 44,* 303–312.

Hetherington, E. M. (1989). Coping with family transitions: Winners, losers and survivors. *Child Development, 60,* 1–4.

Hetherington, E. M., Clingempeel, W. G., and Associates. (1992). Coping with marital transitions. *Monographs of the Society for Research in Child Development, 57*(2–3), Serial No. 227.

Kantrowitz, B., and Wingert, P. (1990). Step by step. *Newsweek, 94*(27), 24.

Meyer, D. R., and Garasky, S. (1993). Custodial fathers: Myths, reality, and child support policy. *Journal of Marriage and the Family, 55,* 73–85.

Olson, D. H., McCubbin, H., Barnes, H., Larsen, H., Muxen, A., and Wilson, M. (1983). *Families: What makes them work?* Beverly Hills, CA: Sage.

Parke, R. D., and Buriel, R. (1998). Socialization in the family: Ethnic and ecological perspectives. In W. Damon (Ed.), *Handbook of child psychology* (5th ed., Vol. 3). New York: Wiley.

Pasley, K. (1985). Stepfathers. In S. M. H. Hanson and F. W. Bozett (Eds.), *Dimensions of fatherhood* (pp. 288–306). Beverly Hills, CA: Sage.

Pasley, K., Dollahite, D. C., and Ihinger-Tallman, M. (1980). *Problems and problem-solving strategies in remarried families: Final Report.* Pullman, WA: Grant-in-Aid Program, Washington State University.

Pasley, K., Dollahite, D. C., and Ihinger-Tallman, M. (1993). Bridging the Gap: Clinical applications of research findings on the spouse and stepparent roles in remarriage. *Family Relations, 42,* 315–322.

Quick, D. S., McKenry, P. C., and Newman, B. M. (in press). Social psychological factors related to the quality of the stepmother–adolescent relationship. In K. Pasley and M. Ihinger-Tallman (Eds.), *Stepparenting: Issues in theory, research and practice.* Westport, CT: Greenwood.

Robinson, J., and Spitze, G. (1992). Whistle while you work? The effect of household task performance on women's and men's well-being. *Social Science Quarterly, 73*(4), 844–861.

Rutter, V. (1994). Lessons from stepfamilies. *Psychology Today,* (May–June), pp. 30–33, 60, 62, 64, 66, 68–69.

Sanrock, J. W., and Sitterle, K. A. (1987). Parent-child relationships: Stepmother families. In K. Pasley and M. Ihinger-Tallman (Eds.), *Remarriage and stepparenting: Current research and theory* (pp. 273–299). New York: Guilford.

Schwebel, A. I., Fine, M. A., and Renner, M. A. (1991). A study of perceptions of the stepparent role. *Journal of Family Issues, 12,* 43–57.

Shaw, D., Emery, R., and Tuer, M. (1993). Parental Functioning and children's adjustment in families of divorce: A prospective study. *Journal of Abnormal Child Psychology, 2,* (1), 119–124.

Stern, P. N. (1978). Stepfather families: Integration around child discipline. *Issues in Mental Health Nursing, 6,* 89–103.

Visher, E. B., and Visher, J. S. (1979). *Stepfamilies: A guide to working with steparents and stepchildren.* New York: Brunner/Mazel.

Visher, E. B., and Visher, J. S. (1988). *Old loyalties, new ties: Therapeutic strategies with stepfamilies.* New York: Brunner/Mazel.

Vuchinich, S., Hetherington, E. M., Vuchnich, R. A., and Clingempeel, W. G. (1991). Parent–child interaction and gender differences in early adolescents' adaptation to stepfamilies. *Developmental Psychology, 27,* 618–626.

U.S. Bureau of the Census. (1993). *Statistical Abstract of the United States, 1993.* Washington, D.C.: U.S. Government Printing Office.

U.S. Bureau of the Census. (1994). *Current Population reports. Series P20-509.* Washington, DC: U.S. Government Printing Office.

U.S. Bureau of the Census. (1995). *Statistical Abstract of the United States, 1995.* Washington, DC: U.S. Government Printing Office,

U.S. Bureau of the Census. (1998). *Current population reports,* P20-509. Washington, DC: U.S. Government Printing Office.

U.S. Bureau of Labor. (2000). *Labor statistics: News 2000.* Washington DC: U.S. Government Printing Office.

U.S. Department of Agriculture. (1993). Agricultural Research Service. Family Economic Research Group. *Expenditures on a Child by Families, 1992.* Hyattville, MD: The Department.

Routes to Parenting

All parents need appropriate support, but their need for support varies.

*P*eople become parents under different circumstances. Some are very young and face the emotional and financial challenges of parenting along with those of being a teenager. Other individuals are parents for the second time, assuming the responsibility for raising a grandchild. Some individuals assume the temporary responsibility of caring for a child as a foster parent. Others, through adoption, assume the legal responsibility of a child who is not their biological child. In addition, there are parents who are gay or lesbian raising a child without the approval of the majority of society. Each of these groups of parents and children need special understanding and specific support because of their circumstances.

Teens as Parents *Early Childbearing: A threat or an appealing option?*

"Parenthood before adulthood" characterizes teenage pregnancy. This takes on special meaning in the United States where adolescent childbearing is by far the highest among industrialized countries and over eleven times higher than Japan's rate. In 2000, the birthrate for teenagers ages fifteen through nineteen was 48.7 births per 1,000. Although this figure is high, it is a decline of 22 percent since 1991 and 2 percent lower than in 1999. The birth rates for black teenagers declined most dramatically (31 percent) but birthrates for Hispanics and Blacks still remain the highest of all the racial/ethnic groups. Although teenage birthrates have declined, the proportion of these births to unmarried teenagers has steadily increased. In 1999 and 2000, the unmarried teenage birthrate was at an all-time high, representing **78.7 percent of all teenage births.** The teenagers who do marry have fewer children (Ventura, Mathews, and Hamilton, 2001).

Societal Conditions

Although complex, a number of conditions has been identified as contributing to teenage pregnancy and parenthood.

1. **Poverty** is a major condition contributing to early pregnancy and childbearing (Northeastern University's Center for Labor Market Studies, 1994; Children's Defense Fund, 1994). Fully 83 percent of adolescents who become teen mothers are from economically disadvantaged homes (Alan Guttmacher Institute, 1996). A 1997 research study by Hotz showed that poverty, dysfunctional families, and abuse very early in children's lives set the stage for teen pregnancies and/or poverty to continue in their adult lives (Cooper, 1997).

2. **Weak basic academic skills** make youth vulnerable to pregnancy. Education failure is one of the strongest predictors of becoming pregnant (Kreinen, 1999). The National Longitudinal Survey of Youth in 1994 shows that three out of eight teens with the weakest academic skills become teen mothers compared to one out of twenty with the strongest academic skills (Children's Defense Fund, 1995).

3. **The high rate of teen unemployment and low hourly wages** for teens when working tend to make teens pessimistic about their future. These conditions are particularly true for African Americans and Hispanic Americans. Lacking a career incentive, many teens do not postpone sexual activity, pregnancy, and childbearing (Children's Defense Fund, 1994).

4. **Greater societal acceptance** of pregnancy out of marriage exists today along with very few negative consequences for male partners. As recently as the 1950s, teen pregnancy was a condition of shame, often hidden by a visit to a relative in another town and an arranged clandestine adoption. In the 1950s, schools expelled girls who were pregnant. In contrast today, many school districts provide special programs for pregnant girls and teen mothers.

   In one school in the late 1980s, the unmarried sixteen-year-old daughter of the PTA president gave birth. Her mother made a huge banner to hang over the entrance to the school: "Belinda has a boy!"

   The decline in the number of teenage pregnancies since 1991 may be due in part to society's changing attitudes toward premarital sex for teenagers and to the public and private efforts over the last ten years on pregnancy prevention both through abstinence and responsible behavior.

5. **Sexuality in the media** is a subconscious force in teen pregnancy. Pornographic movies are now available for home viewing. Television, books, and billboards give the viewer the message that sexual freedom is enjoyable and equally acceptable for both sexes. Overall rising social and cultural pressures encourage early sexual activity (Children's Defense Fund, 1994, 1997).

6. **Inadequate family life or sexual education.** Many young adolescents have reported that they received little or no sexual information from either parent. Ideas leading to unintended pregnancies include "I can't get pregnant the first time I have intercourse" or "to take the pill is to plan to have sex, which would be wrong, but sex in a moment of romantic passion may be excused."

7. **Unsupervised free time** for teens has increased due to working parents, anonymity in neighborhoods, a shorter school day, and unemployment.

   A student of the author was shocked to learn that her fifteen-year-old son and his girlfriend were largely unsupervised the many weekends the girlfriend's parents had invited him to stay at their new house. During intercourse, they had been using plastic sandwich baggies in an attempt to protect her from becoming pregnant.

8. **Availability of an automobile** has given young people more privacy and mobility than in the past.

9. **Drug use** that reduces inhibitions has been rising. The percentage of twelfth graders reporting the use of an illicit drug rose from 14.4 percent in 1992 to a high of approximately 53 percent in 1997. In 2000 this declined to 48 percent (University of Michigan, Institute for Social Research, 1994, 2000). The number of youth "binge" drinkers (over five drinks in succession) is shocking. Within the previous two weeks of their interview, 31 percent of twelfth

graders, 26 percent of tenth graders, and 15 percent of eighth graders reported binge drinking (Children's Defense Fund, 2001).

10. **The failure of parents to communicate with children** makes children vulnerable to outside pressures and advice from peers or others. Many girls feel the need for love and the adult status of being a mother. When asked why they became pregnant, some girls replied, "I wanted someone to love me" (Trinchero, 1983).

Structure

Teen parents may be a part of a nuclear family, a single-parent family, or a subfamily with their parent or parents. Over half of the school-age mothers live with their parents (58 percent) in a subfamily. Another 12 percent live with their husbands and another 12 percent with other adults, including their adult sexual partners (Children's Defense Fund, 1997). This leaves approximately 18 percent in single-parent households.

ROLES OF MOTHERS   The adolescent who lives with her parent(s) may find her mother or parents taking over the parenting role of her child. Although this allows her time for work, school, or other activities, she often resents her mother's involvement with her child. On the other hand, the girl's parents often want their own free time and resent their daughter's socializing in addition to school or work. They may even feel that this socialization represents neglect of their grandchild.

The single mother living on her own has different problems. She has more freedom to choose her own lifestyle but is responsible for all parental roles. This twenty-four-hour-a-day responsibility, along with other difficulties faced by many single parents, can be very stressful.

ROLES OF FATHERS   Some fathers marry their teenage partner and share the responsibilities of parenthood. The young fathers who do not marry the mother are still affected by the existence of the baby, both psychologically and often financially. Even in the cases of abortion or adoption, there is a psychological cost to most fathers. Because fatherhood can be proven by blood tests, fathers as young as fourteen have been successfully sued for child support. This is legally binding until their child is eighteen years old or adopted. If the girl chooses, fathers eighteen or older can be charged with statutory rape if she is under eighteen.

Challenges for Parents, Children, and Society

PARENTS

1. Teen parents usually lack sufficient knowledge and skills in parenting, and some of the most basic safety, health, and nutritional needs of their children may be neglected. Most teenage mothers and fathers are not prepared

emotionally or financially for the responsibilities and challenges of parent-hood (Ventura, Mathews, and Hamilton, 2001).

2. Education is cut short for many parents so that they can earn money and care for their babies. Teen mothers are three times more likely to drop out of school than teens without a child (Children's Defense Fund, 1995), although the number of teen mothers completing high school has increased in recent years. In 1996, seven in ten teen mothers did complete high school but were less likely to go on to college compared to those who delayed pregnancy (Alan Guttmacher Institute, 1996).

3. Income is low because their educational level limits their job qualifications. When the father is older, the economics and stability of the home often improve.

4. Rapid childbearing, plus the additional stress of caring for and supporting their babies, are hard on the physical and mental health of the mother. During 1996–1999, 17 percent of first time-teen mothers had another child each year during their adolescence (Ventura, et al., 2001; Alan Guttmacher Institute, 1996).

5. Normal stresses in adolescence are intensified by parenthood, creating frustration, anger, and depression. The young mother's frustrations may lead to child abuse. Statistically there is a higher rate of child abuse and neglect among teen mothers than mothers over age nineteen (Kreinin, 1999).

   Many girls who have carried through the pregnancy and maintained their children afterwards were themselves abused as children or have had very serious disturbances in their own family life. It is evident that these young parents are unable to pass on to their children what they themselves haven't had. Hence, the risks for a new generation are frightening (Trinchero, 1983).

6. Family arrangements for teen parents will probably change within five years of giving birth. For those who wed, marriage is a fragile condition. When mothers under age fifteen marry, the divorce rate is twice that of the population as a whole (Levering, 1983).

CHILDREN   Compared to children born to mothers ages twenty to twenty-nine, children born to teenage mothers are more likely to have serious health problems surrounding their birth as well as long-term consequences. In 1999, 14.1 percent of teenage mothers gave birth to preterm babies and 9.7 percent to low birth weight (under 5.5 pounds) babies (Ventura, et al., 2001). Low birth weight infants are twenty times more likely to die at birth. Those who survive are at greater risk for lifelong disabilities such as mental retardation, blindness, deafness, cerebral palsy, and other health problems (Children's Defense Fund, 1995). In large part, this is due to conditions during the prenatal period. In 1999, over 40 percent of teenage mothers did not have early prenatal care and some mothers no prenatal care. In addition, 18 percent of teenage mothers smoked during their pregnancy (Ventura et al., 2001).

Children of teenage mothers experience more difficulties in their physical, emotional, and intellectual development than children of parents twenty years or older. This affects their success in school (Sipe, Batten, Stephens, and Wolfe, 1995). In particular, children born to parents age seventeen and younger have lower cognitive scores than children born to parents eighteen and older (Baldwin, 1981).

Although there is controversy over intelligence variations, the children of teenage parents appear to be at a disadvantage because of the inadequate conditions for many of these children both before and after birth. Poor nutrition, living with only one parent or substitute parent, low or poverty level income, and parents with a low educational level all have a negative effect on a child's intellectual development (Sipe, et al., 1995).

Adolescent children of teenage parentage continue to be at risk even in adulthood. They have a greater chance of experiencing behavioral problems, doing poorly in school, participating in delinquent or criminal activities, becoming sexually active at a young age, and becoming teenage parents themselves than children of older parents (Kreinin, 1999; Sipe, et al., 1995). Kreinin, who is the director of state and local affairs for the National Campaign to Prevent Teen Pregnancy, reports that 70 percent of the prisoners in the United States are children of teen mothers (1999). According to the *National Health Interview Survey—1992 Supplement*, the educational level of the parents is linked to a girl's chances of having sexual intercourse by age fifteen. For the girls whose parents did not complete high school, the sexual activity rate at age fifteen was 25 percent, but for those whose parents were college educated, the rate was only 11 percent.

CHALLENGES FOR SOCIETY   Teenage parenthood is very costly to society. The 1996 report, *Kids Having Kids: A Robin Hood Foundation Special Report on the Cost of Adolescent Childbearing*, estimated that the annual public cost of adolescent childbearing is $6.9 billion for welfare and food stamps, lost tax revenue, correctional costs, and additional foster care expenses alone (Children's Defense Fund, 1997).

Many children born to teen mothers also suffer a multitude of medical problems that are costly to treat. For example, it costs more to care for children born too early, too small, or with learning disabilities than for full-term healthy babies. Special education is expensive. In addition, some of these children with special needs simply do not enjoy full participation in society and society also loses. Prenatal damage and its costly consequences could be greatly reduced if mothers would have early prenatal care and abstain from tobacco and drugs.

Supportive and Preventive Programs   Most professionals see the problem as twofold. Preventive measures are needed to help teens make more responsible choices regarding abstinence, sexual activity, contraception, and pregnancy, avoiding the damaging consequences of too early and/or unintended pregnancies. Supportive measures are vital to the health and welfare of teenage parents and their children. When government, social groups, religious organizations, schools, and families work together, it is most effective.

Preventive measures need to deal with the total picture including the motivations for sexual activity and its consequences. Reducing the teen pregnancy rate requires a comprehensive strategy that includes early intervention, sexuality education, counseling, health services, and youth development. This means giving youth an adequate education with access to a good job. The media, often accused of stimulating sexual activity, could be used to educate our youth.

Educational programs examining sexual feelings, conception, contraception, and parenthood, along with ways to withstand pressures for sexual activity, are essential for junior high and high school students and their parents. Developmentally appropriate and culturally sensitive courses covering family life education, sometimes referred to as complete health education, need to be a part of the elementary school curriculum in all grades (Children's Defense Fund, 1996). The Sexuality Information and Education Council of the United States (SEICUS) believes that sexuality education is a lifelong process that includes the biological, sociocultural, psychological, and spiritual dimensions of sexuality from the cognitive, affective, and behavioral perspectives (2001).

Family life education programs in schools have grown in number. In 1986 only three states required sexuality education in their schools and in 2002 twenty states required sexuality education and thirty-seven states required HIV and STD Education (SEICUS, 1994, 2002). In fifteen states the programs must teach abstinence-only until marriage. These programs are not in every district in the state. In addition, the quality and content of these programs vary as well as the qualifications of the teachers in charge.

Preventive programs are being sponsored by various organizations that often work with the schools and the parents. A program called **Human Maturity** was initiated by the Lullaby Guild in Los Angeles in 1979 and further developed by the Children's Home Society of California. It has been used over the years in junior and senior high schools. This six-week course deals with biological maturity, developing personal relationships, self-esteem, problem solving in marriage, budgeting, and the problems of teen marriages and parenting. During the parenting sessions students may be given a hard-boiled egg and told to be "egg sitters" for a week. There are incidents of egg abuse, egg adoption, and egg accidents. One young student came to class crying. "My mother told me to tell you that I left the egg alone for four hours," she explained to the teacher. The program teaches both the responsibilities and burdens of parenthood. The current material available to schools is more comprehensive than their earlier material (Children's Home Society, 1996).

Many nongovernmental organizations over the years have worked to prevent teenage pregnancy. **Girls' Inc.,** formerly **Girls' Clubs of America,** has been working with girls for years trying to help them develop the skills that they need for healthy development. These include avoiding unwanted and too early pregnancies. Today they serve over 350,000 girls. Their current teen pregnancy program, which began in 1985, teaches girls between the ages of eight and eighteen ways to take care of their own lives. The first phase concentrates on the communication of values between children ages eight and ten and their parents. Girls from ages

eleven through fourteen learn about "will power/won't power" through role playing and building of decision-making skills. The program for fifteen- to eighteen-
year-old girls, "Taking Care of Business," helps them to concentrate on career and
life planning. This includes issues such as whether or when a baby would fit into
their plans. In order to evaluate the effectiveness of their total program, Girls'
Inc. completed a three-year study of girls in high-risk regions. Compared to girls
of similar backgrounds not in their programs, the younger girls who completed
phase one of the program were half as likely to have sex, and the older girls who
completed the total program were half as likely to become pregnant while still
an adolescent. Mrs. Plough, the director, says, "Empowering girls to take charge
of their life works. Punishment doesn't" (Chittum, 1995; Children's Defense
Fund, 1995).

Advocates for Youth, a nongovernmental organization based in Washington,
DC, believe that an effective program to prevent teenage pregnancy must provide
access not only to information about pregnancy but also to contraceptives. According to Margaret Pruitt, the director of this advocacy group, most of the teenagers
they work with avoid pregnancy by practicing contraception (Chittum, 1995; Children's Defense Fund, 1995).

Heart of OKC is one of thirteen local teen pregnancy prevention projects
funded by the Centers for Disease Control and Prevention and coordinated by the
Oklahoma Institute for Child Advocacy. It promotes positive youth development
and encourages them to avoid negative risk-taking behavior, including becoming
pregnant. It reaches diverse groups by working with organizations such as the
United Indian Tribal Youth and the Latino Community Development Agency
(*School Board News*, 1999).

Teens: Effective Models and Teachers   *Teen Summit* is a weekly program for teens
on the Black Entertainment Television (BET) cable network. Teens work with adults
on the programming, suggesting program topics. Issues include healthy relationships, sexually transmitted diseases, and teen pregnancy. Teachers can request
videotapes and a teacher's guide for classroom use (*School Board News*, 1999).

Supportive Measures   Once the baby is conceived, support is needed for the
mother before birth and for the family after birth, especially if adoption is not an
option. Available and affordable prenatal care is essential to the birth of a healthy
baby and access to a well-baby clinic is important to keep the baby healthy. Young
parents need guidance in providing appropriate care for their baby and in meeting the financial costs. Continuation of schooling, especially the completion of high
school, is essential for the future income capabilities of the parent.

Many school districts offer teen mother programs with the mothers attending
high school classes while their babies receive care on or near the premises. These
mothers also learn about their babies' needs while helping in the nursery. This is
critical because many of these young parents' expectations of their children's
behavior is not always developmentally appropriate.

Teen Mother Reads to Her 19-Month-Old Baby

In this Teenage Pregnant Parent Program, the mother attends high school classes and spends time twice a day with her baby in the child care facility. Teachers expect the parents to read to their child every day. This 19-year-old mother will graduate next month and plans to enroll in a medical assistant program.

Current Trends

BUDGET CUTS: PUNITIVE VERSUS SUPPORTIVE OR PREVENTIVE MEASURES Large spending cuts occurred in the mid-1990s as a result of legislators trying to balance the federal budget along with states trying to live on declining funds and escalating needs. This was especially true for those programs giving money to the unemployed and to mothers having children while on welfare. In California, effective January 1996, no additional money was given for a child born while the family was on welfare. The 1996 Federal Welfare Reform Bill, called the *Personal Responsibility and Work Opportunity Reconciliation Act of 1996*, eliminated *Aid to Families with Dependent Children (AFDC)*. This was an open-ended federal entitlement program that had been in place for decades. *AFDC* was replaced by a new program, *Temporary Assistance for Needy Families (TANF)*, which provides time-limited cash payments to needy families for a maximum lifetime limit of five years. States have flexibility on eligibility, benefit levels, and the short-term and overall length of welfare. For example, some states limit assistance to a maximum of twelve months at any period with twelve months of work before reapplying for assistance. This would present a problem for many teen mothers who are trying to complete high school or college.

Another measure in the 1996 welfare legislation eliminates the requirement of states to provide money for sex education concerning contraception and instead focuses on abstinence until marriage. This may actually increase unintended pregnancies and sexually transmitted diseases including HIV/AIDS. Some people strongly believe that the social climate appears to favor punitive cost-saving measures over services to pregnant teens and to their babies (Chittum, 1995; Children's Defense Fund, 1997).

Teen pregnancy is a growing national concern for a variety of reasons. Teen childbearing is seen by many as a link to multigenerational poverty. In May 1997, a coalition of liberals and conservatives formed the **National Campaign to Prevent Teen Pregnancy.** They educate the public on the devastating problems surrounding adolescent pregnancy. Their goal is to reduce the teen pregnancy rate by one-third by the year 2005 (Cooper, 1997). If Joseph Hotz's recent study is correct, delaying pregnancy will not solve some problems for many of these adolescents. These problems stem from poverty, abuse, and a dysfunctional family life in their early and formative years (Cooper, 1997). This reinforces the need for society to support our young families so that their children will grow up healthy. There are many forms in which this support can take place.

The teenage birth rate has been declining since the mid-1990s, perhaps due to the increasing effectiveness of education and other prevention campaigns. These programs need to be intensified and directed to boys as well as girls (Children's Defense Fund, 1998). Efforts are needed to reduce the use of alcohol and other drugs among teens as well as to provide more out-of-school programs and available jobs during unsupervised hours. A positive sign for the viability of the teenage family is the increase in the number of mothers finishing high school. Caring adults and support programs help teenagers take responsibility for their actions and for their future.

Foster Parents

Foster parents provide a home to children whose parents, for various reasons, are unable to care for them. Many of these parents do not want to give up their children for adoption. Often children are removed from homes where there has been abuse or neglect. They are placed in foster care while the parents are in rehabilitation programs. Foster care usually involves children of the poor because their families have fewer options in finding substitute care.

As of September 30, 1999, **581,000 children** were in foster care, representing an increase of 48.3 percent in the last ten years. This is due to the increased length of time children spend in foster care and not in the number of children entering the system. Infants continue to be the largest group entering foster care and stay there the longest (U.S. Department of Health and Human Services, 2001). For example, in urban areas in four states (Illinois, Maryland, New York, and Ohio), an estimated five in every one-hundred infants between birth and three months enter foster care shortly after birth (Chapin Hall Center for Children, 1999). In 1999, 60 percent of the children in foster care were of color (not White) and almost 40 percent of these children were Black (U.S. Department of Health and Human Services, 2001).

The goal is to reunite children with their families as soon as the courts determine that the children will receive appropriate care. Often this does not happen and children spend periods of time in foster care. Many times these children move from one family to another. Approximately 27 to 30 percent of the children who leave foster care the first time return within six months. The rate of reentry is the highest for children in group homes and the lowest for those in relative foster care homes (Children's Defense Fund, 2001). Three-quarters of foster care children are in less than one-third of the states. The average time in foster care for children also varies greatly among the states (Children's Defense Fund, 2001). Black children remain in foster care far longer than those from other racial or ethnic groups (Chapin Hall Center for Children, 1999).

An alternative permanent plan must be provided for each child if reunification with the child's family cannot be achieved within a set time. There is a monetary incentive given to states who increase their number of adoptions in a given year over a previous period (see Adoptions). A permanency hearing is now required for each child who has been in foster care for twelve months. In most cases, termination of parental rights proceedings begins once a child has been in foster care for fifteen of the most current twenty-two months. A child being fostered in a relative's home may be exempt from this process (U.S. Department of Health and Human Services, 2001).

History of Foster Care

In the nineteenth century, children who could not be cared for by their parents often were sent to poor houses. When they were old enough to work, they were sent out as indentured servants. One woman born in 1895 was ten years old when her mother died. The five children were either put in orphanages or "assigned" to families. This woman was sent to a farm, where each morning she was required to fix a large breakfast for twenty farmhands and then clean up. She walked five miles each way to school and then in the evening was required to prepare supper. "I was too tired to study much," she apologized. During her six years on the farm she never received a cent for her labor and was not considered a member of the family.

By the mid 1800s, the Children's Aid Society was created in New York City. In 1855, the Society sent children on "orphan trains" to farms in the Midwest. It was believed children would have a proper moral upbringing and develop good work habits. In the latter part of the nineteenth century and into the twentieth century, the churches created foundling homes and orphanages for the protection of children without parental care. With the increase in divorce in the twentieth century, the government was forced to intervene with new laws and ultimately created its own agencies for children needing care. In 1909, the first White House Conference on Children was held. This led to the establishment of the federal Children's Bureau in 1912. By the 1960s, governmental agencies began to shift from the institutional approach to a system of foster homes. This reflected society's belief that children fare better living in a home as opposed to an institution (Children's Defense Fund, 2000).

The funds for foster care come from federal, state, and local governments. Rising costs and increasing numbers of children in foster care led to federal and state permanency laws mandating periodic reviews of children in foster care. There is debate among social workers as to whether current legislation allow parents enough time to become acceptable parents in the eyes of the court.

Roles of Foster Parents and Children

Foster parents are surrogate parents who take in children on a temporary basis and nurture and care for them in a stable environment. They help foster children adjust to their new home and family. Foster children and the foster family's own children often need help in understanding each other.

Foster parents try to minimize or repair the damaging effects on the child's emotional health caused by the child's parental home environment, the sudden separation from their parents, and the uncertainty of their return. Like any parent, foster parents are responsible for overseeing the growth and development of their foster children, which includes their health and education.

Foster children need to fit into their foster family's lifestyle. They are to follow their foster parents' rules for living. This may be as simple as following the family's time schedule for waking, eating, and going to bed or as complex as learning appropriate ways to behave. Children may also have household tasks depending on their age and capabilities.

Because they are new and temporary members of this family, children have little input in family decision making. They also need to adjust to the rules and expectations for activities outside the home. This may be in their new classroom, child-care program, or in activities with new friends.

Challenges for Foster Parents, Children, and Society

FOSTER PARENTS   Foster parents may choose to take in children because of a genuine desire to help and/or to have a child in their own lives. Often these families need the small amount of money the state pays for the child's care. They find, however, that the money does not cover the costs involved, both material and emotional. One foster mother said:

> They may pay you for the food and the child's shoes, but there is never enough to cover the wear-and-tear on your home or the way your towels and sheets wear out. You are left alone with these kids and it would be nice to have a break sometimes and be alone with your family.

The emotional demands placed on foster parents are particularly heavy. Foster children bring with them their emotional, behavioral, and even physical problems. The foster parents must also cope with the reactions of their own children and inevitable changes in family life. Visits from the natural parents of the foster children are usually stressful on all sides, especially if there has been a pattern of heavy conflict within that family. Foster parents may feel a sense of competition with the natural parents for the affection of the child or may not want the additional stress.

Social agencies tend to put additional pressure on foster parents by their inspections to insure that the regulations are being adhered to and that they are doing a good job. The uncertainty of when the child will be taken from them can be stressful, especially when bonds begin to form. On the other hand, some foster families may feel that they can no longer cope with the problems of their foster child. Foster parents are rarely trained to meet many of the severe problems they encounter and support services may not be adequate to improve the situation. To compound the problem, foster parents may have health or emotional problems of their own. They may come to the difficult decision of asking for the child to be placed elsewhere.

CHILDREN'S CHALLENGES Because the breakup of their natural family is usually sudden, foster children have little or no time to adjust to the foster family prior to moving in. To understand and accept their new roles is very difficult. Foster children may already feel that in some way they have caused the death, illness, divorce or other circumstances that brought them here. They may even believe that separation from their family is punishment for some kind of bad behavior on their part. There is always ambivalence toward the natural parents, in which anger and resentments are in conflict with an inborn desire for parental approval and love.

When combined with a sense of alienation from being thrust into a new home, this ambivalence may deepen into depression, with feelings of distrust, personal worthlessness, and a great fear of their uncertain future. The crying, tantrums, and school problems can, in extreme cases, turn into destructive behavior with property, physical violence, and suicide threats (Kates, Johnson, Rader, and Strieder, 1991). Sadly, about one-third of foster children find themselves being moved from one family to another. Often these children have severe emotional or physical disabilities (Fein, 1991). In addition to all these problems, occasionally children are abused by foster parents. Two books revealing some of the problems of life in foster care are *The Lost Children of Wilder* (Bernstein, 2002) and *Finding Fish: A Memoir* (Fisher, 2002).

Although visits from natural parents sometimes upset children in foster care, they also provide a release valve for emotions suppressed. One of the most serious things that happens to foster children is their repression of grief and rage, which can affect their personality for life.

Children need stability, well-defined social roles, and a reasonable opportunity to achieve success. Foster homes by their nature are temporary. Children never know when they will be returned to their homes, if ever, or when they will be moved to another foster home. If foster parents are unable to keep a child, that child's sense of rejection, along with the emotional stresses in shifting from one family to another, only intensifies the child's problems. This is very damaging to the child's sense of self-worth.

In some cases the child's parents may not make the necessary changes, or may get their children back and then repeat the very same behavior that originally caused the removal of their children. In this case, the children are once again returned to the foster care system. The physical, mental, or emotional problems that these children often have make it difficult to find a foster home able to keep them or an adoptive home if they become adoptable.

Health   Many foster children have unmet health-care needs that sometimes are not even identified. Younger children often lack preventive care like immunizations and routine medical visits. A 1995 report by the U.S. General Accounting Office identified the following conditions:

1. One out of three children had no immunizations and one out of eight no routine health care.
2. Three out of five young children had serious health problems and over three out of five were drug babies.
3. An estimated 78 percent were at high risk for HIV, yet only one in ten had been tested (Children's Defense Fund, 1996).

SOCIETY'S CHALLENGES   The nation's child welfare system is faced with serious challenges. The length of stay for children has increased while the number of foster families has dropped. Fewer than 50 percent of the children needing temporary care are placed in foster families. Large numbers of children, including infants, are placed in group care or with relatives who often find it difficult to care for them. This is especially true in many of our largest cities. Those that become free for adoption often have to wait long periods to be adopted (Chapin Hall Center for Children, 1999).

On September 30, 1999, approximately 127,000 children living in foster families and group care settings were waiting to be adopted. This included children whose parental rights had not yet been terminated. These children waiting for adoption had been in continuous foster care, as of September 30, 1999, for an average of forty-four months. Their average age was 7.9 years (U.S. Department of Health and Human Services, 2001).

TABLE 4.1	Children Leaving Foster Care in 1999		
Reunited with parent(s) of primary caretaker		59%	147,640
Living with other relative(s)		10%	24,953
Adopted		16%	38,944
Emancipated (old enough to leave on their own)		7%	18,544
Placed under guardianship		3%	7,396
Transferred to another agency		3%	7,714

U.S. Department of Health and Human Services (2001).
http://www.act.dhhs.gov/programs/cb/publications/afcars/2001.htm

There were 251,000 children who exited foster care in 1999. Their average age was ten years and their average stay in foster care was twenty-two months. Table 4.1 provides data for the next phase of these children's lives.

Societal Support Services

A stable foster home and adequate support services for all parties can reduce the initial negative effects on children separated from their family and placed in a foster home (Fein, 1991). Social caseworkers are usually available for counseling for both foster parents and the natural parents. A vital part of their job is to see that the children receive the medical, dental, and psychological help they need, all of which is paid for by the state.

The natural parents are given help so that they can provide an acceptable home for their children. There are required programs such as counseling, alcohol and other drug rehabilitation, or job assistance, depending on their needs. When children are returned to natural parents, and often before they are removed, support services such as relief child care, homemaker services, and family counseling are available.

The **National Association of Foster Parents** provides a support system for foster parents. Local chapters hold weekly or monthly meetings in many cities and provide periodic newsletters. Often different local members will be designated to provide specific help to other foster parents such as a source for suitable baby sitters, specific clothing or equipment, and articles or references for a particular problem.

CASA (Court-Appointed Special Advocate), a volunteer organization, was founded in 1977 in Washington by Superior Court Judge David Soukup to protect the interests of children in crisis. Today there are 50,000 volunteers, each focusing on an individual or a small group of children placed in foster care because of child abuse. Volunteers work in over 900 cities and represent one-third of the nation's foster children. The volunteer monitors all parties involved with the child. The task may be as crucial as finding a missing piece of paperwork. For example, the adoption of a six-year-old child, abused as a baby, could not be completed because of a missing document. The CASA volunteer who had been following the case for four years was able to locate it (Glasheen, 2000).

ASSISTING OLDER YOUTHS TRANSITIONING FROM FOSTER CARE   The **John H. Chafee Foster Care Independence Program** was established under the **Foster Care Independence Act of 1999.** This legislation was named for the late Senator John H. Chafee, a champion of children's causes. Approximately 20,000 youths transition out of foster care each year who are not reunited with their natural parents or adopted and need the support that most youth get from their parents. These youths continue to have physical and mental health needs and housing costs. They also may want more education. The long-term goal of the Chafee Foster Care Program is to integrate independent living support into the overall child welfare system for foster children. Former foster care youth and other graduates of the child welfare system were very active in getting this Act passed. Youth continue to be a part of the implementation of this vital program (Allen and Nixon, 2000).

The Foster Care Independence Act also expands Medicaid so that youth leaving or having left foster care at eighteen will be automatically eligible for Medicaid until they are twenty-one, regardless of their income (English and Grasso, 2000). In 2000, Congress also expanded eligibility to youths aging out of foster care for housing assistance under the Family Unification Program available to communities (Children's Defense Fund, 2001).

Current Trends

Neighborhood support systems, such as the Family-to-Family model, would keep children in foster families in their own neighborhood. These foster families would be able to provide more support for the natural parents. Another approach to improve the quality of foster homes and to provide care for a number of children is the development of planned communities of foster homes with support groups.

FAMILY-TO-FAMILY INITIATIVE   In 1992, the Annie E. Casey Foundation launched the Family-to-Family Initiative. This exciting and large undertaking responds to the compelling need to improve the care and support of these children and their at-risk families. Representatives of various service systems, especially those who are already serving some of these children, are involved in this project. With the help of citizens and professionals from different fields, the Casey Foundation set up system-wide goals that form the basis for communities to redesign their foster care system. A few of the more innovative goals are:

1. make the family foster care network neighborhood based and culturally sensitive;
2. help the family foster care home be a neighborhood resource for children and families;

3. determine what services the natural family would need to keep their children safely in their home and the services each member would require if the children were removed from their home;
4. involve the foster families as team members in family reunification efforts;
5. reduce the use of institutional, shelter, hospital, psychiatric center, and group home care by expanding relative and family foster care;
6. invest in the communities or neighborhoods needing help by training and recruiting local foster families and support groups.

The Casey Foundation is working with selected communities and states across the country providing human and financial resources to help them reorganize their whole approach to foster care. The Foundation helps communities and states with a portion of the costs in planning and implementing innovations in their services for children and families. Programs must show how they could continue their work after the project is completed. The Casey Foundation plans to share the results with local communities, and state and federal governments. Successful programs can be models for future programs (Annie E. Casey Foundation, 1992).

FOSTER CARE VILLAGE: HOPE MEADOWS Foster care for abused and neglected children in an intergenerational, interracial community was accomplished in 1996 by utilizing part of a closed military base, resources of a nearby university, local retired "grandparents," and other volunteers. This new concept of community foster/adopt care in family homes was inspired by University of Illinois professor and child psychologist, Brenda Krause Eheart. With a few other individuals and support from President Clinton, they were able to purchase from the federal government this twenty-two-acre parcel of land and buildings for $225,000.

Foster children, who previously had been abused or neglected, now live in nuclear foster families. Each family is paid $18,000 for one parent to stay home with the children. There are many activities in the Hope Meadows community, including a swimming pool. There are professionals to counsel, guide, and see that the physical, emotional, and educational needs of these foster children are met. The goal is for these children to become adoptable. This community will also be a research and educational setting for the University of Illinois. Other Hope Villages opened in 1996 in Florida and in Oregon (Lynn, 1996).

Effective efforts must be made to reduce both the numbers of children in foster care and their length of stay. This requires both preventive and supportive programs. A high priority for the federal *Support for Families and Children Program* is to target at-risk families and support them before children need to be removed from their home. Obviously, some parents need help providing a safe and healthy home for their children. This support is especially important after children are reunited with their parents. Other programs, such as Hope Village, are needed to place children who cannot be returned to their homes, in environments where they can flourish with the ultimate goal of adoption.

Certain family characteristics (see Chapter 6) are related to children's emotional and social adjustment. Little is known about supportive traits of foster families. Longitudinal studies are needed to determine which characteristics of foster parents or conditions in the foster home exacerbate children's poor functioning, which minimize children's existing behavioral or emotional problems, and which ones appear to stabilize children's lives (Orme and Buehler, 2001).

Adoptive Families

> *Adoptive families are tied together by bonds beyond genes.*
> — *(Wegar, 2000)*

Adoption fulfills a need for the biological parents who want a home for their child, the adoptive parents who want to have a child, but, most importantly, the children who need the love, care, and legal status that only a family can provide. Hawaiians call adoptive parents "the feeding parents" (Sorosky, Baran, and Panner, 1979). Adoption is the legal method for transferring an individual's membership from the family of birth to a new family with all legal rights including inheritance. Working-class couples are more likely to adopt children of relatives, while middle-class couples are freer to adopt nonfamily members (Sorosky, et al., 1979).

History of Adoption

One of the earliest records of adoption is that of Moses, who was adopted by the daughter of the Egyptian pharaoh. Originally, adoption was designed to serve the needs of adults without children rather than the children in need of parents. In other words, adoption provided these childless adults with the children that they needed to create a family and to have an heir for their estate or title. Adoption was not created for children who needed a home. In fact, in some places (Greece, Spain, and Latin America) adoption still is not permitted if it might interfere with the inheritance rights of biological heirs (Sorosky, et al., 1979).

In the United States, adoption is designed primarily for the welfare of the child who needs a family. For example, not just anyone who needs or wants a child can adopt one. Prospective parents must prove to the court that they will be able to nurture and care for that child in such a way as to promote the child's healthy development. The court sees that children are not taken from their biological parents unless they are truly unable to care for their children safely or choose to release them for adoption.

Children are available for adoption for various reasons. Many are born outside of marriage or come from married parents who feel they cannot adequately care for another child. Sometimes children's parents die or become incurably ill. Many children live in one or more foster homes before adoption.

In recent years, there has been a shortage of babies in the United States for adoption. This is especially true in the case of healthy White infants. This shortage is the result of a large decrease in single mothers releasing their babies for adoption as well as an increase in abortions. Efficient contraception methods have also cut down on unwanted pregnancies. The waiting time for the adoption of an infant through an agency may be from two to five years or longer, which discourages many couples. Consequently, couples are adopting infants from other countries. The *Child Citizenship Act of 2000* confers automatic and retroactive citizenship on all foreign-born children under eighteen admitted to the United States as lawful permanent residents and in the legal and physical custody of one parent who is a U.S. citizen.

Family Structure

The adopted family is different from the traditional biologically related nuclear family. As a family form, adoptive families are connected to another family, the birth family, which may include different racial, ethnic, and/or national groups. Adoption separates the biological from the nurturing part of parenting. This characteristic is also present for stepparents, for at least one partner in a gay or lesbian family, and in families formed through the use of donors (March and Miall, 2000).

It is very difficult to acquire data on adopted families because of the lack of a comprehensive federal system for registering adoptions. According to 1991 estimates, 1.1 million children live with at least one adoptive parent. They live in different family forms, but half (54 percent) of all adopted children live with both adoptive parents. Almost one-third (30.5 percent) live with one biological and one adoptive parent while nearly one-eighth (11.8 percent) live with one parent. White children represent 75.8 percent of all children adopted while only 12.2 percent of the children are Black and 6.1 percent are Hispanic of any race (U.S. Bureau of the Census, 1994).

Both domestic and intercountry adoptions by single parents have increased (Feigelman and Silverman, 1997). For example, in 1999, single parents adopted 33 percent of the children adopted from Foster Care (U.S. Department of Health and Human Services, 2001). Most single parents adopted "special needs" children. This included those who were older, minority, and/or handicapped (Feigelman and Silverman, 1997). In a comparison study of couples and single parents who had adopted a "special needs" child before 1988, the single-parent families experienced fewer problems and also were more likely to evaluate their adoption as being very positive (Groze and Rosenthal, 1991).

Some adoptive families have the birth mother and perhaps her relatives as part of an "extended" family. In this case, they do not share the same household but share parts of each others' lives. With young birth mothers, often the birth grandparents are the ones who keep steady contact with the adoptive family.

Birth Mother, Adoptive Parents, and Child

When children grow up knowing something about their birth mother, they are able to develop a more complete identity and may feel extra love in their life. As adolescents, they do not need to search for their biological identity.

Challenges of Parents and Children

Most parents who adopt children believe that they are infertile. Disparaging attitudes in our society toward infertility and childlessness appear not to have changed (Wegar, 2000; Griel, 1991). In a 1994 study on attitudes toward infertility, Miall found that motherhood, in sharp contrast to fatherhood, was viewed as biologically based and that infertility among women was seen primarily as psychological in nature. For many reasons, women may grieve over their inability to create life. Trouble looms when they use adoption to avoid dealing with this sense of loss.

Parents often fear the genetic unknown of their children. Many fear that the biological mother was an alcoholic or on drugs that damaged the fetus. Other adoptive parents have concerns about the unknown genetic/medical histories of their internationally adopted children. The increasing emphases on geneticization, or linking genetic causes or contributors to later illness, disease, and behavior contributes to adoptive parents' concerns.

In North American culture, the blood bond traditionally has been the basis for the family kinship system. This has been reflected in clinical, research, and social policy literature viewing adoptive family ties as "second best" and adoptive children as "second choice" (Bartholet, 1993; Kirk, 1964, 1981; Miall, 1987, 1996; Modell, 1994).

Some parents find that their adoptive children face prejudices from other children. Adoptive parents have to help their child deal with prejudices about adoption. When their child has a different cultural, racial, or ethnic background, parents need to find ways to help their child form a positive self-identity. Adoptive parents may have to deal with their child's need or desire to meet their biological parent(s), especially during adolescence when youths are searching for their identity. Many of these problems are avoided in open adoptions when children have seen or know about their biological parent(s).

CHALLENGES OF ADOPTED CHILDREN   Children hear subtle negative messages about adoption in many settings in society, even in the home. They may hear questions similar to these. Why didn't your real mother or parents want you? Perhaps you are damaged in some way. One brother wrote the following message which he attached to his sister's birthday gift.

> *I love you, Sis, and even if you were adopted, I'd still love you . . . well, you don't look like Mom or Dad, but don't worry about it. We all love you, even if your real parents don't. Happy Birthday, Sis!*

Adopted children may be more vulnerable to emotional problems than other children. Special problems can occur for children adopted after bonding takes place with the biological or foster parents. Some children bear the scars of neglect or mistreatment that occurred before and/or after their birth. Some adopted children are affected by the biases in community attitudes, media images, and adoption research and practice (Wegar, 2000). However, many adopted children grow up to be well adjusted and emotionally healthy adults. A study by Borders and her coworkers compared the current functioning and pyschosocial well-being of adult adoptees in midlife and their nonadoptee friends of a comparable age. Basically, the overall adjustment reported by each group was very similar. Interestingly, there were more differences reported within the adoptee group than between the two groups. The adoptees, who desired more biological background information, reported stronger emotions of anger, frustration, and a sense of powerlessness over their lack of access to this information (Borders, Black, and Pasley, 1998).

Adopted children need to know how they became a member of their family just as biological children do (Brodzinsky, Singer, and Byaff, 1983). Most experts say that children should be told about adoption in simple terms between two and four years of age, even though they have little understanding of the birth process and even less of the concept of adoption. This is comparable to parents who begin religious training in the toddler and preschool years rather than waiting for a child to be able to understand the concepts. Parents who keep a personal scrapbook for their child help the child and others understand her or his personal history.

Children, especially at times of conflict, may have a fantasy that things would be better if they were with their natural parents. A child might say, "My real mother wouldn't treat me this way." If the adoptive mother, hurt and angry, replies, "Your real mother is a no-good . . . ," the stage is set for tragedy. Good communications are difficult in all families, but may be especially so in adoptive ones. One adult remembers the following from her childhood:

> After the novelty of having a baby wore off, my adoptive mother was very cold. She would apologize for my behavior by reminding people that I was not her child. I was very lonely and unhappy. Nobody wanted their sons dating me because 'who knows what bad blood may be in me' (Mandell, 1973).

The successful adoption is quite different. One boy wrote:

> My parents are super. I have always felt like I really belonged to the family. My younger sister was born to my parents but I think I was their favorite child. I don't see how my natural parents could have made my life as happy. I have no regrets (Mandell, 1973).

During adolescence, when youth are establishing their identity, many want to learn more about their roots and their birth parents. Children may feel that their biological parents represent some part of their psychological self and not just their genetic makeup. If adoptive parents thwart this by being hurt or unsupportive, children are left to fantasy. On the other hand, knowledge of their heredity and cultural heritage can help them in their identity and resolve many questions. One child, after meeting his biological mother and having all his questions answered, said, "For the first time in my life I no longer feel adopted" (Mandell, 1973).

A recent study of 190 adoptions, ranging from confidential to fully open, reported the feelings of all parties in the adoption triangle regarding the adoption. The children interviewed were from four to eight years of age. All of the 171 children in both closed and varying degrees of open adoptions wanted more information about their birth mother. Children with little information about their birth mother wanted to know about her health, well-being, and what she looked like. Children who had more information or contact wanted to know when they would see the birth parent again, what the parent had been doing, and information about birth siblings. Young children seemed to benefit from contact with the birth mother.

> One eight-year-old child stated: I asked if my birth mother still loved me and my mom goes, 'Of course she does' and I believe her, because every time my birth mother comes up to see us, she's always hugging me and stuff (McCoy, Grotevant, and Ayers-Lopez, 1995).

Types of Adoption

All adoptions are governed by state laws except for those of Native American children. Although adoption laws vary from state to state, they are written to protect children, natural parents, and adoptive parents. There is a movement to achieve uniformity in state adoption laws, but the states lack consensus on a number of major issues (Hollinger, 1993).

Native American children must have the approval of their tribe to be adopted. Their adoptions are also governed by the U.S. Indian Child Welfare Act (ICWA). The tribe may choose to be involved in the selection of the adoptive parents. If prospective parents are from another tribe or a non-Indian family, the Superior Court must be petitioned for a variance on the placement order. This procedure can be accomplished through most adoption agencies.

TRADITIONAL AND OPEN ADOPTIONS   Traditional or closed adoption records are sealed to protect the privacy of all parties. This process was developed to make the arrangement more permanent for adoptive parents and children, with no chance for anyone to change his or her mind. However, it is estimated that today, 90 percent of the persons who search find their birth parents or children (Roberts, 1995). Most of the fears and concerns of biological parents, adoptive parents, and adoptees with respect to unsealing of adoption records are unfounded (Sachdev, 1989).

Today there is an increase in "open" adoptions in which the birth parent(s) knows who the adoptive parents are and often has arrangements for continuing contact with them either directly or through an agency. Open placement means that the birth parent participates in the selection of the adoptive parents. Usually they meet, but they may or may not share information about their identity or have ongoing contact.

Openness is looked at as a direction and not as an absolute. Openness with no parameters can be destructive. An adoption needs to be designed in which all parties feel comfortable with the parameters. The contract should be written so that new parameters can be defined as the relationship builds or changes, preferably with the help of a third party. Adoption information that is needed by some children and both sets of parents may not be relevant to others. Information that a doctor or a teacher should know to serve the child better needs to be considered.

Sources of Adoption

Adoptions may be accomplished through licensed adoption agencies or directly from the mother to the adoptive parents. Some states allow an adoption "broker" to arrange the adoption. Although this method can produce quick results, protection is at a minimum. Another program, Fost-Adopt, places a child with a licensed foster family who wishes to adopt the child if the child becomes free for adoption.

AGENCY ADOPTIONS   Governmental adoption agencies operate at state and county levels. In addition, private and religious agencies also place children. Agency adoptions may be closed or open. In either case, the child is relinquished to the agency by the birth parent(s). In a closed adoption, the agency is free to choose the adoptive parents. In open adoptions, the agency works with both sets of parents and helps them design a plan for future contacts.

Reflecting changes in society since the 1970s, agency adoptions today include more options, even individualizing adoption documents. Approximately 80 percent of agencies now include the option of open adoptions or open placements. The agencies who do not offer these options are mainly the ones that have a five- to ten-year waiting period for infants (Roberts, 1995).

Some argue that child welfare agencies rather than independent adoption agents are better able to find the best home for children as opposed to finding suitable children for prospective parents (Emery, 1993). An agency offers the following advantages over nonagency adoptions:

1. the child is legally free for adoption. The birth mother has usually received help through counseling.
2. the child's physical and mental health have been assessed.
3. child and adoptive family are often matched. Character, motivation, age, and ethnic, racial, and religious backgrounds are considered.
4. continuing agency services are provided to help the adopting family with the adjustment and with legal completion through court proceedings.
5. often continuing help in the future is available such as medical information or even opening records.

INDEPENDENT ADOPTIONS   The majority of adoptions in the United States are arranged between the biological parents and the adoptive parents. These independent adoptions provide more options to adoptive and biological parents than many agencies do (McDermott, 1993). Adults who seek nonagency adoptions often do not meet an agency's qualifications, or the waiting time is too long, or no child at the age they want is available. Independent adoptions are costly financially. They may be even more costly emotionally, because many or all of the above agency guarantees may not be met. The birth parent(s) places the child directly with the adoptive parents. State laws must still be met before the adoption is final. This may take up to 180 days. While this process is taking place, the birth parent(s) can legally reclaim the baby.

DIFFICULT-TO-PLACE CHILDREN   Children who are difficult to place, because of age, disabilities, minority status, or membership in a sibling group, need special help in locating adoptive parents. In 1967 the Child Welfare League established an adoption resource exchange that brings hard-to-place children to the attention of adoption agencies across the nation. These children are difficult to place for both financial and psychological reasons. Many of the hard-to-place children who are adopted have multiple disabilities according to North American Council on Adopted Children. To compensate for the additional financial costs, the *Federal Adoption Assistance Program* has special funds available, including Medicaid. This adoption assistance program not only helps to provide permanent homes for children but saves taxpayers money over the costs of foster care. (Children's Defense Fund, 1996).

The *1997 Adoption and Safe Families Act* was passed in part to help find adoptive homes for the large number of children in foster care waiting to be adopted. This legislation added new fiscal incentives to states for every child from foster care adopted above their baseline (number adopted the past year). In 1996, only 28,000 foster care children were adopted. With incentive moneys available in 1999, the number increased to 46,000 children. Every state, including the District of Columbia and Puerto Rico, was eligible for the incentive money (Children's Defense Fund, 2001; U.S. Department of Health and Human Services, 2001).

However, there is still inadequate psychological support for adoptive families, especially for those who adopt difficult-to-place children. Taking on an instant family of two or more children does present a challenge for new parents but a bonus for siblings. They have more security and are able to maintain their sibling bonds. Parents who adopt children of different racial and/or ethnic backgrounds also have additional challenges. Children need to know their rich cultural heritage and develop a positive self-identity. Children of mixed races and/or ethnic groups present a more complex problem both in terms of self-identity and of the racial group with which the family should identify. For example, who would be best suited to adopt a child who is half Black and half Chinese? One girl placed for adoption had four ethnically different grandparents: Black, Indian, Jewish, and White. However, everyone in the family can be enriched by learning about and valuing other cultures.

Some states and organizations are beginning to look at the ongoing needs of adoptive families and are providing postadoption support. For example, the Maine Adoption Guides Program offers ongoing support to families who adopt special needs children. They provide for respite care, short- or long-term therapy, access to an adoptive support group, and advocacy within schools (Children's Defense Fund, 2001).

NATIONAL ADOPTION DAYS   Since 1998, the Alliance for Children's Rights in Los Angeles has reduced the waiting period for many children by coordinating groups of pro bono and staff attorneys who process the paper-work for children already free for adoption. In 2000, Los Angeles County held four Adoption Saturdays, finalizing a total of approximately 1,200 adoptions. This expanded to other counties in the state and, in November 2000, National Adoption Days were held in five other states and the District of Columbia (Children's Defense Fund, 2001).

Societal Responsibilities

The majority of approaches or theoretical models used to study children's adjustments to adoption disregards the impact of social and cultural factors In addition, studies showing successes of adoptive families, such as the long-term study by

Borders, Black, and Pasley (1998), have been slow to reach adoption practitioners. The mass media still shows negative or biased images of adoptees and will continue to as long as they feel the audience is responding favorably (Wegar, 2000).

It is crucial that adoptive families and those persons working with them recognize these biases and understand the damage they do. The public can be educated on the facts by publicizing research supporting the well-being of adoptive families. Research shows that those who have personal experiences with adoption and/or higher education generally have positive attitudes toward adoption (The Evan B. Donaldson Research Institute, 1997). The antibias and the multicultural curriculums in child-care centers and schools also help prevent biases. They teach children to value those that may be different from them in some way. Above all, society needs to view the adoptive family as a viable and potentially healthy family form, just as they do the nuclear family or any other family form.

Current Trends in Adoption

Dramatic changes in adoption practices have occurred in the United States and in other Western countries. These trends are due in part to a greater acceptance of differing lifestyles and the decreased stigma of illegitimacy. The move is away from confidentiality toward more openness (McCoy, et al., 1995). This includes a move to "open the books" or unseal the records on previous adoptions. Kansas and Alabama, which never closed records to adult adoptees, have *lower abortion* rates and 50 percent to 70 percent *higher adoption* rates than the national averages. Oregon, Tennessee, and Delaware have passed laws allowing the opening of records to adult adoptees with a few restrictions and other states are considering similar bills (Samuels, 2001). *Rutgers Law Review* (2001) has a detailed history of access to birth records.

The ethical and legal debate is between the rights of adoptees to know their origin as do all other citizens, and the rights of birth parents to maintain their privacy. In twenty-seven states "mutual consent registries" are assisting adoptees and birth mothers in their searches. A few states allow "confidential intermediaries" to contact adoptees or birth parents for the purpose of obtaining permission to release names or to set up appointments. These intermediaries are usually appointed by the state or a court. Court orders to obtain needed medical records are usually granted but without revealing the identity of the birth families.

Proposed alternatives to unsealing records completely include making available medical and cultural information on the biological parents. Another arrangement might be the registration of biological parents and adopted children; when the child reaches maturity, the records would be made available if the child, the biological, and the adoptive, parents agreed. Yet another possibility would be for the biological parent and adoptive parents to negotiate at the time of adoption the right of periodic contact, probably with correspondence through the agency. This trend for more openness is reflected in Americans' search for their biological roots. The tremendous interest in Alex Haley's story of his own quest for his African tribal background was seen in the popularity of his book *Roots* and the televised version.

In the last decade, search groups have helped adult adoptees locate information about their background. ALMA (Adoptees' Liberation Movement Association) and the American Adoption Congress, an open-records advocacy group, are two examples. The immediate past president of the American Adoption Congress, Jane Nast, believes that adoptees need to know everything about their birth parents that is necessary for their health and well-being and this supercedes the rights of the birth parents to confidentiality (Nast, 2002). The following story of a successful search for roots was told to the author.

> *A college student, with children of her own, met a sister whom she never knew she had. This younger sister had been given up for adoption twenty-five years earlier. After years of searching, this sister located her biological parents, brothers, and sisters. This reunion has produced much joy for the entire family, including the biological parents who felt they could not afford to raise another child at the time of her birth.*

Not all reunions are happy occasions. Some biological parents want to remain anonymous for various reasons. Some children are disturbed by what they learn about their biological parents. When adoptions have a degree of openness from the beginning, such traumas are minimized or avoided.

A number of benefits might derive from individualizing adoptions by designing a contract to meet the needs of each member of the adoption triad (both sets of parents and the child). More openness could reduce the number of adopted children requiring psychological help. Genetic or medical information would be available. Allowing adoptive parents and children to meet the birth parents would test their respective fantasies. Many birth mothers are requesting some choice in selecting the adoptive parents. Overall, there is an increase in the number of birth mothers, adoptive parents, and children contacting agencies to obtain confidential information (McCoy, et al., 1995).

Longitudinal studies are needed comparing the effects of traditional and more open adoptions on the members of the adoption triangle. Only then will researchers be able to look at the long-term effects of the various methods of adoption and evaluate the need for choice.

Adoptive families need pre- and postadoption support for positive ways of dealing with existing societal biases and ways to strengthen their family. In the African American family, the definition of family and kinship relationships is based more on behavior and function (acting like a family member) than on blood ties (Furstenberg, 1995; Lempert, 1999). Adoptive families, like gay–lesbian families, are tied together by bonds beyond genes. A broader, more inclusive definition of the family would support all families in their search for acceptance and identity.

Grandparents as Parents: Kinship Care

Trying to do a better job the second time around.

The vast majority (94 percent) of older adults with children have grandchildren (Kornhaber, 1996). Most grandparents look forward to visits from their grandchildren. Some believe that they have the best of both worlds when they are able to enjoy and spend time with their grandchildren but are also free to leave. Today, this is not true for many grandparents, who are either raising their grandchildren or helping to raise them in an extended family with the child's parent. There are 3.7 million children living with a grandparent or 5.4 percent of all children under eighteen (Saulter, 1996; Hudnall, 2001). This is a 62 percent increase from 1989 to 1996 (U.S. Bureau of the Census, 1997). In over half of these households, the children's parent is not present (Kornhaber, 1996; Hudnall, 2001). *Kinship care* refers to children in the care of a relative. In 1996, over 2 million children lived *without a parent* in a household headed by a relative, two-thirds of these being grandparents (U.S. Bureau of the Census, 1997). The majority of these grandparents are grandmothers.

Although grandparents raising their grandchildren represent all socioeconomic and ethnic groups, they are 60 percent more likely to live in poverty (U.S. Bureau of the Census, 2000). At least 27 percent of children in grandparent-headed households live in poverty (Hudnall, 2001). Most grandparents live in an urban setting and have less than a high school education. Over half (57 percent) of these families live in the south (Turner, 1995). Black children (13 percent) are much more likely to be living in a grand parental home than are White (3.9 percent) or Hispanic (5.7 percent) children (Takas, 1996).

Grandparent Households

Historically, grandparents have raised their grandchildren in times of family crisis. The increase in the number of families living in crisis situations has contributed to the current number of grandparents assuming parental responsibilities (Rothenberg, 1996). The vast majority of children living with a relative (72 percent) have been removed from their home because of parental drug abuse or neglect (American Association of Retired Persons, 1995). In other situations, a parent or parents may die, suffer terminal illness or divorce, be a teenager, in prison, unemployed, never-married, mentally ill, or abandon their child. The AIDS epidemic has contributed to this trend. The Orphan Project of New York City estimates that in the year 2000 between 75,000 and 125,000 children will have lost their mother due to HIV/AIDS (Orphan Project of New York City, 1995).

Recent legislation has enabled more relatives to care for their kin. The amended 1995 Social Security Act specifies that adult relatives must be the state's first foster care option. The Kinship Act of 1996 places grandparents first in line as potential foster care or adoptive parents when children have been removed from their parents' home for safety reasons. Many grandparents choose to raise their grandchild rather than have this child placed with a stranger in foster care or in an adoptive family (Rothenberg, 1996). The *National Family Caregiver Support Act of 2000,* (2000) provides funds for support services to grandparents and other relatives age sixty or older raising children. The first of these funds were distributed to each state in February 2001 for counseling, respite, and other support services.

Challenges for Grandparents and Grandchildren

Although most grandparents raising their kin find it rewarding, they have serious challenges as well. Accepting the responsibility of raising a grandchild brings many changes in lifestyle. No longer do they have the same time, freedom, or money for themselves. There are both physical and emotional costs for grandparents. Relationships with their spouse, grandchild, and their own child, if living, will be changed. For example, a mother may have ambivalent feelings about her parents raising her child even when she knows it is best for the child. Often, conflict occurs when the child's parent is living in the same household. When the child's parent is not living in the household, relationships among grandparent(s), mother, and child can be supportive for all (Rothenberg, 1996).

Grandparents, like most parents, are concerned with health care, child care, education, supportive services, and legal custody of their grandchildren. Many relative caregivers find the lack of money a problem and do not realize that they may be eligible for health benefits for their grandchildren under CHIP (the Children's Health Program), enacted in 1997.

Specific concerns of grandparent caregivers shared at Grandparents Who Care support meetings include:

1. behavioral problems of their grandchildren;
2. their own child's drug use;
3. dealing with bureaucracy, often having two or three caseworkers from the same agency involved in their grandchildren's care;
4. their personal needs (e.g., an electric wheelchair, medical condition, general exhaustion);
5. the need for peer support;
6. monetary needs;
7. respite needs (Kinship Support Network, 1998).

Changes in their family can be a traumatic experience for children. When their parent is not a part of this new household, children may feel rejected and full of anger. Children may also feel a sense of abandonment even though they are grateful to their grandparents (Saltzman and Pakan, 1996). Young children may believe that they caused the situation. During this family transition, children need help in developing a sense of well-being, stability, and love in their new family. For example, children under considerable stress or in crisis often exhibit forms of acting-out behavior (Minkler and Roe, 1993: deToledo and Brown, 1995). Grandparents may need help in responding appropriately. In some instances, the grandparent's housing is not oriented to children's needs, especially for play space, having friends over, and, in general, being able to make noise.

Society's Response

State and community agencies and state legislators are responding to the unmet needs of this growing nontraditional family. The U.S. Department of Health and Human Services estimates that one-third of all children in foster care and one-half of foster children in California are living with relatives. California, Missouri, and South Carolina, in particular, are using new approaches to support relative caregivers, both in terms of financial assistance and legal support (Children's Defense Fund, 1998). At a national conference on kinship care in 1998, kinship caregivers, professionals in social, legal, and health services, educational professionals, researchers, and policymakers from the United States and seven other countries explored ways to support these families (AARP, 1998). The conference was sponsored by the Child Welfare League of America, Edgewood Center for Children and Families, American Association for Retired Persons (AARP), and Generations United. In order to support these vulnerable families, Congress mandated that the 2000 Census collect information on kinship families (U.S. Bureau of the Census, 2000).

SUPPORT GROUPS Community and faith-based organizations are working together to strengthen kinship care families. For example, over forty national community and faith-based organizations held a symposium (May, 2001) to build new strategies for meeting the needs of kinship caregivers. The event was sponsored by the Children's Defense Fund, AARP, and Generations United, and funded by the David and Lucile Packard Foundation (Troope, 2001).

In order to reach and support minority grandparents, the Ford Foundation (1997) awarded the Grandparent Information Center (GIC) a three-year grant to develop a Minority Grandparent Program. GIG conducted a national survey and found that African American grandparents wanted the support group for their emotional support, ways to make friends, and learning the skills that they needed to be parents again. On the other hand, Hispanic grandparents wanted the support group to provide speakers on specific topics and preferred not discussing their personal problems with strangers but would accept a referral for their problems. This Minority Grandparent program operates at limited sites in partnerships with local agencies

The Kinship Support and Resources Program, and most other kinship support groups, usually provide services and support that are not addressed in public social service programs. They also help kin caregivers locate available assistance. The Grandparent Information Center (GIC) in Washington, D.C., sponsored by

AARP (American Association of Retired Persons), provides publications and informational resources for grandparents and children and interested citizens.

Most programs find that these grandparents need respect, recreation, and respite as well as support in other areas.

Respect: The need for respect is basic for good emotional health. Grandparents whose children have been unfit parents are often asked, "Why would you be able to do a better job the second time around?" It is important that support groups help grandparents recognize and appreciate the vital role they play. The Edgewood Kinship Support Program in San Francisco not only helps grandparents succeed in their caregiving but provides frequent recognition for their commitments. For example, they honor these grandparents at an annual luncheon with well-known speakers, such as the governor. To make the occasion even more festive, grandparents are assisted with their costume for the luncheon.

Recreation: Both grandchildren and grandparents need recreation. Some of the support groups provide weekly activities and outings for both the children and the grandparents. Lillian Johnson, former director of the Kinship Support Network in San Francisco, said, "If you could hear the words of advice, concern, and wisdom that are shared as these grandparents are stitching squares for a quilt, you would realize how important these times are for them." Beyond weekly activities, the children often attend a special summer camp (Children's Defense Fund Annual Conference, 1998).

Respite: Every human being needs a break from responsibilities no matter how committed he or she is. Time is arranged periodically for grandparents to enjoy a movie or another activity (Kinship Support Network, 1998). A parishioner, upset with his preacher over taking a vacation, said to him, "The devil never takes a vacation." The preacher retorted, "That's why he is the devil."

The support that grandparents need varies with their individual situation. Their grandchild may come to them with emotional problems beyond the grandparent's ability to help. Also, grandparents often need help in understanding the school or classroom requirements, teacher–parent conferences, or the homework material (Smith, Dannison, Vach-Hasse, 1998). One grandparent, not responding to any of the teacher's requests, was unable to read. For most grandparents, however, it is just understanding how they can help (see Chapter 8 on schooling).

Many grandparents live in housing where, in addition to lack of space, stairs are a problem. Some grandparents have to struggle up one or more flights of stairs with baby carriages, laundry, and groceries. There are instances of grandparents, living in senior housing, being evicted when they take in their grandchild (AARP, 1997–1998). Responding to this problem, the Housing Resource Services of Boston Aging Concerns-Young and Old United (BAC-YOU) and the Women's Institute for Housing and Economic Development in Boston designed a GrandFamilies house.

BOSTON'S GRANDFAMILIES HOUSE

This model housing development is a first in the nation. It has 26 apartments with space designed for grandparents raising grandchildren such as childproof features, physical supports for older adults, and a playground in an easy to watch area. The lower level is for programs for both generations. The YWCA of Boston offers an after-school program promoting math, science, and computer skills. Grandparents have an exercise program, but the most important thing for many residents is their sense of community. Many grandparents feel a sense of isolation bringing up their grandchild, but here they have the friendship and support of their peers. Funding for the 4 million dollar facility comes from many sources, including state and city funds, the Local Initiatives Support Corporation, private foundation funds, and loans (AARP, 1998).

Current Trends

States continue to seek appropriate ways to facilitate the placement of children (legally removed from their parents) into relatives' care as an alternative to foster care. This would include guardian monthly payments. Foundations are funding more kinship projects. For example, the Brookdale Foundation Group is financially supporting a broad range of relative caregivers and state agencies. Schools are being asked to determine the special needs of this family and provide appropriate support. For example, schools can provide special help so that grandparents and relative caregivers understand lesson assignments and the overall school program.

Lesbian and Gay Parents

The ability to nurture is not related to sexual orientation, nor is it related to where a parent resides.
— *American Academy of Pediatrics*

In a growing number of families, one or both of the child's parents acknowledges being lesbian or gay (Baptiste, 1987; Bozett and Sussman, 1990; Pies, 1985). Although these families have existed in many forms for centuries, their numbers have increased along with the openness of homosexual adults. This is the first time in recent history that society has had to deal with such a large group of self-acknowledged lesbian or gay families (Patterson, 1992). The legal definition of a family is being questioned as are laws regarding adoptions and custody cases involving lesbian and gay individuals. In some instances, laws have been modified. Society has been forced to change its definition of the family in order to encompass its many nontraditional families.

History

The vast majority of research in the United States has focused on two-parent families. The most favorable home environment was considered to be the nuclear family, with only the father employed outside the home. It was assumed that both parents were heterosexual (Patterson, 1992). These assumptions were reflected in custody cases and in popular beliefs. However, in the last twenty years, researchers in several fields have investigated lesbian and gay families along with other non-traditional family forms. In 2002, the American Academy of Pediatrics declared that lesbian and gay parents were able to nurture their children as well as other parents (American Academy of Pediatrics, 2002). Studies have found that in each family form there are healthy environments that support a child's growth and develop-ment (Harrison, Wilson, Pine, Chan, and Buriel, 1990; Hetherington and Arasteh, 1988; Hoffman, 1984; McLoyd, 1990; Spencer, Brookins, and Allen, Eds, 1985; Cole, 1988; Elder, 1986; Rogoff, 1990). The key is to identify these healthy environments found in diverse home settings and use this information to support other families.

Estimates of the number of children with lesbian or gay parents range from six to fourteen million (Peterson, 1984: Schulenberg, 1985; Bozett, 1987; Editors of the *Harvard Law Review,* 1990). It is impossible to obtain an exact figure because many lesbians and gays conceal their sexual orientation. They fear discrimination in many areas of their life. Because the majority of their children were born while they were in a heterosexual relationship (Falk, 1989), losing child custody, and/or visitation rights, or even rejection by their own children are very real concerns (Lyons, 1983; Pagelow, 1984; Dunne, 1987; MacPike, 1989; Robinson and Barret, 1986).

Family Structure

Both lesbian and gay families contain great diversity. This includes family form, socioeconomic status, ethnicity, race, and in the avenues to parenthood. In addition to becoming a parent while in a heterosexual relationship within marriage, some individuals become parents after "coming out." Lesbians are bearing children in connection with donor insemination (Pies, 1985, 1990; Steckel, 1985; Rohrbaugh, 1988; Van Gelder, 1988; Wolf, 1990). Gay men are also becoming fathers after "com-ing out" (Ricketts and Achtenberg, 1990). Men may become biological parents through sexual intercourse or donor insemination, and some choose to co-parent their child with a single woman of either sexual orientation, a lesbian couple, or a gay partner. Other gays are becoming foster or adoptive parents (Patterson, 1992).

Some gays and lesbians form single-parent families and others are coupled with a same-sex partner in a family where one or both act as parents. Some gay or lesbian parents are custodial while others are noncustodial parents. Lesbian or gay stepparents may live in a household where their same sex partner is the biologi-cal or adopted parent of a child. The child may live in the household or just visit. Many openly gay and lesbian families form a community with other homosexual families, giving all members a support group. This is also true of many single-parent families.

The roles of family members are similar to those of heterosexual families liv-ing in the same family form. In a single-parent family, the one parent fulfills all the roles. In a blended family, the stepparent assumes a parenting role on different levels, often depending on how long this family has existed. The ability to nurture is not related to sexual orientation, nor is it related to where a parent resides.

Challenges for Lesbian and Gay Families

Lesbian and gay parents must deal with the predominant heterosexist and homophobic views of society. Heterosexists believe that everyone is or should be heterosexual. Homophobia deals with prejudices and fears against lesbians and gays. Until the 1980s, families were always depicted in literature or the other media as heterosexual and the vast majority of families still are (Green, 1982). Children grow up absorbing the prejudice of heterosexists. Until children are aware of their parent's true sexual orientation, they do not see this as directed toward them. This differs from the experiences of children of racial or other minorities who become aware much earlier of their differences and many of society's prejudices.

Not only are lesbians and gays confronted by the prejudices of society at large, but by past assumptions and prejudices found in traditional theories of psychology and in discrimination found in court decisions. Past court decisions ruled that lesbian and gay homes were not a favorable place to raise children. Current research has determined that these assumptions are not scientifically true (Falk, 1989; Green, Mendel, Hotvedt, Gray, and Smith, 1986; Kleber, Howell, and Tibbits-Kleber, 1986; Editors of the *Harvard Law Review,* 1990; Hitchens and Kirkpatrick, 1985; Finkelhor and Russell, 1984; Jones and McFarlane, 1980; Sarafino, 1979; Groth and Birnbaum, 1978). Indeed, the challenges for all parents are remarkably similar. Other studies are cited later in this chapter.

One issue that lesbian and gay parents must deal with is the decision to reveal or conceal their sexual orientation. Sexual identity is very much a part of one's self-concept. Having validation or acceptance of one's lifestyle by significant others is important to one's sense of psychological well-being. Research has shown that lesbian mothers, whose ex-husbands, current employers, and/or children understand or accept their sexual orientation, have a stronger sense of psychological well-being than those who are not open or whose sexual orientation is rejected (Rand, Graham, and Rawlings, 1982). It also appears to benefit the parent and child (especially daughters) if the parent is involved in a healthy couple (partner) relationship (Kirkpatrick, 1987; Huggins, 1989). However, there may be consequences for those who "come out." Some gays and lesbians have been denied rights in many areas of their life because of their homosexuality. Many have been denied child custody and visitation rights on this basis (Basile, 1974; Polikof, 1990).

A big decision for gay or lesbian families is how open to be with child-care or school personnel. To what extent do they want their family form to be recognized along with other family forms? Do they insist that their child refer to both parents as "Mama" as they do at home? Some teachers and parents have difficulty accepting the gay/lesbian family as a healthy family form in which to raise children. It is easier for these teachers and parents to accept and value the children than their parents.

Research on Children of Gay and/or Lesbian Families

Researchers have compared children of homosexual parents to children of heterosexual parents in many areas of personal and social development. There is no evidence in current research that children of gay or lesbian parents or families have any more problems than do children of comparable circumstances in heterosexual families (Patterson, 1992; Golombok, 2003). Both groups fall within normal patterns.

Specifically, there are no significant differences between these two groups of children in sexual identity. This includes gender identity, gender role behavior, and sexual orientation or preference. Gender identity refers to a person's self-identity as male or female. Gender role behavior identifies a person's activities, toys, or occupation as masculine or feminine according to a person's culture. Sexual orientation refers to a person's choice of sexual partners, which could be heterosexual, homosexual, or bisexual (Patterson, 1992; Patterson and Chen, 1997). In twelve studies of over 300 children of gays and lesbians, no evidence was found for significant disturbances of any kind in their sexual identity (Patterson, 1992). The fear that these children are more vulnerable to sexual abuse either by their parent or parent's acquaintances is not valid (Finklelhor and Russell, 1984; Jones and McFarlane, 1980; Sarafino, 1979; Groth and Birnbaum, 1978).

Other areas studied included self-concept, locus of control (meaning internally or externally motivated), development of moral judgment, and intelligence. None of this research showed any significant differences between children of gays and lesbians and children of heterosexual parents (Huggins, 1989; Green, et al., 1986, Patterson, 1992).

Social relationships, both with adults and with their peers, showed no significant differences between the two groups (Patterson, 1992; Golombok, Spencer, and Rutter, 1983; Green, et al., 1986). However, a study on children's social relationships with their noncustodial fathers showed that most children of lesbian mothers had some contact with their fathers while most children with heterosexual mothers had not seen their fathers within the year (Golombok, et al., 1983). In addition, Kirpatrick (1987) found that lesbian mothers and their children interacted with more adult male family friends, including relatives, than did heterosexual single mothers and their children.

When children are given accurate information about their parent's sexual orientation in early childhood, they make a better adjustment and their self-esteem is higher (Huggins, 1989). Early to middle adolescence is an especially difficult time to deal with this or any other identity problem (Paul, 1986). In a survey of young adults, many responded that they had never known anyone else with a gay, lesbian, or bisexual parent (Paul, 1986). Obviously, children in nontraditional families have some different experiences from children in mainstream families just as do children growing up in cities or rural areas or in diverse climates and terrains. Children of lesbian or gay parents were found to be more tolerant and more comfortable in a multicultural environment than children from heterosexual families (Clay, 1990). Perhaps their different experiences contributed to their greater acceptance of differences.

Most of the research has been limited to groups of lesbian mothers and their children in the United States, mostly White, well educated, and middle to upper-middle class. They have been compared to single divorced heterosexual mothers and their children of *similar* circumstances. However, a new study comparing lesbian-mother-familes with both two-parent and one-parent heterosexual families found children in the lesbian families to be well-adjusted and their findings were similar to previous research.

Challenges for Society

Research has shown that court decisions regarding child custody, visitation rights, foster care, or adoption in no way should be based on the parent's or adult's sexual orientation, but on a number of criteria as it is with adults in other family forms (Falk, 1989; Green, 1982; Polikoff, 1986, 1990). The "best interests of the child" demands that the courts and legislative bodies acknowledge the realities of life in lesbian and gay families and other nontraditional families (Falk, 1989; Green, 1982; Polikoff, 1990; Editors of the *Harvard Law Review,* 1990; Ricketts and Achtenberg, 1990). For example, when two lesbian parents, who have been involved in raising their child, separate, the law only recognizes the biological parent as having parental rights (Ricketts and Achtenberg, 1990). Judicial and legislative reforms are needed that would include a change in the legal definition of *parent* (Polikoff, 1990). Only a small number of families have been able to obtain second-parent adoptions (Ricketts and Achtenberg, 1990). This allows the nonbiological parent to legally adopt the child, without the biological parent losing his or her rights (Patterson, 1992).

Lesbian and gay families need to be recognized by society as a legitimate family form and a viable place to raise children. In addition to legal and judicial reforms, public opinion of these families should be based on scientific facts rather than myths. Schools and colleges can help legitimize these family forms by including information on these families. Some family life educators are now including gay populations in their curriculums (Allen and Baber, 1992). School-based support groups for minor and college-age children could help reduce stress by providing a forum to discuss issues.

Counselor training programs are now including counseling for lesbians and gays (Buhrke and Douce, 1991; Iasenza, 1989; Ritter and O'Neil, 1989). It is important that the workplace acknowledge and support lesbian and gay families, as they should all families. For example, when spouses are invited to company events, these families should have their partners included. Industry could also acknowledge the stepparent status of any of their lesbian or gay workers.

Current Trends

Nontraditional families are a growing part of society. All nontraditional family forms would be better understood and supported by having research on the process of their family life and on the diversity within these families. Some studies should be longitudinal so that long-term effects can be ascertained. Research can identify and describe conditions, interactions, and relationships found with favorable outcomes as well as unfavorable outcomes for children in lesbian and gay families.

No family exists in isolation. We need to research the interactions between lesbian and gay families in other settings such as neighborhood, peer group, childcare facilities, schools, community agencies, religious organizations, the workplace, the legal system, and society at large. How can and should society support these and all families?

Key Points

Teens as Parents

1. The United States has the highest teenage birth rate of all industrialized countries. In 2000, 78.7 percent of U.S. teenage births were to unmarried teens.
2. Most school-age teen mothers (58 percent) live with their parents, 12 percent with their husbands, 12 percent with other adults, and approximately 18 percent in a single-parent household.
3. Teen mothers have a higher rate of abusing and neglecting their child. Throughout life, they have less education and earning power than do mothers who marry after age 19.
4. Teen fathers who do not marry the mother are affected psychologically and often economically, such as being required to pay legally mandated child support.
5. Babies of teen mothers have a higher rate of prematurity, low birth weight, birth defects, infant mortality, and a higher risk for life-long disabilities. As children, they have more difficulties in their physical, emotional, and intellectual developmental than children born to parents age twenty and older.
6. Both governmental agencies and private organizations provide preventive programs for early pregnancy and support programs for teen mothers and their babies.

Critical Thinking Questions

1. In what ways do you think that a teen–baby program in a high school would discourage other girls from becoming pregnant and in what ways encourage them?
2. Discuss how society expresses its biases against various nontraditional family forms?

Key Points

Foster Care

1. Foster parents provide a home for children whose parents are unable to care for them safely. Foster parents receive some money, counseling, and other support services. Foster children have free medical, dental, and psychological services.
2. Over 580,000 children are in the foster care system. Infants are the largest age group and the majority are children of color.
3. The foster care system is to return the children to their parent(s) as soon as they are able to care for them safely. All foster children must have a permanency plan within one year.
4. Foster children are removed from their homes suddenly and do not know when they will return causing fear, anger, guilt, rejection, and lower self-esteem.
5. The Foster Care Independence Act of 1999 supports the transition from foster care for youths

at age eighteen without parental support with health-care and housing assistance until age twenty-one.

Critical Thinking Questions

1. How do you think one could minimize the risks of returning children to their home before safe conditions have been stabilized?
2. What are the advantages and disadvantages of having the foster home and the natural parents' home located in the same neighborhood?

Key Points

Adoption

1. Adoption legally transfers an individual's membership from the family of birth to a new family with all legal rights, including inheritance.
2. Licensed agency adoptions provide additional protections and services, while independent adoptions usually cost more and have greater risks, but offer more options for birth and adoptive parents. Special funds are available in the adoption of special needs children.
3. State laws govern all adoptions except for Native American children, whose adoptions are governed by the U.S. Indian Child Welfare Act. Laws are written considering the welfare of the child first.
4. Current research shows open adoptions can benefit all members of the adoption triad. There are many degrees of openness.
5. There is a move to open up adoptions currently sealed so children can know their biological roots for medical and psychological reasons.

Critical Thinking Questions

1. What would you do as the adoptive parent to help your child of mixed-race parentage understand and value his or her heritage?
2. What do you think are the advantages and disadvantages of open adoptions to the adoptive child and parents and the biological parent?

Key Points

Grandparents as Parents

1. In 1996, over 4 million children were cared for by relatives, mostly grandparents, because their parent(s) abused drugs, abused or neglected them, were unemployed, divorced, died, or had a mental or physical illness.
2. Grandparents face many challenges including financial need, legal custody, finding multiple supportive services, health care, child care, and education for their grandchildren.
3. Support groups for kin care are essential to the health and success of this family. Boston's Grand-Family House, a model program, is designed to meet the needs of both the grandparents and the grandchildren in these families.
4. Kinship support groups are working with private foundations and state legislators to provide for the needs of these families.

Critical Thinking Questions

1. How would you respond to the question often asked of grandparents, "What makes you think that you will be a better parent and not make the same mistakes the second time around?"
2. How might the grandparent's role as the responsible caregiver be affected if her daughter, the child's mother, were also living in her home?

Key Points

Lesbian and Gay Parents

1. An estimated 6 to 12 million children are in lesbian and gay families.
2. Lesbian or gay parents can be single or coupled, and custodial or noncustodial parents. The quality of step relationships affects the happiness of any blended family.
3. Lesbian and gays have been denied rights in areas of their life such as child custody, child visitation, adoption, and foster care because of their sexual orientation.

4. Current research shows that children of lesbian and gay parents have no more problems in their gender identity, behavior, sexual orientation, or their personal and social development compared to other children.

5. When told in childhood of their parent's sexual orientation, children adjust better and their self-esteem is higher than when told in early to middle adolescence.

6. Future research needs to look at differences within the gay or lesbian family and their interactions in different settings surrounding their family life.

Critical Thinking Questions

1. What terminology could lesbian and gay parents use to describe their family to teachers and friends and how might this affect their children's degree of acceptance by others?

2. How would you, as a teacher or parent whose personal religious beliefs and ethnic values were condemnatory of homosexuality, interact with these families and their children? Where could you go for advice?

Resources and References

AARP Grandparent Information Center
http//www.aarp.org/getans/consummer/grandparents.html
Adopt a U.S. Kid
http://www.ADOPTAUSKID.org
American Adoption Congress
http://www.aac.org
Annie E. Casey Foundation
http://www.aecf.org
Department of Health and Human Services
http://www.act.dhhs.gov/programs/publications
Generations United-Grandparent Caregivers
http//www.gu.org/
Institute for Social Research, University of Michigan
www.monitoringthefuture.org/
National CASA Association
www.nationalcasa.org

SIECUS: Sexual Education and Information Council of the United States.
www.siecus.org
U.S. Department of Health and Human Services (2001)
http://www.act.dhhs.gov/programs/cb/publications/afcars/2001.htm
Waugh, M. (2002). *Statement of the President of the American Adoption Congress.* Washington, DC: American Adoption Congress.

■ Related Readings

Bernstein, N. (2002). *The Lost Children of Wilder.* Pantheon Books: New York.
Fisher, A. Q. (2002). *Finding fish: A memoir.* William Morrow: New York.

■ References: Teen Families

Alan Guttmacher Institute. (1996). *Facts in brief: Teen sex and pregnancy.* New York and Washington: The Allan Guttmacher Institute.
Baldwin, W. (1981). *Adolescent pregnancy and childbearing: Rates, trends and research findings.* Baltimore, MD: National Institute of Health.
Brown, S., and Eisenberg, L. Eds. (1995). *The best intentions: Unintended pregnancy and the well-being of children and families.* Washington, DC: National Academy Press.
Carnegie Foundation. (1992). *A matter of time: A risk and opportunity in the non-school hours.*
Children's Defense Fund. (1988). *The state of America's children yearbook.* Washington, DC: Author.
Children's Defense Fund, (1994). *The state of America's children yearbook.* Washington, DC: Author.
Children's Defense Fund, (1995). *The State of America's children yearbook.* Washington, DC: Author.
Children's Defense Fund. (1996). *The state of America's children yearbook.* Washington, DC: Author.
Children's Defense Fund. (1997). *The state of America's children: Yearbook 1997.* Washington, DC: Author.
Children's Defense Fund. (1998). *The state of America's children: Yearbook 1998.* Washington, DC: Author.
Children's Defense Fund. (2001). *The state of America's children: Yearbook 2001.* Washington, DC: Author.
Children's Home Society of California. (1996). *Human maturity.* Los Angeles, CA: Author.
Chittum, Samme. (1995). Good news/bad news on teen motherhood in the United States. *NGO*

Action for Children, July–September. New York: UNICEF.

Cooper, R. T. (1997). *Contrary take on teen pregnancy. Los Angeles Times,* May 24.

Furstenberg, F. F. (1976). *Unplanned parenthood: The social consequences of teenage childbearing.* New York: MacMillan.

Garbarino, J. (1982). *Children and families in the social environment* (2nd ed.). New York: Aldine de Gruyter.

Kreinin, T. (1999). Forum on preventing teenage pregnancy: In curricular programs to curb teen pregnancy. *Education Digest, 64*(7), 38–41.

Levering, C. S. (1983). Teenage pregnancy and parenthood. *Childhood Education, 59*(3), 182–185.

Moore, K. A., and Stief, T. M. (1991). Changes in marriage and fertility behavior: Behavior versus attitudes in young adults. *Youth and Society, 22,* 363–386.

National Household Survey for Drug Abuse. (1994). Washington, DC: U.S. Government Printing Office.

Northeastern University's Center for Labor Market Studies. (1994). *National Longitudinal Survey of Youth* in the *State of America's children yearbook, 1996.* Washington, DC: Children's Defense Fund.

School Board News. (1999). Curricular programs to curb teen pregnancy. *Educational Digest, 64*(7), 38–41.

SEICUS. (1994). *National study.* Washington, DC: Sexuality Education and Information Council of the United States.

SEICUS. (2001). *Sexuality education.* National School, Health, Education Clearinghouse Online. Available: www.seicus.org/school/index/html

Sipe, C., Batten, S., Stephens, S., and Wolfe, W. (1995). *School-based programs for adolescent parents and their young children: Overcoming barriers and challenges to implementing comprehensive school-based services in California and across the country.* Bala Cynwyd, PA: Center for Assessment and Policy Development.

Trinchero, A. (1983). *Executive director's annual report,* Florence Crittendon Home for Girls, Santa Ana, CA.

University of Michigan Institute of Social Research. (1994). *Monitoring the future.* Ann Arbor, MI: University of Michigan. On-line. Available: www.monitoringthefuture.org/data/00

——— (2000). *Monitoring the future.* Ann Arbor, MI: University of Michigan. On-line. Available: www.monitoringthefuture.org/data/00.

Ventura, S. J., Mathews, T. J., and Hamilton, B. E. (2001). Births to teenagers in the United States. *National Vital Statistics Reports, 49*(10). Hyattsville, MD: Department of Health and Human Services, Centers for Disease Control and Prevention, National Center for Health Statistics (PHS) 2001-1120.

■ References: Foster Care

Allen, M. L., and Nixon, R. (2000). The foster care independence act and John H. Chafee foster care independence program: New catalysts for reform for young people aging out of foster care. *Clearinghouse Review Journal of Poverty Law and Policy, 34* (July–August), 196–216.

Annie E. Casey Foundation. (1992). *Family-to-family initiative.* Baltimore, MD: Annie E. Casey Foundation. Available: http://www.aecf.org

Bernstein, N. (2002). *The Lost Children of Wilder: The epic struggle to change foster care.* New York: Pantheon Books.

Chapin Hall Center for Children at the University of Chicago. (1999). *Foster Care Dynamics: An update from the multistate foster care data archive, 1983–1997.* Chicago: University of Chicago.

Children's Defense Fund. (1994). *The state of America's children yearbook.* Washington, DC: Author.

Children's Defense Fund. (1995). *The state of America's children yearbook.* Washington, DC: Author.

Children's Defense Fund. (1996). *The state of America's children yearbook.* Washington, DC: Author.

Children's Defense Fund. (2000). *The state of America's children: yearbook 2000.* Washington, DC: Author.

Children's Defense Fund. (2001). *The state of America's children yearbook.* Washington, DC: Author.

Eheart, B. K. (1996). *Foster village.* Urbana, IL: University of Illinois.

English, A., and Grasso, K. (2000). The foster care independence act of 1999: Enhancing youth access to health care. *Clearinghouse Review Journal of Poverty Law and Policy, 34,* 217–232.

Fein, E. (1991). Issues in foster care: Where do we stand? *American Journal of Orthopsychiatry, 6*(4), 578–583.

Fein, E., Maluccio, A. N., and Kluger, M. (1990). *No more partings: An examination of long-term foster care*. Washington, DC: Child Welfare League of America.

Fisher, A. Q. (2002). *Finding fish*. New York: William Morrow.

Garbarino, J. (1982). *Children and families in the social environment* (2nd ed.). New York: Aldine de Gruyter.

Glasheen, L. K. (2000). Score one for foster children. *Modern Maturity*, July–August, 29.

Kates, W. G., Johnson, R. L., Rader, M. W., and Strieder, F. H. (1991). Whose child is this? Assessment and treatment of children in foster care. *American Journal of Orthopsychiatry, 61*(4), 584–591.

Lynn, Andrea. (1996). Hope for the children. *Illinois Quarterly, 8,* 7–9.

Mandell, B. R. (1973). *Where are the children?* Lexington, MA: Lexington Books.

Orme, J. G., and Buehler, C. (2001). Foster family characteristics and behavioral and emotional problems of foster children: A narrative review. *Family Relations, 50*(1), 3–15.

U.S. Department of Health and Human Services. (2001). *The AFCARS Report: Interim FY 1999 Estimates as of June 2001(6)*. Adoption and Foster Care Analysis Reporting Children's Bureau. On-line. Available: http://www.act.dhhs.gov/programs/cb/publications/atcars/2001.htm

■ References: Adoption

Bartholet, E. (1993). *Family bonds: Adoption and the politics of parenting*. Boston: Houghton Mifflin.

Borders, L. D., Black, L., and Pasley, K. (1998). Are adopted children and their parents at greater risk for negative outcomes? *Family Relations, 47,* 237–241.

Brodzinsky, B., Singer, L. and Byaff, A. M. (1983). *The adopted child's understanding of adoption*. Paper submitted at the Society for Research in Human Development, Detroit.

Children's Defense Fund. (1996). *The state of America's children: yearbook 1996*. Washington, DC: Author.

Children's Defense Fund. (2001). *The state of America's children: yearbook 2001*. Washington, DC: Author.

Day, D. (1979). *The adoption of Black children,* Lexington, MA: Lexington Books.

Emery, L. J. (1993). Agency versus independent adoption: The case for agency adoption. *Future of Children, 3*(1), 139–145.

The Evan B. Donaldson Adoption Institute. (1997). *Benchmark adoption survey: Report on the findings*. Princeton: Princeton Survey Associates.

Feigelman, W., and Silverman, A. R. (1997). Single-parent adoption. In *The Handbook for Single Adoptive Parents* (pp. 123–129). Chevy Chase, MD: National Council for Single Adoptive Parents.

Furstenberg, F. (1995). *Fathering in the inner city: Paternal participation and public policy*. Thousand Oaks, CA: Sage.

Groze, V. K., and Rosenthal, A. R. (1991). Single parents and their adopted children: A psychosocial analysis. *Journal of Contemporary Human Services, 130*–139.

Hollinger, J. H. (1993). Adoption Law. *Future of Children, 3,* 43–61.

Kirk, D. (1964). *Shared fate: A theory and method of adoptive relationships*. Washington, DC: Ben Simon.

Lempert, L. B. (1999). Other fathers: An alternative perspective on African American community caring. In R. Staples (Ed.), *The black family: Essays and studies* (pp. 189–201). Belmont, CA: Wadsworth.

Mandell, B. (1973). *Where are the children?* Lexington, MA: Lexington Books.

March, K., and Miall, C. (2000). Adoption as a family form. *Family Relations, 49,* 359–362.

McCoy, R. G., Grotevant, H. D., and Ayers-Lopez, S. (1995). Adoption. *Adoptive Families,* January–February, 14–17.

McDermott, M. T. (1993). Agency versus independent adoption: The case for independent adoption. *Future of Children, 3*(1), 146–152

Melinkoff, E. (1983). Private and public adoption agencies strive for the right combinations. *Los Angeles Times,* May 19, 1983.

Miall, C. (1987). The stigma of adoptive parent status: Perceptions of community attitudes toward adoption and the experience of informal sanctioning. *Family Relations, 36,* 34–39.

Miall, C. (1996). The social construction of adoption: Clinical and community perspectives. *Family Relations, 45,* 309–317.

Modell, J. S. (1994). *Kinship with strangers: Adoption and interpretations of kinship in American culture*. CA: University of California Press.

Nast, J. (2002). Adoptees right to know about their birth mother supercedes the rights of birth parents. E-mail message 10/23/02.

Roberts, C. A. (1995). *Openness, honesty and trust: The benefits of open adoption.* Los Angeles, CA: Children's Home Society of California.

Rutgers Law Review, 367 (2001). Available: Americanadoptioncongress.org. Accessed October 28, 2002.

Sachdev, P. (1989). The triangle of fear: Fallacies and fact. *Child Welfare, 68* (5), 491–503.

Samuels, E. J. (2001). The idea of adoption: An inquiry into the history of adult adoptee access to birth records. On-line. Available: Americanadoptioncongress.org. Accessed October 28, 2002.

Sorosky, A. D., Baran, A., and Pannor, R. (1979). *The Adoption Triangle.* New York: Doubleday-Anchor.

U.S. Bureau of the Census (1994). *Statistical Abstract of the United States.* 121st edition, Washington, DC: Government Printing Office.

U.S. Department of Health and Human Services. (2000). *The AFCARS Report: Interim FY 1999 as of June 2000.* Adoption and Foster Care Analysis. Available online at www.act.dhhs.gov/programs/ab/publications/atears/2001.htm

Wegar, K. (2000). Adoption, family ideology, and social stigma: Bias in community attitudes, adoption research, and practice. *Family Relations, 49,* 363–370.

■ References: Grandparents as Parents

American Association of Retired Persons. (1993). *Grandparents raising their grandchildren: What to consider and where to find help.* Washington, DC: Author.

American Association of Retired Persons. (1995). Presentation at Children's Defense Fund Annual Conference, Los Angeles, 1998 by Lillian Johnson, Director of Edgewood Center for Children and Families. *Statistics from kinship facts, 1995.* Washington, DC: Author

American Association of Retired Persons. (1997–1998). *Reaching and assisting minority grandparents. In parenting grandchildren: A voice for grandparents* (p. 4). Washington, DC: Author

American Association of Retired Persons. (1998). *Parenting grandchildren: A voice for grandparents.* Washington, DC: Author.

Children's Defense Fund (1998). *The state of America's children: Yearbook 1998.* Washington, DC: Author.

deToleda, S., and Brown, D. E. (1995). *Grandparents as parents: A survival guide for raising a second family.* New York: Guilford.

Hudnall, C. E. (2001). "Grand" parents get help. *AARP Bulletin, 42*(10), 9, 12, 13.

Kinship Support Network. (1998). *Supporting grandparents and other kin caring for children.* Presentation at the Children's Defense Fund Annual Conference, Los Angeles, 1998.

Kornhaber, A. (1996). *Contemporary grandparenting.* Thousand Oaks, CA: Sage.

Minkler, M., and Roe, K. (1993). *Grandmothers as caregivers.* Newbury Park, CA: Sage.

Orphan Project of New York City. (1995). *Orphans of the HIV epidemic.* New York: Author.

Rothenberg, D. (1996). Grandparents as parents: A primer for schools. *Eric Digest,* EDO-PS-96-8. Champaign, IL: University of Illinois.

Saltzman, G. and Pakan (1996) Feeling in the grandparent raising grandchildren Triad. *Parenting Grandchildren: A Voice for Grandparents 2* (1, Winter): 4–6.

Saulter, A. (1996). *Marital status and living arrangements.* Washington, DC: National Center for Health Statistics.

Smith, A. B., Dannison, L. L., and Vach-Hasse, T. (1998). When "Grandma" is "Mom": What today's teachers need to know. *Childhood Education, 75*(1), 12–15.

Takas, M. (1996). *Grandparents raising grandchildren: A guide to finding help and hope.* Crystal Lake. IL: National Foster Parent Association.

Troope, M. (2001). Grandparents and other relatives raising children—Project report. *Generation United Newsletter, 6*(2), 10–11.

Turner, L. (1995). Grandparents–Caregivers: Why parenting is different the second time around. *Family Resources Coalition Report, 14,* 6–7.

U.S. Bureau of the Census (1997). March Current Population Surveys for 1986–1996.

U.S. Bureau of the Census (2000). *Statistical Abstract of the U.S.,* 121 ed. Washington, DC: Government Printing Office.

■ References: Gay and Lesbian Families

Allen, K., and Baber, K. (1992). Starting a revolution in family life education: A feminist vision. *Family Relations, 41,* 378–384.

Baptiste, D. A. (1987). Psychotherapy with gay/lesbian couples and their children in "stepfamilies": A challenge for marriage and family therapists. In E. Coleman (Ed.), *Integrated integrity for gay men and lesbians: Psycho-therapeutic approaches for emotional well-being* (pp. 223–238). New York: Harrington Park.

Barret, R. L. (1990). *Gay Fathers.* Lexington, MA: Lexington Books.

Basile, R. A. (1974). Lesbian mothers: I. *Women's Rights Law Reporter, 2,* 3–25.

Bozett, F. W. (1987). Children of gay fathers. In F. W. Bozzett (Ed.), *Gay and lesbian parents* (pp. 39–51). New York: Praeger.

Bozett. F. W., and Sussman, M. B. (Eds.), (1990). *Homosexuality and family relations.* New York: Harrington Park.

Buhrke, R. (1989). Incorporating gay and lesbian issues into counseling training: A resource guide. *Journal of Counseling and Development, 68,* 77–80.

Buhrke, R., and Douce, L. (1991). Training issues for counseling psychologists in working with lesbian women and gay men. *Counseling Psychologist, 19,* 216–234.

Clark, C., and Fields, J. (1999). Evaluation of relationship, marital status, and grandparents. Items in the Census 2000 dress rehearsal. Fertility and Family Statistics Branch, Population Division, U.S. Census Bureau. Washington, DC: U.S. Government Printing Office.

Clay, J. (1990). Working with Lesbian and Gay parents and their children. *Young Children, 45*(3), 31–35.

Cole, M. (1988). Cross-cultural research in the sociohistorical tradition. *Human Development, 31,* 137–57.

Dunne, E. J. (1987). Helping gay fathers come out to their children. *Journal of Homosexuality, 13,* 213–222.

Editors of *Harvard Law Review.* (1990). *Sexual orientation and the law.* Cambridge, MA: Harvard University Press.

Elder, G. H., Jr. (1986). Military timing and turning points in men's lives. *Developmental Psychology, 22,* 233–245.

Falk, P. J. (1989). Lesbian mothers: Psychosocial assumption in family law. *American Psychologist, 44,* 941–947.

Finkelhor, D., and Russell, D. (1984). Women as perpetrators: Review of the evidence. In D. Finkelhor (Ed.), *Child sexual abuse: New theory and research* (pp. 171–181). New York: Free Press.

Golombok, S. et al. (2003). Children with lesbian parents: A community study. *Developmental Psychology, 39*(1), 20–33.

Golombok, S., Spencer, A., Rutter, M. (1983). Children in lesbian and single-parent households: Psychosexual and psychiatric appraisal. *Journal of Child Psychology and Psychiatry, 24,* 551–572.

Green, R. (1982). The best interests of children with a lesbian mother. *Bulletin of the American Association for Psychiatry and Law, 10,* 7–15.

Green, R., Mandel, J. B., Hotvedt, M. E., Gray, J., and Smith, L. (1986). Lesbian mothers and their children: A comparison with solo parent heterosexual mothers and their children. *Archives of Sexual Behavior, 15,* 167–184.

Groth, A. N., and Birnbaum, H. J. (1978). Adult sexual orientation and attraction to underage persons. *Archives of Sexual Behavior, 7,* 175–181.

Harrison, A. O., Wilson, M. N., Pine, C. J., Chan, S. Q, and Buriel, R. (1990). Family ecologies of ethnic minority children. *Child Development, 61,* 347–362.

Hetherington, E. M., and Arasteh, J. D. (Eds.). (1988). *Impact of divorce, single parenting, and stepparenting on children.* Hillsdale, NJ: Erlbaum.

Hitchens, D. J., and Kirkpatrick, M. J. (1985). Lesbian mother/gay fathers. In D. H. Schetsky and E. P. Benedek (Eds.), *Emerging issues in child psychiatry and the law* (pp. 115–125). New York: Brunner/Mazel.

Hoffman, L. W. (1984). Work, family, and socialization of the child. In R. D. Parke (Ed.), *Review of child development research:* Vol. 7, *The family* (pp. 223–282). Chicago: University of Chicago Press.

Huggins, S. L. (1989). A comparative study of self-esteem of adolescent children of divorced lesbian mothers and divorced heterosexual mothers. In F. W. Bozett (Ed.), *Homosexuality and the family* (pp. 123–125). New York: Harrington Park.

Iasenza, S. (1989). Some challenges of integrating sexual orientations into counselor training and research. *Journal of Counseling and Development, 68,* 73–76.

Jones, B. M., and MacFarlane, K. (Eds.). (1980). *Sexual abuse of children: Selected readings.* Washington, DC: National Center on Child Abuse and Neglect.

Kirkpatrick, M. (1987). Clinical implications of lesbian mother studies. *Journal of Homosexuality, 13,* 201–211.

Kirkpatrick, M., Smith, C., and Roy, R. (1981). Lesbian mothers and their children: A comparative survey. *American Journal of Orthopsychiatry, 52,* 545–551.

Kleber, D. J.. Howell, R. J., and Tibbits-Kleber, A. L. (1986). The impact of parental homosexuality in child custody cases: A review of the literature. *Bulletin of the American Academy of Psychiatry and Law, 14,* 81–87.

Lyons, T. A. (1983). Lesbian mothers' custody fears. *Women and Therapy, 2,* 231–240.

MacPike, L. (Ed.). (1989). *There's something I've been meaning to tell you.* Tallahassee: Naiad Press.

McLoyd, V. (1990). The impact of economic hardship of black families and children: Psychological distress, parenting, and socioemotional development. *Child Development, 61,* 311–346.

Nast, J. (2002). *Rights of adopted children.* Interview with author October 21, 2002.

Orme, J. G., and Buehler, C. (2001). Foster family characteristics and behavioral and emotional problems of foster children: A narrative review. *Family Relations, 50*(1), 3–15.

Pagelow, M. D. (Ed.). (1984). *Review of child development research: Vol 7: The family.* Chicago: University of Chicago Press.

Patterson, C. J. (1992). Children of Lesbian and Gay Parents. *Child Development, 63,* 1025–1042.

Patterson, C. J., and Chen, R. W. (1997). In M. E. Lamb (Ed.), *The role of the father in child development* (3rd edition, pp. 245–260). New York: Wiley.

Paul, J. P. (1986). *Growing up with a gay, lesbian or bisexual parent: An exploratory study of experiences and perceptions.* Unpublished.

Peterson, N. (1984). Coming to terms with gay parents. *USA Today,* April, 30.

Pies, C. (1985). *Considering parenthood.* San Francisco: Spinster/Aunt Lute.

Pies, C. (1990). Lesbians and the choice to parent. In F. W. Bozett and M. B. Sussman (Eds.), *Homosexuality and family relations* (pp. 137–154). New York: Harrington Park.

Polikoff, N. (1986). Lesbian mothers, lesbian families, legal challenges. *Review of Law and Social Change, 14,* 907–914.

Polikoff, N. (1990). This child does have two mothers: Redefining parenthood to meet the needs of children in lesbian mother and other nontraditional families. *Georgetown Law Journal, 78,* 459–575.

Rand, C. D., Graham, L. R., and Rawlings, E. I. (1982). Psychological health and factors the court seeks to control: Lesbian mother custody trials. *Journal of Homosexuality, 8,* 27–39.

Ricketts, W., and Achtenberg, R. (1990). Adoption and foster parenting for lesbians and gay men: Creating new traditions in family. In F. W. Bozett and M. B. Sussman (Eds.), *Homosexuality and family relations* (pp. 83–118). New York: Harrington Park.

Ritter, K. Y., and O'Niel, C. W. (1989). Moving through loss: The spiritual journey of gay men and lesbian women. *Journal of Counseling and Development, 68,* 9–15.

Robinson, B. E., and Barret, R. L. (1986). Gay fathers. In B. E. Robinson and R. L. Barret (Eds.), *The developing father: Emerging roles in contemporary society* (pp. 145–168). New York: Guilford.

Rogoff, B. (1990). *Apprenticeship in thinking.* New York: Oxford University Press.

Rohrbauagh, J. B. (1988). Choosing children: Psychological issues in lesbian parenting. *Women and Therapy, 8,* 51–63.

Sarafino, E. P. (1979). An estimate of nationwide incidences of sexual offenses against children. *Child Welfare, 58,* 127–134.

Schulenberg, J. (1985). *Gay parenting: A complete guide for gay men and lesbians with children.* New York: Anchor.

Spencer, M. B., Brookins, G. K., and Allen, W. R. (Eds.). (1985). *Beginnings: The social and affective development of black children.* Hillsdale, NJ: Erlbaum.

Steckel, A. (1985). *Separation-individuation in children of lesbian and heterosexual couples.* Unpublished doctoral dissertation, the Wright Institute Graduate School, Berkeley, CA.

Van Gelder, L. (1988). Gay gothic. *Plain Brown Wrapper, 2,* 5–12.

Wegar, K. (2000). Adoption, family ideology, and social stigma: Bias in community attitudes, adoption research, and practice. *Family Relation, 49,* 361–370.

Weisner, T. S., and Wilson-Mitchell, J. E. (1990). Nonconventional family life-styles and sex typing in six-year-olds. *Child Development, 61,* 1915–1933.

Wolf, M. (1990). Checking out the sperm bank. *Gaybook,* Winter (Book 9), 8–13.

Wicke, E. (1993). Penny's Question: "I will have a child in my class with two moms—What do you know about this?" *Young Children, 48,*(3), 25–28.

Child Rearing

A Challenge for Parents and for Society

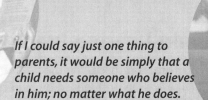

5

If I could say just one thing to parents, it would be simply that a child needs someone who believes in him; no matter what he does.
— **Alice Keliher**

*C*hild rearing is the way parents respond to their children's behavior, thoughts, and feelings in an attempt to socialize them according to parental and societal values. How parents love, nurture, and discipline their children and the types of experiences they provide or allow are based to some extent on the parents' philosophy of life. Child rearing, often referred to as parenting, is a lifelong process.

Parenting involves nurturing, guiding, and protecting a child in all areas of growth and development. Nurturing involves love and caring appropriately for one's child but also providing emotional security and a sense of belonging. A healthy attachment and unconditional love are key for the child's healthy growth and development (see Chapter 2). Understanding each child's special needs is important and easier to accomplish if the child's interests and temperament are close to that of the parent. Parents provide activities that affect their child's self-concept and competence in life's tasks. Ideally, all relationships among family members are based on love.

Parents have the responsibility to help their children grow and develop year by year so that, as adults, they can realize their full potential. This sounds like an impossible task, and it is without the support of others. Society plays a vital role in the types of resources and supports it provides parents and families.

Influences on Child-Rearing Practices

How parents love, nurture, and discipline their children and what types of experiences they provide or allow are influenced by a number of factors. The temperament of each child and of each parent influences their interactions. Other factors include the way the parents were raised, their religious beliefs, ethnicity, and socioeconomic status. Conditions within the family affecting parenting are the age, gender, and developmental stage of each child, the spacing of children, family size, and the physical and emotional health of each member. Relationships of family members may be biological, adopted, or step. Popular press and scientific information on child rearing and general conditions of society at large also affect parenting practices.

Temperament

Temperament is a broad term that includes an individual's predisposition to certain moods and reaction styles. The child's temperament affects the parent's responses to the child and how the child reacts to the parent's actions. Each of their responses is influenced by the previous response (see Chapter 2). Remember the old adage: A good baby makes a good parent, which makes a good baby.

Parental Child-Rearing Experiences

The ways in which parents were raised have a strong influence on how they respond to their children. For some parents, their childhood experiences may provide the only method of child rearing they know. Education gives many individuals other options, but it is difficult to put new ideas into practice.

Religious Beliefs

Parenting practices are influenced to varying degrees by religious beliefs about gender roles, sexual behavior, marriage, divorce, birthrates, dress, and diet. A religious institution's doctrine can have a powerful effect on its followers. The use of birth control allows for family planning, which affects the timing and number of children. However, the Roman Catholic doctrine declared by the present Pope forbids artificial contraception and encourages large families. In Japan, many families of the Shinto faith dedicate their last born son to becoming a priest. The Church of Jesus Christ of Latter-Day Saints forbids the use of alcohol, tobacco, and caffeine and designates Monday as Family Night (see religion in Chapters 1 and 13).

Cultural and Ethnic Groups

Each parent's cultural and ethnic group holds values that influence the way their children are raised (Caldwell, Green, and Billingsley, 1994). Different cultures vary in their approach to communication, displays of affection, control of behavior, and skills to be emphasized. For example, is it appropriate for men to hug, boys to cry, or girls to fight back physically? It is important that educators and researchers understand what constitutes effective parenting within and across cultural groups.

The major ethnic groups in the United States are European Americans, African Americans, Hispanic Americans, Asian Americans, and Native Americans. In order to understand a family's culture, one must know the country of origin for each parent. For example, European Americans trace their cultures to different countries in Europe while Hispanic Americans trace their culture to Mexico and many other countries. In addition, some families have been in the United States longer than others and often have adopted many child-rearing practices of mainstream American culture.

Socioeconomic Status

The parents' socioeconomic status (income and wealth, occupation, and education) affect their child-rearing patterns. For example, lower-class families, struggling to provide the bare necessities, live with stresses and anxieties that increase the use of punitive, inconsistent, authoritarian, and less supportive child-rearing methods (McLoyd, 1990; Dodge, Petit, and Bates, 1994). Many studies show that, as a family's economic situation worsens, discipline becomes increasingly inconsistent and nurturing decreases (McLoyd and Wilson, 1991). Compared to families of high economic status, families of low economic status tend to emphasize obedience, neatness, and conformity. Parents of higher socioeconomic status tend to be more democratic, reason with their children, show more warmth and affection, and model more complex language (Hoffman, 1984).

Parents often raise their children to have the same skills that they use in their own jobs. Parents who work in a factory on an assembly line often stress obedience and disapprove of questioning authority. They want their children to be able to follow orders and to conform. Parents whose jobs demand that they come up with new ideas and be self-directed want their children to learn to raise questions and to think creatively (Kohn, 1977; Kohn, Naoi, Schoenbach, Schooler, and Slomczynski, 1990). How are child-rearing practices affected when a child's parents each work in jobs demanding different behaviors or using different talents? Crouter and McHale (1993) suggest that there could be differences in each parent's child-rearing practices.

Scientific and Popular Media Information

The findings of psychologists such as Watson, Freud, Erikson, Piaget, Skinner, Bandura, and Bronfenbrenner have influenced child-rearing trends. Watson, in the 1920s, saw children as being molded and shaped by forces in the environment. In his book, *Psychological Care of Infant and Child*, Watson (1928) recommends that parents withhold cuddling and affection to prevent spoiling and dependent behavior. He wrote:

> There is a sensible way of treating children. Treat them as though they were young adults. . . . Let your behavior always be objective and kindly firm. Never hug or kiss them, never let them sit on your lap. If you must, kiss them once on the forehead when you say good night. Shake hands with them in the morning. Give them a pat on the head if they have made an extraordinary good job of a difficult task (pp. 81–82).

These households were parent-centered and children adapted to the needs of the family.

Influenced by the teachings of Freud, many parents in the 1930s and 1940s moved from the strict habit training of Watson to a more relaxed approach to child rearing. Schedules became more flexible with babies fed on demand. Toilet training began when the child was ready. Freud believed that children needed some freedom to express their natural impulses and that repression of these impulses would cause internal conflicts. In general, children were given more freedom of expression as families became child-centered.

In the 1950s, there was a move away from excessive parental permissiveness. This was based partially on studies reporting the long-term effects of permissive parenting and other studies showing that children needed limits in order to develop into socially responsible and happy adults (Spock, 1957). This belief was reflected in the authoritative or democratic parenting style. Child-rearing practices during the last century moved from parent-centered to child-centered and finally to a more balanced approach, reflecting the needs of each family member.

Skinner (1957) expanded Watson's behaviorism and formulated the popular approach to learning known as operant conditioning. Skinner believed that the individual operates or acts due to the environment. When a person's actions are reinforced either positively with a pleasant stimulus or by removing an unpleasant stimulus, they are more likely to be repeated. Behavior modification is based on the principles of reinforcing the actions you want repeated and ignoring or providing a punishing consequence for the actions to be extinguished. Parents use behavior modification consciously and unconsciously. For example, they smile when they are pleased with a child's behavior and may frown when they are displeased.

Bandura's (1986) social learning theory shows how the human personality learns from observing others and using or adapting these images in their future interactions. Children observe the behavior of family members and friends. They pay attention to the important features of an interaction and can recall them. Once the behavior is imitated, it must be reinforced by the principles of operant conditioning if it is to be repeated. The old adage, "Do as I say and not as I do," is ineffective. Developmental psychologist Bandura (1977) and his colleagues believe that learning through observations accounts for much of our learning.

Freud's theories (based on his patients' responses) and the research findings of Erikson and Piaget show that children develop according to stages and are affected by their interactions in the environment. At each age and developmental stage, a child is ready to learn or develop certain skills and behaviors. Research findings on the stages of growth and development in the physical, social–emotional, and cognitive areas can help parents understand the needs and behaviors of their children. For example, the need of toddlers to develop independence and to use the word *no* reflects their normal struggle for autonomy rather than misbehavior.

Piaget's research reveals many differences between a child's thinking and an adult's logic. Children proceed through predictable stages in cognitive development. During each stage, they interpret their environment differently. Children need to interact with people and objects during their development (Piaget, 1983).

Bronfenbrenner's ecological theory shows how actions in all areas in society affect the functioning of the family (Bronfenbrenner, 1979). A family systems approach to child rearing looks at all of the relationships and roles within the family as having an effect on the child's growth and development. This approach is reflected in the philosophy of parenting courses that deal with the entire family.

Societal Conditions

The values and conditions in society at large affect the timing and number of children a family has as well as their child-rearing practices. Living during times of war, depression, or economic growth all influence family decisions differently. The system of government also has an impact. A democracy stresses the rights of the individual and the benefits of competition, whereas a socialist system focuses more on the needs of the group and on cooperation and sharing of the wealth.

Changing Roles of Parents

The roles of fathers and mothers in the lives of their children are changing. With a majority of mothers employed outside the home, mothers are spending less time with their children. Employed mothers have the responsibilities for child care and homemaking tasks along with the responsibilities of their employment. Traditionally, fathers, as the sole or major breadwinner, spent time playing with their children but little time with child-care tasks. Today there is pressure for fathers to assume more child-care responsibilities. When this does occur, it relieves some stress for the mother and gives the child time with both parents. When the expectations of a father's' involvement in child-care tasks are greater than his actual participation, it causes marital conflict and increases the tension between the needs of family and work (LaRossa, 1988; McBride and Mills, 1994).

Fathers in Today's Families

Many fathers in the last two decades in the United States have attended birthing and parenting classes, participating in the birth of their children and bonding very early to their babies. However, few are experienced in taking care of young children (Palm and Palkovitz, 1988) and lack the same degree of socialization for nurturing that women have experienced (Berman and Pedersen, 1987). Recent data suggest that fathers, compared with mothers, participate less in child-care tasks and spend more

Sharing and Caring: Dad Helps with the Care of Their Daughter

Dad shares caring for the baby when he is not at work, even if the mother is at home. When both parents are involved in child care tasks, children are able to spend more time with each parent.

of their time playing with infants (McBride and Mills, 1993; Lamb, 1997). However, since 1977 men have increased their weekly hours of child care by two hours to 9.4 hours while mothers still spend 14.4 hours each week (Bond, Galinsky, and Swansberg, 1998). There are increasing numbers of men who report the joys and humanizing experiences of spending time caring for their children, just as many women report finding special rewards in the work world.

Redefining and Supporting Fatherhood

Margaret Mead and others have observed that the supreme test of any civilization is whether it can teach men to nurture their offspring
— (Blankenhorn, 1997).

The role of the father began to be reexamined in the 1970s, along with other issues in our society. Michael Lamb wrote the following in the second edition of *The Role of the Father in Child Development,* (1981) "since the first edition was published in 1976, the paternal role has elicited a great deal of attention from both theorists and researchers . . . so great that it has been necessary to prepare a revision." In Europe and America since 1970, there has been increased involvement of fathers in the direct care of their children, according to Barry Hewlett (1992).

A new "ideal" role for fathers has been emerging both in developed and developing countries. It encourages the father to:

1. be present at the birth of his children;
2. have close relationships with his children;
3. cooperate with his partner, sharing in child care and household tasks.

The ideal role is not necessarily the actual behavior of the majority. How fathers define their role is influenced by the expectations of those in their personal network and in their culture (LeVine, 1999). Does the mother want the father to be more involved with their baby or the household chores and if so, does she want an *assistant* or an *equal partner* in deciding how the task is to be done? Do the health-care providers expect the father to be present at birthing classes or prenatal doctor appointments?

Men often lack the support they need to be more nurturing or involved. Many times they feel that their job limits their participation in family responsibilities, such as parent–teacher conferences. Businesses traditionally are more supportive of mothers, in their schedules for child rearing, than for fathers. Whatever the reasons, many noncustodial fathers are spending little time with their children.

SUPPORT FOR FATHERS   In a move to support the family, the federal government, through the Department of Health and Human Services, focused on the needs of fathers. The *Fatherhood Initiative* emerged in June 1995. This directive, issued by former President Clinton, requested that every government agency recognize and support the role of fathers. Three of the project's guidelines for developing specific activities or services are:

1. Men should receive the education and support necessary to prepare them for parental responsibilities.
2. Parents are partners even if they are *not* living in the same household.
3. Government can encourage and promote safe father involvement through its own programs and its workforce policies (U.S. Department of Health and Human Services, 2000).

The Federal Interagency Forum on Child and Family Statistics is responsible for the publication, *Nurturing Fatherhood: Improving Data and Research on Male Fertility, Family Formation, and Fatherhood* (1998). This informative publication represents the efforts of more than a hundred researchers, policy analysts, and public officials. It is also available on line at http://www.fatherhood.hhs.gov/

Benefits from Fathers' Involvement in Child Rearing

A father's active participation with his children benefits the children and the family. The child's self-esteem, gender identity, social and emotional development, and behavior are all improved (Baruch and Barnett, 1986; United Nations Population Fund, 1996; Lamb, 1986). A father also benefits personally from a closer relation-

Dad and Son Enjoy Books and Each Other

Dad practices at home what he teaches to college students in child development classes.

ship with his children. When he nurtures his children, violence in the home is reduced (United Nations Population Fund, 1996). A high level of positive paternal involvement is important to the child's well-being.

David Blankenhorn, chairman of the "National Fatherhood Initiative," and his supporters work to encourage fathers to be more involved with their children. Blankenhorn believes that fatherlessness is the most harmful demographic trend of this generation (1995). In the United States, about 40 percent of children are living in homes without their fathers and over half of all children will have lived without a father at some period by the time they are eighteen (Blankenhorn, 1995). Blankenhorn and his supporters say that this reflects a diminishing role for the father.

Worldwide Interest in the Role of Fathers

The interest in fathers' participation with their children goes beyond the United States. Researchers worldwide recognize the benefits of nurturing fathers to the family. However, practice does not necessarily follow. A review of research in 186 societies found that only 2 percent of fathers in these societies have regular, close relationships with their infants. Both the actual and expected duties of the father vary greatly throughout the world due in large part to economic and cultural factors. For example, in some parts of West Africa, contact between men and young children is taboo (United Nations Population Fund, 1996).

Practice is slow to change for a variety of reasons:

1. It challenges traditional notions of fatherhood held by both men and women.
2. It may increase men's vulnerability in the workplace if they request paternity leave or refuse to work late because of child-care arrangements.
3. Male role models, policies, and programs to promote men's involvement in fathering are inadequate (United Nations Population Fund, 1996).

Most of these nations are trying to change the attitudes of their people toward the roles of fathers and mothers and boys and girls. Attitudes are affected by many things including government policies, educational programs, and the media. Each could send messages of the importance of fathers as nurturers in the lives of their children and as equal partners with their wives. When men and women experience some of the benefits of men's nurturing roles in the family, fears often diminish, allowing change to occur more rapidly.

Programs in some schools in Africa are teaching boys as well as girls to be nurturing and to care for children and each other. Boys and girls need to be educated to be equal partners in families. Community programs teaching fathers and young children how to interact and develop close bonds have been successful (United Nations Population Fund, 1996). Some countries have had media programs supporting this new role for men. The availability of paternity leave for men is increasing, but in the United States and Sweden, studies show that few men take advantage of this leave (United Nations Population Fund, 1996).

Children's Developmental Stages

How parents develop emotional ties with their children and guide and modify their behavior, thinking, and feelings should be appropriate for their children's developmental stage(s). Erikson provides guidelines in the area of psychosocial development. This involves individuals' interactions with and understanding of each other and of themselves. Other theorists enable parents to understand their children's growth and development in different areas (see Chapter 2).

Erikson's Eight Stages of Psychosocial Development

The development of personality, according to Erikson, is determined by the child's genetic makeup and interactions with the environment during eight distinct stages of life. An individual also is socialized into a given culture. Meeting basic developmental crises at each stage provides a foundation for succeeding stages. The successful resolution of the crisis or challenge allows for the development of a healthy relationship with the world and good feelings about one's self. Many times the resolution of the crisis is incomplete. Experiences at each stage affect ego (rational part of the personality) development. However, experiences in later stages can undo the effects of earlier periods both for better and for worse.

Erickson's Eight Stages

Trust versus mistrust: First year of life

Babies are extremely vulnerable to parents and caregivers who, ideally, provide a dependable environment in which the child's basic needs are met in a timely fashion. Are the baby's cries or smiles responded to consistently and appropriately? Babies need to know that they have some control in their environment. It is important that parents coordinate policies with the child's other caregivers. With sensitive, nurturing, and appropriate care, infants will experience pleasure and trust. If their needs are inadequately met, infants will experience some degree of fear and mistrust. This will affect their relationships with others and how or if they approach certain activities.

Autonomy versus Shame and Doubt: Ages One to Three

Toddlers have a need to develop their independence and to explore their surroundings. Parents and caregivers often thwart the development of autonomy because of their concern for the child's safety. They may also want the toddler to show the same dependence they did in infancy rather than struggling for independence. Children develop autonomy best in a safe setting where they are able to make some choices in their activities. For example, children can choose which clothes to wear from an acceptable selection. This helps them feel good about themselves. Children need to learn and follow some basic rules but limits should not overwhelm or deflate them. Failure to develop necessary autonomy produces shame and doubt. In this case, during the next stage children will use some of their energies attempting to gain autonomy. This reduces their efforts to acquire skills for exploring their environment.

Initiative versus Guilt: Ages Three to Five

Children learn through play, exploration of their environment, and observing adults and older children. They use their physical and mental skills to explore their environment. When this environment is appropriate and stimulating, children are encouraged in their discoveries. Thought-provoking, open-ended questions further their thinking skills. Helping children to be pleased with their efforts as well as their accomplishments, encourages them to feel good about themselves. On the other hand, criticism and punitive parenting or caregiving discourage their initiative and encourage feelings of guilt and a sense of unworthiness.

Industry versus Inferiority: Ages Six to Puberty

Children are ready to learn more about their world and develop skills such as reading and math. They are ready for rules to understand objects and relationships and to learn how to function in larger society. It is important for children to have a sense of competence and success at school, in the neighborhood, and at home. Children need adults to support their efforts. At times, they need help in finding an effective way to accomplish a task. Praise for improvement and effort is important. Praise is better if it helps them feel good about what they accomplish and not how pleased the adult is with the accomplishment. Accomplishments outside the classroom in other areas, such as dance, sports, or music, help children feel competent. When they do not have a sense of competence, they feel to some extent that they are a failure. A sense of inferiority comes from the feeling that parents, teachers, and/or peers see their performances as below standard or not good enough. Parents who are perfectionists can damage their children's self-image by always wanting them to do a little better.

Identity versus Identity Diffusion: Puberty to age eighteen

Intimacy versus Isolation: Age eighteen to middle adulthood

Generativity versus Stagnation: Middle adulthood to late adulthood

Integrity versus Despair: Late adulthood to death (Erikson, 1963;1964).

Stages of Parenthood

Parenting is a process by which parents and children grow and develop, each influencing the other throughout their lives. Parents move through a series of six stages from pregnancy, when they prepare for parenthood and the birth of their child, to the time when their child leaves home to enter the adult world (Galinsky, 1981). Parents assess their success as a parent during each of these stages.

Expectations for their child's behavior and development are measured against the child's actual behavior and development; a parent's self-image may shift as he or she moves through the different stages of parenthood. This information is based on Galinsky's interviews with over 200 couples (Galinsky, 1981). For better or for worse, being a parent changes an individual forever.

Galinsky's Six Parental Stages

Parents with more than one child can be in more than one stage at the same time. Adoptive parents and stepparents become parents after the first stage.

Image-making stage: Pregnancy

Parents prepare for changes in themselves, for new relationships with each other, and the responsibilities of this new life. Many questions are discussed. What will our baby need in terms of equipment, supplies, and space? How will our current schedule and general lifestyle be altered to support our baby's growth and development? Will we have any time for ourselves? How would we cope if our baby has cholic or serious health problems?

Nurturing stage: Birth to 18–24 Months or Autonomy

The major task at this stage is forming bonds of attachment with the baby. Parents attempt to meet the needs of the baby and balance this with other responsibilities involving spouse, jobs, and friends. Parents make decisions about child care. Do work schedules require child care or are work schedules flexible, allowing one of the working parents to be at home, or does one parent stay home full-time?

Authoritative stage: Two to four or five years

Parents nurture, guide, and discipline their child. Parents evaluate their effectiveness in establishing limits, communicating and enforcing rules, and allowing enough freedom for each child to grow and develop. Parents often restrict the child for his or her safety, but other times it may be for the safety of the parents' valued objects.

Interpretive Stage: Preschool Years through Adolescence

Parents teach their child about life and help him or her interpret the actions of others such as their teachers and peers. Parents are concerned with the increasing influences of peers and help their child to understand the consequences of his or her actions. When parents' expectations are different from the actual behavior of their child, they question the effectiveness of their parenting methods or themselves as parents.

Interdependent Stage: During adolescence

Parent–child relationships continue to evolve. Parents involve their teenager in more decisions. Ultimate responsibility still rests with the parent. This is a stressful time for the adolescent, who is searching for identity and independence from parents and for parents struggling to give up enough control to facilitate their teenager's move toward independence and still support and protect their child.

Departure Stage

Parents begin the process of evaluating their roles as a parent and a person as their child prepares to leave home. New relationships emerge between parent and child when the adult child leaves home. Parents need to redefine their own identities.

Styles of Parenting

As soon as parents believe that their child is able to understand social rules, they begin socializing their child in a variety of ways. This usually starts when their child approaches the end of infancy. Most parenting styles can be described by the degree of control parents exert, and the degree of affection they display. In addition, parents operate on different levels of anxiety or concern, which is not addressed in this text.

In a series of studies, Diana Baumrind observed the child-rearing practices of parents and their preschool children in home and laboratory settings. The families were White, middle-class, two-parent, and suburban. Two broad behavioral dimensions emerged. One dimension was the degree of control parents exerted. At one end of the continuum, parents set and demanded very high standards for their children while, at the opposite end, parents demanded very little and rarely redirected their children's behavior. The second dimension measured parents' responsiveness to their children. The degree of responsiveness ranged from parents who were highly responsive, accepting, and supporting their child to those parents who were aloof, ignoring, and/or rejecting their child (Baumrind, 1967).

Using various combinations of control and responsiveness, four parenting styles emerged. Baumrind focuses on three styles: authoritarian, permissive, and authoritative parenting. The fourth style, the uninvolved or permissive–indifferent parent, evolves from Baumrind's permissive style but refers to parents who are uninvolved in their children's lives (Maccoby and Martin, 1983).

Baumrind's Four Basic Parenting Styles

Authoritarian
Shape and control children's behavior
Use of punitive, forceful measures to control behavior
Enforce parental standards with lack of explanations
Stress obedience, respect for authority and tradition

Permissive
Parents are facilitators
Exert very little overt control
Nurture and accept child (rejections fall under uninvolved parent)
Can be indulgent

Authoritative
Firm control but with explanations
Responsive and supportive
Children and parents discuss situation
Respect for parents' and children's needs
Help children understand rules and internalize their own set of values

Uninvolved Parent or Permissive–Indifferent	Use very little control, children free to make their own decisions
	Frequently ignore children
	May show hostility or resentment of children

Effects of Parenting Styles on Children's Behavior

Each of these parenting styles appears to have certain influences on children's behavior. However, culture also influences the outcome, especially for school success. The majority of parents fall into one of these categories most of the time. When parents are inconsistent in their parenting approach, it is very damaging to their children because they do not know what to expect.

AUTHORITARIAN PARENTING   The use of punitive and forceful measures to enforce proper behavior causes anger, resentment, and deceit and impairs wholesome parent–child relationships (Bettelheim, 1985). In Baumrind's 1967 research, preschoolers with authoritarian parents are withdrawn and unhappy. They appear anxious and insecure with peers and react hostilely if frustrated. Baumrind's 1971 research shows girls to be dependent and lacking in motivation and boys much more likely to be angry and defiant. In addition, children of authoritarian parents are less likely to internalize (accept as their own standard) society's unacceptable behaviors (Grusec and Goodnow, 1994), and are more likely to have low self-esteem (Coppersmith, 1967). These children often model their parents' inflexible thinking (Dekovic, Gerris, and Janssens, 1991).

Baumrind's 1971 description of authoritarian parenting emphasizes parents demanding certain behaviors without explaining why and often not listening or providing adequate emotional support (Chao, 1994). In addition, some authoritarian child rearing practices have been linked with an evangelical effort (Smut and Hagen, 1985), stressing domination of the child or breaking the child's will (Dobson, 1992).

PERMISSIVE PARENTING   Parents who are nonpunitive, loving, and accepting of the child often have children who lack independence and are selfish because they are not taught how their actions affect others. These children tend to be impulsive, aggressive, and low in taking responsibility.

UNINVOLVED OR PERMISSIVE–INDIFFERENT PARENTING   The combination of permissiveness and indifference or rejection in varying degrees has detrimental effects on children. In the extreme, it becomes neglect, which is a form of child abuse (Egeland and Stroufe, 1981). Children with few rules who are ignored or living with hostility are noncompliant and aggressive. They have low self-esteem and display anger toward others. Many exhibit antisocial behavior and may end up as criminals (Straus, 1994; Brophy, 1977).

AUTHORITATIVE PARENTING   Parents who are nurturing and set, discuss, and enforce developmentally appropriate limits are the most successful in helping their children become autonomous, independent, self-controlled, self-confident, and cooperative (Grusec and Lytton, 1988; Baumrind, 1969; 1971). These children also are more likely to have high levels of competence and high self-esteem during middle childhood and adolescence (Coppersmith, 1967; Loeb, Horst, and Horton, 1980). They also have internalized moral standards (Holmbeck, Paikoff, and Brooks-Gunn, 1995) and their academic performance in high school is superior to that of children from either authoritarian or permissive homes (Dornbusch, Ritter, Leiderman, Roberts, and Fraleigh, 1987; Steinberg, Dornbush, and Brown, 1992).

Cultural Differences in Parenting Styles

As a group, Chinese American and most Asian American parents exert much more parental control than do European American middle-class parents (Chao, 1995; Dornbusch, et al., 1987; Steinberg, et al., 1992) However, in the Chinese or Asian homes influenced by the teaching of Confucius, the control parents exert is not to dominate the child, but to promote harmonious relations with others and within the family (Lau and Cheung, 1987). In addition, as soon as the child enters school, the mother's love and support focus on promoting specific social responsibilities and school success. These findings help to explain why Chinese and Asian students from homes judged authoritarian and controlling have been performing in U.S. schools at a higher level than European American students from authoritative homes (Kim and Chun, 1995; Sue and Able, 1988). In a 1987 comparison study by Dornbusch, a group of Asian American high school students coming from authoritarian homes attained higher grades than White high school students from authoritative homes.

Dornbusch also found that Mexican American and African American adolescents do not have the same school achievement relationship to parenting style as do Anglo American youth. More research is needed comparing different ethnic groups for both short- and long-term effects of parenting styles.

Ethnic/Racial Child-Rearing Patterns

Ethnic minority groups, who survive or thrive in a dominant culture, have varying degrees of support from the extended family. They also have flexibility in their family roles and a spiritual orientation to life. Many ethnic families successfully integrate their family's culture with the American-dominant culture. (Harrison, Wilson, Pine, Chan, and Buriel, 1990).

The ways in which families express affection, communicate, and control their children's behavior as well as the particular skills they teach their children are influenced by their ethnic background and their degree of assimilation into the dominant culture. The length of time a family has lived in the United States influences their assimilation.

African American Families

African American families have flexibility in their roles and receive strength through their extended family. Their extended family includes relatives living in the household as well as unrelated persons in the community who are involved in the life and function of the family. People who are unrelated by biology or law may take on family roles and often have the same privileges with the children as do the children's blood kin (Ahmeduzzaman and Roopnarine, 1992; Manus, 1981; Stack, 1974). Sometimes each adult provides a specific role in the child's life. One person may provide money, another spiritual direction, and others clothing and financial or human resources (Lewis, 1989; Lewis and Kissman, 1989; Taylor, Chatters, Tucker, and Lewis, 1990). In this open and extended family, men contribute along with women.

Spiritual values provide strength to the African American family. A blend of traditional African religions and American Christianity influence their cultural values (Hale-Benson, 1991). Perseverance, realism, faith, and personal dignity are important values for their children (Hale, 1991). A rich oral tradition is a key feature of West African life and culture (Hale-Benson, 1986). Their folktales help children to survive. Values, including those of the American slavery experience, are transmitted from generation to generation. African Americans' language differs from traditional European languages. It has its own grammatical structure and moves freely from topic to topic (Hale-Benson, 1991). The use of verbal intonations and rhythmic verbal interplay are important to their communications.

Some parents try to raise their children with a neutral attitude regarding race. Spencer (1985) believes that this does not provide the children with a sufficiently strong sense of self. Because the predominant sociocultural forces place African American children at a disadvantage, it is important for the family to help them develop and maintain a healthy self-esteem. One way to accomplish this is to foster their appreciation of the cultural history and achievements of African Americans (Semaj, 1985).

Asian American Families

The term *Asian American* covers diverse groups of people who differ in language, religion, and customs. There are four major groups of Asian Americans. East Asians include Chinese, Japanese, and Koreans; Pacific Islanders include people from Fiji and neighboring islands; Southeast Asians include Thai and Vietnamese, and South Asians include Indians and Pakistanis (Pang, 1990; Feng, 1994). Diversity exists among the four major Asian Americans groups and also within national groups. This is due to their reasons for migration, the number of generations in the United States, and their degree of assimilation. Some arrive as refugees with very few skills, little education and money, while others bring with them many talents and resources (Brand, 1987).

There are a few common cultural characteristics, values, and practices in which most Asians, especially East and Southeast Asians, differ from those of the dominant American culture. Asian families generally are patriarchal. Children are taught respect for elders, deferred gratification, and discipline often based on Confucian ideals. This religion also emphasizes maintaining harmonious relationships with others. Compared to American children, Asian American children place family welfare over individual wishes and tend to be more dependent. As infants, they are nourished and given much freedom but by school age, discipline becomes stricter. The father is usually the authority figure and disciplinarian. Children are quiet and often self-effacing. Teachers are given high status. Children are comfortable with structure and organization and often confused by the informality in school classrooms in the United States. Children are pressured to perform in school for the family. Asian American parents view school failure as a lack of will and respond by increasing parental restrictions. Children suffer shame and guilt if they do not succeed or if they behave in any way to dishonor the family. Dependence and cooperation in the group and family are valued. In contrast, American schooling stresses independence, individualism, and competition.

Hispanic American Families

Child-rearing practices vary among Hispanic Americans in the United States because of their diversity. This includes their socioeconomic status, race, age, country of origin, and the nature and timing of immigration (Nicolau and Ramos, 1990). Mexican Americans represent 59 percent of the 35 million Hispanic Americans living in the continental United States (U.S. Bureau of the Census, 2000). The majority of Hispanic Americans (17 million) speak Spanish in the home (U.S. Immigration and Naturalization Service, 1993).

Hispanic American parenting styles and values in general differ from those of the dominant culture in the United States. Hispanic American children are taught to love, honor, be loyal, and support their immediate and extended family. Interactions are warm and very personal. Family roles are traditional, based on gender and age. Children often play with their siblings rather than with neighbors. They are taught obedience and respect for adult authority. The parenting style is authoritarian. Rules are stressed without emphasizing the reason. The father is the absolute authority figure. The mother is the nurturer. The communications between mother and child are usually directive with little give-and-take in conversations. Many children have few early literacy experiences. The language children hear is simple and direct rather than elaborated speech (Espinosa and Lesar, 1994; Linotos, 1992). There is a relaxed sense of time. Variations in parenting styles occur in part due to the degree of assimilation and the educational level of the parents.

The roles of parent and teacher are separate. Children are taught that the teacher and the school personnel have absolute authority at school (Espinosa, 1995). They are to cooperate and support their group and their community. They are also encouraged to adapt to a problem rather than change the conditions. In contrast, the predominant culture in the United States stresses individuality, independence, and competition. The teaching style of most American teachers is task-oriented.

Native American Families

Native Americans come from over 500 different groups or tribes and represent over half of the languages and cultures in the United States (Reese, 1996). In order to understand a family, the customs of its particular tribe need to be studied. The following values are meant only to provide a framework for understanding many of these children and their families. Native American parents respect their children. Children usually grow up in extended families and are surrounded by many adults who give them attention and approval. Cousins may be as close as brothers and sisters. Children are taught to respect their elders, who pass on their cultural heritage to the younger generation. Children are encouraged to share and cooperate rather than to compete (Gilliland, 1988). Time is in the present with less concern for the future compared to mainstream society. Time is loosely structured so that it is not rude to be "late" for an appointment, it is expected. According to their traditional cultures, mild disapproval is shown by a frown or by ignoring the behavior and physical discipline is to be avoided, which is not always true today. Shaming and group pressure are used while verbal praise is at a minimum.

Each tribe has distinct differences. The Navajo family, traditionally, is matrilineal. The mother heads the household with the husband and children belonging to the mother's side of the family. The mother's oldest brother may discipline the children and control family finances. Modern influences have somewhat altered this pattern, but their family structure remains different from mainstream society (Soldier, 1992).

Most Native Americans believe that one should live in harmony with nature. They also believe in the supernatural, mythology, and nonscientific explanations for their concerns. Children are taught spirituality. Ceremonials and "sings" are important events. For example, the Navajos believe that illness is an imbalance that can be healed only by restoring harmony within the body. Legends may be told or sung to the patient. Traditionally, they do not believe that bacteria cause illness so they may not be as concerned with cleanliness and related health standards as those who do (Soldier, 1992).

Today, Reba Walker is a member of the Bismark, North Dakota United Church of Christ (UCC) and the United Church of Christ executive council. She helped the UCC General Synod in Kansas City in 2001 pass the **Resolution on the Preservation of the Mandan, Hidata, and Arikara Languages of the Three Affiliated Tribes.** The resolution acknowledges the damage that suppression of their indigenous languages did and proposes a pilot program to preserve and expand the three languages spoken today by members of the UCC Bismark church living on the Fort Berthol, North Dakota reservation (Walker, 2002).

5.1 "Kill the Indian and Save the Man": Indian Assimilation

This was the educational philosophy of Captain H. Pratt, the army officer who founded Carlisle Indian Industrial School in 1879 in North Dakota. The goal of this school and others was Indian assimilation, to be achieved by discrediting the students' traditional ways of living. Moccasins were replaced by laced shoes and long hair and braids had to be cut off. The most devastating directive according to Reba Walker, who attended a mission boarding school, was to prohibit children from speaking their native languages because this was *savage* and *wrong*. At her school, the children would find a time when the matrons were sleeping in order to speak in their native language and talk about their customs and values (United Church of Christ, 2002).

Boarding schools were established in the late 1800s, and children were taken from their families and tribes and forced, until recently, to attend these schools. The Bureau of Indian Affairs and not the tribe was in charge of the schools. In addition to being cut off from their culture, many Native Americans today feel that boarding schools denigrated Native American beliefs and practices. These Anglo American style schools taught Christianity, English, basic skills, and some vocational training.

Some Native American families have serious personal problems that they attribute to "forced living conditions" over the years. Some believe that the loss of traditional positive parenting approaches resulted from boarding school education experiences. Alcoholism is a problem, as is child maltreatment. Parents Anonymous leaders have been working with Native American families in Arizona since 1988. In an attempt to strengthen and empower these families, Parents Anonymous leaders have reintroduced some Native American positive traditional values into their current child-rearing strategies. These techniques also help enhance self-esteem (Bresnahan, 1993).

Parenting a Child with Special Needs

All children have special needs at some time but some children have special needs all the time. These needs or conditions deviate from what society considers typical or the norm. These children might have physical handicaps, learning disabilities, or learning abilities that surpass the norm. They may have an emotional disturbance, chronic illness, antisocial behavior, or a combination of these conditions. Physical impairments are usually identified at birth but psychological impairments may not be identified until the child is older. Damage can be caused by heredity or prenatally from environmental conditions such as drugs taken by the mother. Other children suffer damage later due to child abuse, severe neglect, or an accident. This discussion will focus on children's impairments rather than on special gifts.

Parenting any child is a difficult task but parenting a child with special problems is even more challenging. There are additional stresses on all family members. How they cope with these challenges depends to some extent on how healthy each of these family relationships was before the special needs child was diagnosed. Some reactions are detrimental to healthy development:

1. attempting to compensate for the condition by overindulging the child;
2. reacting at times with hostility or even rejection; and
3. focusing on the disability.

Some actions of parents are helpful:

1. finding out all you can about the disability, treatments, and resources available for the child;
2. developing a support system;
3. being kind to one another and not taking out your anger or frustration on loved ones; and
4. viewing the whole child with his or her strengths and weaknesses. This child, like all children, needs to develop a positive self-image and achieve as much as realistically is possible.

Initial Adjustments

Parents' initial responses to a child's disability vary greatly (Meadow-Orlans, 1995). Most parents are shocked. Any dreams they had for their child seem shattered. For some, the initial response is denial, which may be followed by depression. There is anger, guilt, sorrow, and often helplessness, but never joy (Batshaw, 1998). According to Kubler-Ross's research, parents may go through the stages of anger, denial, bargaining (to make conditions right), depression, and final acceptance (1962). It is important for parents and siblings to understand and then accept the nature of the disability. Guilt, anger, and blame are counterproductive. Love, setting realistic goals, and seeking needed professional help is the best course.

Siblings need special help in their understanding of the situation. Young children need simple and clear explanations. For example, "Your sister cannot learn as quickly as other children or understand as much. We can help her." Young children usually ask more questions when they are ready for more information. On the other hand, older children need accurate and more complete information about the disability. Not knowing only intensifies their feelings. They may think, "Why won't you tell me?" "How bad is it?" or "You don't trust me to know" (Batshaw, 1998).

Siblings experience a range of emotions. They may be embarrassed, resentful, or feel guilty that they are so healthy. Young children may feel that they caused the problem because they had some negative thoughts about the baby. Siblings may feel resentful when much of their parents' energy, time, and money go to helping the special needs child. In addition, they may feel guilty for these negative feelings (Trout and Foley, 1989). They also have to cope with their peers' reactions to their sibling's condition.

Children with disabilities need to come to terms with their special or limited abilities. In addition, they must adjust to the reactions of other children and adults to their problem. Any child who deviates considerably from the norm has more difficulty in establishing a positive self-image.

Support Systems

Family members with special needs children have many demands placed on them that are stressful. Not only can personal health suffer but these families have a higher percentage of divorces (Batshaw, 1998). Support systems are crucial in maintaining a healthy family. These support systems put parents and family members in touch with scientific information and other parents with similar problems who share experiences and valuable resources. Support groups are usually formed around a particular disability. Seeking and accepting help from extended family members, their place of worship, and/or the community provides additional relief. It is important for parents to have some free time.

Many parents find satisfaction in networking to provide help for their child or other children. Parents have been active in the legislative process to support children and families with disabilities. In the 1950s, parents helped establish the National Association of Parents and Friends of Mentally Retarded Children, now called the Association for Retarded Citizens. Parents also helped to establish other support groups such as the United Cerebral Palsy Association and the National Society for Autistic Children. See Chapters 8 and 9 for legislation affecting children with disabilities.

Acceptance

After months and sometimes years, most parents can replace the anger, guilt, and/or blame with a degree of acceptance. However, it is difficult when one parent comes to terms with a child's condition before his or her spouse. Occasionally the spouse may never get to this point, remaining in a state of denial or grief. This makes it more difficult for this person (and the family) to cope (Batshaw, 1998).

Certain periods in the child's life will reignite the sense of pain and loss. Batshaw (1998) suggests that these events often include starting school, placement in special education, the period when most children start dating, or late adolescence, when many children go to college, find a job, leave home, and/or marry. When both parents and siblings have reached the stage of acceptance, family life can begin to have a sense of "normalcy" and members are freer to experience the many joys in life. Life is put into a broader perspective.

Parenting Education

Parents find information on child rearing through the popular press, the Internet, parenting courses, and talking with friends. The complexity of modern society and of parenting, and the availability of scientific information have stimulated this interest in parenting.

Opinions as to what constitutes effective parenting vary greatly. Many differences relate to culture. Most parents want their children to behave appropriately, according to cultural values. The assumption that Western, middle-class, child-rearing practices are universal and desirable for all children is considered ethnic bias (Ambert, 1994). It is important for researchers and educators to understand what constitutes desirable or appropriate behavior across and among the cultures (Caldwell, Green, and Billingsley, 1994; Kagan, 1995). What practices are common in a particular culture but not in most other cultures? What practices are universal? Feeding or comforting a distressed infant is universal in parenting, but how we accomplish this may be culture-specific. Parents in all cultures share certain basic goals for their children, which include:

1. physical health and survival;
2. economic self-sufficiency;
3. fully functioning human beings according to cultural values (LeVine, 1974, 1977, 1988).

In the United States most parents, especially middle-class parents, value in their children:

1. good behavior;
2. competence in basic skills, including skills for economic self-sufficiency;
3. good relationships in and outside the family;
4. positive self-image (Jaffe, 1997).

Parenting Programs for Enhancement, Remediation, and for Fathers

Parenting programs focus either on the prevention or remediation of problems. The prevention approach, known as parenting education, is voluntary, and supports parents who are at low risk for parenting failure. The programs involving remediation, known as parent training, are working with high-risk parents with a number of problems. Many of these parents have been mandated by the courts to change behavior that is inappropriate and damaging to their children.

Both programs often look at the total family environment, including outside forces such as poverty, unemployment, child care, and schools. The goal is to give the parents information and support that prevents or changes damaging ideas of child rearing and enables parents to provide a healthy environment for their children.

PARENTING EDUCATION PROGRAMS   Parenting education programs enhance parents' overall competence and knowledge of child development. This helps to prevent some problems and to deal more effectively with minor and often age-related problems. Most programs are based on parents' input and needs. Participation is voluntary. In general, these programs focus on prevention rather than treatment, the family rather than the individual, increasing parental strengths rather than overcoming weaknesses, and nurturing cultural diversity (Dunst and Trivette, 1994). Parenting education programs have a variety of sponsors, funding sources, degrees of intensity, and evaluation components (Kagan, 1995). Families with more money have a wider selection of programs than do those with less income.

PARENT TRAINING PROGRAMS   Parent training programs work to identify and remediate the particular deficit or deficits the parent has. The current focus is to build on the parents' strengths rather than concentrating on their deficits. However, programs often focus on a particular problem such as abusive behavior. This may include drug and child abuse. Parents receive support from other parents in the program who are at varying stages of change. Most parents benefit from knowing they are not alone.

Some of these programs are reaching out to high risk parents before they are in serious trouble. These parents include those who are very young, poor, or emotionally troubled as well as those with chronically ill or disabled children. Gelles (1989) found that mothers who are economically deprived and single are more likely to physically abuse their children than mothers with either more income or who are married. One cause for child abuse among young single mothers is an unrealistic expectation of how their baby or young child should behave. In addition, premature and low birth weight babies born into poverty have a poorer prognosis of functioning within normal ranges compared to those not born into poverty (Bradley, et al., 1994). When conditions in these families are improved by parent training or family support services, immediate and continued benefits for children, siblings, and families are seen (Roberts and Wasik, 1990; Seitz and Apfel, 1994). For example, these programs educate parents about *prenatal care, immunizations, positive communication skills, and positive discipline methods.* Parents receive information on what behaviors to expect from their baby or child. The most successful programs are those that help parents change their family environment and their parenting ideas and skills during the first years of the child's life (Benasich, Brook-Gunn, and Clewell, 1992; van den Bloom, 1995). Although family support programs are usually open to anyone, they most often are located in low-income areas.

PARENT EDUCATION PROGRAMS FOR FATHERS   Men and women bring different strengths and concerns to the parenting situation. Issues that concern men are not addressed in traditional parenting programs. Even today, there are very few programs for fathers. Women, on the other hand, have an elaborate structure of formal and informal support systems that help them in adapting to parenthood and child rearing. When such support is offered to men, more of them take an active parenting role (Riley, 1990; Turbille, Umbarger, and Guthrie, 2000).

By observing their children's child-care program or attending parenting classes, fathers find ways to stimulate acceptable behavior in their children and discover play activities that are fun and developmentally appropriate.

One father, who had been visiting the college child study center, asked the author, "How did you get Brian to come here so quickly from his outdoor play." "Oh, I just said to Brian, can you hop like Snowy our bunny rabbit all the way to the door?"

The **McBride Intervention Program Model for Dads** provides an opportunity for them to become involved with their preschoolers in two-hour sessions for a series of ten Saturdays. Fathers and children share an hour of play time with structured and unstructured activities. While the children continue to play, a discussion hour helps fathers understand their child's developmental needs and provides an opportunity for them to share their concerns (McBride, 1990). Many fathers mention that they now feel closer to and have more fun with their child. The findings from these three studies suggest that the fathers improved their parenting skills and assumed more child-rearing responsibilities (McBride, 1990). In addition, these fathers report that they now spend more time with their children on nonworkdays and experience fewer feelings of isolation and parental stress (McBride, 1991a, 1991b). Fathers are no different from mothers in finding comfort and help from support groups. The **National Center on Fathers and Families** (**NCOFF**) is an excellent support center.

Discipline and Punishment

Concepts of discipline vary. The conventional elementary school concept of discipline is based on obedience (Gartrell, 1997). Many parents and teachers see punishment as a part of discipline. However, some educators view discipline as a "neutral" term that can exclude punishment (Marion, 1995). Discipline in this chapter is considered to be different from punishment both in its intent and consequences. It may be referred to as positive discipline or guidance.

Positive Discipline:

✔ is guiding and teaching;
✔ is done with a child;
✔ requires understanding, time, and patience;
✔ teaches problem solving and builds a positive self-image;
✔ develops long-term self-control and cooperation.

Punishment:

✔ is control by fear, power, and coercion;
✔ is done to the child;
✔ elicits anger, guilt, resentment, and deceit;

- ✔ impairs communication and wholesome parent–child relationships;
- ✔ stops undesired behavior in the specific situation temporarily, but behavior often is exhibited in other ways.

All parents discipline their children by teaching them appropriate ways to behave. However, discipline is interpreted by some parents as correcting or punishing children in order to stop the reoccurrence of unacceptable behavior. Discipline comes from the Latin word *disciplina,* meaning instruction or teaching to correct, strengthen, or perfect. Obviously, the leader models the ideas or principles to be followed. Disciples respect and care for the messenger. If parents want their children to behave in caring and appropriate ways, they must show them how. *The ultimate goal of discipline is to have children responsible for their own actions.*

Punishment is the use of physical or psychological force or action that causes pain in an attempt to prevent undesirable behavior from recurring. Scolding, threats, deprivations, and spanking are all forms of punishment. Physical punishment of children by parents and teachers is legal in most states and most countries. It is *outlawed* in Austria, Norway, Denmark, Sweden, and Finland (Straus, 1994). Back in the nineteenth century, Froebel wrote that the use of punishment was a good way for adults to make a child "bad." If the goal for the child is the development of morality, of making good choices on his or her own, then punishment should not be involved. Conditions should be created that not only allow but strongly induce children to be or become moral and disciplined individuals who can make good choices on their own (Bettelheim, 1985; Ramsburg, 1997).

Punishment teaches a child that those who have the power can force others to do what they want them to do (Bettelheim, 1985; Samalin and Whitney, 1995). In addition, punishment, such as spanking, does not teach a child an acceptable alternative way to behave (American Academy of Pediatrics, 1995). Punishment is the least effective form of changing behavior and may have long-term consequences. The child feels humiliated, often hides mistakes, tends to be angry and aggressive, and fails to develop self-control. Punishment stops behavior temporarily, but the behavior is often repeated in other settings.

Forms of punishment with fewer negative consequences than physical or psychologically demeaning punishment include ignoring the behavior, showing a mild disapproving look, the use of time out, especially to gain control of one's emotions, and taking away a privilege. Ignoring the behavior can be very effective in eliminating its repetition, especially if it is a new action and not reinforced by someone else. Time out has been overused in recent decades as a way to change children's behavior. Although experts disagree about its use (Ucci, 1998; Schreiber, 1999), it can have negative effects such as embarrassment, anger, or confusion. More importantly, by itself it does not teach a child how to behave differently. It is more effective if time out is followed with a discussion of the actions and support to help the child learn how to behave appropriately. *Gartrell (2001, 2002) believes that time out should be replaced with teaching children how to solve social problems rather than punishing them for their behavior over problems they have not yet learned how to solve.*

If punishment is used, a number of conditions can increase its effectiveness. It should occur immediately after the problem. It is also more effective when the child is punished by a nurturing person (Baumrind, 1978). There should also be consistency in being punished for an offense. The punishment should include an explanation and allow the child some control over the situation. For example, in using time out, the child should be helped to decide when he or she is able to follow the rules and return to play. During time out, the child must be removed from all forces reinforcing the unacceptable behavior.

Physical Punishment of Children

Physical punishment includes spanking, slapping, grabbing, shoving (with more force than needed to move the child), and hitting a child with an object (Straus, 1991). Spanking is the most controversial method of discipline and continues to be used as an acceptable form of "discipline." Some parents define spanking as slapping a child on the buttocks (Straus, 1995), while this and other reports use spanking to cover any corporal punishment that does not cause injury. Many parents believe spanking will teach children not to repeat forbidden behavior while other parents spank because they are not aware of more effective ways of changing behavior. Some parents do not believe that nonphysical forms of punishment, such as denial of privileges, are effective. In 1994, a parental opinion poll conducted by the National Committee for the Prevention of Child Abuse showed for the first time that a majority of parents reported not spanking their children in the previous year. Denying privileges was used by 79 percent, confinement to a room by 59 percent, 49 percent spanked or hit their child, and 45 percent insulted or swore at their child. (Straus, 1995).

DOES PHYSICAL PUNISHMENT LEAD TO CHILD ABUSE AND LATER VIOLENCE?

Social science researcher, Murray Straus, and professor of criminology, Joan McCord, agree that physical punishment during childhood often leads children to violence when they are teenagers and adults. However, McCord believes that *all* punishment accounts for later violence in adults (DelCampo and DelCampo, 1995). Straus reports that, as adults, the children whose parents spanked them, compared to children who were not spanked, have higher rates of juvenile delinquency, spouse abuse, drug and alcohol abuse, and lower economic achievements (Straus, 1994). McCord reports that a study on criminals found that the largest number of criminals came from punitive and unaffectionate homes. The next highest number came from punitive but affectionate homes and the fewest came from nonpunitive homes. McCord believes that the use of reward and punishment models the norm of self-interest over the welfare of others while Straus argues that the act of spanking sends a message that the use of violence is a legitimate way to solve problems (DelCampo and DelCampo, 1995).

Societal Norms Supporting Punishment and Violence

Physical punishment has always been a part of European American religious and legal traditions (Straus, 1991). One definition of *violence* is any act carried out with the intention or perceived intention of causing physical pain or injury to another person (Straus, 1991). Not only is some physical punishment legal, so is some violence. Society models violence in many ways.

One can legally use violence or force to defend oneself and, in some cases, one's property. The law in most states permits capital punishment. When violence increases in our society, the response is to increase punishment. For example, California enacted a law placing convicted third-time offenders in jail for life. It's known as "Three Strikes and You're Out." The age for trying youth offenders for specific violent crimes under the adult penal system has been lowered in many states and in recent federal legislation (Children's Defense Fund, 1998, 1999).

ABC's of Good Parenting

The following guidelines emerged over years from the author's parenting classes. ABC stands for *always be consistent*. The term *guidance* is used in place of *discipline*. Parents in these classes wanted to find more constructive or effective methods of guiding their children. For some parents, it was a move away from reacting after the act to encouraging and praising appropriate behavior. Of many guidelines, three general principles stand out. Always be consistent, be positive, and praise the behavior you want repeated.

1. **Always be consistent.** The younger the child, the more difficult it is for him or her to understand why a rule changes from one day to another. From the parents' perspective, it may make sense to tell the children that they cannot play with clay or certain toys in the house because company is coming. To a young child this is especially confusing. Consistency means modeling what you tell your children to do. "Always tell the truth" may be stressed. What message is heard if the parent asks a child answering the phone to tell the caller that mother or dad is not home? If parents tell children to make their bed in the morning and the parents do not make their bed, the children will probably do as they see rather than do as they hear. There needs to be consistency in the parents' expectations of each child within developmentally appropriate limits. If the parent asks one child to pick up toys and lets another child play without putting things away, it can cause resentment, overall confusion, and lower self-esteem.

2. **Always be positive.** Most young children want to please. Encourage this by telling children exactly *what to do* rather than *what not to do*. Say, "You need to walk in the house because . . . If you want to run, you may go outside." If

a child needs help in achieving a goal, this positive approach relays the message that the parent has trust or confidence in the child wanting to do the right thing.

3. **Praise good behavior.** It is so easy for parents to ignore children's desirable behavior because it is causing no problem. Two sisters are playing close to where their mother is finishing a project. The two-year-old begins to fuss and points to a toy that the four-year-old has. The older sister says, "Here, Susie, you can have this one." The play goes on amicably. The mother continues her work, either not noticing the incident or not wanting to interrupt her activity. A more positive response would be, "Susie, wasn't that nice of your sister to give you that toy?"

4. **Love needs to be unconditional.** This means that children are loved regardless of their actions. You may not like a child's actions, but you still love that child. To say, "If you love Mommy, you will pick up your room," bases your love on the child's actions.

5. **Discuss the child's action and not the child's trait or personality.** To label the child as naughty, lazy, selfish, or sloppy is harmful to the child's self image. To talk about actions, such as not hanging up clothes or not sharing toys, is easier for the child to deal with and to correct.

6. **Provide limits.** These should be developmentally appropriate, understood by all, open to discussion, and enforced with love. By allowing children to have some voice in a rule, they will more likely comply. By giving children a choice, you are giving them some control over the situation.

Parent's Helper: Cooking and Clean-Up Is Fun for Boys and Girls

Four-year-old son is helping in the meal preparation and clean-up before dinner. When children help with a project, they feel important, learn new skills, and are being supervised while parent is busy.

7. **Help children to control their own behavior.** Help them understand their actions and accept certain ways of behaving. Eventually they will be able to control their own behavior from within rather than externally or based on outside forces. Help children understand how their actions affect the other person. Ask them how they could have expressed their feelings in another way.

8. **Communications should be open, honest, clear, and appropriate.** Children must

be allowed to express their feelings. They often need help in how to release their feelings in an acceptable manner (see Chapter 6).

9. **Spend time with children.** Listen and be sensitive to a child's needs. Be supportive of those needs while helping the child meet the demands of parents, family, and the environment. Have fun with your child!

10. **Provide an environment where children are able to succeed.** This includes providing activities that are challenging but attainable. It is often easier for a child to accomplish one small part of a task at a time than to tackle the whole project. Praise, encouragement, and help are important to success.

Key Points

Child Rearing

1. Child rearing is the way parents respond to their children's behavior, thoughts, and feelings in teaching them parental and societal values.

2. Child-rearing practices are influenced by the way the parents were raised, religious beliefs, culture, ethnicity, socioeconomic status, scientific information, and societal conditions.

3. The age and temperament of the children and parents, the sex, birth order, and age differences, their biological, adopted or step relationships, family size, and the physical and emotional health of each member influence child-rearing practices

4. Today parenting roles are broader and more nurturing for fathers. The majority of mothers are employed and contributing economically.

5. Authoritarian, authoritative, permissive-caring, and permissive-indulgent parenting styles represent different degrees of control and of affection that parents exert.

6. In the dominant culture, authoritative parents tend to raise independent, self-reliant, and self-disciplined children with a positive self-image. Parents exert control but explain rules and are supportive. Asian American families using a culturally based authoritarian parenting style have results similar to Baumrind's authoritative parents.

7. African American families gain strength from their extended families, role flexibility, and spir-

itual beliefs. Close family ties, oral communication and nonverbal gestures are important. Language has its own grammatical rules.

8. Asian American parents teach children to respect their elders, delay gratification, have self-discipline, cooperate in a group, and achieve academically.

9. Hispanic children are taught to support their immediate and extended families, respect father and adult authority, have group cooperation, and a relaxed sense of time.

10. Native Americans have extended families, close relationships and a belief in supernatural healing powers. They focus on the present and have a relaxed sense of time. Children are taught to cooperate and respect elders.

11. Discipline is guiding and teaching, resulting in self-control, cooperation, and a stronger self-image. Punishment is control by fear, power, and coercion, resulting in anger, guilt, resentment, closed communications, and lower self-esteem.

12. Basic rules for good guidance: be consistent, positive, and give unconditional love.

Critical Thinking Questions

1. How do you view the right of parents to raise their children as they see fit and society's right to protect children from harmful situations?

2. How do you feel about state laws making parents responsible for their child's antisocial behavior?

3. How do you think teachers could help children to communicate more effectively with their parents and siblings?

 Resources and References

National Center for Fathering
  http://www.fathers.com
National Parenting Network
  http://www.npn.org
Nurturing Fatherhood
  http://www.fatherhood.hhs.gov/

■ References

Ahmeduzzaman, M., and Roopnarine, J. (1992). Sociodemographic factors, functioning style, and fathers' involvement with preschoolers in African American families. *Journal of Marriage and the Family, 54,* 699–707.

Ambert, A. (1994). An international perspective on parenting: School change and social constructs. *Journal of Marriage and the Family, 56,* 529–543.

American Academy of Pediatrics. (1995). *Caring for your school-age child: Ages 5–12.* New York: Bantam.

Bandura, A. (1977). *Social learning theory.* Englewood Cliffs, NJ: Prentice-Hall.

Bandura, A. (1986). *Social foundations of thought and actions: A social cognitive theory.* Englewood Cliffs, NJ: Prentice-Hall.

Baruch G. K., and Barnett, R. C. (1986). Fathers' participation in family work and children's sex-role attitudes. *Child Development, 57,* 1210–1223.

Batshaw, M. (1998). *Your child has a disability: A complete sourcebook of daily and medical care.* Baltimore, MD: Brookes.

Baumrind, D. (1966). Effects of authoritative control on child behavior. *Child Development, 37,* 887–907.

Baumrind, D. (1967). Child care practices anteceding three patterns of preschool behavior. *Genetic Psychology Monographs, 74,* 43–88.

Baumrind, D. (1968). Authoritarian vs. Authoritative parental control. *Adolescence, 3,* 255–272.

Baumrind, D (1971). Current patterns of parental authority. *Developmental Psychology Monograph, 4*(1).

Baumrind, D. (1978). Parental disciplinary patterns & social competence in children. *Youth & Society, 9,* 239–276.

Baumrind, D., and Black, A. E. (1967). Socialization processes associated with dimensions of competence in preschool boys and girls. *Child Development, 38,* 291–327.

Benasich, A. A., Brook-Gunn, J., and Clewell, B. C. (1992). How do mothers benefit from early intervention programs? *Journal of Applied Developmental Psychology, 13*(3), 311–312.

Berman, P. W., and Pedersen, F. A. (1987). Research on men's transitions to parenthood: An integrative discussion. In P. W. Berman and F. A. Pedersen (Eds.), *Men's transitions to parenthood: Longitudinal studies of early family experience* (pp. 217–242). Hillsdale, NJ: Erlbaum.

Bettelheim, B. (1985). Punishment versus discipline. *Atlantic Monthly,* November, 51–59.

Blankenhorn, D. (1995). *Fatherless America: Confronting our most urgent social problems.* New York: Basic Books.

Blankenhorn, D. (1997). Life without father. In *Early Childhood Education 97–98: Annual Editions.* (pp. 62–64). Guilford, CT: Dushkin/McGraw-Hill.

Bond, J., Galinsky, E., and Swanberg, J. (1997). *The 1997 National Study of the Changing Work Force.* New York, Families and Work Institute.

Bradley, R. H., Whiteside, L., Mundfrom, D., Casey, P., Kelleher, K., and Pope, S. (1994). Early indications of resilience and their relations to experiences in the home environments of low birthweight premature children living in poverty. *Child Development, 65,* 346–360.

Brand, D. (1987). The new wiz kids. *Time, 130*(9) 42–51.

Branham, A. M. (1992). Hispanic culture interwoven into American life. *Children's Horizons,* Fall, p. 9.

Brophy, J. (1977). *Child development and socialization.* Chicago: Science Research Associates.

Bresnahan, Rita. (1993). Parenting programs target Native Americans. *Children's Horizons,* Spring, p. 7.

Bronfenbrenner, U. (1979). *The ecology of human development: Experiments by nature and design.* Cambridge, MA: Harvard University Press.

Caldwell, C. A., Green, A., and Billingsley, A. (1994). Family support in Black churches: A new look at old functions. In S. L. Kagan and B. Weissbourd

(Eds.), *Putting families first: America's family support movement and the challenge of change* (pp. 137–160). San Francisco: Jossey-Bass.

Chao, R. K. (1994). Beyond parental control and authoritarian parenting style: Understanding Chinese parenting through the cultural notion of training. *Child Development, 65,* 1111–1119.

Chao, R. K. (1995). *Beyond authoritarianism: A cultural perspective on Asian American practices.* Paper presented at the Annual Meeting of the American Psychological Association, New York, August.

Children's Defense Fund (1998). *The state of America's children: Yearbook 1998.* Washington, DC: Author.

Children's Defense Fund (1999). *The state of America's children: Yearbook 1999.* Washington, DC: Author.

Coppersmith, S. (1967). *The antecedents of self-esteem.* San Francisco: Freeman.

Crouter, A. C., and McHale, M. S. (1993). The long arm of the job: Influences of parental work on childrearing. In T. Luster and L. Okagaki (Eds.), *Parenting: An ecological perspective.* Hillsdale, NJ: Erlbaum.

Dekovic, M., Gerris, J. R. M., and Janssens, J. M. A. M. (1991). Parental cognitions, parental behavior, and the child's understanding of the parent–child relationship. *Merrill-Palmer Quarterly, 37*(4), 523–541.

DelCampo, R. L., and DelCampo, D. S. (1995). *Taking sides: Clashing views on controversial issues in childhood and society.* Guilford, CT: Dushkin.

Demo, M. H., Sweitzer, M., and Lawritzen, P. (1985). An evaluation of group parent education: Behavioral, P.E.T., and Adlerian programs. *Review of Educational Research, 55,* 155–200.

Dobson, J. (1992). *The new dare to discipline.* Wheaton, IL: Tyndale House.

Dodge, K. A., Petit, G. S., and Bates, J. E. (1994). Socialization mediators of the relation between socioeconomic status and child conduct problems. *Child Development, 65,* 649–665.

Dornbusch, S., Ritter, P., Leiderman, P., Roberts, D., and Fraleigh, M. (1987). The relation of parenting style to adolescent school performance. *Child Development, 58,* 1246–1257.

Duncan, G., Brooks-Gunn, J., and Klevanov, P. (1994). Economic deprivation and early childhood development. *Child Development, 65*(2), 296–318.

Dunst, C., and Trivette, C. M. (1994). Aims and principles of family support programs. In C. Durnst, C. M. Trivette, and A. G. Deal (Eds.), *Supporting and strengthening families: Vol. 1: Methods, Strategies, and Practices* (pp. 30–48). Cambridge, MA: Brookline Books.

Egeland, B., and Stroufe, L. A. (1981). Attachment and early maltreatment. *Child Development, 52,* 44–52.

Erikson, E. H. (1963). *Childhood and society.* New York: Norton.

Erikson, E. H. (1964). *Human strength and the cycle of generations.* In Erik Erikson (Ed.), *Insight and responsibility* (pp. 109–157). New York: Norton.

Espinosa, L. (1995). Hispanic parent involvement in early childhood programs. *ERIC Digest,* May. EDO-PS-95-3. Urbana, IL: University of Illinois.

Espinosa, L., and Lesar, S. (1994). *Increasing language-minority family and child competencies for school success.* Paper presented at the Annual meeting of the American Educational Research Association, New Orleans, April 4.

Feng, J. (1994). Asian American children: What teachers should know. *ERIC Digest,* EDO-PS-94-4. Urbana, IL: University of Illinois.

Galinsky, E. (1981). *Between generations: The six stages of parenthood.* New York: Times Books.

Gartrell, D. (1997). Beyond discipline to guidance. *Young Children, 52,* 34–42.

Gartrell, D. (2001). Replacing time-out: Part One: Using guidance to maintain an encouraging classroom. *Young Children, 56,* 8–16.

Gartrell, D. (2002). Replacing time-out: Part Two: Using guidance to maintain an encouraging classroom. *Young Children, 57,* 36–43.

Gelles, R. J. (1989). Child abuse and violence in single-parent families: Parent absences and economic deprivation. *American Journal of Orthopsychiatry, 59,* 492–501.

Gilliland, H. (1988). A culturally relevant education. In H. Guilland and J. Reyhner (Eds.), *Teaching the Native American* (pp. 1–3; 37–46). Dubuque, IA: Kendall/Hunt.

Grusec, J., and Goodnow, J. (1994). Impact of parental discipline methods on the child's internalization of values: A reconceptualization of current points of view. *Developmental Psychology, 30*(1), 4–19.

Grusec, J. E., and Lytton, H. (1988). *Social development: History, theory and research*. New York: Springler-Verlag.

Hale-Benson, J. E. (1986). *Black children: Their roots, culture and learning styles*. Baltimore: John Hopkins University Press.

Hale-Benson, J. E. (1991). The transmission of cultural values to young African American children. *Young Children, 46*(6), 7–15.

Harrison, A., Wilson, M., Pine, C., Chan, S., and Buriel, R. (1990). Family ecologies of ethnic minority children. *Child Development, 61*, 347–362.

Hewlett, B. (1992). *Father–child relations: Cultural and biosocial contexts*. New York: Aldine de Gruyter.

Hoffman, L. W. (1984). Work, family, and the socialization of the child. In R. D. Parke (Ed.), *Review of child development research, 7, The family*. Chicago: Chicago University Press.

Holmbeck, G. N., Paikoff, R. L., and Brooks-Gunn, J. (1995). Parenting Adolescents. In M. H. Bornstein (Ed.), *Handbook of parenting* (Vol. 1). Mahwah, NJ: Erlbaum.

Jaffe, M. (1997). *Understanding parenting* (2nd ed.). Boston: Allyn and Bacon.

Kagan, Sharon. (1995). The changing face of parenting education. *ERIC Digest*, May, EDO-PS-95-7. Urbana, IL: University of Illinois.

Kim, U., and Chun, M. (1995). Educational "success" of Asian Americans: An indigenous perspective. *Applied Behavioral Development*, retrieved online.

Kohn, M. L. (1977). *Class and conformity: A study in values*. Chicago: Chicago University Press.

Kohn, M. L., Naoi, A., Schoenbach, V., Schooler, C., and Slomczynski, K. M. (1990). Position in the class structure and psychological functioning in the United States, Japan, and Poland. *American Journal of Sociology, 95*(4), 864–1008.

Kubler-Ross, E. (1969). *On death and dying*. New York: MacMillan.

Lamb, M. E. (1981). *The role of the father in child development* (2nd ed.). New York: Wiley.

Lamb, M. E. (1986). The changing role of fathers. In M. E. Lamb (Ed.), *The father's role: Applied perspectives*. New York: Wiley.

Lamb, M. E. (1997). *Fathers and child development: An introductory overview and guide*. In M. E. Lamb (Ed.), *The role of the father in child development*. (3rd ed., pp. 1–18). New York: Wiley.

LaRossa, R. (1988). Fatherhood and social change. *Family Relations, 37*, 451–457.

Lau, S., and Cheung, P. C. (1987). Relations between Chinese adolescents' perception of parental control and organization and their perception of parental warmth. *Developmental Psychology, 23*(5), 726–729.

Levant, R. F. (1988). Education for fatherhood. In P. Bronstein and C. P. Cowan (Eds.), *Fatherhood today: Men's changing role in the family* (pp. 253–275). New York: Wiley.

LeVine, J. (1999). Interview with James LeVine. In J. B. Brooks (Ed.), *Processing* (5th ed, pp. 116–117). Mountain View, CA: Mayfield.

LeVine, R. A. (1974). Parental goals: A cross-cultural view. *Teachers College Record, 76*, 226–239.

LeVine, R. A. (1977). Child rearing as a cultural adaptation. In P. H. Leiderman, S. R. Tulken, and A. Rosenfeld (Eds.), *Culture and Infancy*. New York: Academic Press.

LeVine, R. A. (1988). Human prenatal care: Universal goals, cultural strategies, individual behavior. In R. A. LeVine, P. M. Miller, and M. M. West (Eds.), *Parental Behavior in Diverse Societies*, San Francisco: Jossey-Bass.

Lewis, E. (1989). Role strain in Black women: The efficacy of support groups. *Journal of Black Studies, 20*, 155–169.

Lewis, E., & Kissman, K. (1989). Factors in ethnic sensitive feminist social work practice. *ARETE, 14*(2), 23–31.

Lilley, I. M., Ed. (1967). *Froebel: A selection from his writings*. London: Cambridge University Press.

Linotos, L. B. (1992). *At-risk families and schools: Becoming partners*. ERIC:ED 342055.

Loeb, R., Horst, L., and Horton, P. (1980). Family interaction patterns associated with self-esteem in pre-adolescent girls and boys. *Merrill Palmer Quarterly, 26*, 203–217.

Maccoby, E. E., and Martin, J. A. (1983). Socialization in the context of the family: Parent–child interaction. In E. M. Heatherington (Ed.), *Handbook of child psychology: Vol. 4, Socialization, personality, and social development* (4th ed.). New York: Wiley.

Manus, W. (1981). Support systems of significant others in Black families. In H. MaAdoo (Ed.), *Black Families* (pp. 115–130). Beverly Hills, CA: Sage.

Marion, M. (1995). *Guidance of young children* (5th ed.). Columbus, OH: Merrill.

Martin, G., and Pear, J. (1996). *Behavior Modification: What it is and how to do it* (5th ed.). Upper Saddle River, NJ: Prentice-Hall.

McBride, B. A. (1990). The effects of a parent education/play group program on father involvement in child rearing. *Family Relations, 39,* 250–256.

McBride, B. A. (1991a). Parent education and support programs for fathers: Outcome effects on paternal involvement. *Early Child Development and Care, 67,* 73–85.

McBride, B. A. (1991b). Parental support programs and paternal stress: An exploratory study. *Early Childhood Research Quarterly, 6,* 137–149.

McBride, B. A., and Mills, G. (1994). Variations in parental involvement: Implications for parent education and support programs for fathers. *Early Childhood Research Quarterly.*

McCord, J. (1991). Questioning the value of punishment. *Social Problems, 38*(2), 167–176.

McLoyd, M. C. (1990). The impact of economic hardship on black families and children: Psychological distress, parenting, and socio-emotional development. *Child Development, 61,* 311–346.

McLoyd, V. C., and Wilson, L. (1991). The strain of living poor: Parenting, social support, and child mental health. In A. C. Houston (Ed.), *Children and poverty: Child development and public policy* (pp. 105–135). New York: Cambridge University Press.

Meadow-Orlans, K. P. (1995). Parenting with a sensory or physical disability. In M. H. Borstein (Ed.), *Handbook of parenting* (Vol. 4). Mahwah, NJ: Erlbaum.

Nicolau, S., and Ramos, C. L. (1990). *Together is better: Building strong relationships between schools and Hispanic parents.* New York: Hispanic Policy Development Project.

Palm, G. F., and Palkovitz, R. (1988). The challenge of working with new fathers: Implications for support providers. In G. F. Palm and R. F. Palkovitz (Eds.), *Transitions to Parenthood* (pp. 357–376). New York: Haworth.

Pang, V. O. (1990). Asian American children: A diverse population. *Educational Forum, 55,* 49–66.

Piaget, J. (1983). Piaget's theory. In P. H. Mussen (Ed.), *Handbook of child psychology:* Vol. 1: *History, theory and methods.* New York: Wiley.

Ramsburg, D. (1997). The debate over spanking. *ERIC Digest,* EDO-PS-97–13. Urbana, IL: University of Illinois.

Reese, D. (1996). *Teaching young children about Native Americans.* ERIC Digest, EDO-PS-96-3.

Riley, D. (1990). Network influences on father involvement in childrearing. In M. Cochran, M. Larner, D. Riley, L. Gunnarsson, and C. Henderson (Eds.), *Extending families: The social networks of parents and their children* (pp. 131–153). New York: Cambridge University Press.

Roberts, R. N., Wasik, B. H. (1990). Home visiting programs for families and children birth to three: Results of a national survey. *Journal of Early Intervention, 14*(3), 274–284.

Sailor, D. 1998. Report to the World Organization for the Education of Young Children, World Congress, Copenhagen, DK. August 10–16.

Samalin, N., and Whitney, C. (1995). What's wrong with spanking? *Parents, 70,* 35–36.

Schreiber, M. E. (1999). Time-outs for toddlers: Is our goal punishment or education? *Young Children, 54*(4), 22–25.

Seitz, V., and Apfel, N. (1994). Parent-focused intervention: Diffusion effects on siblings. *Child Development, 65*(2), 677–683.

Semaj, L. (1985). Africanity, recognition and extended self-identity. In M. Spencer, G. Brookins, and W. Allen (Eds.), *Beginning: The social and effective development of Black children.* Hillsdale, NJ: Erlbaum.

Sipes, D. S. B. (1993). Cultural values in American Indian families. In N. Chavkin (Ed.), *Families and schools in a pluralistic society* (pp. 157–173). Albany, NY: State University of New York Press.

Skinner, B. (1957). *Verbal behavior.* New York: Appelton-Century-Crofts.

Smut, A. B., and Hagen, J. W. (1985). History of the family and of child development: Introduction to Part 1. *Monographs of the Society for Research in Child Development.* 5094-5, Serial No. 211).

Soldier, L. L. (1992). Building optimum learning environments for Navajo students. *Childhood Education, 68,* 145–148.

Spencer, M. B. (1985). Cultural cognition and social cognition as identity correlates of Black children's personal-social development. In M. Spencer, G. Brookins, and W. Allen (Eds.), *Beginnings: The social and effective development of Black children,* Hillsdale, NJ: Erlbaum.

Spock, B. (1957). *The pocket book of baby and child care.* New York: Pocket Books.

Stack, C. B. (1974). *All our kin.* New York: Harper and Row.

Steinberg, L., Dornbusch, S., and Brown, B. B. (1992). Ethnic differences in adolescent achievement: An ecological perspective. *American Psychologist, 47*(6), 723–727.

Straus, M. A. (1991). Discipline and deviance: Physical punishment of children and violence and other crimes in adulthood. *Social Problems, 38*(2), 134–144.

Straus, M. A. (1994). *Beating the devil out of them: Corporal punishment in American families and its effects on children.* Boston: Lexington Books/Macmillan.

Sue, S., and Abe, J. (1988). *Predictors of academic achievement among Asian-American and White students* (Report No. 88–11). *College Board Report,* 148.

Taylor, R., Chatters, L., Tucker, B., and Lewis, E. (1990). Developments of research on Black families: A decade review. *Journal of Marriage and the Family, 52,* 993–1014.

Trout, M., and Foley, G. (1989). Working with families of handicapped infants and toddlers. *Topics in Language Disorders, 10*(1), 57–67.

Turbille, V. P., Umbarger, G. T., and Guthrie, A. C. (2000). Fathers' involvement in programs for young children. *Young Children, 55,* 74–79.

Ucci, M. (1998). "Time-outs" and how to use them. *Child Health Alert, 1,* 2–3.

United Nations Population Fund. (1996). *A new role for men: partners for women's empowerment.* New York: United Nations Population Fund.

U.S. Bureau of the Census. (1993). *The Hispanic population in the United States: March 1993.* Washington, DC: U.S. Government Printing Office.

U.S. Bureau of the Census. (2000). *The Hispanic population in the United States. Statistical abstract of the United States* (121st ed.). Washington, DC: U.S. Government Printing Office.

U.S. Department of Health and Human Services. (2000). *Fatherhood Initiative,* June 15. http://www.fatherhood.hhs.gov/

van den Bloom, D. C. (1995). Do first-year interventions endure? Follow-up during toddlerhood of a sample of irritable Dutch infants. *Child Development, 66*(6), 1798–1816.

Walker, R. (2002). *"Kill the Indian and save the man." United Church of Christ Sunday Bulletin,* June 2, 2002. Cleveland, OH: United Church Press.

Watson, J. B. (1928). *Psychological care of mother and child.* New York: Norton.

Zuniga, R. (1992). Latino Families. In E. W. Lynch and M. J. Hanson (Eds.), *Developing cross-cultural competence.* Baltimore, MD: Brookes.

Family Strengths and Stressors

6

A family can be a noose around a child's neck or a springboard to success in life.

*T*his chapter looks at the characteristics of healthy and unhealthy families and the process of encountering and handling stresses. Some families are healthy, helping each of their members to grow, develop, and cope successfully with daily life, while other families are disturbed and dysfunctional, unable to meet each member's needs or cope successfully with the outside world. Most families are functioning somewhere between these two extremes. Many families function adequately until crises occur. What traits make the difference in how families deal with everyday life and crises such as divorce and death which produce major changes in the family? Children learn ways to deal with problems from the significant adults in their lives. Some coping methods are more successful than others.

Healthy and Unhealthy Family Characteristics

Very little is written about the everyday life of healthy families because good news seldom makes the headlines. Less data is also available because these families have dealt with fewer social agencies and courts. On the other hand, considerable information is available about dysfunctional families. Comparing family characteristics of these two groups, families who are considered healthy appear to have many similar traits, while families in trouble lack some of these traits. The following eight qualities may be used to distinguish between healthy and unhealthy families.

Healthy Families	Unhealthy Families
1. Stability	1. Instability
2. Clear, open communication	2. Confused and closed messages
3. Nurturing and mutuality	3. Neglect and isolation
4. Individuality	4. Enmeshment
5. Complementary and realistic roles	5. Poorly defined and unrealistic roles
6. Ability to solve problems and cope with stress	6. Disintegration
7. Establishment of clear values and standards	7. Inconsistent or confused values and rules for living
8. Strong ties with friends and community	8. Lack of support and involvement outside the home

(Curran, 1983; Barnhill 1975)

Families have these characteristics to varying degrees and changes occur during different periods in a family's life. The system of support is crucial in times of chronic or extreme stress.

Sense of Stability or Instability

Stable families continue to function day after day and year after year. They face changes and difficulties. They grow and adapt and can meet each other's needs. There is a sense of structure and continuity in these families, and they manage both internal and external conditions that affect them.

Unstable families lack control over their own destinies. Insecurity often results because members don't know what to expect from each other. They may lack trust in each other because of unmet promises. Internal problems include poor mental or physical health, drug abuse, or lack of sufficient intelligence to carry out family functions. The instability of marriages also contributes to dysfunctional families. In many such families, the children's needs are pushed aside in favor of the concerns of adults, with resulting negative effects.

External problems also have a strong influence on the internal workings of the family. Chronic poverty may leave parents apathetic and lacking self-respect. The loss of a job, and the inability to replace it with one of comparable value, can be devastating to the individual and the family.

Clear, Open Communication or Confused, Closed Messages

Communication is the ability to give and to receive messages, a complex process. Messages consist of words and intonation as well as body language such as facial expression, body position, and muscle tone. In addition, internal attitude, timing, and the setting affect communications (Satir, 1988). For example, parents may say to their child, "It's time to go to bed." Their tone of voice may be firm, indicating that there is no room for negotiation, or their tone might sound hesitant, sending the message of flexibility. On the other hand, the parent may be tense and the body language may be interpreted as showing anger or impatience. The body may be relaxed, conveying pleasure in giving this message. Overall the parent may convey either a feeling of wanting time free from the child, or wanting the child's company, but knowing that the child should be in bed. Timing of these messages and the setting will also determine how the request is received. Is it the appropriate bedtime hour or is it a holiday or a special occasion with company present? In good communications, the parent's voice, body language, and feelings come across in a direct or congruent manner. The timing and setting are appropriate.

Because communication is both sending and receiving messages, parents need to listen to their children's remarks. A four-year-old son of the author once accused his mother of not listening to him. "I am," was her response. The child then said, "But Mother, you're not looking at me."

In families with good communications, not only are the messages clear, but all members are free to express themselves, whatever the ideas or feelings may be. Permission is given to say things out in the open so that they can be discussed and resolved. These families are able to handle disagreements and try to respect differing viewpoints. Free expression is a vital element in the healthy development of one's individuality. Emotional health throughout society is better if feelings can be expressed, respected, and negotiated.

Listening skills are essential. They are fostered by not interrupting and by clarifying what was said. A response such as, "You said that. . . ." allows the sender to

Special Moments: Sharing Thoughts with Grandpa

Listening is key to good communications and to building caring relationships.

confirm or correct the message. For a problem, it is often helpful to ask how the person thinks the problem could be solved, or who should be involved in making the decision.

Good communication requires effort. When family members are having fun together and are in agreement, communication is easy. When there is a problem, it becomes more difficult to tell others what you mean and equally difficult to hear what is being said. It is important to keep personalities out of the discussion and deal with the problem. For example, saying, "You are such a slob leaving your clothes all over the house," accuses the person of being a slob and does not deal with the problem of clothes scattered around. Communication can also be thwarted by the listener. If a member brings home a problem and a family member dismisses it or tries to solve it, communication is cut. For example, a child says to a parent, "I don't have any friends!" The parent replies, "That's not true, you have many friends. What about Trudy or Jane?" The child has not had the chance to talk about her or his feelings or to feel understood and usually walks away. If the mother says, "Tell me about it," or "I'm sorry you feel that way," the child is encouraged to respond.

Successful families have devised ways to plan together for their needs and the use of their resources. Some families have regular family meetings in which all members are able to express their ideas and to discuss and plan for family and individual needs. Other families hold planning sessions on a regular basis as well as responding to problems as they arise. For example, how should we spend our money and our time? Each member's opinion is taken into account but all may not share equally in each decision. One criterion would consider who is affected most by the decision. Whatever the method, it is essential to get everyone's input. In summary, good communication patterns are congruent, open, involve all concerned members, and produce growth.

In troubled families, communications are closed, meaning that children are not free to express themselves, especially to disagree. In other cases, the rules to be followed are unclear. This occurs when the different levels of communication conflict. In this double bind message, the parent may verbally disapprove of the child's behavior in school, but the facial expression may show approval. "Johnny, you know your mother and I don't approve of fighting, even if he did start it." Expression may change. "You say he did get a bloody nose out of it?" Other times parents may be filled with conflict. They do not want to act out their own impulses, consciously or unconsciously, so they give the child permission to do so for them. Unclear messages often result from low self-esteem and fear of rejection.

Families in which the expression of emotions is suppressed are usually troubled. Young children often are made to feel shame when they cry or are unhappy. A mother told her dejected child, "You go back to your room until you can come out with a smile on your face." This is detrimental to their feeling of self-worth.

The repressive family believes the myth that the expression of conflicting feelings suggests a lack of love. Everyone must appear to feel the same about everything. Under these circumstances, children experience emotions as tensions. In closed systems, where opposing opinions cannot be freely expressed, mistakes are often punished harshly. Children learn to cover up their behavior by being secretive or even deceitful. They may learn to deny their feelings even to themselves, and often adapt antisocial behavior or an attitude of not caring.

Nurturing and Mutuality or Neglect and Isolation

The healthy family provides tender, loving care in raising children. Nurturing families care about each other. Parents work to make each child feel special, wanted, and needed. They are sensitive to their child's individual needs within the framework of normal growth and development. (The critical need for nurturing the infant is discussed in Chapter 2.)

Cousins: Feeling Special

Special attention from her older cousin at a wedding reception delights this child. In healthy families, a child is valued and given opportunities to be a part of other adults' lives and special occasions. This mother is also sending the message to her daughter that her mother's cousin and "family" are very important to her.

Caring about each other can be shown in many ways, such as touching, making eye contact, listening, sharing experiences, laughing, and having fun together. Parents take time to be available when needed, to provide that extra encouragement, or make it possible for a child or spouse to participate in a special activity. Nurturing is providing for each member's health and emotional needs. This means an environment that enables each member to grow and develop within the family.

Loving involves forming a special relationship, including a sense of belonging. Love is not "rational" and is not dependent on the individual's response. A love that nurtures is unselfish, or, in the case of a young child, is freely given. The child who is loved feels free to be him- or herself, make mistakes, and find home a safe retreat when things are wrong.

The nurturing family protects each other physically and psychologically. The older brother or sister looks out for younger siblings at school. Parents will support their children just like a lawyer trying to protect a client by working for that person's best interest. This spirit of mutuality, of caring for each other, makes members feel safe.

A key element in nurturing is the ability to respond to the child's signals. These signals can be very clear or difficult to read. The infant who pushes the bottle away does not require any more food. The responsive parent should understand this. On the other hand, a child, desiring more attention from a parent, may be hitting his or her sibling or regressing in toilet training to gain attention. The parent may respond to the behavior and may or may not address the need. Children who are successfully nurtured feel good about themselves and other people. They tend to be enthusiastic about life.

The unhealthy or dysfunctional family does not adequately nurture its members. Some parents have not developed this capacity or the necessary skills. Many of them did not receive sufficient nurturing as a child. In other situations, parents are so stressed in attempting to fulfill their parental roles and/or meet their personal needs that they have insufficient energy or time left to provide the needed emotional support for their children. They do not know where to turn for help. A few parents move frequently and do not leave a forwarding address, thus precluding any follow-up help. Families who lack nurturing skills are also frequently isolated from the outside world.

The lack of nurturing may take the form of neglect. This may turn into other forms of abuse and occasionally abandonment. Children who lack nurturing feel rejected and have a low self-image. As parents, they often lack the ability to nurture their children, thus damaging the next generation.

Individuality to Enmeshment of Members

In healthy families, all members have room to grow and develop. Along with quiet activities, parents see that their children's need for noise and activity are met. The home environment is structured so that each person can be comfortable and grow. For example, a very active child may need more space outdoors to release energy than a quieter child. If the child is hyperactive, a more routine setting with few sudden changes in family plans may be required.

While parents are totally in charge of their children's life at birth, healthy families encourage their children to make decisions and be responsible for some part of their own activities as soon as they are able. Brief separations from their parents foster autonomy and independence. Helping a child adjust to and enjoy a sitter and, later, preschool and elementary school are important steps. Making bedtime or any routine an acceptable and pleasant experience also helps the child grow in independence.

Healthy families prepare their children to enter the adult world as responsible citizens with their own set of values. When these children reach maturity, they can leave their family and live independently or form their own family.

In dysfunctional families, personalities are enmeshed, which does not allow for individual differences. There is a lack of separation between parent and child. A mother may be too dependent on a child and not want the child to move away from her physically or emotionally. Children, under constant supervision and with continued dependence on their mother, often develop a passive-dependent personality. As adults, they still may want a mothering figure.

Fathers seldom encourage dependence but may discourage children from achieving goals. Some fathers, who have failed to achieve in their own lives, may unconsciously adopt child-rearing patterns that prevent their sons from succeeding in school or a career. They may give their sons messages such as, "All I ask is that you get by. It doesn't make any difference later on what you do in school anyway."

Roles: Complimentary and Realistic to Poorly Defined and Unrealistic

Parents in successful families are good role models. They are consistent in their behavior and in what they expect of their children, who accept many of their ideas and values. Parents are comfortable with their roles as mother or father: they clearly define everyone's responsibilities in the family and help each child to understand his or her role. Responsibilities are appropriate for the children's ages and abilities and they are given some voice in the tasks they assume.

In unhealthy or dysfunctional families, parents are not only poor role models but assign their children unclear and/or unrealistic roles. Such parents often expect their children to behave in certain ways but model the opposite behavior. They may not understand how children view these inconsistencies or they may even fail to realize what they are doing. Some parents who want a child of a particular gender cannot get over their disappointment. Perhaps they wanted a boy to carry on the family name or business. One girl said, "My parents have never forgiven my sister for being a girl. She is nineteen years old and they still talk about how they wished they had a boy."

In an unhealthy family, when the balance of roles in the family fails, the parents begin to assign inappropriate roles to their children in an attempt to achieve equilibrium. These roles may be that of a rescuer, pacifier, worrier, or troublemaker. However, instead of achieving balance, additional stresses occur from these inappropriate role assignments.

Values and Standards: Clear and Consistent or Inconsistent

A family's values influence the development of each child. Individual families vary in the kinds of ideals they cherish and their relative importance. Some families value achievement highly while others may place more emphasis on athletic abilities, especially for their sons. Some families say hard work is more important than achievement. Others say honesty comes first or kindness is very important. Some parents teach children to follow the rules while other parents teach their children that some rules may not be just and need to be challenged and changed. Each family has its own set of values to which members may be deeply committed. Families vary in their ability to grow and modify their values as conditions change. This may include accepting some of their children's values.

In healthy families, parents model a clear set of personal values so that their children understand them. Flexibility is one of the values that allows adjustments to be made if circumstances change. For example, information on obesity shows that fat cells in children remain throughout life. A rule like, "Eat up all your food," could change to, "Take only what you can eat." Another example would be the adage, "Cleanliness is next to Godliness." Perhaps washing one's car would not be the best use of water in a drought.

Healthy families show respect for individual differences. As their children grow and develop, they are encouraged to think increasingly for themselves and to acquire their own value system and rules for living. In most successful families, children's values eventually do not differ greatly from their parents, especially on ethical issues.

In unhealthy families, the value system may be inconsistent or unclear, as are the rules for behavior. Discipline is often harsh, nonexistent, and/or inconsistent. As reported in Chapter 3, single mothers are often inconsistent in their discipline, oscillating between being permissive and authoritarian. This is confusing and ineffective for children. Unhealthy families often resist their children having different values or priorities, which they see as threatening.

Solve Problems Coping with Stress or Disintegration

Successful families do have their share of problems, resulting in varying degrees of stress, but have learned successful ways to cope with their problems. By solving small problems within the family through compromise, taking turns, or agreeing to disagree, they have learned to work together. These coping skills are then used and further developed in dealing with problems outside the home. Family members show respect for each other in their interactions. They support each other, but most members find additional strength from an outside support system. Above all, they look at crises and problems optimistically and search for solutions to deal effectively with the situation. It may be a long-term illness or the need to change jobs. Family members would ask, "What needs to be done to help, what can each of us do, and where can we find additional help if needed?"

Unhealthy or dysfunctional families often fail to handle crises. These families often encounter difficulties at developmental stages in family life such as marriage, child bearing, their child starting school, and facing the empty nest. The statistics on family breakups due to illness in the family, loss of a job, and other major problems show how damaging stress is to their family life. A family that has been merely surviving in good times will usually disintegrate in times of major crises.

> *Peter had worked at a local factory for three years. Without warning, he was one of a group of employees laid off. His wife, Mary, took care of two children along with their own baby for extra money. Both parents handled frustration very differently. Peter's typical reaction to problems was to eat or drink, depending on the degree of the problem. He did not like to talk about problems, whether they were family or work-related. Mary was quick to anger, pointing out problems, but rarely with feasible solutions. The lack of income and frustrations over Peter's unemployment compounded other stressful conditions. Peter's need for extra food treats increased and drinking resulted. Mary's frustration mounted with Peter at home while she was trying to manage her responsibilities. Their family was in jeopardy.*

Strong Ties with Friends and Community or Lack of Outside Involvement

Successful families are flexible, open to new ideas, and involved in activities outside of their family. It may be helping with a Girl Scout troop or a neighborhood project. These families have networks of social relationships that include extended family and friends. Children can bring their classmates home to play.

In our pluralistic society, successful families can live with those whose values and religious beliefs differ greatly. They realize that their children will be interacting with children from diverse backgrounds at their child-care center, at school, or in their neighborhood. They want their children to be able to benefit from healthy relationships. Their children are taught that not all people think or believe alike, and they need to respect each other, look for commonalities, and work for the common good. Diversity is accepted and not seen as threatening. The family's involvement with others not only enriches the children's experiences but provides a support system in times of need. The successful family views the world as enticing, predictable, manageable, and understandable.

Children whose parents are isolated from the community experience narrow views of the world. They lack the necessary

Contemplating Her Place in the World

This 12-year-old is experiencing new surroundings with caring adults who have been in her life since infancy. Supportive adults provide nurturing and a broader view of the world.

skills to cope successfully with many situations in life. When crises occur, these families generally do not seek or receive help. Conditions often deteriorate. The dysfunctional family views the world as unorganized and threatening. They see no laws or rules for explaining environmental events. Life is outside of their control.

Stress

Stress is a part of everyday life from birth to death. Hans Selye (1982), the "father of stress research," defines *stress* as any demand on our body that produces disequilibrium in the homoeostatic, physiological system. More simply put, *stress is an exposure to any event that requires a physiological response beyond the basic functions of breathing, thinking, or maintaining a neutral emotional state.* We all experience stress in daily life, but the kinds and degrees of stress, how they are perceived, and strategies for coping with stress vary greatly. One factor is the differences individuals have in their support systems both internally (from within the body) and externally (from outside sources).

The body usually adjusts to stress such as that involved in learning to walk, talk, or ride a bicycle easily. However, when children or adults are exposed to life situations that threaten their security, significant physiological changes take place that, in turn, lead to a lowering of the body's resistance to disease. Children living in poverty, homeless, or in an abusive home are heavily stressed and get sick more often than those living with average everyday stresses.

Children need their family to provide them physical and emotional security and developmentally appropriate challenges. Sometimes parents are unable to provide this stability or appropriate experiences because of their problems or conditions in society at large. Most parents try to protect their children from physical dangers and sources of psychological distress, although this is not always possible.

Types of Stressors

Some stressors are internal such as cholic or asthma. Other stressors come from outside sources. These external stressors could be the anticipation of the first day of school or going to the hospital. Sociocultural stressors soften, impede, or alter the individual's actions. Examples of stressors include not being allowed to play in a neighborhood because of the risk of violence, or hearing an unusual or loud noise. Individual reactions to these two situations vary.

Acute stressors occur suddenly in a child's life and are of short duration like a dislocated finger joint that is quickly relocated. Chronic stressors impact a child over a period of time and cause both short- and long-term problems. Living with an alcoholic parent or in a home where one is constantly diminished in value can cause long-term damage to even the most well-adjusted child.

Stages of Stress and Coping Strategies

Stress is part of being alive. Although stress elicits various emotions and actions, all stress follows the same pattern. Zegans (1982) describes the following stages.

1. *Stage of Alarm.*
   The first reactions are involuntary physical changes. This can be an increase in heart rate, the flow of certain hormones, and/or changes in galvanic skin responses. Here, adrenalin is secreted for energy.

2. *Stages of Appraisal*
   How the stress is interpreted depends on the person's psychological makeup, experiences, and age. An invitation to play on the team may be exciting for one person while for another it would arouse the fear of failing.

   Susie and Julie, each age ten, went to the mountains with Susie's dad for a fun day in the snow. They were coming down the mountain road near sunset when one of the tires lost its air. They pulled safely off the shoulder. Susie's dad said he would put another tire on. As he went to the trunk to get the spare tire and equipment, Susie ran after him and said, "Oh, let me help." They looked at Julie and she was crying softly, When asked what was wrong, she said, "But what if we don't get home? It's getting dark and no one might see us here." Each girl appraised the situation differently.

3. *Search for Coping Strategies*
   Infants attempt to control the situation by crying, spitting out the food, or, if all else fails, falling asleep. As children grow, they can think more about the situation and similar situations. They recall past experiences and how people reacted. They learn coping skills from those around them. Some strategies help the child to adapt to the situation while other techniques are counterproductive.

   When the people around children use positive coping plans, it helps children to choose more successful plans such as ignoring an unpleasant situation, compromising, or finding acceptable substitute satisfactions (Honig, 1986).

   When children learn and use inappropriate techniques such as swearing or hitting, they often encounter additional stresses rather than resolving the existing problem. This is particularly true when an inappropriate behavior from home is taken into the child-care center or school or from school to home.

4. *Stage of Implementation*
   Defense mechanisms used by some children distort the situation, resulting in denial. Children may exhibit compulsive behavior and not want to try anything new.

   Children who **externalize** *the situation blame others or fate as the cause of the problem. They often respond aggressively and show little empathy for the children they may have hurt. Their actions and refusal to accept some personal responsibility are not very effective in adjusting to stress.*

   Children who **internalize** *the situation to the degree that they accept some responsibilities for their actions are more successful in adjusting to and dealing with that situation and future stress.*

The process of successful coping involves the following responses:

a. flexibility and creative responses;
b. open consideration of options;
c. thinking about reality and future consequences;
d. rational and purposeful thinking;
e. direction and control over disturbing negative emotions (Haan, 1982).

Younger children will not be able to solve problems and reason the way older children can. It is crucial that adults in children's lives understand the help and support they need. Society, through its laws, agencies, and institutions, must also protect children. Children thrive best in environments low in stress and with adults who are positive models. These adults guide them to become competent in coping with life's stresses. *It seems that children's ability to cope with everyday stresses is more important in determining their well-being than the type or amount of stress that they experience* (Hardy, Power, and Jaedicke, 1993).

Family Stressors and Coping Skills

Families have always lived with stress but the kinds of stresses and the degrees of stress vary. Stress is affected by societal conditions. Change produces stress and today's families are living in a society affected by many changes. These include the roles of parents, the choices in family forms, increased options for women in the work world, the need for child care, pressure for increased income, and the lack of affordable housing or health care. These changes can provide exciting opportunities for families but they can also be overwhelming. Feelings of helplessness or lack of control may occur. The ways in which a family handles everyday and disastrous conditions either minimize or escalate their stress.

Expectations for family life, needs of family members, societal demands, the availability of support systems, and a family's ability to deal with stressful conditions affect the health and well-being of the family. Stress of any family member affects all family members. Long-term **poverty** is one of the most devastating stressors because of its ramifications. It affects health, nutrition, medical care, housing, education, and parental attention. Parents' time is often spent struggling to gain needed resources. **Loss of employment** is devastating in economic terms but also has emotional costs. Adult roles in the family change and other problems such as drug use may occur. Other common stressors include the **birth or adoption** of a baby, **moving, changing jobs,** an **accident, illness,** or living with or observing **violence.** The child who is pressured to learn skills too early or forced to grow up too fast is under repeated stress, as mentioned in Chapter 1 (Elkind, 1984, 1994). In addition, there are **natural disasters** such as earthquakes and fires. This chapter will discuss divorce and death of a parent. **Violence** in the lives of children and their families is the subject of Chapter 11.

Divorce

Divorce is an adult decision that traumatically affects all members of the family. Children, who need a secure, consistent, and caring environment, are living in the middle of anger, hurt, and the breakup of their family. Children live in conditions before, during, and after a divorce. Longitudinal studies show that some children continue to experience the effects of childhood divorce for a number of years, some even into adulthood (Wallerstein and Kelly, 1980; Chase-Landsay, Cherlin, and Krieman, 1995). Wallerstein and Kelly (1980) reveal that one-third of the children in their study continue to encounter open parental discord even five years after the divorce.

Divorce is very hard for children to accept and adjust to because of its many consequences. The loss of one parent from their home is generally the hardest to understand and accept. Many children also face changes in their housing and neighborhood, child care, school, friends, and activities. Family income will be reduced and a parent may have to increase her or his work schedule.

Children react to divorce with fear, anger, and resentment. Young children fear that if one parent leaves, the other parent might, too. If parents no longer love each other, maybe they will stop loving their children. Younger children question why a parent would leave if he or she really loves them. Children old enough to understand that their parents caused their distress are angry with their parents, and "guilt-restoration fantasies" may even be more powerful and last longer for children of divorce than bereaved children (Wallerstein and Kelly, 1980).

Phases of Divorce

The process of divorce has three distinct phases to which all parties need to adjust.

1. **The Acute Phase.** The deteriorating relationship reaches the point where one parent moves out of the house. In addition to the hurt, anger, and resentment, there is the loss of one parent in the home. The custodial parent tends to become less competent (Hetherington, Cox, and Cox, 1978; Wallerstein, 1983). Disorder in the household increases not only due to the custodial parent's fatigue and overload but also to this parent's feelings of rejection (Wallerstein, 1983). Discipline is inconsistent and goes from permissive to authoritarian. Single mothers tend to be less authoritative and provide less discipline and supervision than do married parents. This can contribute to their children functioning poorly in the emotional, cognitive, and behavioral areas (Dornbusch, et al., 1985; Cole, 1998).

2. **The Transitional Phase.** Economic hardship often occurs, necessitating changes in housing, work schedule, child care and/or school, and their overall lifestyle. All the basic roles in maintaining and supporting the family must be restructured. Child–parent relationships change with the intimate bond now being between parent–child and not between the parents. Older

children have more responsibilities. The success of this transition period for all members affects the children's adjustment to their new lifestyle. This process takes from two to three years or longer to deal with all the changes and attain stability and balance in family functioning (Hetherington, 1989a, 1989b; Wallerstein and Kelly, 1980).

3. **The Stabilizing Phase.** The post-divorce family makes adjustments and becomes a stable functioning family (Wallerstein, 1983). The family roles have been redefined and the family has established daily routines as individuals and as a family.

What to Tell Children

1. Together parents should tell the children about their decision to divorce. Parents should present the divorce as a rational decision, and say they are sad that the marriage did not last. This allows the children to mourn.
2. Wallerstein (1983) suggests that parents tell the children that they had expected to be married and love each other forever, but one or both of them is unhappy. They do not love each other and cannot get along living together. It is better to divorce and stop the fighting. Neither parent is blamed nor are the problems discussed.
3. Parents must reassure their children that they both love them, are committed to them, and will care for them. This will not change. The only change is that they will live separately. Parents can say that they are sorry for all the hurt and concerns the children have.
4. Parents should ask their children how they feel, what they are worried about, or what questions they have. They need to assure each child that they will try to answer his or her questions. Each child needs help to express feelings and actions in ways that are not damaging to the child or others. *Dinosaurs Divorce* is an excellent book for parents and children to read together and separately (Brown and Brown, 1986). It helps children understand what is happening in the lives of their parents and their family. What will happen to them, how they feel, and what they can do about their feelings are expressed through the dinosaur characters.

Coping with Divorce

Children, like adults, need help, support, and counseling the same as adults do to try to understand their feelings and the changes that will occur for them and their parents. The pain and confusion during this period in a child's life can be eased with appropriate support. Wallerstein and Blakesley (1989) have identified seven psychological tasks that children need to master to make a healthy adjustment to divorce. Younger children will only be able to deal with these tasks based on their developmental level.

1. Acknowledge the marital conflict.
2. Separate from the marital conflict and resume your customary activities.
3. Adapt to the loss and overcome feelings of rejection.
4. Forgive your parents and resolve your blame and anger.
5. Work out your feelings of guilt (which are especially strong in young children).
6. Accept the permanence of the divorce. (Most children want their parents to get back together.)
7. Achieve realistic ideas of relationships. This is only possible after working through the previous tasks.

Visitation patterns can help a child in dealing with the grief over one parent leaving the home and in coming to terms with the partial or total loss of that parent. When the visitation is not what the child expects or wants, the child feels rejection and unworthiness, affecting his or her self-esteem. This lower self-esteem interferes with school learning and peer relationships.

Both Hetherington, Cox, and Cox, (1978) and Wallerstein (1983) found that girls in female-headed homes adjusted much better than boys in the first couple of years after the divorce. Hetherington and her colleagues believe that boys receive less support from their mothers, teachers, and peers than girls (Hetherington, 1988, 1989a, 1989b). Girls and boys tend to respond differently to divorce. Girls internalize their feelings more and become less aggressive. Their expressions of sadness or crying elicit help. Boys externalize their feelings and become more aggressive, willful, and disobedient during the period surrounding separation and divorce.

Custody battles are particularly damaging to children. Some children hear one parent blaming the other or they are even asked to take sides or spy on one parent. These conditions make it impossible for children to achieve the task of "forgiving their parents."

Joint Custody

Joint legal custody includes a variety of custodial arrangements which allow both parents to make joint decisions for their child. Joint physical custody refers to the physical custody of the child being shared in some predetermined way (Bender, 1994). Joint custody, compared to sole custody, provides better access for both parents and grandparents, easier collection of child support, and above all a more unified parenting plan that benefits the child. Children are better able to keep their attachments to both parents (Bender, 1994; Kelly, 1988; Schwartz, 1987).

Often the child lives in both parents' homes for designated periods. Problems can occur when children live with each parent for parts of each week or according to certain monthly arrangements. School-age children find difficulties with homework schedules and being with their best friend or friends unless the residences are in the same neighborhood. Shifting households has been shown to affect both school performance and relationships with friends (Francke, 1983).

Death of a Parent

A parent is the source of life, a primary attachment figure, a nurturer, and a protector in a child's life. The death of a parent is a profound loss. Terminal illness and death bring about many changes in a child's life. These include additional caregivers, a grieving parent, and economic losses. In addition, there may be a change in housing and an additional member living with the family. The age and gender of the child, the temperament, the internal and external supports available, and the conditions that follow the death all affect the child's short- and long-term ability to adjust.

Children's Reactions

Children respond to a parent's terminal illness and death in a variety of ways. Some typical reactions include denial, anger, intense attachment to the surviving parent, idealizing the lost parent, fantasizing the parent's return, personal suffering to force the return of the parent, and regressive behavior. Children may demand to be cared for and feel anger against the world (Adams-Greenly and Moynihan, 1983).

AGE   The loss of a parent is more confusing and difficult for the young child whose cognitive functioning does not allow adequate processing of the situation (Furman, 1974). Children five and under have a limited conception of death and do not see death as final. They see the world from an egocentric viewpoint (Piaget, 1963). They often think that they have caused the death by making too much noise, saying a cruel word to their parent, or even having a bad thought. For young children, cause and effect are based on two things that occur at the same time called transductive thinking. For example, a loud thunderstorm the night a parent dies could be the cause of the death.

Children from six to eight or nine recognize that death happens and is final, but think of it as happening to someone else. Their sense of reality is limited. Terms requiring abstract thinking, like heaven, are confusing, as discussed later in this chapter. The death of a parent greatly intensifies children's sense of helplessness (Furman, 1974).

The immediate grief reactions of young children are milder and of shorter duration than those of adolescents, but the long-term consequences of psychiatric disturbances are greater for young children (Rutter, 1984). When children under

6.1   Reflections of a Seven-Year-Old on Dying

Before my mom was diagnosed with cancer, we had a good life living in Fullerton with my mom and dad. In 1994 my sister Sephanie was born ...

The next year I was in Mrs. Alleman's first-grade class. My Mom had her first seizure in a meeting at her school ... Going through cancer in the family was bad and not talking about it was even worse ... I finally found a counselor I liked. Counselors really help. You need to talk to people about your feelings, it is good to get them out.

If you are feeling alone (I've had that feeling) then think about going up to a family member and asking them if they want to cuddle or tell jokes ... here's a few that you can tell. (Jokes followed) ...

When my dad came home, my sister and I told him about my mom being in the hospital (again) and all that. My dad had a look of fright on his face that scared me even more. There was an awful storm that night with lightening and thunder so we were also scared from that.

There was a picture on the wall in our house that you could see when you were on the couch. I took it down and when my mom came home we hung it back up together ... Though my mom was sick for 3½ years straight, she always had a positive attitude. She would laugh and laugh even though she knew that she was going to die that very day. Try not to forget your parents' smiles and laughs. I think her positive attitude kept her (alive) extra time. Make an effort to keep all the adults around you happy and not too sad and miserable.

Grade four. When my mom was on medicine, it made (her) really round and big. She had a really puffy back and stomach. She gained a lot of weight over the last three years. I was embarrassed to take her places for two reasons. First, because she was really big and rounded. Second, because she was partly bald ...

Before my mom died, I told my class about my mom's illness. It felt good to know that people won't still ask why I was going up to the office or why I was leaving school early. They all felt sorry for me ...

At the funeral I got to sing "My Heart Will Go On" by Celine Dion. My grandpa chose it. I also read a letter that I wrote to my mom the night before.

I hope this book helped you through this hard time! I am sorry about what is going on in your life! Remember that time will make change. It will make things better! Believe in yourself and good luck on the rest of your life! Have fun!

age eleven lose the same-gender parent, they are at risk for emotional problems all of their lives. Boys have a higher rate of emotional pathology than girls (Institute of Medicine and the National Academy of Sciences, 1984).

When the death is caused by murder, children feel intense rage and often want revenge. They may express terror in their environment (Turkington, 1984). In particular, when the killer is not apprehended, emotional pathology is more likely.

What to Tell Children

The parent is a model for the child. What the parent says and how he or she acts during this period sets the stage for the child's feelings, behavior, and adjustment. It is important for the parent to listen to the child, try to answer questions, even to say that he or she does not know, and to show love and concern. The teacher can assist parents in finding the appropriate resources to help their child.

The child should be an active participant in the family's changing activities and schedules occurring before, during, and after the death. Unusual telephone calls and visitors should *not* be kept a secret for the child to worry about. If the parent is ill before dying, children should know what is happening at a level of their understanding. Maybe say, "Mommy is very sick. We will try to see what we could do to help. What do you think you could do? Maybe you could read her your storybook." It is important for the child to be able to see or visit the ill parent, just as it is for adults. What you tell children and how you answer their questions vary with the situation. When young children want to know more, they usually ask. This is not always true for older children.

The parent is truthful but uses words and phrases that are understandable to each child. It is confusing to younger children to say that Mommy went to heaven. They will wonder what heaven is and where it is. Some children may wonder if Mommy will be floating up there and looking down on them. Will this become a punishing conscience for a child? A youth may understand as much as an adult about heaven, but will be disturbed by any discrepancy in what the parent says and what he or she believes. And of course, never say that the parent was so good that God wanted her or him in heaven. If death is equated with sleep, the child may be afraid to go to bed. The Christian prayer, *Now I lay me down to sleep, I pray the Lord my soul to keep, if I should die before I wake, I pray the Lord my soul to take,* can cause concern even for a young child who has not just lost a parent.

Resilient Children

Some children emerge from unhealthy families with emotional strengths and intellectual competence (Werner and Smith, 1992). Originally these children were labeled *invulnerable* (Anthony, 1974), but the term *stress resistant* is more accurate (Garmezy and Telegren, 1984).

About one-half to two-thirds of children growing up in dysfunctional families or in a violent neighborhood develop into "competent, confident, and caring adults" according to a number of international, cross-cultural, and longitudinal studies (Werner and Smith, 1992; Benard, 1995; Garmezy, 1993).

This does not mean that resilient children will be unaffected in adulthood by their potentially damaging childhood experiences. Werner, who followed a group of "at-risk" Hawaiian babies into adulthood, found that marrying a caring person helped them to overcome their past experiences (1993).

6.2   **Resilient Children**

In a longitudinal study of 505 babies in 1955 on the Hawaiian Island of Kauai, Werner found that approximately half of the babies were born into poverty, often in homes with alcohol and abuse. Werner, a pioneer in the study of resiliency, followed these at-risk babies through childhood and into adulthood. Werner reported that about one-third had done well in school, were into good careers, and thought of themselves as competent adults (1993).

Resilient children have qualities that help them develop social competence, problem-solving skills, a critical awareness of conditions, autonomy, and a sense of purpose (Benard, 1995). **Social competence** includes responsiveness to others and the ability to elicit responsiveness from them, flexibility, sensitivity to others who are different, communication skills, and a sense of humor. **Problem-solving skills** involve the ability to plan, elicit help from others, and think critically. **A critical awareness** allows individuals to reflect on damaging conditions in their environment, such as an abusive parent, and develop strategies to cope constructively with these situations. **Autonomy** includes a sense of identity, the ability to act independently, and to have some control over their environment. The autonomy of resilient children is strengthened by their ability to ignore or reject negative messages, thus detaching themselves from parental dysfunction. Resilient children have **goals, persistence, and optimism** in meeting their challenges successfully.

No child is invulnerable, but resilient children seem to share some commonalities.

1. They are calm, easy-going, sociable, and will take the initiative.
2. They usually have a warm, close relationship with one parent, which is facilitated by the child's temperament.
3. There is a strong bond between the child and a neighbor or relative, often in the child's first year of life. This adult models positive coping skills.
4. They are optimistic, seeing their glass as half-full rather than half-empty.
5. They are helpful to siblings and classmates.
6. They have a hobby on which they focus (This helps them escape quarrels at home or school).
7. They have a sense of humor.
8. They tend to be more intelligent than their siblings or peers (Werner, 1995, 1984; Garmezy, 1989, 1993).

Characteristics of Supportive Environments

Children are influenced profoundly by conditions in their family, child-care center or school, and their community. Caring relations, high expectations, and opportunities for children to participate in a variety of activities or projects benefit their healthy growth and development and can mitigate the effects of damaging conditions in their lives (Benard, 1995).

CARING RELATIONSHIPS   All children need caring relationships outside the home, but especially children whose family members are unable to provide sufficient nurturing. A relative, a neighbor, teacher, or person involved in a child's life can provide the crucial caring, valuing, respect, and support essential for healthy growth and development. Studies over forty years show that the teacher is the most frequently mentioned positive role model outside the family in the lives of resilient children (Werner and Smith, 1992). Teachers who listen to and enjoy a child become a role model for that child in developing personal traits. A special teacher often motivates children to succeed. When children feel that the school, in general, is a place where many people know and care about them, their relationships with others are more caring. Their academic work also improves.

HIGH EXPECTATIONS AND OPPORTUNITIES FOR PARTICIPATION   When parents or other adults notice that a child has potential or certain talents and provide support, the child is more likely to accomplish the goal. It also raises the child's self-confidence. When a school and a teacher believe that all their children can succeed and they provide necessary support, their children will try harder and are more likely to achieve. There are also fewer behaviorial problems (Rutter, 1984). In China, a teacher once said to the author, "I expect all of the children in my class will be able to do the math assignment."

The child-care center or school that advocates success for each child provides an environment that respects individual learning styles, strengths, interests, and experiences. Classroom activities that promote inclusion, cooperation, shared responsibility, and a sense of belonging promote resilience in children. Teachers' accurate evaluations of children based on information from multiple intelligences and children's self-reflection also foster resilience (Benard, 1995). It may be helpful for parents and teachers to encourage a child to find a hobby or something of interest to explore and focus on.

Recent research on resilience shows a relationship between heredity and environment. Parents and teachers can examine children's abilities to cope with stresses and the conditions in which this process takes place. Frequently, problems in a child's life can be reduced in one or more of the child's settings by providing caring and appropriate experiences. Often a timely intervention program can save both vulnerable and resilient children from damaging stress. Children also need help in strengthening their coping skills.

Current Trends

Community efforts continue to reach out to families to involve them in their children's different settings. When adults working with children understand the family's culture, the family feels more comfortable and is more likely to participate. Professionals also realize that they must understand and support the family in order to fully support the children.

How can people in the lives of children and society help more children survive the environmental risks of poverty, negative family interactions, parental divorce and death, job loss, mental or physical disabilities, and drug and family abuse so they can become competent adolescents and adults?

Key Points

1. Successful, healthy families are stable in their daily functioning, have clear, open communication, are nurturing and support each other, allow for individual needs, have clear, consistent values and standards, solve their problems by coping with the stresses, and have strong ties with friends and the community. Dysfunctional or unhealthy families are missing some of the strengths of healthy families.

2. Stress is an exposure to any event that requires a response beyond the basic functions of breathing, thinking, or maintaining a neutral emotional state. Everyone experiences stress daily, but the types and degrees of stress, how they are perceived, and strategies for coping vary greatly.

3. Internal coping strategies such as accepting some responsibility for their actions give children more control over the present and future situations. External coping strategies such as blaming others do not.

4. Acute stressors occur suddenly and are of short duration. Chronic stressors, such as living with an alcoholic parent, impact children causing short- and long-term damage.

5. Divorce is an adult problem and very difficult for children to understand and finally accept. Age and gender affect their responses to divorce.

6. In divorce, children suffer from the loss of a parent living in the home, less income, inconsistent discipline, and often changes in houses, schools, and friends.

7. It takes two to three years minimum for family members to deal with their feelings, all the changes, and to stabilize their family.

8. The death of a parent is the loss of a primary attachment figure, a nurturer, and a protector. Children experience many other changes.

9. Children's typical reactions include denial, anger, intense attachment to the remaining parent, idealizing the lost parent, fantasizing the parent's return, and regression.

10. Children need truthful and appropriate information. They should be a part of daily family activities surrounding their parent's death and allowed to grieve.

11. Resilient children can spring back from adversity. They have common personal traits such as being calm, easy-going, sociable, optimistic, independent, and intelligent. They always have social support from someone outside the immediate family.

Critical Thinking Questions

1. How could a parent or a teacher help a child acquire some of the traits of resilient children? Which of these characteristics would be difficult to teach a child?

2. How would you help the children in your classroom to understand and support a classmate who is experiencing divorce or the death of a parent?

3. How would you prepare yourself as a teacher to help children in your classroom and their parents deal with some of the stresses discussed in this chapter?

Resources and References

■ Resources

Hopkins, A. (2002). Children and Grief: The role of the early childhood educator. *Young Children, 57*(1), 40–47.

■ Nonfiction for Children Ages 5 to 12

Blackburn, L. (1992). *I know I made it happen: A book about children and guilt.*

Heegaard. M. (1992). *When someone very special dies.* (A workbook to express grief). Minneapolis, MN: Woodland.

Mellonie, B. and Ingpen, R. (1987). *Lifetimes: The beautiful way to explain death to children.* (Life cycles of plants, animals, and people). New York: Bantam.

■ Fiction for Children Ages 3 and Up

Brown, M. (1995). *The Dead Bird.* New York: Harper Trophy.

Brown, L. K. and Brown, M. (1986). *Dinosaurs divorce: A guide for changing families.* Little Brown and Company: Boston: MA.

Joslin, M. (1999). *The goodbye boat.* (Visually represents the stages of grief). Grand Rapids, MI: Eerdmans.

■ References

Adams-Greenly, M., and Moynihan, R. T. (1983). Helping children of fatally ill parents. *American Journal of Orthopsychiatry, 53*(2), 219–229.

Anthony, E. J. (1974). The syndrome of the psychologically invulnerable child. In E. J. Anthony and Koupernik (Eds.), *The child and his family 3: Children at psychiatric risk.* New York: Wiley.

Barnhill, L. R. (1975). Healthy family systems. *Family Coordinator,* 94–99.

Benard, B. (1995). Fostering resilience in children. *ERIC Digest,* EPO-PS-95-9. Urbana, IL: University of Illinois.

Bender, W. N. (1994). Joint custody: The option of choice. *Journal of Divorce and Remarriage, 21*(3/4), 115–130.

Brown, L. K., and Brown, M. (1986). *Dinosaurs divorce: A guide for changing families.* Waltham, MA: Little Brown & Company.

Chase-Landsay, P. Sh., Cherlin, A. J., and Krieman, K. E. (1995). The long-term effects of parental divorce on the mental health of young adults: A developmental perspective. *Child Development, 66,* 1614–1634.

Cole, M. (1998). *Cultural psychology: A once and future discipline.* Cambridge, MA: Belknap Press.

Curran, D. (1983). *Traits of a healthy family.* Minneapolis, MN: Winston Press.

Curran, D. (1985). *Stress and the healthy family.* Minneapolis, MN: Winston Press.

DeToledo, S., and Brown, D. E. (1995). *Grandparents as parents: A survival guide for raising a second family.* New York: Guildford.

Dornbusch, S. M., Carlsmith, J. M., Bushwall, S. J., Ritter, P. L., Liederman, H., Hastorf, A. H., and Gross, R. T. (1985). Single parents, extended households, and the control of adolescents. *Child Development, 56,* 326–341.

Elkind, D. (1984). *The hurried child.* Reading, MA: Addison-Wesley.

Elkind, D. (1994). *Ties that stress: The new family imbalance.* Cambridge, MA: Harvard University Press.

Furman, F. (1974). *A child's parents dies.* New Haven, CT: Yale University.

Garmezy, N. (1993). Children in poverty: Resilience despite risk. *Psychiatry, 56, 127–136.*

Garmezy, N., Masten, A. S., and Tellegren, A. (1984). The study of stress and competence in children: Building blocks for developmental psychopathology. *Child Development, 55*(1), 97–111.

Garmezy, N., and Tellegren, A. (1984). Studies of stress-resistant children: Methods, variables, and preliminary findings. In F. Morrison, C. Lord, and D. Keating (Eds.), *Advances in applied developmental psychology.* New York: Academic Press.

Haan, N. (1982). The assessment of coping, defense, and stress. In L. Goldberg and S. Brezner (Eds.). *Handbook of stress: Theoretical and clinical aspects.* New York: The Free Press.

Hetherington, E. M. (1988). Family relations six years after divorce. In K. Pasley and M. Inhinger Tallman (Eds.), *Remarriage and stepparenting: Current research and theory.* New York: Guildford.

Hetherington, E. M. (1989a). Coping with family transitions: Winners, losers, and survivors. *Child Development, 60,* 1–18.

Hetherington, E. M. (1989b). Divorce: A child's perspective. *American Psychologist, 44,* 303–312.

Hetherington, E. M. (1993). An overview of the Virginia longitudinal study of divorce and remarriage with a focus on early adolescence. *Journal of Family Psychology, 7,* 39–56.

Hetherington, E. M., Cox, M., and Cox, R. (1978). The aftermath of divorce. In J. H. Stevens, Jr. and Mathews (Eds.), *Mother-child relations.* Washington, DC: NAEYC.

Hardy, D. F., Power, T. G., and Jaedicke, S. (1993). Examining the relation of parenting to children's coping with everyday stress. *Child Development, 64,* 1829–1841.

Honig, A. (1986a). Stress and coping in children, Part 1. *Young Children, 41*(4), 50–63.

Honig, A. (1986b). Stress and coping in children, Part 2. *Young Children, 41*(5), 73–84.

Institute of Medicine (1984). *Report on bereavement.* Washington, DC: National Academy of Sciences.

Kelly, J. B. (1988). Longer-term adjustment in children of divorce; converging findings and implications for practice. *Journal of Family Psychology, 2,* 119–140.

Piaget, J. (1963). *The origins of intelligence in children.* New York: Norton.

Rahe, R. H., Meyer, M., Smith, M., Kjaerg, G., and Holmes, T. H. (1964). Social stress and illness. *Journal of Psychosomatic Research, 8,* 35–44.

Rump, M. (2002). Involving fathers of young children with special needs. *Young Children, 57*(6), 22–30.

Rutter, M. (1984). Resilient children: Why some disadvantaged children overcome their environments, and how we can help. *Psychology Today, 18*(3), 57–65.

Satir, V. (1988). *The new people in the making.* Mountain View, CA: Science and Behavior Books.

Schwartz, L. L. (1987). Joint custody: Is it right for all children? *Journal of Family Psychology, 1,* 120–134.

Selye, H. (1982). History and present status of the stress concept. In L. Goldberger and S. Breqnitz (Eds.), *Handbook of Stress.* New York: Free Press.

Turkington, C, (1984). Support urged for children in mourning. *APA Monitor,* December, 16–17.

Wallerstein, J. S. (1983). Children of divorce: Stress and developmental tasks. In N. Garmezy and M. Rutter (Eds.), *Stress, coping, and development in children.* New York: McGraw-Hill.

Wallerstein, J. S. (1987). Children of divorce: Report of a ten-year study of early latency children. *American Journal of Orthopyschiatry, 57*(2), 199–211.

Wallerstein, J. S., and Blakeslee, S. (1989). *Second chances: Men, women, and children a decade after divorce.* New York: Ticknor and Fields.

Wallerstein, J. S., and Kelly, J. B. (1980). *Surviving the breakup: How children actually cope with divorce.* New York: Basic Books.

Werner, E. E. (1984) Resilient children. *Young Children, 4,* 68–72.

Werner, E. E. (1993). Risk, resilience, and recovery: Perspectives from the Kauai Longitudinal Study. *Development and Psychopathology, 5,* 503–515.

Werner, E. E. (1995). Resilience in development. *Current Directions in Psychological Science, 4,* 81–85.

Werner, E. E., and Smith, R. S. (1992). *Overcoming the odds: High risk children from birth to adulthood.* Ithaca, NY: Cornell University Press.

Zegans, L. S. (1982). Stress and the development of somatic disorders. In Golberger and S. Breznitz (Eds.), *Handbook of stress: Theoretical and clinical aspects.* New York: Harper and Row.

Early Education and Care
New Challenges

7

Every child should have the opportunity to grow up in a setting that values children, that provides conditions for a safe and secure environment, and that respects diversity. Because children are both the present and the future of every nation, they have needs, rights, and intrinsic worth that must be recognized and supported.

— Global Guidelines for Early Childhood
Education and Care in the Twenty-First Century
International Symposium, Switzerland, 1999

*T*he need for high-quality, affordable, and available early childhood education and care for infants, toddlers, preschoolers, and school-age children is more important than ever before. The quality of a child's environment in and outside the home affects that child's growth and development. Recent research findings on critical brain development emphasize the importance of a child's experiences during the first years of life (Shore, 1997; Bruer, 1999). The nutrition, stimulation, environment, and overall care interacting with the child's genetic endowment affect growth and development. The "I Am Your Child Campaign," a widespread 1997 public education initiative, has publicized these findings and continues to advocate for better care, especially for babies and toddlers (Children's Defense Fund, 1998). Many parents try to choose high-quality child care, but often find it is not affordable or available.

Today, the majority of mothers with young and school-age children are employed outside the home. In 1973, only 30 percent of mothers with children under age six were in the workforce. Recent U.S. Bureau of Labor Statistics show that 62.8 percent of married mothers and 65.3 percent of all mothers of children under age six work outside the home (Children's Defense Fund, 2000). Over half of the mothers return to the workforce before their infant is one year old (Children's Defense Fund, 2001).

Since the 1970s, changes in family structure, along with recent economic conditions, have placed more mothers with young and school-age children in the workforce, and relatives are often not available for chlid care. Many of these mothers are single parents who must work. Many other women work because their family needs two incomes to meet current expenses or to have money for their children's education. In addition, recent changes in welfare legislation have moved many welfare mothers into a work-training program or a job. Consequently, the number of economically disadvantaged children who are eligible for programs such as Head Start has greatly increased.

Society has always recognized paid employment as a validating experience for men, but today more women are finding careers a fulfilling part of their lives. Many of these women fear that taking a period of time off for child rearing will reduce their future career options.

Effects of Early Childhood Education and Care

The effects of early childhood education and child care on children's development continue to be the focus of research projects and debates. Although there is ambiguity regarding the effects of child care among scholars, most have concluded that *high-quality* early childhood education and care have beneficial effects on children (Love, 1998). Many find it is particularly good for children from lower-income homes (Children's Defense Fund, 2000).

In assessing the effects of early childhood education and child care on children's aggressive behavior, characteristics of the child and the family need to be considered. Both temperament and gender affect children's degree of prosocial and aggressive behaviors. In addition, low family socioeconomic status and low-quality child care programs are related to increased aggressiveness in children (Bates, et al., 1994; Dodge, Pettit, and Bates, 1994; Farrington, 1991; Patterson, et al., 1990; Rutter, 1981). Parents with low income levels typically place their children in lower-quality child care settings, which could explain why children from these low-income families often show more aggressive behavior than children from middle- or higher-income families (DiLalla, 1998). These factors are often not considered in the research.

Many of the studies are hard to compare because of differences in their subjects, evaluation methods, and definition of terms. It is particularly difficult to judge the quality in the environments of home-reared children for comparisons. In addition, all of the conditions in the family surrounding the mother's employment have largely been overlooked when assessing the effects of early childhood education and care.

Researchers continue to study the effects of maternal separation on infants' social, emotional, and cognitive development. Other research is examining the immediate and long-term effects of child care on the young child's social, emotional, and cognitive development.

Effects of Mothers' Employment on Children's Development

The impact of a mother's employment on her children is influenced by a number of interrelated variables. They involve:

1. the mother's satisfaction with work;
2. the father's family involvement;
3. the conditions of early childhood education and care;
4. the characteristics of the child.

The reasons a mother has for working outside the home, her attitude toward and satisfactions from work, her degree of autonomy at work, relationships with coworkers and individuals outside the home, educational level, and job status affect her family roles. In addition, her adjustment to the demands of work and family roles, the father's or other family adult's relationship and involvement with the child, the divisions of housekeeping tasks, and the mother's overall stress level all play an important role in how her employment affects the socialization and development of the child (Belsky and Eggebeen, 1991; Desai, Chase-Lansdale, and Michael, 1989).

Key to how a mother's employment affects her children is the quality and the type of child care (relative, center-based or family child care). In addition, the mother's feelings about the separation on her child and the ability of others to provide good care for her child are vitally important. Does this mother feel guilty and see her child as suffering from her absence or does she see her child benefiting from experiences at substitute care? Most studies showing advantages of child care on a child's development focus on high-quality center-based care. Very few studies have compared the effects of different types of child care on a child's development.

The effects of a mother's employment appear to vary with the child's age, sex, race, ethnicity, family form, and socioeconomic status. Considerable research focuses on the age of the child when the mother enters the workplace. However, researchers do not always agree. For example, using the same National Longitudinal Survey on Youth data, Nasal Baydar and Jeanne Brooks-Gunn (1991) reported that White preschoolers whose mothers worked during infancy did not do as well on cognitive and behavioral tests as did White preschoolers with mothers who stayed home.

Preschoolers whose mothers waited until their second three months to return to work tested lower than those whose mothers returned to work during their first three months. Perhaps the first three months are an easier time for infants to separate from their mother. This could relate to the developmental stage of the attachment process from three to six months and person permanence. After the first year of life, these authors found that maternal employment had no significant negative effect. In general, girls were less vulnerable than boys to their mothers' working and to their substitute child care. Other studies also found that girls appeared to benefit more than boys from mothers' employment, especially in middle-class families (Bogenschneider, 1990; Desai, et al., 1989). Boys appeared to do better if a grandmother or some relative (not their father) cared for them (Baydar and Brooks-Gunn, 1991).

On the other hand, Vandell and Ramanaen (1992), using the same research data but studying *only low-income* families, found that both early and recent employment of mothers had been beneficial to their children who scored higher in second grade compared to children from similar families whose mothers had not worked. Higher math scores were best predicted by early maternal employment while recent employment was a better predictor of higher reading achievement. In addition, children whose mothers were unemployed in their infancy were more likely to be living in poverty in second grade compared to children whose mothers were employed at that time.

Mothers are going to continue to be employed, even with very young children. The question is how to minimize any detrimental effects on the development of children and how to maximize any benefits this has for them.

Infants

The concern of most researchers is the effect of infant care on the mother–child attachment. The majority of studies in the 1970s were based on laboratory settings using the Strange Situation to assess the infant's separation from and reunion with the mother. Over the years, the results of studies on mother–child attachment have varied.

The National Institute of Child Health and Development (1997) conducted a study of the effects of infant child care in the first year of life on infant–mother attachment security. They compared 1,153 infants and their mothers with and without child-care experience using the Strange Situation attachment classifications. These children were observed periodically at home and in child-care. They then were tested and observed in the laboratory and child care at twenty-four and thirty-six months. *There were no significant effects of the child-care experience (quality, amount, age of entry, stability or type of care) on attachment security or avoidance.* However, infants were less likely to be secure when low maternal sensitivity/responsiveness was combined with poor-quality child care. (There was a gender difference. Boys with many hours of child care and girls with fewer hours were somewhat less likely to be securely attached). This study corroborates other studies that *the nature of the attachment relationship itself is primarily dependent on the nature of the ongoing interactions between mother and child* (Ainsworth, 1973; Sroufe, 1988). The NICDH study is continuing to follow these children.

In 1998, the NICHD studied children enrolled in their NICHD Study of Early Child Care at twenty-four and thirty-six months as to the effects of child care on self-control, compliance, and problem behavior. The results showed that mothering was a stronger and more consistent predictor of child outcomes than child care. This agrees with their previous research on infant–maternal attachment. However, in determining the effects of child care on children, the quality of care was the most consistent *child care* predictor. Higher-quality care was related to social competence and cooperation and less problem behavior at both two and three years of age. More experience in groups with other children also predicted more cooperation and fewer problems at both two and three years of age (NICHD, 1998).

For *high risk* infants, the quality of the mother–infant attachment appears to modify the short- and long-term effects of child care. Child care has a positive effect on high risk infants who are insecurely attached and a negative effect for those with a secure mother–child attachment. Infants in child care who were insecurely attached to their mothers were less withdrawn at forty-two months and infants in the secure group were more negative and avoidant at forty-two months and aggressive in kindergarten than children reared at home. However, both groups of child-care children were more aggressive than the home-reared children in kindergarten. These differences disappeared later in school (Egeland and Hiester, 1995).

For infants living in poverty the picture is different. Over half of the infants in center-based care showed both positive mother–infant interactions and positive social development (Benasich, Brooks-Gunn, and Clewell). Almost all programs report enhanced cognitive functioning through the preschool years (Lazaar and Darlington, 1982). None of these studies showed the mother's reasons for working. In some cases, the money from a mother's employment could lift the family out of poverty. It is also possible that a mother's employment could add to the stresses associated with living in poverty and in a single-parent home.

Preschool and School-Age Children

Children who attend child-care centers experience life with other children. It is not surprising that children who have attended more child care and/or began at a younger age interact more with their peers both prosocially and aggressively than children in home care (DiLalla, 1998). Preschool children who attend child-care centers or nursery schools have been found, on the average, to be more self-confident, more outgoing, and more socially competent with both peers and adults than home-care children (Clarke-Stewart, 1989). Various studies show that center-care children, compared to home-reared children, know more about the social world, gender roles, perspective-taking, labels for feelings, and how to solve social problems. Center-care children are also less stereotyped and more sophisticated in their play as well as more realistic about their achievements. In general, children of employed mothers tend to have less stereotyped gender roles (Zaslow and Hayes, 1986).

The relationship between child care and later aggression is ambiguous (DiLalla, 1998). Some studies show no effects of child-care experience on aggression or social problems (Bates, et al., 1994; Belsky and Eggebeen, 1991; Burchinal, Ramey, Reid, and Jaccard, 1995; Clarke-Stewart, 1989; Howes, 1990; McCartney and Rosenthal, 1991; Moore, 1996; NICHD Early Child Care Research Network, 1997; Scarr, 1991, Vandell, 1991; Vandell and Corasanti, 1990). However, other research shows that child-care children are more aggressive, assertive, and rebellious than home-care children both in the preschool years and in elementary school (Rutter, 1981). Two studies in other countries, Sweden and England, also found child-care children to be more aggressive in school (Haskins, 1985).

In a study of aggression in public schools, Ron Haskins (1985) followed fifty-nine children for two to three years after they entered elementary school. The children had varying degrees of child-care experience. Children who spent the most time (about five years) in child care in a cognitively oriented program were the most aggressive in public school. The group with almost as much child-care experience (thirty-six to fifty-three months) from licensed centers that did not emphasize intellectual development showed less aggression. In fact, their level of aggression was similar to the amounts shown by the other two groups with even less child care. Interestingly, the aggressive children were liked by the elementary teachers and were not considered more difficult to manage. These aggressive children were considered more intelligent in first grade than the children in the three other groups with less child care. Furthermore, the degree of aggression in school declined each year for the children with the most child care, while children from the other groups showed a modest gain in aggression over time.

Aggression in children can be reduced by teachers' practices that promote positive social behavior. Seven aggressive children from Haskins' original research were part of such a study. After their participation in the study, these children had such a dramatic, immediate, and continued decrease in aggressive behavior that they had to be dropped from Haskins' study.

Two crucial questions remain. How do we define aggression? Some teachers may use the term *aggressive* while others would label the same behavior *assertive*. Some may say that the child shows *perseverance* and others may say *aggression*. Secondly, does this "aggressive" behavior remain stable later in the school years? There is some evidence that the home-reared children become more aggressive during the first years of school.

Child-Care Options

Child care refers to the care of a child by any adult other than the parent. For some families, these choices are limited because of cost or availability. Some children are cared for in their own home by a relative or another adult. Many children, especially infants and toddlers, go to another person's home for care. This is referred to as a family child-care home and may or may not be licensed. Other children attend center-based programs. Regulations for family child-care homes and centers are discussed later in this chapter.

Family Child-Care Homes

Family child care is care provided in a person's home for a limited number of children. The states usually limit the size of the group to six or eight (including the caregiver's children) but some homes are licensed for twelve and require an additional adult. Many parents choose family care for very young children. Because the group is small, it is usually informal. Infants and younger children as well as some older children need the extra individual attention possible in a smaller group. They do better with fewer children and less stimulation. A home setting can be an excellent place for young children to learn about real-life activities. However, most providers lack education in early childhood (Clarke-Stewart, Allhusen, and Clements, 1995).

TABLE 7.1 Who's Minding the Kids?
1995 Child Care Arrangements for Children under Five with Working Mothers
25.1% were in child care centers
23.5% in family child care homes
21.4% with relatives
4.9% in home care and unrelated caregivers

Source: Kristin Smith, *Current Population Reports*, P70-70, Bureau of the U.S. Census, 2000.

Often the family child-care provider has more flexibility to meet a family's time schedule or special needs than the staff in a center. Sometimes an ill child can be safely cared for in this home setting. On the other hand, coordinating the caregiver's vacation with the family's needs can be a problem. Also, when only one adult is present, there is no one to monitor the caregiver's behavior or to provide assistance in an urgent situation.

Center-Based Programs

Programs housed in centers vary as to their funding sources, purpose, and type of sponsorship. Some programs are funded with local, state, or federal monies and fees based on parents income. Others are supported with private funds and tuition. There are also private–public partnerships. About 10 percent of child-care centers are nonprofit and half of the for-profit centers are owned by chains (DeBord, 1991). Centers are operated by private individuals or groups, churches or other faith-based organizations, public or private schools, colleges, universities, government agencies, research institutes, and industry.

Preschool and Nursery School Programs

These programs are designed to meet the educational and socialization needs of young children from two and a half or three to five years of age. The children's social, emotional, physical, intellectual, and creative needs are met through their play activities. They usually provide half-day programs, often two or three days a week. Their schedule is related to the school year as opposed to the calender year. Their popularity has declined with the increase of mothers in the workforce.

Parent Cooperatives

These nonprofit cooperative preschools are initiated, financed, and run by parents who set policies, plan or approve the curriculum, participate in the daily routine, and hire staff. Many are half-day enrichment programs. Parents participate in various ways to reduce the costs of the program and learn from their experiences. These parent cooperatives may be entirely parent-initiated and include a professional director (Hewes, 1998). Parents participating in these organizations form bonds and often lifetime friendships as indicated by the title of Hewes' book, *"It's the Camaraderie"—A History of Parent Cooperative Preschools.*

Employer-Supported Child Care

Employers can choose to support child care for employees in a number of ways. It can be direct financial assistance to a program on or near their premises, resource and referral services, and/or child-friendly work policies such as flextime, job sharing, and the use of employees' sick leave for an ill child. A Dependent Care

Assistance Plan is a salary reduction plan that allows the employer to set aside a portion of the employee's salary to pay for the employee's child-care costs out of "pretax" dollars.

Full-Day Child-Care Centers

These centers provide education as well as care for young children. Some centers include infants and toddlers while others include out-of-school programs for school-age children. A few centers operate multiple programs offering half-day as well as all day programs.

Infant Centers

These centers serve infants from birth to two years of age. Full-day programs provide care and activities for children of parents who are working or in a training program.

Head Start

Head Start is a comprehensive, federally funded, intervention program serving children mainly from three to five years of age from families with an income below a certain level. It is a comprehensive program that meets the needs of the child and supports the family, staff, and community. Typically, the Head Start programs are half-day, but full-day programs are becoming more common. Since 1972, 10 percent of Head Start children served are disabled physically, emotionally, socially, or mentally (Amendment to the 1965 Economic Opportunity Act). Head Start programs are designed to provide children with a special environment so that they can enter kindergarten with many experiences similar to those of children from middle-income families. Emphasis is on increasing specific cognitive and language skills, self-concept development, and social and emotional competencies. Home visits by teachers are mandated and parents are involved in the program. In addition, some health, nutrition, and psychological services for children and their families are available. Head Start programs only have space for three out of five eligible preschool children (Children's Defense Fund, 2002).

Early Head Start

The importance of brain development in the first three years on later development (Newberger, 1997), along with the shortage of home care for infants and toddlers, and the poor quality of much of the existing care (Helburn, 1995) forced government action. In 1994, the federal government began funding Early Head Start (EHS) programs for low-income families with pregnant mothers or infants and toddlers. These programs have goals similar to Head Start. They provide a setting and activities promoting all areas of the child's development. They support fami-

Look at This Teacher: Home Visit

A teacher's visit to the home makes the child feel special. It helps the teacher relate to the child's conversation at school and understand the family's goals for the child.

lies and help them to provide for the healthy development of their infants and toddlers. Each family has an individualized family development plan. The staff and administrator work with community agencies building collaborative relationships. EHS programs also provide ongoing staff development.

According to the final report of the seven-year national evaluation of Early Head Start, participating children performed significantly better in cognitive, language, and socio-emotional development than their peers who did not participate. The study also showed positive effects on many aspects of parenting, the home environment, and parents' progress toward economic self-sufficiency.

The number of Early Head Start Programs has grown from 68 in 1995 to over 600 by 2001, serving about 45,000 families (Buell, Hallam, and Beck, 2001). As more families transition from welfare to work or to job-training programs, the need for affordable full-day, full-year, high quality, infant–toddler programs becomes more urgent (Buell, et al., 2001). Innovative partnerships with existing child-care programs are essential to provide sufficient space for child development and family support programs (Koppel, 1995; Poersch and Blank, 1996).

Child Care–Early Head Start Partnerships appear to reinforce each other in providing needed resources for their programs. Child-care programs usually have

| TABLE 7.2 | Child Care Options | | |

Type	Sponsors	Income	Characteristics
PRIVATE: For Profit			
Family Child Care Home	**Individual**	Tuition	Small number of children in home atmosphere. Less monitoring of and support for provider.
Center	Individuals	Tuition	Limited resources; freedom in type of program
Center	Corporation	Tuition	Chain of schools. Goals set by corporation; share resources in purchases, financial management, and curriculum
Employer sponsored	Employer— business, hospital, government agency	Tuition	Parents can visit when on-site or nearby. Possible tax advantage. Business hierarchy must approve general operation.
PRIVATE: Nonprofit			
Religious or philanthropic organization	Religious or philanthropic organization	Tuition Fund-Raising, In-Kind Church Contributions	Religious Child Care board determines policies. Share church facilities. Lower tuition.
Parent Cooperative	Family Members	Fees and Fund-Raising	Parents operate school, usually hiring a director. Parents learn and see their child in relation to others. Low fees.
Laboratory	College or University	Tuition Intuition Support	Model program to provide training for students and quality program for children. Hours and yearly schedule meets institution's needs.
PUBLICLY FUNDED			
Child Care Centers	Local School Districts	Government funds. Tuition— sliding scale	School district hires director and school board sets policy. More money for program and salaries.
Head Start and Early Head Start	Public or private	Government funds, nonprofit agencies	Comprehensive program providing health, education for preschool low-income children and families. Parents' participation required. Better money for program materials and salaries. Higher teacher requirements.

Adapted from Phyllis Click (2000). *Administration of Schools for Young Children*, p. 49–50, important records on their children and families and experience with infants and toddlers. They also provide full-day and full-year programs, which families in job-training programs require. On the other hand, EHS programs provide resources that can enhance the quality of care in these centers, offer professional development, and additional family support. The new programs must meet the performance standards of EHS, and often blend both operations in very creative ways (Buell, et al., 2001).

The **Quality in Linking Together Education Partnerships Project (The Quilt Project)** is cosponsored by the Child Care and Head Start Bureaus in the Administration on Children, Youth and Families. QUILT promotes partnerships between early education programs by providing national and regional training, forums, meetings, and publications (Buell, et al., 2001). There is also Web site assistance (www.quilt.org).

The Nanny Program

The United States nanny is a trained in-home child care specialist. The International Nanny Association (INA) is the oldest nanny organization in the United States. Since 1987 it has worked to educate and train its members to be qualified professionals with high ethical standards, child development knowledge, and the ability to fit into a family, being sensitive and respecting its values. The nanny may live with the family or go to her own home after work. Today the emphasis is for the nanny to be a part of the family. Wages for the nannies are better than for child-care teachers. Many upwardly mobile families employ nannies.

The INA provides support services for their nannies and their references to interested families. The organization consists of nanny employers, placement agencies, and their own educators for the training program.

Contrasting Curriculums: Approaches to Learning

Not only are there a variety of centers for early education and care but the programs in these centers vary according to their beliefs about how children learn best. A model is a framework for content, teaching methods, and evaluation. Different models or programs can be grouped according to the roles given to the teacher and to the child in the learning process. The teacher's role may be that of an initiator who plans and directs the curriculum. The child's role would then be that of a receiver who responds to the teacher's directions and information. In another model, these roles are reversed. The child is the initiator, picking up cues from the environment with the teacher responding, taking cues from the child. Another group of programs represents an interactive approach in which both the teacher and child share, to varying degrees, the initiator role. Each of these approaches has a number of variations. In addition, some curriculum models are designed to improve the overall quality and predictability of early education and care for mainstream programs and other models are designed to improve early education and care for children from low-income families.

Teacher-Initiated Approaches

Teachers plan programs for children using the principles of behaviorism and Skinner's doctrine (Skinner, 1957; see Chapter 7). Children learn from observations and tend to repeat tasks that are reinforced. Children learn or respond to the values and information from adults. These programs have been criticized for a lack of creativity and for a negative effect on children for incorrect answers. The researchers have partially corrected for children's mistakes by teaching the correct responses in a program before the children need the information, reducing errors to approximately 10 to 15 percent. Bereiter and Engelmann developed the DISTAR model at the University of Illinois (1966). This curriculum was designed especially for low-income preschoolers and is found in academic preschools.

Child–Teacher-Initiated Approaches

This open framework encourages both the child and adult to initiate activities that use play as a vehicle for learning. Children learn through direct contact with their environment. They are encouraged to question what is happening and to solve problems. Rather than telling the child that what she or he said about something is wrong, the child might be asked, "What makes you think that?" Often this approach is referred to as cognitive developmental, based on Piaget's theory of cognitive development. Two early models emerged based on Piaget's theory, the Kamii-DeVries approach and the High-Scope Curriculum. Both Kamaii and DeVries studied under Jean Piaget and colleagues at the University of Geneva in 1966 to 1967. The Kamii-DeVries approach relied solely on Piaget's ideas in the beginning whereas the High Scope Curriculum also incorporated the ideas of non-Piagetians (Goffin and Wilson, 2001).

The High-Scope Curriculum was developed by David Weikart and his colleagues, working in Ypsilanti, MI. Their preschool curriculum emerged in 1962 and the K–3 curriculum in 1978, with the hope of alleviating the academic disadvantages of some of Ypsilanti's children (Goffin and Wilson, 2001). This model not only encourages creativity, decision-making skills, and taking responsibility for one's problems, but also lays the foundation for moral development. Other examples of the teacher–child-initiated approach are the British Infant and Primary Schools and Susan Gray's Demonstration and Research Center for Early Education, known as DARCEE.

Child-Initiated Approaches

The Developmental-Interaction approach focuses on the whole child, both the cognitive and the emotional parts. It recognizes the complexity of the child's develop-

Creative Self-Expression and Growth through Play

The child is able to pursue his interests in this child-initiated activity. The teacher is available if the child needs assistance.

ment and interactions with the environment (Goffin and Wislon, 2001). Children choose their own activities and what they want to learn. Teachers act as facilitators and provide a safe and stimulating environment for them, responding to individual needs. Creative self-expression and growth through play are valued. Children's self-confidence and emotional, social, and intellectual development are stressed.

This approach has been influenced by the teachings of Freud, Erikson, and cognitive developmental psychologists such as Piaget, all of whom believe in a stage theory of development. Educational theorists and practitioners such as John Dewey also contributed to this approach (Goffin and Wilson, 2001). The word *model* is avoided because the approach is never static, but open to change. The Bank Street School for Children reflects this approach. Other slight variations are the Tucson Early Educational Model and Nimnicht's Responsive Program.

The Montessori program, based on children's individual self-paced interaction with specially designed materials, is considered child-directed. However, it does have more teacher control than most child-initiated programs. It is based on Marie Montessori's philosophy of respect for children as individuals who must educate themselves rather than adults giving them their ideas. Yet, the materials that children choose are to be used in a specific way and in order of difficulty. Montessori believed that the prepared environment with an emphasis on freedom provided a setting where children could respond to their inner forces without being stifled (Montessori, 1917/1965).

COMPARISON OF PROGRAMS   Schweinhart (1997) believes that recent research suggests that preschool programs based on child-initiated learning activities contribute to children's short- and long-term academic and social development, while those based on teacher-directed lessons produce a short-term advantage in children's academic development but sacrifice the long-term contribution to their social and emotional development.

Findings from the High-Scope Preschool Curriculum Comparison Study (Schweinhart and Weikart, 1997), the Louisville Head Start (Miller and Bizzell,

TABLE 7.3	Contrasting Curriculums: Approaches to Learning	
Teacher-Initiated Direct Instruction	Child-Teacher-Initiated Cognitively Oriented	Child-Initiated Developmental Interaction
Goals and Activities:		
Determined by adults. Programmed materials and curriculum guides researched and sequentially packaged in kits.	Activities and environment set up by teacher according to the interests of the children. Children choose and adapt the activities.	Goals, knowledge, skills determined by the child. Natural activities are encouraged.
Method:		
Teacher directs learning, often in small groups, for desired responses. Rote memory encouraged.	Teacher provides resources, activities, interpersonal support, raises questions, and encourages interactions with the environment.	Child chooses kind and sequence of activities with minimal direction and stimulation from teacher. Teacher is the facilitator and encourages success and self-worth. Child explores and experiments with much freedom.
Motivation:		
External rewards, tangible and intangible.	Child's natural curiosity and some extrinsic rewards.	Primarily intrinsic; child initiated.
Evaluation and Major Learning Results:		
Teacher-made or widely standardized test of specific knowledge. Outcome predictable and high similarity.	Use interviews, behavioral tests, and observational methods. Learner is compared to self primarily and then to peers. Objective skills and knowledge vary.	Essentially self-evaluation based on learner's own goals. Teacher uses descriptive assessment of learner's performance. No peer comparisons. High variability.

1983), and the University of Illinois Study (Karnes, Schwedel, and Williams, 1983), include outcomes for the different approaches to curriculum. Each of these studies includes programs with direct-instruction models and child-initiated models with minimum to moderate teacher direction. The High-Scope programs have more teacher input than do the nursery school models. Table 7.4 shows outcomes for participants in each model.

These studies suggest that preschool programs based on a child-initiated approach with some teacher directions facilitate children's short- and long-term academic and social development whereas programs based on teacher-directed activities show short-term but not long-term academic advantages and fewer emotional or social developmental gains. Other researchers see a cultural influence. For exam-

TABLE 7.4 Long-Term Effects of Curriculum Models			
Participants: Preschoolers to Early Adults	High- Scope	Nursery School	Direct Instruction
1. treated for emotional problems	6%	6%	43%
2. did volunteer work	43%	44%	11%
3. arrested for a felony	10%	NA	39%
4. arrested for a property crime	0%	NA	38%
5. reported over 10 acts of misconduct	23%	NA	56%
6. married and living with their spouse	31%	NA	0%
7. planning to graduate from college	70%	NA	36%
8. arrested for felony at ages 22–23	NA	9%	34%
9. suspended from work	NA	0%	27%

J. Schweinhart and D. P. Weikart. (1997). *Early Childhood Research Quarterly, 12*(2), 117–143. Reprinted with permission from the High/Scope Educational Research Foundation.

ple, some African American and Asian American children appear to learn better in a direct instruction approach to teaching (Delpit, 1995). Perhaps the key to success is not the instructional approach but the commitment of the teacher to a program with clearly defined educational goals and parents who support the program.

The Reggio Emilia Approach to Early Childhood Education *Observation, Documentation, Community Involvement, and the Environment as a Teacher*

The infant–toddler centers and preprimary schools of Reggio Emilia began almost fifty years ago in Italy. The philosophy, teaching methods, and the interests and needs of the children, parents, and the community provide the framework for a program that is always sensitive to current conditions. Teachers are keen observers of the children and involved with parents and the community in exploring the possibilities for new and exciting learning experiences for their children. Children are viewed as having limitless possibilities. The environment is seen as a teacher. The Reggio Emilia philosophy cannot be put in a box with other curriculums. It is not a model and cannot be replicated in a different environment. However, the Reggio Emilia approach to learning and the role of the child, teacher, and community in this process can be adapted to each individual setting (Goffin and Wilson, 2001).

Reggio Emilia schools are part of the public system in the community of Reggio Emilia. They support the child's right to grow and learn in a favorable environment surrounded by caring, professional adults. In addition, their schools support the social needs of families and are an integral part the community (Gandini, 1997).

Interest in the Reggio approach to early childhood education continues to grow in the United States. The National Association for the Education of Young Children has a Reggio Emilia track at their annual conferences. In addition, there are newsletters, publications, conferences, and a quarterly journal, *Innovations in Early Education: The International Reggio Exchange.*

Quality Care

How can children have a high-quality environment in child care? What constitutes high-quality care and how can it be measured? Individual interpretations of quality tend to be subjective and influenced by culture. Parents, teachers, educators, and legislators need to know what the components of "high quality" are, and the relationship between the quality of child care and outcomes for children.

Quality is determined by both its **structural** and **process** characteristics (Kontos, Howes, Shinn, and Galinsky, 1995). The structural components involve the teacher–child ratio, size of the group, staff training, indoor and outdoor space, safety, and facilities. These components set the stage for the process conditions, which involve the experiences and interactions within the child-care center. These conditions include the child's interactions with humans, the materials, and the environment. The support of the staff and the support and interactions of the parents are also part of the process dimension.

Certain features of child care are related to high-quality care and to healthy development. An early national study initiated by the federal government found that the centers with smaller groups, lower adult–child ratios, and teachers with early childhood training were associated with certain children's behaviors such as cooperation, verbal initiative, involvement, and less hostility (Ruopp, Travers, Glantz, and Coclen, 1979) Studies during the 1990s showed a significant correlation between program quality and children's behavior such as cooperative play, sociability, creativity, ability to solve conflicts, self-control, and language and cognitive development (Love, 1998). Other research confirms that high-quality early education and care experiences improve academic performances of all children, but especially low-income children and others at-risk for school failure (Schulman, Blank, and Ewen, 1999).

The National Institute of Child Health and Human Development's (NICHD) study found that the high quality of the provider–child interactions, including the language used, were related to better cognitive and language scores and more positive mother–child interactions for the first three years of life (Love, 1998). The infant–adult ratio was found to be related to the infant's communication skills and high quality was related to his or her cognitive development (Burchinal, Roberts, Nabors, and Bryant, 1996). High-quality care is important for all children regardless of income (Love, 1998).

The National Association for the Education of Young Children has been instrumental in establishing guidelines for high-quality early childhood education and child care. In their 1997 revision of *Developmentally Appropriate Practice in Early Child-*

hood Programs Serving Children Birth through Age 8, editors Bredekamp and Copple have expanded the definition of developmentally appropriate practice to include:

1. the predictable stages of children's development and related skills and capabilities;
2. each child's individual strengths, interests, and needs;
3. respect for the child's cultural background.

A developmentally appropriate curriculum is one in which learning experiences are appropriate for the child's physical, social-emotional, cognitive, and creative needs and it reflects the child's cultural heritage.

Multicultural Environment

Children live in a global society. A quality environment therefore must reflect a culturally sensitive setting where each child is valued for who he or she is. All children learn to appreciate others and their differences and develop a positive self-concept. The setting and everyday materials should reflect different cultures and lifestyles, especially those of the children in the classroom and their community. The environment should be one where children and adults learn to settle their

Look, the Clay Matches Poetri's Arm

Multicultural activities are a part of the daily curriculum at this college lab school. Children see themselves in the curriculum and experience children and teachers from diverse racial/ethnic groups.

TABLE 7.5	Opposing Cultural Values	
■ Independence is the primary goal	■ Interdependence is the primary goal
■ Individual achievement is supported	■ Working together for group achievement is stressed
■ Activities for children are object-oriented	■ Activities for children are people-oriented
■ Provide educational toys for learning	■ Children learn from daily activities with people
■ Lay babies on the floor or set toys in front of babies	■ Babies are held much of the time
■ Child-centered learning is valued	■ Academic preparedness is valued
■ Children learn through play and activities	■ Children are taught academic skills and the value of work
■ Discipline is to teach self-control	■ Discipline is to teach respect for authority
■ Adults help children gain inner or self-control	■ Adults teach what is acceptable behavior, monitor child's actions, and use external rewards
■ Encourage children to solve problems	■ Adults usually adjudicate conflicts
■ Encourage open expression of emotions	■ Encourage regulation and control of emotions
■ Express feelings, learn acceptable behavior, and discuss feelings with adults	■ Control emotions and subordinate feelings to the harmony of the group

Source. J. Bromer. (1999). Cultural variations in child care: Values and actions. *Young Children, 54*(6), 72–75. Used by permission.

conflicts in peaceful ways. (This is developed in Chapter 12 on *Violence . . . and Peaceful Alternatives.*)

Values for socialization vary in different cultures as do the practices supporting these values. In our multicultural society, child-care teachers will encounter many differences in parental expectations for their children. Some cultural values are similar, some mutually exclusive, while others differ but could be held simultaneously. Table 7.5 lists contrasting pairs of values that parents or teachers support to varying degrees.

Anti-Bias Environment

Louise Derman-Sparks and the ABC Task Force of early childhood educators provide ideas for an anti-bias curriculum. Their book, *Anti-Bias Curriculum: Tools for Empowering Young Children* (1992), helps teachers create an environment that is rich in possibilities for exploring gender, race/ethnicity, and different-ableness. Societal stereotyping and bias affect children's self-concept and attitudes toward others. An anti-bias curriculum helps them and their teachers develop critical thinking and problem-solving skills. Four anti-bias curriculum goals from this book should be reflected in the daily activities in a developmentally appropriate way (1992).

ANTI-BIAS EDUCATION GOALS   The underlying intent of anti-bias education is to foster the development of children and adults who have the personal strength, critical thinking ability, and activist skills to work with others to build caring, just, and diverse communities and societies for all.

(1) **Nurture each child's construction of a knowledgeable, confident self-only concept and group identity.**
This goal means creating the educational conditions in which all children are able to like who they are without needing to feel superior to anyone. It also means enabling children to develop biculturally—to be able to interact effectively within their home culture and the dominant culture.

(2) **Promote each child's comfortable, empathic interaction with people from diverse backgrounds.**
This goal means guiding children's development of the cognitive awareness, emotional disposition, and behavioral skills needed to respectfully and effectively learn about differences, comfortably negotiate and adapt to differences, and cognitively understand and emotionally accept the common humanity that all people share.

(3) **Foster each child's critical thinking about bias.**
This goal means guiding children's development of the cognitive skills to identify "unfair" and "untrue" images (stereotypes), comments (teasing, name-calling), and behaviors (discrimination) directed at one's own or others' identities (be they gender, race, ethnicity, disability, class, age, weight, etc.), *and* having the emotional empathy to know that bias hurts.

(4) **Cultivate each child's ability to stand up for her- or himself and for others in the face of bias.**
This "activism" goal includes helping every child learn and practice a variety of ways to act: (a) when another child acts in a biased manner toward her or him, (b) when a child acts in a biased manner toward another child, (c) when an adult acts in a biased manner. Goal four builds on goal three: Critical thinking and empathy are necessary components of acting for oneself or others in the face of bias.

These goals are for *all* children and interact with each other. The specific tasks and strategies used will depend on children's backgrounds, ages, and life experiences. Permission from Louise Devman Sparks, Co-Director of Equity Alliance (2002).

SPECIAL NEEDS CHILDREN   In 1992, the American with Disabilities Act (ADA) became law. One of its provisions prohibits all public accommodations, including nursery schools, child-care centers, and family child-care homes from discriminating against any individual because of a disability. Chapter 9 considers the inclusion of special needs children.

How Can High-Quality Care Be Measured?

As a profession, we have been slow to formalize the criteria to be used in determining a high-quality program for young children. All fifty states and the District of Columbia have minimum legal requirements for center programs for young children, but these requirements vary greatly. For example, thirty-two states do not require teachers in child-care centers to have any early childhood training prior to serving children, even though approximately 1,500 hours of training at accredited schools is required to be a licensed hair cutter or manicurist (Children's Defense Fund, 1999). Although minimum legal requirements help, they are not criteria for high quality.

We need a national policy for minimum standards for child care. Beyond this, there must be national guidelines for assessing the level of the quality of care. Most professionals agree on certain basic conditions and have been working through professional organizations to establish these conditions.

Voluntary Accreditation of Child-Care Programs

In 1984 the NAEYC (National Association for the Education of Young Children) formed a new division, the **National Academy of Early Childhood Programs,** to provide a national voluntary accreditation system for center-based programs. The accreditation system is based on a three-step process:

1. self-study by the center's director, teachers, and parents;
2. a validation visit by academy-trained local professionals;
3. the accreditation decision by a three-person commission of nationally recognized childhood educators who are from diverse backgrounds and have practical experience.

The accreditation process involves most aspects of the program. It includes interaction among staff, parents, and children, parent involvement, the curriculum, staff qualifications and continuing training, staff–child ratios, health and safety, nutrition and food service, and administration. This accreditation should help parents choose a high-quality center.

The **National Association for Family Child Care (NAFCC)** has provided a voluntary accreditation process for Family Child Care Providers since 1988. First, the provider must meet all state licensing requirements. The process involves a self-study portion for the provider and parents, and validators' observation. The evaluation includes an assessment profile for the family child-care provider, parent

TABLE 7.6	Ratings of Centers
The Cost, Quality, and Child Outcomes Study (CQO, 1995) rated 400 centers in four states.	
Infant care classrooms:	8% rated good or excellent and 40% rated poor
Preschool classrooms:	24% rated good or excellent and 10% rated poor
Child-care staff:	36% bachelor's degree or higher.
Infant childcare providers:	18% had bachelor's degree or higher and 33 1/3% had no specialized training in child development

(National Institute of Child Health and Human Development, 1996).

questionnaires, and a provider's report. The accreditation is for three years with annual updates.

High-quality, affordable, and available early education and care must be a high priority for society in order for conditions to change. This would require basic government regulations for child-care centers and family child-care homes. It is not sufficient to have this on a voluntary basis. High-quality programs cost money. In order to find competent students willing to invest in an early childhood education, teachers must have adequate salaries to support themselves now and in the future. The wages and benefits for staff are among the lowest of all U.S. workers. It is easy to understand why the staff turnover rates each year range from 25 percent to 50 percent (Love, 1998). Liability insurance for child-care providers must be available and affordable. It will take parents, teachers, businesses, volunteer groups, and government working together to promote high-quality care and find the moneys needed.

Military and Nonmilitary Child Care

The Department of Defense is the largest employer-sponsored child-care provider in the nation, serving 200,000 children worldwide. Their child care services were criticized ten years ago but today military child care is superior to that in any state (Campbell, Applebaum, Martinson, and Martin, 2000). In the last ten years, the Department of Defense has built a comprehensive system of child-care centers, family child-care homes, and resource and referral services for military families. When space is available, civilian employees are also eligible.

In 1989, the Military Child Care Act mandated the development of a system of quality child-care services. Money was appropriated for this every year. The military focused on quality rather than quantity, even though it meant fewer children at first. For quality, they used the guidelines of the NAEYC's National Academy for Early Childhood Programs. Today, over 95 percent of their child-care centers are accredited by the National Academy. Each center has a curriculum specialist

TABLE 7.7	Military and Non-Military Child Care	
	Military	**Nonmilitary**
Accreditation	95% of all centers	8% of all centers
Starting pay	$8 an hour, raised to $10 in two years; full benefits	Average wage in centers is $7.40 an hour, benefits vary
Training	Basic preservice training and 13 additional course units linked to pay increases	No pretraining required in 31 states in centers and 41 states for family child-care homes
Fees	Sliding scale fees. $3,640 average annual fee. Subsidies to all parents to cover costs	Annual average ranges from $3,342 in Birmingham, AL to $7,904 in Boston

Sources: National Women's Law Center.

whose only job is to provide staff training and monitor the quality of the program. Because staff stability is important, the military restructured and raised staff salaries and provided health benefits. Instead of 300 percent staff turnover, military facilities now have 30 percent, largely due to transfers. Their programs are supported by parent fees based on a sliding scale and a Department of Defense annual subsidy. The military believes that supporting children and families is not only vital to the future lives of these children but also to enlisting and maintaining people in the military (Campbell, Applebaum, Martinson, and Martin, 2000).

Although there are differences between the private sector and the military, there are many common problems both sectors face. The military has a Web page listing many of their best practices. They also have established a speakers' bureau.

Parent Involvement

Parents are an essential component of any child-care arrangement but are an integral part of a high-quality program. When parents can work with the teachers and caregivers, it is possible to provide an integrated twenty-four-hour plan for their child's continuous and optimal development. Parents, teachers, caregivers, and the child each support the responses and actions of the other. Valuing each of these partners allows for a more appropriate and supportive environment for the child and a more satisfying feeling of accomplishment for each. See Chapter 9 for extensive information on parent involvement in the school and parent–teacher partnerships.

To encourage fathers' involvement in child-care programs, fathers' interests and concerns must be addressed. According to a survey taken in four different types of

NAEYC-accredited child-care programs in six states, fathers participated the most in family activities. This was followed by Daddy and Me programs, activities for both parents to learn about their children, activities for both parents about child development, and sporting events (Turbiville, Umbarger, and Guthrie, 2000). Fathers also liked being asked personally to participate in some part of the program and to know that their efforts were appreciated (Turbiville, et al., 2000).

Building Blocks for Good Relationships between Parents and Teachers

Will parents consider the teacher their adversary or their colleague? Building good relationships takes effort and time. The quality of the communication is central to the quality of the relationship. Being able to share information freely is important for parents, teachers, and children. The process is like playing ping pong. Two or more players take turns hitting and returning the ball. When one player dominates, the game is soon over, with the winner possibly feeling superior. How does the loser feel and will that person continue to play?

When both parties agree, it is easier to talk about a problem or a course of action. Sometimes what may be a serious problem or the best course of action to one person may be seen very differently by the other person. When parents and teachers disagree, it is difficult but crucial that, in the end, each one feels understood and the solution reflects both of their feelings. The following are guidelines for teachers in working with parents:

1. **Establish contacts on different levels.** Learn the parents' names and information on which to comment. This shows your interest in the parents and family.
2. **Work on establishing trust.** Parents need to rely on information and agreements the teacher or the school makes. They need to feel that the teacher has their child's best interests in mind when making curriculum decisions or adjudicating peer problems. Writing out messages or agreements can avoid misunderstandings.
3. **Develop an appreciation and respect for every parent.** Communicate your feelings to each parent with appropriate comments and take time to listen. Treat parents as equal partners.
4. **Establish open communications.** Parents and teachers are able to be honest in their discussions. They are free to agree or praise, which is easy, but they must also be able to disagree and criticize. It is essential that both parties listen to each other. Teachers should use descriptive language rather than language that is judgmental.
5. **Jointly identify and work on common goals for the child.** If parents' ideas are a part of the plan for change, they are more likely to carry it through at home. In addition, this helps the parents to work out their own solutions in the future.

6. **In discussing a problem, convey to the parents your concern for their child's welfare.** Use descriptive language in explaining behavior. "This behavior leads to other children's responses that are not good for Johnny. I would like to help Johnny find ways, other than hitting, to convey anger . . . I also do not want any child to be hit."

Stumbling Blocks

The following actions will close down communications. Often anger and hurt feelings occur.

1. **Blaming** each other for the problem, either verbally or through body language, blocks communication. Teachers may identify with the child and fail to see the situation from the family's eyes, while parents may see the problem only from their position.
2. **Power struggles** result in winners and losers. This creates additional problems for the winners as well as the losers.
3. **Distrust** of someone or not believing their promises makes it difficult to work together effectively.
4. **Language** that is confusing causes misunderstandings. The teacher's use of educational jargon is a quick way to turn off a parent. Words and gestures can have different meanings in another culture.

Parent–Teacher Conferences

Most schools require individual parent–teacher conferences to be arranged periodically to discuss a child's academic progress, social development, and special behavior problems. (The term *parents* will be used to include parents, stepparents, and parent substitutes.) Some parents dread these conferences for various reasons. If they see the child as an extension of themselves, they take any criticism personally. Parents may be shy, or feel inadequate about their language or educational level. They may also be reluctant to express themselves critically for fear of conscious or unconscious reprisals to their child. Perhaps calling these conferences progress report meetings and beginning with areas of strength would help. It is important that the parents be asked to bring their questions. The following are suggestions for a successful conference:

1. Prepare ahead of time. Collect samples of work, develop an agenda and time line, allowing time for parents' responses and concerns.
2. Choose a time convenient for parents.
3. Find a comfortable setting away from interruptions and power symbols such as a desk. Watch your body language. For example, leaning forward and open hands show listening and concern or approval in mainstream culture but maybe not in the parent's culture. Eye contact should be at the parent's comfort level.

4. Greet parents with appreciation for their coming and say something positive about the child.
5. Show concern for the parents and child.
6. Share the agenda and time line and ask if they have any additions.
7. Be simple, direct, and explain the program or project that is being discussed. Use descriptive language and avoid being judgmental. Share backup material to support comments.
8. Work out a joint plan with the parents to deal with a problem or to promote further progress. Set up guidelines including a time table and method for follow-up. If parents share ideas, including what could be done at home, incorporate as much as feasible into the plan. If parents help develop the plan, they are more likely to follow through. This also empowers parents to solve other problems.
9. Again ask parents if they have other items they would like to discuss now or at another time.
10. Sum up what was covered and what each person is to do.
11. Share some positive things about the child, thank the parents for their help, and express your pleasure in working together for their child's success.
12. Evaluate and record the conference immediately afterward or as soon as possible. Were all topics covered? What was the comfort level of each parent? List possible improvements or suggestions for the next meeting. Include any work plan for parents and teacher.

What Parents Should Look for in Child Care

GOOD HUMAN RELATIONSHIPS AMONG STAFF, CHILDREN, PARENTS   Basic to the type of care children receive are the personal traits and educational background of the caregivers. A warm, nurturing adult who has a knowledge of how children grow and develop, and an understanding of the needs and interests of individual children, is essential for high-quality care. Children are valued for themselves and not for what they do or how they look. Good caregivers tend to view children positively and help them learn what to do rather than focusing on what not to do. They help children learn to take responsibility for their own actions and eventually develop self-discipline. Rules should be reasonable, consistent, and well explained. Children are treated with respect. When caregivers view themselves positively and feel good about their work, they model a good self-image for the children.

It is essential for caregivers and teachers to help parents feel a part of the program. Home and school should share information in order to understand more fully a child's needs and provide the best coordinated twenty-four-hour schedules for the child. Parents can share important family values, goals for their child, methods of discipline, and changes in the child's home environment while teachers can share the program goals, special activities for the child, weekly plans, and how they believe children learn. Teachers should utilize appropriate community resources for the school and help parents find needed resources. (Parent–Teacher relationships are discussed in Chapter 9 on schooling.)

Good relationships among staff members are important. If the children see adults working together cooperatively and solving problems successfully, they will learn to use some of these skills. All staff members must maintain professional ethics, which includes protecting the privacy of the children and families in their program.

REGULATIONS, FACILITIES, AND PROGRAM ACTIVITIES   Licensing of child-care centers and family child-care homes gives parents some protection. To determine which regulations apply in the area, contact the local or state department of health or social welfare. States vary in their requirements for the facilities and the staff. Criminal clearance of caregivers, health and safely regulations, and child–adult ratios are usually included. Many states have no special educational requirements for their family child-care providers and, as mentioned earlier in this chapter, thirty-two states require *no* prior training for teachers in centers (Children's Defense Fund, 1998).

The adult–child ratio affects the individual attention given to each child and the group size affects the interactions of children. The National Academy of Early Childhood Programs accreditation advocates the following standards. Ages of children are followed by adult-to-child ratio and group size.

Age	Adult–Child Ratio and Group Size
Infants and toddlers 0 to 24 mo.	1:3 for 6 children; 1:4 for 8 children One teacher and one assistant for each group
Two-year-olds	1:4 for 8 children; 1:5 for 10; 1:6 for 12
Two- and three-year-olds	1:5 for 10 children; 1:6 for 12; 1:7 (14)
Three-year-olds, four-year-olds, or four- and five-year-olds	1:7 for 14 children; 1:8 for 16; 1:9 for 18; 1:10 for 20
Five-year-olds	1:8 for 16 children; 1:9 for 18; 1:10 for 20
Six- to eight-year-olds (school-age)	1:10 for 20 children; 1:11 for 22; 1:12 for 24

Multi-age grouping is permissible and often encouraged. The staff–child ratio and group size requirements are based on the age of the majority of children, but when infants are included, ratios and group size for the infants must be maintained (NAEYC, 1984).

It is essential that parents visit a center and talk with the director, teachers, and children before enrolling their child. The school should welcome unannounced visits. The parents must check for safety in the total environment. Is the equipment appropriate and in good condition? Are gates latched so children cannot get out? Are activities well supervised? The child should also visit the program before being enrolled.

There should be a variety of developmentally and culturally appropriate activities as well as equipment and materials so that each child can develop in all areas—physical, social, intellectual, emotional, and creative. Physical development includes large and small motor skills and health issues. Particular attention should be paid to routines such as eating, toileting, and resting. Intellectual development involves the acquisition of language skills as well as general knowledge about one's "world" and how to function in daily tasks.

Children need opportunities to play and work with other children as well as to play and work alone. Activities should be balanced between active and quiet play both indoors and outside. Some activities should be teacher-directed while others should be selected by the child. The transition times between activities should be relaxed and provide pleasant learning experiences.

Learning centers should reflect children's families, cultures, and interests. Learning centers should include table-top activities with manipulative materials, activities with housekeeping props, dramatic play, books and quiet corner, music and movement, art and creative activities, cooking and science areas, and a block area. Look for outdoor climbing equipment, space to run, wheel toys, sensory motor activities such as obstacle courses, balls, beanbags, and hoops. Children need carpentry, gardening, and ample sand, water, and mud play. There should be nature walks and trips away from the center. (See *How to Choose a Good Early Childhood Program* by the National Association for the Education of Young Children, 1990.)

CHILDREN'S VIEW OF A CHILD-CARE CENTER OR A CAREGIVER'S HOME   Who will take care of me? Will I be safe? What will I eat? Where will I go to the toilet? Where will I sleep? Who will be my friend? Judging the quality of a program from a child's point of view is what Lillian Katz calls from the bottom up approach (Katz, 1993).

Homeless Children and High-Quality, Comprehensive Child Care

Homeless young children need health care, a safe and permanent living space, and quality comprehensive child care where they relate to other adults and children while engaging in developmentally appropriate activities. They need to make choices, internalize healthy values, and experiment in a safe supportive environment. A comprehensive program helps the family meet the needs of their children.

An effective child-care program must be sensitive to the needs and concerns of the parents. Many homeless parents are reluctant to enter the system for fear their children will be removed from them on abuse or neglect charges. This concern must be addressed. Teachers should have an empathetic and understanding view of homeless families. Parents' sensitivity to many routine questions must also be respected. Homeless parents and all parents should interact with the school to share in their child's educational needs. Parents should be exposed to positive ways to discipline.

Many homeless parents need help in finding a job or a job-training program, temporary or permanent housing, and medical care. Often other agencies or groups in a community will provide such assistance. Coordination of agencies is essential.

Health care is crucial to the child's success in preschool. Most homeless children have unmet medical needs. Some need immunizations. A transition room in the child-care center has been found to be helpful in meeting the physical and emotional needs of these children. In a transition room the children can become comfortable in this new environment, receive individual attention, and reduce some of their fears about school. In some of these model programs, children from the regular classrooms visit the children in the transition room. This helps homeless children make a more successful adjustment to the preschool program. Since 1992 Head Start has enabled some homeless children in shelters to attend a Head Start program. Providing transportation has been essential, including transferring the child to another Head Start program when the family moves.

Can Early Childhood Education Intervention Make a Lasting Difference?

High-quality early childhood education intervention does make a difference in the performances and lives of children from poor families, but it took broad-based longitudinal studies to prove this. The early studies (1964–1970) compared children from low socioeconomic homes in various Head Start programs with control groups from similar backgrounds but without preschool experience. (See Head Start programs in this chapter.) Although the purpose was to measure changes in behavior or development in children, the early studies concentrated on children's IQ scores. The children in the experimental preschool programs showed IQ gains compared to the control group without preschool experience but these gains lasted for only one to three years after the program (Schweinhart and Weikart, 1997).

The short- and long-term effects of high-quality early childhood education and care for poor children was validated by the Consortium on Developmental Continuity Study (Lazar, 1977; Lazar and Darlington, 1982), along with studies by Schweinhart and Weikart detailed in *Children Grow Up* (1980), and by Gray and colleagues in *From 3 to 20* (Gray, Ramsey, and Klaus, 1982). These longitudinal studies, which began in the 1970s, were much broader in scope than earlier ones measuring IQ Lazar's study, which included material from Gray's and Weikart's works, followed participants from a number of experimental infant and preschool programs in the 1960s. In 1977, as many of these children as could be found were retested on the Wechsler Intelligence Test and interviewed extensively. In the majority of the projects, there was no IQ difference in the test scores between the adolescents who had this preschool experience and those who did not. However, there were other differences in their school performances. *Only a small percentage of children in these experimental preschool programs ever repeated a grade in school or were placed in a class for mentally retarded (special needs) children compared to a much higher percentage of children from the control group.*

There was some limited evidence that children's motivation, values, aspirations, and coping styles were influenced and that these families increased their aspirations for their children. None of this was found for the control children. Although the curriculum approaches differed, there was a strong parent component in all these programs

Those who have worked in programs with young children never doubted the value of high-quality preschool experience for children, but the general public and legislators needed to see their value as more than "baby sitting."

School-Age Children and Out-of School Care

Latchkey or Self-Care Children

Latchkey children are those left alone regularly for some portion of the day. The term *latchkey* comes from the use of a tool to lift the latch to open a door. Almost 7 million children ages five to fourteen care for themselves regularly without adult supervision (Snyder and Sickmund, 1999). Nearly one in ten children between ages five and eleven goes home after school to an empty house during some part of each week (Children's Defense Fund, 2001). Latchkey children are vulnerable to delinquency, vandalism, drug use, injury, and even rape (Collins, Harris, and Susman, 1995). Those children who are restricted to their home without a friend lack normal after-school activities and socialization. Latchkey children compared to their peers report feeling afraid regardless of their age, abilities, or assurances by parents (Long and Long, 1982).

Today the term *self-care* is used rather than *latchkey*. Self-care includes children who stay home alone, stay home with siblings, and, in some statistics, those who stay in public places such as the library or a park, without any adult responsible for their supervision. Some families feel that they have no choice but self-care for their children, even when they are very young or fearful when alone. Usually the choice of self-care is related to the child's own characteristics including age, family circumstances, and safety of the neighborhood. In interviews with parents and children, Belle (1997) found that a number of factors were involved in choosing self-care. These included the child's preferences, the absence of age-appropriate programs, and availability of extended family.

Children frequently in self-care include children whose parents feel that they are quite capable, have few fears, and don't want structured programs. Boys more often than girls are in self-care. Self-care is more likely in White, non-Hispanic families with higher incomes and more educated mothers. On the other hand, low-income, employed single mothers use sibling care as the most common form of child care, even for four- to seven-year-old children (Miller, O'Connor, and Sirignono, 1995).

Self-care is usually introduced gradually. Typically the time children are left alone during the week increases with the age of the child. It starts with approximately ten minutes for first graders to two hours a week for fifth graders (Posner and Vandell, 1994). For many children, it is not until middle school that self-care becomes their primary care arrangement (Vandell and Su, 1999).

SELF-CARE AND DEVELOPMENTAL OUTCOMES   According to recent research, the effects of self-care are especially detrimental to children who are younger, with a history of problems, from low-income families, left unsupervised with peers, or living in unsafe neighborhoods (Marshall, et al., 1997; Pettit, Laird, Bates, and Dodge, 1997). In a study of 466 sixth graders, those children who, according to parents, had spent more time alone in first and third grades were less socially competent and had lower grades and achievement test scores in sixth grade compared to their classmates who had spent less time unsupervised in grades one and three. Having unsupervised time with peers in first and third grades was also related to problem behaviors at the time and in sixth grade. The amount of self-care in fifth grade was unrelated to children's behavior or school performance. The amount of time in sibling care showed no effects on children's adjustment (Pettit et al., 1997). Older children and adolescents who spend time unsupervised with peers have consistently been linked to problem behavior and misconduct (Vandell and Su, 1999).

Parents, schools, and communities have been working together to aid children who spend time at home alone. Often hotlines are available for self-care children. Some services require them to check in when they arrive at home and their parent is only notified when there is a problem. There are manuals on how to be safe at home and how to deal with emergencies or problems. In some cases, neighbors may be available if needed.

School-Age Child Care or Out-of-School Care

During World War II, after-school care was provided for children whose mothers worked, children of families with low incomes, and those in high crime areas. Although these same conditions have existed for over twenty years, only recently has the concern for age-appropriate and affordable out-of-school care been in the national spotlight.

Besides meeting the needs of children of employed parents, society is turning to out-of-school programs for help with education, socialization, and safety. Out-of-school programs are seen as one way to improve the school performances of many children and protect them from perpetrating or being victims of crime during the high-crime after-school hours. Education reform has increased pressure on schools and communities to do a better job of educating all children.

A powerful group working for out-of-school services is the National Institute on Out-of-School Time (NIOST) at the Center for Research on Women at Welles-ley College. Since 1979, they have been educating the public and federal, state, and local governments of the need for out-of-school programs. The NIOST group has been instrumental in many improvements. In 1997, a White House Conference on out-of-school care brought people together from diverse backgrounds to brain-storm the need for out-of-school services for children.

School-age child-care programs may be center-based, home-based, school-based, or through parks and recreation departments. Their programs may be before and/or after school hours, during holidays, or summer vacation. Some are enrich-ment programs while others combine homework and a variety of activities. The school setting has been popular because of the indoor and outdoor space and equipment. Some communities use empty classrooms for a combination of all-day child care for preschoolers and programs for school-age children. Some private preschools have expanded to include programs for older children. Religious insti-tutions and other philanthropic groups such as the YWCA or YMCA also provide out-of-school programs for older children.

Funding and Partnerships

> After-school care costs approximately $3,000 per child per year.
>
> Each new juvenile correction facility costs approximately $102,000 per bed to build.
> — Children's Defense Fund, 1998

Most funding for out-of-school or enrichment programs has been through tuition and fees. This prevents children from low-income families partic-ipating unless they can be subsidized. In 1998 the U.S. Department of Education distributed $40 mil-lion in grants to schools or school districts nation-ally for out-of-school programs. Federal funds for school-age care are also available through the Child Care and Development Block Grant and the new 21st Century Community Learning Centers (CCLC) for School-Age Services. CCLC programs work in collaboration with other public and private agencies and schools serving over 1.2 million children in every state. The 2003 federal fund-ing was frozen at $1 billion and, in 2002, only 11 percent of the grant requests could be funded (Juvenile Justice and Delinquency Prevention Coalition, 2002). In addi-tion, some states have enacted legislation providing financial support and regula-tions for the safety and quality of out-of-school programs. Recent efforts of the private sector to provide money and to form partnerships have increased the num-ber of slots available and in some cases raised the quality of programs.

Since 1993, the DeWitt-Wallace-Reader's Digest has supported school-age care in Boston, Chicago, and Seattle. The Fund's *Making the Most of Out-of-School Time (MOST)* initiative has increased the number of slots available in these three cities and focused on guidelines for quality and affordability, Their funds are used to expand current programs and develop new ones. They are involved in an extensive evaluation project.

SAN DIEGO'S AFTER-SCHOOL PROGRAMS   The city of San Diego is offering a before and after school program in each of its 194 elementary and middle schools. The 6 A.M. to 6 P.M. program began in 1998 serving 2,000 children and in the fall of 2001 served approximately 25,000 children. The activities include help with homework, tutoring and mentoring, arts and crafts, music, drama, sports programs, and other recreational activities. The funds come from California's After-School Learning and Safe Neighborhoods Partnership program, which requires city matching funds, tobacco funds, the city's general fund, and the federal 21st Century Community Learning Centers matching funds (Children's Defense Fund, 2001).

Defining High Quality in School-Age Child Care

Children benefit from a high-quality program. A number of research studies have linked certain characteristics of a program to children's school performance, behavior, and self-esteem. Perhaps the most important predictor of positive effects on children is the nature of the interactions between staff and children. Rosenthal and Vandell (1996) found this crucial for improving reading scores and self-esteem. Other studies found that low adult–child ratios, individual attention from caring adults, and more frequent participation in programs produced positive results in school performance and behavior (U.S. Department of Education and Justice, 1998). Low-income children in formal after-school programs showed greater academic achievement and social adjustment than their peers in their mother's care, babysitter/other adult in child's home, or self-care (Posner and Vandell, 1994).

The National School-Age Care Alliance (NSACA) has identified standards for high-quality programs and developed a national accreditation program. Under each of these standards are a number of criteria for quality.

STANDARDS OF HIGH-QUALITY CARE AND ACCREDITATION
Human Relationships: Staff members must be able to relate to the children and their parents and coordinate the needs of families, children, and the center into the program. Beyond this, they have the communication skills to enable the children to interact positively with each other.

Environment: Both indoor and outdoor space is available for chlidren to pursue a variety of activities that stimulate both intellectual and physical needs at their skill levels. There are opportunities for individual and group experiences as well as private time.

Activities: Children have a variety of choices and a flexible schedule to pursue hobbies, learn new skills, do homework, or read quietly as needed.

Safety, Health, and Nutrition: Provide a safe, secure environment where children have adequate supervision to pursue activities and staff members have first-aid training. Children are given healthy, appealing snacks.

Administration: Provide staff members with access to training and professional development regarding the program, human resources, community resources, and financial aspects of the program.

A major problem for quality care is the shortage of qualified staff and the high (35 percent) staff turnover each year. In 1999, the wages for most staff members range from $5 to $7 per hour and for coordinators and directors $8 to $15 per hour, with few if any benefits. Many colleges, especially community colleges, offer degree or certificate programs for out-of-school child-care (after-school). A few states require a school-age teaching credential while other states are working on some form of credentialing (Nilsen, 1999).

Accreditation: Using these standards for quality, NSACA developed a national accreditation program. Their accreditation program is based on a process of program assessment and of self-improvement (National School-Age Care Alliance, 1997).

In the fall of 1998, the first out-of-school programs received NSACA accreditation. Perhaps accreditation and new or future state requirements will force a more equitable wage scale for the staff and, therefore, a more stable program.

Community Planning

School-age child care has no single home or agency responsible for it at any level of government. It may be attached to child care, the public school system, or private entities. Many private and public groups and agencies must work together for a community to develop integrated system of out-of-school services for school-age children. An effective plan starts with an assessment of the out-of-school needs of families and school-age children and proposes a variety of programs to meet these needs. Sources of funding are included and directions for monitoring the programs in terms of fostering children's developmental needs and not just their safety (Seligson, 2001).

Providing high-quality child-care programs for all ages is the responsibility of all citizens in the community. Quality care/education benefits the children and their families as well as the community.

Early Childhood Education and Care for the Twenty-First Century

The early education component of child care needs to be stressed. Progress has been made in promoting child care for working parents, but the overall quality of care must be improved. Strong research shows the importance of both the early

7.1 The Teapot Curriculum of the Wisconsin Child Care Information Center

The Wisconsin Child Care Information Center (CCIC) provides a statewide special electronic library offering information and multicultural resources in early child care and education for professional development. It also supports informal continuing education curriculums through the quarterly newsletter. The free CCIC lending service credits child-care workers using the library materials with continuing education hours toward child-care relicensing (Haddal, 2001).

years on learning and of high-quality child care. Next to the family, child care is the setting in which children spend much time and learn (Shonkoff and Phillips, 2000; Bowman, Donovan, and Burns, 2000). In addition, increased emphasis must be placed on recognizing and promoting the importance of family support (Lombardi, 2001). Research also shows the benefits of outside support. Although there have been recent increases in federal funding through the Child Care Development Fund, Head Start, and other programs, it is crucial to find other funding sources and develop more partnerships. High staff turnover for child-care programs will only change if the staff can consider this a viable career with adequate pay, professional development, and security. Lombardi (2000) lists four components essential to redesigning child care for the twenty-first century:

1. neighborhood learning programs;
2. a community support system for high-quality care;
3. reinvented financial assistance; and
4. a career development system.

The state of Wisconsin is supporting child-care professionals, families, and children through the projects of the Wisconsin Child Care Information Center.

If early childhood education and care became a high priority in our society and families could find high-quality child care that was accessible and affordable, the results would be **healthier children, families, and society.**

Key Points

1. Recent research on brain development in the first years of life has increased the awareness and need for high-quality, affordable early education and care.
2. The impact of a mother's employment on her children is affected by the quality of and her satisfaction with the child-care program, her relationship to her job, and the roles of the father or other family members in the home.
3. Children who attend child-care centers are generally more self-confident, outgoing, socially competent, and more aggressive with peers and adults than home-care children.
4. High-quality early childhood education intervention programs improve the performances (not on IQ tests) and lives of children from low socioeconomic families.
5. A family child-care home serves a limited number of children including the caregiver's children and often is not licensed. Programs in

child-care centers are licensed and have teachers with varying units of early childhood education. They differ in purpose, funding sources, and type of sponsorship.

6. Head Start is a comprehensive, intervention program serving children ages three to five from low-income families. Early Head Start comprehensive programs provide child care and family support for infants and toddlers.

7. Programs differ in their approach to learning according to the roles of the teacher and child. A teacher may initiate, plan, and direct the curriculum and the child responds. In other programs, the child initiates the activities to varying degrees and the teacher is the facilitator. Outcomes for children vary.

8. High-quality child care depends on low adult–child ratios, qualified teachers, good human relationships, and safe but challenging facilities with a variety of appropriate equipment and materials. Activities should be developmentally and culturally appropriate. Military child-care facilities have higher standards than the private sector.

9. The National Academy of Early Childhood Programs provides a voluntary accreditation system for center-based programs.

10. High-quality school-age child-care programs provide a safe environment, a variety of activities, and a setting encouraging good behavior and improving academic skills and self-esteem.

Critical Thinking Questions

1. What do you think are some positive things to do when a teacher/caregiver faces a cultural conflict among the children?

2. Discuss practical ways in which the community can provide resources for teachers and/or parents.

3. How might your cultural background affect your role as a teacher and how you relate to the children?

4. What are some steps that could be taken to lead to child care and education systems with

high quality, accessibility, affordability and where the staff has equitable compensation?

 ## Resources and References

BrainWorks: Helping Babies Grow and Develop
http: www.zerotothree.org/brain/wonders/index

Educational Resources Information Center's Clearinghouse on Elementary and Early Childhood Education (ERIC/ECE)
http://ericccec.org/

Families and Work Institute
http://www.familiesandwork.org

International Nanny Association
http//www.nanny.org

Military Child Care
http://dticaw.dtic.mil/milchild

National Association for the Education of Young Children
http://www.naeyc.org/naeyc/

National Association for Family Child Care
http://www.nafcc.org/

National Child Care Information Center
http://nccic.org/abtnccic.html

National Institute on Out-of-School Time
http://www.wellesley.edu/WCW/CRW/SAC

National Women's Law Center
info@nwlc.org

Quality Afterschool Learning
http://www.ed.gov/pubs

World Organization for Early Childhood Education (OMEP)
http://omepusnc.org

■ Related Readings

Andrews, J. (1998). *Very last first time*. Aladdin (grades P–2).

Bodrova, E., and Leong, D. J. (1996). *Tools of the mind: The Vygotskian approach to early childhood education*. Columbus, OH: Merrill/Prentice-Hall.

Boocock, S., Barnett, W., and Frede, E. (2001). Long-term outcomes of early childhood programs in other nations: Lessons for Americans. *Young Children, 56*(5), 43–50.

Cartwright, S. (1999). What makes good preschool years? *Young Children, 54*(4), 4–7.

Edwards, C., Gamdini, L., and Forman, G. (Eds.). (1998). *The hundred languages of children: The Reggio Emilia approach—advanced reflection* (2nd ed.). Greenwich, CT: Ablex.

Fromberg, D. P. (2002). *Play and meaning in early childhood education.* Boston: Allyn and Bacon.

McLead, J., and Kilpatrick, K. M. (2001). Exploring science at the museum. *Educational Leadership* (April), 59–63.

■ References

Ainsworth, M. (1973). The development of infant–mother attachment. In N. B. Caldwell and H. Ricciuti (Ed.), *Review of child development research, vol. 3.* Chicago: University of Chicago Press.

Bates, J. E., Marvinney, D., Kelly, T., Dodge, K. A., Bennett, D. S., and Pettit, G. S. (1994). Child-care history and kindergarten adjustment. *Developmental Psychology, 30,* 690–700.

Baydar, N, and Brooks-Gunn, J. (1991). Effects of maternal employment and child-care arrangement on preschoolers' cognitive and behavioral outcomes: Evidence from the children of the national longitudinal survey on youth. *Developmental Psychology, 27.*

Belle, D. (1997). Varieties of self-care: A qualitative look at children's experiences in the after-school hours. *Merrill-Palmer Quarterly, 43,* 478–496.

Belsky, J., and Eggebeen, 1991. Early and extensive maternal employment and young children's socioemotional development: Children of the National Longitudinal Survey of Youth. *Journal of Marriage and the Family, 53,* 1083–1110.

Benasich, A., Brooks-Gunn, J., and Clewell, B. (1992). How do mothers benefit from early intervention programs? *Journal of Applied Developmental Psychology, 13*(3), 311–362.

Bereiter, C., and Engelmann, S. (1966). *Teaching disadvantaged children in the preschool.* Englewood Cliffs, NJ: Prentice-Hall.

Bogenschneider, K. 1990. *Maternal employment and adolescent academic achievement: Mediating, moderating and developmental influences.* Unpublished doctoral dissertation, Department of Child and Family Studies, University of Wisconsin.

Bowman, B. T., Donovan, M. S., and Burns, M. S. *Eager to learn: Educating our preschoolers.* Washington, DC: National Academy Press.

Bredekamp, S. (Ed.). (1986). *Developmentally appropriate practice in early childhood programs serving children from birth through age eight.* Washington, DC: National Association for the Education of Young Children.

Bredekamp, S., and Copple, C. (Eds.). (1997). *Developmentally appropriate practice in early childhood programs* (Rev.ed.). Washington, DC: National Association for the Education of Young Children.

Bromer, J. (1999). Cultural variations in child care: values and actions. *Young Children, 54*(6), 72–75.

Bromer, J., Modigliani, K., and Callahan, C. (1999). *NAFCC Accreditation, Observer Trainers' Manual.* Des Moines, IA: National Association of Family Day Care.

Bruer, J. (1999). *The myth of the first three years: A new understanding of early brain development and lifelong learning.* Riverside, NJ: Simon and Schuster.

Buell, M. J., Hallam, R. A., and Beck, H. L. (2001). Early Head Start and child care partnerships: Working together to serve infants, toddlers, and their families. *Young Children, 56*(3), 7–12.

Burchinal, M. R., Ramey, S. L., Reid, M. K., and Jaccard, J. (1995). Early child care experiences and their association with family and child characteristics during middle childhood. *Early Childhood Research Quarterly, 10,* 3361.

Burchinal, M. R., Roberts, J. E., Nabors, L. A., Bryant, D. M. (1996). Quality of center child care and infant cognitive and language development. *Child Development, 67,* 606–620.

Campbell, N. D., Applebaum, J., Martinson, K., and Martin, E. (2000). *Be all that we can be: Lessons from the military for improving our nation's child care system.* Washington, DC: National Women's Law Center.

Carnegie Foundation. (1994). *Carnegie Population Reports.* New York: Author.

Children's Defense Fund. (1990). *The state of America's children: Yearbook 1990.* Washington, DC: Author.

Children's Defense Fund. (1998). *The state of America's children: Yearbook 1998.* Washington, DC: Author.

Children's Defense Fund. (1999). *The state of America's children: Yearbook 1999.* Washington, DC: Author.

Children's Defense Fund. (2000). *The state of America's children: Yearbook 2000.* Washington, DC: Author.

Children's Defense Fund. (2001). *The state of America's children: Yearbook 2001.* Washington, DC: Author.

Children's Defense Fund. (2002). *The state of children in America's union: A 2002 action guide to leave no child behind.* Washington, DC: Author.

Clarke-Stewart, K. A. (1989). Infant day care: Maligned or malignant? *American Psychologist, 44,* 266–273.

Clarke-Stewart, K. A., Allhusen, V. D., and Clements, D. C. (1995). Nonparenting caregiving. In M. H. Borstein (Ed.), *Handbook of parenting* (Vol 3). Mahwah, NJ: Erlbaum.

Collins, W., Harris, M., and Susman, A. (1995). Parenting during middle childhood. In M. H. Bornstein (Ed.), *Handbook of Parenting,* (Vol. 1). Mahwah, NJ: Lawrence Erlbaum.

DeBord, K. (1991). Selecting child care: The quality question. In *Community based Child Care: An Action Manual for Communities Addressing Child Care. 350-038, 9-11.* Blacksburg, VA: Virginia State University Extension.

Delpit, L. (1995). *Other people's children: Cultural conflict in the classroom.* New York: The New Press.

Desai, S. P., Chase-Lansdale, P. L., and Michael, R. T. (1989). Mother or market? Effects of maternal employment on the intellectual ability of 4-year-old children. *Demography 26,* 545–561.

Derman-Sparks, L., and the A. B. C. Task Force. (1992). *Anti-bias curriculum: Tools for empowering children.* Washington, DC: National Association for the Education of Young Children.

DeWitt-Wallace-Reader's Digest Fund. (1998). *Focus: School-age care.* New York: Author.

DiLalla, L. F. (1998). Daycare, child, and family influences of preschoolers' social behaviors in a peer play setting. *Child Study Journal, 28,* 233–245.

Dodge, K., Pettitt, G., and Batres, J. (1994). Socialization mediators of the relation between socioeconomic status and child conduct problems. *Child Development, 54,* 1386–1399.

Egeland, B., and Hiester, M. (1995). The long-term consequences of infant day-care and mother–infant attachment. *Child Development, 64,* 474–485.

Farrington, D. (1991). Childhood aggression and adult violence: Early precursors and later-life outcomes. In D. J. Pepler and K. H. Rubin (Eds.). *The development and treatment of childhood aggression, 5–29.* Hillsdale, NJ: Erlbaum.

Gandini, L. (1997). Foundations of the Reggio Emilia approach. In J. Hendrick (Ed.), *First steps toward teaching the Reggio way* (pp. 14–25). Upper Saddle River, NJ: Prentice-Hall.

Gerstein, R., and Keating, T. (1987). Improving high school performance of "at-risk" students: A study of long-term benefits of direct instruction, *Educational Leadership, 44,* 28–31.

Goffin, G., and Wilson, S. (2001). *Curriculum models and early childhood education: Appraising the relationship* (2nd ed.). New York: Merrill Prentice-Hall.

Gray, S. W., Ramsey, B. K., and Klaus, R. A. (1982). *From 3 to 20 The Early Training Project.* Baltimore: University Park Press.

Haddal, L. (2001). *The Teapot Curriculum of the Wisconsin Child Care Information Center.* Presented at the 2001 National Association Conference at the OMEP session. Anaheim, CA.

Haskins, R. (1985). Public school aggression among children with varying day-care experience. *Child Development, 56,* 689–703.

Helburn, S. (Ed.). (1995). *Cost, quality, and child outcomes in child care centers.* Public Report. Denver: Department of Economics, Center for Research in Economics and Public Policy, University of Colorado at Denver.

Hewes, D. (1998). *"It's the Camaraderie"—A History of Parent Cooperative Preschools.* Davis, CA: University of California, Center for Cooperatives.

Hock, E. (1980). Working and non-working mothers and their infants: A comparative study of maternal care-giving characteristics and infant social behavior. *Merrill Palmer Quarterly, 46,* 79–101.

Howes, C. (1990). Can the age of entry into child care and the quality of child care predict adjustment in kindergarten? *Developmental Psychology, 26,* 292–303.

International Symposium Participants. (1999). *Global guidelines for early childhood education and care in the 21st century.* Olney, MD: Association for the Education of Young Children International and World Organization for the Education of Young Children.

Juvenile Justice and Delinquency Prevention Coalition. (2002). 21st CCLC Fact Sheet, May.

Karnes, M. B., Schwedel, A. M., and Williams, M. B. (1983). A comparison of five approaches for educating young children from low-income homes. In Consortium for Longitudinal Studies, *As the twig is bent: Lasting effects of preschool programs* (pp. 133–170). Hillsdale, NJ: Erlbaum.

Katz, L. (1993). Multiple perspective on the quality of early childhood programs. *Eric Digest, EPO-PS-92-2*. Urbana, IL: University of Illinois.

Kontos, S., Howes, C., Shinn, M., and Galinsky, E. (1995). *Quality in Family Child Care and Relative Care*. New York: Teachers College Press.

Koppel, S. G. (1995). *Head Start and child care: Partners not competitors*. Lumberville, PA: Support Services for Child Care Professionals.

Lazar, I. (1977). The persistence of preschool effects: A long-term follow-up on fourteen infant and preschool experiments. *Final report to the administration on children, youth and families*. Washington, DC: Office of Human Services, U.S. Department of Health, Education, and Welfare.

Lazar, I., and Darlington, R. B. (1982). Lasting effect of early education: A report from the consortium for longitudinal studies. *Monographs for the Society for Research in Child Development, 47*, 2–3.

Lombardi, J. (2001). It's time to redesign child care to create 21st century early education. *Young Children, 56*, 74–77.

Long, T. J., and Long, L. (1982). *The handbook of latchkey children and their parents*. New York: Arbor House.

Love, J. (1998). Quality in child care centers. *Educational Digest, 63*, 51–53.

Marshall, N. L., Coll, C. G., Marx, F., McCartney, K., Keefe, N., and Ruh, J. (1997). After-school time and children's behavioral adjustment. *Merrill-Palmer Quarterly, 43*, 497–514.

McCartney, K., and Rosenthal, S. (1991). Maternal employment should be studied within social ecologies. *Journal of Marriage and the Family, 53*, 1103–1107.

McCartney, K., Scarr, S., Phillips, D., Grajek, S., and Schwartz, J. C. (1982). Environmental differences among day care centers and their effects on children's development. In E. F. Ziegler and E. W. Gordon (Eds.), *Day care: Scientific and social policy issues* (pp. 126–151). Boston: Auburn House.

Miller, B. M., O'Connor, S., and Sirignono, S. W., 1995. Out of school time: A study of children in three low-income neighborhoods. *Child Welfare, 74*, 1249–1280.

Miller, L. B., and Bizzel, R. P. (1983). The Louisville experiment: A comparison of four programs. In The Consortium for Longitudinal Studies, *As the twig is bent... lasting effects of preschool programs* (pp. 171–199). Hillsdale, NJ: Erlbaum.

Montessori, M. (1965). *The advanced Montessori method: Spontaneous play in education.* (F. Simmons, Trans.). New York: Schocken. (Original work published in English in 1917).

Moore, D. R. (1996). Substitute child care at different ages: Relationship to social-emotional functioning in preschool. *American Journal of Orthopsychiatry, 66*, 305–308.

National Association for the Education of Young Children (NAEYC). (1984). *Accreditation criteria and procedures of the national academy of early childhood programs.* Washington, DC: Author.

National School-Age Care Alliance. (1997). *NAFCC Accreditation Observer Trainers' Manual*, Eds. Mogigliani, Lutton, Bromer, and Wright. Boston, MA: National School-Age Care Alliance.

Newberger, J. (1997). New brain development research: A wonderful window of opportunity to build public support for early childhood education! *Young Children, 52*(4), 4–9.

Nilsen, E. (1999). *The road to professionalism: Emerging models, trends, and issues in credentialing.* Wellesley, MA: National Institute on Out-of-School Time, Center for Research on Women, Wellesley College.

National Institute of Child Health and Human Development (NICHD), Early Child Care Research Network. (1996). Characteristics of infant child care: Factors contributing to positive caregiving. *Early Childhood Research Quarterly, 11*, 269–306.

National Institute of Child Health and Human Development, Early Child Care Research Network. (1997). The effects of infant child care or infant–mother attachment security: Results of the NICHD study of early child care. *Child Development, 69*, 860–879.

National Institute of Child Health and Human Development, Early Child Care Research Network (1998). Early child care and self-control, compliance, and problem behavior at twenty-four and thirty-six months. *Child Development, 69*, 1145–1170.

Patterspn, C., Kupersmidt, J., and Vaden, N. (1990). Income level, gender, ethnicity, and household composition as predictors of children's school-based competencies. *Child Development, 61*, 485–494.

Petit, G. S., Laird, R. D., Bates, J. E., and Dodge, K. A. (1997). Patterns of after-school care in middle childhood: Risk factors and developmental outcomes. *Merrill-Palmer Quarterly, 43*, 515–538.

Poersch, N. O., and Blank, H. (1996). *Working together for children: Head Start and child care partnerships.* Washington, DC: Children's Defense Fund.

Posner, J., and Vandell, D. (1994). Low-income children's after-school care: Are there beneficial effects of after-school programs? *Child Development, 65,* 440–456.

Rosenthal, R., and Vandell, D. L. (1996). Quality of care and school-age child care programs: Regulatable features, observed experiences, child perspectives, and parent perspectives. *Child Development 67,* 2434–2445.

Ruopp, R., Travers, J., Glantz, F., and Coclen, G. (1979). *Children at the center: Final results of the national day care study.* Cambridge, MA: Abt Associates.

Rutter, M. (1981). The city and the child. *American Journal of Orthopsychiatry, 51,* 610–625.

Sargent, P. Under the glass: Conversations with men in early chldhood education. *Young Children, 57*(6), 22–30.

Scarr, 1991. On comparing apples and oranges and making inferences about bananas. *Journal of Marriage and the Family, 53,* 1099–1100.

Schulman, K. (2000). *Issue brief: The high cost of child care puts quality care out of reach for many families.* Washington, DC: Children's Defense Fund.

Schulman, K., Blank, H., and Ewen, D. (1999). *Seeds of success: State preschool initiatives, 1998–1999.* Washington, DC: Children's Defense Fund.

Schweinhart, L. J. (1994). *Lasting benefits of preschool programs.* ERIC Digest-EDO-PS-94-2. Urbana, IL: University of Illinois.

Schweinhart, L. J. (1997). Child-initiated learning activities for young children living in poverty. *ERIC Digest EDO-PS-23.* Urbana, IL: University of Illinois.

Schweinhart, L. J., Barnes, H. V., and Weikart, D. P. (1993). *Significant benefits: The High-Scope Perry Preschool Study through age 27.* Monographs of the High-Scope Educational Research Foundation, 10. Ypsilanti, MI: High-Scope Press.

Schweinhart, L. J., and Weikart, D. P. (1997). The High-Scope Preschool Curriculum Comparison Study through age 23. *Early Childhood Research Quarterly, 12*(2), 117–143.

Shore, R. (1997). *Rethinking the brain: New insights into early development.* New York: Families and Work Institute.

Skinner, B. F. (1957). *Verbal Behavior.* New York: Appleton-Century-Crofts.

Smith, K. (2000). Who's minding the kids? Child care arrangements: Fall 1995. *Current Population Reports,* P70-70. Washington, DC: U.S. Bureau of the Census.

Smith, L. 2000. Operation: Superior child care. *Los Angeles Times,* June 4, E1, 3.

Snyder, H., and Sickmund, M. (1999). *Juvenile Offenders and victims: 1999 National Report.* Washington, DC: U.S. Department of Justice, Office of Juvenile Justice and Delinquency Programs.

Sroufe, L. (1988). A development perspective on day-care. *Early Childhood Research Quarterly, 3,* 283–291.

Turbiville, P., Umbarger, G., and Guthrie, A. (2000). Fathers' involvement in programs for young children. *Young Chlidren, 55,* 74–78.

U.S. Department of Education and Department of Justice. (1998). *Safe and smart: Making after-school hours work for kids.* Washington, DC: U.S. Government Printing Office.

Vandell, D. L. (1991). Belsky and Eggebeen's analysis of the NLSY: Meaningful results or statistical illusions? *Journal of Marriage and the Family, 53,* 1100–1103.

Vandell, D. L., and Corasanti, M. A. (1990). Child care and the family: Complex contributors to child development. In K. Martney (Ed.), *New Directions in child development research* (pp. 23–37). San Francisco: Jossey-Bass.

Vandell, D. L., and Ramanen, J. (1992). Effects of early and recent maternal employment on children from low-income families. *Child Development, 63,*(4), 938–949.

Vandell, D. L., and Su, H. (1999). Child care and school-age children. *Young Children, 54,* 62–71.

Zaslow, M. and Hayes, C. (1986). Sex differences in children's response to psychosocial stress: Toward a cross-context analysis. In M. Lamb and B. Rogoff (Eds.), *Advances in Developmental Psychology, 4,* 289–337. Hillsdale, NJ: Erlbaum.

Schooling

8

Schools have become a place for solving problems to which society itself has failed to find an answer.

— Giovanni Gozzer, 1990

THE WORLD

Society looks to its schools to solve problems that children bring to school. How can the community provide support for its schools in their struggles to educate and help children to succeed? This chapter examines the role of schools, teachers, parents, and the community at large in the lives of its children. Education is the major institution in our society that transmits its knowledge, skills, and values from one generation to another. Education takes place informally in many settings, such as the family, the peer group, and mass media. Education is also pursued formally through schools. Schooling usually occurs in a classroom setting. Some system of education is present in all societies, but in societies with limited technology, education is largely informal. In complex societies, such as the United States, education is both elaborate and formal.

In ancient Greece, Socrates, Plato, and Aristotle instructed aristocratic males in philosophy and science. In ancient China, the famous philosopher Confucius also taught a privileged few (Rohlen, 1983). Historically, most schooling has been directly linked to the world of work. Even today, schooling that is not tied to work is generally available only in affluent societies.

All major institutions are interrelated. Education is closely linked to the family and shares with it the tasks of socializing children and teaching them many skills. Education and religious organizations teach children values and ways of behaving. Most religious organizations have worship or special classes for children and some have their own private schools. Decisions about education and its funding are made on local, state, and national levels, which also tie the educational system to both political and economic institutions.

The American Education System

America's early settlers came from European countries, where public schooling was exclusive. Our educational system was built on the premise that schools should be open to all children, allowing them to advance in society according to their abilities. Even before the American Revolution, Americans viewed public schooling as fulfilling functions vital to preserving their democracy. Education was, and to some extent still is, seen as the key to eliminating poverty and crime. One example of this is Head Start, a comprehensive child development program giving children of low-income families experiences similar to those of many middle-income children. The goal is to enable these children to begin school with a "head start" (see Chapter 7).

Today, we have a multitude of educational programs designed to include all children in the educational process. Educational opportunities were much more limited in America's early history. For example, in 1850, only about half of the children between the ages of five and nineteen were enrolled in school. Not until mandatory education laws were enacted in every state did (practically) all children

TABLE 8.1

Educational Achievement in the United States, 1971–1999

Percentage of 25–29-year-olds who have completed high school

	ALL			WHITE			BLACK			HISPANIC		
March	Total	Male	Female	Total	Male	Female	Total	Male	Female	Total	Male	Female
1971	77.5	79.1	76.5	81.7	83.0	80.5		56.7	60.5	48.3	51.3	45.7
1999	87.8	86.1	89.5	93.0	91.9	94.1	88.7	88.2	89.2	61.1	57.4	65.9

Percentage of 25–29-year-olds high school completers with a bachelor's degree or higher

March	Total	Male	Female	Total	Male	Female	Total	Male	Female	Total	Male	Female
1971	22.0	25.8	18.1	23.1	27.0	19.1	11.5	12.1	10.9	10.5	15.4	5.8
1999	32.1	31.2	33.0	36.1	34.8	37.3	16.9	14.9	18.6	14.4	13.0	15.8

National Center for Educational Statistics, 2000.

attend school. In 1918, Mississippi joined the other states making formal education to the age of sixteen or completion of the eighth grade mandatory throughout the United States (Cremin, 1961). In the last thirty years, graduation rates from high schools and colleges have increased as shown in Table 8.1 (National Center for Educational Statistics, 2000).

Functions of Education

> *Education is experience:*
> *The rest is only*
> *information.*
>   *—Albert Einstein*

The central functions for American schools are transmitting knowledge and skills training, social and political integration, cultural transmission, talent selection, and socialization.

TRANSMITTING KNOWLEDGE AND SKILLS TRAINING

An important function of schools is and always has been to teach children the basic skills of reading, writing, and arithmetic. Currently society is concerned about the many children unable to read by the end of third grade. Functional illiteracy occurs when society fails to educate their children in reading and writing to a degree that allows them to do basic tasks. For example, some of our youth and adults cannot read simple documents such as a voting ballot, or communicate a simple message in writing. Overall, about one-fourth of the adults in the United States are functionally illiterate and the proportion is higher among the elderly and minorities (Kozol, 1985).

Today, society is more complex because of technological advances and globalization. It is increasingly important that children can use these basic skills to think (to reason or solve problems) and not just to memorize facts. Both children and adults need to use their mental skills to solve new problems. Schools need to provide knowledge and skills necessary for current and future jobs and for technological innovation.

CULTURAL TRANSMISSION   Every society teaches children its values, norms, and accumulated knowledge. Some teachings perpetuate tradition while others allow for new ideas, promoting varying degrees of growth and change in society. Many cultural norms are taught or reinforced in school by requiring appropriate behavior. These norms include punctuality, respect for authority, and obedience to rules. In the United States, the values of competition, individualism, fair play, and success are seen in many games that children play, and in the ways in which they work together and learn. Chess and spelling bees are two examples of individual competition. Measurement of school success is based on the individual's performances rather than that of the group.

In contrast, when this author visited schools in China and the Soviet Union in the 1970s and 1980s, the teachers were concerned that their activities might be misinterpreted or judged according to American values. The first thing that a teacher or director wanted her to understand was that their children were taught that the group came first and the individual second. After that concept was understood, the visit proceeded smoothly. Although some societies are subtler in their teachings than others, children are taught their values, customs, and traditions directly and indirectly.

In the past the United States was seen as a "melting pot" although it never really was (see Chapter 1). The goal of education was to teach the English language and the values of mainstream society. This viewpoint was dominant from the mid-nineteenth century until the late 1960s (Light and Keller, 1981). With changes in society, the goals for education have been modified. Instead of trying to transmit only the dominant cultural norms, many schools now attempt to share information about the distinct cultural backgrounds of their children. Multicultural education for all children began to gain acceptance in the 1980s. Although schools in the twenty-first century are still teaching English and mainstream culture, many schools now are also providing information about other cultures. Some families are searching for their roots and helping their children learn and become proud of their culture. This changing philosophy looks at the United States more as a "salad bowl" with many cultures all valuable and necessary to make the best "salad," or society. However, there is still criticism that schools are ignoring the history and contributions of African Americans, Native Americans, Hispanic Americans, other ethnic minorities, and women. In response, many schools do include some of these topics in their literature, music, art, and other activities.

Social and Political Integration   Formal education helps students from diverse backgrounds to integrate both socially and politically into the mainstream culture. It teaches a common language, a national identity, and general characteristics of American society. For example, the value of patriotism is portrayed with the appropriate flag, the pledge of allegiance to the country, and portraits and stories of political and national heroes. Public education in the United States attempts to teach its students appropriate behavior and responsibilities for good citizenship. Schools teach about American political and economic systems, forms of family life, and basic values. This information is part of classroom curriculums and is also found in many school activities.

IDENTIFYING TALENT OR RECRUITMENT TO OCCUPATIONS   Formal education historically has been a major avenue to upward mobility. It provides special hope to those beginning life with social disadvantages based on sex, race, ethnicity, or social class (Hurn, 1978). Equal opportunity for every individual to succeed as a result of talent and hard work, regardless of social status at birth, is the first of the ten ideal values in the U.S. culture listed in Chapter 1. Ideally, the schools should provide that opportunity to all students. Able students, regardless of status, would rise to the top. These students eventually would be guided into the most challenging and advanced studies or tracks while the others would be guided into educational programs leading to occupations compatible with their talents. Advocates believe this process enhances meritocracy, which links social status to personal merit. Although tracking is based on an individual's talents or performance rather than social status, more students in the most rewarding tracks come from higher socioeconomic backgrounds. Students from affluent families score higher on the standardized tests used to measure students' performance levels (Macionis, 1997). Opponents of this type of tracking believe that it is detrimental to educational meritocracy and increases the segregation of the privileged and disadvantaged students (Bowles and Gintis, 1976; Persell, 1977; Davis and Haller, 1981; Hallman and Williams, 1989; Oakes, 1982).

SOCIALIZATION   Although socialization begins in the family, the school plays an important role in this process. At school children are introduced to others who judge them by performance rather than relationship, as in the family. Children meet others from diverse backgrounds, often with different values and ways of behaving. They are introduced to a system of rules and learning that is impersonal. This experience may be a child's first opportunity to live with impersonal authority. In school, children learn to adjust to a hierarchial institution in which power and privileges are distributed impersonally and often unequally. These unwritten and written rules help prepare children for larger society. Children are socialized into culturally approved gender roles. Some instructional activities for boys and girls differ. Boys engage in more physical activities while girls are more sedentary, often helping the teacher with housekeeping chores (Best, 1983).

ADDITIONAL RESPONSIBILITIES OF SCHOOLS   As society's needs change, so do the roles of its schools and all of its institutions. The dramatic changes in the American family over the last several decades have affected the schools. For example, the high divorce rate, the increase of mothers in the workforce, and the increases in single and blended families have produced conditions stressful to many of our children. Some parents are unable to supervise or guide their children adequately. This may be because of time constraints or other problems with which the parents are coping. Because virtually all children attend school, many see the school as the best place to reach children outside of the family.

A number of conditions affecting children are addressed by the schools. Topics on divorce, blended families, changing roles in a family, and discipline or guidance are often part of the curriculum. Many children are unsupervised before and after school while their parents work. In response, many school districts provide out-of-school child-care programs to reduce the risks of self-care. As more mothers enter the workforce, pressure on the schools for extended child care increases.

In order to improve the immunization rates of children for some of the childhood diseases, the schools generally require proof of these immunizations before school enrollment. Our society is also concerned with child abuse, teen pregnancy, children's use of drugs, the spread and prevention of the disease AIDS (acquired immune deficiency syndrome), moral values, and children's self-image. Therefore, many schools are including these and similar topics in their curriculums.

With the emergence of these additional subjects, the school has become a place for solving problems for which society has failed to find an answer (Gozzer, 1990). This socio-therapeutic education has the best chance of being effective if it is an integral part of a more traditional subject and not just preventive message education. For example, anti-drug education would be more effective if taught as a part of a health class.

Sources of Funding and Control for Schools

Public primary and secondary education is largely funded by state and local governments. The amount of money per student for educational expenditures varies greatly in different states and even within each state. The federal government makes some funds available (approximately 6.5 percent of the total expenditure) to state and local communities under specific categories (National Center for Educational Statistics, 2000). For help in funding certain programs, teachers and school districts look to Title 1 of the Elementary and Secondary Act, the largest federal aid program to states. The Fund for the Improvement and Reform of Schools and Teaching (FIRST) was created in 1988 to seek, encourage, and reward innovative projects and reforms to improve primary and secondary education. For example, this fund provides federal money to local education agencies for Family/School Partnership innovative projects (Cross, 1993).

The control each community exerts over its school system varies from state to state according to the current political climate within the state. In California and most other states, there is a move to shift more control to the local school or school district. This is based on the theory that the local school knows better what their children need. Although school curriculums are decided at the local level, in practice, primary education programs have been very similar.

Conditions Affecting the Functions of Schools

Many conditions contribute to the overall quality of the school and the type of education that each child receives.

1. Schools are funded at different levels within a state and in other states.
2. Parental, neighborhood, and community participation in schools differs widely.
3. Standardized tests appear to favor some groups over others.
4. The hidden curriculum may not be the same for different individuals or groups.
5. Teachers may have different expectations for individual children.

Schools vary greatly in their financial resources within a community and across the country. Schools with fewer resources most often are in poorer neighborhoods with poorer families. They support schools less than their wealthier counterparts. According to recent data, parent involvement in schools increases with higher household income and level of education. In addition, White parents are more likely than Black or Hispanic parents to participate in school activities (National Center for Educational Statistics, 2000). Children coming from lower socioeconomic families and neighborhoods achieve less in school than their counterparts and are less likely to be chosen for college preparatory classes. Though standardized testing has been corrected for apparent biases, it is still argued by some that standardized testing favors children from higher socioeconomic backgrounds because of familiar vocabulary and examples used (Owen, 1985; Macioni, 1997). Some teachers have higher expectations for middle- and upper-class children (Owen, 1985).

The formal curriculum involves written plans for the activities and experiences of the children each day. The hidden curriculum, which often goes unrecognized, deals with the socialization of children for appropriate school behavior and attitudes. The hidden curriculum involves the subtle presence of cultural or political ideas in the classroom. Compliance, punctuality, discipline, and competition are considered part of the hidden curriculum (Macioni, 1997). In the hidden curriculum, attitudes and personality traits such as decisiveness, questioning, compliance, and acceptance may be encouraged or discouraged. For example, particular traits may be encouraged in children to prepare them for particular jobs. Students from middle- or higher-class families, usually attending suburban schools, may be given opportunities to develop decision making and critical thinking skills, whereas students from lower-class families are often encouraged to learn obedience and respect for authority. Middle-level jobs require workers to be methodical, predictable, and persevering (Bowles and Gintis, 1976). Curriculums in lower tracks include more memorization and classroom drill and emphasize punctuality and respect for authority figures.

A larger percentage of children from higher socioeconomic homes are selected for the tracks leading to more prestigious jobs or careers. Children who spend more time in higher tracks see themselves as bright and capable while children in the lower tracks have lower ambitions and self-esteem (Bowles and Gintis, 1976; Kilgore, 1991). The "Pygmalion" effect also showed that children's performances were influenced by teachers' expectations. In this study, teachers gave their students a test and told them that it was to identify students who were potential high performers. The researchers gave the teachers a random list of potential high performers that was shared with the students. Eight months later the students were retested with the same IQ test. The test scores of the students on this random list actually showed significant intellectual gains, especially students in the first and second grades (Rosenthal and Jacobsen, 1968). The study was criticized for its methodology.

Differences in student performance may be influenced by hidden factors or subtle expectations due to cultural or political values and not based on the individual capabilities or talents of the child. Children may or may not take up their parents' type of work. Because teachers' expectations can influence the outcomes of children, teachers must be very careful in their comments to children and in their overall evaluations of their abilities.

Children come to school with many inequalities. An equal opportunity means that all of them should have the appropriate treatment and opportunities to succeed. When parents can work with teachers on certain goals, the outcome for children is better. However, schools usually do not succeed in fully compensating for the inequities some children bring with them. Our society requires credentials or degrees for most higher-paying occupations. Because more students from middle and higher socioeconomic classes receive college degrees, social-class differences are perpetuated.

8.1 I Think I Can!

A fifth-grade teacher wanted to encourage her students to achieve so she created a class motto, "I think I can," and had the class repeat it every day. She reminded them of the book, *The Little Engine That Could.* She also tried to spend more individual time with her students and, every chance she could, told them how wonderful they were. The majority of her students improved their performances (Younger, 1999).

Teachers' Influences

Teachers play a crucial role in children's school experiences and in their lives. Teachers provide the classroom environment and the motivation for learning. Elementary school children spend more time with their teacher during the school year than with any other adult except a parent. An elementary school teacher may have as many as one thousand interpersonal exchanges with pupils in one day.

Roles of Teachers

Teachers are *leaders, nurturers, role models, decision makers, interpreters, classroom managers, and authority figures.* When teachers are able to guide and encourage children to solve a problem or to be more successful in their tasks or relationships, children come closer to reaching their full potential according to Vygotsky (1978), who viewed human development as having both a biological and a cultural dimension. Teachers help children develop by guiding their participation in culturally valued activities (Goffin and Wilson, 2001).

TEACHERS AS LEADERS. Teachers have various styles of leadership involving different degrees of control and warmth or responsiveness. Styles range from direct instruction, in which the teacher tells the children what she or he wants them to learn, to the teacher's role of facilitator, encouraging the children to decide what they want to do and learn. Between these two positions on control is an authoritative or democratic approach in which the teacher plans the day with the help of the children. An authoritative teacher sets goals and maintains control, but with warmth, explanations, open communications, and the opportunity for pupil participation. These leadership styles follow the teachers' roles described in the three curriculum models in Chapter 7 on Child Care and Baumrind's parenting styles in Chapter 6. Each method affects the socialization and learning of children differently. As mentioned in Chapter 7, teachers should be aware that some African American and Asian American students learn better when the teacher uses a direct learning style with them (Delpit, 1995).

TEACHERS AS NURTURERS. Teachers nurture children by showing interest, concern, support, and praise for them. Nurturing teachers are sensitive to their needs academically, socially, and emotionally, finding ways to provide appropriate experiences for all of them. For example, nurturing teachers try to identify children's learning styles and interests and provide some activities that utilize them. These teachers respond with extra attention and support when children experience crises such as their parents divorcing or being a victim or witnessing violence.

TEACHERS AS ROLE MODELS. Teachers are effective role models when they are both nurturing and exhibit the traits they are preaching. Children benefit when teachers feel good about themselves and value their work. Effective teacher–student relationships usually develop from an authoritative or democratic leadership style just as they do in parenting. Effective teachers are respectful of children and parents, flexible, patient, open, positive, and competent. Teachers who avoid labeling children while supporting and gently pushing them to a higher level of achievement will promote a positive self-fulfilling prophecy for them. By the very nature of their roles, teachers help their students define who they are.

TEACHERS AS DECISION MAKERS.   Teachers constantly make decisions about the curriculum, the organization of the classroom, a child, or the best way to deal with a parent. Teachers interpret the curriculum, monitor and evaluate behavior, and facilitate peer group experiences. They help children to understand the curriculum, themselves, and other children's behaviors. Teachers interpret the policies of the school, which reflect the social values and norms of the community, as well as their own values.

TEACHERS AS CLASSROOM MANAGERS AND AUTHORITY FIGURES.   The successful manager is organized and remains calm. Children have freedom at times to work with other children. The effective manager can organize the classroom so that individual children have developmentally and culturally appropriate learning environments that provide challenging but realistic goals for each of them.

> Teach children to solve problems rather than punish children for problems they cannot solve
> *(Gartrell, 1997).*

The effective teacher is in control of the classroom, working with the children to establish goals, rules, and activities. As an authority figure, the effective teacher articulates clear rules, regulates the time schedule for different activities, and provides smooth transitions between activities. Effective teachers use intervention methods that are solution oriented such as a peaceful conflict resolution approach (see Chapter 11). The teacher helps the children develop positive social and life skills, Teachers build partnerships with other adults, including parents, realizing that it takes teamwork to be successful. The goals of good guidance or discipline are for children to learn to "get along with others, solve problems using words, and express strong feelings in acceptable ways. These are (also) the goals for citizens of a democratic society" (Gartrell, 1997).

Children's Learning Styles

One size (style) does not fit all. Effective teachers try to understand how individual children take in and process information. They realize that not all children learn the same way. Learning styles describe the ways in which individual children acquire information, evaluate it, and then examine their findings. Learning styles in general are applicable to all content areas and settings. Effective teachers try to present materials in ways that will interest children and help them to absorb the information. Understanding a child's learning style helps accomplish this.

Most theories of learning styles, beginning with the theory of Carl Jung in 1927, focus on the personality and motivation of the individual. Most learning style theories place individuals into four groups of learners, with approximate percentages for each group. The following model by Silver, Strong, and Perini (1997) is a good example.

- ✔ **Mastery Style Learners:** Absorb information concretely step by step. They value practicality and clarity (35 percent).
- ✔ **Understanding Learners:** Work with ideas and abstractions using methods of questioning and reasoning. They value logic and evidence (35 percent).
- ✔ **Self-Expressive Learners:** Learn through feelings and seeing images in materials. They value originality (12 percent).
- ✔ **Interpersonal Learners:** Work with others using concrete ideas. Results should be of social value. They are the future humanitarians or volunteers (18 percent).

Currently, most learning style theorists believe that individuals become more flexible in the ways they approach learning as they gain knowledge and experience. Eventually most individuals will have a favored learning style but will use other learning styles when necessary. Teachers can help children develop a profile of their preferred learning style but should also encourage them to utilize other ways to process information. This will give them more options in the future.

Multiple Intelligence Theory

Understanding what is meant by intelligence or trying to separate intelligent from unintelligent behavior is difficult. There are many different theories. According to Wechsler (1975), intelligence is the capacity to understand the world, think rationally, and use resources effectively when faced with challenges. Gardner (1993), a Harvard theorist, defines intelligence as "the ability to solve problems, or to fashion products that are of consequence in a particular setting or community." Gardner (1983) does not define intelligence as a single broad-based domain, but describes nine distinct intelligences: linguistic, logical-mathematical, spatial, bodily-kinesthetic, musical, interpersonal, intrapersonal. naturalist, and existential. The first seven are described and integrated with learning styles in the next section. Each of these intelligences is relatively independent, but can combine with any other intelligence depending on the activity (Gardner and Hatch, 1989). This theory is based on research in physiology, anthropology, and personal and cultural history (Silver, et al., 1997). Individuals show different aptitudes in each of these content areas but no one is highly gifted in all areas. It is often easy to identify someone who is gifted in one area such as music, sports, or writing, but many times it is not so obvious. Consulting with parents helps teachers find children's strengths.

Integrating Learning Styles with Multiple Intelligences

Each of these theories presents us with different information about children's learning. Gardner's multiple intelligences theory provides cognitive information about the various content areas and the products of learning. Learning styles look at how individuals may differ in the ways in which they process information. By combining both learning styles and multiple intelligences theories, one can understand the different ways in which individuals process information as well as look at how this occurs in the different content areas and contexts (settings).

The following chart shows seven of Gardner's multiple intelligences and how each of the four learning styles operates within a particular intelligence. It includes possible vocations people might choose. Individuals utilize their particular talents differently based on their learning style preference. For example, a journalist, lawyer, playwright, and salesperson all use their linguistic skills differently because of their different learning styles. **Learning Styles are Mastery, Understanding, Self-Expressive, and Intrapersonal.**

Linguistic Intelligence: the ability to produce and use language
> **Mastery:** Uses language to describe events. Jobs: journalist, technical writer, administrator
> **Understanding:** Uses logical arguments and rhetoric. Jobs: lawyer, professor, philosopher
> **Self-Expressive:** Uses metaphoric and expressive language. Jobs: playwright, poet, ad writer, novelist
> **Interpersonal:** Uses language to build trust and rapport. Jobs: salesperson, counselor, member of the clergy

Logical-Mathematical Intelligence: Ability to solve problems and think scientifically
> **Mastery:** Uses numbers to compute and document. Jobs: accountant, bookkeeper, statistician
> **Understanding:** Uses mathematical concepts for conjectures, proofs, and other applications. Jobs: computer programmer, scientist, logician
> **Self-Expressive:** Sensitive to the patterns, symmetry, logic, and aesthetics of mathematics. Solves problems in design and modeling. Jobs: composer, engineer, inventor, designer
> **Interpersonal:** Uses mathematics in everyday life. Jobs: tradesperson, homemaker

Bodily-Kinesthetic Intelligence: Ability to use parts or the whole body to solve problems, to construct products or displays
> **Mastery:** Uses the body and tools to act, construct or repair effectively. Jobs: mechanic, trainer, craftsperson
> **Understanding:** Develops strategic plans and critiques the actions of the body. Jobs: physical educator, sports analyst, professional athlete, theater or dance critic
> **Self-Expressive:** Appreciates and uses the aesthetics of the body to create new forms of expression. Jobs: sculptor, choreographer, actor, dancer, puppeteer
> **Interpersonal:** Uses the body to build rapport, console, persuade and support others. Jobs: coach, counselor, salesperson, trainer

Spacial Intelligence: Uses visual and spatial configurations
  Mastery: Views the visual-spacial world accurately. Jobs: artist, guide, photographer
  Understanding: Interprets and graphically represents visual or spacial ideas. Jobs: architect, icongrapher, computer graphics designer, art critic
  Self-Expressive: Uses visual and spacial ideas creatively. Jobs: artist, inventor, model builder, cinematographer
  Interpersonal: Uses color, space, line, form and space to meet the needs of others. Jobs: illustrator, artist, guide, photographer
Musical Intelligence: Uses skills involving music
  Mastery: Understands and develops musical technique. Jobs: technician, music teacher, instrument maker
  Understanding: Interprets musical forms and ideas. Jobs: music critic, aficionado, music collector
  Self-Expressive: Creates expressive and imaginative performances and compositions. Jobs: composer, conductor, individual/small group performer
  Interpersonal: Works with others and uses music to serve others. Jobs: choral, band, and orchestral performer or conductor
Interpersonal Intelligence: Interacts with others, sensitive to their moods, temperament, motivations, and intentions
  Mastery: Effective communicator and organizer of people. Jobs: consultant, politician, evangelist
  Understanding: Interprets differences in interpersonal clues. Jobs: sociologist, psychologist, psychotherapist
  Self-expressive: Creates imaginative and expressive performances and compositions. Jobs: composer, individual or small-group performer
  Interpersonal: Works with others to use music to meet the needs of others. Jobs: coach, counselor, salesperson, or trainer
Intrapersonal Intelligence: Understands one's own feelings and emotions
  Mastery: Accesses and uses one's own weaknesses, strengths, talents, and interests to set goals. Jobs: planner, small business owner
  Understanding: Develops concepts and theories based on self-examination. Jobs: psychologist
  Self-expressive: Creates and expresses a personal vision based on inner moods, intuitions, and temperament. Jobs: artist, religious leader, writer
  Interpersonal: Uses understanding of self to serve others. Jobs: counselor, social worker

This integrated plan for understanding the acquisition and use of knowledge can help:

1. Teachers individualize learning in a manageable way.
2. Children acquire the specific skills that society requires.

3. Children acquire information and an appreciation of each intelligence by exploring it through their personal learning style.
4. Children identify and develop their special talent or talents (Silver, et al., 1997).

(From: "Integrating Learning Styles and Multiple Intelligences," by H. Silver, R. Strong, and M. Perini, September 1997, *Educational Leadership*, 55(1), pp. 22–27. Copyrighted 1997 by the Association for Supervision and Curriculum Development. Reprinted with permission of ASCD. All rights reserved.)

Family School Involvements

By the year 2000, every school will promote partnerships that will increase parental involvement and participation in promoting the social, emotional, and academic growth of children (U.S. Department of Education, 1994).

The family's support of its children's classroom teachers and the school is so vital to children's learning that it was chosen at the Educational Summit in 1990 as one of the six national educational goals for the year 2000. According to a review of sixty-six studies, when parents supported their children's teacher and classroom or school activities, their children showed one or more of the following benefits (Henderson and Berla, 1997):

1. higher grades and test scores;
2. better attendance and regularly completed homework;
3. fewer placements in special education or remedial classes;
4. more positive attitudes and behavior in school;
5. higher graduation rates;
6. greater enrollment in postsecondary schools such as colleges and universities.

The concept of parent involvement is much broader today. The 1970s approach was to have parents help in the classroom. In the 1980s, the emphasis was on parents and teachers forming partnerships and working together. In the 1990s, this concept of forming partnerships expanded to include the community (Goldring and Hausman, 1996). For example, businesses have worked with the schools in securing funds and developing out-of-school programs. These community and school partnerships are covered in Chapter 13.

It is far more effective for parents and teachers to work together rather than separately. Success requires mutual commitment, trust, understanding, and reaching out. Some parents are afraid that, if they upset the teacher, their child might suffer. Parents often feel uncomfortable or unequal in their relationships with teachers. Similarly, teachers who see themselves as the authority figure in the child's formal education can be threatened when parents become involved in the school. These teachers see parents as usurping part of their power. *When power is directed to provide support and facilitate student success, power is no longer an absolute to be divided, but a force that increases.* Empowering parents should not diminish the power of the teacher or school but should strengthen everyone's position. For this partnership to take place, a plan or program needs to be developed at each school to help teachers and parents develop a common understanding of family–school relations (Coleman, 1997).

The following sections on parents and teachers working together are designed to identify areas of concern and to provide suggestions for dealing with various issues.

Encouraging Parent Involvement

How do teachers, school administrators, and the community motivate parents to become involved in their children's learning at school? It is essential that the schools are motivated to promote parent involvement for this process to be effective. Schools must go out of their way to be inviting to parents. Teachers, with the support of school administrators, can take the first steps. Before school starts, they can invite parents to participate in a workshop on family–school activities. During the year, teachers could send home notes or telephone parents with positive comments about their child. This prevents the first message a parent receives from the teacher being one involving a problem. Strong partnerships must be nurtured, encouraged, and adapted to current needs.

When classroom teachers and school administrators reach out to learn more about each of their students' families and their concerns, parents are more likely to become involved. A few parents remember unpleasant experiences when they were in school. Some parents have a problem understanding English. Other parents, often from the upper-middle or upper classes and with some college education, are eager to participate (Berger, 1995). Knowledge of a parent's cultural background, family form, commitments to family and work, free or unscheduled time, and their attitudes toward school help teachers relate appropriately. It also reveals parents' expectations of teachers as well as their ability to participate.

UNDERSTANDING CULTURAL BACKGROUNDS   Parents and teachers often have different backgrounds. Increasing numbers of the children's parents come from minority cultures while the majority of teachers are White, middle-class, Euro-American, and female. Our schools and our institutions are also based on the dominant culture, which is Euro-American. Although there are efforts to provide a multicultural environment in our classrooms, many programs have only a minimal approach to this concept. These programs often include ethnic stories, music, food, and celebrations of some holidays. Because these activities are limited and occur at special times and not throughout the curriculum, this approach to multiculturalism is often referred to as a tourist's exposure.

Parents from other cultures often differ from those of the dominant culture in some of their values and priorities for their children. They may fail to reinforce certain school goals such as independence, self-reliance, creative thinking, and reasoning because they are unfamiliar with them. Other times they do not reinforce a school goal because it differs from what they are teaching at home. The family's teachings are affected by their degree of assimilation or their adoption of values of the dominant culture. It is important for the teacher to share with all parents the basic goals in the classroom. The following questions will help teachers to identify cultural differences and respond appropriately.

1. **Greetings:** How do parents prefer greeting others, including teachers?
2. **Seeking Information:** How are parents comfortable in obtaining information or expressing concerns? What do they see as the role of the teacher and parent?
3. **Giving Information:** How do parents prefer being asked for information? Are they comfortable answering direct questions?
4. **Nonverbal Communication:** How do parents interpret body actions such as direct eye contact, smiling, leaning forward, folding one's arms, distance between participants, and touching?
5. **Time Orientation:** How important is it to parents for them or their children to be on time for a meeting or for school? How do they feel about delayed gratification and planning for future events? Are they more comfortable if school projects have a completion date rather than an open time line for finishing the task?
6. **Basis of Success for Children:** Do parents socialize their children to be competitive or to work cooperatively on the task? What is the relative importance of striving for an individual identity versus a group identity?
7. **Motivation:** Do parents primarily give their child external or internal rewards? For example, do parents give their children money for good grades or are their children encouraged to feel good about themselves for their achievements.
8. **School Progress:** How is the failure or success of the child in school seen by the child's family? Is school failure a disgrace to the child's family?

FAMILY FORM AND PARENT INVOLVEMENT The structure of the family often affects parents' options in school involvement, including parent–teacher conferences (See family forms in Chapter 3). Questions for teachers to consider are:

1. How many adults are in the family?
2. How many parents in the household work outside the home?
3. What support outside of the family do parents have?
4. What are the ages and the number of children in the family? Does anyone have special needs?

5. Does a parent living outside the home need to be included in the communications?
6. Who needs to be included in the communications in an extended family household?
7. What are the special needs of foster parents and children?
8. What may be the special concerns of gay or lesbian families?

PARENTAL WORK SCHEDULES AND TIME COMMITMENTS   Teachers must be accessible for all parents to have the option of participating in parent–teacher conferences and other activities. The administration can support teachers for working after school hours in terms of extra pay or released time.

Parent–Teacher Relationships

In every relationship, there are some common interests and needs that bring the parties together. To understand and modify any relationship, it is necessary to understand each person's perspective. What does the parent want and need from this relationship? What does the teacher want and need from the parent? How do their goals differ and how are they similar? Realistically, what can each do? What type of support systems are available for the parent–teacher relationship?

PARENTS' GOAL: SCHOOL SUCCESS   Most parents want their children to do well in school both in academics and in their behavior. Parents vary in their beliefs about how this is to be achieved, especially their responsibility in the process.

INTERESTS OF TEACHERS AND PARENTS   Teachers and parents have mutual concerns for children, primarily their education and socialization needs. Both have been given the responsibility of preparing children for adulthood. Neither can fully achieve this without the help of each other. Teachers and parents need each other for support, recognition, and success.

Parenting can be lonely, stressful, and often without external rewards. If teachers understand and recognize the efforts of parents, then the parents are going to feel successful. In turn, teachers often feel unappreciated or perhaps not as successful as they wish in promoting children's learning. Parents who send a thank-you note or acknowledge their child's improvement can make a teacher feel that the job is worthwhile. *Teachers and parents need recognition and validation.* Children need parents and teachers combining forces for their success.

ROLES OF PARENT AND TEACHER   The roles of parents and teachers have become more diffuse in recent decades. The teacher may be a parent surrogate in times of crisis, especially for the young child. Children and their families are often supported by teachers during times of divorce, death, remarriage, or acts of violence.

TABLE 8.2	Parents' and Teachers' Different Approaches to Children	
Roles	Mothers	Teachers
Scope of Functions	Diffuse and Limitless	Specific and Limited
Intensity of Effect	High	Low
Attachment	Optimum Attachment	Optimum Detachment
Rationality	Optimum Irrationality	Optimum Rationality
Spontaneity	Optimum Spontaneity	Optimum Intentionality
Partiality	Partial	Impartial
Scope of Responsibility	Individual	Whole Group

L. Katz. 1980. *Topics in Early Childhood Education.* Vol. 3., Figure 1, p. 49. Aplex Publishing Corp.

Parents are ultimately responsible for their children's care, but the teacher is also concerned with the welfare of children who arrive early at school or linger unsupervised after school.

Parents and teachers have been assigned different tasks by society, which affect their perspectives on these roles. Parents are ultimately responsible for their children's welfare so their role is broad. The parent–child attachment makes parents highly protective and emotionally involved when viewing situations concerning their child. The teachers' role is specific and limited. They are responsible for the education, broad socialization, and objective evaluation of each child. Teachers will form attachments to the children in the classroom but will need to release some energies to form new attachments to different children each year. Parents see things from their child's perspective. Teachers provide a more accurate picture of each child's group behavior and school progress than do the parents. Parents are responsible for helping their child be accepted and accept and respect the other children. The teacher is responsible for integrating children of different cultures and special needs into the classroom, helping all children to understand and respect each other. The child, on the other hand, can see his or her behaviors in terms of both school and peer expectations. Katz (1980) helps us look at some differences between parents' and teachers' approaches to their children.

Ways to Communicate with Parents

Schools and families can share information in a variety of ways. Each method differs in what can be accomplished such as the type or depth of information, the relationship it fosters, and the opportunities for participation. Some messages, like written communiqués, are one way in that one party is sending information to others. Two-way messages, such as conversations, involve responses of both parties. Methods of communication include the following:

1. **Visits.** These can take place at school, home, and a neutral setting such as a park. The park has the advantage of being neither the teacher's nor the parents' territory. Visits should take place before the start of school and at regular intervals.

2. **School Handbook.** This gives parents information on the school, its policies, and schedules. It includes holidays, short days, parent–teacher conferences, workshops, and parent participation opportunities. Providing information about the child's teacher, the curriculum, homework policies, and how to contact the teacher is also helpful.

3. **Written communiqués.** These can be sent to an individual or to a group of parents. They are informational, perhaps requesting help, giving the progress of a student or duplicated messages to a group related to an activity, homework assignment, or school policies.

4. **Smile-o-grams or messages of appreciation.** A "thank you" could be for helping with homework, helping with a special task, or sharing an idea. When parents feel appreciated, they are more willing to continue their efforts.

5. **Telephone calls.** They can be brief and at a time convenient to both teacher and parents. Relaying a positive message is helpful for the first telephone call; in other situations, begin the telephone call with a positive phrase.

6. **Informal face-to-face chat.** It can take place as a parent delivers or picks up a child. It is helpful for bonding with the parent and an opportunity to share something positive that the child did.

7. **Formal meetings and parent–teacher conferences.** Each provides different information. Conferences provide for parents' input. Times need to vary so as to be workable for all parents.

8. **Group meetings and open houses.** Group meetings could focus on a problem or a project for the school or on a topic such as safety, drugs, or discipline. An Open House gives children an opportunity to show off their projects and helps parents gain an understanding of classroom performances.

9. **Parent bulletin boards.** This is a place for teachers and parents to post messages and obtain information. Parents may want a home for three baby kittens. Teachers have announcements or articles for parents to read. For example, posted outside two kindergarten classroom doors in Acapulco, Mexico, were colorful posters on two articles from the UN Convention on the Rights of the Child. Information on one door dealt with the equal rights to education for girls and boys. The other poster discussed alternatives to spanking. Parents who had arrived early to pick up their children were reading them (Sailor, 1994).

10. **Resource library.** Materials are available for families to borrow or to use on-site. This could include children's books or toys or items for parents. Infor-

mation on social services, family support groups, and immunization opportunities are helpful.

11. **Newsletters.** Contributions come from parents, teacher, and children. A parent can collect the information from other parents and the teacher and help edit the paper. The teacher can share exciting activities in the classroom or school as well as community events. Most newsletters are sent biweekly or monthly. The maximum length should be two pages.

12. **Media.** Parents can find out about school activities through the local newspaper, radio, television, and cable stations. An announcement before or following a sporting event could also reach many parents.

Methods to Support Parental Involvement in Schools

A parent involvement program considers the needs of the teachers, school, and children, and the interests and talents of the parents participating. It involves recruiting parents and providing the appropriate training, supervision, support, and evaluation. Ideas from successful school models are helpful but ultimately the school personnel and families must develop their own plan. Parents can contribute as visitors, volunteers, paid classroom aides, advocates, or/and support their children's learning activities at home.

Visitors: The key is to make parents feel welcome at school, whether it is for scheduled visits, observations, or just to drop in. Many schools provide an orientation program for the families of children entering school. Written material is available in the parents' native language. A reception area for visitors and a welcome sign invites their participation.

Volunteers: A volunteer program can recruit and train parents according to their available time, skills, talents, interests, and teacher or school needs. Scheduling must be flexible.

Decision Makers: Recruiting parents who represent the diversity of the school and *training* for each job contributes to parents' effectiveness. Techniques for problem solving, decision making, and communicating can be helpful. Parents are involved in making decisions in parent–teacher organizations, on advisory councils, as representatives on a board of directors, as members of planning teams for classroom curriculums or new programs, and on interview committees for hiring school personnel. Some public or private-funded programs require parent representation on their board of directors or advisory board. Not only do parents have good ideas but they can gain the support of other parents.

Parent participation in decision making in their children's school provides the following benefits:

1. Parents represent the concerns of other parents in policies affecting their children's education.
2. Parents feel in control of their child's learning environment.

3. Parents' and children's rights are better protected.
4. Teachers and staff become aware of parents' perspectives for developing school policies (Epstein, 1988).

Advocates: People who work to improve conditions for children are child advocates. Advocacy involves identifying conditions that need to be changed, educating the public about the problems, and working with others to affect changes. School personnel can inform parents and community members of these conditions and what needs to be done. It helps in recruiting parents if there is a reasonable chance of success.

School personnel can provide informational and training workshops on being a school advocate. Parents and teachers can learn how to identify candidates for the school board, city council, and state legislature who either have supported children's education in the past or seem sensitive to improving specific conditions in the schools. They can invite candidates to talk to their school groups and tell them which issues are important to parents and teachers. People who help to get out the vote for a supportive candidate and/or vote for these candidates are advocates. Advocacy tasks include telephoning, distributing a petition, holding or attending meetings, and/or joining another group with the same goal.

Some school advocates attend school board meetings, special city council sessions, or advance an educational cause. Other advocates support particular programs such as school lunches, extracurricular activities, tutoring, or before- and after-school care. Some parents work for causes such as seat belts in school buses and smaller class sizes. Others help as language interpreters during conferences or translate messages or books. Supporting a family literacy program or a health clinic available on the school site helps school families. Organizing a computer class for parents at the school would also help the school support the needs of parents. A crucial part of advocacy is knowing who or what body is the source of power able to affect change. On school matters, the source of power for change may be the principal, the superintendent, the school board, or the state legislature. Wanting a traffic light at a school crossing would ultimately require the approval of the city council or city legislative body (see Chapter 12).

FAMILY SUPPORT OF HOMEWORK.   Parents often do not understand their children's homework assignments. It is helpful if the school sends home the weekly or monthly homework assignments in the language the parents understand. It is important to include directions and resources for assistance. At one elementary school in Tempe, Arizona, teachers were perplexed when a few parents were not even signing the paper acknowledging that their child brought home a book. Most of these parents were found to be functionally illiterate. In districts where this is a problem, a family literacy program at a school helps parents and their children.

Homework hot lines for parents and children are available at some schools. They are staffed by volunteers or paid personnel, but paid personnel are usually more effective. The use of call forwarding allows personnel to work out of their homes. Taped messages are also available. Schools and teachers determine what information is most needed. If there are hot-line specialists for specific subjects, teachers can give parents the particular problems students will be attempting.

Difficult Problems: Irate Parents and Chronic Complainers

There is always a particular situation that triggers an irate response from a parent or parents. A few parents are chronic complainers. These situations can challenge even the most experienced and skilled problem solver. When a parent explodes, the first thing a teacher should do is to take a deep breath and remain calm. Second, the teacher listens and writes down key points. Third, the teacher repeats what the parent has said for clarification. The teacher can then ask, "What do you think should be done." Finally, the teacher schedules a time for his or her response and further discussion. Usually twenty-four hours is sufficient time for parents to cool off and the teacher to gather all the facts and any assistance needed in forming the response. Remember to:

1. **Keep calm, then listen, record, and repeat.**
2. **Delay response to get all the facts and allow parents to cool off.** Children benefit from seeing teachers and parents resolving conflicts with both parties agreeing. They model skills for children to use in solving their conflicts.

EVALUATION OF POLICIES AND PROGRAMS   Effective family involvement models recognize the mutually supportive roles that the parents, teachers, and school personnel play in children's education and development. Knowing which activities are benefiting students, parents, and/or the school and what changes are needed can best be determined by all parties jointly evaluating the different components of their programs. Are the goals realistic and is there sufficient administrative support in terms of training, time, and money? Some forms of parent involvement may take too much supervision to be practical. Healthy family–school involvement requires continual assessment and implementation of necessary changes.

Kindergarten

Today all states provide public kindergarten for five-year-old children. Nearly as many children attend kindergarten as first grade (Smith, et al., 1994). Kindergarten is crucial because it is the initial year of elementary school for 98 percent of all children (West, Denton, and Germino-Hausken, 2000). These kindergarten experiences affect children's attitudes toward school and formal learning. A good transition between home and kindergarten or home, preschool, and kindergarten will facilitate the child's adjustment to school.

School Readiness

A major concern for preschool teachers and parents is a child's school readiness. What knowledge and skills should children possess when they enter kindergarten in order to meet the social, emotional, and academic demands of kindergarten? School readiness involves both academic and noncognitive factors. During their preschool years, children acquire many skills that prepare them for reading, writing, and arithmetic (see Chapter 7).

Noncognitive factors are equally or more important than academic skills are for school success. They include a child's physical health and motor coordination, emotional well-being, and social skills such as cooperation, curiosity, and eagerness to learn (West, Germino-Hausken, and Collin, 1993; National Association for the Education of Young Children, 1990; Kagan, 1990; Kagan, Moore and Bredekamp, 1995).

CHILDREN'S ACADEMIC, SOCIAL, EMOTIONAL, AND PHYSICAL SKILLS ON ENTERING KINDERGARTEN   The U.S. Department of Education's Early Childhood Longitudinal Study, Kindergarten Class of 1998–1999 (West, et al., 2000) is the first direct assessment of a large and nationally diverse group of kindergartners. It measures the knowledge, skills, health, and behavior of these kindergartners on school entry and plans to follow these children through fifth grade (Zill and West, 2000).

This initial assessment shows that children enter kindergarten with a wide range of knowledge and skills. Most children can recognize both upper- and lowercase letters and two or more characteristics about English print such as reading from left to right and from the top to the bottom of the page. Most children are in very good health, are reasonably well behaved, and exhibit a positive approach to classroom tasks. Most children have basic skills leading to reading, mathematics, and appropriate social behavior. However, there are too many children who fall below these levels. In comparing these children by age, ethnicity, gender, where they live, and other characteristics, this study reveals differences within each category.

CHILDREN FROM AT-RISK FAMILIES   In the ECLS-K study, nearly half of all entering kindergartners came from families with one or more risk factors for school achievement. Children from families with certain risk factors were more likely to do poorly in reading, mathematics, general knowledge, and have more behavior problems than children from families without these conditions. Risk factors were linked negatively to the child's social development and health but not to impaired growth or coordination. Of course, some children did well despite these factors. The Kids Count Family Risk Index includes similar conditions, except for health care, as risk factors for children's success (Casey Foundation, 2001). For the ECLS-K study, four high risk factors were considered:

1. having a mother with less than a high school education;
2. living in a family that receives food stamps or cash welfare payments;
3. living in a single-parent household;
4. having parents whose primary language is not English.

Two-thirds of the kindergartners from large cities (population over 250,000) were at risk compared to approximately one-third from the suburbs. Minority children were also more likely to be at risk. Nearly 75 percent of the children from Black or Hispanic families had one or more risk factors compared to 29 percent of those from White families. The proportion of children in two or more risk categories was five times larger among Hispanics and four times larger among Blacks than among Whites. Asian children ranked about the same as White children for two or more risk factors. It is interesting to note that none of the six-year-old kindergartners were in all of the risk categories and only 10 percent of them had two or more risk factors.

AGE-RELATED AND GENDER DIFFERENCES IN SCHOOL READINESS   The ECLS-K findings support other research that showed older children, age five and a half to six and older, often had advantages with respect to reading skills, math skills, and general knowledge compared to younger kindergartners. In this study, older children had more advanced motor skills, were more persistent, more socially adept, and less prone to problem behaviors than the younger kindergartners. However, not all younger kindergartners performed below the older ones. A small percentage of children under age five and also between age five and five and a half scored as high as the older children.

Although previous studies found that girls matured earlier than boys (Gullo and Burton, 1992), this study showed no appreciable differences in their knowledge or in most skills. However, boys experienced more developmental difficulties than girls in articulating words clearly and in paying attention for sustained periods. There were also behavior differences. Boys were much more active than girls while girls were more prosocial and less prone to problem behaviors. For example, girls were reported more often to be comforting or helpful to classmates than were boys.

Although many older children do better in kindergarten, and perhaps throughout their school years, Grosser (1998) cautions against teachers and parents making decisions to delay entry to kindergarten based largely on age and not on all indicators of school readiness (Zill and West, 2000).

Developmentally and Culturally Appropriate Programs

Historically, kindergarten curriculums emphasized social competence over academic competence. In the last three decades, there has been a greater emphasis on academic skills, such as children learning to read earlier (Shephard and Smith, 1988; Walsh, 1989). How can parents and school administrators find the most effective ways to help children acquire specific skills that foster their reading and mathematic readiness as well as social skills?

A developmentally appropriate curriculum is one in which learning experiences are appropriate for the child's physical, social-emotional, cognitive, and creative needs as well as supportive of their cultural needs (see Chapter 7). Children at this age learn through hands-on experiences. For example, by playing with different size unit blocks they are experiencing mathematical concepts. In using the tools of literacy (paper, pencil, books), they are acquiring skills for reading. Other prereading skills involve sensory or perceptual activities such as working with puzzles using different shapes or activities practicing left-to-right concepts. Helping children develop a sense of story and the ability to understand decontextualized language (understand words out of context) also develop emergent literacy skills. It is important for many activities in kindergarten to involve small groups of children, allowing for more child input. Child-led activities encourage them to follow their interests and their ideas. A variety of manipulative materials should be available but worksheets are not appropriate. Young children need space for their activities and their energies.

Children in inappropriate settings show behaviors such as fingernail biting, inappropriate laughter, pencil tapping, and overall stress (Burts, et al., 1992; Maxwell and Eller, 1994). A national survey of kindergarten classrooms found both developmentally appropriate and inappropriate kindergarten activities. Unfortunately, 93 percent of teachers in this survey reported that they and *not* the children usually determined the classroom learning activities. This certainly limited opportunities for providing learning activities that met individual interests and needs. In addition, 80 percent of these teachers divided the curriculum into separate subjects rather than integrating various subjects into the children's activities (Love, Logue, Trudeau, and Thayer, 1992).

FULL-DAY OR HALF-DAY PROGRAMS   Many districts offer both half- and full-day kindergarten and in about half of these children attend classes for a full day. Children who are minority and/or living in poverty comprise a large percentage of the children in full-day kindergarten. State and federal monies for at-risk students is often used in funding these all-day classes (Fromberg, 1992; Housden and Kam, 1992). Full-day programs eliminate the cost of buses and crossing guards midday. They also help working-parent families by eliminating the need to coordinate transportation between kindergarten and child care and reducing transitions for children.

Recent research supports the effectiveness, both academically and behaviorally, of full-day developmentally appropriate kindergarten (Cryan, Sheehan, Weichel, and Bandy-Hedden, 1992; Karweit, 1992; Holmess and McConnell, 1990; Rothenberg, 1995). The environment is more relaxed and the teacher has more time to get to know and work with individual children. Of course, there are excellent half-day kindergarten programs.

Private Schooling

Paralleling the public school system are two private school systems: private religious schools and independent private schools. Most religious schools are parochial or Catholic schools. Although there are fewer Protestant schools, the fun-

Give Me a Book: Baby Brother Telling Sister What Book He Wants

When children see parents or older siblings enjoying books, they want books also.

damentalist Protestant schools are increasing in number. Independent private schools have higher tuition and many enroll students from the upper classes as well as scholarship students. These schools, often referred to as preparatory schools, provide an education and a network that enable many of its children to further their education in prestigious private colleges and universities. Funds for these private schools come from tuition and private resources.

Compared with public schools, private schools have smaller classes, greater parent participation and influence, less violence, more control, fewer discipline problems, and personal curriculum options such as religion. Private schools can choose their students and expel those who do not conform to their basic rules. The socialization in private schools is limited. Children in public schools experience more diverse cultures, socioeconomic groups, and more children with special needs.

Teachers in private schools receive less salary, fringe benefits, and job security than those in public schools. Although some private school teachers are credentialed, legally they do not have to be. They often have less education than public school teachers. Most private schools have fewer resources. This means they often have limited academic offerings. In particular, most private schools are not able to have as many expensive labs for the sciences or options for sports, especially in secondary schools.

Magnet Schools

As an effort to meet the needs of bright students and to provide racial balance, magnet schools were established in the 1970s by many school districts in inner cities. They offer their students special facilities and programs that promote educational excellence. There are now more than a thousand magnet schools, mostly in urban areas, providing intensive learning in subjects such as science, math, foreign languages, or computer science and the arts. Students are high achievers with very low absenteeism. Magnet schools can choose their students and some even have admission tests. In contrast, the local neighborhood school must accept all students (Nathan, 1998). Sometimes magnet schools receive more money per pupil than the local public school. In order to provide voluntary desegregation, they have tried to make these inner-city magnet schools attractive to more affluent White students with mixed success.

Home Schooling

Home schooling is an alternative to public schooling in which parents take the responsibility for educating their child at home. Home schooling was the norm in the early years of our nation but with mandatory education in all the states by 1918, it declined rapidly. In the 1960s parents searched for school choices through alternative schools. After most of these schools closed, public interest in home schooling began to escalate. In 1990, approximately 500,000 children were schooled at home, representing a tenfold increase in a decade (*Time*, 10-22-1990). Currently, it is estimated that as many as one million children are being home schooled and, by 2010, it is predicted that there will be five million children (Gorder, 1996; Ray, 1997). Most parents are motivated by religious convictions and/or by concerns over the quality of the education and discipline problems in the schools. Although individual parents vary in their motives, all feel that they can do a better job of educating their children.

The home schooling movement of the 1960s and 1970s went through periods of contention followed by court battles over its legality. By the 1980s, attitudes of both the parents and the schools had changed and they began to cooperate. In the last fifteen to twenty years, the movement has grown so that parents are able to form networks. These networks provide them with

---

8.2   Community Home Education Program

In 1988, the Orange County Department of Education in California began an alternative kindergarten through eighth grade public education program for families who home-school. This Community Home Education Program (CHEP) is a support system to parents as well as school districts. It offers access to public education for students K-8 who are out of the regular school system and involved in a home-study program. Parents are offered a complete curriculum, testing, tutoring, and legal accountability. Conferences, a hot line for students and parents, and many extracurricular activities are available.

information from publications, workshops, and a wider range of curriculum programs. Many schools are responding with innovative plans ranging from providing counselors and computer resources to options to attend some classes and school activities such as field trips (Knowles, 1989; Lines, 1995)

Because of state mandatory education laws, each state has criteria for accepting home schooling in place of public or approved private schooling. Michigan, Iowa, and North Dakota have rigid requirements for home schooling, which include filing a curriculum plan with the superintendent showing proof of equivalency and requiring the home school teacher either to be certified or to be supervised by a credentialed teacher. Other states require a curriculum plan but testing, proof of equivalency, or certification is not required (Deckard, 1996; Gorder, 1996; Lines, 1991).

Data on the effectiveness of home instruction is insufficient and often hard to measure. Concerns often involve missing socialization skills, especially those needed to be effective in the larger world. Others worry whether the parent is able to cover a broad enough range of subjects and has access to necessary equipment, especially in science. However, students returning to the public school after home schooling often do well both academically and socially in school (Colfax and Colfax, 1992). The states that require home-schooled children to take the same tests as other students find that those in home school score academically as well as or even better than those in regular public schools (Lines, 1995).

Schooling for Special Needs Children

Changes in attitudes and legislation have affected the education of children with special needs. From World War II until 1975, most disabled children were segregated in "special education" classes. Now, mandatory education laws not only require children to attend school, they also express the obligation of society to provide a basic education to everyone. The Education for All Handicapped Children Act of 1975 mandated that all children be educated in the least restricted environment meeting their special needs. Putting this into practice was very slow. Many parents did not realize their legal rights. In 1985, legislation extended these mandates to cover children ages three to five with special disabilities.

In 1990, Congress changed the title of the 1975 Education for All Children Act to the Individuals with Disabilities Act (IDEA) and amended it. Children ages three to five with disabilities must be placed in the Least Restrictive Environment (LRE) in which the individual child can learn. It includes the provisions in the 1975 legislation and the 1985 law covering ages three to five. In 1992, infants and toddlers were included. Part C of IDEA is a grant program helping states in developing early intervention programs for infants and toddlers with disabilities in settings as similar as possible to regular settings. The latest revision of this act was in 1997.

Each child is required by law to have an individualized educational plan or IEP. The necessary specialists meet with an administrator, the classroom teacher, and the parents to diagnose the child's educational needs and prepare a plan of instructional activities to meet these needs. This plan is evaluated and adjusted periodically.

In 1992, the Americans with Disabilities Act became law (ADA). One of its provisions prohibits all public accommodations from discriminating against any individual because of a disability. This includes nursery schools, child-care centers, and family child-care homes.

Inclusion or Full Inclusion

Should inclusion in the regular classroom be for all students regardless of the disability or its severity or only for some special needs children? For over two decades, educators around the world have been debating what is the least restrictive environment that meets the needs of an individual with disabilities. Some educators believe in inclusion while others advocate full inclusion. The difference in these two positions is the degree to which children with special needs should be included in the regular classroom.

Inclusion	Full Inclusion
Inclusion is only for some students	Inclusion is for *all* students.
Inclusion can be full-time in general education classes or can combine some time in general classrooms with some time in specialized learning centers.	Inclusion means full-time placement in general education classrooms.
Inclusion must result in useful academic learning to be considered successful.	Inclusion can focus primarily on social learning and friendship for some disabled students.
Inclusion must be a positive experience for students without disabilities.	Full inclusion may be detrimental for students without disabilities.
Many special educators are opposed to full inclusion.	Many general educators are opposed to inclusion.
The evidence does not support full inclusion.	The evidence does support inclusion.

Reprinted by permission of Philip M. Ferguson and Diane L. Ferguson, *Childhood Education, 74*(5), and the Association for Childhood Education International. Copyright © 1998 by the Association.

Each group of educators advocates for different groups of children. Most inclusionists represent children with common disabilities, such as learning disabilities, behavior disorders, and mild mental retardation. They focus on these children receiving appropriate academic instruction. Most full inclusionists represent children with severe mental retardation such as the Association for Persons with Severe Handicaps. Their primary concern is for these children to develop healthy relationships even if their academic skills suffer. Professional organizations supporting the least restrictive environment that meets the child's needs include the Council for Learning Disabilities, Learning Disabilities Association of America, and the National Joint Committee on Learning Disabilities. They argue that full inclusion may not provide appropriate services for some students with disabilities. There is also a concern about the impact of full inclusion on general education teachers and all students (Ferguson and Ferguson, 1998; Fuchs and Fuchs, 1998).

In recent years there appears to be a more moderate approach to educational placement by many full inclusionists. This moderated movement has been referred to as "responsible inclusion" or supported education (Polloway and Patten, 1997). Smith (1995) states that responsible inclusion means:

1. *children with disabilities should be included in general classrooms as much as possible;*
2. *the education of children with disabilities should be shared among special and general educators;*
3. *children with disabilities should be included in all facets of the school;*
4. *children with disabilities need to have a place and be welcomed in regular classrooms.*

Table 8.3 shows options for children from the regular classroom to hospital or residential placement.

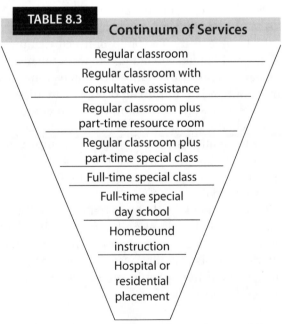

TABLE 8.3 **Continuum of Services**

Regular classroom

Regular classroom with consultative assistance

Regular classroom plus part-time resource room

Regular classroom plus part-time special class

Full-time special class

Full-time special day school

Homebound instruction

Hospital or residential placement

D. Fuchs and L. S. Fuchs. (1998). *Childhood Education, 74*(5), p. 311. Reprinted by permission of Douglas Fuchs and Lynn S. Fuchs and the Association for Childhood Education International. Copyright © 1998 by the Association.

JUST HOW INCLUSIVE ARE CURRENT PRACTICES AND HOW EQUALLY ARE THEY APPLIED?   A recent report to Congress on the implementation of the Individuals with Disabilities Act for the 1993–1994 school year showed that 5.5 million children between the ages of six and twenty-one were served under Part B of IDEA. Approximately 43 percent of these children spent at least 80 percent of their time in general education classrooms. However, this varied considerably with different disabilities, ages, and geographical locations. Only 8 to 10 percent of children with significant disabilities were in inclusive placements and 60 percent of children labeled mentally retarded spent most of the school day in self-contained classrooms (U.S. Department of Education, 1996; Ferguson and Ferguson, 1998).

The Charter School Experiment

Over twenty years ago, a New England teacher promoted the idea of local school boards granting small groups of teachers a "charter" or contract to explore new approaches to education. This included changes in curriculum, school calender, administration, teaching styles, and requirements for students and their families. The current charter school movement emerged in Minnesota in 1991 with the passage of the first state charter school law. This school movement has grown from one school in one state in 1992 to approximately 1,100 schools in thirty-three states and the District of Columbia by late 1998 (Nathan, 1998; Children's Defense Fund, 1999). A state or local school board, university, or city council issues the charter, usually for five years. The philosophy, curriculum, staffing, and requirements for students and parents are tailored to meet the needs of those involved.

Charter schools are founded by three groups: educators, parents, or organizations (profit and nonprofit) all of whom are dissatisfied with their current choice or choices and want freedom to create an alternative public school. Families and teachers choose charter schools primarily for educational reasons: high academic standards, small classes and school size, emphasis on teaching and learning, and an educational philosophy that is compatible with theirs (Manno, Finn, Bierlein, and Vanouerki, 1998). Parents of older children often express the desire for a safe, drug-free school.

Because these schools are given no more state money per pupil than regular schools and rarely capital outlay money, they have been innovative in seeking alternative funding, especially for their capital outlay. In 1995–1996, 54.4 percent of charter schools operating were startups (began as charter schools), 32.5 percent were converted from regular public schools, and 11.1 percent were once private schools (Manno, et al., 1998).

Freedom, Responsibility, and Accountability

1. Charter schools are free of most educational code regulations in order to design and operate a school to meet the needs of an individual group of par-

ents and children, teachers, staff and administrators. No teaching credentials are required. School personnel and families elect to participate in the
program.

2. The school personnel accept responsibility for the achievement of their students. Parents and children also make certain commitments.

3. All participants are accountable. If schools do not show student achievements within three or five years, they will be closed. However, the evaluation methods they use vary. If parents or students do not meet their
obligations, they may be asked to leave. Teachers, staff, and administrators
are hired on a performance basis. Teachers have no tenure.

Charter Schools: A Smorgasbord of Schools

Most charter schools average 150 students with small numbers of children per
class. Generally their students reflect the same ethnic/racial and income levels as
students in their district. In fact, one-third of the charter schools are more likely to
have students of low-income and color than schools in their district (Children's
Defense Fund, 1999). They are nonsectarian and prohibit admission tests. They
require that the average per-pupil funding follow students to their schools, along
with appropriate funds such as Title I and special and compensatory education
money. They are mandated by Congress to accept children with disabilities as are
other publicly funded schools.

A national two-year study, "Charter Schools in Action" (Manno, et al., 1998),
showed literally dozens of approaches to learning. These included individualized
learning, project-based and hands-on learning, foreign languages in the early years,
unconventional approaches to special and bilingual education, and an array of
assessments, both packaged and locally developed. These schools were organized
in different ways. They often combined grades. Some had self-contained classes
while others had teams of teachers responsible for large groups of children. In the
multiyear houses, some teachers and children stayed together in the same space
for two or more years and some teachers moved with their students each year.

The leadership and governance of charter schools are rarely the traditional
principal and assistant principal team. There may be an executive director, director of instruction, or other leaders with different titles. Some charter schools are
headed by teachers, a few have a charismatic principal, while other schools contract outside management for all or part of their operations. These outside management groups may be nonprofit or for-profit. Still other schools have a strong
authoritative board that makes or approves decisions.

Staffing selection and arrangements are quite diverse. There are master teachers, performance-based pay, and teachers both with and without state teacher credentials. One charter school shares teachers and rents space from a private
parochial school. Charter schools have found many ways to involve parents and
the community. Parents or family members are often required to contribute a minimal number of hours during the school year. Beyond this, parents may be used

as instructors and school sites may have a social-service center. Some schools offer classes for parents and community members.

Charter schools have different schedules and calendars from regular public schools. In general, they have more hours per day and more days of school per calendar year. A higher percentage of these schools compared to other public schools have before- and after-school programs. Detroit's Sierra Leone Academy operates 210 days from 9 A.M. to 5 P.M., while City Academy in St. Paul operates year-round from 7 A.M. to 8 P.M.

Many charter schools take advantage of technology to support their instructional programs. There are home computers, E-mail addresses, and homework hot lines. A two-way interactive distance-learning system allows two schools several hundred miles apart to share instructors. However, the most advanced uses of technology are employed to create "virtual" schools. The Choice 2000 On Line School started in 1994 and is open twenty-four hours a day for its students. Often a few teachers are on the school site but much of their teaching is from their homes (Manno, et al., 1998).

Evaluation of Charter Schools

Many charter schools have shown positive performances using their own tests, which were not necessarily standard tests from the school district. These results include positive performance scores from some charter schools serving children with previous school problems and/or dropouts. Many of these schools have reached out to low-income, minority, and disadvantaged families who otherwise have few options. A small number of charter schools have already had their charters renewed because of improved student achievements (Manno, et al., 1998).

A few schools have been closed for financial mismanagement. The biggest criticism or debate has been over the achievement of individual schools and not on the impact of the charter movement. However, some believe that charter schools remove committed families from the traditional public school system.

Whatever else can be said about charter schools, they have provided many innovative ideas and models of schooling. Some models will fall by the wayside, others will survive with fine tuning, and a few may become so popular that they are reproduced on a large scale. An important message that this movement is sending is that *no one model is best for all children in our diverse society.*

Educating and Supporting Homeless Children

Homelessness is a way of life for an estimated 100,000 children each night (Children's Defense Fund, 1997). Homeless children live on the streets and in cars, abandoned buildings, public places, and shelters (Alker, 1992; McCormick and Holden, 1992). Not only has homelessness increased greatly in the past decade but there has been a significant demographic shift in the population. In the past, the alcoholic man or the slightly deranged "bag lady" was the stereotypical homeless person (Bassuk, 1990; Jones, Levine, and Rosenberg, 1991). In recent years, families with children, mostly headed by women, are the fastest growing group of homeless persons. In 1992, homeless families represented approximately 33 percent of the homeless population. In 2001, homeless families had increased to 40 percent of all homeless people and 67 percent of these were single-parent families (U.S. Conference of Mayors, 2001).

Needs of School-Age Homeless Children

The inadequate living conditions of homeless children usually result in their developmental impairment (Rafferty and Shinn, 1991). Many of the children have severe emotional and social deficits, with over half of these children testing high for depression (Menke, 1998). Homeless children, compared to housed children, have many more health and educational problems (Bassuk, Weintraub, Dawson, Perloff, and Bruckner, 1997; Bassuk and Rubin, 1987).

Homeless children need to attend school regularly. Education, both informal and formal, is necessary preparation for a child's success in the adult world. During the school years, all children need to develop both cognitive and social competencies. The McKinney Homeless Assistance Act of 1987 (PL 100-77) and amendments of 1990 and 1994 provide funds for programs and guarantee homeless children access to education. This law requires every state to have a coordinator to help in assessing homeless children and developing appropriate programs. It also removes residency requirements that had kept children out of school. States vary greatly in their implementation of this act (First, 1992). It is estimated that 43 percent of homeless school-age children are not in school at any one time. According to a survey by the U.S. Mayors (2001), 12 percent of homeless children are denied access to school despite federal law.

Homeless children need temporary shelter and transportation in order to attend school regularly. They must have their medical records, including the necessary vaccinations. Many children need medical attention and school clothing. Community agencies are often able to help these children and their families. If society does not provide help for homeless children, they will *not* become productive adult members of society. In strictly monetary terms, it costs far *more* to provide for dysfunctional adults than to provide the necessary help for these children now.

Assessment of Public Schools

A comprehensive study of the academic quality of education was prepared by the National Commission on Excellence in American Education. Their 1983 report, *A Nation at Risk,* found deterioration in the quality of education based on a number of studies. They reported a high functional illiteracy rate among secondary school graduates. Approximately one out of every eight children completing secondary school did not read or write well enough for basic societal functions. For minorities, it was one in three. The report also claimed that nearly 40 percent of youth aged seventeen could not draw inferences from written material, 80 percent could not write a persuasive essay, and 66.6 percent could not solve mathematical problems requiring several steps.

The average scores on standardized achievement tests, including the Scholastic Aptitude Test (SAT), began to decline in the early 1960s with a slight rebound in the 1980s. However, SAT scores in recent years are not comparable to the scores in the mid-1970s when only a small percentage of our population—our elite—took the SAT. For example, more than three and one half times as many students take Advanced Placement examinations for college credit today as compared to 1976 figures. Also each subgroup taking the test (Whites, Blacks, Hispanics) has increased its score. According to Houston, the decline is due to the increase in minorities now taking the test, who, as a group, score lower (1992).

Whatever the case, education has not improved at the rate needed to prepare many of our children for the complex and changing society that they will navigate. Society has not closed the minority achievement gap nor overcome the grinding problems created by poverty. A number of students are abused, ill-fed, and poorly clothed. An increasing number of students are minorities and they have lower scores and a lower rate of completing high school than White children. The correlations are strong between minority status and income and between income and achievement.

Test scores for United States children in science, math, and reading are lower than scores for children in many of the industrialized countries. Shootings and violence in our schools are shocking. In an attempt to improve our schools, national educational goals were developed and funded along with a number of federal initiatives.

National Goals for Education by the Year 2000

In 1990 President Bush held an Educational Summit with the governors of all the state. They adopted six educational goals to be achieved by the year 2000. Two additional goals were added. In March, 1994, the **Goals 2000: Educate America** became law. The federal government gave states and communities financial support for projects to meet these standards.

1. *All children will start school ready to learn.*
2. *The high school graduation rate will increase to at least 90 percent.*
3. *Students will leave grades four, eight, and twelve having demonstrated competency in English, mathematics, science, history, and geography, and be prepared for responsible citizenship, further learning, and productive employment in our modern economy.*

4. *U.S. students will be the first in the world in science and mathematics achievement.*

5. *Every adult will be literate and possess the knowledge and skills necessary to compete in a global economy and exercise the rights and responsibilities of citizenship.*

6. *Every school will be free of drugs and violence and will offer a disciplined environment conducive to learning.*

7. *The nation's teaching force will have access to programs for the continued improvement of their professional skills and the opportunity to acquire the knowledge and skills needed to instruct and to prepare all American students for the next century.*

8. *Every school will promote partnerships that will increase parental involvement and participation in promoting social, emotional, and academic growth of children (U.S. Department of Education, 1994).*

The last goal was further supported by President Clinton in 1996 with the *America Reads Challenge.* This initiative calls for schools to involve the community organizations and the home to help all children learn to read by the end of third grade (Mitchell and Spencer, 1997).

Most educators agree with these broad goals but argue over what they really mean and how they can be achieved. Does the first goal mean that school readiness depends on adequate health care and nutrition and freedom from abuse as prerequisites to learn? Goal three involves accountability, but many would not agree on a single national competency test and the implications of this in the curriculum.

By the year 2000, many gains were made but none of these goals was met. Revised educational goals are to be achieved by 2005. Teachers were not a part of the 1990 Education Summit. Educators, parents, businesspeople, communities, and politicians will need to work together to bring about significant improvements in the educational system (Houston, 1992). "Schools are not and cannot be parents, police, hospitals, welfare agencies or drug treatment centers" (U.S. Department of Education, 1991). The families and communities will have to replace their own missing pieces.

Computers, the Internet, Schools, and the Twenty-First Century

The computer revolution has entered the schools and increased options for learning. Computers are already used in virtually every occupation. By 1993, more than 95 percent of public schools reported having instructional computers, with an average of one computer for sixteen students (U.S. Bureau of the Census, 1993). In 1999, 69 percent of all children ages eight to eighteen had a computer in their household (Kaiser Family Foundation, 1999). However, only 28 percent of Black and Hispanic students had computers in their household compared to 70 percent of White students (U.S. Bureau of the Census, 1998). White children have approximately twice as much access to the Internet at home as low-income, Black, and Hispanic children. It is important for children to have access to computers and the Internet at school.

Schools Help Equalize Access to Computers

The value of computers for classroom instruction depends on how and to what extent computers are used in the daily curriculum (Haugland, 1999). When computer activities are integrated into the curriculum, children demonstrate gains in conceptual understanding and problem solving and develop or improve their abstract thinking (Haugland, 1992). Ideally, computers allow children to progress at their own speed, obtain information, and record or document their findings. This enables them to reflect on the data later. Computers provide a vehicle for self-expression in a variety of ways such as creative stories, drawings, and /or scanning pictures into a document. Computers allow students who are unable to use a pencil to use the keyboard to participate.

How are computers used at school? Are they used only for programmed learning activities or are they used in open-ended activities in which students use the computer to gather information, solve problems, and create their own projects? The most promising uses of the computer have nothing to do with programmed learning, such as drill-and-practice sheets, but with open-ended programs. Children using open-ended software have made significant gains in general intelligence, nonverbal skills, structural knowledge, long-term memory, complex manual dexterity, and self-esteem (Haugland, 1992, 1996). Other studies show that open-ended programs, such as Logo, benefit children in many ways. These include developing subject-matter knowledge, problem-solving and socio-emotional competencies, and increasing their creativity (Natasi and Clements, 1994; Clements, Nastasi, and Swaminathan, 1993).

The Computer: An Integral Part of Her Life at Age 8

Children can contribute information to their class Web site. Children also use the computer for research and homework assignments as well as for pursing their personal interests. Parents can access information from the Web site pertaining to homework, meetings, holidays, and special messages.

FIGURE **8.1**   **COMPUTER USE**   **The impact of school on income differentials in computer use. In a typical day . . .**

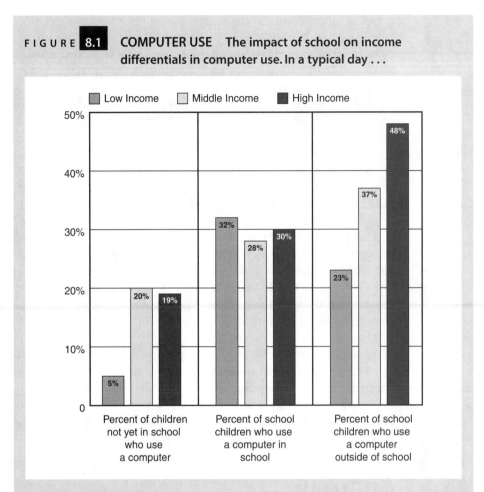

Income categories are based on the median income of the zip code in which a child lives (among 2–7-year-olds) or attends school (among 8–18-year-olds) and represent the following ranges: "Low Income," less than $25,000; "Middle Income," $25,000 to $39,999; "High Income," $40,000 or more.

Source: Kaiser Family Foundation, Kids and the Media at the New Millenium, November 1999.

REGGIO-EMILIA SCHOOLS AND TECHNOLOGY   The use of technology in the Reggio-Emilia Schools in Italy is impressive. They have long-term projects during which children can explore a topic from many perspectives over an extended period of time (Katz and Chard, 1989; Trepanier-Street et al., 2001). In their long-term projects, the children and teachers use computers, various software packages, digital cameras, video printers, scanners, and Internet connections to find, examine, organize, and document their experiences. Teachers use this documentation to determine children's interests, progress, and any confusions on the topic. Assessment of individual children is more accurate, their curriculums are more appropriate, and communications with parents are more accurate (Trepanier-Street, Hong, and Bauer, 2001).

In the past few years, many new early childhood software packages have been added to the market. In order to identify and encourage the use of developmentally appropriate software, Developmental Software Awards have been given to publishers based on eight categories: creativity, language, math, multicultural, multipurpose, problem solving, thematic focus, and nonviolence. The category nonviolence was recently added because of the increase in the violence found in early childhood software (Haugland, 1997).

The Internet is now a part of many young children's experiences. Increasing numbers of children have access to information both helpful and damaging. The Internet is used by teachers and students to find information for classroom activities. Teachers can check out various Web sites on a topic and give appropriate sites to the children to use. Teachers can help them prepare questions to research. Teachers can help them develop a class Web page and parents can access information about class activities, meetings, and events.

The computer will never take the place of a qualified and motivated teacher interacting with the child. Teachers are needed not only to assist in computer learning but to help children understand, value, and work with each other. After all, our major problems in society stem from humans not being able to live peacefully with each other rather than humans not having sufficient scientific knowledge to cope with the earth's resources. Computers will continue to shape education and the roles of teachers in this twenty-first century.

Current Trends

Parents have more options in choosing a primary school for their children. They have choices within the regular public school system and through its charter schools. Private schools remain an option for some, but an increasing number of parents are choosing to home-school their children.

The local school has more freedom in developing its curriculum based on the principal, teachers, parents, and community representatives working together. Parent-teacher partnerships will be formed creatively, enabling more parents to participate. Increasing numbers of parents and teachers will work together to plan their children's programs. Special partnerships will be formed to increase out-of-school care programs for children.

Private schools may see increases in government funding. Private companies are proposing to operate more schools. Chris Whittle, head of a large media company that provides educational TV for classrooms, leads the movement for private companies to provide management teams for public schools (Macioni, 1997).

The movement for private school vouchers will continue. Private school vouchers allow public funds to be used by students to attend private schools, including religious schools. Supporters believe vouchers allow some parents to escape failing schools for their children. They say it stimulates change in public schools through this competition. The Children's Defense Fund (1999) has the following concerns:

1. It would siphon money from the already inadequately funded public schools.
2. Vouchers provide for only a small number of students, leaving many children behind.
3. Private schools can be selective unlike public schools, which must take all children.
4. Private schools lack the same accountability to the voters that public schools have through school board elections or election of officials who appoint leadership. Private school teachers are not required to have a teacher's credential or, in some cases, a college degree. Private schools are not required to meet the same educational code requirements as public schools, although many of them choose to do so.

The United States, along with all nations, is increasingly a multi-ethnic and multicultural society. Any educational policy endorsing a nationalistic and single culture curriculum does not meet the needs of today's children (Gozzer, 1990; Domenach, 1990).

Key Points

1. Education is seen as the key to preserving democracy and reducing poverty and violence. Its basic functions include teaching skills, cultural transmission, political and social integration, talent selection, socialization, and dealing with some of the problems of children.
2. Teachers are leaders, nurturers, role models, decision makers, interpreters, and classroom managers
3. Learning styles involve the ways in which different individuals process information while multiple intelligences focus on the different settings or contexts in which this takes place.
4. Kindergarten readiness includes academic and noncognitive skills such as a child's physical and emotional well-being, ability to cooperate, and eagerness to learn.
5. Developmentally appropriate programs consider each child's developmental skills, capabilities, interests, and cultural background.
6. Private schools charge tuition, have smaller classes, less diversity, different curriculum choice, less violence, fewer discipline problems, fewer expensive labs, and teachers receive lower pay and are not required to have a teaching credential.
7. An estimated 1 million children are home-schooled, generally for religious reasons, concerns over academic standards, and for school discipline problems. Many school districts encourage these families to use some of their resources.
8. The *current* Individuals with Disabilities Act (IDEA) includes the rights and benefits of all disabled children between ages three to

twenty-one and the rights and services for children under age three. Full inclusion is defined as full-time placement of all children in regular classrooms, while inclusion means the least restrictive environment that meets the academic needs of each student.

9. Charter schools are given a charter to design a school and operate for a limited period of time as a public school, but free of most state regulations. All participants voluntarily choose this setting and are responsible for the outcome.

10. Computers using interactive and developmentally appropriate software increase children's options for learning.

11. Current trends include more parent choice in schools and an increase in parent and community partnerships to improve schools.

Critical Thinking Questions

1. What are the advantages and disadvantages of tracking in schools?
2. Choose a unit of study for your classroom and suggest ways it could be presented to support children with different learning styles.

Resources and References

Eric Clearinghouse on Elementary and Early Childhood Education
http://www.ericsp.org/ or www.ericece.org/
Federal Resources for Educational Excellence (Free)
http://www.ed.gov/free/
The Homeless Information Exchange
1830 Connecticut Avenue, NW
Washington, DC 20036
Homework Helper site
http://school.discovery.com/homeworkhelp/bjpinchbeck
National Center for Educational Statistics
http://www.ed.gov/NCES/pubs/D
National Coalition for the Homeless and Poverty
http://www.nlchp.org
US. Conference of Mayors
http:/www.NLCHP.org

U.S. Department of Education
http://www.ed.gov

Related Readings

Fogarty, R., and Bellanca, J. (Eds.) (1995). *Multiple Intelligences: A collection.* Arlington Heights, IL: IRI/Skylight Training and Publishing.

References

Alker, J. (1992). Modern American homelessness. In C. Solomon and P. Jackson-Jobe (Eds.), *Helping homeless people: Unique challenges and solutions* (pp. 7–14). Alexandria, VA: American Association for Counseling and Development.

Bassuk, E. L. (1990). The problem of family homelessness. In E. L. Bassuk, R. W. Carmen, L. F. Weinreb, and M. M. Herzig (Eds.), *Community care for homeless families: A program design manual* (pp. 7–11). Newton Center, MA: Better Homes Foundation.

Bassuk, E., and Rubin, L. (1987). Homeless children: A neglected population. *American Journal of Orthopsychiatry, 57*(2), 279–286.

Bassuk, E. L., Weintreb, L. F., Dawson, R., Perloff, J. N., and Bruckner, J. C. (1997). Determinants of behavior in homeless and low-income housed preschool children. *Pediatrics, 100,* 92–100.

Becker, H. J. (1990). How computers are used in United States schools. *Journal of Educational Computing Research, 7,* 385–406.

Berger, E. H. (1995). *Parents as partners in education: Families and schools working together.* (4th ed.). Columbus, OH: Merrill.

Best, R. (1983). *We've all got scars: What boys and girls learn in elementary school.* Bloomington: Indiana University Press.

Bowles, S., and Gintis, H. (1976). *Schooling in capitalist America: Educational reform and the contradictions of economic life.* New York: Basic Books.

Bowles, Samuels. (1972). Schooling and inequality from generation to generation. *Journal of Political Economy, 80,* 219–251.

Bredekamp, S., and Couple, C. (1997). *Developmentally appropriate practice in early childhood programs. (Rev. ed.).* Washington, DC: National Association for the Education of Young Children.

Burts, D., Hart. C., Charlesworth, R., Fleege, P., Mosely, J., and Thomasson, R. (1992). Observed activities and stress behaviors of children in developmentally appropriate and inappropriate kindergarten classrooms. *Early Childhood Research Quarterly, 7*(2), 297–318.

Calvery, R., Bell, D., and Vaupal, C. (1992). *The difference in achievement for home schooled and public schooled children for grades four, seven, and ten in Arkansas.* Paper presented at the annual meeting of the Mid-South Educational Research Association Knoxville, TN. (Eric Document Reproduction Service No. ED354248).

Casey (Annie E.) Foundation. (2001). *Kids Count data book: 2001.* Baltimore, MD: Author.

Cazden, C. B., and Mehan, H. (1989). Principles from sociology and anthropology: Context, code, classroom, and culture. In M. C. Reynolds (Ed.), *Knowledge base for the beginning teacher* (pp. 47–57). New York: Pergamon Press.

Children's Defense Fund. (1997). *The State of America's Children: Yearbook 1997.* Washington, DC: Author.

Children's Defense Fund. (1999). *The state of America's children: Yearbook 1999.* Washington, DC: Author.

Clements, D., Natassi, B., and Swaminathan, S. (1993). Young children and computers: Crossroads and directions in research. *Young Children, 48*(2), 56–64.

Coleman, M. (1997). Families and schools: In search of common ground. *Young Children, 52*(5), 14–21.

Colfax, J. D., and Colfax, M. (1992). *Hard times in paradise.* New York: Warren.

Collins, Allen. (1991). The role of computer technology in restructuring schools. *Phi Delta Kappan, 73*(1).

Comer, J. P. (1993). *School power: Implications of an intervention project.* New York, NY: Free Press.

Cremin, L. A. (1961). *The transformation of the school: Progressivism in American education, 1876–1957.* New York: Knopf.

Cross, Christopher, La Pointe, Allen, and Jensen, Karl. (1993). The First Grants: Federal leadership to advance school and family partnerships. Office of Educational Research and Improvement, U.S. Department of Education. *Phi Delta Kappan, 73.*

Cryan, J., Sheehan, J., Weichel, J., and Bandy-Hedden, I. G. (1992). Success outcomes of full-day kindergarten: More positive behavior and increased achievement in the years after. *Early Childhood Research Quarterly 7,* 187–203.

Davis, S. A., and Haller, E. J. (1981). Tracking, ability, SES: Further evidence on the 'revisionist-merito-cratic debate'. *American Journal of Education, 89,* 283–304.

Deckard, S. (1996). *Home schooling laws and resource guide for all 50 states.* (9th ed). Ramona, CA: Vision.

Delpit, L. (1995). *Other people's children: Cultural conflict in the classroom.* New York: Teachers College Press.

Domenach, Jean-Marie. (1990). *Ce qu'il faunt enseigner,* 1999. Paris: Seuil.

Epstein, J. L. (1988). How do we improve programs in parent involvement? *Educational Horizons, 66*(2), 58–59.

Ferguson, P., and Ferguson, D. (1998). The future of inclusive educational practice: Constructive tension and the potential for reflective reform. *Childhood Education, 74,* 302–308.

First, P. F. (1992). The reality: The status of education for homeless children and youth. In J. H. Stronge (Ed.), *Educating homeless children and adolescents: Evaluating policy and practice.* Newbury Park, CA: Sage.

Fromberg, D. P. (1992). Implementing the full-day kindergarten. *Principal, 71,* 26–28.

Fuchs, D., and Fuchs, L. (1998). Competing visions of educating students with disabilities: Inclusion versus full inclusion. *Childhood Education, 74,* 309–316.

Gardner, H. (1983). *Frames of mind: The theory of multiple intelligences.* New York: Basic Books.

Gardner, H. (1993). *Multiple intelligences: The theory in practice.* New York: Basic Books

Gardner, H., & Hatch, T. (1989). Multiple intelligences go to school. *Educational Researcher, 18*(8), 4–10

Gartrell, D. (1997). Beyond discipline to guidance. *Young Children, 52,* 34–42.

Ginsberg, H. P. (1989). *Children's arithmetic: How they learn it and how you teach it.* Austin, TX: Proed.

Goldring, E., and Hausman, (1996). Empower parents for productive partnerships, Streamlined Seminar, 15, *National Association of School Principals.*

Gorder, C. (1996). *HOME Schools: An alternative: You do have a choice!* (4th ed.). Tempe, AZ: Blue Bird.

Goffin, G., and Wilson, S. (2001). *Curriculum models and early childhood education: Appraising the relationship* (2nd ed.). New York: Merrill/Prentice-Hall.

Gozzer, Giovani. (1990). School curricula and social problems. *Prospects, 20*(1), 9–19.

Grosser, S. (1998). He has a summer birthday: The kindergarten entrance age dilemma, *ERIC Digest,* EDO-PS-98-7, Urbana, IL: University of Illinois.

Gullo, D. F., and Burton, C. B. (1992), Age of entry, preschool experience, and sex as antecedents of academic readiness in kindergarten. *Early Childhood Research Quarterly, 7,* 175–186.

Hallman, M. T., and Williams, R. A. (1989). Interracial choices in secondary schools. *American Sociological Review, 54*(1), 67–78.

Haugland, S. (1992). The effect of computer software on preschool children's developmental gains. *Journal of Computing in Childhood Education, 3*(1), 15–20.

Haugland, S. (1996). Enhancing children's sense of self and community through utilizing computers. *Early Childhood Education Journal, 23*(4), 227–230.

Haugland. S. (1997). Outstanding developmental software. *Young Children, 24,* 179–184.

Haugland, S. (1999). What role should technology play in young children's learning? Part 1 Young Children, 54(6), 26–34.

Haugland, S., and Wright, J. (1997). *Young children and technology: A world of discovery.* Boston: Allyn and Bacon.

Heaviside, S., and Farris, E. (1993). *Public school kindergarten teachers' views of children's readiness for school.* Washington, DC: U.S. Department of Education, NCES, (NCES 93-410).

Henderson, A. T., and Berla, N. (1997). A new generation of evidence: The family is critical to student achievement. *Education Digest, 2,* 5–7.

Holmes, C., and McConnell, B. (1990). *Full-day versus half-day kindergarten: An experimental study.* ED 369540.

Housden, T., and Kam, R. (1992). *Full-day kindergarten: A summary of the research.* Carmichael, CA: San Juan Unified School District/ED 345 868.

Houston, Paul D. (1992). What's right with schools. *American School Board Journal, 4,* 179.

Hurn, C. (1978). *The limits and possibilities of schooling.* Boston: Allyn and Bacon.

Jencks, C. (1972). *Inequality: Reassessment of the effect of family and schooling in America.* New York: Basic Books.

Jones, J. M., Levine, I. S., and Rosenberg, A. A. (1991). Homeless research, services, and social policy. *American Psychologist, 46,* 1109–1111.

Jung, C. (1927). *The theory of psychological type.* Princeton, NJ: Princeton University Press.

Kagan, S. I., Moore, E., and Bredekamp, S. (1995). *Reconsidering children's early development and learning: Toward communications and vocabulary.* Washington, DC: National Education Goals Panel.

Kagan, S. L. (1990). Readiness 2999: Rethinking rhetoric and responsibility. *Phi Delta Kappan, 72,* 272–279.

Karweit, N. (1992). The kindergarten experience. *Educational Leadership, 49*(6), 82–86.

Katz, L. (1980). *Topics in Early Childhood Education.* Aplex.

Katz, L., and Chard, S. (1989). *Engaging children's minds: The project approach.* Norwood, N.J.: Aplex.

Kilgore, Sally. (1991). The organizational context of tracking in schools. *American Sociological Review, 56*(2) 189–203.

Knowles, J. G. (1989). Cooperating with home school parents: A new agenda for public schools? *Urban Education, 23,* 392–411.

Kornhaber, M., Krechevsky, M., and Gardner, H. (1991). Engaging intelligence. *Emotional Psychologist, 25,* 177–199.

Kozol, Jonathan. (1985). *Illiterate America.* Garden City, NY: Anchor/Doubleday.

Light, Donald, Jr., and Keller, S. (1981). *Sociology.* New York: Knopf.

Lines, P. (1987). An overview of home instruction. *Phi Delta Kappan,* March, 5–12.

Lines, P. (1991). *Estimating the home school population* (Report No. OR 91-537). Washington, DC: Office of Educational Research and Improvement. (GPO ED1.310/2:337903.)

Lines, P. (1995). Home schooling. *Eric Document, No. 95.* (Gov. Doc. ED 1 310//2:381849).

Love, J. M., Logue, M. E., Trudeau, J. V., and Thayer, K. (1992). *Transitions to kindergarten in American schools: Final report of the national transition study.* Washington, DC: U.S. Department of Education, Office of Policy and Planning.

Maxwell, K. L., and Eller, S. (1994). Children's transition to kindergarten. *Young Children, 49*(6), 56–63.

Macionis, John J. (1997). *Sociology.* Englewood Cliffs, N.J.: Prentice-Hall.

Manno, B. V., Finn, J., Bierlein, C., and Vanoueri, L. (1998). How charter schools are different: Lessons and implications from a national study. *Phi Delta Kappan,* March, 489–498.

McCormick, L., and Holden, R. (1992). Homeless children: A special challenge. *Young Children, 57*(6), 61–67.

Menke, E. M. (1998). The mental health of homeless school-age children. *Journal of Child and Adolescent Psychiatric Nursing, 11,* 87–104.

Mitchell, C. J., and Spencer, L. M. (1997). *21st century community learning centers program.* Washington, DC: U.S. Department of Education, Office of Educational Research and Improvement.

Nathan, J. (1998). Heat and light in the charter movement. *Phi Delta Kappan,* March, 499–505.

National Association for the Education of Young Children. (1990). NAEYC position statement of school readiness. *Young Children, 46,* 21–23.

National Center for Educational Statistics. (1998). *Digest of educational statistics, 1998.* Washington, DC: U.S. Government Printing Office.

National Center for Educational Statistics. (2000). *The condition of education 2000.* Washington, DC: U.S. Government Printing Office (NCES 2000-06).

National Commission on Excellence in Education. (1983). *A nation at risk: The imperative for educational reform.* Washington, DC: U.S. Government Printing Office

Natasi, B., and Clements, C. (1994). Effective motivation, perceived scholastic competence, and higher order thinking in two cooperative computer environments. *Journal of Educational Computing Research, 10,* 241–267.

Oakes, J. (1982). Classroom social relationships: Exploring the Bowles and Gintis hypothesis. *Sociology of Education, 55*(4), 197–212.

Owen, D. (1985). *None of the above: Behind the myth of scholastic aptitude.* Boston: Houghton Mifflin.

Parsons, T. (1959). The school class as a social system: Some of its functions in American society. *Harvard Educational Review, 1*(4), 297–318.

Patton, J., Polloway, E., and Smith, T. (1997). *Strategies for teaching learners with special needs* (6th ed.). Columbus, OH: Merrill.

Persell, C. H. (1977). *Education and inequality: A theoretical and empirical synthesis.* New York: Free Press.

Polloway, E., and Patten, J. (1997). *Strategies for teaching learners with special needs* (6th ed.). Columbus, OH: Merrill.

Rafferty, Y., and Shinn, M. (1991). The impact of homelessness on children. *American Psychologist, 46,* 1170–1179.

Ray, B. (1997). Home education across the United States. *Home School Court Report, 13,* 11–16.

Rohlen, T. P. (1983). *Japanese high schools.* Berkeley, CA: University of California Press.

Rosenthal, R., and Jacobsen, L. (1968). *Pygmalion in the classroom: Teacher expectation and pupils' intellectual development.* New York: Holt, Rinehart & Winston.

Rothenberg, D. (1995). Full-day kindergarten programs. *ERIC Digest* EDO-PS-95-4.

Shapiro, J., and Doiron, R. (1987). Literacy environments: Bridging the gap between home and school. *Childhood Education,* April, 263–270.

Shephard, L. A., and Smith, M. L. (1988). Escalating academic demand in kindergarten: Counterproductive policies. *Elementary School Journal, 89,* 135–145.

Shonkoff, J. P., and Phillips, D. A. (Eds.). (2000). *From neurons to neighborhoods: The science of early childhood development.* Washington, DC: National Academy Press.

Sider, J. (Ed.). (1991). America 2000: An educational strategy. *Outlook, 1*(4), 5–7.

Silver, H., Strong, R., and Perini, M. (1997). Integrating learning styles and multiple intelligences. *Educational Leadership, 55*(1), 22–27.

Smith, J. (1995). Inclusive school environments and students with disabilities in South Carolina. *Occasional Papers, 1,* 1–5.

Smith, T. G., Rogers, N., Alsalam, M., Perle, T., Mahoney, R., and Martin, V. (1994). *The conditions of education.* Washington, DC: National Center for Educational Statistics.

Trepanier-Street, M. L., Hong, S. B., and Bauer, J. C. (2001). Using technology in Reggio-inspired long-term projects. *Early Childhood Education Journal, 28*(3), 181–188.

U.S. Bureau of the Census. (1993). *Statistical abstract of the United States, 1993* (112th ed.). Washington, DC: U.S. Government Printing Office.

U.S. Bureau of the Census. (1998). *December and October current population surveys 1998.* Washington, DC: U.S. Government Printing Office.

U.S. Conference of Mayors. (2001). *A status report on hunger and homelessness in America.* Washington, DC: Author.

U.S. Department of Education. (1991). *America 2000: An education strategy.* Washington, DC: Author.

U.S. Department of Education. (1994). *Goals 2000, educate America.* Washington, DC: U.S. Government Printing Office.

U.S. Department of Education. (1996). *To insure the free appropriate public education of all children with disabilities.* Eighteenth annual report to Congress on the implementation of the Individuals with Disabilities Act. Washington, DC: Author.

U.S. Department of Education. (2000). *The condition of education, 2000.* Washington, DC: U.S. Government Printing Office.

Updyke, J., and Gilmore, J. (1986). Pupil age at school entrance: How many are ready for success? *Young Children, 1,* 11–16.

Vygotsky, L. S. (1978). *Mind in society: The development of higher psychological processes.* Cambridge, MA: Harvard University Press.

Younger, M. (1999). I think I can. *Instructor.*

Walsh, D. J. (1989). Changes in kindergarten: Why here? Why now? *Early Childhood Research Quarterly, 4,* 377–391.

Wechsler, D. (1975). Intelligence defined and undefined. *American Psychologist, 30,* 135–139.

West, J., Denton, K., and Germino-Hausken, E. (2000). *Findings from the Early Childhood Longitudinal Study, kindergarten class of 1998–99.* Washington, DC: U.S. Government Printing Office.

West, J., Germino-Hausken, E., and Collins, M. (1993). *Readiness for kindergarten: Parent and teacher beliefs.* Washington, DC: U.S. Government Printing Office.

Zill, N., and West, J. (2000). *Entering kindergarten: A portrait of American children when they begin school in the U.S.* Washington, DC: U.S. Government Printing Office.

Siblings, Peers, and Friends

9

The single best childhood predictor of adult adaptation is how well a child gets along with other children.

— Willard Hartup, 1991

*T*his chapter explores the interactions of children with their siblings, peers, and friends. These relationships help children develop their self concept and personality. They also learn valuable social skills and acquire a broader view of the world. The various roles that children play in each others lives are an important part of their growth and development.

Sibling's Special Place

For Better or for Worse, Siblings Are for Life!

Siblings are an integral part of each other's lives. Most siblings develop a strong emotional tie to each other, second only to that with their parents. Biological siblings are the closest genetically of all relatives with their genes coming from the same two people. The family environment of siblings is never the same, even for identical twins, but it is closely shared. Their parents and relatives, and often schools, toys, and bedrooms, are shared. However, siblings have many different experiences, even within the home, that contribute to the differences in their personalities. Siblings normally provide companionship, help, and emotional support but also challenges and conflicts. "I love you, I hate you," are two familiar phrases exchanged by siblings. The social, emotional, and cognitive skills learned from each other are fundamental to their overall development.

Qualities of Sibling Relationships

Sibling relationships vary as to the degree of closeness and affection, relative power and status, conflict or harmony, and rivalry or cooperation (Furman and Buhremester, 1985). The warmth–closeness characteristic appears greater between same-sex siblings and increases with the closeness of their ages. Physical intimacy between opposite-sex siblings, as with peers, appears to be affected by taboo (Furman and Buhremester, 1985). The power and status each sibling feels may range from one of superiority to one of being controlled and subordinate. When siblings have very different temperaments, there is more conflict. This is especially true when the older child has the more difficult temperament (Dunn, 1995). The dimension of rivalry, especially when children are young, is stronger in sibling relationships than other relationships. According to Newman, siblings in most families coexist peacefully with only occasional rivalry (1994). Many conditions, including age differences, sex, number and spacing of children, temperaments, and relationships in the home, along with parental employment and socioeconomic status, affect each of these qualities.

Influences on Sibling Relationships

The family constellation, or structure of the family, the relationships within the family, and the characteristics of the individual children all impact sibling relationships. Family constellation refers to the number and sex of the adults and children including the birth order, type of relationship (biological, adopted, stepparent or sibling), age, and spacing of the children. Although all relationships in the family are important, the parent–child relationships have the greatest impact on sibling relationships. Individual differences among siblings also impact their relationships. When children are younger, temperament is important in sibling relationships but for older children, relationships are influenced by their personality and social and cognitive skills. Family life varies greatly and many factors influence the outcome for children.

Birth Order

The relationship between birth order and an individual's personality has been debated since Alfred Adler (1928) described specific characteristics of children according to their birth order. He also coined the phrase "sibling rivalry." Although a number of factors affect the outcomes for children, many authorities believe that children's birth order plays a special role in their destiny.

FIRSTBORN CHILDREN   Firstborn children, who are often surrogates for their parents as caregivers, teachers, and models, enjoy a greater status/power position in relationship to their younger siblings. This difference becomes more pronounced as the age gap increases for at least up to four years. In children's eyes, status/power is conferred most heavily on the eldest son (Furman and Buhremester, 1985). Older girls are more often good teachers and nurturers for younger children (Cirirelli, 1972). Older boys, on the other hand, tend to be better stimulators and models (Cirirelli, 1972). The oldest sibling feels more rivalry over the birth of the second child than other birth orders do toward a new baby. This is because the firstborn has had the full attention of parents and now has to share their affections. The adverse effects of this dethronement can be modified if parents prepare the older child for the changes and give her or him special attention after the new baby arrives. In this case, the older sibling often becomes protective of the new family member (Adler, 1928; Teti, Sakin, Kucera, Corns, and Eiden, 1996).

Firstborn children tend to have distinct personality traits. Many studies depict these children as more adultlike, achievement-oriented, verbal, conservative, controlling of subordinates, and displaying a higher self-concept, but more anxious and less popular with peers than children born later (Lahey, Hammer, Crumrine, and Forehand, 1980; Zajonc, 1983). Success seems to fit firstborn children. Many firstborns show leadership qualities. Alfred Adler said firstborns were in a favorable position being larger and stronger, but, to keep their position, they also had to be more clever (1928). In studies as early as Galton's *English Men of Science* (1874), disproportionate numbers of firstborns have achieved eminence. A higher percentage of firstborn children have become scientists, professors, presidents, Rhodes scholars, and astronauts. More firstborns have been finalists in the National Merit Scholarship tests compared to any other birth order (Muzi, 2000). This advantage may be explained by the fact that firstborns have only adults for language models and social interactions in the most formative period while their siblings are influenced by their predecessors in the family.

ONLY CHILDREN   It is not surprising that only children have many of the characteristics of firstborns with siblings (Falbo and Polit, 1986). Their relationship to their parents is similar and both are responsive to adults. Parents provide an adult intellectual environment for these children. In the case of the only child, this environment remains unchanged by the presence of younger children.

Although both groups surpass other birth orders in intellectual and academic achievements, only children, as a group, score higher than other firstborns. They also complete about three additional years of schooling, achieve higher occupational prestige, and earn more money than firstborn children with siblings (Blake, 1989; Falbo, 1984; Falbo and Polit, 1986). However, a study on birth order by Steelman and Powell (1985) shows no correlation between birth order and academic success.

Only children miss the experiences of sibling relationships and of having to share their parents with siblings. However, the stereotype of only children as more lonely, selfish, spoiled, and maladjusted than children with siblings is not true. A study of only children placed them into three groups. Some were normal and well adjusted, others were impulsive and acting out, and others were similar to the stereotype of only children (Rosenberg and Hyde, 1993).

MIDDLE CHILDREN   Middle children are more sociable and harder to classify than the firstborns. They are sometimes called the "overlooked child." It is more difficult to be the middle child when all siblings are of the same gender. If second-born children are closer in age to the oldest, they tend to take on some of these characteristics. This is especially true when the second-born is the oldest girl in a large family. On the other hand, middle children tend to be less adaptive to parental values, perhaps because they want to avoid competition with the older child. Because firstborn children mirror their parents in searching for their identity, middle children turn to peers, often adopting some of their values. In contrast to the first-born the middle child may be more friendly, cheerful, placid, and less studious with lower self-esteem. According to Adler (1928), the middle child is ambitious, rebellious, envious, and better adjusted than either the first born or the youngest child.

YOUNGEST CHILD   When growing up, the youngest child is smaller, weaker, less knowledgeable, and less competent compared to older siblings, and often turns to attention-seeking. At a very early age, the youngest are more outgoing, exploring toys, making responses to people, and initiating more play with strangers. Youngest children are significantly more successful socially than other birth orders (Steelman and Powell, 1985). The younger or youngest sibling is more dependent on others for help. Their dependency, however, deprives them of status/power and may lower their self-esteem.

Spacing, Gender, and Age

Most children are born within two or three years of the last sibling's birth (Dunn; 1995). Spacing of less than two years or five or more years is beneficial for the child's adjustment to a new sibling (Dunn, 1995; Teti, et al., 1996). A child under age two cannot realize all the implications of another sibling to their special position. In addition, young children closely spaced spend more time together than with their parents during these years and learn to understand each other intimately (Jaffe, 1997). After age two, resentment and rivalry increase until children reach age five or six. By this time their world outside the family has expanded and they are better able to cope with and/or avoid some of these feelings (Dunn, 1995). All children, including the newborn, benefit from larger intervals between births. Parents have time to give them more individual attention.

Age differences, gender, and the ages of children in the family account for differences in the quality of their sibling relationships. Younger siblings admire most their siblings who are four or more years older. As already mentioned, the warmth–closeness characteristic appears greater between same-gender siblings and increases with the closeness of their ages. (Furman and Buhremester, 1985). On the other hand, conflict and competition are also more intense when siblings are close in age and, particularly, the same gender. Sibling rivalry is most intense in the early years and diminishes, at least on the conscious level, as siblings approach maturity.

Family Size

There are differences in growing up in a small family (one or two children) as opposed to a large family (over four children). The larger the family, the greater is the number of relationships for a child to experience, which can be enriching or frustrating or both. Discipline in large families is more rule oriented, less individualized and there is more corporal punishment (Wagner, Schubert, and Schubert, 1985). Children in small families have fewer experiences in relationships but do have more individual time with their parents. According to some studies, they also have slightly higher test scores, more schooling, and achieve more academically and in their occupation than children from large families (Blake, 1989; Hauser and Sewell, 1985).

Parent–Child Relationships

The quality of the relationship between each child and parent and between parents affects the sibling relationships. Parents who are constructively responsive to their children foster good feelings and cooperative behavior among their children (Furman, 1995; Bryant and Crockenberg, 1980). In homes where fathers are affectionate and helpful, there are more positive sibling interactions. On the other hand, conflict between mother and each child is associated with increased sibling conflicts (Volling and Belsky, J., 1992). The child's temperament, sex, health, or hereditary traits also affect sibling relationships. Parents sometimes understand one child better than another. The child's temperament, gender, health, or hereditary traits affect this relationship. When children perceive parental partiality, it increases feelings of competition, conflict, and jealousy among siblings. Most children believe that their parent has a favorite child, which may not be true (Zervas and Sherman, 1994).

Sibling rivalry is a normal emotion growing out of the need to share biological and affectional ties of the two most important people in a child's world, his or her parents. When a baby comes along, a child's world changes greatly. The child or children in the family need to know about this ahead of time and be given special attention. The new baby does take time and energy from the parents and the other child or children do not receive the same kind of attention from parents, relatives, and friends as before. The author at age three-and-one-half said to a relative fussing over her new baby sister, "Aunt Olive, you can go home now and you don't need to come back again!"

A child development student told the following story about herself as a baby.

> Her five-year-old brother asked their mother to bring his new baby sister to kindergarten for "show and tell time." Holding her, he told the class what a good baby she was and how cute she was. He then proceeded to say to his classmates: "I'm looking for a good home for her."

This dethronement may best be understood by the following illustration:

> The husband said to his wife, "Darling, I love you so much that I am going to bring home another wife. You will have someone to love and have fun with. You can share your clothes and jewels and let her drive your sports car. I won't love you any less, I'll just open up my heart and love you both the same."

Through expressions of sibling rivalry, children are reacting to the denial or felt denial of their needs for dependence and the affection of their parents. To punish children for these acts of jealousy tends to confirm their feelings of loss and resentment. When parents try to treat each child as an individual and avoid making sibling comparisons, they reduce sibling rivalry. These actions also support each child's self-image. Parents can also do much to foster good sibling relationships by their responses to sibling conflicts. In children's arguments, parents should listen to both children, but never take sides. Parents should support children and help *them* find an acceptable solution. It is helpful when adults model good conflict resolution skills around children. Even though parental intervention may have a more equitable outcome, children do not experience how to resolve conflicts for themselves. Of course, violence should be prevented.

The roles that parents consciously or unconsciously assign to each child affect the qualities of the sibling relationship. This includes the degrees of warmth–closeness, status/power, cooperation or conflict, and rivalry each sibling feels. Is the older sibling given frequent and considerable responsibilities in caring for the younger ones or just an occasional role? Is the younger child given certain responsibilities or helped to develop talents that are different from the older siblings? Do parents label one child the troublemaker, another child the responsible one, and yet another one the baby? Children will tend to fulfill the role assigned to them.

Baby Brings Opportunities for Everyone

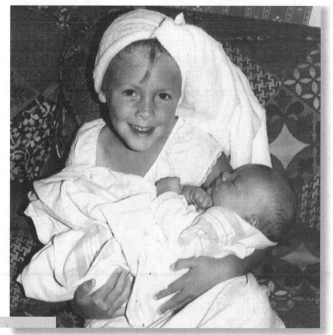

When the older sibling has some responsibility in caring for the new baby, she or he feels important and the process of bonding with the new brother or sister takes place. Sibling rivalry is reduced.

Parenting Tips to Reduce Sibling Rivalry

1. Consistent, positive, and developmentally appropriate rules
2. Nurture each child as a valued individual and spending individual time daily
3. Avoid sibling comparisons
4. Avoid taking sides in sibling conflicts but support them in resolving their disputes

---

Individual Children's Characteristics and Sibling Relationships

As in any relationship, individual characteristics shape the nature of the sibling relationship. Some research has shown that temperament and sociability can influence the qualities of the relationship (Kendrick and Dunn, 1983). Do two siblings enjoy doing things together? Are many or few of their interests the same? Are both outgoing, wanting to be with other people or adventurous, trying new things?

Would they rather spend a sizable amount of time alone reading or working on a hobby? Does one like to take the lead and the other one follows? Is one or are both children moody, unable to deal with frustration, or poor sharers? Sharing experiences, whether failures or successes, bring siblings closer together. Having fun or helping each other also strengthens sibling bonds. Later in life, reminiscences are important. All this affects the short- and long-term closeness, power/status, cooperation/conflict, and rivalry in each relationship.

Sibling Interaction on Development

Children's personalities, social and cognitive skills, self-concepts, values, and sense of protection from the outside world are influenced by their sibling relationships. Siblings also affect children's roles in peer groups, in selecting friends, and in the larger world. The interests and skills children develop in their sibling relationships are often repeated later in choosing an occupation, mate, or deciding on the number of children to have. Siblings influence all sorts of competencies. This is particularly true in their play, especially the dramatic play of children under age six. One example is the close similarity of siblings in tests of creative thinking.

Children's self-image and gender role is first formed in the family. How children interpret the way parents and siblings see them affects what they think about themselves. A sibling is like a looking glass in which a child's thoughts and values are reflected. "Is this behavior acceptable?" "Are my ideas good or bad?" Older siblings are gender models for behavior and attitudes. An older brother becomes particularly important to a young boy in a home where there is no father.

Siblings protect each other outside the family and provide an emotional anchorage to each other in times of stress or crisis. Although relationships change over the years and distance may limit contact, siblings find strength in each other in times of crisis or celebrations like funerals or weddings. For better or for worse, sibling relationships are for life!

Peers

Throughout childhood, some of the most important relationships involve peers or people of roughly equal age and maturity. Relationships with children other than peers vary because of the age differential of the children involved. Older children tend to help, teach, comfort, and protect younger children whereas younger children watch, imitate, ask, and are dependent on older children. When children are close to the same age and similar in developmental levels, their relationship involves reciprocity, sharing, negotiation, rule construction, and aggression regulation. Peer status tells the extent to which a child is accepted or rejected by their peers while friendship is a mutually formed relationship between two specific children (Vandell and Hembree, 1994). Social relationships and friendships become more complex and involved with age.

Development of Peer Groups

The development of peer groups begins on a very impromptu basis. A child's attraction to another child the same age can be seen in infancy. One baby will look at another one in a stroller or both will move toward each other in a play area. Babies will gaze, smile, and coo at other infants in much the same way they do with their parents. These responses to parents and peers develop at the same time (Field and Roopnarine, 1982; Vandell, 1980). Babies as young as four months will respond to another infant's cry. Between 9 and 12 months they give and receive toys from another infant they know and play social games such as crawl and chase (Endo, 1992). Around 12 months, they will imitate each other (Russon and Waite, 1991). By 13 or 14 months, infants will pat or hug the crying baby and by 18 months they will offer specific kinds of help like giving the baby a toy (Dunn, 1985). Between 6 months and one year, infants will start to recognize certain children as someone with whom to play. They touch, look at, and vocalize with another child (Brownell, 1990). By 2 years children enjoy playing with or next to each other and by age 3 or 4, they often choose to play with peers over adults. This process begins on a very impromptu basis and develops to the point at which children have a definite preference for specific peers.

During the preschool years, children increase their language and social skills and develop a sense of taking another's perspective. These new skills enable them to spend more time in peer group activities. By 5 years of age, most children engage in cooperative play.

Boys and girls form the same-gender peer groups during the elementary school years. Girls' peer groups are smaller, more exclusive, and more intimate than those of boys (Adler, Kless, and Adler, 1992; Gottman, 1986). Boys play in larger groups, often involving a game or sports activity. Time spent with peers increases steadily during the middle years. By late elementary school, about half the time children spend in social interactions is with their peers. Peer pressure also increases from the ages of 7 to 14. For example, fourth-graders report that they rely on parents more frequently than peers for help. Seventh-graders reply that same-gender friends are their most frequent source of support (Furman and Buhremester, 1992). This pressure to conform declines though the rest of adolescence (Gottman, 1986). By the end of adolescence, most young people conform to conventional adult standards.

Age, Gender, Race/Ethnicity, and Culture

Many factors are involved in peer-group membership. Age, gender, race/ethnicity, and culture play key roles.

AGE Often children choose their peers from the child-care center or the classroom where their classmates are of similar age. Although school children say that they prefer to play with children the same age, many spend between one-fourth and one-half of their time with children either 2 years older or younger. In mixed age groups, the younger children receive help from the older ones and the older children show nurturing behavior (French, 1984). In comparing mixed-age to same-age groups, children in mixed-age groups tend to be less sociable but help more while in the same-age groups, children tend to be more sociable but give and receive less practical help and get into conflicts more frequently (Furman and Buhremester, 1992). In developing countries, mixed-age grouping is the norm.

GENDER   Children as young as 10 months may show a preference for a same-sex playmate. This increases with age (La Freniere, Strayer, and Gauthier, 1984). In preschool free play, children tend to interact more with those of their own gender, especially in their choice of a best friend. Young elementary school children, during free play, interact four times as often with children of their own gender as with the opposite gender (Maccoby and Jacklin, 1987). By fifth grade, almost all peer groups are one gender. As children move toward adolescence, there is an increase in cross-gender friendships (Shrum and Check, 1987).

However, research suggests that children choose a play partner more on the basis of the toys rather than the gender of the child. As early as 15 months and increasingly afterwards, children show a preference for gender-specific toys (O'Brien, 1992). Preschool girls prefer more cooperative play while preschool boys are more competitive and like rough and tumble play (Maccoby, 1990). In another study of six- to eight-year-olds, both girls and boys report that they choose playmates on the basis of their style of play and their toys rather than their gender (Alexander and Hines, 1994).

RACE, ETHNICITY, AND CULTURAL DIFFERENCES   Racial and ethnic preferences increase during middle childhood until children reach junior high school (Shrum, Cheek, and Hunter, 1988; Singleton and Asher, 1979). Same racial or ethnic peer groups could represent prejudice or a combination of causes. In schools that are very diverse, children can interact with those who differ from them. Cooperative learning experiences in the classroom can provide cross-racial group experiences. When children form relationships and peer groups with children from different backgrounds, they may find that they do not live near each other. When children's classmates live in different neighborhoods, it becomes difficult to sustain relationships. Sports groups or club meetings after school help bridge the gap.

The behavior of human beings is shaped by their culture. Culture defines what may be shared and to what extent (Cairns, 1986). What kinds of topics are appropriate to discuss, how feelings should be expressed, and how and when individuals should touch. For example, when can boys cry and when can girls hit? Some cultural groups teach children to fight back if attacked while others look for a less violent way to defend their possessions or themselves. Teachers need to be aware of the basic norms, values and expectations of the cultural groups of the children in their classrooms.

Good multicultural programs in schools and child-care centers promote respect and appreciation for each other. The most effective multicultural academic and extracurricular elementary school programs include parents and members of the community in their activities. These programs help children develop a better understanding of each other and foster peer acceptance among students of different racial, ethnic, and cultural backgrounds (Bojko, 1995).

Functions of Peer Groups

Children's interactions with their peers are essential to their happiness and overall development. Scientific studies show that peer relations can greatly benefit children in their social and intellectual development (Hartup, 1983, 1991; Youniss, 1980). The effect of peers on children's behavior can be positive or negative. Families often blame peers rather than themselves for their child's antisocial behavior. Children who engage in antisocial behavior with their peer group often have conflict and poor relations with their parents (Patterson, Reid, and Dishion, 1992).

Build Social Competence

Social competence is the individual's ability to initiate and sustain satisfying relationships with peers at a level that is developmentally appropriate. It involves a complex interplay of feelings, thoughts, and skills developed over a long period of time (Katz and McClellan, 1997). Learning how to get along with others with approximately similar social experiences and skills is quite different from learning how to get along with parents and adults. Early social competence is so important that some researchers believe that we should shift our educational emphasis from the three R's to the four R's: **reading, 'riting, 'rithmetic,** and **relationships** (Katz and McClellan, 1997). Research also suggests that, as early as kindergarten, the quality of social competence accurately predicts children's social and academic competence in later grades (Pellegrini and Glickman, 1990).

Social competence includes emotional regulation, social knowledge, social understanding, and the necessary social skills. The ability of children to control and use their emotions appropriately is crucial for peer-group membership and status and the development of friendships (Denham, Renwick-Debardi, and Hewes, 1994; Fox, 1994). For example, a significant achievement for children is to learn appropriate ways to deal with frustration. Children learn to choose from a variety of emotions and at times to delay spontaneous reactions. Children move from depending on adults for regulating their responses to self-regulation of their emotions.

Social knowledge is understanding basic rules, social customs, and appropriate language for their group and society. Children who are successful in the group can predict the responses and feelings of others, and anticipate their preferences.

Social competence at any age involves a variety of skills. Initially, an individual must be able to gain access to the activity or a group. These social approach skills are often learned in the preschool years. A 4-year-old boy complained to the teacher that the children wouldn't let him in the (pretend) food play group. Teacher said, "Juan, did they have any sweet rolls or muffins?" Juan replied, "I don't think so." Teacher suggested that Juan might want to bring them some bakery goods to eat. Juan picked up some items and went to the group and quietly said, "Who wants a doughnut?" " I do," said one girl. Juan was now accepted into the group.

Other social skills include praising others, giving positive attention, thanking them for their help, or asking for their advice during play. For example, "Is it all right to put this block here?"

A peer group helps children overcome their egocentrism and learn to understand the views of others (Piaget, 1963). Sullivan (1953) emphasizes the value of peer relationships in fostering skills in the art of compromise, cooperation, and competition, and in promoting emotional health. Peer interactions are critical to children's understanding of fairness, their self-esteem, their proclivities toward sharing and kindness, their mastery of symbolic expression, their acquisition of role-taking and communication skills, and their development of creative and critical thinking.

Children benefit from a variety of peer-group activities. Different activities seem to foster different social and emotional skills in children. Noncompetitive activities, such as hanging out and watching TV, help children in socializing and in relationships while competitive activities, such as noncontact sports, enable children to evaluate their own skills and abilities. Participation in team sports may help children learn important skills needed later in the workplace.

Relationship-oriented activities, such as baby sitting or talking on the telephone, aid the development of skills for establishing intimacy. Boys participate more often in the competitive activities and girls more in the relationship oriented activities (Seifert and Hoffnung, 1997; Zarbatany, Hartmann, and Rankin, 1990).

Peer group leaders and members model what they consider appropriate behavior, ways of thinking, and values. Peers influence each other's actions by reinforcing the behavior they approve and punishing or rejecting undesirable behavior. Peers also teach each other various skills though practice and demonstration.

Provide Companionship

Peer groups fulfill the basic need to belong. Peers enable children to participate in activities that cannot be accomplished alone, such as building a fort or playing a game. It is also fun to share activities. Elementary school children like hanging out, walking to school, talking on the telephone, listening to music, playing games, and just acting silly. Sharing attitudes and some intimate feelings become important to children as they approach adolescence (O'Brien and Bierman, 1988; Zarbatany, et al., 1990).

Testing for One's Identity

"Who am I?" Unlike the family, peer membership has no legal status. It is emotionally less intense and voluntary. Children are accepted for themselves and their actions and not because of family membership. Children share ideas, thoughts, and values with peers. They also compare their ideas and accomplishments. They are sensitive to the responses of their peers regarding their attire and their interactions. Children can also gain status through their group membership. These experiences influence their self-concept development.

Explore Behavior, Morals, and Values

Children learn which behaviors are right or acceptable and which ones are wrong (morals) through experiences with their peers. They also can test their fundamental attitudes or values with those of their peers. A child may discover that his or her behavior at home does not work with children outside the home. Here, there are no family or kinship ties and no adults to set and enforce the rules. Most children have to make some adjustments for peer-group membership. For many children the adjustments are minimal, but for others they are more extensive. Some children may completely change their behavior while others form two or more codes of behavior, one for peers, one for school, and one for family. *Adults often want children to obey while peers want ideas, perseverance, and self-assertion.*

Children learn how to treat one another from peers. This may be how to show fairness or ways to comfort another person or how to hurt someone. Peers provide support for individual members, especially in dealing with the adults in their lives.

Children learn about sexual behaviors and feelings from parents, peers, school, and the media. Peers influence children's gender role behavior. They also share their knowledge of sex. This knowledge is never complete and often full of misconceptions, partially due to their limited cognitive development. **Children are keen observers of those in their environment.** Parents can help them deal with sexual input and other information from peers and the media by providing accurate and developmentally appropriate information throughout childhood. Above all, it is crucial for parents to be available and maintain open communications with their children.

Teach Peer Culture

Peers transmit childhood culture, which includes what to wear, what language to use, music to enjoy, games to play, and what to think. Peers also model and talk about appropriate gender role behavior. A boy who had played dolls with his sister might be told by girls at preschool, "Boys don't play with dolls." Peer culture is influenced by many forces in present-day society but also forces from the past. Some childhood games are centuries old. Where did you learn the game "Scissors-Paper-Stone," or to chant the ditty "Step on a Crack and Break Your Mother's Back"? Because peer groups are often similar in ethnicity, age, and gender, their understanding and openness to those children who differ may be limited.

Facilitate Personal Independence

The peer group provides support for children's ideas as well as a refuge from home and the adult world. They share material objects, give advice, and provide comfort and companionship. Many elementary school children have a secret meeting place such as a fort where they and a friend or friends meet. No one knows their "secret" even if the dog trails after them. Here, special friends discuss ideas, keep out unwanted children, and store treasures. One college student's secret fort when she was 7 and 8 years old was a narrow space hidden by bushes between her house and the neighbor's. "My mother never let on that she knew where we were."

Peer groups promote emotional health by helping children understand the emotional biases they learn from their families. They may see that not all adults have the same temperaments or stress the same activities for their children. For example, a child whose parents value athletic activities may find that some parents feel other things are more important. A peer group facilitates a child's need for autonomy and independence in preparation for adulthood.

Facilitate Learning about the Adult World and Societal Values

In the elementary years, children continue to learn how to cooperate, share, be generous, and also to be competitive. Their attitudes and behaviors are affected by the values of their society. For example, in the dominant culture, American children are taught that winning is important and individual rights are valued, whereas in countries such as the People's Republic of China children are taught that the group comes first and the individual second.

In societies like Mexico, individual assertion and competition are not stressed as much as in the United States. There, children are encouraged to develop prosocial behaviors such as helping each other achieve success. When children from this culture are placed in a classroom in the United States, they are not as assertive as their classmates in raising their hand to respond to the teacher's questions. A teacher, not understanding their culture, might think that they do not know the answer. In classrooms in the United States, boys are more likely to be rewarded for competitiveness while girls are rewarded more for cooperation. This is reflected in their respective behaviors (Mussen & Eisenberg-Berg, 1977). American society's values of competition and winning are reflected in children's sports, games, and the school's grading system.

Skills Facilitating Peer Acceptance

Even in infancy and toddlerhood, some children in a group are approached by peers while others may be ignored. Researchers have identified three basic skills that promote peer acceptance in young children (Asher, Renshaw, and Hymel, 1984).

1. **Initiation skills.** Children who are socially successful find ways to be accepted, such as mentioning interests in common or offering to bring something different to the play (Gottman, 1983). For example, they may say to another child, "We both are using red paint." Another child, wanting to join the group playing with blocks, may say, "Here is a truck we can use on your block road." Room is made for Johnny to join them.
2. **Conflict Resolution.** Conflicts occur frequently in the play environment. Successful children learn how to react nonviolently to these conflicts. One way to deescalate the disagreement is for the child to provide a reason for her or his position and/or offer another idea. Mary might say to her friend, "That was my toy. I will get you another truck" or "As soon as I finish playing with the puppet, I will give it to you. " Another way would be to compromise: "You can play with this if I can have . . . "
3. **Maintenance.** Children who are positive, show affection, exchange ideas, and have an attitude *of we-ness* will tend to maintain the play activity and form and maintain friendships (Gottman, 1983). Mary might say to her friends, "Do you think I should put different clothes on the doll?" A verbal request is much better than a physical demand. "Can I put these pajamas on your baby doll?"

Bierman and Furman (1984) reports that training in social skills seems to increase children's popularity with peers. Preschool children, unable to play successfully with their own age group, have been helped when placed in a group of children approximately one year younger. They gain social skills and often return successfully to their age group in a short period of time.

Adult Support in Development of Peer Acceptance and Friendships

Secure parental attachments, good parental relationships, and healthy parental emotional expressiveness in the home are linked with good peer relationships (Cassidy, Parke, Butkovsky, and Braungart, 1992). Infants who are securely attached at age one show greater social skills during their preschool years than those infants who are not. These securely attached children approach other children more freely, are more empathetic, and show greater leadership (Lieberman, 1977). Peer acceptance is a predictor of later social and emotional adjustment and cognitive adequacy (Hartup, 1991). Parents foster healthy social development in their children when they are affectionate, show interest in their children's feelings, support and express parental pride in their activities and accomplishments, and provide support during times of stress (Moore, 1992). Authoritative parents usually are nurturing and enforce moderate levels of control over their children's behavior. These parents praise good behavior and try to model positive social responses.

Peer conflict is an important form of social interaction and can contribute to children's development (Rende and Killen, 1992; Ross and Conant, 1992). Teachers can help children develop strategies for resolving conflicts without needing adult intervention. During conflicts, teachers help children understand their own actions and help them explain their behavior to each other. Adults' praise for children's positive social actions also reinforces this behavior.

Competition in a group increases the likelihood of aggressive behavior. Teachers who provide cooperative learning tasks in the classroom give children an opportunity to work with others and experience prosocial behavior. Teachers can model prosocial behavior in their actions with children, other teachers, and parents.

Adult-Sponsored Activities That Build Peer Relationships

Adult-sponsored peer groups differ from those that children form. Children's peer groups are informal and casual, with rules that they construct as needed. They provide interactions without an adult's close supervision. Adult-sponsored groups are formal and are organized for a purpose. The sponsor designates the purpose and promotes specific values and skills. Adults define appropriate behavior. Children can pursue the activities of the group within the defined rules and purposes of the group. Children interact with other children who would not necessarily be available to them in an informal peer group. This often gives many children, including those who are shy, skills and experiences that will help them in the group and in other situations (Bierman and Furman, 1984). For some children, there are leadership possibilities.

There are many organizations for children including Boy and Girl Scouts of America, 4H clubs, school clubs, and religious groups. Each has its own orientation and set of rules and values. Some of these groups stress building character, cooperation among members, and support for all individuals to achieve. The adult leadership affects the benefits for various children. For example, is winning the main goal, or is it the ability to work together, helping each child to improve? Ideally, every child who puts forth the effort will gain from participation in the group.

Sports and Recreational Programs

Cities, schools, and religious groups sponsor sports and recreational programs for children. These are either individual or team activities and are competitive and/or cooperative activities. Sports are very popular in the United States. Large numbers

Batter Up: City Softball Team Picture

The city sponsors softball leagues for various age groups. These programs often bring children together from diverse backgrounds. Children learn the skills of the particular sport, team work, competition, and with the help of competent adults, cooperation and good sportsmanship.

of people attend or watch sporting events and many professional sports organizations pay their top players extremely high salaries. Some children believe that a sport such as professional basketball or football is a way out of poverty. Statistically this is rare. A few professional athletes do provide help for low-income youth. Tiger Woods, the top-rated golfer in the PGA in 2000, has set up a foundation to provide golfing opportunities to children in low-income neighborhoods.

Participation in a sports program can have many beneficial effects. Children can learn teamwork, competition, cooperative relationships, and loyalty. They can learn about themselves and others, their capabilities, develop particular skills, improve their physical fitness, and have fun. Children and youth in these programs often have an opportunity to participate with others from diverse neighborhoods and backgrounds.

What children gain from these experiences depends on the actions and values of the adults in charge and the reactions and support of the parents who are the fans. Some children improve their self-esteem from these experiences but others are hurt and humiliated. Is team winning the number one goal or is it for all team members to play and do their best? Can each child win if he or she has improved in individual skills and team effort? The author can remember Little League games where a few parents would shout at the umpire over a decision at home plate and take a picture to prove he was wrong. (Additional information is provided in Parks and Recreation Programs in Chapter 13).

Friends

Friendships are vital to children' s healthy development. Friendship, very possibly, is even more important than popularity for children's mental health and the quality of life throughout the life span (Katz and McClellan, 1997). A person may be very popular, getting along with many people, but not able to form very close relationships with a few friends. Healthy friendships involve openness and freedom while unhealthy friendships are restrictive.

Development of Friendships

Friendship begins with two children liking each other and moves to a mutual involvement with each child providing affection, satisfaction, enjoyment, respect, and a sense of importance. Selecting one's friends and forming relationships is a developmental process that becomes more complex and stable with age. Infants show concern for other infants while children as young as 2 report needing and wanting a friend (Bullock, 1992). During the preschool years, children begin to choose a few friends, usually of the same age and sex. These friends are valued for their material possessions and for being in close proximity (Selman, 1981). Selman and Selman (1979) call this momentary playmateship. The amount of contact that children have with other children affects their development of friendships and their own personality.

Understanding of Friendships

Rubin (1980) has identified three dimensions in understanding friendships that evolve with age and social experience. Children's answers to the same question reveal their level of understanding.

1. Children shift from a preoccupation with themselves to an awareness of other persons and their ideas and feelings. Very young children are egocentric and see the world and other people in terms of their needs. By age 5, most children play cooperatively with others. By 8, they look to friendship as benefiting each person. Consequently, children of different ages will answer these questions differently. "Who is your best friend?" "Why?"

    Sammy, age 3, says, "Tom is my friend. 'Cause he has a new fire engine with a ladder, and he has lots of toys." Sammy likes the material possessions of his friend.

    Sally, age 5, says, "Christy is my friend. Friends like each other. Christy invites me to her house." Sally did not mention reciprocity.

    Enrique, age 8, says, "Tom is my friend because we both like to play ball and we help each other become better catchers." Here friendship goes beyond liking each other to being mutually beneficial.

2. Young children look at friends in terms of surface attributes and gradually move to an awareness of their friends' deeper psychological characteristics.
    Question: How would you describe your best friend?
    Juan, age 4, replies, "Tom, he has black hair, cowboy boots and Star Wars' toys."
    John, age 13, says, "Tom is kind and has lots of ideas and if he tells you something, he can be counted on."

3. Young children think that friendships are brief interactions while older children think about friendships as lasting over time.
    Question: "How do you feel about your friend who moved away?"

Sally, age 3, said, "Tom moved away. He is not my friend."

Sheila, age 14, replied, "Tom and his family moved. I miss him but we talk on the phone. We are planning ways to spend time together this summer."

Basis for Selection

The process for selecting friends is based on proximity, surface features, and/or deeper characteristics depending on the child's level of development. Proximity is the most basic feature because it requires only location. The next level of selection is based on visible features of others such as sex, age, or race/ethnicity (see peer-group selection). The third level involves deeper features of others such as individual personality traits or values (Epstein, 1983a and b).

The selection process is also affected by the environment of the person's home, neighborhood, school, and community. The organization of the environment as well as the proportion of cross-age and cross-race friends affect children's interactions with others or limit their interactions (Epstein, 1983a and b).

LEVEL ONE: PROXIMITY   Friends are chosen to some degree on the basis of shared space. The home, neighborhood, community, and child-care or school settings establish boundaries for shared space. The definition of space broadens with age.

Friends Celebrate

These children are friends because their families see each other frequently. The two-year-old enjoys the festivities at her four-year-old friend's birthday party. In mixed-age groups, older children help and nurture younger ones. The younger child learns from older role models.

For infants, toddlers, and preschoolers, there is complete reliance on physical proximity for the selection of friends. This space is chosen for them by the adults in their lives. Proximity for infants and toddlers means security and familiarity, but for preschoolers it can have the added meaning of "play and shared space" (Maccoby and Jacklin, 1974). However, other research shows that toddlers (18 to 24 months) in group settings use their shared space to select a friend for play and not just to coexist (Vandell and Mueller, 1995).

As children grow older, proximity or the geographical area or areas from which they meet children and choose friends increases as does the child's whole environment. Children from grades six to twelve choose their friends from increasingly wider boundaries within the school setting (Epstein, 1983a and b).

LEVEL TWO: SURFACE ATTRIBUTES   As children grow and develop, the selection process gradually becomes more complex. but still involves proximity. At level two, children consider visible features in each other in choosing friends such as their age, gender, and race or ethnicity. For 5- to 7-year-olds, friendships are based on shared activities or doing things with someone and having fun (Berndt and Perry, 1986). Children age 8 to 12 increasingly recognize the importance of friends meeting each other's needs and possessing desirable traits. They want friends to be nice to each other and share both interests and things. During elementary school, there is an increase in cross-gender choices of best friends (Epstein, 1983a and b).

Numerous studies have examined the influence of age in selecting friends. School-age children are considered the same age if they are within 12 months of each other. More recent studies support older findings that approximately 65 percent of children's interactions in and out of school are among friends who differ 12 or more months in age. Ladd (1983) reports considerable mixing of grade levels in activities on school playgrounds. Although children play predominantly with children in their same grade, popular children interact more with older children and "rejected" children spend more time with younger children (Ladd, 1983).

LEVEL 3: DEEP SURFACE FEATURES   As children mature, they look for other characteristics in choosing a friend. At this level, personality traits and similarities and differences give depth to relationships (Epstein, 1983a and b). Although children between age 8 and 11 mention possessing desirable traits, they are more likely to say that friends are nice to each other and share interests and things. Around age 12, friends have empathy for each other's problems and share intimacies (Damon, 1977). Friends are chosen from wider social settings and friendships last longer even when youth move. Perhaps this is because of the deeper relationships.

Environmental Conditions Affecting the Selection of Friends

Environmental conditions in the home, neighborhood, child-care setting, school, and community affect the parameters of proximity, the need for certain kinds of interactions, and the number of friends. Organization of space and activities, demographics, and climate also affect the selection of friends.

In the home, the space for children's activities with their friends and the types of family activities that include children's friends limit or encourage the development of friendships. It may be a game room or a swimming pool that brings children together. Parents may carpool children to their practice games or include friends for occasional meals or family outings.

Characteristics of neighborhoods affect the number and kinds of friends available. The types of housing, apartments, townhouses, or single-family dwellings, and the physical setting—urban, suburban, or rural—each provide different opportunities for meeting and making friends. There are additional factors of safety and access that affect children's opportunities for interaction. A cul-de-sac provides physical safety but perhaps limits proximity to other children. Some housing units have common play areas and some neighborhoods have a park close by that brings children and adults together. In the Netherlands, for example, an outdoor multipurpose open area serving all ages is a part of every large apartment complex built. Activities include children playing soccer and adults walking their dogs.

According to Epstein (1983a and b), five major conditions in schools affect the interaction of the students.

1. Architectural features of the classrooms, play yards, and other spaces encourage or discourage the size and diversity of groups working or playing together.
2. The types of equipment and supplies and their availability and placement indirectly affect their usage. Some setups encourage individual use, others shared use, while still other situations stimulate crowding and aggression. A teeter-totter requires sharing, a swing does not. If there are too few balls available, children may crowd around and push to get a ball.
3. Teachers' instructional methods allow or preclude children from working together on various tasks or helping each other on individual projects.
4. Demographic factors in the classroom and the entire school, such as gender, ages, races, and social classes of children, affect children's opportunities for diversity in their friends.
5. Organization of nonacademic activities before, during, or after school can limit or encourage children of similar interests and talents to get together.

Characteristics of Popular, Rejected, and Ignored Children

In addition to environmental factors, the characteristics of a child affect that child's ability to form friendships. Popular children differ from their unpopular counterparts in a number of ways. A study of young children, 43 to 66 months old, shows that the children who are liked have superior communication skills in a variety of settings and with all children in their groups. They initiate conversation clearly and speak and respond to all children involved. They are also able to reenter the group if rejected (Hazen and Black, 1989).

In general, popular children tend to reinforce their peers through praise and affection (Moore, 1967; Rubin, Bukowski, and Parker, 1998). Popular children are friendly and outgoing, and possess good conversational skills (Biennan and Furman, 1984). Boys and, especially, girls are generally more physically attractive and both genders are mature for their ages (Adler and Adler, 1998; Langlois, 1986; Ritts, Patterson, and Tubbs, 1992; Moore, 1967). Popular children tend to do well in school or excel in valued activities such as sports (Adler and Adler, 1998).

Later-born children tend to be more popular than firstborn children because they develop superior skills in relating to peers, although not to adults. This trend holds true in spite of the fact that firstborns tend to earn higher grades in school (Epstein, 1983).

Children living in homes with troubled family relationships often have poor peer relationships, low self-images, and limited alternatives in choosing friends. They also show signs of social defiance in early childhood (Hartup, 1996). Research shows that popular and unpopular children construe social goals differently. For example, aggressive boys interpret social situations in ways that preclude prosocial solutions. Children who are rejected by their peers are more likely to show aggressive behavior and disrupt group activities (Asher and Renshaw, 1981; Dodge, 1983). Although peer pressure to conform is strong, children who are rejected rarely change their behavior. Most of these children either remain on the fringes of the

TABLE 9.1 Characteristics of Children

Popular	Unpopular
Good family relationships	Poor family relationships
Superior communication skills	Poor communication skills
Initiate conversation clearly	Put people down
Speak and respond to all children in a group	Low self-image
Reinforce peers with praise and affection	Limited alternatives for friends
Friendly, outgoing	Interpret social situations in ways that preclude prosocial reaction
Do well in academics	
Often excel in valued activities, sports for boys	Aggressive—disruptive of group activities
Often physically attractive, especially girls	Defensive
Physically mature	Do not change behavior

group or alone. A few join deviant groups whose values and goals differ from the mainstream of society.

Loneliness in Children

Loneliness is a significant problem among younger and older children with immediate and long-term consequences. Only recently have researchers understood that young children articulate feelings of being lonely (Cassidy and Asher, 1992). By age 5, children are sensitive to the needs of others and some will express concern about being lonely (McAfee and Leong, 1994). Young children's loneliness has meanings for them that are similar to those of older children and adults. Kindergarten and first-grade children have described loneliness in the following ways.

1. Definition: It is "being sad and alone."
2. Cause: "Nobody to play with."
3. Solution: "Find a friend" (Cassidy and Asher, 1992).

Contributing Factors and Consequences

Situations contributing to loneliness include family problems, neighborhood conflicts, loss of a friend or a pet, and moving to a new school or neighborhood. In the school setting, loneliness includes being or feeling rejected by peers or lacking the social skills and knowledge needed to make friends. This is particularly true in middle childhood when peer group membership is so important (Renshaw and Brown, 1993). Children who are or have been victimized by peers have more difficulties in making friends (Kochenderfer and Ladd, 1996). Friendless children coming from low socioeconomic status homes show loneliness more often or more intensely than friendless children from average or high socioeconomic status homes (Renshaw and Brown, 1993)

Lonely children have poor peer relationships and few friends. They therefore miss the experiences and lifelong skills developed in peer groups. Low self-esteem may be both the cause and the consequence of lack of friends.

Strategies for Teachers

The problem of loneliness is complex. Teachers have to focus on the individual child, try to identify the contributing factors, and then work with the child in developing needed social skills. The teacher may work with the parents in helping the child find release for damaging emotions through an activity in school or pairing the child with another child who might be helpful. The teacher can take charge of the situation if someone is picking on the child and restructure the classroom setting to increase interactions among all students. Working on a task cooperatively in small groups often helps.

Shy or Withdrawn Students

Some children in child care or elementary school are quiet in the classroom. Often they don't get the attention they may need because the teacher is busy with the aggressive or demanding children. Some quiet children are well adjusted socially and do well academically, but tend to play or work by themselves. Other children are shy or inhibited, lack self-confidence, and are socially anxious. Still other children are withdrawn and may be unresponsive, uncommunicative, or possibly off in their own world daydreaming (Brophy, 1996). A few may be problematically shy or withdrawn to the point where professional intervention is necessary.

Contributing Factors and Consequences

Shyness or withdrawal can be due to a new or stressful situation or may appear to be a personality trait. Shyness is normal when a child encounters a new situation such as the first day of school or the first time at a scout meeting. Some children are stressed if they don't know what to say, how to read a story well out loud, or play a game. There is some evidence that shyness can be inherited (Fox, 1994). However, a genetic or temperamental basis for shyness accounts for only a small portion of shyness and it can be modified (Hyson, 1987).

Social anxiety can grow out of repeated failure, mistreatment, or rejection from adults or peers. If children are labeled as shy or withdrawn, they may internalize this and see this as normal for them. If their behavior becomes worse, their discomfort around others will increase, and they will be even more reluctant to enter social situations.

Social withdrawal in the early years limits children's opportunities to develop adequate social skills, which leads to further withdrawal (Hymel, Rubin, Rowden, and LeMare, 1990). Certain personal characteristics, such as shyness, anxiety, being withdrawn or inhibited, and low self-esteem often make it more difficult to develop friendships (Bullock, 1998; Renshaw and Brown, 1993; Asher, Parkhurst, Hymel, and Williams, 1990).

Strategies for Teachers

Determine the interests of this child with the help of parents, the school librarian, and others who know him or her.

1. Determine, with professional help if necessary, the reasons for the child's shyness or withdrawal and where the child appears to be the most comfortable. Find specific ways to help by working with parents as much as possible.
2. Minimize situations where the child might be embarrassed.
3. Choose a topic that interests the child, such as rocks or butterflies. If the child has a collection, encourage the child to show it to classmates. The

teacher and the parents could help the child to share certain features of the collection. The teacher could ask, "Is there another avid collector in the classroom? What do all collectors have in common?" Provide occasions when each child's work or talents is recognized.

4. Pair the shy or withdrawn child with a similar but more popular or outgoing student for small projects. Promote a friendship with another child. For example, at preschool, placing a child in a carpool often helps her or him to get to know another child and also to enter the classroom together. Parents could invite a child over on a Saturday or take a possible friend with them on a fun family activity.

5. Give the shy or withdrawn child a job to do that places the child in a social activity with a few others in the classroom or at recess time. For example, feed fish with another child or carry out balls for recess activities.

6. Teach the child basic social skills such as how to greet someone and to look at another child when talking. The teacher could suggest the shy child offer to help another child with something, or how to use phrases such as, "What do you think about . . . " or "I am sorry that you were sick yesterday." Encourage, without embarrassing, the child to speak up (assertively) and say what she or he would like.

7. Perhaps a shy or withdrawn child could be a tutor or teach a younger child how to play a game.

8. The child could possibly benefit from an adult-sponsored peer group like Brownies or Cub Scouts or a soccer team.

9. Help the child who appears to be noncommunicative and daydreaming to stay on-task by checking frequently what she or he is doing and praising any progress.

10. Stop frequently, even if it is brief, and talk to the child.

These strategies should help children to feel better about themselves and feel more comfortable with other children. Some of the strategies were adapted from the work of other researchers (Brophy, 1996).

Problems in Relationships

Aggression

Aggressive behavior is one of the most challenging problems for parents, teachers, and children (both the aggressor and the victim). Any act that intentionally hurts another person physically or psychologically is aggression. At times, adults differ in their definition of aggression with some calling certain behaviors assertive (taking charge but not hurtful) and others labeling the same behaviors aggressive. Two common types of aggression are reactive aggression and proactive aggression.

In reactive aggression, a child is responding defensively and with a show of anger to a perceived provocation. In proactive aggression, the child often has a goal in mind and may not show overt signs of anger. Their actions may be to obtain an object or a position of power. The bully is attempting to intimidate or dominate another person (Schwartz, Dodge, and Cole, 1993). When children express aggressive behavior in the peer group, it usually reduces their acceptance. For example, a study by Dodge (1983) showed that boys who exhibited inappropriate, disruptive, antisocial, and aggressive play behaviors were often unpopular.

Inappropriate aggression may be due to a lack of appropriate social skills and/or having too high a level of anger to be able to control it. When children do not know how to express their feelings or needs effectively, they need help. Adults can teach or model for these children appropriate words, ways to approach someone for an object or a turn, and how to defend assertively and not aggressively the objects in their possession. Children need to practice these skills. In the process, children require adult support until these responses become part of their social repertoire. When children are successful, their anger is also reduced.

Some children are aggressive because they cannot cope with their high levels of anger and frustration. Their actions often escalate both their levels of anger and frustrations. It is crucial to help these children to respond in ways that reduce the anger and not cause them to get into more trouble. They need techniques for taking control of their feelings and for using socially acceptable ways to release them. Pounding clay, kicking a ball, running, hitting a nail into wood, and water play all can substitute for inappropriate aggression. Again, children need adult support while they are attempting to behave in an acceptable manner.

Teasing

Teasing is generally defined as persistent behavior intended to irritate, provoke, confuse, or otherwise annoy someone (Katz and McClellan, 1997). However, not all teasing is harmful. Some teasing can be fun and even the target of the teasing can laugh. This kind of teasing is often reciprocal. Our concern is over the harmful teasing that occurs, causing the person being teased to feel hurt, sad, humiliated, or angry. Some young children who are teased learn effective social skills that will help them in dealing with teasing later in life (Ross, 1996).

REASONS FOR TEASING   Children tease for a number of reasons.

- ✔ **Attention.** Children want attention even if it is negative.
- ✔ **Imitation.** These children may mimic teasing that they see around the house, in the schoolyard, or they may be victims of teasing by older siblings. Their parents may also use aggressive discipline.
- ✔ **Feelings of superiority or power.** They may feel superior or powerful when putting someone down (Olweus, 1993)

☑ **Peer acceptance.** They may feel teasing is cool and may help them to be accepted by the popular children.

☑ **Misunderstanding differences.** Some children target anyone who is different rather than trying to understand them. This could have to do with physical, emotional, learning, cultural, or ethnic differences.

☑ **Media influences.** Children experience teasing, putdowns, sarcasm, and a lack of respect on many children's television programs (Freedman, 1999).

How Parents and Teachers Can Help

Parents should listen to their child and try to see the situation from the child's eyes. Show concern rather than an overreaction so as not to escalate the child's fear or anger. Teasing cannot be prevented and children cannot control what others say to them, but they can control their reactions and become less vulnerable.

Some strategies to teach children are:

☑ **Self-talk.** Encourage children to plan what they can think about or say to themselves to remain calm when they are being teased (Bloch, 1993).

☑ **Ignore.** Help the victim to avoid reinforcing the teaser by getting angry, crying, or showing any reactions of concern. Tell the child not to look at the teaser in the face and walk away if feasible. However, if a pattern of teasing is well developed, ignoring the behavior may not help initially.

☑ **Visualization.** Help children visualize a way to prevent the words from getting to them. What kind of a protective shield could they imagine to be encompassing them? Help children have the power to ignore the message, at least outwardly.

☑ **Agree with the facts.** Have the child say to the teaser, "You're right" or "That was a stupid thing for me to say" to take the wind out of the teaser's sails. This may be one of the easiest ways to diffuse the comment (Cohen-Possey, 1995).

☑ **The child could say, "So?"** The child is telling the teaser that it does not matter or that he or she could care less. Bill Cosby, in *The Meanest Thing*, uses this concept.

WHEN OR HOW A TEACHER SHOULD INTERVENE   The intent of teasing and its effects vary. Teachers must look at the setting in which the teasing is taking place, the relationship between teaser and the teased, whether or not there is reciprocal teasing, and the tone or intention. Does the teasing occur in front of a group of children rather than in play with a friend? Does the teasing have a hostile tone with an apparent intention to inflict psychological pain? Are there overtones of racism, sexism, or any stereotyping (Katz, 1997)?

Teachers can intervene in many ways. When teachers assess the setting, such as the playground, they may find that there are not enough interesting activities available, or the supervision may be poor, or the area may be too crowded. If the teasing involves any kind of stereotype, this is an opportunity for a discussion or antibias activities in the classroom. The recipient of the teasing might be helped to react in ways to defuse the situation.

Bullying   *What if bullies had to wear dresses?*

Bullying in schools is a worldwide problem affecting the general school environment and not just the students involved. Although bullying occurs in other settings, such as summer camps and playgrounds, most research has focused on the school setting. Bullying is the act of teasing, taunting, threatening, hitting, and stealing to intimidate or damage a victim or victims. Bullying can be physical, like pushing another child off a swing or taking a child's lunch money. It can be verbal, such as making a derogatory comment on the appearance or skills of a child. In bullying, the physical and/or psychological intimidation occurs repeatedly over time, creating an ongoing pattern of harassment and abuse (Batsche and Knoff, 1994; Olweus, 1993).

Sometimes bullying is indirect and devious such as spreading rumors. This causes the victim to be hurt psychologically and possibly socially isolated or ostracized. Bullying can leave emotional scars for life (Banks, 1997). Bullying affects the ability of the students to learn. All students need a safe and fear-free learning environment.

Approximately 15 percent of students are regular victims or bullies (Olweus, 1993). The bullying role begins early in life but it becomes more intense around fourth grade. By the upper elementary grades, it is a well-developed pattern and difficult to change. Bullying peaks in junior high years. Physical bullying decreases with age while verbal bullying remains constant into adult life (Banks, 1997; UCLA Child Care Services, 1996).

Characteristics of Bullies and Victims

Bullies have a need to feel powerful and in control. They appear to find satisfaction in inflicting injury and suffering on others. More boys than girls are bullies and victims. Boys usually engage in direct bullying behaviors while girls tend to use more subtle, indirect methods (Banks, 1997; Ahmad and Smith, 1994; Smith and Sharp, 1994). Bullies often come from homes where physical punishment is used, children are taught to defend themselves physically, and parental involvement and warmth are frequently lacking (Banks, 1997; UCLA Child Care Services, 1996). Bullies are often defiant or appositional toward adults, antisocial, and apt to break school rules. According to many researchers, bullies show little anxiety and possess high self-esteem (Batsche and Knoff, 1994; Olweus, 1993). However, Katz and McClellan disagree, saying that bullies may feel unlikable and suffer from low self-esteem (1997). In either case, their aggressive behavior pattern is highly stable over time and predictive of later difficulties in life (Parker and Asher, 1995). Many bullies end up with criminal convictions or legal problems as adults (Banks, 1997).

Victims are typically anxious, cautious, and suffer from low self-esteem. They rarely defend themselves or retaliate when confronted by bullies (Schwartz, Dodge, and Cole, 1993; Slaby, Roedell, Avezzo, and Hendrix, 1995). They want to avoid school even when the victimization ends (Kochenderfer and Ladd, 1996). An article in the *American School Board Journal* reports that 160,000 children stay home from school *every day* because they are afraid of being bullied (Vail, 1999). Many victims lack social skills and friends. Some children who witness an incident do not support the victim for fear of becoming victims themselves or losing peer status. A few children feel that victims bring some of this treatment on themselves. This thinking is similar to blaming the abused spouse because she (or he) did not leave. Victims tend to be close to their parents, who often are overprotective. Victims are physically weaker than their peers but no other physical characteristics such as weight or eyeglasses appear to correlate. Being a victim lowers self-esteem and often leads to depression, which can last into adulthood (Batsche and Knoff, 1994; Olweus, 1993).

Intervention Programs

Bullying is a complex problem, often undetected or underestimated by teachers and parents. Even when teachers are present, they often ignore the incident, as reported in the K–3 study just sited. Students usually don't get involved and, when they do, they don't know how to help (Charach, Pepler, and Ziegler, 1995). Effective intervention programs must involve the entire school community and the parents.

Intervention programs should begin when children are young, before their attitudes turn into bullying behavior. At a young age, children need to understand that teasing and bullying behavior hurts everyone and is unacceptable (see the antibias program in Chapter 7). In working with young children, one technique is to use a stuffed animal to tell a story relating to an incident that occurred. For example, if some children are excluding a child, at storytime the frog may say, "I don't like you, you are not my friend!" Children often respond in very perceptive ways. Sometimes the children who are being hurtful are the ones who come up with very sensitive answers. In child care, teachers often are able to work more closely with parents than in elementary school. Sometimes parents unconsciously are modeling inappropriate behavior or attitudes. Perhaps these parents can be helped to understand that the goal is for young children to learn to value and respect each other and that adults need to be good models.

A comprehensive intervention program developed by Olweus and colleagues involves parents, school administrators, teachers, and students (Olweus, Limber, and Mihalic, 1999; Olweus, 1993). Interventions take place at the school, in individual classrooms, and with individual students. Schools implementing this program report reducing bullying incidences by 50 percent.

1. Questionnaires are sent to students and adults to make them aware of the extent of the problem.
2. A parental awareness campaign reaches parents though a variety of means.
3. Classroom activities include developing rules against bullying and role-playing activities to experience the different roles, including how to help victims and alternatives to bullying.
4. Individualized programs with bullies and victims, classroom activities to reduce social isolation such as cooperative learning tasks, and improved adult supervision during vulnerable times in the school are put into practice.

Bullying in Schools provides an excellent resource list. It contains articles, children's books, guides, videos, posters, and Internet resources (*Bullying in Schools*, 2001).

Current Trends

Communities are increasingly aware of the importance of developing close, healthy relationships in families and the consequences when this does not occur. For example, sibling relationships form the basis for peer relationships and friendships. Communities also realize that many families lack the time and/or knowledge to help their children develop close and healthy relationships. More programs in the community are needed to support these vulnerable families and provide community activities supporting all children.

Informal peer groups need safe places to play under watchful eyes of adults in the community. Adults in leadership roles for organized peer groups need special training. Nurturing and authoritative leaders promote prosocial behaviors in children. Teachers and schools need help in their efforts to support unpopular, shy, lonely, and aggressive children. More schools need to adopt one of the successful programs to reduce bullying at their school. Ideally, it would become a policy for the school district.

 **Key Points**

Siblings

1. Sibling relationships vary greatly in the qualities of power and status, warmth and closeness, conflict or harmony, and rivalry or cooperation.
2. Qualities of sibling relationships are affected by the composition of the family, individual char-

acteristics of each sibling, and family relationships.

3. Sibling rivalry is a normal emotion arising out of the need to share their parents, the two most important people in their lives. There is more rivalry when siblings are younger, close in age and the same sex, competing in similar activities, and in large families.

4. Parents promote healthy sibling relationships when they are nurturing, appropriate and consistent in their rules, treat each child as an individual, and avoid comparisons and taking sides in sibling conflicts.

5. Sibling interactions shape personality, socialization, values, and self-concepts.

Critical Thinking Questions

1. In what ways could a parent promote feelings of warmth and friendship among siblings?

Key Points

Peers and Friends

1. Children's social relationships and friendships become more complex, stable, and interactive with age.

2. Peer relationships involve reciprocity, sharing, negotiation, rule construction, and aggression regulation. They predict later social and emotional adjustment.

3. Peers provide companionship, transmit childhood culture, and are a testing ground for behavior, ideas, values, and self-identity.

4. Adult-sponsored peer groups are formal, organized, and supervised by adults for a specific purpose.

5. Friendship is a mutual relationship providing affection, respect, and enjoyment that becomes more complex and stable with age.

6. Popular children compared to their unpopular counterparts reinforce their peers with more praise and affection, are more friendly and outgoing, have better conversational skills, are more physically attractive and mature, get better grades in school, and excel in valued activities such as sports.

7. Bullying is the physical or psychological intimidation of a victim(s) causing harassment and abuse with lifelong consequences for bullies and victims.

Critical Thinking Questions

1. What do you think parents and /or teachers could do to help the victim of a bully be less vulnerable?

2. How could the teacher help a lonely child interact more easily with others in the classroom and at recess?

Resources and References

Bullying in Schools. ERIC Clearing House on Counseling and Student Services
http://ericcass.uncg.edu/virtuallib/bullying/bullyingbook.html
No Bully Web Site.
http://www.nobully.org.nz

■ Children's Books

Rigby, K. (1998). *Bullying in the schools and what to do about it.* Markham, Ontario, Canada: Pembroke.

Romaine, T., and Verdick, E. (1997) *Bullies are a pain in the brain.* Minneapolis, MN: Free Spirit.

■ References: Siblings

Adler, A. (1928). Characteristics of first-, second-, and third-born children. *Children, 3,* 14–52.

Banks, R. (1997). Bullying in schools. *ERIC Digest, EDO-PS-97-17.* Urbana, IL: University of Illinois.

Blake, J. (1989). Numbers of siblings and educational attainment. *Science, 245,* 32–36.

Bryant B. K., and Crockenberg, S. B. (1980). Correlates and dimensions of prosocial behavior: A study of female siblings and their mothers. *Child Development, 51,* 529–544.

Cirirelli, V. G. (1972). Concept learning of young children as a function of sibling relationships to the teacher. *Child Development, 43,* 282–287.

Dunn, J. (1985). *Sisters and brothers.* Cambridge, MA: Harvard University Press.

Dunn, J. (1995). *From one child to two.* New York: Ballentine.

Falbo, T. (1984). *The single-child family.* New York: Guilford.

Falbo, T., and Polit, D. (1986). Quantitative review of the only child literature: Research evidence and theory development. *Psychological Bulletin, 100*(2), 176–189.

Furman, W. (1995). Parenting siblings. In M. H. Berstein (Ed.), *Handbook of parenting* (Vol. 1). Mahwah, NJ: Erlbaum.

Furman, W., and Buhremester, D. (1985). Children's perceptions of the qualities of sibling relationships. *Child Development, 56*(2), 448–461.

Furman, W., and Buhremester, D. (1992). Age and sex differences in perceptions of networks of personal friendships. *Child Development, 63,* 103–115.

Furman, W., and Masters, J. C. (1980). Affective consequences of social reinforcement, punishment, and neutral behavior. *Developmental Psychology, 16,* 100–104.

Galton, F. (1874). *Englishmen of science: Their nature and nurture.* London: McMillan.

Hauser, R. M., and Sewell, W. (1985). Birth order and educational attainment in full sibships. *American Journal of Educational Research, 22,* 1–23.

Jaffe, M. L. (1997). *Understanding parenting* (2nd ed.). Boston: Allyn and Bacon.

Kendrick, C., and Dunn, J. (1983). Sibling quarrels and maternal responses. *Developmental Psychology, 19*(1), 62–70.

Lahey, B. B., Hammer, D., Crumrine, P. L., and Forehand, R. L. (1980). Birth order: Sex interaction in child behavior problems. *Developmental Psychology, 16,* 608–615.

Muzi, M. (2000). *Child Development.* Upper Saddle River, NJ: Prentice-Hall.

Newman, J. (1994). Conflict and friendship in sibling relationships: A review. *Child Study Journal, 24*(2), 119–152.

Rosenberg, B. G., and Hyde, J. S. (1993). The only child: Is there only one kind of only? *Journal of Genetic Psychology, 154*(2), 269–282.

Steelman, L. C., and Powell, B. (1985). The social and academic consequences of birth order: Real, artifact, or both? *Journal of Marriage and the Family, 47,* 115–125.

Teti, D. M., Sakin, J. W., Kucera, E., Corns, K. M., and Eiden, R. (1996). And baby makes four: Predictors of attachment security among preschool-age firstborns during the transition to siblinghood. *Child Development, 67,* 579–596.

Volling, B., and Belsky, J. (1992). The contributions of mother-child and father-child relationships to the quality of sibling interaction: A longitudinal study. *Child Development, 63,* 1209–1222.

Wagner, M. E., Schubert, H. J., and Schubert, D. S. (1985). Family size effects: A review. *Journal of Genetic Psychology, 146*(1), 65–78.

Zajonc, R. B. (1983). Validating the confluence model. *Psychological Bulletin, 93,* 457–480.

Zervas, L. J., and Sherman, M. F. (1994). The relationship between perceived parental favoritism and self-esteem. *Journal of Genetic Psychology, 155*(1), 25–33.

■ References: Peers and Friends

Adler, P. A., and Adler, P. (1998). *Peer power: Preadolescent culture and identity.* New Brunswick, NJ: Rutgers University Press.

Adler, P. A., Kless, S. J., and Adler, P. (1992). Socialization to gender roles: Popularity among elementary school boys and girls. *Sociology of Education, 65,* 169–187.

Ahmad, Y., and Smith, P. K. (1994). Bullying in schools and the issue of sex differences. In John Archer (Ed.), *Male violence,* London: Routledge.

Alexander, G. M., and Hines, M. (1994). Gender labels and play styles: Their relative contributions to children's selection of playmate. *Child Development, 65,* 869–879.

Always, D. (1993). *Bullying at school: What we know and what we can do.* Cambridge, MA: Blackwell.

Asher, S. R., Hymel, S., and Renshaw, P. D. (1984). Loneliness in children. *Child Development, 55,* 1456–1464.

Asher, S. R., Parkhurst, J. T., Hymel, S., and Williams, G. A. (1990). Peer rejection and loneliness in childhood. In S. R. Asher and H. D. Cole (Eds.), *Peer rejection in childhood* (pp. 253–273). New York: Cambridge University Press.

Asher, S., Renshaw, O., and Hymel, S. (1984). Peer relations and the development of social skills. In S. G. Moore and C. R. Cooper (Eds.), *The young child: Review of research, 3.* Washington, DC: National Association for the Education of Young Children.

Asher, S., and Renshaw, P. (1981). Children without friends: Social knowledge and social skills lacking. In S. Asher and J. Gottman (Eds.). *The development of children's friendships,* pp. 273–296. New York: Cambridge University.

Banks, R. (1997). Bullying in schools. *ERIC Digest,* EDO-PS-97-17.

Batsche, G. M., and Knoff, H. M. (1994). Bullies and their victims: Understanding a pervasive problem in the schools. School Psychology Review, 23(2), 165–174.

Berndt, T. J. (1988). The nature and significance of children's friendships. In R. Vasta (Ed.), *Annals of child development*, (5, 155–186). Greenwich, CT: JAI Press.

Berndt, T., and Perry, T. (1986). Children's perceptions of friendships as supportive relationships. *Development Psychology, 22*, 640–648.

Bierman, K. L., and Furman, W. (1984). The effects of social skills training and peer involvement on the social adjustment of preadolescents. *Child Development, 55*, 151–162.

Bojko, M. (1995). The multicultural program at O'Brien Elementary School. In K. L. Seifert and R. J. Hoffnung (Eds.), *Child and Adolescent Development* (p. 414). Boston: Houghton Mifflin.

Bloch, D. (1993). *Positive self-talk for children: Teaching self-esteem through affirmations.* New York: Bantam.

Brophy, J. (1996). Working with shy or withdrawn students. *ERIC Digest,* EDO-PS-96-14, Champaign, IL: University of Illinois.

Brownell, C. A. (1990). Peer social skills in toddlers: Competencies and constraints illustrated by same-age and mixed-age interaction. *Child Development, 61*, 838–848.

Bullock, J. (1992). Children with friends. *Childhood Education, 69*(2), 92–97.

Bullock, J. (1998). Loneliness in young children. *ERIC Digest,* May, EDO-PS-98-1.

Bullying in Schools (2001). Resource List (September) ERIC ericece@uiuc.edu.

Cairns, R. B. (1986). Contemporary perspectives on social development. In *Children's social behavior* P. Strain, M. Guralnick, and H. Walker (Eds.), Orlando, FL: Academic.

Cassidy, J., and Asher, S. R. (1992). Loneliness and peer relations in young children. *Child Development, 63*(2), 350–365.

Cassidy, J., Parke, R. D., Butkovsky, L., and Braungart, J. M. (1992). Family–peer connections: The roles of emotional expressiveness within the family. *Child Development, 63*(3), 603–618.

Charach, A., Pepler, D., and Ziegler, S. (1995). Bullying at school: A Canadian perspective: A survey of problems and suggestions for intervention. *Education Canada, 35*(1), 12–18.

Cohen-Possey, K. (1995). *How to handle bullies, teasers, and other meanies.* Highland City, FL: Rainbow Books.

Cosby, B. (1997). *The meanest thing to say.* New York: Scholastic.

Damon, W. (1977). *The social world of the child.* San Francisco: Jossey-Bass.

Denham, S. A., Renwick-Debardi, S. and Hewes, S. (1994). Emotional communication between mothers and preschoolers: Relations with emotional competence. *Merrill Palmer Quarterly 40*(4), 488–489.

Dodge, K. A. (1983). Behavioral antecedents of peer social status. *Child Development, 54*, 1386–1399.

Ellis, S., Rogoff, B., and Cronner, C. (1981). Age segregation in children's social interactions. *Developmental Psychology, 17*, 399–407.

Endo, S. (1992). Infant–infant play from 7 to 12 months of age: An analysis of games in infant-peer triads. *Japanese Journal of Child and Adolescent Psychiatry, 33*, 145–162.

Epstein, J. (1983). Selection of friends in differently organized schools and classrooms. In J. L. Epstein and M. Karweit (Eds.), *Friends in school.* New York: Academic.

Field, T., and Roopnarine, J. (1982). Infant–peer interactions. In T. Field (Ed.), *Review of human development.* New York: Wiley.

Fox, N. A. (1994). Introduction to Part 1. In N. A. Fox, (Ed.), *The development of emotion regulation: Biological and behavioral considerations, Monographs of the Society for Research in Child Development, 59*(2–3). Chicago: University of Chicago Press.

Freedman, J. (1999). Easing the teasing: How parents can help their kids cope. *Early Childhood* (Spring), 1–4.

French, D. C. (1984). Children's knowledge of the social functions of younger, older, and same-age peers. *Child Development, 55*, 1429–1433.

Furman, W., and Buhremester, D. (1992). Age and sex differences in perceptions of networks of personal friendships. *Child Development, 63*, 103–115.

Gottman, J. M. (1983). How children become friends. *Monographs of the Society for Research in Childhood Development, 48*(3).

Gottman, J. M. (1986). The world of coordinated play: Same and cross-sex friendship in young children. In J. M. Gottman and J. G. Parker (Eds.), *Conversations of friends: Speculations on effective development* (pp. 139–191). Cambridge, UK: Cambridge University Press.

Gropper, N., and Froschl, M. (1998). *The role of gender in young children's teasing and bullying behavior.*

Paper presented at the American Educational Research Association Annual Meeting, 19–23 April 1999, Montreal, Quebec, Canada.

Hartup, W. (1983). Peer relations. In P. Mussen (Ed.), *Handbook of child psychology* (Volume 4, pp. xxx). New York: Wiley.

Hartup, W. (1991). Having friends, making friends, and keeping friends: Relationships as educational contexts. In Institute of Child Development (Ed.), *Early Report*. Minneapolis, MN: Center for Early Education and Development.

Hartup, W. (1996). The company they keep: Friendships and their developmental significance. *Child Development, 67,* 1–13.

Hayden-Thomas, L., Rubin, K. H., and Hymel, S. (1987). Sex preferences in sociometric choices. *Developmental Psychology, 23,* 558–562.

Hazen, N., and Black, B. (1989). Preschool peer communication skills: The role of social status and interaction context. *Child Development, 60,* 867–876.

Hymel, S., Rubin, K. H., Rowden, L., and LeMare, L. 1990. Children's peer relationships: Longitudinal prediction of internalizing and externalizing problems from middle to late childhood. *Child Development, 61,* 2004–2021.

Hyson, M. C. (1987). The shy child. *ERIC Digest,* EPO-ps-87-3. Champaign, IL: University of Illinois.

Katz, L. G., and McClellan, D. E. (1997). *Fostering children's social competence: The teacher's role.* Washington, DC: National Association for the Education of Young Children.

Kochenderfer, B. J., and Ladd, G. W. (1996). Peer victimization: Manifestations and relations to school adjustment in kindergarten. *Journal of School Psychology, 34*(2), 267–283.

Ladd, G. (1983). Social networks of popular average and rejected children in school settings. *Merrill Palmer Quarterly, 29,* 283–307.

La Freniere, P., Strayer, F. F., and Gauthier, R. (1984). The emergence of same-sex affiliative preferences among preschool peers: A developmental/ethological perspective. *Child Development, 55,* 1958–1965.

Langlois, J. (1986). From the eye of the beholder to behavioral reality: Development of social behavior and social relations as a function of physical attractiveness. In C. P. Herman, M. P. Zanna, and E. T. Higgins, (Eds.). *Physical behavior: The Ontario Symposium,* Vol. 3. Hillsdale, NJ: Lawrence Erlbaum.

Lieberman, A. Preschoolers' competence with a peer: Relations with attachment and peer experience. *Child Development, 48,* 1277–1287.

Maccoby, E. E. (1990). Gender and relationships: A developmental account. *American Psychologist, 45,* 513–520.

Maccoby, E., and Jacklin, C. (1974). *The psychology of sex differences.* Stanford, CA: Stanford University Press.

Maccoby, E. E., and Jacklin, C. N. (1987). Gender segregation in childhood. *Advances in Child Development and Behavior, 20,* 239–287.

McAfee, O., and Leong, D. (1994). *Assessing and directing young children's development and learning.* Boston: Allyn and Bacon.

Moore, S. G. (1967). Correlates of peer acceptance in nursery school children. In W. W. Hartup and N. L. Smothergil (Eds.), *The young child,* Washington, DC: National Association for the Education of Young Children.

Moore, S. G. (1992). The role of parents in the development of peer group competence. *ERIC Digest,* EDO-PS-92-6. Urbana, IL: University of Illinois.

Mussen, P., and Eisenberg-Berg, N. (1977). *Roots of caring, sharing, and helping: The development of prosocial behavior in children.* San Francisco: Freeman.

Muzi, M. J. (2000). *Child development: Through time and transition.* Upper Saddle River, NJ: Prentice-Hall.

O'Brien, S. F. (1992). Gender identity in sex roles. In V. B. Van Hasselt and M. Hersen (Eds.), *Handbook of social development: A life-span perspective,* New York: Plenum.

O'Brien, S. F., and Bierman, K. L. (1988). Perceptions and perceived influence of peer groups: Interviews with preadolescents and adolescents. *Child Development, 59,* 1360–1365.

Olweus, D. (1993). *What we know and what we can do.* Cambridge, MA: Blackwell.

Olweus, D., Limber, S., Mihalic, S. (1999). Blueprints for violence prevention, book nine: Bully prevention program. Center for the Study and Prevention of Violence, University of Colorado at Boulder, IBS #10, Campus Box 439, Boulder, CO 80309-0439.

Parker, J. G., and Asher, S. R. (1995). Peer relations and later personal adjustment: Are low-accepted children at risk? *Psychological Bulletin, 102,* 357–389.

Patterson, G., Reid, J., and Dishion, T. (1992). *Antisocial boys.* Eugene, OR: Castilia.

Pelegrini, A. D., and Glickman, C. D. (1990). Measuring kindergartners: Social competence. *Young Children, 45*(4), 40–44.

Piaget, J. (1963). *The origins of intelligence in children.* New York: Norton.

Ranch, P. D., and Brown, P. J. (1993). Loneliness in middle childhood: Concurrent and longitudinal predictors. *Child Development, 64,* 1271–1284.

Rende, R. D., and Killen, M. (1992). Social interactional antecedents to conflict in young children. *Early Childhood Research Quarterly 7*(4), 551–563.

Renshaw, P. D., and Brown, P. J. (1993). Loneliness in middle childhood: Concurrent and longitudinal predictors. *Child Development, 64,* 1271–1284.

Ritts, V., Patterson, M. L., and Tubbs, M. E. (1992). Expectations, impressions and judgments of physically attractive students: A review. *Review of Educational Research, 62,* 413–426.

Rizzo, T. A., and Corsaro, W. A. (1995). Social support processes in early childhood friendship: A comparative study in enacted support. *American Journal of Community Psychology, 23*(3), 389–415.

Ross, D. M. (1996). *Childhood bullying and teasing: What school personnel, other professionals, and parents can do.* Alexandria, VA: American Counseling Association.

Ross, H. S., and Conant, C. L. (1992). The social structure of early conflict: Interaction, relationships and alliances. In C. Shantz and W. Hartup (Eds.), *Conflict in Child and Adolescent Development* (pp. 153–185). Cambridge, UK: Cambridge University Press.

Rubin, K. H., Bukowski, W., and Parker, J. G. (1998). Peer interactions, relationships, and groups. In W. Damon (Ed.), *Handbook of child psychology* (5th ed., Vol. 3). New York: Wiley.

Rubin, Z. (1980). *Children's friendships, 1–11.* Cambridge, MA: Harvard University Press.

Russon, A. E., and Waite, B. E. (1991). Patterns of dominance and imitation in an infant peer group. *Ethology and Sociobiology, 12,* 55–73.

Schwartz, D., Dodge, K. A., and Cole, J. D. (1993). The emergence of chronic peer victimization in boys' play groups. *Child Development, 64,* 1755–1772.

Shrum, W., and Cheek, N. (1987). Social structure during the school years: Onset of the degrouping process. *American Psychological Review, 53,* 218–223.

Shrum, W., Cheek, N., and Hunter, S. (1988). Friendships in schools: Gender and racial homophily. *Sociology of Education, 61,* 227–239.

Seifert, K. L., and Hoffnung, R. J. (1997). *Child and adolescent development.* Boston: Houghton Mifflin.

Selman, R. L. (1981). The child as friendship philosopher. In S. Asher and J. Gottman (Ed.), *The development of children's friendships,* New York: Cambridge University Press.

Selman, R. L., and Selman, A. P. (1979). Children's ideas about friendship: A new theory. *Psychology Today, 12*(4), 71–80.

Singleton, L. and Asher, S. (1977). Peer preferences and social interaction among third-grade children in an integrated school district. *Journal of Educational Psychology, 69,* 330–336.

Slaby, R. G., Roedell, W. C., Arezzo, D., and Hendrix, K. (1995). *Early violence prevention: Tools for teachers of young children.* Washington, DC: National Association for the Education of Young Children.

Smith P. K., and Sharp, S. (1994). *School bullying: Insights and perspectives.* London: Routledge.

Sobol, M. P., and Earn, B. M. (1985). Assessment of children's attributions for social experiences: Implications for social skills training. In B. H. Schneider, K. H. Rubin, and J. E. Led Ingham (Eds.), *Children's peer experiences: Issues in assessment and intervention* (pp. 93–109). New York: Springer-Verlag.

Sullivan, H. (1953). *The interpersonal theory of psychiatry.* New York: Norton.

University of California at Los Angeles Child Care Services. (1996). Bullies and victims: How parents can help. *Working Parents Newsletter,* 11.

Vail, K. (1999). Words that wound. *American School Board Journal, 186*(9), 37–40.

Vandell, D. L. (1980). Sociability with peers and mothers in the first year. *Developmental Psychology, 16,* 355–369

Vandell, D. L., and Hembree, S. E. (1994). Peer social status and friendship: Independent contributions to children's social and academic adjustment. *Merrill-Palmer Quarterly, 40*(4), 461–467.

Vandell, D., and Mueller, E. (1995). Peer play and friendships during the first two years. In H. C. Foot, A. J. Chapman, and J. R. Smith (Eds.), *Friendship and social relations in children* (pp. 181–208). New Brunswick, NJ: Transaction.

Wheeler, E. J. (1994). Peer conflicts in the classroom. *ERIC Digest,* EDO-PS-94-13. Urbana, IL: University of Illinois.

Youniss, J. (1980). *Parents and peers in social development: A Sullivan-Piaget perspective.* Chicago: University of Chicago Press.

Zarbatany, L., Hartmann, D. P., and Rankin, D. B. (1990). The psychological functions of preadolescent peer activities. *Child Development, 61,* 1067–1080.

Mass Media and Technology

10

Mass Media: A Force to Be Understood

Children, age 2 to 18, spend the equivalent of a full-time work week, over 38 hours, using media not including school and homework.
— Kaiser Family Foundation, 1999.

*T*hrough mass media, or mass communication, information reaches large groups of people quickly. Print media is one way to distribute information, but electronic media accelerates this process. Today the Internet provides a wealth of information at the discretion of the "surfer" or user.

Each medium has a different impact. Print media require readers to put their own images to the printed messages. Radio allows listeners to hear the voices with expression, but requires them to visualize what is taking place. Television, videos, movies, and the Internet are multisensory, giving their messages in words, pictures, and sounds. Unlike books, most television programs and movies are passive activities for viewers. The exceptions are radio or TV call-in talk shows, which are interactive for their callers. Computer programs and the Internet can be interactive depending on the software.

Changes in technology in the last 15 years provide many more options for communication, information, and entertainment. How we use technology with children is a critical issue facing parents, teachers, and child advocates. There is concern over the accuracy of some information and whether or not it is appropriate for children and supports their developmental needs. What control does an individual or a family have in utilizing the media to their benefit? Who decides the contents of the media and what are the influences of mass media on children and families? Parents and adults need effective ways to monitor their children's exposure to the media. The role of private and government forces in monitoring what is available to children, especially during their prime viewing time, is of concern to many.

Role of Mass Media

Mass media transforms our lives and socializes our children. The various forms of mass media educate, entertain, and inform large groups of people. They are particularly powerful because of the size of their audiences and how quickly they reach people. They affect attitudes and behavior. However, individuals and families can choose how they will use the various media. Some families appear to let the media, especially television, dictate to them while others decide what the best choices are for their family.

Provide Formal and Informal Education

Books, periodicals, newspapers, radio, television, educational films, the computer, and the Internet provide education. Each medium can be used in the classroom or by individuals informally. Specific ways in which children gain knowledge through the various media are discussed throughout this chapter.

Provide Entertainment

A major focus of the media is entertainment. The movie industry and the theater work to amuse, divert, and provide pleasure to their audiences. Radio and television broadcast a wide range of programs to entertain their audiences. The recording industry and many books, magazines, and sections in the newspaper, such as the comics, also provide entertainment. Television produces many of its own programs but also broadcasts live events. Viewers may enjoy sporting events or musical concerts from many different perspectives. The various camera angles and the commentary each add a different perspective. On the other hand, when present at an event, individuals view the event through one pair of eyes and ears.

Provide a Broader View of the World

Mass media give their audiences information about the world. They cover local, national, and global events, actions of U.S. and foreign governments, weather, and disaster news. The arts, nature, science, and scenes from everyday life are reported. News from other countries is gathered by U.S. and local newspersons and reported by the media. Many countries produce programs and printed materials that are seen, heard, or read elsewhere in the world. People around the world can take a glimpse at each other's lives and culture.

Reflect Ideas, Values, and Problems of a Society

The popular ideas of each generation can be found in their literature, music, art, television, and movies. For example, individuals tend to bond with the type of music that was popular during their adolescence. A daily newspaper, a monthly magazine, a radio or television talk show, and the weekly TV or movie guide reveal some of the thoughts and concerns of the people they cover. Letters to the editor and news broadcasters allow for dissenting opinions.

Shape Behavior and Social Values

The media shape behavior in a multitude of ways. Advertisers spend an enormous amount of money each year in the belief that, through the media, they can shape the buying behavior of the public. School-age children are prime targets for advertisers, as evidenced by the greater number of commercial breaks for children's programming compared to commercial time for any other group. Politicians also spend vast amounts of money for media exposure to capture votes.

The media give people messages about acceptable behavior and values. Various forms of the media advocate which foods people should eat, which clothes they should wear, or which toys they should buy. Clothing, toys, food, and entertainment for children are multibillion dollar markets. Young children are particularly vulnerable to television messages because they have difficulty distinguishing facts from fiction and also have fewer life experiences from which to draw. For example, a concerned Indiana School Board issued an advisory to young children that there were no such things as Teenage Mutant Ninja Turtles. Children had been crawling in the storm drains looking for them (Centerwall, 1992).

Criticism of any medium occurs when the values portrayed, the language used, or the information given is inaccurate or offends people or certain groups of people. In the past, radio broadcasting was criticized for "sanitizing" its programs, restricting both language and content, while at the same time promoting racial stereotypes. The very popular radio program in the 1940s and 1950s called "Amos and Andy" depicted urban "Negro" life in a demeaning way and its Black characters were actually played by non-Blacks. When an effort was made to convert this program to a television program, it was accused of being racially demeaning and misleading and was rejected for TV.

Television is criticized for fostering materialism and moral superficiality. It is accused of creating stereotypes for groups of people according to gender, race, ethnicity, age, sexual orientation, physical ableness, and family form. What are the roles given to each gender and racial, ethnic, or age-group in programs or commercials? How are individuals with varying degrees of physical or mental abilities portrayed? Often messages are given by omission. What children do and do not experience influences their behaviors and expectations in life.

Gender stereotyping was examined in a study of television programs in the 1990s. The study showed that the roles of women were more often nurturing and dependent, while the roles of males displayed more leadership, aggression, and decision making. Under increasing pressure from the feminist movement and other groups, the television industry has been slowly shifting the portrayal of women in shows such as *Murphy Brown, Oprah,* and *Judging Amy* to suggest a wider range of options for jobs and acceptable behavior.

Recognizing the problem of ethnic bias, CNN Broadcasting Network in Atlanta has a separate newsroom and studio for news from around the world and encourages their reporters to provide information from that nation's perspective. For example, care is taken to identify the nation by name and the word *foreign* cannot be used.

Control of the Media

In some countries, the government controls the media through censorship. In the United States and other democratic countries, there is freedom of speech, with very few restrictions. In the United States, the First Amendment of the Bill of Rights guarantees this. The freedom of the press has been strongly maintained throughout U.S. history. This is in spite of serious objections by some individuals over the rights of others to make or write certain remarks. For example, many consider language and messages found in some of the tabloids to be offensive. However, there are a few regulations to protect the public, especially in the areas of safety. One cannot cry "fire" in a crowded theater.

Regulations and Laws Governing the Media

The print media do *not* have a regulatory agency guiding and limiting publications as the broadcasting industry does. In the 1930s, at the beginning of the broadcasting era, Congress declared that the airwaves belonged to the public. Consequently, the Federal Communication Commission (FCC) was formed to regulate broadcasting according to "the best interests, convenience, or necessity" of the people. This federal agency assigns frequencies, controls the transmitting power and time schedules, and sets other regulations for radio and television. In addition, there are state and local laws. Cable television and videocassettes do not use public airwaves, so are not subject to FCC regulations.

In 1984, the FCC responded to the general political climate to reduce government intervention and to deregulate television in certain areas. The FCC lifted some of the restrictions affecting advertising time and content from children's programs. For example, this permitted the advertising of specific toys by the "hero" or main character often seen on the show. The FCC also lifted certain restrictions on scheduling violent and adult programs during children's prime viewing time. The idea was that the free marketplace would be "in the best interests" of children. In reality, children's programs had less educational content and increased advertising after deregulation.

Action for Children's Television (ACT), an advocacy group formed in 1969, and other advocates for children, opposed the 1984 deregulation as harmful to children. An alarming increase in violence was seen among the first group of children to enter middle school and high school after deregulation (Carlson-Paige and Levin 1994). After years of pressure from ACT and others, Congress passed the *Children's Television Act of 1990*. Television commercials were limited to 10.5 minutes for each hour of children's television during the week and 12 minutes per hour during the weekends. Pressure continued on the FCC to improve children's television through additional regulations. In 1995, the FCC required broadcasters to provide a minimum of three hours a week for educational programs (Murray, 1997).

By 1997, most of the television industry agreed on and began implementing a rating system giving parents information about the degree of violence, foul language, and sexually suggestive material in a program. The television industry used their definitions of violence and their criteria to evaluate programs.

Congress passed a law that requires manufacturers to install V-chips in all new television sets. V-chips are also available for existing sets. Parents can decide what their children can watch and set the chip accordingly. This built-in electronic lock is similar to the device television sets have for closed caption circuitry.

Who Controls the Messages of Mass Media?

Private enterprises operate most of the newspapers, movie companies, television networks, radio stations, and publishing and recording houses. Because these enterprises and their stockholders operate to make a profit, they choose program material that will generate money from advertisers and other sources. Companies buy time to advertise their products or services in a newspaper, on a TV show, or other places where there will be a receptive and sizable audience. The advertisers use the power of the media to persuade consumers to buy their product or services.

Consequently, **consumers** determine media content by their choices of newspapers, books, TV shows, movies, videos, musical events, or theater productions. When game shows such as *Who Wants to Be a Millionaire?"* are popular similar game shows will be produced until the market becomes saturated. If enough people express their objections to a program, a movie, a TV show, or a recording and boycott it, changes will be made. The ultimate power lies with the reader, viewer, or listener.

Private and Public Television and Radio

Most television and radio broadcasting companies using the public air waves are private and, as already mentioned, are funded by advertisers and are broadcast free to the public. However, some television is available through cable or satellite. Private companies provide the equipment necessary to produce or broadcast programs to a local area via cable or satellite and charge households for these services. A flat monthly fee provides basic services and additional fees purchase special monthly packages such as movies. The viewer can also order pay-per-view and receive special programs. Cable or satellite provides all the regular TV networks shows plus additional channels and services, with the advantage of giving the viewers a consistently clearer picture. For some rural and urban areas with a weak or nonexistent signal, this may be their only choice.

The **Public Broadcasting Service** (PBS) is an alternative to commercial television and radio. The Public Broadcasting Act was passed in 1967. Programming on public television and radio represents the viewers' interests free of the approval of advertisers. Public stations depend on the Corporation for Public Broadcasting, subscribers, and corporate or private grants to supply the majority of funding needed. Credits of corporate sponsors or foundations contributing to a particular program are listed during the showing. Public television and National Public Radio (NPR) represent a small portion of these media.

Programs are selected to reach specific groups of adults and children and provide the best in the arts, sciences, and news for education and entertainment. This is costly. With the reduction of federal funds, private and viewer contributions are crucial. Children's programs such as *Sesame Street, Barney,* and *Mr. Roger's Neighborhood* are enjoyable, educational, and promote healthy development. The NPR series, *Science Friday Kids Connection*, provides curriculums for middle school students.

 # Television, Video Games, Computers, and the Internet

Children today are surrounded by media. How they use various media and the amount of time involved are of growing concern to adults. What messages are children getting from the children's media? The Kaiser Family Foundation designed and conducted the first national study on media use by over 3,000 children, ages 2 to 18. It includes TV, movies, computers, the Internet, music, video games, radio, magazines, books, and newspapers. Professor Roberts from Stanford University and Harris, Inc., formerly the Harris Poll, were consultants.

Children's Use of Media

1. Children ages 2 to 18 spend over 5¼ hours a day using media. Children ages 2 to 7 use the media 3½ hours a day. 16 percent of children age 8 to 18 are heavy media users, spending over 10½ hours daily using media.
2. Very little parent supervision of children's media use is reported. Many children have media in their bedroom. The percentages of children age 2 to 7 with media in the bedroom are: 42 percent with radio, 36 percent with tape recorder, 32 percent with TV, 16 percent with VCR, 14 percent with CD player, 13 percent with video game player, 6 percent with computer, and 2 percent with Internet access.
3. Boys and girls spend approximately the same amount of time using the media but girls listen to more music and boys watch more TV and play more video games.
4. Children living in or attending school in lower-income neighborhoods spend significantly more time using media, except for computers, than children in wealthier neighborhoods.
5. Children in urban and rural areas are similar in the amount and kinds of media that they use. Children in the suburbs use media less overall, but more (74 percent) have computers at home compared to children in urban (66 percent) or rural (63 percent) areas, and more (51 percent) have Internet access at home compared to children in urban (41 percent) or rural (39 percent) areas.
6. Black and Hispanic children spend significantly more time using media, especially TV, than White children.
7. The use of new media supplements rather than decreases the use of traditional media.
8. Children still read for fun or are read to for forty-five minutes daily (Kaiser Family Foundation, 1999).

Television and Children

Television has become a babysitter, a friend, an entertainer, and a substitute for a wealth of activities for children including reading books. In the mid-1940s, very few homes had television, but by 1977, 99 percent of U.S. homes had at least one television (Liebert and Spravkin, 1988). Television viewing for children decreased slightly during the 1990s because of the time spent with computer games and on the Internet. The two concerns regarding the effects of television on children are the content of the programs and the number of hours they spend watching TV. In fact, children spend more time watching television than they spend on school-work, reading, and playing (Van Evra, 1998).

Influence of TV on the Developmental Needs of Children

Children need environments conducive to healthy growth and development of their physical, social, emotional, cognitive/language, and creative selves. Much of what children watch on television does not support healthy development in one or more areas of development (Carlsson-Paige and Levin, 1994).

TABLE 10.1 Television and Video Viewing
99% of all homes have TV and 28% have 3 or more sets.
Children ages 2 to 7
3 hours per day (49 minutes with parents watching TV and 29 min watching videos or movies prerecorded)
81% of time—no adult supervision
32% of homes have TV sets in children's bedroom
School-age children, ages 8 to 18
23 hours per week
Over 95% of time—no adult supervision.
65% of homes have TV sets in children's bedroom
50% of children have no rules about how much and what kind of TV programs they watch
TV is always on in 42% of homes
TV is usually on during meals in 58% of the homes.
Children in single-parent homes watch more TV than those in two-parent homes.

(*Kids and the Media at the New Millenium.* Kaiser Family Foundation, Nov. 1999. Reprinted with permission.)

PHYSICAL DEVELOPMENT Healthy physical development for young children requires activities in which they use their large muscles, such as running, jumping, and climbing, and small muscles, involving eye–hand and –finger coordination. The coordination of sensory and fine motor skills are crucial before kindergarten. Children of all ages need exercise from physical activities. Sitting in front of the television does not accomplish this. In addition, good health requires eating healthy foods. Many food products advertised on TV have too much sugar and calories with few, if any, of the nutrients children need. This is often referred to as junk food.

LANGUAGE AND COGNITIVE DEVELOPMENT Children need to learn how to think, reason, solve problems, and be creative. This requires interactions with others and making choices. Young children learn through active play with other children, using materials and objects in their environment (Piaget, 1962). Children explore their surroundings, create or pretend that they are other people or animals in an attempt to make sense of their particular settings. Children learn through solving conflicts and through failure and reorganization of their activities.

Children in the preoperational thinking stage (approximately age 2 to 7) have one level of reality (Piaget, 1962) so it is difficult and often impossible for *younger* children in this group to separate fantasy from reality. Young children often believe that animals in their cartoons, who are hurt and pop back to life with full strength, represent what does or should take place in the real world.

Based on this information, researchers in child development are concerned that too much television watching by children interferes with much-needed first-hand experiences. While watching television, children are passively taking in what others have done for them. *Teach the Children,* a documentary presented by the Public Broadcasting System, examined the impact of television programs on children's behavior and attitudes. They found that too much watching of television was related to aggressive behavior and a shortened attention span in children, as well as diminished cognitive abilities. Many of the TV programs that children watched were geared for the adult viewer and contained sex, violence, and anti-intellectualism (Carlsson-Paige and Levin, 1994). Other research showed an increased fearfulness of the world among the children who were heavy TV watchers without adult mediation (Murray, 1997).

School-age children need to become competent readers. When so much entertainment is available on TV, it diminishes the incentive and the available time to read for pleasure. Books foster a child's images of the story, while TV leaves little to the imagination. The language children read in books is also more complex than that heard on television. Studies show that children who watch the most television get lower grades in school compared to children who watch TV less than the "average" time (Arendell, 1997). It is difficult to know which is cause and which is effect.

Educational TV and cognitive development *Sesame Street* and *Mr. Rogers' Neighborhood* are two TV shows watched by children and studied by researchers over the years. *Sesame Street* was designed in the mid-1960s to provide information and cognitive skills for preschool children identified as "disadvantaged." It was used as the cognitive part of the daily program for some of the early Head Start Centers and research programs. *Sesame Street* stresses cognitive skills such as using letters and numbers, solving problems, reasoning, and understanding one's physical and social environment.

A review of several studies showed that frequent viewers of *Sesame Street* improved the most on the particular skills of focus in the program compared to the children who seldom or never watched the program. The 3-year-olds improved more than 5-year-olds (Friedrich and Stein, 1973). "Disadvantaged" children who watched frequently gained as much as "advantaged" children who watched infrequently, but when both these groups watched infrequently, advantaged children gained more than the disadvantaged ones. Evidently, "advantaged children," unlike the "disadvantaged" ones, had other sources for learning. By comparison, children who watched mostly cartoons were at a learning disadvantage by the time they were age 7 (Wright and Huston, 1995).

SOCIAL DEVELOPMENT   Healthy social development requires that children interact with both adults and children. Children need to play with others, taking turns, sharing, and resolving conflicts. They pick up and imitate ideas from their experiences. Children need props that can change as their play evolves. The content of most TV programs that children imitate during play reflects violence and adult ideas of a subject. This can be confusing for young children. The most popular program in 1994 for 2- to 11-year-old children was *Mighty Morphin Power Rangers*. This program focuses on a group of villains who threaten to take over the world (Bickelhaupt, 1994). Another popular show, *Teenage Mutant Ninja Turtles*, finds human-size turtles mutated by radiation and living in a city sewer. "When themes that are removed from children's experiences and understanding become the basis for children's play, the play is usually superficial and imitative." This is because children have difficulty transforming these themes into elaborate play episodes (Carlsson-Paige and Levin, 1994).

The toys marketed with these shows are highly realistic and encourage imitative and often aggressive play. According to one survey, over 90 percent of the teachers reported that watching the *Mighty Morphin Power Rangers* led to increased violence in their children's play (TRUCE—Teachers for Resisting Unhealthy Children's Entertainment, 2000). Because of the aggressive actions of children using these toys, many directors refused to let children bring them to preschool (Sailor, 1995).

Conflict resolution on TV typically is quick and simplistic and uses physical force. Violence against "bad guys" is condoned. The best way to gain power and control is through physical force. Other forms of power in relationships are rarely shown. For example, the use of language, assertive behavior, and compromise to solve problems is often missing. Children need to see ways of negotiating a solution to a conflict where both parties feel that they have gained something.

TABLE 10.2	I'm Okay, You're Dead! TV and Movies Suggest Violence Is Harmless

Popular Culture

1. Every four minutes, scenes of serious violence confront TV viewers and moviegoers. Music videos average one scene of serious violence per minute.
2. The majority of high violence TV shows and movies have PG ratings, acceptable for teens.
3. The most serious violence is often portrayed as harmless or justified.
4. All violence is often portrayed as laudable, necessary, or relatively harmless.

These findings are based on the most extensive study of controversial content across entertainment genres. The sample included the top-grossing films in theaters and 284 episodes of original fictional television series on broadcast and cable networks or in first-run syndications, 50 made-for-television movies and 189 music videos on MTV during the 1998–1999 season. Later these will be analyzed for sexual content and crude language. Violence is defined as the deliberate use of physical force.

Center for Media and Public Affairs (CMPA), a nonpartisan, nonprofit research organization. (www.cmpa.com/pressrel/violence99.htm) On-line: accessed 12/15/01.

Social responsibility. Children are developing a sense of right and wrong behavior for themselves and others. Young children especially tend to put an action into a good or bad category without thinking about the motivation behind it (Kohlberg, 1968; Gilligan, 1982). Cartoons show a simplistic view of morality by categorizing characters as "good guys" or "bad guys" (Hesse, 1989) which only intensifies this propensity in children. As children grow older, they can understand a more complex view of behavior and relationships. Children need to see TV characters face moral dilemmas and try to find the right thing to do.

EMOTIONAL DEVELOPMENT AND SELF-CONCEPT FORMATION   Young children ideally are learning to develop a healthy understanding of their emotions and acceptable ways of releasing feelings. They also are learning to understand the feelings of other people and reasons for their behavior. During Erikson's first stage of development, the infant and young child establish a sense of trust and must be able to count on the people around them to meet their needs. TV programs showing how adults and others are consistently there for children promote a sense of trust. In *Mr. Roger's Neighborhood* each person is listened to and respected. Mr. Rogers ends every program by telling his friends that he will be back with them. Children feel good about themselves when they can trust others around them. Many children's TV programs show that some people can*not* be trusted and that weapons are used to protect oneself against the enemy (Carlsson-Paige and Levin, 1994).

Erikson's second stage—developing autonomy or a sense of independence and some control over one's body or immediate environment—is a difficult task. The child's need is for independence but with a growing bond among human beings. Children need to see adults or children being independent but also caring for each other. TV portrays independence often with aggressiveness and not with helping or caring for others. (Carlsson-Paige and Levin, 1994).

Young children need to form a positive self-identity, valuing their gender, race, ethnicity, family, and their own abilities. Children also need to respect and value others, understand and appreciate differences, and be able to form a positive group identity, allowing each individual to value his or her gender, race, ethnic group, and physical and mental ableness (Derman-Sparks, 1989). The diversity of the characters in *Sesame Street* and *Barney and Friends* shows children how valuable it is to be a part of a diverse group of friends (Carlsson-Paige and Levin, 1994). On the other hand, children's cartoons often depict the "good guys" as mainstream White Americans and the "bad guys" as those who are different, often foreigners with distorted dehumanized voices (Carlsson-Paige and Levin, 1994). Perpetuation of these values and stereotypes sends children a biased view of differences.

A crucial part of one's self-concept is one's gender identity. In developing their gender role, children need to see many options in life for their gender and many commonalities between the genders. On TV, gender roles are most often highly stereotyped, depicting boys as competent, in control, and aggressive and girls as helpless and, often, as victims.

A 4-year-old boy reported the following episode to his teacher:

> 'There was a guy and he raped this girl on TV last night,' Matt said in a cheerful voice. The teacher murmured, 'How terrible! That must have hurt the girl and scared her awfully.' 'Oh, no,' assured Matt, 'my sister's boyfriend was watching with us and he said that girls love rape. You just don't know about that,' the four-year-old reported in superior tones (Honig, 1983).

CREATIVITY After manipulating and exploring their settings, children from 4 to 6 years of age are ready to develop creatively (Erikson, 1950). Children must be free to use materials in meaningful ways whether they are art materials, science objects, or blocks. Meaningful play, as discussed under cognitive development, encourages children to think of many ways to use materials or many answers to problems. In contrast, television programs tend to give quick, one-answer solutions, often superficial, and frequently based on the use of force to solve conflicts and maintain control or power. The realistic toys advertised on TV programs promote imitation and not creativity.

Programs Enhancing Learning and Providing Healthy Entertainment

Educational television (ET) comes into some classrooms to supplement the regular curriculum. Many of these programs are a free service provided by corporations that, in return, advertise their products on the show. The quality of the programs and the supplementary materials for the teachers are considered excellent. The problem for many teachers and parents is allowing advertising in the classroom.

Television can be a powerful tool for teaching children how to get along, to have fun, to appreciate each other, and to discover things about the world in which they live. Prosocial television appears to have an even greater impact on children's behavior than violent television does (Hearold, 1986). A cable channel for children, Nickelodeon, provides programs for children age 2 to 15. They air a variety of programs including songs, adventure stories, and talk shows, depending on the ages of their audience. Children's programs such as *Barney, Sesame Street,* and *Mr. Roger's Neighborhood* have already been mentioned. *Teletubbies,* a show on educational TV, premiered in the United States in 1998. Four teletubbies, who look like alien babies waddling around in neon-color pajamas, help children learn language, expand their knowledge, increase creativity, improve listening skills, and promote affection. Children can easily identify with them. Teletubbies are criticized for their use of short ungrammatical phrases.

The major commercial stations, along with PBS, have specials that take the audience into the world of science, or introduce them to new places and terrains. National Geographic sponsors such programs. TV introduces children to the world of music. There are history specials and programs responding to current events. For example, after the September 11, 2001 tragedies, some programing gave information on religious and cultural differences and similarities among Islam, Christianity, and Judaism. Television can help children and adults gain perspective on an event.

Television Violence and Children's Aggressive Behavior

Many researchers believe that television violence is partly responsible for the rise in violent crimes. Children often imitate in life what they observe on television and some even carry violent behavior into adulthood (Centerwall, 1992). Others argue that children who watch more aggressive television are more aggressive to begin with. These social scientists also believe that certain parent–child relationships are a much more influential force for violence than the violence on television. Children with non-nurturing parents or children who identify the least with their parents tend to be more aggressive (Silano, 1994). Because there are so many forces in children's lives, it is difficult to prove that it is television violence and not other things or a combination of conditions that causes the aggressive behavior.

The majority of studies only compare children's behavior shortly after watching a particular TV show. Those watching a program with aggression show more aggresive behavior compared to more prosocial behavior of a similar group of children after watching a program like *Mr. Rogers' Neighborhood.* More impressive are the longitudinal studies comparing groups of children who have watched varying amounts of aggressive television as children. Some studies showed changes in the

10.1 TV Viewing and Physical Aggression

Notel, Canada

In 1973, a remote rural town in Canada was first able to receive television. Prior to the introduction of television to Notel, researchers observed 45 first- and second-grade children in Notel and two other similar communities who already had television. All children were observed for inappropriate physical aggression. Two years later, a new group of researchers observed the same children. The data collected showed an increase of 160 percent in the rate of aggression of the group in Notel with an increase occurring among both boys and girls and passive and more aggressive children. There was no change in levels of aggression in the two control communities who already had television (Williams, 1986). Another study was conducted from 1960 to 1981 (Eron and Huesman, University of Illinois, Chicago) of 875 children living in a semi-rural U.S. county. Researchers found that the amount of television watched by a group of boys and girls at age 8 predicted the seriousness of criminal acts for which they were convicted by age 30. This held after correcting for the children's baseline aggressiveness, intelligence, and socioeconomic status. Second-generational effects were also witnessed. When the children who watched a lot of television at age 8 became parents, they punished their own children more severely than did the parents who had watched less television as children (Centerwall, 1992).

behavior of children shortly after the introduction of television to their area while others report the doubling of violent crimes ten to fifteen years later.

Seven U.S. and Canadian studies of children with prolonged exposure to television showed a positive relationship between television watching and physical aggression. Three different Surgeons General reports, the American Medical Association, the American Academy of Pediatrics, and the American Psychological Association have spoken about the dangers of television violence. The critical period is pre-adolescence and younger (Centerwall, 1992) (see Figure 10.1 on Notel, Canada).

The relationship between television viewing and the homicide rates in different countries and in various areas in the United States shows an increase in homicide rates after television is introduced. Other factors such as economic growth, civil unrest, age distribution, urbanization, alcohol consumption, capital punishment, and availability of firearms are controlled for or explained. Both in the United States and Canada it took ten to fifteen years after the introduction of television for the homicide rates to double among the targeted groups. The actual increase in homicide rates from 1945 to 1974 was 92 percent for Canada, 93 percent for the U.S. White population, and a decline of 6 percent for the White population in South Africa. In South Africa, television was not permitted until 1975. Again, there was a lag of ten to fifteen years before the homicide rate doubled among their White population. *This period of time coincides with the number of years that it takes for children to become adults.*

THE RESPONSE OF THE TELEVISION INDUSTRY In the 1960s and 1970s, top TV executives all testified that TV violence reduced aggression in viewers by bleeding or draining off aggressive motivations (Slaby, 1994). In the mid to late 1970s, NBC, CBS, and ABC broadcasting networks each did their own research on television and violence. The CBS research, *Television, Violence, and the Adolescent* (1982), investigated 1,565 teenage boys for aggressive behavior. Controlling for over 100 variables, the study showed that the teenagers who had watched above-average quantities of television before adolescence were committing crimes of assault, rape, major vandalism, and abuse of animals at a rate 49 percent higher than teenage boys who had watched below-average quantities of television violence. ABC conducted two surveys of young male felons imprisoned for violent crimes. In the first survey, 22 percent, and in the second, 34 percent, reported consciously imitating crime techniques from TV shows. This was especially true for the more violent crimes. All felons reported watching five to six hours of television daily as children (Centerwall 1992).

During the 1980s and 1990s, top TV executives changed their claims that TV violence reduces aggression. Instead, they told Congress and the public that TV violence had no effect on viewers. At this same time, the television industry was earning several billion dollars a year from advertisers who believed that television did affect the behavior of viewers (Slaby, 1994). TV network executives changed their statements after considerable pressure from public interest groups and government leaders, including the President. At a press conference in July 1993, the executives admitted that TV violence did contribute to problems of violence. They agreed to place advisories for parents at the beginning of violent programs and in TV listings.

Challenge for Change: Whose Responsibility?

It is everyone's responsibility to see that our children are exposed to less TV violence and to more developmentally appropriate programs. The television industry cannot be expected to stop profitable programing on their own, any more than the tobacco industry will voluntarily stop selling tobacco. Social responsibility and quality programming will rarely take precedence over profits. As long as violence in programs holds large audiences, it means money that the industry does not want to lose.

PARENTS AND TEACHERS   Parents and educators have a responsibility to help children learn to monitor their own TV viewing. Children need adults to explain the reasons for their views about specific programs, television time limits, and their overall daily schedule. Children must be free to express their thinking. They need to understand why certain portrayals of the world are inaccurate and why violent solutions to problems are not the best. They need to know what to look for in programs. Why should television time or time for any other activity be limited? Children need to be part of the decision-making process as much as possible. This will help them to become critical viewers.

Grandma and Spencer Selecting TV Programs for the Week

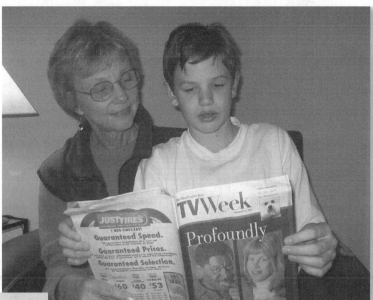

By discussing the qualities of a program, Spencer, age 11, is learning how to make good TV choices and to plan his TV time wisely. His daily schedule also includes homework and all media time.

KIDSNET is a national resource for children's television and radio programs. It includes a media guide to programs and support materials for preschool through high school students. It also includes program ratings from the new voluntary broadcast industry's program rating system. KIDNET selections are based on one or more of the following criteria. The program must

- contain educational/informational material to benefit children's learning;
- include material that improves fundamental intellectual skills in academic discipline;
- teach skills in conflict resolution and critical thinking;
- encourage awareness and understanding of prosocial behavior and relationships, issues of motivation/self-esteem, and/or an appreciation of multiculturalism;
- reflect creativity, originality and innovation;
- include information on health and/or social issues for children;
- not reflect gratuitous violence or inappropriate sexual activity. http//www.kidsnet.org/ (2002).

FIGURE  **MEDIA IN BEDROOM**

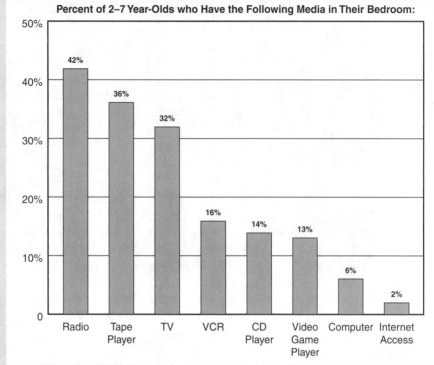

Source: Kids and Media of the New Millenium, Kaiser Foundation, November 1999.
Reprinted with permission.

PARENTAL INVOLVEMENT   There is a strong consensus that parents **should monitor, discuss, view together, and set limits with children** on children's TV viewing. Parents need to:

1. know the contents of the program, the commercials, and available ratings;
2. watch and listen to children's responses;
3. discuss with children the programs and the amount of viewing time and set
   limits;
4. discuss the content, taking advantage of concepts to be stressed or to be
   questioned;
5. use children's television viewing time for enjoyment and valuable learning
   experiences;
6. help develop a well-rounded schedule of play, reading, homework, athletics,
   and the arts.

New technology makes it possible for parents and children to choose ahead of
time what TV programs they want to view. Using a video recorder allows selected

programs to be viewed at another time. An electronic lock (the V-chip) permits parents to preset the channels and times available.

EDUCATION OF THE PUBLIC BY PROFESSIONALS   Educators, public health leaders, and researchers can provide the public with information on the hazards of television violence. The American Academy of Pediatrics has guidelines available for parents to follow in choosing and monitoring their children's TV viewing. They believe limiting children's exposure to television violence should be part of a public health agenda along with automobile safety seats, bicycle helmets, immunizations, and good nutrition (Centerwell, 1992).

Congress needs to pass legislation to reduce violence in children's programs that does not violate First Amendment rights. First Amendment scholars have some positive proposals. The FCC (Federal Communications Commission) needs to reduce the violence seen in children's programs. The link-up of children's programs with toys must be banned as it was before the 1984 deregulation. Advocacy groups need to keep informing the public of the current issues involved. Together they can continue to pressure the television industry, Congress, and the FCC for effective regulations on violence in children's programs and all programs seen during children's prime viewing hours.

The public must let the television industry and their advertisers know what programs and products they support and what programs and advertised products they oppose or boycott.

CONCLUSION   Television continues to be a powerful force in society. What kind of a teacher will the viewers allow it to be? Will television programs continue to *glamorize* violence, either in children's programing or in "entertainment" programs? Will television programs continue to give children misleading solutions to conflicts, or will they show a variety of accurate and more effective solutions? Will the industry provide higher quality educational programs?

In its role as an educator, will television give us more information on health and public safety issues? Television can be a good educator. For example, it did present the hazards of smoking. Will television be used to inform the public of the harm for children and for society of watching too much TV or too violent programs? Will programs show a more accurate view of men and women in today's society with a greater range of opportunities for women as well as men? Will individuals from diverse backgrounds be shown on TV working together and appreciating each other's differences? In general, will television programs give a more accurate picture of the world and U.S. society? **Do the air waves really belong to the people, or do they belong to the networks and/or the advertisers?**

Video Games

Video games are interactive, combining television and the computer. Video games emerged in the 1970s and became very popular within a few years, especially with boys. More boys (25 percent) ages 2 to 7 play video games than girls (7 percent). More than a *third of all children have a video game player in their bedroom* (Kaiser Family Foundation, 1999). The 2- to 7-year-old children who play video games spend an average of 50 minutes a day (Kaiser Family Foundation, 1999). Video games can be used as an educational tool, but many are for entertainment including the two most popular video games, Nintendo and Poke/mon. Two major concerns are the amount of violence and gender-role stereotyping in these games (Dietz, 1998; Cesarone, 1994). Women are most often the characters being acted upon and not the initiators of action. They are sometimes even depicted as the victims. In addition, the games are usually rule bound and stress autonomous actions rather than cooperation (Cesarone, 1994).

Based on a study of seventh- and eighth-grade students, the two most popular categories for video games were fantasy violence and sport games containing some violence. This was followed by general entertainment and human violence categories. Only 2 percent of the students preferred educational games. More males (77 percent) played video games than females (63 percent) at home and also more males played in arcades (Funk, 1993).

The National Coalition of Television Violence (NCTV) has a rating system for video games that ranges from XUNFIT and XV (highly unfit) to P and PG. However, the Nintendo company uses the same rating system as the Motion Picture Association of America (Cesarone, 1994). One problem is the subjectivity in defining violence. The behavior of game characters is either absolutely right or absolutely wrong and rarely do the characters reflect on their actions (Provenzo, 1992).

Playing violent video games has harmful effects on normal children and adolescents according to the findings of 9 out of 12 research studies (NCTV, 1990; Funk, 1993). Although many studies show connections between children's playing violent video games and later aggression, it is not proven whether violent games help children in releasing aggressive feelings or actually in encouraging them. However, playing violent games does contribute to children's acceptance of violence as a method of solving problems (Levin, 1998).

As a result of research and pressure from professionals, parents, and citizens, the government protects children against unsafe toys, play equipment, food additives, and medicine and requires the use of bicycle helmets and safety car seats. However, it has failed to protect children against the violence found in video games such as *Mortal Kombat, Lethal Enforcers, Doom, Night Stalker, Street Fighter,* and many others which can be even more dangerous to their healthy development (Kemm, 1995).

Computers and the Internet

SURFING THE INTERNET: A TWO-EDGED SWORD   The interactive use of computers with CD-Roms and modems gives children access to more information than is available at the Library of Congress in Washington, DC. Some of this information is very beneficial to learning, encourages creativity, and provides healthy entertainment, but some information is not appropriate and can be damaging to children (see Chapter 8).

Over 1 out of every 5 children age 2 to18 has Internet access from their own room and almost 45 percent of children have access to the Internet at home (Kaiser Foundation, 1999). This means that they may have access to chat groups, computer conferences, bulletin boards, and a multitude of Web sites. Through E-mail children are able to communicate with others. They can develop virtual relationships. This becomes unhealthy if virtual relationships replace real relationships. Some of the entertainment and information is adult-oriented. Children who state that they are age 18 or older have access to pornography and other inappropriate information. Children can be introduced to hate groups and some even have a "children's friendly" Web site.

Parents can limit access to undesirable Web sites through filtering systems, as can schools and libraries. For the home computers, Cyber Space and Net Nanny are useful. WebBlocker is installed in many school and some library computers.

Print Media and Children

Books Give Us Wings
— Center for the Book,
Library of Congress.

An Avenue to the World: People communicate using visual symbols, sounds, and touch, but written language enables communication on many levels. Books, periodicals, posters, and newspapers provide access to the world using written language and static images to describe their messages. It is more personal than pictorial media, where visual images are present. Children, as readers or being read to, must put these words into visual images. Children interpret the content differently depending on their vocabulary, reading ability, and knowledge or experiences. At an early age children benefit from experiences with the many different forms of literature such as prose, poetry, stories, proverbs, and riddles. Literature provides an avenue to the world.

Books contribute to children's language development, thinking skills, and information about life and events in the past, the present, and possibilities for the future. The print media enable children to compare other people's feelings and behavior with their own. Printed materials socialize children in the ways of society, contributing to their values, attitudes, and behavior. Books, indirectly and directly, affect children's development.

Adults take more control over children's early experiences with print media than with television (Van Evra, 1998). The books and printed materials chosen by parents,

10.2 Reading for Fun

Children ages 2 to 7 and 2 to 18 read for fun or are read to 45 minutes a day. Reading for fun, especially of books, drops off between ages 14 to 18.

(Kaiser Family Foundation, 1999.)

teachers, and librarians generally reflect family and community values. However, some books and printed materials available to children contain excessive violence, stereotyping, confusion of reality with fantasy, and quick-fix solutions. These elements are detrimental to children's healthy development just as they are in TV.

Influence on the Developmental Needs of Children

Books, magazines, and other print media need to be appropriate for the child's developmental level. Young children who are in Piaget's preoperational level of thinking (approximately ages 2 to 5–7) will only be able to comprehend one idea at a time, one time period, one role for a person, and a very simple plot, especially those in the early preschool years. Young children often confuse fantasy with reality. As children move into the concrete operational stage (age 7 or earlier), their thinking becomes flexible and reversible. They are able to move in and out of time periods and to understand more complex relationships. However, not until the stage of formal operational thinking, which may occur between ages 11 and 15, are children able to think logically and abstractly. At this age, many children can interpret abstract symbols and analyze books.

PHYSICAL DEVELOPMENT   Books, magazines, pamphlets, and newspapers provide information on healthy living. Parents and children can read articles on health and nutrition, exercise, how to play certain sports, and teams to join. They can learn the dangers of unhealthy life practices such as smoking or using drugs including alcohol. The print media may also promote unhealthy lifestyles, especially through advertisements. For example, the media makes junk food sound and look good to eat.

LANGUAGE AND COGNITIVE DEVELOPMENT   The print media help children become literate. Literacy, or the ability to read and write, is essential in modern society. Adults facilitate this process when they read to children and provide them with the tools of literacy such as paper, pencils, crayons, and books (Shapiro and Dorian, 1987). Most parents expose their children to the tools of literacy, but vary in the types of literacy activities with their children as well as in their attitudes and personal use of books (Bus and Van Ijzenndoorn, 1995). When parents interact with their children in activities such as taking a child to the library to check out a book, children's interest in books increases. Modeling the use of writing includes simple activities such as making a shopping list with the child, writing a check, writing down a telephone number or address, or sending a greeting card.

The process of reading stimulates thinking to a different degree than does viewing pictorial media, because children are actively involved in deciphering the words, thinking about the meaning, and using their imagination to produce the visual images. Books provide concepts as well as information. They help children solve problems. Books can develop plots to a greater extent than TV. For example,

Listen to Me Read: 7-Year-Old Reading to Her Aunt

Listening to children read encourages their desire to read. In reading, children learn new words, improve their language skills, use their imagination to depict the story, and learn more about themselves and their world.

when an act of violence takes place, the motives of the characters involved are often discussed.

SOCIAL AND EMOTIONAL DEVELOPMENT   The print media are powerful agents of socialization because children actively participate in the process. Books and other printed material show them how to behave, think, and feel. Books provide information about their daily lives from eating, dressing, and sleeping to playing. Books talk about life and objects in their environments. Books can reaffirm children's beliefs and attitudes or they can challenge them with different ideas. They learn about relationships and their own identity through books and magazines. They learn about different gender roles. These may be more traditional or more expansive (androgynous) according to the books they read or adults read to them. Print media help them to understand their present and past cultures.

Parents and teachers help children understand what they have read or heard by listening to their comments and asking open-ended questions. What is happening to the characters in the book? How would you describe the characters in a book or their specific actions? Adults can also encourage children to explore and understand their feelings about what they read.

Young children's books changed during the 1980s and 1990s. They went from representing narrow segments of society and stereotyped roles to a broader view of society, including gender roles. These changes were encouraged by the demand for nonsexist and anti-bias books in child-care centers and for children's literature to reflect more options and role models. These views were reinforced by early childhood professional organizations.

CREATIVITY   Some books encourage creative thinking and most books can be used creatively. In storytelling, the teacher could ask, "What would be another way that the story could end? or, What if . . . ?" Children can make up new stories, poems, songs, and games. Expose them to different kinds of stories and different ways of telling a story. The use of puppets or flannel-board characters and different shapes encourages imagination and is fun. Children enjoy using a tape recorder to tell stories.

Minimizing Effects of Violence, Advertising, and Stereotyping

Children are exposed to some of the same negative conditions or situations in books and comics as they are on television. Violence from storybooks, comics, and fairy tales, just as from television programs, stimulates children's aggressive behavior (Neuman, 1991). Violence, as already mentioned, can desensitize children to real-life violence and send the message that violence is the way to settle problems or can be a viable solution to an injustice. However, books are better able to view the motives of the various characters and the consequences of their behavior. Children can learn how to evaluate situations when adults ask stimulating questions. "How do you think the person felt who was teased? Can you think of another way to influence your friends than by using force? Do you think that the hero was the 'good guy' or the 'bad guy' and why?" "What actions of the hero were good or helpful and which ones were harmful?"

Advertisers target children to buy their goods, regardless of their value to them. Magazines contain many advertisements for their readers. Some of their messages are not conducive to healthy development, such as promoting unhealthy foods or certain toys. In France, a resolution to protect children worldwide from advertisers and commercialism was submitted by their national OMEP (World Organization for the Education of Young Children) committee to the OMEP World Council in Chile (Sailor, 2000). Adults can lobby to reduce these commercial messages in printed materials and on television that target children. Above all, adults can help children evaluate their reading materials, including advertisements. Ultimately children should be able to interpret commercial messages and choose and evaluate their reading material wisely.

Textbooks in the classroom vary as to their accuracy in content, in representing various groups accurately, and in being open to students' opinions. Supplementary material often provides a good balance. Children's books may be

TABLE 10.3	Ten Quick Ways to Analyze Children's Books for Ethnicity and Gender*

1. Check the illustrations for stereotypes, tokenism (not a genuine representation of a minority), and the roles of the characters.
2. Check the story line for an unbiased standard for success and resolving problems, and equitable roles of women.
3. Look at the lifestyles depicted for minorities and other cultures and see that differences are not shown in a negative way or made to look as if they represent the whole group.
4. Weigh the relationships between people to be sure that non-Whites and females are not just in supporting roles and be sure the roles in the family are accurate for that racial/ethnic group.
5. Examine the heroes and heroines to see if minority heroes and heroines represent their concepts and struggles for justice and not that their behavior has pleased or benefited White people.
6. Consider the effects of the material on a child's self-image to see if it is supportive of all skin colors, both genders, and physical characteristics such as weight.
7. Consider the author's or illustrator's background, ethnicity, culture, and gender to see if he or she is qualified to create the book.
8. Check out the author's perspective to see if it is biased regarding ethnicity, gender, or culture. Check for Eurocentric and middle-class biases.
9. Watch for loaded words with insulting overtones such as *savage, primitive, lazy, docile, backward,* the use of *man* to represent both genders, or words like *chairman* instead of *chairperson.*
10. Look at the copyright date for books on minorities. In the late 1960s and the 1970s, books began to be written by minority authors and to reflect the realities of a multicultural society and gender equity.

*Council on Interracial Books for Children, 1841 Broadway, New York, NY.

evaluated for representing gender and ethnic/racial groups accurately by using the chart in Table 10.3.

Current Trends

Mass media continue to be a powerful force in the lives of children and society. The media can be used to facilitate healthy development and provide enjoyment. Significant adults in the lives of children need information on what is available, how to evaluate materials, and ways to help children make positive choices.

Families, schools, libraries, and support groups are finding strength in networking for better television programming, well-written books, and other conditions to provide children with a wider range of appropriate learning and entertainment opportunities through the media.

Key Points

1. Mass media transmit information quickly to large groups of people in various ways. Mass media broaden people's view of the world, reflect the ideas, values, and problems of a society, and shape individuals' views, social values, and behavior.
2. Advertisers enable media to operate, but consumers have the ultimate power over media content by their choices.
3. Children, age 2 to 18, spend the equivalent of a full-time work week using media, excluding school and homework. Those who watch more violent TV than the average viewer are most likely to behave aggressively as children and, later, as adults.
4. Violence by the "good guys," stereotypical roles, and quick and aggressive ways of solving conflicts are common in children's TV programs and damaging to healthy development.
5. The Internet gives children access to a wealth of information. The use of a filtering system can block out pornography and unwanted sites.
6. Books socialize children in the ways of society, contributing to their values, attitudes, language development, literacy, thinking skills, and social and emotional development.
7. Parents who monitor and discuss media use with children contribute to positive experiences. Families, schools, libraries, and support groups need to network for improved television programming, well-written books, and other conditions to provide children with better learning and entertainment opportunities.

Critical Thinking Questions

1. How could books be used to enhance the value of children's TV programs? How would you encourage children to tell or write a different ending to an episode that they have viewed?
2. What additional regulations for children's TV programs could the FCC pass that you think would not interfere with First Amendment rights?
3. How could you help parents assume more responsibility for their children's use of the various media?

Resources and References

American Advertising Federation
  http://www.aaf.org
American Library Association
  http://www.ssdesign.com
Federal Communications Commission (FCC)
  http://www.fcc.gov/
Kaiser Family Foundation
  www.kkf.org
KIDSNET
  http://www.kidsnet.org
Motion Picture Association of America
  http:www.mpaa.org/
The National Television Violence Study
  www.ccsp.ucsb.edu
Public Broadcasting Service
  http://www.pbs.org/

■ Related Readings

Cassell, J., and Jenkins, H. (Eds.). (1999). *From Barbie to mortal combat: Gender and computer games.* Cambridge, MA: MIT Press.
Haugland, S. W., and Wright, J. L. (1997). *Young children and technology: A world of discovery.* Boston: Allyn and Bacon.
Spitz, E. H. (1999). *Inside picture books.* New Haven: Yale University Press.

■ Children's Books

Bender, R. (Ed.). (2000). *Lima beans would be illegal: Children's ideas of a perfect world.* New York: Dial.
Sandford, L., and Halstead, V. (1996). *Ten-second rainshowers: Poems by young people.* New York: Simon and Schuster.

■ References

Arendell, T. (1997). A social constructionist approach to parenting. In T. Arendell (Ed.), *Contemporary parenting: Challenges and issues:* Volume 9: Understanding families (pp. 1–45). Thousand Oaks, CA: Sage.

Bickelhaupt, S. (1994). "Power Rangers" muscles its way to the top of kid's TV. *The Boston Globe,* January 5.

Bus. A. G., and Van Izendoorn, M. H. (1995). Mothers reading to their 3-year-olds: The role of mother–child attachment security in becoming literate. *Reading Research Journal Quarterly, 30*(4), 998–1014.

Carlsson-Paige, N., and Levin, D. E. (1990). *Who's calling the shots? How to respond effectively to children's fascination with war play and war toys.* Philadelphia: New Society.

Carlsson-Paige, N., and Levin, D. E. (1991). The subversion of healthy development and play. *Daycare and Early Childhood Education, 19*(2), 14–20.

Carlsson-Paige, N., and Levin, D. E. (1992). Making peace in violent times: A constructivist approach to conflict resolution. *Young Children, 48*(1), 4–13.

Carlsson-Paige, N., and Levin, D. E. (1994). Position paper on media violence in children's lives. *Young Children, 50*(5), 18–21.

Carter, D., and Strickland, S. (1977). *TV violence and the child: The evolution and fate of the surgeon general's report.* New York: Russell Sage Foundation.

Centerwall, B. S. (1992). Viewing television in the United States, Canada, and South Africa. *Journal of the American Medical Association.*

Centerwall, B. S. (1993). Television and violent crime. *The Public Interest, 111,* 56–71.

Cesarone, B. (1994). Video games and children. *ERIC Digest* EDO-PS-94-3. Urbana, IL: University of Illinois.

Derman-Sparke, L. (1989). *Anti-bias curriculum: Tools empowering young children.* Washington, DC: National Association for the Education of Young Children.

Dietz, T. L. (1998). An examination of violence and gender-role portrayals in video games: Implications for gender socialization and aggressive behavior. *Sex Roles, 38,* 425–442.

Erikson, E. (1950). *Childhood and Society.* New York: Norton.

Eron, L. & Huefmann, L. (1986). Aggressiveness in children: A cross-cultural study. In L. Huefmann and L. Eron (Eds.). *Television and the aggressive child: A cross-national comparison.* Hillsdale, NJ: Erlbaum.

Friedrich, L. K., and Stein, A. H. (1973). Aggressive and prosocial television programs and the natural behavior of preschool children. *Monographs of the Society for Research in Child Development, 38*(4, Serial No. 151).

Funk, J. B. (1993). Reevaluating the impact of video games. *Clinical Pediatrics, 32*(2), 86–90.

Gilligan, C. (1982). *In a different voice: Psychological theory and women's development.* Cambridge, MA: Harvard University Press.

Hearold, S. (1986). A synthesis of 1043 effects of television on social behavior. In G. Comstock (Ed.), *Public communications and behavior* (Volume 1, pp. xxx). New York: Academic Press.

Hesse, P. (1989). *The world is a dangerous place: Images of the enemy on children's television.* Videocassette. Cambridge, MA: Center for Psychology and Social Change.

Honig, A. S. (1983). Television and young children. *Young Children, 38*(4), 63–76.

Kaiser Family Foundation. (1999). *Kids and media and the new millennium.* Menlo Park, CA: Author.

Kamii, C. (1984). Autonomy: The aim of education envisioned by Piaget. *Phi Delta Kappan, 65*(6), 410–415.

Kemm, B. (1995). Video-game violence. *Young Children, 50*(5), 53–55.

KIDNET. (2000). Criteria for program selections. http//www.kidsnet.org/

Kohlberg, L. (1968). A cognitive-developmental analysis of children's sex-role concepts and attitudes. In E. Maccoby, (Ed.), *The development of sex differences,* Palo Alto, CA: Stanford University Press.

Levin, D. E. (1998). *Remote control childhood? Combating the hazards of media culture.* Washington, DC: National Association for the Education of Young Children.

Liebert, R. M., and Spravkin, J. (1988). *The early windows: Effects of television on children and youth* (3rd ed.). New York: Pergamon.

Murray, J. P. (1997). Media violence and youth. In J. D. Osofsky (Ed.), *Children in a violent society* (pp. 72–97). New York: Guilford.

National Association for the Education of Young Children. (1990). NAEYC position statement on media violence in children's lives. *Young Children, 45*(5), 18–21.

National Coalition on Television Violence. (1990). Nintendo tainted by extreme violence. *NCTV News 11*(1–2, Feb–Mar): 1, 3–4.

Neuman, S. B. (1991). *Literacy in the television age: The myth of the TV effect.* Norwood, NJ: Ablex.

Pearl, D. (Ed.) (1982). *Television and behavior: Ten years of scientific progress and implication for the eighties: Vol. 1, Summary Report.* Washington, DC: U.S. Government Printing Office.

Piaget, J. (1962). *Play, dreams, and imitation* (C. Gattegno and F. M. Hodgson, Trans). New York: Norton. (Original work published in 1951).

Postman, N. (1992). *Technology: The surrender of culture to technology.* New York: Vintage.

Provenzo, E. J., Jr. (1992). The video generation. *American School Board Journal, 179*(3), 29–32.

Reno, J. (1993). Reno warns TV industry to curb TV violence. *Congressional Quarterly Weekly,* Rep (51), 2885.

Sailor, D. (1995). Banning Mutant Ninja Turtle toys from centers: Reports from selected child care centers in Orange County. Unpublished report.

Sailor, D. (2000). *Report to the OMEP World Council.* London: OMEP.

Shapiro, J., and Dorian, R. (1987). Literacy environments: Bridging the gap between home and school. *Childhood Education, 63*(4), 263–269.

Silano, B. (1994). Frankenstein must be destroyed: Chasing the monster of TV violence, *The Humanist, 54*(1). The American Humanist Association.

Slaby, R. C. (1994). Closing the gap on TV's "Entertainment" violence. *Chronicle of Higher Education,* 11, B1–B2.

Singer, J. L. (1984). Family patterns and television viewing as predictors of children's beliefs and aggression. *Journal of Communications, 34,* 73–89.

TRUCE, Teachers for Resisting Unhealthy Children's Entertainment. (2000). See through violence in the media effort. In D. Levin and C. Gerzon (Eds.), *Violence in the Media.* Boston, MA: Massachusetts Medical Society and Massachusetts Violence Prevention Task Force, Department of Public Health.

Van Evra, J. (1998). *Television and child development* (2nd ed.). Mahwah, NJ: Erlbaum.

Wright, J., and Huston, A. (1995). *Effects of educational TV viewing of lower income preschoolers on academic skills, school readiness, and school adjustment one to three years later.* Lawrence, KS: Center for Research on the Influence of Television on Children.

Violence in the Lives of Children and Peaceful Alternatives

11

"We believe that violence in America is an epidemic and a public health emergency"
— C. Evertt Koop.
Former Surgeon General

*V*iolence in the United States has increased, making this country the most violent of all industrialized countries, leading these countries in homicides, rapes, and assaults (Dodd, 1993: Weiner, 1990). Violence occurs in affluent suburbs and on inner-city streets. It knows no social, economic, racial, or geographic boundaries (Dodd, 1993). Violence has become more lethal with the increase in the use of guns over fists and knives.

Violence is the physical or psychological harm or threat of harm to a person, animal, or object. Violence touches the lives of every child, but some children more than others. Children experience violence in the family, peer group, neighborhood, school, media, and community at large. Violence may be seen by children indirectly as in the media or directly as witnesses, victims, or perpetrators. A group of young children was asked by their teacher, "What is violence?"

A four-year-old says, 'It's guns and blood.'
Another chimes in, 'It's gangs and police.'
Still another, 'It's knives.'
A soft-spoken child whispers, 'It's getting dead.' (Parry, 1993).

Roots and Consequences of Violence

Both poverty and discrimination are seeds for violence. Since 1980, the numbers of the poor and of the wealthy have increased, leaving a smaller middle class. The discontent among the poor and minorities is also more vocal. Other conditions, such as unemployment, substance abuse, and the proliferation of guns, also contribute to violence in our culture. The media contribute to and reflect the violence in society.

When children experience violence, they feel a sense of helplessness and vulnerability. It is particularly damaging when children realize that their parents are not always able to protect them. Young children, trying to establish a sense of trust and security, are particularly vulnerable. A sense of helplessness affects their motivation and self-image and ultimately their achievements. When children believe that they have some control over what happens to them, they are freer to concentrate on acquiring skills for healthy growth and development. For example, they can concentrate on play activities and schoolwork.

Violence is a learned response. Children learn their behaviors and emotions from those around them but particularly from those in their home. When their only models use force to solve problems, children act in aggressive ways (Garbarino, Dubrow, Kosteiny, and Pardo, 1992). In fact, children who live with violence often see force as the best response to get what they want and to survive. When they are victims of or witnesses to violence, they become angry. When this anger is added to anger from normal conflicts, it can lead to a lack of self-control in their responses, and can limit peaceful or prosocial solutions. This anger can become a part of their personality.

When children live where they are often concerned with their safety, they run a high risk of becoming victims or perpetrators of violence. The impact of chronic violence on many children produces a post-traumatic stress disorder similar to symptoms identified with some Vietnam war veterans (Garbarino, et al., 1992). Children who are traumatized by violence often have diminished dreams about their future and expectations of future disasters (Terr, 1983). A common response to trauma is to return to an earlier period in life to feel safe. While regression may temporarily help the healing process, long-term regression limits growth and development.

Effects of Violence on Development

Children living with violence are at risk for pathological development. It is difficult for them to establish trust, autonomy, and social competence (Wallach, 1993). The effects of violence, however, are modified by their age and temperament as well as the reactions to violence and stress of those close to them. Children who experience an initial trauma before the age of 11 are three times more likely to develop psychiatric symptoms than children first exposed to a trauma in their teens (Davidson and Smith, 1990).

The effects of violence on development are influenced by children's particular stage of life. According to Eric Erikson, children have different tasks at each stage (Erikson, 1963, 1964; see Chapter 5 on Erikson's Eight Stages of Psychosocial Development). The fulfillment of earlier tasks is particularly important to succeeding stages of development. A primary need of infants is to develop a sense of trust. This means that they learn to rely on their parents and other significant adults to protect, nurture, and care for them. Babies must have their basic needs met on a consistent basis for healthy development. Developing a sense of trust is essential for positive self-esteem and for success in the next stage of development. Parents who are preoccupied with keeping their family safe from violence may lack sufficient energy to meet their infants' needs.

When children move into toddlerhood, the shift is away from being dependent to developing independence and autonomy. Toddlers need safe environments to explore and make choices while using their new motor skills such as walking, climbing, and jumping. Toddlers who live in a violent neighborhood or are homeless do not have safe physical environments to explore. Normal restrictions due to socialization and basic safety are enough to frustrate toddlers without additional restrictions on their movements due to a violent environment. Frustrations can lead to temper tantrums and poor family adjustments.

Preschool children are ready to venture outside the family to make new friends and to learn about their world. They are particularly vulnerable when violence in their neighborhood limits their ventures (Spock, 1988). Their explorations may be further limited and fears increased if their child-care center is located in a dangerous area.

School-age children have crucial academic and social skills to master. These experiences set the stage for their adult life. If children are afraid on the playground, en route to and from school, or in the classroom, their energies are drained and their school performances are diminished (Craig, 1992). Those traumatized by violence can have distorted memories and compromised cognitive functions (Terr, 1983).

Forms of Violence

Violence takes many forms, often interrelated. Family violence includes child maltreatment, spouse or domestic abuse (adults), substance abuse, and gun violence. Some type of child abuse or neglect is usually present with spouse abuse. Substance abuse of a family member often leads to other forms of abuse or neglect in the family. Gun violence is never an isolated incident. Parental negligence often contributes to gun violence or accidents. For example, in many homes with children, parents store their guns either loaded or with the ammunition near the gun (Schuster, et al., 2000).

Ideally, the family is the place where children are protected, nurtured, and guided from infancy into adulthood. Yet, individuals are more likely to be killed, injured, or physically attacked in their own home by someone to whom they are related than in any other social context. Child maltreatment and family violence between spouses have far-reaching effects in other relationships. It can affect siblings' relationships and, later in life, affect the relationships between adult children and their aging parents (Gelles and Cornell, 1990).

Family violence exists among all social classes, races, and ethnic groups. Historically, family violence was considered a family problem. Today, children and adults who are abused are protected by laws, when these laws are successfully enforced. Women who fear harm from an abusive spouse or ex-spouse can obtain court protection. Since 1990, about half of the states have passed stalking laws prohibiting a partner or an ex-partner from following or threatening a (former) partner. However, it is often difficult to provide adequate protection from a determined and aggressive stalker.

Child Maltreatment: Abuse and Neglect

The term *child maltreatment* has been used in recent years to refer to child abuse and neglect. Maltreatment by parents and others is the intentional or avoidable endangerment of a child. It includes physical, sexual, and psychological abuse and physical and psychological neglect. Abuse involves actions while neglect is adults' inactions. A broader definition of maltreatment includes anything that interferes with a child's optimal development.

Physical abuse is intentional physical injury to the child. Repeated abuse is often referred to as the **battered child syndrome** (Kempe, Silverman, Steele, Droegemueller, and Silver, 1962).

Psychological abuse includes both actions and omissions that cause a child's behavioral, cognitive, emotional, or psychological functioning to be damaged. Children's self-esteem and emotional and social well-being are attacked. One or more types of psychological abuse is present in physical abuse cases; **rejecting the child with disdain** include labeling the child as inferior, shaming, ridiculing, humiliating, and singling out the child for criticism. Examples of **terrorizing** the child are threatening to punish or abandon the child and leaving the child in an unsafe setting. **Isolating the child** includes locking the child in a room or keeping the child away from others. **Being emotionally unresponsive** includes a failure to express affection or being detached and uninvolved. **Exploiting** or **corrupting** a child includes promoting aggression, sex, delinquency, or substance abuse and degrading a child who is racially or ethnically different (Hart and Brassard, 1994).

Sexual Abuse is any kind of sexual contact between a child and an adult or an older person. It includes fondling, exposing or touching the genitals, photographing, commenting verbally to, and engaging in sexual exploitation of a child. Incest is particularly devastating because of the closeness of the relationship and the violation of trust.

Child neglect is a form of physical, emotional, and/or medical deprivation of a child's needs including lack of supervision. Physical neglect includes inadequate food or nutrition, clothing, physical exercise, and/or health care.

Child maltreatment has both short- and long-term consequences for children. Rather than a single behavioral or emotional result, the consequences vary. Abuse is particularly destructive when parents misuse their power to undermine the child's self-worth. Derogatory and accusatory statements such as "You are no good" or "You always cause a problem" become part of the child's self-concept. Children begin to believe the abusive statements about themselves and feel that they deserve what is done to them. Their damaged self-image affects their relationships and school performance. As adults, many abused girls become victims of spouse abuse and many of the boys become spouse abusers (Stark and Flitcraft, 1996; Hotaling and Sugarman, 1986). They are also at risk for abusing their own children. In addition, abused children are more likely than other children to become aggressive, delinquent, or criminals in adulthood (Dodge, Bates, and Pettit, 1990).

CHILD MALTREATMENT REPORTS   From 1985 through 1995, the number of child abuse and neglect reports increased by 61 percent and substantiated reports by 36 percent. The number of seriously injured children quadrupled between 1985 and 1993 (Children's Defense Fund, 1997). Many cases go unreported.

In 1999, an estimated 2,974,000 individual reports were sent to the National Child Abuse and Neglect Reporting system for processing (Administration for Children and Families, 2001). Their summary report included the following information for 1999.

✔ An estimated 826,000 children were victims. This is an average of 11.8 children out of 1,000 children, down slightly from 12.6 children for every 1,000 in 1998.

✔ An estimated 1,100 children died of abuse and neglect. This is 1.62 deaths per 100,000 children. 2.1 percent of the deaths occurred in foster homes. In 1998, approximately 1,500 children died.

✔ Almost three-fifths of the victims suffered neglect, one-fifth physical abuse, and over one-tenth (11.3 percent) sexual abuse. Over one-third of all victims were reported earlier for other or additional types of maltreatment.

✔ The highest victimization rates were from the 0–3 age group. Rates declined with age.

✔ Most types of maltreatment were similar for males and females with the exception of sexual abuse. This was 1.6 per 1,000 for female and .04 for male children.

✔ Three-fifths of the perpetrators were female, with 41.5 percent younger than 30 years of age. More men were perpetrators of sexual abuse than women.

✔ Almost nine-tenths of all victims were maltreated by at least one parent.

✔ Victimization rates by race/ethnicity ranged from the low of 4.4 Asian/ Pacific Islander victims per 1,000 children to 25.2 African American victims per 1,000 children (Administration for Children and Families, 2001).

✔ A different report showed that children in families earning under $15,000 are twenty-five times more likely to be identified as abused than are children whose family incomes are $30,000 and up. This report was based on interviews of professionals working with children including child-care workers, teachers, health and mental care agency staff, and police (Children's Defense Fund, 1997).

Child Protective agencies provide services to these victims and their families to try to remedy the damage already done and to prevent future harm. They also help children and families who are considered at risk for abuse.

Causes and Conditions Surrounding Child Maltreatment

A number of conditions, often interacting, can increase the risks of child maltreatment. Certain personal traits and the background of the adult, the health, temperament, special needs of the child, and some conditions in the family and the neighborhood all can contribute to child abuse. Other factors include the interactions or lack of contact of the family with other settings, such as child care, workplace, and the community. Cultural values, laws allowing such actions as corporal punishment, and customs also affect the chances of abuse. One or more of the following factors is present in many situations of abuse and neglect.

✔ Parent was abused as a child and/or lived in an abusive home as a child.

✔ Parent is often unrealistic about her or his child's abilities and becomes abusive when the child fails to meet the expectations.

✔ Parent suffers from a mental or emotional disorder or addiction. Parent suffers from depression or is unable to control aggressive impulses.

✔ Parent is under considerable stress, such as loss of a job, and often without social supports.

☑ Parent lacks appropriate parenting skills. Discipline is harsh and spanking may become abusive.

☑ Parent is a single parent and/or isolated from other people.

☑ Conditions of poverty, violence in the neighborhood or home, large number of children in family, with children often a year apart, a child with special needs (including those born prematurely, and extreme notions of individual rights and/or family privacy are often present.

SOCIETAL CONDITIONS   Looking at the macrosystem, a number of factors can offset maltreatment while others often lead to abuse. A culture that promotes a sense of shared caring for children and their families, opposes violence, and promotes economic prosperity minimizes the risks of abuse. On the other hand, cultural and legal acceptance of corporal punishment, a view of children as possessions, and economic depression place children at risk. In countries where physical punishment is illegal, child abuse is rare (Zigler and Hall 1989; see corporal punishment in Chapter 7). Violence in our society, the neighborhood, and the media not only is stressful and dangerous, but it sends the message that violence is the way to deal with certain situations.

What are the rights of children and their parents according to American society? Children, considered by many the property or the possession of their parents, are the only people that it *is* legal to hit except in self-defense. Although the Eighth Amendment to the United States Constitution prohibits cruel and unusual punishment for criminals, the United States Supreme Court, in *Ingraham v. Wright* (1997), ruled for the second time that school personnel may strike disobedient children. On the other hand, every state has child abuse/neglect laws intended to protect children from maltreatment.

REPORTING SUSPECTED CHILD ABUSE   State laws and federal regulations and guidelines require that suspected cases of child abuse be reported within a specified period of time. States vary in the wording of their laws and in reporting procedures. Copies of the law are available at social service and licensing agencies, law enforcement agencies, and city, county, state, and district attorney's offices.

Individuals and institutions responsible for some aspect of the child's health and welfare are required to report suspected cases of child abuse including:

1. physician, hospital intern or resident, nurse, pharmacist, laboratory technician, dentist, and chiropractor;
2. teacher, caregiver, and child-care and school personnel;
3. psychologist, therapist, social worker, marriage and family counselor.

Individuals who report a suspected case of child abuse in good faith are protected by the law against civil or criminal prosecution. Reporting suspected child abuse is still very difficult to do. It makes the accused parent angry, and that anger may be taken out on the child or the school. A teacher may feel that it is up to the administrator to report abuse. The administrator may not want to anger the parent or lose a family from the program. Also, there may have been frustrating experiences in the past with Child Protective Services when no action was taken. In addition, because of privacy laws, the person who reports the case may never learn what is happening to the child. After an incident is reported, a social worker and/or a police officer visits the home of the accused and possibly the child's school. If the child is in immediate danger, the child is put into protective custody until the case is heard in court, which is usually within seventy-two hours.

Parents who abuse their children are required to get help, and, in extreme cases, may be convicted of a crime. The child can be temporarily removed from the family and placed in foster care until the home is deemed a safe environment. If the risks of more harm are not too great, the child may remain in the home while the family is receiving help.

Community, State, and National Resources

Local communities have various programs that provide services for children and families. Some programs try to strengthen the "at risk" family and provide activities that reduce the risks of violence. Other programs provide protection and/or treatment for victims such as domestic abuse shelters. Some local parenting classes offer positive discipline and basic child development information for parents before abusive behavior occurs while other classes provide therapy to change harmful behavior.

PARENTS ANONYMOUS SUPPORT GROUP　Parents Anonymous is a support group for parents who have a problem with child abuse. It was founded in 1970 by a woman who had been abused herself as a child and abused one of her children. She told a college class at Fullerton College (California) that the child she abused reminded her of herself (Sailor, 1972). Parents Anonymous has grown with chapters throughout the United States and in other countries. Parents share their problems and learn effective ways to release frustrations and more positive methods of guiding their children. Above all, they have a common bond. Each person has been there, although all are at different levels of change. Parents are there to help and support each other. For example, they have a telephone network for assistance.

The Child Abuse and Prevention Act passed in 1974 provides government funds for research on preventive programs. States can apply for funds for various preventive programs as well as for treatment of its victims. Since 1974, there has been a National Center for Child Abuse and Neglect, which provides information and support. In addition, the Resource Center on Child Protection and Custody and the National Resource Center on Domestic Violence provide information and materials. Two other resources are the Clearinghouse on Child Abuse and Neglect Information, and the National Committee of Prevention of Child Abuse.

Domestic Violence

Domestic violence is about **power** and **control.** Whenever one person uses force to control or hurt another physically or psychologically, it is battering and illegal. Force can be a threat or it can be a physical action. Overwhelmingly, its victims are women, but it also affects the lives of their children. It is estimated that nine million, or one in six, spouses suffers some form of violence each year. This abuse results in serious injuries for one to two million spouses, mostly women (Straus and Gelles, 1986). The cycle of abuse continues to escalate in frequency and intensity without extensive intervention. After a serious attack, and especially if the spouse is hospitalized, the abuser will promise that it will never happen again, and, indeed, there will be a honeymoon period before the violence recurs.

Women stay in abusive situations for many reasons. They believe that the abuser will change and things will be better. This is reinforced by the "honeymoon" period. The victims' self-esteem has been shattered and they usually have been stripped of access to their resources—family, friends, and credit cards. Many abused women live with the fear that they or their children will be harmed if they try to leave or tell anyone. They feel they have no options but to stay. In reality, most laws are inadequate in protecting abused women and enforcing sanctions against abusers.

Often there is a **community shelter** where a woman with her children can find sanctuary and counseling for a short period of time, usually two months. Children attend the local school. Women's options are explored, including their safety and economic survival if they choose to live with their children separately from their spouse. Women are told that the only hope for a safe reunion with their spouse is if he goes through long-term counseling and can change well-established behaviors for dealing with frustration and anger. Yet many women, believing conditions somehow will be better, end up reuniting with their spouses only to find that the abuse returns.

Children suffer from spouse abuse both at the time and in the future. They experience fear and anger over the abuse and often suffer physical or psychological abuse themselves from either or both parents (Gelles and Cornell, 1990). In addition, the parent, who is the victim, may not have the energy to nurture or be available for the children all the time because of abuse or threats of abuse. Years later, when these children are in adult relationships, they often repeat the behavior they lived with when they were children.

Substance Abuse in the Family

Substance abuse is a family problem. Chemical dependency—the physical or psychological dependence on mind-altering drugs—is a chronic, progressive, and potentially fatal disease with identifiable symptoms and a predictable progression.

In physical dependence, the drug is used to feel normal. In psychological or emotional and cognitive dependence, it is used to deal with stress, interpersonal relations, and other needs. Once chemicals cause problems in any area of the user's life, the user is considered dependent. Alcohol is a drug, although it is often put into a separate category; it depresses the central nervous system. Alcoholism is also a chronic, progressive, and potentially fatal disease.

The majority of Americans drink alcoholic beverages on occasion, but for some there is no such thing as a social drink. As with other types of substance abuse, when alcohol interferes with any area of the user's life, the user is an alcoholic. Alcoholism in the family has serious consequences for all family members: children, spouse, and user. For the alcoholic, it is a disease. A recent report by the American Academy of Child and Adolescent Psychiatry revealed that one out of five adults in the United States lived in an alcoholic home as a child (1999).

Most children of alcoholics grow up in a dysfunctional home because alcoholism disrupts the normal functioning of the family. The uncertainty of when the next drinking binge will take place and what kinds of abuse will occur can be devastating. These children are more likely to experience physical and sexual abuse than the children of nonalcoholics (Mathew, Wilson, Blazer, and George, 1993). They are at risk for psychological problems such as depression, anxiety, phobias, attention deficit disorder, and substance abuse. It also affects their self-esteem. As adults, children of alcoholics have a higher risk of becoming alcoholics themselves or compulsive gamblers, spenders, or sex or drug addicts. Eating orders are also common. *No child can live for any length of time in an alcoholic home and leave unscathed.*

A family systems approach to alcohol and other drug addictions involves all family members and the roles they take (Parke and Buriel, 1998). Most family members or close friends work to keep the family secret because they are ashamed, embarrassed, or fear losing a vital source of income. The cover-up begins with members assuming increasing responsibilities for the user. Family members become co-dependents and begin to exhibit compulsive behavior themselves. The more the enablers shield the user, the more they enable the dependence to continue. As the drinking intensifies, the enablers have to take on more and more responsibilities. The survival skills become so engrained in these individuals that they become hard patterns to change.

Dysfunctional Family: Compulsive Behavior and Survival Roles

Sharon Wegscheider (1981) studied the role responses of family members in alcoholic families, and identified four roles that children fulfill and how each affects the child.

Chief Enabler: This person is often the spouse or parent on whom the user is most dependent. The chief enabler compensates for failures of the user by taking on the unfulfilled jobs, making more choices, and assuming the burden alone.

The Hero: Often the oldest child tries to improve things by being an overachiever. This person also helps the nonalcoholic parent. Later in life, this child often experiences chronic feelings of guilt and inadequacy.

The Scapegoat: This child's role is to provide distraction from the family problems, usually by acting in an irresponsible or self-destructive way. This is often due to repressed anger. The scapegoat often turns to drugs or alcohol use at some point.

The Lost Child: This child withdraws from family conflict. The child is quiet, unassuming, and a loner, receiving little or no nurturance or support. The child may appear to be independent but covers up feelings of worthlessness and a deep fear of depending on others.

The Mascot: This child becomes the family comedian, providing simple fun and humor in an attempt to minimize problems. The child experiences some control in this chaotic environment but often fails to develop mature coping skills (Wegscheider, 1981).

These roles often vary with individual children. It is possible for a role to change with the progression of the disease or the ages and stages of development of the children or friends. The important thing is that help is needed so that each individual can return as a healthy functioning family member or friend. Family members can seek individual psychotherapy but some may prefer group treatment. If the alcoholic is not ready for help, the other parent and the children can get help. Alcoholics Anonymous is a worldwide organization. Their program is based on a sequence of steps that provides the basic structure for recovery. Al-Anon is their support group for family and friends of alcoholics. Al-Anon sponsors a special group for children of alcoholics, called Al-Ateen.

Teachers and the school can help if they are aware of the problem. The American Academy of Child and Adolescent Psychiatry (1999) has a pamphlet on Children of Alcoholics. Although children try to keep their family's secret, it is difficult when they are really hurting and confused. Some may show the following behaviors, depending on the family role they are assuming:

- ✔ school failure; truancy;
- ✔ withdrawal from classmates; lack of friends;
- ✔ complaints of headaches or stomachaches;
- ✔ aggression toward other children;
- ✔ risk-taking behaviors;
- ✔ abuse of drugs or alcohol;
- ✔ depression or suicidal thoughts.

If teachers can identify potentially serious problems, they can assist the child and the family get the support and help they need. The sooner children understand that they don't need to be responsible for their "adult" role, the better their prognosis is for a healthier life. Children can then become free to behave like a child, form better social relationships, and concentrate on their school work.

Gun Violence

Guns are used by adults to kill and wound children and by children to kill themselves and others. According to the Centers for Disease Control and Prevention, deaths by firearms for children under age 15 are almost **12 times higher** in the United States than in **twenty-five other industrialized nations combined** (Children's Defense Fund, 2001). In 1998, 58 percent of all gun deaths of children were homicides, while 33 percent were gun suicides and 7 percent gun accidents (Children's Defense Fund, 2001).

The number of children who died by gunfire each year nearly doubled between 1983 and 1995, while the children murdered by gunfire tripled between 1984 and 1995. Despite the recent reduction of 35 percent in the number of youth killed by firearms in 1998, 10 children died every day as a result of gunfire. This was more than all the children and teens who died from cancer, pneumonia, influenza, asthma, and HIV/AIDS **combined.**

ACCESS TO GUNS   Both the increase in the number of guns and their availability to youths and adults have contributed to the rise in violence by firearms these last two decades. A firearm in the home is an undeniable risk for accidents and suicide (Children's Defense Fund, 2001). Today, nearly 200,000,000 guns are held by private citizens and approximately 43 percent of the households with these guns have one or more children (Hart, 1998). A study reported in the *American Journal of Public Health* revealed that 1.4 million homes with 2.6 million children had firearms that were **stored unlocked, either loaded or unloaded but stored with ammunition** (Schuster, Franke, Bastian, Sor, and Halson, 2000). Another study revealed that parents who stored firearms loaded or unlocked believed that their child could safely handle a gun and knew the difference between toy and real guns (Farah, 1999). In addition to easy access for many children, most guns cost less than $100 and military rifles less than $300 (Children's Defense Fund, 1996).

In 1998, nearly one million students took guns to school, according to the Parents Resource Institute for Drug Education (American Academy of Child and Adolescent Psychiatry, 2001).

PROTECTING CHILDREN FROM GUNS   The *Asking Saves Kids* is a campaign to educate the public about the risks to children when a gun is in the household. It was launched in 1999 by the American Academy of Pediatrics and PAX: The Movement to End Gun Violence. For example, parents are urged to ask adults if there is a gun in their home before letting their child visit. Ways to approach this and other information on guns in the home are available (Children's Defense Fund, 2001).

Under pressure from the federal government, Smith and Wesson, the nation's largest gun manufacturer, began in 2002 to include internal locking devices on all new handguns. It also pledges money to develop "smart gun" technology (limiting gun use to the owner or authorized user). State legislatures in some states have passed gun legislation to help prevent deaths and injuries caused by firearms. In Maryland, the state legislature voted to require all guns in Maryland to have a built-in trigger lock by 2003, along with better enforcement of gun laws and research for "smart gun" technology. Citizens are becoming more active in pressing legislators to pass gun protection legislation. In 2000, citizens of Colorado and Oregon were successful in lobbying state legislators to include the purchase of guns at gun shows in their state's waiting period requirement.

School Violence

Although still a problem, school violence is declining. Significantly fewer students are carrying a weapon or fighting on the school grounds. Theft accounts for the majority of crimes against students and teachers (U.S. Department of Education and U.S. Department of Justice, 1999). According to this same *Annual Report on School Safety*, there is one chance in a million that a student will suffer a violent death from a school incident. However, multiple homicides at schools are up.

Although schools are statistically safer than children's homes, the number of children reporting feeling unsafe at school increased between 1989 and 1995 with more fourth and eighth graders feeling *very* unsafe. In fourth grade the number of Black (9 percent) and Hispanic (6 percent) students reporting feeling *very* unsafe was higher than the number of White (2 percent) students.

Reacting to tragic school shootings, many schools have responded with zero tolerance for certain offenses. The vast majority of these schools expel a student for carrying a weapon to school (U.S. Department of Education, 2000). There is concern among some educators and child advocates that such a rigid policy does not allow for individual circumstances. They also feel that expelling or suspending students places many of them on the streets where they are unlikely to get the help that they need. A disproportionately higher number of Black students is suspended from school than White students (Children's Defense Fund, 2000). No comprehensive data is available on the impact of zero tolerance on suspensions or expulsions (Children's Defense Fund, 2001).

The *Safe Schools/Healthy Students Initiative* of the Department of Justice suggests that the most effective strategies for reducing violence in the schools involve the education, justice, social service, and mental health systems working together. One of their joint guidelines is to create early childhood psychosocial and emotional development programs. Another is to ensure students access to school or community mental health preventive treatment and intervention services. Some funds are available to communities that are following their guidelines. (U.S. Department of Education and U.S. Department of Justice, 1999).

Juvenile Offenders

What conditions make children vulnerable to violent antisocial behavior? The book *Lost Boys: Why Our Sons Turn Violent* by Garbarino (2000) provides insight into the lives of juvenile offenders. It was written after the murderous episodes of 1998 but before the Columbine High School killings and based on the author's work with boys who end up in a juvenile detention facility or death row. Many of the boys in the study have lived under conditions that put them at risk. These include the failure of an early attachment, a difficult temperament, physical, sexual, or psychological abuse, life in a toxic environment that offers violence as entertainment, and adults modeling violence as a way of life. In addition, their peer experiences encourage antisocial activities. Often they join gangs that provide needed security, friendship, and access to guns and crime. Guns are often used in their crimes. Crime provides money for material items needed for status. Guns are also seen as protection. When asked what would make him safe, one eight-year-old, responded, "A gun of my own."

The increase in juvenile crime since the 1980s causes great public concern. Between 1985 and 1994, juvenile arrests for murder, forcible rape, robbery, and aggravated assault rose 75 percent. The good news is the 23 percent drop in the arrests of juveniles for violent crimes since 1995 and the decline in the murder arrest rate by 55 percent in the last ten years (Children's Defense Fund, 2001). Less than 10 percent of juvenile crime involves serious, habitual, violent offenders. Most juveniles are involved with property offenses (Children's Defense Fund, 2001). The vast majority of violent crimes by youth have taken place in severely stressed communities (Children's Defense Fund, 1997).

Helping Children Cope with Violence

Family Influences

Children who live in a stable family with nurturing parents are better able to deal with stress and minimize the effects of violence in their lives. The kinds of coping skills that children learn from their parents affect their feelings and actions. When parents take some responsibility for dealing with stressful conditions in their environment, it helps them and their children to cope with or minimize these stresses and dangers more effectively (Garbarino, et al., 1992; see Chapter 6 for effective coping skills).

Children need parents to listen to their fears and help them understand traumatic or stressful experiences. Parents often minimize the impact of violence on their children because they misinterpret children's reactions and explanations of the situation (Richters and Martinez, 1993). It is important for parents to understand how and when children might express their feelings and be sensitive to these signs. Children who appear unaffected by an incidence of violence may have a delayed reaction to the situation. It is important for adults to listen and reflect or repeat what children are saying so that it is clear to them both. Encourage children to take as much responsibility as possible for finding healthy solutions, but also support them and provide needed help.

Child Care, School, and Recreational Program Staff Influences

How the children's parents, teachers, and recreational leaders handle stress or violence themselves and how these adults relate to the children and their experiences affect the children's responses. Do the caregivers, teachers, and staff assume they

Drawing of 9-11 Tragedy by Second Grade Girl One Year Later Drawing

Claire's teacher talked about 9/11 that morning. Claire and two other children each drew a picture about the event during their free choice time. This drawing also gave Claire's parents an opportunity to talk about her feelings.

have some control over the violence they experience and take actions to minimize it? Do they provide their children with a safe and caring environment with opportunities for emotional outlets? Do they work with the families?

To minimize the effects of violence, it is essential that children who experience it have relationships with nurturing adults in nonviolent settings. Often children can be helped to develop positive social relationships and constructive ways of dealing with conflict through experiences in their child-care center, school, recreational program, or other adult-led group activities. When teachers or leaders and parents work together to create a supportive environment for children, it enables some parents to provide a more positive home environment.

PARTNERSHIP WITH PARENTS PROJECT   This project helps children and parents cope successfully with the effects of violence and prevent future violence. Children, through their play with others, learn to value differences and solve conflicts cooperatively. In addition, teachers and program staff help parents identify children's reactions to stress or to violence so that they can minimize the negative effects. This project can be adapted to the ages of the children and their setting.

The first step is for the teachers or recreational program staff to complete an extensive self-evaluation to find and eliminate any abrasive or violent behavior in their interactions, in their program, or in the overall setting. In doing so, teachers and staff work to increase their cooperation and respect for each other, the children, and their parents, and to resolve all differences peacefully.

The next step is to develop the program with the help of parents, utilizing each person's special knowledge. The following roles emerged for teachers, leaders, and staff members: interpreters, coordinators, and facilitators.

As **interpreters,** teachers or program staff share their expertise with parents on typical childhood behaviors relating to trauma. Parents share what violent or frightful experience their child has had and how they interpret his or her reactions. Teachers can help parents understand the degree of violence with which children are exposed and its possible effects. Parents need encouragement to express their concerns and offer solutions. Remember that parents are the experts concerning their children and should be encouraged to share pertinent information. Both teachers and parents need to discuss any behavior that might relate to current stresses or fears.

As **coordinators,** teachers and other program staff work with parents to develop compatible programs to be used outside school to help a child deal with stresses and violence. A major concern is how to support the child in the healing process after a traumatic experience. Other joint efforts concentrate on ways to reduce violence in the child's life at home and in outside settings. In place of violence, the child needs to experience success in peaceful interactions and problem solving. Sharing basic information in these areas with parents is helpful. This includes suggestions for positive discipline or guidance (see Chapter 7).

As **facilitators,** teachers and other program staff help parents and children find successful ways to solve their problems and ways to gain a feeling of having some control over conditions in their lives. Parents may need references for appropriate professional help such as a child mental health professional, therapeutic play group, or family counselor.

Facilitators encourage the parents to try to find some positive way to respond to the violence, such as working to reduce it. Parents could participate in a neighborhood or community group advocating against violence in their neighborhood or in the media. The issue might be violent toys or the illegal distribution of guns or drugs. This work allows parents to be part of the process **for reducing violence and gaining power in controlling what happens in their family's life** (Zero to Three, 1992).

Peaceful Alternatives to Violence

The very concept of civilization has at its core the protection of children. Families, child-care centers, schools, public and private agencies, youth organizations, local, state, and federal governments, religious institutions, businesses, and all citizens need to work together and agree to make serious changes in what is acceptable behavior, which values or cultural norms are to be supported, and, above all, to model peaceful ways of dealing with conflict.

Societal Responses

A recent approach to reducing violence is through partnerships. Religious organizations, citizens in neighborhoods, government officials, community members at large, and youth themselves are joining forces with some success. The emphasis is on prevention. Numerous strategies have been developed to combat violence. These include new laws, tougher penalties, more rigorous prosecution, rehabilitation programs, and many preventive measures. For example, the Providing Safe and Stable Family Programs are working with at-risk families or with families in at-risk neighborhoods before crime forces punitive actions by adapting services to work best with families or neighborhoods rather than making them fit into an existing help system (see Chapter 12).

Prevention Programs and Peaceful Alternatives

In both developed and developing countries, there are many programs working with men to change traditional roles of masculinity and fatherhood. Some programs help fathers and their infants or young children to develop close relationships.

11.1   NAEYC's Position Statement on Violence in the Lives of Children, adopted July 1993

The National Association for the Education of Young Children's position paper addresses the problem of violence, the effects of violence on children, and actions to take.

1. Advocate for public policies and actions that prevent violence. Allocate resources to the prevention of crime. The number of inmates doubled from 1980 to 1990 partially because of tougher punishment, but the crime rate still increased 12 percent. Criminal justice measures must be combined with even more prevention programs targeted to support families with young children and poor children. Revitalize neighborhoods, ensuring peacekeeping by providing human services such as job training, parent education, and health care.

2. Commit the early childhood profession to helping children cope with violence in their lives and promoting their resilience through partnerships with parents; early childhood programs and curriculum; and professional preparation, development, and support.

Teacher certification standards should require violence-prevention training and the teaching of alternatives to violence. Create in-service teacher-education programs on helping children cope with violence in their lives with special emphasis on the therapeutic strategies of children's play and art. (Excerpts from NAEYC's Position Statement by permission of NAEYC.)

Other programs help boys and men to resolve conflicts in nonviolent ways. Some countries have used the media to send messages for nonviolence and for men and women to nurture and protect their children and each other. These programs appear to reduce men's violent treatment of women and children (United Nations Population Fund, 1996).

UN INTERNATIONAL DECADE FOR THE CULTURE OF PEACE AND NONVIOLENCE, 2001–2010   On a global level, the United Nations General Assembly declared the **year 2000 the International Year for the Culture of Peace** and 2001–2010 the **International Decade for the Culture of Peace and Nonviolence for the Children of the World.** A group of Nobel Prize Peace laureates drafted Manifesto 2000, an international pledge for peace, on the occasion of the 50th anniversary of the Universal Declaration of Human Rights. Individuals around the world signed this pledge for peace declaring that in their daily life, family, work, community, country, and region they would:

1. **Respect all life**—without discrimination or prejudice.
2. **Reject violence**—in all its forms: physical, sexual, psychological, economic, and social and support the most deprived and vulnerable such as children and adolescents.
3. **Share with others**—put an end to exclusion, injustice, and political and economic oppression.
4. **Listen to understand**—defend freedom of expression and cultural diversity.
5. **Preserve the planet**—respect all forms of life and preserve the balance of nature on the planet.

6. **Rediscover solidarity**—contribute to the development of their communities, the full participation of women, and respect for democratic principles (UNESCO, 1999).

BOSTON VIOLENCE PREVENTION PROJECT   The city of Boston, through the development of a broad-based coalition, public education, money, human efforts, and new and enforced laws, has made its city a much safer place. The coalition, which began in 1982 with a few concerned individuals, initially provided a training program in violence prevention. Hundreds of people were trained and went on to work with existing programs or to develop initiatives in their communities to reduce violence.

One of the strengths of this coalition in recent years is its broad-based membership, which provides a wide range of expertise. The mayor's office is actively engaged in securing money for the project. Today the police and other agencies, such as probation officers and social service workers, and the communities are effectively working together. It is essential that the police be involved to curb violence. By working with other agencies, the police have been able to identify at-risk youths and respond more appropriately to a neighborhood's particular needs. In 1993, right after the passage of the Brady Bill, the community was able to secure federal support to curtail the flow of illegal guns into Boston. As a result of all these efforts, children in Boston live in safer neighborhoods. **The number of Boston children murdered has declined from 16 in 1993 and six in 1994 to one in 1995.** However, the roots of violence must be attacked in order to reduce all forms of violence against children now and in the future (Children's Defense Fund, 1997).

CHOOSING NON-VIOLENCE (CNV)   The **Rainbow House** is a comprehensive social service agency in Chicago providing shelter and support services for women and children who are victims of domestic violence. In an attempt to understand and stop the cycle of systemic violence, they developed an educational abuse prevention mini-course called Choosing Non-Violence (CNV) for high school juniors and seniors. The organizers found that many of these youth already had been in violent relationships and defined males in terms of violent domination over women. The decision was made to reach out to younger children and the CNV program was redesigned for children in primary schools. When these younger children were asked how they would express their very strong feelings, their answers were shockingly violent.

In 1988, **Choosing Non-Violence (CNV)** became a training program for Head Start and Title XX child-care teachers. The five-week teacher training program covered violence and its effects on children, gender role stereotyping and its relationship to violent responses, stress, discipline, classroom management, and classroom application. Rather than developing a new curriculum for their program, teachers use their current activities but teach them with a nonviolent approach. For example, when reading the story of Cinderella, the teacher now would ask, "How do you think Cinderella felt being spoken to so cruelly? How would you feel if someone spoke to you like that?" Another teacher, taking children on a nature walk to look for beautiful things, would also have children look for people helping each other.

Teachers can help children to:

1. *understand and identify violence in their lives, toys, and their choices;*
2. *realize that they have the power to choose and control how they act and how they will be;*
3. *learn the power of language and use words to say how they feel and to protect and defend themselves without being violent;*
4. *understand that violence can hurt or destroy any person, place, or thing. "Feelings are okay, but how we act on these feelings becomes important. There are alternatives to a violent response." (Parry, 1993).*

CNV also has a parent-training component. Many parents report using these methods at home. Parents are taught to help their children use words to express their feelings and solve problems without violence. Teachers and parents are reinforcing each other but it takes time to make major changes (Parry, 1993).

The CNV project expanded. By 1993, 263 Head Start and child-care teachers had completed their training and were working with over 6,000 children and 3,000 parents throughout Chicago. This program has partnerships with other programs such as substance abuse, clinical counseling, and job-training opportunities in order to be more effective in stopping violence.

ORANGE COUNTY PEACE CAMP: A CIRCLE OF FRIENDS   This one-week camp for children entering first grade through high school has evolved into a more elaborate child-driven program since its inception in 1993. Approximately 75 children and adults come together for one week each summer to get to know each other, build a sense of trust, and work on some very difficult issues. Beyond creating a peaceful community at camp, they struggle to find ways to build a more peaceful environment in their homes, schools, with friends, and in the world. The Women's International League for Peace and Freedom, Orange County Association for the Education of Young Children, and Fullerton College Child Development and Family Life Department (Fullerton, CA) sponsor this program. A youth leadership program has emerged from this project.

MAKING A DIFFERENCE   A study, released in 1995 by Public/Private Ventures, showed that children who had Big Brothers or Big Sisters were less likely to abuse drugs, have trouble in school, or hit another person. They also improved their relationships with family and friends. A key to the success of these programs is their training and support of their volunteers (Children's Defense Fund, 1997).

A RAND CORPORATION STUDY   It is far more cost-effective to work with delinquent youth, hold them accountable, and provide rehabilitation when needed than it is to take punitive approaches such as "three-strikes-and-you're-out" laws. Three

Building Community at Peace Camp

This mixed-age group of children comes from diverse backgrounds, but all want to understand each other and resolve problems peacefully. The focus for the 2002 Peace Camp was A Circle of Friends: Growing Leaders for Tomorrow.

intervention programs were compared to the results from the "three-strikes-and-you're-out" laws. The intervention programs offered training to parents struggling with delinquent youths and provided financial incentives to graduate from high school. They worked with youth who had just become delinquent. The result was that graduation incentives averted 250 serious crimes for every million dollars spent compared with just 50 crimes averted by three-strikes laws (Children's Defense Fund, 1997).

SAFE CORRIDORS   In Chicago, Beth New Life, Inc., of Bethel Lutheran Church, instituted a "Take Back the Streets" campaign to reduce drug trafficking, shootings, and other violence. This project united the Garfield Park community. Citizens created safe corridors for children outside their local school. They held a march to signal drug buyers to stay away from Garfield Park and to seek help for drug abuse. Citizens proceeded to clean up vacant lots, install lighting, and fence off buildings that were heavy drug-trafficking sites. They then held prayer services and family fun nights in the streets that had been controlled by drug dealers (Children's Defense Fund, 1996).

In Irvine, California, Physicians for Social Responsibility and some medical students from the University of California at Irvine formed a coalition and forced a manufacturer of handguns, known as Saturday Night Specials, to close down operations and move out of the community. Sadly, the gun death of a youth was the catalyst for the movement.

THE OAKLAND MEN'S PROJECT   This project in California is an example of a group working toward the eradication of male violence, racism, and homophobia. Males are taught to be nurturers and to work for equality in relationships with women. Boys are taught by male mentors that violence is unacceptable and men should not be tough, aggressive, and in control over women, children or others (Children's Defense Fund, 1996).

Children need a safe environment at home and in their neighborhood where they can play, explore, and form relationships. Those who experience this are more likely to grow up to become competent adults (Garbarino, 1992). It is crucial that these efforts to promote peaceful alternatives to conflicts are effective. Is the approach and are the projects of individuals and organizations working? If not, why continue to repeat the same actions? Are violence or threats of violence used as a means to end violence either in their actions or words? Even some words representing violence and force are used in ordinary conversation. "If looks could **kill,** you would be **dead** now," "I'm just **dying** to see that movie," or "Don't jump the **gun,** just wait." Then there's the U.S. War on Poverty. Some groups advocating peace want to change these "deadly" expressions. In any case, let us change our thinking and focus on how to live together peacefully and support those who have difficulties. Let this be known *not* as a War on Violence but a *Movement for Peace or a Culture for Peace.*

Current Trends

More individuals and groups are accepting responsibility and working on solutions to end or greatly reduce violence in the lives of children. Ending violence takes grassroots efforts as opposed to a few individuals in leadership positions coming up with solutions. Everyone, including children and their families, must participate. Children need significant adults in their life to listen to what they are thinking and feeling and give them the best of their understanding and guidance. Currently, poverty and the great gap between the rich and the poor are not being reduced significantly and these underlying causes of violence have to be removed before any permanent changes will take place.

Key Points

1. Poverty and injustice in wealth and status must be reduced before permanent solutions to violence are possible.

2. Violence, a learned response, is the physical or psychological harm or threat of harm to a person, animal, or object.

3. The immediate effects of violence are feelings of helplessness and vulnerability that thwart motivation, lower one's self-image, and reduce general performance. Children living with violence are at risk for pathological development.

4. Family violence includes child maltreatment, domestic abuse, substance abuse, and gun misuse.

5. Child maltreatment includes the physical, emotional, or sexual abuse of a child and the physical and psychological neglect of a child. Abused children's self-image is damaged, which affects their social relationships and motivation for school performance As adults they may be child abusers or involved in spouse abuse.

6. Programs for peaceful alternatives to violence teach nonviolent ways to deal with conflict.

7. Every day 10 children die from gunfire. The annual death toll is higher than deaths of children from guns in five industrial countries combined.

8. The damaging effects of stress and violence in children's lives can be minimized by a supportive family and other significant adults who are sensitive to their experiences and provide peaceful coping skills.

9. A number of programs are available that reduce various forms of violence and offer peaceful alternatives.

10. Families, child-care centers, schools, public and private agencies, youth organizations, religious institutions, government, and all citizens need to work together to reduce violence and to provide children with peaceful alternatives to solve their problems.

Critical Thinking Questions

1. How would you explain the relationships among poverty, parental stress, and child abuse?

2. How would you, as a teacher, help children understand that violence is not a normal or healthy way to respond to conflict?

3. What characteristics seem to make a child more vulnerable to abuse in a family or being bullied?

4. What types of programs would you want in your classroom or child-care facility to model positive conflict resolution?

Resources and References

■ Web Sites or Telephone Numbers

ACT Adults and Children together against violence
http://www.ACTagainstviolence.org
Center for the Prevention of School Violence
http:www.ncsv.edu/cpsv/
Clearinghouse on Child Abuse and Neglect Information (703) 385-7565
National Clearinghouse on Child Abuse and Neglect
http//www.calib.com/nccanch
National Coalition Against Domestic Violence
http//www.ncadv.org
National Committee of Prevention of Child Abuse
http://www.childabuse.org/
National Institute on Alcohol Abuse and Alcoholism
http//www.niaa.nih.gov/
National Resource Center on Domestic Violence (800) 537–2238
Parents Anonymous
http://www.parentsanonymous-natl.org/
Resource Center on Child Protection and Custody (800) 527–3223
UNICEF
www.unicef.org
UNESCO
www.unesco.org

■ Related Readings for Adults

Alexander, L., Duerell, A., Sachs, M., and Agee, J. (1990). *The big book for peace.* New York: E. P. Dutton Children's Books.

Caduto, M. J., and Bruchac, J. (1991). *Native American stories: Told by Joseph Bruchac.* Golden, CO: Fulcrum.

Canada, G. *Fist, stick, knife, gun: A personal history of violence in America.*

Carlsson-Paige, N., and Levin, D. (1990). *Who's calling the shots? How to respond effectively to children's fascination with war play and war toys.* Philadelphia, PA: New Society.

Child Development Division, California Department of Education. (1997). *Reducing exceptional stress and trauma: Curriculum and intervention guidelines: Resources to help staff and children identify and work through trauma, stress, and grief.* Sacramento, CA: Department of Education.

Garbarino, J., Eckenrode, J., and Barry, F. D. (1997). *Understanding abusive families: An ecological approach to theory and practice.* New York: Jossey-Bass.

Kreidler, W. J., and Tsubokawa Whittall, S. (1999). *Adventures in peacemaking: A conflict resolution activity guide for early childhood educators* (2nd ed.). Cambridge, MA: Educators for Social Responsibility.

Lantieri, L. and Diener, S. (2001). Talking to children about violence and other sensitive and complex isses in the world. Adapted from S. Jones and S. Berman, *A discussion guide for parents and educators.* Educators for Social Responsibility: http://www.emotional.org, October 9, 2001.

Smith, C. A. (1993). *The peaceful classroom: 162 easy activities to teach preschoolers compassion and cooperation.* Beltsville, MD: Gryphon House.

■ Books for Children and Youth

Knight, Margy Burns, (1996). *Talking wall: The stories continue.* Gardner, ME: Tibury House. Introduces different stories from around the world by telling the stories of walls, from Maya murals in Bonampak, Mexico, to dikes in the Netherlands.

Stanek, Muriel. (1983). *Don't hurt me, Mama.* Morton Grove, IL: Albert Whitman. A kind, sensitive school nurse finds help for a young victim of child abuse and her mother.

Trottier, M. *A safe place.* Morton Grove, IL: Albert Whitman. To escape her father's abuse, Emily and her mother go to a shelter where they find a safe place to stay with other women and children in similar circumstances.

■ References

Administration for Children and Families. (2001). *Child Maltreatment 1999: Reports from the National Child Abuse and Neglect Data System.* Washington, DC: U.S. Department of Health and Human Services.

American Academy of Child and Adolescent Psychiatry. (1999). *Facts for families: Children of alcoholics. (No. 17).* Http//www.aacap.org/publications/factsfam/

Children's Defense Fund. (1996). *The state of America's children, Yearbook 1996.* Washington, DC: Author.

Children's Defense Fund. (1997). *The state of America's children, Yearbook 1997.* Washington, DC: Author.

Children's Defense Fund. (2001). *The state of America's children, Yearbook 2001.* Washington, DC: Author.

Craig, S. E. (1992). The educational needs of children living with violence. *Phi Delta Kappan, 74,* 67–71.

Davidson, J., and Smith, R. (1990). Traumatic experiences in psychiatric outpatients. *Journal of Traumatic Stress Studies, 3*(3), 459–475.

Dodd, C. (1993). Testimony prepared for the Joint Senate-House Hearing on Keeping Every Child Safe: Curbing the Epidemic on Violence. 103rd Congress. 1st session, March 10.

Dodge, K. A., Bates, J. E., and Pettit, G. S. (1990). Mechanisms in the cycle of violence. *Science, 250,* 1678–1683.

Erikson, E. H. (1963). *Childhood and society.* New York: Norton.

Erikson, E. H. (1964). Human strength and the cycle of generations. In Erik Erikson(Ed.), *Insight and responsibility.* New York: Norton.

Gabarino, J. N. (2000). *Lost boys: Why our sons turn violent and how we can save them.* New York: Anchor Books.

Garbarino, J., Dubrow, N., Kosteiny, K., and Pardo, C. (1992). *Children in danger: Coping with the consequences of community violence.* San Francisco: Jossey-Bass.

Gelles, R. J., and Cornell, C. P. (1990). *Intimate violence in families* (2nd ed.). Newbury Park, CA: Sage.

Farah, M. M. (1999). Firearms in the home: Parental perceptions. *Pediatrics, 104*(5), 1059–1063.

Hammil, J. O. (1999). A model of justice from South Africa. *Concerned Educators Allied for a Safe Environment–Cease News, 19*(1), 4.

Hart, P. (1998). *Parents, kids and guns: A nationwide survey.* October 31, 1998. http://www.handguncontrol.org/press/1998.htm on November 21, 2000.

Hart, S. H., and Brassard, M. R. (1987). A major threat to children's mental health: Psychological maltreatment. *American Psychologist, 42*(2), 160–165.

Hotaling, G. T., and Sugarman, D. B. (1986). An analysis of risk markers in husband and wife violence: The current state of knowledge. *Violence and Victims, 1,* 101–1024.

Jackson, B. R. (1995). Early childhood professionals: Partners with parents helping young children exposed to violence. Redmond, WA: *Child Care Information Exchange.*

Kempe, C. H., Silverman, F. N., Steele, B. B., Droegemueller, W., and Silver, H. K. (1962). The battered child syndrome. *Journal of the American Medical Association, 181,* 17–24.

Mathew, R. J., Wilson, W. H., Blazer, D. G., and George L. K. (1993). Psychiatric disorders in adult children of alcoholics: Data from the epidemiological catchment area project. *American Journal of Psychiatry, 150,* 793–800.

Parke, R. D., and Buriel, R. (1998). Socialization in the family: Ethnic and ecological perspectives. In W. Damon (Ed.), *Handbook of Child Psychology* (5th ed., Vol. 3,). New York: Wiley.

Parry, A. (1993). Children surviving in a violent world: "Choosing non-violence." *Young Children, 48,* 13–17.

Richters, J., and Martinez, P. (1993). The NIMH community violence project: I: Children as victims and witnesses to violence. *Psychiatry, 56,* 7–21.

Sailor, D. (1972). *History of Parents' Anonymous Lecture.* Fullerton, CA. Fullerton College.

Schuster, M., Franke, M., Bastian, A., Sor, S., and Halson, N. (2000). Firearm storage patterns in U.S. homes with children. *American Journal of Public Health, 90*(4), 588–594.

Spock, B. (1988). *Dr. Spock on parenting.* New York: Simon and Schuster.

Stark, E., and Flitcraft, A. (1996). *Women at risk: Domestic violence and women's health.* Thousand Oaks: Sage.

Straus, M. A., and Gelles, R. J. (1986). Societal change and change in family violence from 1975 to 1985 as revealed by two national surveys. *Journal of Marriage and the Family, 48,* 465–479.

Terr, L. (1983). Chowchilla revisited: The effects of psychic trauma four years afer a schoolboy's kidnaping. *American Journal of Psychiatry 140,* 1543–1550.

Tower, C. (1996). *Understanding child abuse and neglect* (3rd ed.). Boston: Allyn and Bacon.

UNESCO. (2000). *Manifesto 2000: For a culture of peace and non-violence.* www.unesco./org/manifesto2000

United Nations Population Fund. (1996). A new role for fathers. New York: UNESCO.

U.S. Department of Education. (2000). *Fast facts: Violence prevention.* National Center for Education Statistics. Http//nces.ed.gov/fastfacts

U.S. Department of Education and U.S. Department of Justice. (2000). *2000 annual report on school safety* (October). Washington, DC: Authors.

U.S. Department of Education and U.S. Department of Justice, *2000 annual report on school safety.* Washington, DC: Authors. On-line. Available: http://www.ed.gov/official/OESE/SDFS/annrept00.plf

Wallach, L. (1993). Helping children cope with violence. *Young Children, 48,* 4–11.

Wegscheider, S. (1981). *Another chance: Hope and health for the alcoholic family.* Palo Alto, CA: Science and Behavior Books.

Weiner, T. (1990). Protective factors and individual resilience. In S. J. Meisels and J. P. Shonkoff (Eds.), *Handbook of early childhood education* (pp. 97–116). Cambridge, England: Cambridge University Press.

Zero to Three. (1992). *Can they hope to feel safe again? The impact of community violence on infants, toddlers, their parents and practitioners.* Arlington, VA: National Center for Clinical Infant Programs.

Zigler, E. F., and Hall, N. W. (1989). Physical child abuse in America: Past, present, and future. In D. Cicchetti and V. K. Carlson (Eds.), *Child maltreatment: Theory and research on the causes and consequences of child abuse and neglect.* New York: Cambridge University Press.

Ziegler, E. F., and Hunsinger, S. (1977). Supreme Court on spanking: Upholding discipline or abuse? *Society for Research in Child Development Newletter,* Fall, p. 10.

Effects of Government and All Social Policies on Children and Families

12

The moral test of a government is the way it treats those who are in the dawn of life, the children; the twilight of life, the elderly; the shadows of life, the sick, needy and the handicapped.

— Hubert Humphrey,
former vice-president of the United States

*T*he extent to which families are able to provide for their children is determined in large part by how successfully society is able to support the family (National Commission on the International Year of the Child, 1980). What is society's attitude toward its children and their families? For example, do all children have a right to adequate nutrition, health care, child care, education, and protection from physical and emotional harm? Societal support is conveyed through its attitudes and in its policies. Policies express principles that guide our actions in every level of society and in every system of the social ecology of the child. Policies come in many forms and under many labels covering cultural norms, laws, regulations, judicial decisions, executive orders, administrative practices, and traditions. **Social policy** is a broad term covering everything from cultural consensus to a particular business policy. **Public policies** refer to social policies that are enacted by government agencies and are enforceable by the police and judicial powers of the local, state, and federal governments. The ramifications of a policy can be so great that people disagree as to whether it should remain or be changed. For example, the United States Supreme Court decision in 1973 on Roe *vs.* Wade regarding abortion rights is still a hotly debated issue.

All public actions and legislation have some impact on families directly or indirectly. Government policies affect housing, health care, education, transportation, social services, environmental regulations, equality of opportunity, employment, insurance, use of public lands, agriculture, nutrition, and taxes as well as judicial decisions. All contribute in varying degrees to the successes or failures in the functioning of a family.

Roles of Government

Americans are divided as to how government should intervene in economic affairs and in their private affairs. There are four schools of thought or ideologies: liberalism, conservatism, populism, and libertarianism. Most individuals tend to belong to one group on most issues but certainly can change positions on individual issues. The majority of Americans are either liberals or conservatives. Liberals favor increased government intervention in the economy but oppose increased limits on personal freedom. Conservatives hold the opposite views. They oppose government intervening in the marketplace unless absolutely necessary but are in favor of the government intervening in private lives for moral purposes. The populists are inclined to favor government intervention in both economics and in personal matters while the libertarians oppose government interference in both areas (Gitelson, Dudley, and Dubnick, 1998). For example, a conservative and a libertarian would be inclined to limit government spending for social and welfare programs whereas a liberal would favor government funding for such programs. A conservative or a populist would favor legislation requiring parental notification by a physician of their minor daughter's pregnancy.

Despite numerous federal, state, and local policies that directly affect children, there has never been a coherent national policy for children (Barbour and Barbour, 2001), with the exception for the state mandated ages at which all children should attend school. Perhaps the lack of a national public policy for children is really our policy. There are at least two reasons for avoiding a comprehensive national policy for children. One reason is the belief in individual rights and another is the fear by some citizens of government controlling their rights, especially on a national level. As a nation, we believe in individual rights first and society's rights second. Socialist countries like China believe in society's rights first and individual rights second. Many other nations have policies in-between these two extremes. In the United States, parents are given freedom to raise their children according to their values. The government will protect the rights of children if the threat is considered damaging to the child but government agencies are reluctant to interfere with parental authority.

Public policy in the last two decades has been to let child care and prenatal care remain largely the family's responsibility. The few regulations governing the care of children outside the home are left to the individual states. Conservatives argue that government's aid in providing health care and child care might rob the family of its incentive and its freedom to care for their children as they see fit. Liberals see the government as failing to support families who lack the freedom or ability to provide essentials like health care and adequate child care (Kenniston, 1977; Sailor, 1982). The nation's responses to health care, child care, and parental leave have a direct and increasingly powerful bearing on the quality of life for children and their ability to lead happy, productive lives.

Policies at the National, State, or Local Level

At what level of government should a particular public policy be established? Should it be at the national, state, or local level? Who knows the issues better? In some cases, like collecting garbage, running the city public library, or hiring teachers, most people would agree that these are local decisions. Issues on foreign policies and defense should be dealt with by the federal government because it affects all citizens. Here, the appropriate federal agency or department can take a broader perspective and has more human and financial resources. However, on many more issues, people disagree.

The current trend is to make local decisions as much as possible although some funding from the federal government may be necessary. In the case of schools, many believe that the local teachers, administrators, and parents know best what their children need. Because our population and communities are so diverse, community interests and local citizen's input are important. However, opponents fear that local citizens lack a larger perspective that could be found at the state or national level. Some believe that national policies, as opposed to local policies, represent the general norms and values of the American people and are less likely to discriminate against racial, religious, and political minorities (Gitelson, Dudley, and Dubnick, 1998).

Legislative, Administrative. and Legal/Judicial Systems

Government includes the institutions and officials that enact, execute, and enforce the laws. Federal, state, and local governments affect families through decisions made by its legislative, administrative, and judicial branches. Legislative bodies, such as Congress on the national level, enact laws and allocate funds for various programs. The administrative branches at each level implement legislative policies and provide services. The federal government, headed by the President of the United States, includes an entire bureaucratic system. Because much legislation is written in general terms, program administrators in the bureaucracy often become powerful policymakers (Garbarino, 1982). The United States constitution allows national, state, and local governments to share power. In a conflict, national law takes precedent.

Families are affected broadly by economic policies expressed in banking regulations, tariffs, taxation, defense policies, the use of public lands such as the National Park system, and an array of environmental policies. Hundreds of federal agencies have direct programmatic impact for children and families. This includes the powerful federal regulatory agencies such as the Federal Food and Drug Administration and the Consumer Protection Agency. Our present reliance, or some would say overreliance, on the federal government can be traced back to 1935 with the creation of the Social Security Act. This Act was part of a safety net to help people during the Great Depression of the 1930s. Today, federal funds given to the states often require matching state funds. Additional government programs are discussed in Chapter 13.

Each level of government has a judicial branch with police to protect citizens by enforcing laws, courts to try cases, and jails to incarcerate suspects and offenders, and for the protection of society. Judicial decisions are interpretations of legislative decisions or legal standards. Every society has laws to protect its members. State laws require parents to protect and provide for their children. The decision to intervene in family life is a response to family failure. Some judicial decisions affect only an individual family, as in a child custody case, while other mandates about family life affect the institution of the family. For example, state laws regulating adoption are written in the "best interest of the child." The Adoption Assistance and Welfare Act of 1980 (PL 96-272) focuses on reuniting families and the Adoptions and Safe Family Act of 1997 promotes adoptions for children waiting in foster care. Foster homes are to be close to children's parental homes to facilitate parental visits. The treatment time of rehabilitation of parents is shorter than in the past and long-range plans for children in foster care are mandated. (See Chapter 4.)

When should a child be removed from the home? One theory is to safeguard family integrity by requiring evidence of quite serious family trouble and proof of undesirable conditions before removing the child. The other theory advocates a lower threshold for removing the child, which allows for early intervention. This early intervention may prevent an eventual family breakup and/or save a child from some abuse.

Children enter the legal system when:

1. their parents divorce or legally separate; both support of the child and custody arrangements are established by the court;
2. parents seek money, such as welfare;
3. abuse, neglect, or abandonment by parents is discovered;
4. there is a permanent removal provision that frees the child for adoption;
5. there is an adoption;
6. there is a reported and substantiated case of child abuse by a professional or person working with the child;
7. there is a willful act by the child, such as vandalism or truancy.

Juvenile Justice System

The juvenile justice system, one part of the legal system, was created to help youth live within the law and, at the same time, protect society from harm. Young people are salvageable and need treatment rather than punishment. In the juvenile justice system, the language of the law and the treatment of the offender is different from the regular courts. The juvenile is referred to as an offender and not a criminal, and the court records remain sealed and cannot be used against the person in the future.

A youth may enter the juvenile system by being arrested, referred by a school, or turned in by parents. A status offense is an act that is against the law only because of the age of the offender. For example, violating a curfew is a status offense. Other offenses are a crime regardless of age. The court looks at the child's offense, general behavior, any emotional problems, and conditions in the family. The judge may release the youth to the supervision of the parents, perhaps requiring family counseling or remove the youth from the home. The offender would then be placed in a foster home or a juvenile facility.

The juvenile justice system varies from state to state. A few federal laws apply, such as juveniles are to be housed separate from adults. However, this law is not always followed. Efforts are being made to develop some standard guidelines for all states, but a number of differences remain. The Juvenile Justice and Delinquency Prevention Act of 1974 was designed to encourage states to improve their juvenile justice systems. In the fiscal year 2001, Congress appropriated $279 million for juvenile justice improvements, but only $95 million was for local delinquency prevention programs (Children's Defense Fund, 2001).

Even though juvenile crime rates declined between 1994 and 2001, states are treating more of their youthful offenders of violent crimes as adults. Children as young as age 13, rather than age 15, may now be tried under the adult jail system for certain violent crimes committed on federal property (Federal 1994 Crime Law). When juvenile offenders are treated under adult laws, they come in contact with and learn from adult criminals. Children in adult prisons compared to those in the juvenile facilities are eight times more likely to commit suicide, five times more likely to be sexually assaulted, twice as likely to be beaten by prison staff, and 50 percent more likely to be attacked with a weapon (Children's Defense Fund, 2001). In the adult judicial system, the death penalty is possible. Since 1973, United States courts sentenced 196 people to death for crimes committed while they were under age 18 and executed 17 under age 18 (U.S. Department of Justice, 2000; Hansen, 2000). The UN Convention on the Rights of the Child (1989) outlaws the death penalty for juvenile offenders.

Federal Programs Supporting Children and Families

Programs for public assistance vary in their concept. **Social insurance** programs are designed to help people help themselves. **Job skills** programs are geared to help individuals acquire the skills that they need for employment. **Welfare** programs provide money, food, housing, and medical care to anyone with low enough income. **Workfare** requires anyone applying for welfare to take job-training classes and/or submit evidence of seeking employment. The current emphasis is on workfare and seeing that individuals on welfare become part of the workforce.

LIVING EXPENSES

Temporary Assistance for Needy Families (TANF) replaces Aid to Families with Dependent Children (AFDC). It provides temporary assistance to families with children but places a lifetime limit on support and requires work or job training for recipients. States vary in their plans.

Social Insurance Programs are designed to help people help themselves. These include unemployment compensation and social security. Recipients have contributed to these programs and in time of need they are eligible for financial help. Unemployment compensation is administered by both federal and state governments.

Supplemental Security Income (SSI) provides a guaranteed minimum income for the aged or disabled.

Social Security Survivor or Disability Benefits are for those individuals who are eligible for social security benefits and who die or become disabled. Benefits are paid to survivors or their dependents.

Veterans Benefits are for veterans and survivors or dependents of veterans who die or are disabled in the service.

HEALTH AND NUTRITION

Medicaid and the Children's Health Insurance Program (CHIP) provide health services to poor children and families.

Food Stamp Program is for food (rent and utilities) for low-income families. Participants pay for the food stamps according to their income and family size. This reduces the cost of the food they purchase.

The Child and Adult Food Care Program (CAFCP) provides funds for child care and food for low-income families. The child-care component has been drastically cut. Many family child-care providers are no longer eligible (Children's Defense Fund, 1998).

Supplemental Food Program for Women, Infants, and Children (WIC) began in 1972 and provides food and nutritional supplements for low-income pregnant and lactating mothers and their at-risk children under age 4.

CHILD NUTRITION SERVICES OR PROGRAMS:

National School Breakfast Program, National School Lunch Program, Summer Food Service Program (SFSP) all provide food for low-income children in poor neighborhoods. Some summer recreational programs for these children are eligible for help from the last program.

CHILD CARE

Title IV and Title XX of the Social Security Act fund child-care programs and related services to low-income children.

Head Start and Title I of the Elementary and Secondary Act fund child care and other social services.

Income deduction of some child-care expenses is available for employed mothers.

SPECIAL NEEDS OF CHILDREN

Child Abuse and Treatment Act of 1974 provides funds to the states to help with their programs for preventing and treating child abuse.

Support for Promoting Safe and Stable Family Programs (originally the 1993 Family Preservation and Support Services): money given to states for funding community programs that support children and families and prevent the need to remove children from the home.

Social Services Block Grant (Title XX) provides various services for low-income children and abused, vulnerable, and neglected children and their families. It includes preventive and support services. Its current funding is very low. This became a block grant in 1981 when the 1974 Title XX Social Services Program had its funding cut. In a block grant, the states have considerable flexibility in how they distribute the funds.

Child Adolescent Service System Program assists youth with serious emotional problems in finding mental health services.

Although these programs are helping many children and families, too many poor children and their families are still suffering from inadequate nutrition, health care, child care, and education. According to the Children's Defense Fund (1998), a number of conditions in society are forcing more families into poverty. Not only is there a high rate of unemployment for minorities but many parents working two jobs are not earning enough money to stay out of poverty. Inadequate education and job training prevent many individuals from getting a job or a decent paying job. In addition, funding in many government programs has been reduced.

Conditions Impacting Children and their Families

Poverty, inadequate and unaffordable health care and child care, inadequate education, inadequate protection from physical and psychological abuse, inadequate, unsafe, or no housing, environmental pollution, inadequate public transportation, and lack of minimum income are all conditions detrimental to children and their families. An increasing number of children have a parent in jail. This group of children often goes unrecognized and is therefore inadequately supported.

The child poverty rate in the United States is one of the highest in the developed world. In a recent study of seventeen developed countries on several continents, the United States had the highest rate of poverty, 50 percent higher than the next highest rate. The percentage of children in poverty ranged from 3 percent in Denmark, Switzerland, and Sweden to 22 percent in the United States (Nelson, 2000).

This high poverty rate for American children is due to both the wide differences in U.S. private sector income and the enormous differences among nations in their governmental efforts to alleviate child poverty. In 1999, only 31 percent of American children living *in poverty* were in a family receiving cash public assistance. Besides the human costs, the lack of investment in American children could put the United States at a competitive disadvantage in the international marketplace in this century (Casey Foundation, 2001).

TABLE 12.1	Where the United States Ranks among Industrial Countries

- 1st in military technology
- 1st in defense expenditures
- 1st in Gross Domestic Product
- 10th in eighth-grade science scores
- 12th in the percentage of children in poverty
- 16th in living standards among our poorest one-fifth of children
- 17th in our efforts to lift children out of poverty
- 17th in low birth weight rates
- 18th in the gap between rich and poor
- 21st in 8th-grade math scores
- 23rd in infant mortality
- **Last** in protecting children against gun violence

(Children's Defense Fund, 2002.)

Children with a Parent(s) in Prison

An estimated 1.6 million children have a parent in prison and 200,000 children have a mother in prison (Seymour, 1998). These mothers often were the sole caregiver. This growing population of children, frequently unrecognized, lacks appropriate support. These children suffer both physically and emotionally from unstable and often abusive conditions before and during their mother's incarceration, and again during the reunion period. The majority of these children live in poverty, frequently moving from one household to another.

Many are unable to visit their incarcerated parent. Approximately one-half of incarcerated parents receive no visits from their children and the others only infrequent ones (Snell, 1994). For children, the traumatic separation from their parent, the continued lack of parental contact, and the social stigma of having a parent in prison, all contribute to their fear, anger, anxiety, guilt, and confusion (Johnson, 1995a, 1995b; Osborne Association, 1993). Without intervention, children of inmates are five times more likely than their peers to become delinquent (CAEYC, 1990).

These families are in need of help even before there is an arrest. Resources from the Promoting Safe and Stable Family Programs (formerly Family Preservation and Support Services Programs) can be used (see Chapter 13). They need assistance in:

1. finding safe and stable placements for children;
2. maintaining relationships with the person in prison;
3. family relationships and parenting skills;
4. dealing with the knowledge of having a parent in prison.

Some parents are afraid to ask for help for fear of losing custody of their child. Government agencies and social-service groups lack coordination. The criminal justice system is involved with the prisoners but does not keep records on the prisoners' children and families. The welfare system is responsible for children needing placement but few child-welfare agencies have policies or programs that specifically deal with the needs of children with incarcerated parents (Child Welfare League of America, 1998). The Prisoner's Advocacy groups tend to focus on providing visitation programs but not on their other needs. A comprehensive plan by all agencies in the justice and social-welfare systems needs to be developed and implemented. Research is needed in this area. What are the effects on children of having a parent in prison? What are the effects on children of their placement(s) and their permanency options during this period? How best can children be supported (Seymour, 1998)?

Support Programs

The following three advocacy projects are making a difference for some of our most vulnerable children, those with a parent in prison.

PRISON MATCH: A MODEL CHILDREN'S CENTER PROGRAM SAN FRANCISCO COUNTY JAIL   Prison Match is a visitation program that enables children to spend quality time with their incarcerated parent every Sunday at a children's center in the prison. This program began over twenty years ago in a Women's Federal Prison and in 1989 moved to San Francisco County to operate at the San Francisco County Jail in San Bruno. Professionals in social work are present to support the families during the visiting hours and at other times for help. A bus provides transportation.

The program encourages children and families to maintain positive family ties. This experience helps children have better emotional and physical health and is a deterrent to delinquent behavior. Family relations are strengthened and better parenting skills are learned. This should contribute to later family stability and serve as a deterrent to recidivism.

Prison Match is a national model for prisons across the country and is visited by delegates from other countries. Prison Match is involved in research and publications, and maintains a clearinghouse for information and support regarding parental incarceration with Pacific Oakes College, Pasadena, CA (California Association for the Education of Young Children, 2001).

CHILDREN VISITING PRISONS: KINGSTON, ONTARIO, CANADA   This program was founded in 1993 to enable children to visit a parent in prison in an environment that is positive for them and their parent. Volunteers provide supervision during scheduled prison visits, promote and monitor toy libraries at local prisons, and occasion-

> *"To his child, a father in prison is a father first."*

ally present information on this project to the public. The fathers have requested and been given books on parenting and related subjects. Appropriate play materials enhance the visiting experiences, building relationships and a sense of trust. A list of books for children and for adults is available on their Web site (Townsend, 2000).

A major sponsor of this program is OMEP, the world organization for the education of young children, founded in 1948 for the purpose of improving the education and welfare of young children worldwide.

GIRL SCOUTS BEYOND BARS   Youth service organizations, like the Girl Scouts, are built on a family model and do not reach some children who could benefit greatly from their programs. This special Girl Scout program reaches children of "zero-parent" families (Carnegie Corporation of New York's Task Force on Youth Development, 1992). Because their mothers are in prison, these children are vulnerable to a number of problems. They are more likely than other girls to experience anxiety, depression, post-traumatic stress symptoms, aggression, attention disorders, truancy, a decline in school performance, and are more likely to become pregnant in their teens (Moses, 1995).

In this program, Girl Scouts from age 5 to 13 can work with their mothers in prison on their Girl Scout projects. These two-hour meetings take place two

Saturdays a month. On the other Saturdays, the girls meet elsewhere in their community where they finish their projects, take field trips, and form friendships with each other. The girls also benefit from the mentoring relationships with Girl Scout leaders (Moses, 1995). In addition to these valuable experiences with their daughters, some programs offer the mothers Girls Scout leadership training, group counseling with a licensed social worker, formal parenting instruction, targeted transitional planning, or after-care services with collaborating agencies.

Key to the success of these challenging projects was the building of partnerships. In Broward County, FL, the Girl Scout executive director and council members forged partnerships with numerous community agencies and institutions in order to meet more needs of the girls and their mothers. Their principal partner was the Broward Correctional Institution. Other participants included the Broward County School District, Mount Bethel Baptist Church, the Florida Department of Health and Rehabilitation, the Broward County Sheriff's Office, Henderson Mental Health Center, Women in Distress, Camber Hakk, and Woodson Psychological Services.

The Girl Scout beyond Bars program began in 1992 as a National Institute of Justice (NIJ) pilot demonstration project at the Maryland Correctional Institute for Women. In November, 1995, the NIJ sponsored their first annual "Girl Scouts beyond Bars" conference. Over eighty participants attended from fifteen states. Currently, the twelve participating sites are funded by private contributions, foundations, and state grants rather than by the NIJ. The Girl Scouts beyond Bars program has also stimulated other correctional institutions and advocacy groups to provide visitation programs for children (Moses, 1995).

Advocacy

Advocacy is standing up for a person, cause, or movement. Child advocacy calls for actions to affect social and political influences on all children. It is a process of educating the public to the needs of children and to society's responsibilities in meeting these needs. It confronts citizens with the tragic consequences of *inadequate* nutrition, prenatal and postnatal health care, child care, education, and protection of children. These consequences are expressed not only in ever-increasing costs to the children themselves, but ultimately to society as a whole, human costs that translate directly into financial costs. Although some may fear that the intrusion of government policy threatens parental freedom to raise children, the child advocate asks, "**What freedom of choice is there for parents, particularly among the poor, who along with their children are imprisoned by poverty, disease, and ignorance?**"

In the United States and other countries with a similar form of government, public attitudes and pressure affect government policies. However, some members of society influence government actions more than others. It is imperative that those who are concerned about *all* children work for government policies and actions that support the healthy growth and development of every child. When some of our children's basic needs are inadequately met, it is important for citizens to take action.

For generations, U.S. interest groups have regularly lobbied legislators to write and vote for laws that would be favorable to their industry such as the oil industry or automobile manufacturers. Since the 1970s, professionals working with children and concerned citizens have become increasingly aware of this process. In 1977, Kenneth Keniston and the Carnegie Council on Children published the report, *All Our Children: The American Family Under Pressure.* This report described the detrimental effects, both human and economic, of specific social polices reaching deep into the fabric of American life.

This report inspired the National Council of Churches of Christ to create the Child and Family Justice Project, which was active for twenty-seven months from 1978–1980. The Carnegie Foundation was the major funding source. This project was designed to educate participants in twenty diverse communities across the nation on how to be a child advocate and how to develop local models for advocacy. The author was a member of the Fullerton, CA Advocacy Group. Each committee had eighteen members from diverse backgrounds, including religious and secular. After extensive investigations, including town hall meetings, each community identified local conditions detrimental to their children. Eventually one condition was chosen by each group as their final project. The final report included the findings of each project and nineteen recommendations for national policies (Sailor, 1982). The Fullerton, CA committee identified the need for late-day child care as the number one condition in which they could make a difference. They used the $500 seed money from the project and found grant money to operate the first late-day child-care center in the area on a sliding scale for fees (Sailor, 1982).

Children need the support of adults because they have no power in society to stand up for themselves. They have no vote and usually no money of their own. Because of their immaturity, they do not even know what they need. If society is to continue and flourish, it needs its children to grow up to be healthy, capable leaders, and contributing members. In addition, parents may need their children, as adults, to provide for them when they can no longer care for themselves.

Advocacy, Coalitions, and Networking

When an individual stands up for an issue, he or she becomes an **advocate.** When individuals join forces for more power, they form a **coalition.** When coalitions work together to reach more people and increase their effectiveness, they form a **network.**

A coalition, often referred to as an advocacy group, may be formed to address a specific problem or it may exist on an ongoing basis to monitor particular issues affecting children. An example of a specific-issue child advocacy group or coalition was the Alliance for Better Child Care. The ABC coalition, as they became known, was formed to get federal legislation passed regulating child care in the United States. Over a five-year period, they educated the public on the conditions of child care in the United States. They networked with other groups like the National Association for the Education of Young Children and the Parent Teacher Association (PTA). The ABC bill was introduced into Congress, and modified to get the support of necessary groups in the child-care field as well as bipartisan support in Congress. On the last day of the 1988 Congress, the bill failed to be passed and died. Many individuals and groups refused to give up their work and eventually were successful. In 1991, Congress enacted similar legislation regarding child care.

HOW TO BECOME AN ADVOCATE   Most individuals who work with children want to make a difference in their lives, but some also feel a responsibility to all children. This project will provide information on the process of advocacy and give you experience as a child advocate. Consider the following suggestions.

1. Educate yourself on issues and existing advocacy groups.
2. Look for issues in professional child development journals such as *Young Children* and for a "Public Policy" or information page.
3. Check professional newsletters for existing advocacy groups.
4. Attend advocacy workshops at conferences and read your newspaper.
5. Listen to the concerns of parents and teachers.
6. Find the conditions around you that are harmful to children. It may be unsafe play equipment, illegal staffing, unhealthy snacks or lunch, an unsafe school crossing, or pending legislation that would lower requirements for staffing or cut funding for child-care centers, social services, or school programs.

Projects can be very small. Often it is easier to obtain approval and funding for a pilot project such as installing seat belts in *some* but not all school busses in your district. Many advocates join groups that are already working on a project.

Student Group Project: A Virtual Project or a Real One

1. Identify a problem and then research the condition to determine if the problem really exists, who is affected, and if anyone or any other group is attempting to meet the need.
2. Organize a core group of supporters and research how changes can be made. Have your facts, identify your power base (who can make the change), and make a detailed plan on how to proceed. List your priorities.
3. Educate the public and particularly other groups who have some power and interest. Place an announcement on public radio, in the local newspaper, the PTA newsletter, in flyers, or hold public meetings.
4. Find outside support. Who would be interested in your project? Would it be members of the local PTA, parents, teachers, a counselor, the vice principal, or members of a community group? Divide up the jobs.

5. Contact those who have the power to make changes and present them with facts and possible solutions. Include how much money would be needed and how it might be raised. The source of power, depending on your project, could be one of the following:
   a. legislators on the federal, state, or local level;
   b. administrative and advisory agencies;
   c. advisory board members—work for the appointment of persons concerned for children;
   d. school board or board of directors;
   e. courts which can take legal action if government or private agencies are not implementing a law or regulations appropriately.
6. Attend and express your concerns at public hearings held by legislative groups, school boards, and administrative and regulatory agencies, if applicable.
7. Mediate, negotiate, and compromise. Rarely are changes made exactly as advocates want.
8. Monitor the project during and after completion, perhaps creating a small standing committee to be sure the project continues to operate. It is very possible to have funds cut or a new bill introduced at the next session to eliminate the project.
9. Recognize all who help make these changes possible. Send notes and accolades to policymakers, media personnel, organizations, and individuals for their support. This contributes to future efforts to improve conditions for children.

Remember that you will become an expert in the area you select. This project should interest you. Enjoy!

Advocacy Groups and Projects

Numerous groups have been established in communities across the United States to improve conditions for children and their families. Some of these groups are formed to accomplish a single objective, while others monitor certain conditions for children over time. Successful groups have continuous sources of funds, a focus for their efforts, a support group, and a paid staff. They improve conditions for children and can monitor their programs' progress. The following are examples of successful groups and their programs.

Fullerton Interfaith Emergency Service (FIES) has been reaching out to the homeless people since 1976. It is a community effort by twenty-four North Orange County (California) congregations, the YWCA of North Orange County, businesses, individuals, and grants from foundations and government agencies. New Vista Transitional Living Center is one of their programs. They also provide other services for the poor or homeless, such as emergency food and vouchers for motels. In 2001, they added a transitional living program for a few employable adults to help them

12.1   Homeless But Not Hopeless

Many agencies, churches, and a community college worked together to provide crucial support for this family.

In 1988, Susan found herself homeless with little education or technical skills and five young children to support. They lived in motels, with friends and family, and finally in parks before entering New Vista Transitional Living Center. This community shelter, sponsored by a nonprofit private agency representing local churches partnering with public agencies, provided a home for Susan's family and helped her find a job and save her money for two and a half months. The family eventually moved into a HUD (government) housing project. Susan, while working part-time, began her college studies at a community college while her children continued their schooling.

By 2002, Susan had earned a teaching credential and a Master's degree in special education and was teaching in an underprivileged community. All five children were attending college. One daughter had been a volunteer for five years working with troubled teens. Her only son was past president of the honor society, a student trustee for the Community College District, and editor of the college newspaper.

Susan is now contributing to her community, grateful for the support her family was given.

"Today I work with empathy and compassion in my community because I too raised my children in tough times. . . . It is important to treat students with dignity, respect, and as competent human beings."

become self-sufficient within the 120-day program. Participating congregations provide housing and food for two-week periods.

Children's Defense Fund (CDF) is a private, nonprofit organization that has provided a strong voice for children since 1973. Its trademark is "Leave no Child Behind" and its goal is "to ensure that every child has a Healthy Start, a Head Start, a Fair Start, a Safe Start, and a Moral Start in life and safe passage into adulthood with the help of caring families and communities" (Children's Defense Fund, 2003). CDF advocates for the poor, the minority, and the disabled. The focus is on programs and policies that affect large groups of children rather than individuals. They research Congressional and other records and educate the public as to the problems. They help organize and support groups to lobby those in power to change specific conditions. They monitor bills regarding children's health and welfare and encourage preventive investments before children get sick, into trouble, drop out of school, or suffer from the breakdown of their family

CDF educates the public on these specific conditions and provides valuable resources. They have a number of publications, including an annual yearbook, *The State of America's Children*. Their Web site includes a legislative action center that provides information on elected officials, current issues and legislation. It also contains a media guide with information on how to contact local and national media. For example, under local media one can find information on individual editors, reporters, and producers as well as locate local newspapers and TV and radio stations.

LEAVE NO CHILD BEHIND: A CHILDREN'S DEFENSE FUND NATIONAL MOVEMENT

Leave No Child Behind, a national movement, was launched at the Children's

Workday at a Transitional Living Center: Respect and overall support are key to the program's success.

On Saturday, families work together to do chores on the premises. These homeless families live here for a short time while the parent, usually single, is able to work and save enough money for housing for the family. Children attend school or child care.

Defense Fund's (CDF) annual conference, May 23, 2001. The mission is to put into action whatever it takes for:

1. every child to enter school ready to learn and to leave school on the path to a productive life;
2. babies most likely to be born healthy and sick children to have the health care they need;
3. no child to grow up in poverty;
4. all children to be safe in their community;
5. every child to have a place to call home;
6. Americans to proudly say "We Leave No Child Behind."

The Children's Defense Fund has organized groups in every state with active volunteers.Their staff and members worked with legislators to draft an omnibus children's bill. The Act to Leave no Child Behind of 2001 was introduced into the Senate and House first in 2001 with specific proposals under twelve headings. CDF members and friends are holding Wednesday meetings in Washington, DC and across the nation to join together advocates and friends of children to make sure all (vulnerable) American children will receive adequate support. This will require continuing massive public pressure on legislators to look at, revise, and vote to pass this act into law (Children's Defense Fund, 2001, 2003).

The Annie E. Casey Foundation, a private charitable organization, has worked for over fifty years to improve conditions for disadvantaged children and their families. They foster public policies, human service reforms, and community support programs. They provide grants to public and private organizations to improve the support services, social networks, physical infrastructure, employment and self-determination, and economic vitality of distressed neighborhoods and communities. They publish an annual data book, *Kids Count,* which measures the status of children state by state. The information covers children's educational, social, economic, and physical well-being. The Casey Foundation's goal is to educate the public so that appropriate pressure can be exerted to effect needed changes. They work to promote public and private initiatives that improve children's lives. Their Web site is http://www.aecf.org

JUVENILE DETENTION ALTERNATIVES INITIATIVE (JDAI)   The Annie E. Casey Foundation established this initiative in 1992 to introduce more effective and efficient systems of juvenile detention. For example, rather than holding all youth awaiting trial in a locked facility, the Juvenile Detention Alternatives Initiative finds a less restrictive way to monitor some youths and also avoid delinquent behavior in the interim. Another objective of the Initiative is to improve conditions in secure detention facilities. The model for this Initiative was the basis for the successful reforms in Broward County, FL, where the average daily population was reduced from 160 to 56 youth over the course of five years. By using innovative policies and programs, this operation saved the taxpayers more than $5.2 million during this period by reducing operating costs, the need for construction of new facilities, and overtime pay (Casey Foundation, 2001).

In 1994, four large jurisdictions, Cook County, IL, Multonma County, OR, New York City, and Sacramento County, CA, began their JDAI programs for juvenile detention reform. Each program has successful strategies to reduce the number of youth in secure detention facilities and to improve their overall system. The progress of these JDAI programs can be found on their Web site and additional material is available through the Casey Foundation (2002).

MAKING CONNECTIONS/STRENGTHENING FAMILIES AND THEIR NEIGHBORHOODS
This Casey Foundation project is based on the premise that children need strong families and families need strong neighborhoods in order to be successful. Although these families have talents, strengths, leadership, and resilience, they are simply overwhelmed by their present conditions. This new approach connects poor, often isolated, families to the resources, opportunities, and supports that they need in order to raise healthy and confident children. It is a combination of economic opportunities, social networks, supports, and services. Economic opportu-

nities alone are not enough. Families need to be connected to networks of people both for support and a sense of belonging. They also need formal supports and services that often are lacking or hard to find in poor urban and rural communities (Nelson, 2000).

The second part to this initiative is the building of nontraditional coalitions representing families, neighborhood leaders, nonprofit institutions, public and private sector leaders, and a wide range of civic, political, grassroots, and faith-based groups. They work together to promote programs, policies, and activities that help make families strong and neighborhoods supportive.

The Making Connections demonstration project is the first component. Neighborhoods in twenty-two cities were chosen based on need and their political will and ability to participate. Their families' talents and strengths were identified and utilized. The Casey foundation is committing half of its grant funds to these projects. They believe that, with the right mix of incentives, investments, and opportunities, neighborhood conditions can be changed in ways that support families and bolster children's chances of beating the odds (Casey Foundation, 2001).

The **Child Welfare League of America (CWLA),** founded in 1920, is an association of more than 1,100 public and private nonprofit agencies that assist over 3.5 million abused and neglected children and their families every year. They look at the broad picture and advocate for all needed welfare policies. Their various programs cover most areas affecting children including health care, mental health, adoption, foster care, child care, generations united, housing and homelessness, children with parents in prison, and other areas of service. Information can be accessed at their Web site (http://www.cwla.org). The CWLA Legislative Agenda, the CWLA Legislative Report Forum, and CWLA Kids Advocate Online all provide information about actions of Congress.

The **National Council of Churches (Child and Family Justice Project),** Black Child Development Institute, National Council of Jewish Women, and Action for Public Television are but a few other advocacy groups working for children and their families. The projects already described that support children with a parent in prison are also effective advocacy programs.

Where America Stands

In the United States people claim that children are their most precious possession. If so, should this not be reflected in how a government allocates its resources? What percentage of the national budget is spent on education, health, transportation, subsidizing industry, defense, and social entitlement programs? How do children's conditions in the United States compare with those of children in twenty-five other industrialized nations? The Centers for Disease Control and Prevention and the Children's Defense Fund provide the statistics in Table 12.1. **From this standpoint, can it be claimed that children really are America's number one priority?**

Current Trends

Government and all social policies affect individuals differently depending on their circumstances such as age, education, talents, health, where they live, and economic resources. Our most vulnerable citizens, our children, the elderly, the sick, and the needy cannot take care of themselves. They need financial and other types of support just as do the families and children of the disaster victims of the September 11, 2001 terrorist attacks. Private and public policies and practices provide varying degrees of support for America's most vulnerable citizens.

If Americans want social policies (including public or government policies) to be supportive of children and families, they must act. This means individuals and groups must identify particular needs, educate the public, form a consensus among groups in the community, and then work together to bring about changes. It will take both government and nongovernmental policies to strengthen our most vulnerable families and provide the necessary preventive and supportive services including:

1. basic health care;
2. high-quality child care and out-of-school programs;
3. schools that can educate all children;
4. safe neighborhoods;
5. lifting families out of poverty.

Will our social policies and actions "leave no child behind"?

Key Points

1. The family's ability to provide for its children depends in part on the opportunities, protection, and support from society.
2. Social policies include everything from cultural norms, laws, regulations, judicial decisions, executive orders, administrative practices, business practices, and traditions. Public policies are social policies enacted by government agencies and enforced by police and judicial powers.
3. The United States has a larger percentage of its children living in poverty, without health insurance, born with low birth weight, and having lower eighth-grade math scores, than children in most industrialized countries.
4. The juvenile justice system is designed to help youth live within the law and protect society from harm.

5. An estimated 1.6 million children suffer emotionally and physically from unstable and often abusive conditions surrounding the incarceration of a parent. Advocacy programs that improve their family relationships also improve children's emotional health and behavior.
6. A child advocate works to identify and improve conditions for children. Advocates join forces to form a coalition. Networking is the working together of various coalitions.
7. Ongoing child advocacy groups include the Children's Defense Fund, the Annie E. Casey Foundation, and the Child Welfare League of America.
8. It will take supportive public and other social policies to provide basic health care, high-quality child care and out-of-school programs, successful schools, and safe neighborhoods.

Critical Thinking Questions

1. To what extent do you think the local, state, or federal government should support a family? How should the private sector support vulnerable children and families?

2. Do you think that the government is run by a few big interest groups looking out for themselves or run by those who are looking out for the benefit of all the people? Support your answers.

Resources and References

Annie E. Casey Foundation
   http://www.aecf.org/kidscount/klc2001
Child Welfare League
   http://www.cwla.org
Office of Juvenile Justice and Delinquency Prevention
   http://www.ojp.usdoj/bjs/
Social Security Administration
   http://www.ssa.gov
The Early Childhood Advocate
   Published quarterly by NAEYC's Public Affairs Division, Washington, DC
Washington Update and Public Affairs columns in each journal issue of *Young Children*
   http://www.naeyc.org

■ Related Readings

Jenson, M. A., and Hannibal, M. A. (2000). *Issues, advocacy, and leadership in early education* (2nd ed.). Boston: Allyn and Bacon.

■ References

Barbour, C., and Barbour, N. (2001). *Families, schools, and communities.* Upper Saddle River, NJ: Merrill/Prentice-Hall.

CAEYC (California Association for the Education of Young Children). (1990). Prison match: A children's center program. *CAEYC Connections, 19*(2), 10–11.

Carnegie Council on Adolescent Development, Task Force on Youth Development and Community Programs. (1992). A matter of time: Risk and opportunity in the nonschool hours. New York: Carnegie Corporation of New York.

Casey (Annie E.) Foundation. (2002). At http://www.aecf.org

Casey (Annie E.) Foundation. (2001). *Kids Count data book: 2001.* Baltimore, MD: Author.

Children's Defense Fund. (1998). *The state of America's children: Yearbook 1998.* Washington, DC: Author.

Children's Defense Fund. (2001a). The act to leave no child behind—brief summary, April 2, 2001. Letter, May 17. Washington, DC: Author.

Children's Defense Fund. (2001b). *The state of America's children: Yearbook 2001.* Washington, DC: Author.

Children's Defense Fund. (2002). *The state of children in America's union.* Washington, DC: Author.

Children's Defense Fund. (2003). *Letter from the President.* Marian Wright Edelman, 1, 13, 03. Washington, DC: Author.

Child Welfare League of America. (1998). *State agency surveys on children with incarcerated parents.* Washington, DC: Author.

Garbarino, J. (1982). *Children and families in the social environment* (2nd ed.). New York: Aldine de Gruyter.

Gilliard, D. K., and Beck, A. J. (1998). *Bureau of Justice statistics bulletin: Prison and jail inmates at midyear 1997.* Washington, DC: U.S. Department of Justice, Bureau of Justice Statistics.

Gitelson, A. R., Dudley, R. L., and Dubnick, M. J. (1998). American Government, 5th ed., p. 18. Boston, MA: Houghton Mifflin Company.

Hansen, M. (2000). Deadly knell for death row? *ABA Journal,* June, 40–48.

Johnson, D. (1995a). The care and placement of prisoners' children. In K. Gabel and D. Johnston (Eds.), *Children of incarcerated parents* (pp. 103–123). New York: Lexington Books.

Johnson, D. (1995b). Effects of parental incarceration. In K. Gabel and D. Johnston (Eds.), *Children of Incarcerated Parents* (pp. 59–88). New York: Lexington Books.

Keniston, K. and the Carnegie Council on Children. (1977). *All our children: The American family under pressure.* New York: Harcourt and Brace.

Moses, M. C. (1995). A synergistic solution for children of incarcerated parents. *Corrections Today, 57,* 124–127.

National Commission on the International Year of the Child. (1980). *Report to the President.* Washington, DC: U.S. Government Printing Office.

Nelson, D. W. (2000). Connections Count: An alternative framework for understanding and strengthening America's vulnerable families. *Young Children, 55,* 39–42.

Osborne Association. (1993). How can I help? Working with children of incarcerated parents. In *Serving Special Children* (Vol. 1). New York: Author.

Sailor, D. (1982). Child and family justice project; A model for advocacy. *Childhood Education, 58,* 216–221.

Seymour, C. (1998). Children with parents in prison: Child welfare policy, program, and practice issues. *Child Welfare, 77,* 469–494.

Snell, T. (1994). *Women in prison.* Washington, DC: U.S. Department of Justice, Bureau of Justice Statistics (special report).

Townsend, J. (2000). *Children visiting prisons, Kingston.* Kingston, Canada.

U.N. Convention on the Rights of the Child. (1989). New York: United Nations.

U.S. Department of Justice, Office of Juvenile Justice and Delinquency Prevention. (2000). *Juveniles and the death penalty.* Washington, DC: Coordinating Council on Juvenile Justice and Delinquency Prevention.

Community:
Its Influence
on Children

13

Democracy is not possible unless all of us are connected as a community.

— *Children of 2010,*
Washington and Andrews, Eds.

*C*hildren grow up in two universal social organizations, a **family** and a **community.** Both the family and the community affect the lives of children immeasurably. The **interaction of the family with the community** is as important an influence on children as each of these microsystems is individually. One of the characteristics of a healthy family is its involvement in the community (see chapter 4).

A community is a designated space where people live and share some sense of belonging. It may be as small as a neighborhood, a residential trailer park, or a particular dock with live-aboard slips in a marina. One may also feel a sense of belonging to and a part of a **global** community. Each community has a set of social norms and values and ways of teaching, modeling, and enforcing them. Norms include folkways, from eating the main meal at noon on Sunday, to more important rules such as appropriate dress. Some norms are so important that they become laws. Values are beliefs or standards by which a community or an individual defines what is desirable or undesirable. Some communities or families may value a college education more than others. For some, respect for elders may be an important value.

A community provides a setting where common interests bring people together. A community provides a protected place to live, the necessities such as food, clothing, housing, household goods, social institutions, a variety of services, and opportunities for employment.

Functions of a Community

A community provides a range of functions that support both individuals and families.

Economic. The community provides many of its members with a means of making a living.

Socialization. The community instills its norms and values in its members through formal and informal methods.

Social control. Control is accomplished both through group pressure and formal laws.

Social participation. Needed companionship can be found in the neighborhoods, churches, schools, recreational facilities, and community functions.

Mutual support. By pooling resources of its members and friends, a community can provide or share parks, a hospital, a library, and other services. Resources include taxes and donations of money, time, and talent (Warren, 1992).

The ways in which communities carry out these functions vary with their size, density, stability (mobility), homogeneity, economic and human resources, and location. Because communities vary, people often choose a community or a neighborhood because of a particular asset such as the quality of schools, affordable housing, mass transportation, proximity to their job, or cultural affinity.

Life in Cities, Suburbs, and Rural Communities

In the United States, three-fourths of the population is concentrated in 1.5 percent of the land. In 2000, 80 percent of Americans lived in metropolitan areas that included central cities and suburbs. Even those individuals who lived in rural areas were influenced in their lifestyles by life in the cities (U.S. Bureau of the Census, 1998, 2000).

Cities

Cities were key elements in ancient Roman and Greek civilizations. The word *civilization* comes from the Latin root ***civis*** ('city dweller'). The Greek word ***polis*** ('city') is also the root for *politics,* which was the core of Greek life (Macionis, 1997). Today, two types of urban areas are identified in the 2000 Census. An *urbanized area* has a central place(s), a minimum population density of 1,000 people per square mile, and a minimum population of 50,000. An *urban cluster* is a densely populated area with a minimum population of 2,500 and less than 50,000 (U.S. Bureau of the Census, 2000). Central cities comprise only 27.6 percent of the metropolitan population; suburbs total 62.4 percent (Woodward and Damon, 2000).

The **postindustrial city** emerged in the last half of the twentieth century. As many cities in the Snowbelt (the Northeast through the Midwest) lost population, cities grew quickly in the South and the West. Many of these Sunbelt cities emerged after urban decentralization began. They sprawled as a city rather than forming many suburbs. These cities still lack a dense center and usually have inadequate mass transit systems.

In postindustrial cities, multinational corporations are very powerful. Many businesses are dependent on the global economy and the electronic flow of information. The decentralization of their production is often outside of the urban area, making conditions worse for the urban poor (Phillips, 1996; Smith and Timberlake, 1993).

Urban Americans are a diverse group. Cities have always been home to immigrants from many parts of the world who settle there and become socialized. Urban dwellers usually settle in neighborhoods where they have something in common with their neighbors. Families with children gravitate to neighborhoods with good schools and large apartments or single-family homes. Some seek neighborhoods with families of similar social standing based on income and prestige, while others seek to live near people of similar race and/or ethnicity (Shevky and Bell, 1955; Johnston, 1976). Some neighborhoods combine more than one of these criteria. Families with few children tend to live in the city's center while families with more children live away from the center.

Sociologist Herbert J. Gans identified five groups of people living in a city.

1. **Cosmopolites,** such as writers, artists, and scholars, who desire its cultural and intellectual benefits.

2. **Unmarried and childless people,** who enjoy the city's active nightlife and varied recreational opportunities.
3. **Ethnic villagers** who want to live in their own ethnic community.
4. **The deprived** who are very poor people with little choice but to live in low-rent and often run-down neighborhoods.
5. **The trapped** who include elderly people living alone or families with limited economic resources or personal limitations (1991:54–56).

Children growing up in cities have different experiences from children growing up in suburbs or rural communities. Children are exposed to a greater diversity of ethnic and racial groups, occupations, ideas, values, and lifestyles. City children generally have better health care, a wider range of recreational activities, a safe water supply, an adequate sewage system, and emergency services. Children in cities, compared to those in suburban and rural areas, are exposed to more pollution, crime, noise, and rapid growth and change. They also live in higher density neighborhoods. However, cities often receive government subsidies to help with poverty, high crime, and racial problems.

Sense of Belonging and Segregation

Children growing up in cities have less sense of belonging to or identity with the community than children in less populated areas. Some sociologists believe that **size** is the key factor affecting one's sense of belonging while others feel that the degree of **mobility** of its members is a more important component.

Toennies (1988, orig. 1938) and other sociologists believed that as a community continues to grow in size, personal relationships outside of primary groups become less intimate and personal identity lessens. Increased size may also facilitate spatial segregation of its members based on race, ethnicity, marital status, or age (Wirth, 1938).

Other sociologists believe that a high degree of transiency in the community or neighborhood and one's newness to the community is far more damaging to a sense of belonging and identity than is size, density, or heterogeneity. Whatever the reasons, people in high-density areas report a lack of privacy and often protect themselves from "unwanted" social contacts. Social withdrawal can precipitate a breakdown in socially supportive relationships.

Individuals find ways to belong to a community. Just as individuals identify with their school or their athletic team, they may also see an organization such as the New York Philharmonic or the Atlanta Braves as a part of their community and part of their sense of identity. If, for example, a sports team moves to another city, their fans often feel angry and betrayed.

SEGREGATION   Pioneering sociologists saw the diversity in the cities as neutralizing the effects of race, class, and sex. More recently, sociologists report that cities often intensify the problems (Spates and Macionis, 1987). Riots in cities in recent years have shown the hatred or resentment some members of one racial/ethnic group have for members of another. Police arrests and court trials often are tainted with accusations of racial prejudice, such as the 1995 O. J. Simpson murder trial that was reported around the world.

Residential segregation has always existed in our cities. People often choose a neighborhood where residents have a similar background. Where people live is also determined by the business practices of real estate agents, actions of home sellers, urban planning initiatives (such as the location for public housing), and the location of businesses. Sociologists Masses and Denton (1993) have called the residential patterns of the nation "American apartheid" (Schaeffer, 2000).

Control over Personal Events or Conditions and Safety

The size and density of the community also impact the sense of power its members may feel over life's events. Individuals living in high-density areas more frequently have a feeling of "learned helplessness" over conditions in their lives whereas individuals in low-density areas more often feel that they have some control over situations and their outcome (Rodin, 1976).

Communities vary greatly in the number of incidences and types of violence that take place. Communities with high density have been found to have higher rates of crime than communities with low density (Limber and Nation, 1998). Children who live in high crime areas are at greater risk of being the object or witness of a crime. For safety, children may be restricted regarding where they can go. Unfortunately, some children may see crime as a way of life and violence as the norm for settling disputes (see Chapter 11). Garbarino, Dubrow, Kostelny, and Pardo (1998) believe that children need a safe environment at home and in their neighborhood where they can play, explore, and form relationships. Those who experience this are more likely to grow up to become competent adults.

Effects of Noise

Exposure to high levels of noise has been found to affect hearing discrimination, reading, language acquisition, math, school achievement tests and scores, stress levels, blood pressure, and behavior (Evans, Lercher, Meis, and Koffer, 2001; Wilensky, 2001; Savage, 1983; Cohen, Glass, and Singer, 1973). Recent studies show that **lower** levels of noise, not damaging to hearing, have many other consequences for children. For example, one body of research links chronic levels of noise to reading ability. This may be due to long-term memory loss and/or deficits in language acquisition, both of which are related to chronic exposure to noise (Wilensky, 2001).

Another study found that even low-level but chronic ambient (surrounding) community noise can cause stress in children and raise their blood pressure. This was based on a study of 115 fourth-grade children with similar family characteristics. Half of the children lived in quiet neighborhoods, where the noise level was below 50 decibels (sound of a clothes dryer), and the others lived in neighborhoods with noise levels above 60 decibels with noise levels (sound of a vacuum cleaner). Those living in the noisier neighborhoods had higher resting blood pressure rates, greater heart rate reactivity to a test, and signs of modestly elevated stress. In addition, girls exposed to high traffic sounds became less motivated. Researchers speculated that this resulted from a sense of helplessness regarding the noise (Evans, et al., 2001).

Another study examined preschool children's reactions to chronic noise in their child-care center and their reactions after the setting was made quieter. The noise was caused by the faulty structural design of the building. The Corning Glass Company built this center in New York in the early 1990s with interesting and attractive spaces and views of the outdoors, but the director, teachers, and even the children complained about the noise. After noise-absorbing acoustical panels were installed near the ceilings, the children's language skills improved. They used longer sentences, spoke to each other and the adults more often, and increased their vocabularies. Maxwell believes that when it is difficult to hear, young children will block out the sounds. Being able to block out some noise is helpful, but the concern is that children may fail to discriminate in blocking out sounds. They may not "hear" their parents or their teachers or be able to listen as well as they should. Evans believes that blocking out noise can also result in a delay in language acquisition (Maxwell and Evans, 2000). In another study, Evans and Maxwell found that chronic exposure to airport noise affected the language acquisition skills of nearby New York City elementary school children (1997).

In the United States, there is no designated resource to fund research or examine public policy on noise levels. Even in child-care facilities where there are some government regulations for the facility and play space, there are no regulations about noise or acoustical levels. The only public policy on noise comes from the regulatory agency for the airline industry. Many European countries have more research on the effects of various levels of noise and have enacted regulations to protect their public (Wilensky, 2001).

Suburbs

A suburb is any community near a large city that is not included in the city population. Suburbs began their growth in the late nineteenth century when railroads and trolley lines allowed people to work in the city and commute from a suburb. The first commuters were wealthy Americans. The growth of suburbs after World War II was due to middle-income Americans, the introduction of mass-produced housing such as prefabs, racial and ethnic intolerance, and increased crime in the cities. The expansion of the nation's highway system and low gas prices in the late 1950s made commuting easier. By the 1970s, more individuals lived in suburbs than in central cities and the suburban mall had replaced downtown metropolitan stores (Rosenthal, 1974; Geist, 1985). The migration of families from the cities to the suburbs continued throughout the 1990's. There was a 60 percent increase in the number of suburban families between 1970 and 1997 compared to the modest 12 percent increase for cities (Woodward and Damon, 2000).

The first suburbs were homogeneous. Suburbs in the l990s grew in racial, ethnic, and income diversity, yet were still less diverse than the cities. One study showed that Asian Americans and Hispanics often lived next to White Americans in similar socioeconomic areas (Logan and Alba, 1995; Palen, 1995). Some higher-income suburbs are affluent bedroom communities largely for commuters, while others are older affluent settled communities that may include business firms. Still other suburbs have residents with middle or lower incomes. Low-income communities with upwardly mobile blue-collar workers are growing. Gangs, crime, and drugs, which suburbanites were trying to escape, are now found in the suburbs.

Suburbs provide for safe water, sewage disposal, and police and fire protection, but offer fewer job opportunities than cities. Therefore, children see fewer adult occupations compared to city children and often have not seen their parent's or parents' work place(s). Most suburbanites work at urban rather than rural jobs.

Rural Communities

The number of people living in towns of 2,500 or less that are not adjacent to a city is dwindling, especially the farm population. In 1993, farm residents represented only 2 percent of the nation's population (U.S. Bureau of the Census, 1993). The farming, mining, and logging industries have all been in decline. However, advances in technology have allowed some workers to live in a rural community and to work at home (U.S. Bureau of the Census, 1993). Although many rural communities are not surviving, others are surviving by making radical changes. The addition of a Wal-Mart or another large discount store has enabled some rural communities to prosper, but many of their local stores had to close.

Many Americans have maintained an idealistic image of rural life. People moving from the city to a rural community often are seeking a safer, more pleasant environment. Some individuals returned to their roots only to find their small town with many retail or service stores closed or closing. There also were inadequate public services such as fire protection, road maintenance, hospital and medical services, and waste facilities.

In a small town, children are likely to know their neighbors and the town businesspeople. They see many residents as they walk down the street. The backgrounds of community members are more homogeneous and values are more commonly held than those of city dwellers. Children are socialized according to a single point of view. Basic values, norms, and customs are informally enforced by the community. There is less reliance on formal law and more reliance on group pressure.

Rural children do not have the anonymity of children in the city. All interactions are more intimate than those in the cities. Everyone knows about each other's affairs and is involved in each other's life whether it is for support or for gossip. The actions of children's relatives often become part of their children's identity, whether or not they and their family approve of their relative's conduct. Even a stranger to the community often hears some of this gossip.

Characteristics Affecting All Communities

Economic Conditions

Communities that are stable and have a good economic climate provide better services for their children. These augmented services include a variety of library

Hands-On Activity at a Children's Museum

This 4-year-old boy is painting a big truck. Children are able to experience various displays at the museum by touching and manipulating objects as well as through their other senses.

activities, museums, parks and recreation programs, better schools, and better health care.

Neighborhoods

Physical characteristics of the neighborhood and the diversity of age, race, ethnicity, and socioeconomic status of its residents affect the activities and socialization of their children. Are houses facing the street or a common play area? Can parents see their young children playing from the house? Does play take place in a backyard, a park, or a school yard? Do children play in a busy street or a cul-de-sac? What rules or values do children learn from their peers? What do children learn about the adult world from the adults they see? These factors affect their choice of playmates, how far they go from home, and the role models they see.

Environmental Problems

Research has shown that members of the lower classes have poorer health than the affluent. Not only are their diets and health care poorer, they often live and work near environmentally hazardous places. According to a study in Los Angeles, the poor, often African Americans, Hispanics, and Native Americans, are most likely to be living near all 82 of the county's recognized environmental hazards (Moffatt, 1995).

AIR POLLUTION   More than one billion people on the earth are exposed to potentially health-damaging levels of air pollution (World Resources Institute, 1998). In the United States in 1995, approximately 18 million children under age 10 lived where they were breathing unhealthy air that did not meet federal air-quality standards. Air pollution can irritate eyes or contribute to lung cancer. In urban areas, the major pollutants are emissions from automobiles, electric power plants, and heavy industries. It is possible to reduce smog from automobile emissions by fitting cars with pollution control devices. This is enforced by passing legislation on clean air as California did in 1963 and 1970. With far more population and four times the number of cars than in 1955, Southern Californians breathed cleaner air in 1998 than in the 1960s (Schaeffer, 2000).

Air pollution and smog as well as other environmental factors such as cigarette smoke, animal hair, and dust mites can trigger **asthma.** Hospitalization and outpatient visits for children with asthma have doubled during the last twenty-five years. Many homeless children also suffer from asthma. The hospitalization and emergency outpatient rates for Black and Hispanic children under age four with asthma are particularly high (Children's Defense Fund, 2001).

LEAD POISONING   Lead poisoning is still one of the most common environmental health hazards to children. Lead poisoning can cause learning disabilities, developmental delays, behavioral problems, and kidney damage. Very high levels can cause seizures and death (Children's Defense Fund, 2001). Although the Environmental Protection Agency (EPA) banned lead from paint and gasoline in the late 1970s, almost 900,000 children under age 5 currently have elevated blood-lead levels. Older houses and schools are more likely to have lead-based paint (Advisory Committee on Childhood Lead Poisoning Prevention, 2000). In 1998, the California Department of Health found lead-based paint in 95 percent of the schools that were inspected. Three out of four of these schools had levels of lead above the EPA's level for mandatory removal (National Resources Defense Council, 2000). The U.S. Department of Urban Housing (HUD) and the EPA are working together to reduce children's exposure to lead and prevent the toxic effects of lead poisoning.

PREVENTION AND TREATMENT   Children are more vulnerable than adults to toxins and other environmental hazards because of their body weight and activities such as playing on the floor and ground. Some children are exposed to potentially damaging chemicals in most of their settings. Lead accumulates in the body, causing irreversible damage. However, with early detection, proper treatment, eating foods that decrease the absorption of lead, and no further exposure to lead, children can be free of its long-term damaging effects (Children's Defense Fund, 2000). It is important to screen children at risk so that early treatment can minimize damage and prevent additional exposure. The American Academy of Pediatrics (1999) has published a handbook on the prevention and the treatment of childhood environmental health problems.

Community Services

Community services are vital to the health, welfare, safety, education, recreation, and enrichment of the community. These services are essential, directly or indirectly, for most of its members and are based on the needs and the economic conditions of the community. Most communities provide welfare and social services, health care, education, civic services, religious services, and information using the media such as community newsletters, newspapers, radio, or cable TV.

If these services are to be effective, they must be affordable, available, and accessible. The national Child and Family Justice Project demonstrated in their two-year study that services could be available and affordable but also had to be accessible. For example, it was not the lack of affordable medical services but the lack of transportation that kept many Appalachian families from getting needed medical care available at low or no cost in the city (Sailor, 1982).

Community services help maintain the physical and emotional health, education, and welfare of community members. Supportive health services provide information concerning health and facilities for physical and emotional treatment. Counseling for individuals or groups can be very helpful. Educational programs provide support for various age groups and interests. They often include "Mommy and Me" activities, programs for job training, retraining, and English as a second language. There are support groups for victims of crime and their families as well as those suffering from specific illnesses. Community development programs improve the welfare of its members.

Community preventive services try to avoid future problems and reduce current stresses. Well-baby clinics or free immunizations prevent some future health problems, including specific diseases. Sanitation and a safe water supply prevent many health problems. Parks and recreational programs give children something constructive to do rather than just hanging out and possibly getting into trouble. They also support children and families by improving the quality of their lives.

Compensatory and rehabilitative services accommodate community members with special needs. Head Start programs were first designed to make up for experiences that certain groups of children were lacking. Providing ramps and elevators for the physically handicapped allow them the same access as others, thus compensating for their physical conditions. Other examples include assistance in finding a job or low-cost housing. Rehabilitative services for individuals with special needs provide treatment and help in developing skills to improve their lives and their productivity. Correction services try to rehabilitate individuals who break the law so that they can become productive, law-abiding citizens or residents. The juvenile justice system is covered in Chapter 12.

In an effort to help families before a major crisis occurs, the federal government enacted the Family Preservation and Support Services Program that is now the **Promoting Safe and Stable Families Program.** These services in the community provide both support for current conditions and prevention of more serious problems. In order to receive federal funding, communities and states, working with representatives from various organizations, must develop a plan of services needed including an assessment of the strengths of the families in their community. The idea is to provide programs to meet the families' needs rather than the traditional approach in which families have to adapt to the available services. This new approach looks at a family's strengths and does not emphasize its deficits. Families and social workers jointly set goals and look for solutions. Programs such as parenting classes are offered to families or a parent-to-be considered at risk for serious problems. Very young pregnant mothers would be in this at-risk category. These participants would be able to share information, look for positive ways to discipline a child, and feel more successful in parenting. The goal is to help them to provide healthy environments for their families.

Central to the success of many of these programs are their partnerships with various community groups and state and federal programs. One community partnership included a group using funding from the federal Children's Mental Health Services Grant Program. The additional expertise and funding increased their range of services (Children's Defense Fund, 1998).

Public and Private Agencies

Both public and private agencies provide services to a community. In general, public agencies are less expensive for the clients and by law must accept all applicants who meet the eligibility requirements. Eligibility cannot be on the basis of race, creed, gender, or sexual orientation. Private agencies are not obligated to take all clients needing their services and may limit their services to a particular group. For example, a Christian adoption agency may require that the client acknowledge faith in Jesus for eligibility.

Public agencies emerged in the depression of the 1930s when voluntary organizations could no longer meet the needs of society. Public agencies are governed by local, state, and/or federal laws and run by an administrator. Most agencies operate at the local level, varying slightly due to local laws. These local laws must be consistent with state and federal laws. Their funds come from taxation and the legislators determine the allocation of funds. Advocates try to influence legislators for funds for a particular cause or service. Legislators are responsive to the wishes of the public who elect them (see Chapter 12).

Private agencies are established by individuals and philanthropic groups to meet specific needs in a community. Private organizations must adhere to local and state laws. They are funded by private and corporate donations, special fund raisers, endowments, trust funds, and, often, United Way moneys. A board of directors is chosen that represents different constituencies in the community. A director is hired by the board and is responsible to that body. The director selects and supervises the staff.

With the current demand for the care of children outside the home, private organizations, such as the YMCA and YWCA, have established child-care programs for infants, preschoolers, and school-age children. For the past 100 years the Children's Home Society, a private child-welfare agency, has served communities throughout California. Their services include programs in child care and development, community education, family support, shelter care, foster family care, and postadoption.

Other organizations provide help for people and their families suffering from a specific problem or disease. This could be dyslexia, alcoholism, spouse or drug abuse, AIDS, cerebral palsy, or cancer. In addition, Alcoholics Anonymous has chapters throughout the country and overseas for alcoholics and special programs for family victims. The Salvation Army serves the homeless and those in need. The American Red Cross helps victims of disaster.

Health Care: A Right or a Privilege?

High-quality, available, and affordable health services in a community are vital to the health and survival of its members. **The United States is the only Western industrialized nation that does not treat health care as a right for all its citizens** (Shaefer, 2000). Health, according to the World Health Organization, is a "state of complete physical, mental, and social well-being, and not merely the absence of disease or infirmity" (World Health Organization Constitution, 1946). "Healthy People 2010" is a national program to improve the health of all citizens. Its goals are to increase the quality and years of healthy living for all the population and to eliminate the health disparities among certain groups of children and adults by 2010. This means that conditions of poverty, inadequate access to quality health services, inadequate prevention programs in schools and communities, and environmental hazards in some homes and neighborhoods must be drastically reduced (Children's Defense Fund, 2001). To address these disparities, the federal Health Care Fairness Act of 2000 created a National Center for Research on Minority Health and Health Disparities at the National Institute of Health.

All industrial nations have experienced escalating health-care costs because of technological advances, increasing medical options, and a growing elderly population. The cost of health care is a burden for many, but especially for low-income, single-parent families, the unemployed, and the underemployed. Unlike most other nations, the private sector provides the majority of health care in the United States. To reduce costs and to serve more patients, the private sector insurance companies have shifted much of their coverage from traditional insurance plans to managed-care plans. By 1997, 85 percent of all workers were covered by managed-care plans (Children's Defense Fund, 1998).

Managed-care plans include the traditional Health Maintenance Organizations (HMO) and the Preferred Provider Organizations (PPO). The HMOs provide medical services for a set monthly fee covering group or individual enrollment plans. Minimum patients' fees for physician visits and medicine vary. The physicians receive salaries. In the PPO model, physicians work out of their own offices. They are part of a number of physicians selected by a company or employers to serve eligible employees and often family members for a fixed fee. Visits to physicians and prescribed medicines have varied patient fees.

Health services available in communities are affected by their population, their residents' socioeconomic levels, and the geographical location. There is an unequal distribution of doctors in the United States. More physicians practice medicine in urban areas (outside the inner city) than in rural areas. More doctors locate their office close to hospitals that are fully equipped for their specialty. A higher proportion of physicians' offices are located near more affluent populations. These conditions affect the number of doctors available for patients. For example, in southeast San Diego, CA, Dr. Butcher has nearly 2,000 patients while in affluent La Jolla, a short distance away, the physician/patient ratio is 1 doctor to 200 or 250 patients. In southeast San Diego, the infant mortality rate is higher than in some third-world countries (Butcher, 1993).

Quality of Medical Care

The medical training and expertise of physicians in the United States are equal to or better than that of any nation. Medical care for a crisis, serious illness, or elective surgery is superb. However, this quality care and choice of services are available to those who can pay for them. The recent cost-cutting and efficiency efforts by both the "for-profit care" and health maintenance organizations (HMO) may reduce the quality of care. The "for-profit care" industry has adopted some cost-cutting practices of corporate America. They are reducing costs by linking hospitals and insurance companies with groups of doctors. HMO's are reducing costs by limiting the time of the doctor's office visit, monitoring access to specialists, and reducing the choice of prescriptions.

Availability of Health Care

The widest selection of medical services can be found in our cities. In some rural areas and on most Native American reservations, there is a lack of medical specialists and expensive facilities. This may mean no neonatal unit for high-risk newborns or laboratory for diagnosing a rare blood disease at any age. Patients often need to be transported many miles for appropriate medical help. In addition, patients on government-assisted health-care plans find that some physicians will not accept the prescribed payments for medical procedures, and they must pay the uncovered costs. In many cities, emergency rooms have been forced to close for lack of funds. Typically, this occurs in poorer neighborhoods where more primary care takes place in the emergency room.

Affordable Health Care

The sharp increase in health-care premiums in the twenty-first century reflects rising costs and insufficient political pressure to keep costs down. A number of Americans no longer can afford health-care insurance or needed health care. Other American workers and their families who have health-care insurance partially paid for by their employer have had their contributions increased.

The Children's Health Insurance Program (CHIP), enacted in 1997, provides health insurance for children in low-income families without coverage. Between CHIP and Medicaid enrollment efforts, the number of uninsured children, ages 18 and under, dropped from a record high of 11.9 million in 1998 to 10.8 million in 1999. However, more than 6 million children who are eligible for health insurance under CHIP or Medicaid are not enrolled (Children's Defense Fund, 2001). A higher proportion of Black (1 out of 6) and Hispanic (1 out of 4) children are uninsured compared to White (1 out of 11) children (Children's Defense Fund, 2001).

Preventive Health Care

The multipayer system of health care in the United States does not provide adequate and affordable preventive health care. For example, many children enrolled in Medicaid's Early and Periodic Screening, Diagnosis, and Treatment (EPSDT) Program are not receiving any or all of the services to which they are entitled (U.S. General Accounting Office, 2000). A dollar invested in immunizations against diphtheria, tetanus, and whooping cough saves $23.00 in future costs. A dollar spent in the Women, Infants and Children (WIC) nutritional program saves spending $3.07 later (Children's Defense Fund, 2001). Not only is preventive care financially prudent, it is crucial to the survival and/or overall healthy development of children.

PRENATAL CARE　Early prenatal care and the mother's health at the time of conception and during her pregnancy affect the health and survival of the newborn and the child's later development. Before conception, the woman should determine her level of health and any damaging conditions such as HIV\AIDS. It is crucial that the mother be free of sexually transmitted diseases, and that she abstain from tobacco and drugs (including alcohol) during pregnancy. Second-hand smoke can also affect a baby after birth.

Monitoring the development of the fetus and the health of the mother contributes to healthy prenatal growth and development and the birth of a healthy

TABLE 13.1	Prenatal Care and Low Birth Weight	
Prenatal Care and Low Birth Weight by Race/Ethnicity of Mother, 1998		
White	84.8% early prenatal care	6.5% low birth weight
Black	73.3% early prenatal care	13.0% low birth weight
Hispanic	74.3% early prenatal care	6.4% low birth weight

(Children's Defense Fund, 2001.)

baby. Risk factors such as hypertension, diabetes, undue stress, and lack of social or other support services for the mother can be minimized. The cost of prenatal care is a fraction of the economic costs to treat conditions in babies that could have been prevented with early prenatal care.

IMMUNIZATIONS   During the 1990s, a dangerous drop in the immunization rate for preschool children occurred. Many parents did not realize the current dangers of diseases that the vaccines prevented and the cost of immunizations increased dramatically. Prices for all the vaccines needed to immunize a child fully escalated from $10.96 in 1970 to $235 in 1993, and this did not include the medical provider's costs (Children's Defense Fund, 1994).

Under the Immunization Initiative, which became effective October 1, 1994, the federal government pays for immunizations for all children who are uninsured, on Medicaid, or Native Americans. States may also buy vaccines from the federal government at their bulk rate for their own state programs. As a result, by 1999 80 percent of two-year-olds were fully immunized against diphtheria, tetanus, pertussis, measles, mumps, rubella, and polio (Children's Defense Fund, 2001). Since 2001, children in California are also required to have a vaccination against chicken pox.

REGULAR CHECK-UPS AND WELL-BABY CLINICS   Both of these programs are cost-effective measures to prevent, diagnose, and treat health problems early, avoiding later damage. The health-care costs for poor children with comprehensive primary and preventive health care are nearly 10 percent lower than for poor children without this care (Children's Defense Fund, 1999).

EDUCATION FOR PREVENTION   Families make many decisions affecting their children's present and future health. Patterns for living, attitudes on diet and exercise, and ways of handling stress are learned in the home and have long-term consequences for children. The public needs information on numerous health issues in order to take responsible action. Information on the causes, prevention, and consequences of diseases, such as the HIV virus, unsafe sex, and early adolescent pregnancy are essential. Often changing people's attitudes, such as respect for their body, are necessary before certain preventive or health-affirming actions are possible.

The National Health/Education Consortium (NHEC) has a multimedia program to educate parents about the connection between their child's health and their education. The importance of prenatal care, immunizations, and periodic health screenings is presented through videos, public service announcements, and on note pads (Cesarone, 1993). Children need access to health care and nutrition and parents need to understand that good health makes a difference in the child's school readiness and performance (Cesarone, 1993).

There is concern about the health and nutrition of many infants, toddlers, and preschoolers. The Carnegie Foundation for the Advancement of Teaching recommends a national network of Ready-to-Learn clinics, fully funded WIC (Women, Infants and Children) programs located near the schools, and comprehensive health education programs in all schools. The Ready-to Learn clinic would include prenatal care for pregnant mothers and a range of health services for preschoolers. These services for preschoolers would include regular checkups, screening for visual and hearing problems, and testing for lead poisoning (Carnegie, 1990).

Some research shows that children who eat an adequate breakfast learn better in the late morning than children with an inadequate or without breakfast (Rothlien, 1991). Other research shows that children with poor health often have cognitive and social-emotional deficits, low scores on developmental and achievement tests, and are inattentive. Programs providing good nutrition can lessen or eliminate these detrimental effects and foster school readiness for preschool children (Cesarone, 1993).

Obesity: A Growing Risk for Children

The percentage of children who are overweight has more than doubled in the last thirty years. Poor diets and lack of exercise have contributed to this. Overweight is determined by the age, sex, and body mass index at or above the 95th percentile. Using this definition, 11 percent of children, ages 6 to 11, are overweight (National Center for Health Statistics, 2000). Many of these overweight children already have a risk factor for heart disease (Children's Defense Fund, 2001).

Children and teens who increase their physical activities improve their health according to a joint report by the Secretaries of Health and Human Services and of Education. Too many children suffer from obesity, diabetes, and have the potential for future heart disease, resulting in devastating increases in health costs. Too many children spend much of their time watching television, using the computer, and being taken places by car rather than engaging in vigorous physical activity or walking or riding their bikes. Activity levels are higher for White students than for Hispanic or Black students. This may be due to unequal access to sports and educational classes and unsafe recreational areas in their neighborhoods. For some children, it may also be unsafe to walk to school. The report recommends an increase in school-based, after-school, and community programs that would allow access for all children. The report also recommends health education programs (U.S. Department of Health and Human Services and U.S. Department of Education, 2000).

Mental Health Care

An essential part of children's overall health is their mental health. Supporting children's mental health requires recognition and treatment of emotional, social, and behavioral problems. The nation is suffering a public crisis in mental health care for infants, children, and adolescents. According to the Report of the Surgeon General's Conference on Children's Mental Health (2000), one in ten children and adolescents suffers from mental illness severe enough to cause some level of impairment (U.S. Department of Health and Human Services, 2000). Only about one in five of these children receives mental health services (Burns, et al., 1995; Shaeffer, et al., 1996).

Children and their families suffer from a lack of effective prevention and early detection. Unfortunately, our health-care system, including federal government programs, does not respond as readily to mental health needs as it does to the child's physical well-being. This is due in part to fragmented services and low priorities for mental health resources (U.S. Department of Health and Human Services, 2000). In addition, stigmas continue to surround mental illness.

Mental health is a critical component of children's learning and general health. Fostering social and emotional health in children must therefore be a national priority. Both promoting good mental health for children and the treatment of mental disorders should be major public health goals. The urgent need for better access and treatment is reflected in the Surgeon General's National Action Agenda for Children's Mental Health (2001).

National Agenda for Public Health

Promote public awareness of children's mental health issues and reduce stigmas associated with mental illness.

Continue to develop, disseminate, and implement scientifically proven prevention and treatment services in the field of children's mental health.

Improve the assessment of and recognition of mental health needs in children.

Eliminate racial/ethnic and socioeconomic disparities in access to mental health-care services.

Improve the infrastructure for children's mental health services, including support for scientifically proven interventions across professions.

Increase access to and coordination of quality mental health-care services.

Train frontline providers to recognize and manage mental health issues and educate mental health-care providers about scientifically proven prevention and treatment services.

Monitor the access to and coordination of quality mental healthcare services.

(U.S. Department of Health and Human Services, 2001.)

The key for improvement is to educate everyone involved with children so that they can identify possible mental health problems and know where to find appropriate help.

> *Mental health care should have the same emphasis, money, and assistance as does physical health care.*

Hospice Care

Hospice comes from the Latin word *hospes* ('host'). A hospice originally was an inn or refuge for travelers usually maintained by a religious order. Today *hospice* refers to the care and support of terminally ill patients and their families at home or in a special facility. Hospice provides for the physical, emotional, and spiritual needs of the dying person as well as those of the family. It enables patients to die at home in a loving environment.

The hospice team usually includes a doctor or medical director, hospice nurse coordinator, registered nurses, home health aides, a licensed clinical social worker, a medical social worker, a registered physical therapist, a registered respiratory therapist, members of the clergy, and volunteers as needed. However, the family is the main care-giving unit, with one family member or friend assuming the main responsibility for care. The patient, family, and attending physician must agree that no prolonging life support measures will be used.

Pain is managed with needed medication. The spiritual values and needs of the family are supported. Often there is additional help at the time of death such as filling out police reports and insurance forms. The family often receives support during the bereavement period. Cost of hospice care is partially covered by Medicare, Medicaid, private insurance programs, and by private donations.

Religious Organizations

Religious organizations in a community provide a place for people to gather. They give meaning to their followers for living. Religious institutions often provide counseling and support to those in need. They provide support for their members and often support for others in the community, whether it is dealing with a natural disaster or the untimely death of a child. They also hold social events and cultural programs, often in connection with their holidays or holy days.

The values of religious institutions usually reinforce those of other social institutions and the social order as a whole. This helps children to accept certain values and ways of behaving. Some religious organizations hold religious and cultural education classes for their children. Many operate child-care centers and private schools.

Christian and Judaic values are a part of the U.S. legal system, business ethics, and everyday living. Some recent immigrants have brought with them religions other than Christianity or Judaism. These religious beliefs will also influence U.S. society. Since the 9/11 disaster of 2001, more attention is being given by various religious organizations and the media to help Americans understand the basic beliefs of Islam and Muslim Americans.

Some religious organizations are involved with social justice issues in their communities. They may support programs for the homeless and the poor with soup kitchens, food pantries, and temporary shelters. Some religious organizations work with community leaders to provide a safer neighborhood or community. They may also offer drug or family counseling services.

Community Play Areas and Parks and Recreation Programs

The freedom, the joys, the right to make noise in outdoor play.

The importance of play, exploration, relaxation, and space for the development of physical, mental, social, and creative skills has always been valued in the United States. In 1660, the first public land to be used for a park was purchased. In 1857, Olmstead, a renowned architect, was engaged to create New York City's Central Park on 843 acres of land for recreation and escape from urban conditions. The first serious play movement in America for young children began in 1886 when piles of sand were dumped in the yards of the Boston Children's Mission (Playground and Recreation Association of America, 1915). The interest in parks and open space grew and in 1906 the Playground Association of America was established. This has become the National Recreation Association and fosters the building and improvement of parks and recreational programs in communities across the country. Their monthly journal, *Parks and Recreation*, features interesting projects.

Parks are operated by federal, state, county, and city governments. There are twenty-nine national parks managed by the National Park Service under the Department of the Interior. National parks protect nature for people to enjoy and preserve areas from being developed. In addition, the Cooperative Extension Service, a federal agency under the Department of Agriculture, works through state agricultural colleges and county agricultural agents. Today it provides information and education to both rural and urban communities. One of its services is the operation of 4-H programs. This began as a service to farmers and their families, but today it serves both rural and urban children. The name 4-H stands for Head, Heart, Hands, and Health. Children choose a project, learn about the subject, and acquire skills needed to see the project through to completion. They then have the opportunity to enter their project in their county fair. The early 4-H projects involved animals, farm crops, and the jobs of a farm family. Today projects also include science, nature, and other topics. Some city children can find the space often provided by high schools to have a horse or raise a farm animal for their project. Children learn interesting facts related to their project but they also become attached to the animals that they raise,

> One city boy raised a steer, then showed and sold it at the county fair. He came to terms with eating beef from someone else's steer, but when his mother served tongue months later, it was too much!

Each state has state parks, regional parks, and community parks. Parks provide space and some equipment for recreation and nature trails. Community parks also offer recreation programs. They have classes to develop physical, social,

4-H County Fair: City Boy Earns Blue Ribbon for Steer He Raised

Children learn many things from their 4-H year's project including responsibility.

and employment skills and to support leisure pastimes and enrichment activities. Activities for children vary but often include arts and crafts, music and dance, sports lessons, physical fitness, reading programs, and education. Some communities sponsor organized sports programs, "Mother and Me" programs and/or After-School programs. There is pressure for after-school programs to support school class assignments. However, many parks and recreational departments believe after-school programs should be enriched recreation and not enriched education where the kids have activities similar to the school day (Alexander, 2000).

Parks and Playgrounds Reflecting the Needs of Children

What do children need in their play area? All children need a safe, developmentally and culturally appropriate place to play. It is important that disabled children have equal access to these areas. Children need space and a variety of materials. Young children especially like to build and take things apart transforming them in

reality or in their imagination. Children should feel comfortable in the play setting. It helps if the area reflects something of their neighborhood. Children need
to be challenged but also to feel successful.

**How do different spaces, structures, and materials affect children's think-
ing and their actions?** **Traditional** playgrounds have swings, a slide, a climbing
structure, and a sandbox, whereas **modern** playgrounds have structures that can
become many different things to suit children's imaginations. The climbing, sliding, and swinging are available on this nontraditional equipment. Materials are
colorful. **Adventure** playgrounds, usually for older children, have different materials and objects for constructing or creating things. There may be old tires, lumber, hammers, nails, glue, c-clamps, and rocks. Projects may take weeks or longer
to complete.

Six New York City Playgrounds

Six diverse New York City playgrounds have been designed to meet the play needs
of children from different backgrounds and physical abilities. All were constructed
about the same time. Each play area also reflects characteristics of its neighborhood.
One setting in Central Park offers children a choice of a traditional flat area playground or a modern playground up the hill. The modern playground is used by
more children. One of the six playgrounds serves the homeless children living in
adjacent Transitional Housing. Another one is for children from Harlem who had
been playing in the streets and in unsafe drug-active parks. Other playgrounds
include one for children attending the United Nations International School, a playground for children in Hudson River Park with a spectacular setting, and a special playground for children with and without disabilities to play together. They
all provide exciting and healthy play choices for the children.

The Harlem Playground, next to Public School 197 in Central Harlem, was
built to keep children off the streets and out of drug-active parks and the hospital
emergency room. (The director of pediatric services at the nearby Harlem Hospital organized this project, considered the first New York City hospital-based injury-
prevention program. The rate of serious injuries for children from Harlem was
reduced by 42 percent for the first four years). The playground reflected things
found in their neighborhood such as equipment looking like a piece of a store or
an apartment house. Colorful structures were challenging for different age groups.
The Red Cross operates the playground.

The Playground for All Children (PAC) was the first playground in the country in which children with disabilities and nondisabled children could play
together. It is a 3½-acre playground in Flushing Meadows-Corona Park in Queens.
All children have access to the play equipment. For example, the ramps allow two
wheel chairs to pass, and there is a pet-facilitated therapy program with dogs
trained to pull wheelchairs or push the right buttons at cash machines (Hiss and
Koren, 1993).

Playgrounds for All: Disabled and Nondisabled Children

Ten years after both the first PAC playground and the Americans with Disabilities Act of 1990, many parks still do not have access for the disabled. This legislation mandates equal access to public facilities

To create barrier-free playgrounds, the equipment and the surrounding spaces are designed so that children in wheel chairs have access. An elevated sandbox allows children to reach it from their wheel chair. Using ramps and transfer points, disabled children can have access to slides and jungle gyms. At the Telephone Pioneer Park in Phoenix, kids can roll their wheel chair up a ramp to a three-sided platform. The fourth side comes up and secures the chair. The whole platform swings from chains just like a regular swing (Vogt, 1998).

Public–Private Partnerships for Play Space

The Trust for Public Land, a national conservation group, the New York City Department of Parks and Recreation, the Supportive Children's Advocacy Network, the Metropolitan Life Foundation, and community residents have worked together to add more play sites to the overcrowded park areas in parts of New York City. The sites are under the jurisdiction of the Department of Parks and Recreation, but local

Everyone Plays Together

At Telephone Pioneer Park in Phoenix, children in wheelchairs roll up ramps while able-bodied children run up. Children in wheel chairs have access to all the play equipment.

community groups sponsor the different sites and have the primary responsibility for long-term maintenance and programming. Funding was also a joint effort. Metropolitan Life provided a large grant to the Trust for Public Land's City Space program along with some funding from the city. Other contributions, including many hours of volunteer time, have made these various projects possible (*New York Amsterdam News*, 1998).

Municipal/corporate partnerships in Phoenix have enabled the city to provide free summer recreational activities for its residents. Six years ago, the City of Phoenix Parks and Recreation and the Library Department joined forces with Cigna Health Care of Arizona to develop a comprehensive water-safety program called Cigna Summer (Parks and Recreation, 1998).

START SMART SPORTS DEVELOPMENT PROGRAM   The Start Smart Program is a program introducing children, ages three and older, into the world of sports. It is a family program that teaches them the motor skills needed for sports and helps parents with parenting skills, such as enhancing communication and promoting positive parent–child relationships. Parents can learn how to support their children and become model spectators. Not all parents provide good role models at competitive children's sports games. For example, in the summer of 2001, two hockey parents got into a fight over some rough play and one of the dads died.

Start Smart programs are part of many parks and recreational programs in the United States. They are also found in a number of other countries (Parks and Recreation, 1999).

Current Trends

Sucessful initiatives will continue to unite different segments of a community to work together to strengthen families and neighborhoods. The old African proverb, "It takes a village to raise a child," is especially true today. Children need a safe and caring community with high-quality child care, schools, libraries, museums, parks, recreation opportunities, and a supportive environment in which to grow and develop. Partnerships among families, schools, social agencies, religious organizations, and all citizens are essential. As citizens participate in activities that make a difference in the lives of children and their families, they will experience a renewed sense of belonging and the power to effect change. As this movement grows, communities will be better places in which to live. It is like the message in the *Little Engine that Could* by Lois Lenski: I think I can, I think I can, I CAN!!!

Key Points

1. The community, the family, and their interactions affect the lives of children immeasurably.

2. A community is a place where people live and share some sense of belonging. It provides economic opportunities, socialization,

social control, social participation, and mutual support.

3. Children in urban areas have broader social experiences and better health care, water supply, sewage system, and emergency services compared to children in rural areas, but have less of a sense of belonging and are exposed to more crime and environmental hazards.

4. Public agencies, funded by taxes, must serve all who meet the requirements. Private agencies, funded by private donations, may limit their services to a specific group.

5. The private sector provides the majority of health care, mostly in managed-care plans either under Preferred Provider Organizations or Health Maintenance Organizations.

6. Many Americans do not have health insurance. The Children's Health Insurance Program (CHIP) of 1997, along with Medicaid, provides health insurance for children in low-income families, but many eligible children are not enrolled.

7. The number of overweight children has doubled in the last thirty years. They are at risk for health problems, including heart disease.

8. One in ten children and adolescents suffers from mental illness severe enough to cause some impairment but only one in five receives mental health services.

9. Parks preserve wilderness and provide space and some equipment for many types of activities that foster physical, social-emotional and mental skills. Playgrounds for All, mandated by law, provide equal access for the disabled.

10. A variety of innovative programs and play spaces around the nation have resulted from public–private partnerships.

Critical Thinking Questions

1. In what ways do you think residents in a large city could improve their sense of community and belonging?

2. Would you rather raise a family in a city, suburb, or a small town, and why?

3. How do you think teachers and parents could better utilize their community's resources?

Resources and References

■ Websites

Boundless Playgrounds (non-profit)
  http://boundlessplaygrounds.org
Center for Disease Control and Prevention
  http://www.cdc.gov/
Environmental Protection Agency
  http://www.epa.gov/
National Alliance for Youth Sports
  http://www.nays.org
National Center for Health Statistics
  http:/www.cdc.gov/nchs
National Institute for Mental Health
  www.nimh.nih.gov
National Resources Defense Council
  http://www.nrdc.org/nrdcpro/ocar/ocarrev.html

■ Related Readings

Frost, J., and Wortham, S. (2002). The evolution of American playgrounds. *Young Children, 43*(5), 19–28.

Rivkin, M. S. (1995). *The great outdoors: Restoring children's right to play outside.* Washington, DC: National Association for the Education of Young Children.

■ References

Advisory Committee on Childhood Lead Poisoning Prevention. (2000). Recommendations for blood lead screening of young children enrolled in Medicaid: Targeting a group at high risk. *Morbidity and Mortality Weekly Report 49,* (December 8), 11.

Alexander, D. (2000). Nothing that lies between play and academics in after-school programs. *The National Institute on Out-of-School Time.* Available: http://www.wellesley.edu/WCW/CRW/SAC/activity.html

American Academy of Pediatrics. (1999). *Handbook of Pediatric Environmental Health.* Health Press Releases 1999. On-line. Available: http://www.aap.org/advocacy/releases/greenbook.htm

Bell, P. A., Greene, T. C., Fisher, J. D., and Baum, A. (1996). *Environmental Psychology* (4th ed.) Fort Worth, TX: Harcourt Brace.

Blackhall, L. J. et al., 1995. Ethnicity and attitudes toward patient autonomy. *Journal of the American Medical Association, 274,* 820–825.

Burns, B. J., Costello, E. J., Angold, A., Tweed, D., Stangl, D., Farmer, E. M. Z., and Erkanli, A. (1995). Data Watch: Children's mental health service use across service sectors. *Health Affair, 14*(3), 147–159.

Butcher, R. (1993, February). *The good doctor. San Diego Magazine,* 56–59, 74–79.

Carnegie Foundation for the Advancement of Teaching. (1990). *Ready to learn: A mandate for the nation.* Princeton, NJ: Carnegie Foundation for the Advancement of Teaching.

Carrese, J. A., and Rhodes, L. A. (1995). Western bioethics on the Navajo reservation: Benefit or harm? *Journal of the American Medical Association, 274,* 826–829.

Cesarone, B. (1993). Health care, nutrition, and Goal One. *ERIC Digest: EDO-PS-93-5.*

Children's Defense Fund. (1998). *The state of America's children: Yearbook 1998.* Washington, DC: Author.

Children's Defense Fund. (1999). *The state of America's children: Yearbook 1999.* Washington, DC: Author.

Children's Defense Fund. (2000). *The state of America's children: Yearbook 2000.* Washington, DC: Author.

Children's Defense Fund. (2001). *The state of America's children: Yearbook 2001.* Washington, DC: Author.

Cohen, S., Glass. D.C., and Singer, J. E. (1973). Apartment noise, auditory discrimination, and reading ability in children. *Journal of Experimental Social Psychology, 9,* 407–422.

Etzioni, A. (1991). Too many rights, too few responsibilities. *Society, 28*(2), 41–48.

Evans, G. W., Lercher, P., Meis. M., and Koffer, W. (2001). Community noise exposure and stress in children. *Journal of the Acoustical Society of America, 109,* 1023–1027.

Evans, G. W., and Maxwell, L. (1997). Chronic noise exposure and reading deficits: The mediating effects of language acquisition, environment, and behavior. *Environment and Behavior, 29,* 638–656.

Gans, H. J. (1991). *People, plans, and policies: Essays on poverty, racism, and other national urban problems.* New York: Columbia University Press and Russell Sage Foundation.

Garbarino, J., Dubrow, N., Kostelny, K., and Pardo, C. (1998). *Children in danger: Coping with the consequences of community violence* (2nd ed.). San Francisco: Jossey-Bass.

Geist, W. (1985). *Toward a safe and sane Halloween and other tales of suburbia.* New York: Times Books.

Hiss, A., and Koren, E. (1993, May 24). Child's play. *New Yorker,* 77–81.

Hollander, P. (1995). We are all (sniffle, sniffle) victims now. *Wall Street Journal,* January 18, A14.

Johnson, D. (1996). Rural life gains new appeal, Turning back a long decline. *New York Times* September 23, A1, B6.

Johnston, R. J. (1976). *Residential Area Characteristics.* In D. T. Herbert and R. J. Johnston (Eds.), *Social areas in cities:* Vol. 1: *Spacial Processes and Form* (pp. 193–235). New York: Wiley.

Kaiser Family Foundation. (1999). *Kids and the media @ the new millennium.* Menlo Park, CA: Kaiser Family Foundation.

Leavell, H. R., and Clark, E. G. (1965). *Preventive medicine for the doctor in his community: An epidemiologic approach* (3rd ed.) New York: McGraw-Hill.

Limber, S. P., and Nation, M. A. (1998). Violence within the neighborhood and community. In P. K. Trickett and C. J. Schellenbach (Eds.), *Violence against children in the family and the community.* Washington, DC: American Psychological Association.

Logan, J. R., and Alba, R. D. (1995). Who lives in affluent suburbs? Racial differences in eleven metropolitan regions. *Sociological Focus, 28,* 353–364.

Macionis, J. (1997). *Sociology,* 6th ed. Upper Saddle River, NJ: Prentice Hall.

Markowitz, M. (2000). *Lead poisoning: Pediatrics in review, 21,* 327–335.

Maxwell, L., and Evans, G. (2000). The effects of noise on preschool children's prereading skills. *Journal of Environmental Psychology, 20,* 91–97.

Moffatt, S. (1995). Minorities more likely to live near toxic sites. *Los Angeles Times* (August 30), B1, B3.

Monmaney, T. (1995). "Ethnicities": Medical views vary, study says. *Los Angeles Times* (September 13), B1, B3.

Mott, L., Fore, D., Curtis, J., and Solomon, G., 1997. *Our children at risk: The 5 worst environmental threats to their health.* New York: Natural Resources Defense Council.

National Center for Health Statistics (2000). *Healthy United States, 2000.* Hyattsville, MD: Author.

National Resources Defense Council. (2000). *Lead paint in schools.* Available: www.nrdc.org/health/

kids/qleadsch.asp, accessed on November 20, 2000.

New playground opens. (1998). *New York Amsterdam News, 89,* 33–34.

Palen, J. J. (1995). The suburban revolution: An introduction. *Sociological Focus, 28,* 347–351.

Parks and Recreation. (1998). Municipal/corporate partnerships make a splash. *Parks and Recreation, 33*(2), 74–79.

Parks and Recreation. (1999). Start smart. *Parks and Recreation, 34,* 27.

Phillips, E. B. (1996). *City lights: Urban-suburban life in the global society.* New York: Oxford University Press.

Playground and Recreation Association of America. (1915). A brief history of the playground movement in America. *The playground, 9*(1), 2–11, 39–45.

Rodin, J. (1976). Crowding, perceived choice and response to controllable and uncontrollable outcomes. *Journal of Experimental Social Psychology, 12,* 564–578.

Rosenthal, J. (1974). The rapid growth of suburban employment. In Lois H. Masotti and Jeffery K. Hadden (Eds.), *Suburbia in transition* (pp. 95–100). New York: New York Times Books.

Rothlein, L. (1991). Nutrition tips revisited on a daily basis, do we implement what we know? *Young Children, 46*(6), 30–36.

Sailor, D. H. (1982). Child and family justice project: A model for advocacy. *Childhood Education, 58*(4), 216–221.

Savage, D. G. (1983, February 15). Freeway noise linked to poorer test scores. *Los Angeles Times,* p. 1 Part 1.

Schaefer, R. T. (2000). *Sociology: A brief introduction* (3rd ed.) Boston: McGraw-Hill.

Shaeffer, D., Fisher, P., Dulcan, M. K., Davies, M., Piacentini, J., Schwab-Wtone, M. E., Lahey, B. B., Bourdon, K., Jensen, P. S., Bird, H. R., Canino, G., and Regier, D. A. (1996). The NIMH Diagnostic Interview Schedule for Children Version 2.3 (DISC-2-3): Description, acceptability, prevalence rates, and performance in the MECA study. *Journal of the American Academy of Child and Adolescent Psychiatry, 35*(7), 865–877.

Shevky, E., and Bell, W. (1955). *Social area analysis.* Stanford, CA: Stanford University Press.

Smith, D., and Timberlake, M. (1993). World cities: A political economy/global network approach. In Ray Hutchinson (Ed.), *Urban sociology in transition* (pp. 181–207). Greenwich, CT: JAI Press.

Spates, J. L., and Macionis, J. J. (1987). *The sociology of cities* (2nd ed.) Belmont, CA: Wadsworth.

Suburbia: the new American plurality. (1971). *Time, 97* (March 15), 14–21.

Taylor, J. (1991). Don't blame me: The new culture of victimization. *New York Magazine* (June 3), 26–24.

Toennies, F. (1988). *Community and society.* Rutgers, NJ: Transaction. (Originally published in 1887)

UNICEF. (2000). *Convention on the Rights of the Child.* New York: Author. Available: www.unicef.org, 2002

U.S. Bureau of Census. (1993). *Statistical abstract of the United States, 1993.* Washington, DC: U.S. Government Printing Office.

U.S. Bureau of the Census. (1998). *Statistical abstract of the United States, 1998.* Washington, DC: U.S. Government Printing Office.

U.S. Bureau of Census. (2000). *Statistical abstract of the United States, 2000.* Washington, DC: U.S. Government Printing Office.

U.S. Department of Health and Human Services (2000). *Report of the Surgeon General's Conference on children's mental health: A national agenda,* Sept. 18–19, 2000. Available: www.surgeon-general.gov/cmh/childreport.htm

U.S. Department of Health and Human Services, Office of the Surgeon General. (2001). *Report of the Surgeon General's Conference on children's mental health: A national action agenda.* Washington, DC: Office of the Surgeon General.

U.S. Department of Health and Human Services and U.S. Department of Education. (2000). *Promoting better health for young people through physical activity and sports: A report to the president from the secretary of health and human services, and the secretary of education.* Washington, DC: Authors.

U.S. General Accounting Office. (2000). *Medicaid and SCHIP: Comparisons of outreach enrollment practices and benefits.* Washington, DC: Author.

U.S. Public Health Service. (2000). Report of the Surgeon General's conference on children's mental health: A national action agenda. Washington, DC: Department of Health and Human Services. Available: http:www.surgeongeneral.gov/cmh/childreport.htm

Vobejda, B. (1993). U.S. ends survey of its dwindling farm population. *Chicago Sun-Times,* (October 9), p. 6.

Vogt, T. (1998). Playgrounds for all. *Sports Illustrated for Kids, Supplement Parents, 10,* 7/8p., 1c.

Warren, R. (1992). The community in America. In R. L. Warren and L. Lyon (Eds.), *New perspectives on the American community.* Homewood, IL: Dorsey Press.

Washington, V., and Andrews, J. (1999). *Children of 2010.* Washington, DC: National Association for the Education for Young Children.

Wilensky, J. (2001). Quiet zones for learning. *Human Ecology, 29*(1), 15–17.

Wirth, L. (1938). Urbanism as a way of life. *American Journal of Sociology, 44,* 1–24.

World Health Organization. (1946). *Constitution of the World Health Organization.* New York: World Health Organization Interim Commission.

World Resources Institute. (1998). *1998–99 World resources: A guide to the global environment.* New York: Oxford University Press.

Woodward, J., and Damon, B. (2000). *Housing characteristics, 2000.* Washington, DC: U.S. Department of Commerce, Economics, and Statistics Administration, U.S. Bureau of Statistics, 2001.

Appendix

Piaget's Stages of Cognitive Development

Sensorimotor	Birth to about 2	Actions are based on what infants see, hear, touch, and put in their mouth. Schemes are based on sensory and motor activities. Object permanence is acquired.
Preoperational	2 to 6 or 7	Use symbols for their discoveries; egocentric view of the world; lack ability to think logically.
Concrete operational	7 to 11 or 12	Logical reasoning but limited to concrete reality; comprehension of conservation and reversibility and multiple classifcations of an object.
Formal operational	11 or 12 to adulthood	Logical reasoning applied to abstract ideas as well as concrete objects; can consider possible outcomes for any problem.

Author Index

Subject Index